Elisabeth Elliot

Elisabeth Elliot

A Life

Lucy S. R. Austen

WHEATON, ILLINOIS

Elisabeth Elliot: A Life

Copyright © 2023 by Lucy S. R. Austen

Published by Crossway
       1300 Crescent Street
       Wheaton, Illinois 60187

Copyright material from *Gold by Moonlight*, *Gold Cord*, *If*, and *Mountain Breezes: The Collected Poems of Amy Carmichael* by Amy Carmichael are used by permission of Christian Literature Crusade, Ft. Washington, PA.

Cover design: Jordan Singer

Cover image: Copyright 1986 Kenneth R. Buck. All Rights Reserved.

First printing 2023

Printed in the United States of America.

Unless otherwise indicated, Scripture quotations are from the ESV® Bible (The Holy Bible, English Standard Version®), copyright © 2001 by Crossway, a publishing ministry of Good News Publishers. Used by permission. All rights reserved. The ESV text may not be quoted in any publication made available to the public by a Creative Commons license. The ESV may not be translated into any other language.

Scripture quotations marked AMP are from the Amplified® Bible, copyright © 1954, 1958, 1962, 1964, 1965, 1987 by The Lockman Foundation. Used by permission. www.lockman.org.

Scripture quotations marked ASV are from the American Standard Version of the Bible, which is in the public domain.

Scripture quotations marked ERV are taken from the Holy Bible: Easy-to-Read Version (ERV), International Edition. Copyright © 2013, 2016 by Bible League International and used by permission.

Scripture quotations marked GNT are from the Good News Translation in Today's English Version—Second Edition. Copyright © 1992 by American Bible Society. Used by permission.

Scripture quotations marked HCSB are taken from the Holman Christian Standard Bible®, Copyright © 1999, 2000, 2002, 2003, 2009 by Holman Bible Publishers. Used by permission. Holman Christian Standard Bible®, Holman CSB®, and HCSB® are federally registered trademarks of Holman Bible Publishers.

Scripture quotations marked KJV are from the King James Version of the Bible.

Scripture quotations marked NEB are taken from the New English Bible, copyright © Cambridge University Press and Oxford University Press 1961, 1970. All rights reserved.

Scripture quotations marked NIV are taken from the Holy Bible, New International Version®, NIV®. Copyright © 1973, 1978, 1984, 2011 by Biblica, Inc.™ Used by permission of Zondervan. All rights reserved worldwide. www.zondervan.com. The "NIV" and "New International Version" are trademarks registered in the United States Patent and Trademark Office by Biblica, Inc.™

Scripture quotations marked PHILLIPS are taken from the New Testament in Modern English by J. B. Phillips. Copyright © 1960, 1972 J. B. Phillips. Administered by The Archbishops' Council of the Church of England. Used by Permission.

Scripture quotations marked RSV are from the Revised Standard Version of the Bible, copyright © 1946, 1952, and 1971 the Division of Christian Education of the National Council of the Churches of Christ in the United States of America. Used by permission. All rights reserved.

All emphases in Scripture quotations have been added by the author.

Hardcover ISBN: 978-1-4335-6591-5
ePub ISBN: 978-1-4335-6594-6
PDF ISBN: 978-1-4335-6592-2

Library of Congress Cataloging-in-Publication Data

Names: S. R. Austen, Lucy, 1982– author.
Title: Elisabeth Elliot : a life / Lucy S.R. Austen.
Description: Wheaton, Illinois : Crossway, [2023] | Includes bibliographical references and index.
Identifiers: LCCN 2021012274 (print) | LCCN 2021012275 (ebook) | ISBN 9781433565915 (hardcover) | ISBN 9781433565922 (pdf) | ISBN 9781433565946 (epub)
Subjects: LCSH: Elliot, Elisabeth. | Missionaries—Ecuador—Biography. | Missionaries—United States—Biography.
Classification: LCC BV2853.E3 E53 2023 (print) | LCC BV2853.E3 (ebook) | DDC 266/.023730866092 [B]—dc23
LC record available at https://lccn.loc.gov/2021012274
LC ebook record available at https://lccn.loc.gov/2021012275

Crossway is a publishing ministry of Good News Publishers.

SH			32	31	30	29	28	27	26	25	24	23
15	14	13	12	11	10	9	8	7	6	5	4	3	2	1

That Nature Is a Heraclitean Fire
and of the Comfort of the Resurrection

Cloud-puffball, torn tufts, tossed pillows | flaunt forth, then chevy on an air-
built thoroughfare: heaven-roysterers, in gay-gangs | they throng; they glitter in marches.
Down roughcast, down dazzling whitewash, | wherever an elm arches,
Shivelights and shadowtackle ín long | lashes lace, lance, and pair.
Delightfully the bright wind boisterous | ropes, wrestles, beats earth bare
Of yestertempest's creases; | in pool and rutpeel parches
Squandering ooze to squeezed | dough, crust, dust; stanches, starches
Squadroned masks and manmarks | treadmire toil there
Footfretted in it. Million-fuelèd, | nature's bonfire burns on.
But quench her bonniest, dearest | to her, her clearest-selvèd spark
Man, how fast his firedint, | his mark on mind, is gone!
Both are in an unfathomable, all is in an enormous dark
Drowned. O pity and indig | nation! Manshape, that shone
Sheer off, disseveral, a star, | death blots black out; nor mark
          Is any of him at all so stark
But vastness blurs and time | beats level. Enough! the Resurrection,
A heart's-clarion! Away grief's gasping, | joyless days, dejection.
          Across my foundering deck shone
A beacon, an eternal beam. | Flesh fade, and mortal trash
Fall to the residuary worm; | world's wildfire, leave but ash:
          In a flash, at a trumpet crash,
I am all at once what Christ is, | since he was what I am, and
This Jack, joke, poor potsherd, | patch, matchwood, immortal diamond,
          Is immortal diamond.

GERARD MANLEY HOPKINS

Contents

Preface

BIOGRAPHERS AT LEAST since Boswell have struggled with varying success against the desire to capture *everything* about their subject. Such a life would take longer to read than to live, so it's probably best that even the most dedicated researcher can't fully satisfy this yearning. Sometimes the source material doesn't tell everything we want to know. Hermione Lee notes, "You can only access [the subject] in as far as you have materials and witnesses to allow you to access them. You are at the mercy of what you can find and read and hear and see. . . . There is always going to be a gap." Sometimes the source material would take lifetimes to fully assess. Robert Caro vividly depicts the moment when, walking through one of four floors in the Johnson Library filled floor-to-ceiling with shelves of boxes of Lyndon Johnson's papers, he realized he would never be able to honor his dictum, "Turn every page."[1]

Elisabeth Elliot's biographer faces both challenges. Any attempt to tell the story of Elliot's life raises questions, some unanswerable. At the same time, to examine the life of a writer and speaker involves examining her work, and Elliot's available work—thirty-one books; twenty-one years of bimonthly newsletter; twelve-and-a-half years of a radio program that ran five days a week; numerous articles, introductions, and pamphlets; and dozens upon dozens of transcripts and recordings from a fifty-year speaking career—is massive. Though time and space have precluded addressing everything, I have relied heavily on Elliot's published work in surveying her thinking over the course of her life.

Elliot knew the biographer's urge to preserve the historical record. She was also an inveterate purger. She satisfied these competing desires by donating much of what she purged to the Billy Graham Center Archives at her alma mater, Wheaton College. Since her death in 2015, her widower, Lars Gren, and her daughter, Valerie Elliot Shepard, have made further donations to this collection, which now includes childhood scrapbooks, college photo albums, love letters, home movies, and forty years of family correspondence. The majority of my direct quotations from Elliot's unpublished writing comes from these thousands of letters; original spelling and punctuation are reproduced, except when an error was obviously caused by sticky typewriter keys.

Elliot was also a lifelong journal keeper. This private writing helped her both to mark the moments as they passed and to make meaning of the events of her life. While her complete journals are held by her family and unavailable for scholarship, portions of them are accessible from four sources. Elliot occasionally quoted her journals in her books. Shepard's published account of her parents' relationship, *Devotedly: The Personal Letters and Love Story of Jim and Elisabeth Elliot*, excerpts Elliot's 1948–1955 journals. Elliot's family has commissioned an authorized biography by Ellen Vaughn and given Vaughn exclusive access to the complete journals. The first of Vaughn's projected two volumes (2020) contains quotations from journals up to 1963. Finally, the BGC Archives holds photographs of portions of Elliot's journals donated by *Elisabeth Elliot Newsletter* editor Kathryn Deering:

- A few pages from 1938 and 1951
- January 1957–August 1959
- October–December 1960
- March 1964–September 1965
- June–August 1968
- January 1969–December 1971
- March 1972–December 1973

These cannot be directly quoted, but they shine light on Elliot's thinking during significant times in her life.

Portions of this book deal with the Waorani, who live in the eastern jungle of Ecuador. For many years, it was common practice to call indigenous people by names assigned to them by outsiders. This practice continues today, but was even more prevalent during the 1950s and 1960s, when the paths of the Waorani and Elisabeth Elliot crossed. In the 1950s, the Waorani were largely uncontacted, and the term used for them by the neighboring Kichwa—"auca," meaning, more or less, "savages"—was the only one anyone outside the Waorani knew to use. "Auca" was often assumed to be a proper name and thus was capitalized. As outsiders made progress in learning Wao tededo, the Waorani language, it became apparent that the group called themselves, and preferred to be called, Waorani, "the People." The singular is Wao. There are three primary spellings: Huaorani is the Spanish spelling, while Waodani and Waorani are both used more commonly by the people themselves. Waorani is the spelling most commonly used by English speakers. This book uses "auca" only when dealing with events before outsiders learned the tribe's name or in direct quotations.

The Kichwa are another indigenous group with whom Elliot spent time. In their mother tongue, they are Runa (singular) or Runakuna (plural), and their language is Runashimi. Kichwa is the Runashimi spelling for Quechua, the name Spanish explorers used to describe the people they found in Ecuador's eastern lowlands as they searched for El Dorado in the 1500s. It appears to be a Spanish approximation of the Kichwa word "ghechwa," meaning "temperate valleys," although there are large numbers of Kichwa living in mountain regions as well. Unlike "auca," the origins of the name Kichwa are not derogatory, and it appears that the Runakuna/Kichwa themselves use the names interchangeably. Because of this, and since "Quechua" is the name that appears in source material from the 1950s and 1960s, this book uses the Runashimi spelling of Kichwa in an attempt to both prevent confusion and respect the right of people to decide their own name.

Several people in this book, in keeping with Waorani tradition, have only one name, and many more share the same handful of last names. I largely follow the custom of using an individual's full name once and their last name subsequently in identifying people whom Elliot knew more formally, but have chosen to use a given name or nickname for many in her life—particularly those who share the surnames Howard, Elliot, Leitch, Gren, Shepard, Saint, Fleming, McCully, and Youderian. Elliot went by various names over the course of her life, both last names and versions of her given name. She was most commonly called Betty for many decades, and that is the name I use until she becomes a published author, at which point I revert to the custom of calling her by the surname under which she published. In order to discuss themes important in Elliot's thinking while still respecting the right of living individuals to control the public telling of their own stories, I have in one instance replaced a name with a letter of the alphabet, and in another, avoided naming an individual entirely.

When writing about complex moments and movements in history, space constraints often require a narrow focus. This narrowness can become problematic if we are so immersed in the centered tradition that we forget that the water in which we swim is not the only or even the primary experience of the given historical period. As Catherine A. Brekus, W. Clark Gilpin, et al., have pointed out, scholarly attention in the study of American Christianity has tended to focus primarily on comparing white Protestantism in the United States with white Protestantism in the northern European nations from which early colonists came, rather than comparing American and global Christianity or various Christian experiences within the US.[2] This could lead to the latent assumption that white Protestantism is the American Christian experience, leaving gaping holes in our theology and practice. The cultural setting for this book is largely middle-class, white Protestantism in America from roughly the mid-1800s through the early 2000s because that is the milieu in which Elliot moved. We are the poorer if we fall into thinking that this view of the aquarium accurately represents the whole ocean, or even the largest or most important part of it.

Prologue

To a Watching World

ON MONDAY JANUARY 9, 1956, listeners to HCJB, "the Voice of the Andes," tuning in for the "Off the Record" radio program heard a disturbing news bulletin: five young American missionaries were missing—captured or killed in the jungles of Ecuador. The men had failed to make a scheduled radio check-in after trying to establish friendly contact with an isolated tribe known as "aucas." Over the centuries, "auca" spears had kept out Spanish conquistadors, Jesuit missionaries, nineteenth-century rubber hunters, twentieth-century oil company employees, plantation owners, neighboring tribal people—anyone who got too close to their borders. Their reputation as ferocious killers had reached almost mythic status.

Between them, the five missing Americans—Jim Elliot, Pete Fleming, Ed McCully, Nate Saint, and Roger Youderian—had ties along both coasts and through the heartland of the United States. HCJB continued to broadcast updates, which were quickly picked up in the US by NBC. As people across the country waited and prayed, a search party of neighboring Kichwa men, American missionaries, Ecuadorian soldiers, and a US Air Force air-rescue helicopter crew looked for the missing men by water, land, and air. On Tuesday, the Associated Press picked up the story, reporting that the missionaries' plane had been seen from the air, stripped to the frame. One lance-pierced body lay on the beach nearby. On Wednesday, a second body was spotted, and AP headlines proclaimed, "5 U.S. Missionaries Are Believed Slain." Thursday's headline read, "Four Bodies Found in Ecuador." On Saturday, January 14, the ground search party returned: all five men were dead.[1]

Hope for a rescue came to an end, but interest in what came to be called "Operation Auca" did not. On January 23, *Time* magazine ran a two-column synopsis of the event. On January 29, the *New York Times* published an article running to more than a page of newsprint, which placed the missionaries' deaths against the backdrop of a vast, hostile jungle where "barbaric" tribes fought to survive, relying on violence for self-preservation and living in fear.[2] The next day, *Life* magazine broke the first detailed story on "Operation Auca."

Life's nine-page spread introduced America to the faces of the five men—and the wives and young children they left behind—and told their story using excerpts from their diaries, film from their cameras (including the first photographs of the mysterious "aucas") and a moving photo essay by *Life* photographer Cornell Capa. Hurrying from New York to Ecuador, Capa had arrived just in time to record the last of the bodies being towed through the river, the hasty burial in a common grave, the soldiers nervously fingering rifles as they watched the jungles for signs of attack, and the drawn faces of the widows as they listened to details of the search and burial. Readers learned, in the men's own words, of their unexpected discovery of "auca" settlements during a routine flight, their strong desire to contact the tribe, the weeks of aerial gift drops and attempts to learn a few friendly phrases in the "auca" language, of a promising peaceful contact. Then the text told of harsh deaths, of the quiet strength of the widows in the face of grief, and of their desire that at some point, friendly missionary contact would still be made with the tribe that had killed their husbands. The article opened a window from America's living room into two alien worlds—that of the mysterious "stone-age" Amazonian tribal people and that of America's own evangelical Christian missionaries.

Public fascination with the story continued strong. In August, *Reader's Digest* published an article by Abe Van Der Puy of HCJB radio, called "Through Gates of Splendor." Van Der Puy had planned, at the request of the five widows, to expand that article into a full-length book, but as time went by, decided that his time and talents precluded a project of that scope. The task fell instead to one of the widows, Elisabeth Elliot, who had some background as a writer, and who was already at work compiling her husband Jim's letters and diaries into a biography.

In May 1957, about sixteen months after their first article had appeared, *Life* ran a follow-up article by Capa on the widows, with pictures—Barbara Youderian helping a Jivaro tribal woman learn the alphabet, Elisabeth Elliot teaching Bible classes for the Kichwa, Marilou McCully caring for missionaries' children, Marj Saint preaching in an Ecuadorian prison. The women saw this work as their vocation, with or without their husbands, and were continuing it, while praying that someone, somehow, would still be able to reach the "aucas." The article was timed to coincide with the release of Elisabeth Elliot's book on "Operation Auca," *Through Gates of Splendor*. The biography of Jim, *Shadow of the Almighty*, which had been put on hold while she wrote *Through Gates of Splendor*, was published the next year.

And then in November 1958, shocking the nation, *Life* magazine ran an eight-page article, "Child among Her Father's Killers: Missionaries Live with Aucas." Rachel Saint, sister of one of the dead men, and Elisabeth Elliot, with her three-and-a-half-year-old daughter, Valerie, had been invited to live, were in fact living, with the people who had killed their loved ones. Here were pictures: Valerie standing by one of the killers, Elisabeth cutting an "auca" woman's hair, Rachel and Elisabeth working together over vocabulary files. The article, written by Elisabeth Elliot in a thatched-roof, open-wall hut, described how she and Rachel Saint had been invited to join the tribe, talked about what it was like to live among them, and pondered the nature of God's leading and protection. It was read by approximately eighty-seven million Americans, an astounding 76 percent of adults. This was followed, in 1961, by Elliot's *The Savage My Kinsman*, a large coffee table–style book full of pictures and descriptions of "auca" tribal life and of Elisabeth and Valerie's life in their midst, interspersed with meditations on "auca" and American culture and on Christian faith.

Two years later, Elisabeth Elliot left the "aucas." She brought her daughter, Valerie, back to the United States and built a life for herself as a writer and Christian speaker.

This is how she is best known and most often remembered. It is neither the beginning of her story, nor the end.

PART 1

———————

1926-1952

1

Elisabeth Howard the Great

IN MAY 1927, as Charles Lindbergh soared east over the Atlantic from New York to Paris, a little American family of four, warmly bundled against the ocean breeze, steamed west from Belgium to the United States. They were missionaries, going home on furlough.

The mother of the little family, born Katharine Gillingham, was a slim, pretty woman in her late twenties, vivacious and outspoken. She had grown up with money, thanks to a great-uncle who had cornered the market on lightweight, versatile white pine just before a building boom, then bought stock in Bell Telephone Company at ten cents a share. Her father and grandfather ran a successful lumber business in Philadelphia. Her parents, Ida and Frank Gillingham, had a butler, a cook, two maids, a laundress, and a nanny for little Katharine, who was substantially younger than her two brothers. The family spent summers away from the city, where it was cooler. Katharine's parents held season tickets to the opera and treated their children with lovely things—their little daughter had a fur coat and hat, and a doll with a complete wardrobe, right down to kid gloves and silk stockings, made by her mother's dressmaker.

When Katharine was twelve, Ida Gillingham died, perhaps of pneumonia. Never a demonstrative man, her father withdrew into what Katharine later called a "black despair."[1] Doubly shaken by his grief on top of her own, Katharine tried to comfort her father by putting a brave face on her sorrow.

Although the family had always attended church, Christian faith didn't come alive for Frank Gillingham until, turning the pages of his wife's worn Bible after her death, he saw how much it had meant to her. He began attending Bible studies with Ida's sister, Lizzie, then taking Katharine, the only child still at home, with him to Lizzie's church. It was here that Katharine heard an explication of Christian teaching that rang true and made the faith her own.

Gradually, as the heavy weight of grief lessened, Katharine returned to her interests in school and friends. Frank Gillingham disapproved of college for women, so after high school graduation, she did volunteer work (World War I was in full swing) and spent time with friends. Her father bought her a car, and she was one of the first female drivers in Philadelphia. She must have cut quite a figure, zooming around the city with her fox furs flying.

———

The father of the little family on the steamship was Philip Eugene Howard Jr. Just a year older than his wife, he was tall and thin, thoughtful and well-spoken. Philip had loved to be outdoors from an early age—hiking, fishing, or just standing quietly, hands clasped behind his back, watching birds. As a boy, he could also be something of a harum-scarum. On one occasion he fired his slingshot from a hotel balcony at a wine merchant's display until he broke a bottle. On another, he played with Fourth of July fireworks his parents had forbidden. The resulting explosion cost him his left eye.

Philip's parents did not have a large margin financially. Family vacations were generally spent at an uncle's cottage in the mountains of New Hampshire, an affordable way to enjoy outdoor pursuits. They had one servant, a maid-of-all-work, thought of by many as the bare minimum for middle-class households at the time. And meat was a luxury at their dinner table. But Philip Howard Sr. and Annie Slosson Trumbull Howard were a warm, loving couple with a strong sense of fun and an active interest in people. They enjoyed their family a good deal.

Philip's father was publisher of the *Sunday School Times*, a major provider of Sunday school materials both nationally and internationally. The *SST*, as the Howards called it in their family shorthand, was something of a family business, bought by Philip's grandfather in the 1870s and edited first by the grandfather, then by an uncle, so the family name was fairly well-known within the evangelical world. Although Philip never had a crisis of belief in the religion his parents taught him, he struggled with a sense of failure in trying to live up to the standards he had learned, until one night a long talk with his uncle and a spiritual experience during prayer brought him settled peace. He was eighteen years old. Unable to enlist during the war because of his glass eye, he spent a year with the Pocket Testament League, handing out New Testaments and talking with men in Army camps around the country. Then he enrolled at the University of Pennsylvania. During his senior year he was elected to the prestigious Phi Beta Kappa academic honor society.

———

In the summer of 1918, Philip Howard attended a Victorious Life conference, where he responded to an altar call for missionary work. Among the others who went forward was a young woman named Margaret Haines, with whom Philip became friends. A few months later, Margaret introduced him to her neighbor, Katharine Gillingham. After two years of seeing each other in group settings—drives with friends, eating in company, birthday parties, house parties—Philip proposed. Katharine, who had already turned down several other marriage proposals, was startled; she had thought Philip interested in Margaret Haines. She made him wait six weeks while she thought it over—but he can't have been too worried, because he went home and told his family he was "practically engaged."[2]

His confidence was justified. She said yes on October 18, 1920. The couple took classes together at the Bible Institute of Pennsylvania, and since both had felt before they knew each other that God wanted them to work as missionaries, they prayed together about the where and the how. They eventually decided to join the Belgian Gospel Mission.

Philip and Katharine were married June 14, 1922. Their honeymoon— spent at Gale Cottage, where Philip had vacationed as a boy—was chiefly distinguished by a whole ham that Katharine had unwittingly purchased. She had always had other people to cook for her and hadn't realized that a ham was too large a cut of meat for two people. They ate ham in every form imaginable over the two weeks. Then they went home to pack. They sailed for Belgium a month after their wedding.

———

The Howards moved into a flat fifty-eight steps above a wine shop, with no running water and a bathroom shared with the neighbors. It was furnished with what Katharine later called "a huge and hideous" miscellany of furniture and heated by a single coal stove.[3] They were plunged immediately into work. Philip was made responsible for teaching a group of children from a nearby slum, although he and Katharine had just begun learning French. But despite the hard work, the Howards were happy. Philip bought a canary, and its bright songs cheered their little flat. They made some good friends. And they were young and in love.

In 1923, Katharine got pregnant. The thought of climbing all those stairs with a baby and a stroller was overwhelming. The Howards moved to a three-room flat—with running water!—on the second story of a brick row house. Philip Gillingham Howard was born on December 9, 1923. By this time Philip Eugene Howard Jr. was fluent in French and teaching in a French-language Bible school run by the mission. Katharine cared for little Phil and taught a French-language Bible class as well.

The Christmas Phil was two, Katharine spent most of December in the hospital because of a miscarriage. So the next year, when she was pregnant again and due in December, she talked the doctor into attending her at home. This time the baby was a girl. They named her Elisabeth.

———

Elisabeth Howard was a nice plump baby with a full head of downy blonde hair. Her father called her Betty; her mother, Bets or Bet. Her first memory of her mother was of sitting on Katharine's lap and looking up into her blue, blue eyes. Despite the nondemonstrativeness of her own upbringing, Katharine rocked and sang to her babies and tucked her children in at night with kisses. She was still the cheerful, lively person she had been in girlhood. For Katharine, lights blazed, radios blared, and children clattered around—a tendency toward the dramatic which young Betty picked up. When something tickled Katharine's funny bone she would laugh until tears rolled down her cheeks. She kept a neat house, and though she had come a long way from the honeymoon ham, she was still a no-nonsense cook. Dessert was usually something easy, canned fruit or store-bought cookies. If Betty asked for something more elaborate, Katharine would say, "You just go ahead and do all the fiddling you want."[4]

Betty would later write that as a child, she found her father's presence in their home "comforting."[5] He got back from work at the same time every night, and Betty would hang around the door watching for him, then wrap herself around his knees as he came inside. Philip had a sharp temper and would slam doors or stand up so quickly from the table that he knocked over his chair. He could be passive-aggressive, using his command of language to bait and provoke. But he struggled with himself, increasingly mastered his outbursts over time, and never let a blowup pass without apologizing afterward. And he was a fun daddy. He did sleight-of-hand magic tricks for the children and rode them around on his feet. Sometimes, for a special treat, he would take one of them on the train with him to his office. They would have lunch at a restaurant, and the child would spend the day playing with his paperclips and being fussed over by the staff. On Saturdays, he led long walks or outings to the zoo, the planetarium, the ocean. Philip loved birds, and he taught his children to recognize their calls and songs, to walk quietly and stand still, to identify nests and flight patterns. Every family member had their own bird call with which Philip called them when he wanted them. Betty's was the wood pewee.

———

When the little family of four—Philip, Katharine, three-year-old Phil, and five-month-old Betty—crossed paths with Lindbergh over the Atlantic, the Howards had been five years in Belgium and were taking their first furlough. Back in the States, they did some traveling before settling in to spend the rest of their three-month stay with Katharine's father and his second wife, Katharine's Aunt Lizzie. Then Philip's Uncle Charley, now editor of the *SST*, dropped a bombshell: he wanted Philip to come and work for him as the assistant editor.

The Howards were greatly upset. Philip had always said that if there was one thing he would never do, it was work for the *SST*. Katharine was pregnant again and couldn't imagine having anyone but her Belgian doctor for the delivery. They had been happy and settled in their little flat, with their friends and their work, looking forward to many more years there.

But Uncle Charley, the same uncle whose "wonderful talk" had made such a difference in Philip's spiritual life, must have made a persuasive case.[6] The Howards didn't even want to consider his proposition, but as they wrestled with it, they came to the conclusion that God wanted them to accept it.[7] So they did. Katharine would later write that at the time, it was the hardest decision they had ever faced.

In Belgium they had lived on a $100-a-month missionary salary provided by Katharine's father. When they decided to stay in the US, they had to scramble to find a place to live. They scraped together the money to buy a narrow three-story house with a tiny yard in the Germantown section of Philadelphia. The house needed major repairs—a new roof, which Frank Gillingham paid for, and a new furnace. Only one room was really warm in the winter, and it was that first winter that the baby, christened David Morris Howard, was born. In a humorous reversal of the era's popular Holiness motto, "Not somehow, but triumphantly," Katharine later said that the first year back in the US was survived, "NOT TRIUMPHANTLY, BUT SOMEHOW!"[8]

The next year, the Great Depression hit. The two hundred dollars the Howards had painstakingly saved disappeared when their bank failed. Although Frank Gillingham replaced the lost savings, this marked the beginning of what Katharine later called the days they did without— "Without maids, without money, without new clothes, without a washer, dryer, vacuum cleaner, radio, car—you name it, we didn't have it."[9] Philip's salary was cut. Katharine did the laundry by hand. Phil, Betty, and eventually Dave walked the 2 miles to school in all weathers, then home again at noon for a hot lunch. Katharine taught the children the maxim "Wicked waste makes woeful want."[10] They practiced many small economies—turning off the water, turning out the lights, using a tiny dot of toothpaste, saving the slivers of soap from the end of a bar in a small wire basket to be swished in dishwater. Betty was embarrassed by all the hand-me-downs they wore. But their house was furnished with beautiful oriental rugs and sterling silverware passed down from the Gillingham family, and they always had money to give—in the offering at church, to missions, to the down-and-out who came to their back door. It was not until she was in her teens that Betty began to realize that not everyone had those things.

Spiritual disciplines provided the framework for life in the Howard home. Philip rose early every morning for private prayer. Breakfast was at 7:00, and the children quickly learned that they were to be washed, dressed, and in their chairs by 6:55. After breakfast came family prayers—a hymn, a page from Hurlebut's *Story of the Bible*, Philip's short prayer for the help each needed for that day, and the Lord's Prayer—before everyone went their separate ways. After that, Katharine went to her rocking chair with her Bible, hymnbook, and prayer notebook. Dinner always ended with Philip reading aloud the day's selection of Bible verses from *Daily Light*, and with prayer.

Sunday was treated as a special day. The children had Sunday clothes, which they did not change out of after church. They played quietly and often went to noon dinner at Frank and Lizzie Gillingham's house—where they reveled in roast beef and chocolate cake—or had company to dinner. Meals at home were simpler, both because of Katharine's cooking and because of financial constraints. Soup and macaroni-and-cheese made regular appearances on the table, and there wasn't something different when company came, just more of it. But regardless of what was on the menu, hospitality was important. The children met many different people, often missionaries, from a wide range of backgrounds, and heard their stories. Dinner guests like Chinese missionary Leland Wang, with his motto, "no Bible, no breakfast," and the American Betty Scott Stam, who was later beheaded in China, made lasting impressions on Betty.[11]

Philip and Katharine ran an orderly household in other ways as well, teaching by example that there was a place for everything, and that things were to be in their places when not in use. Katharine cleaned the kitchen as she worked; Philip cleared his desktop before stopping work for the day. There was a switch over the door in every room. The parents looked a child in the eyes and gave a command, then moved for the switch if the child didn't obey. Betty had the courage of her convictions from infancy; she was stubbornly committed to her own courses of action, and she often refused to cry when spanked. She got more licks than Dave, who had figured out that punishment ended sooner if he howled right away. The children were expected to show respect—for adults, for authority, for private property—and to tell the truth. This teaching had its effect on Betty's conscience. When she was seven or eight years old, she decided she wanted to see what it was like to do something wrong and began looking for an opportunity. One day, leaving a friend's house, she found a Mickey Mouse watch lying on the newel post of the stairs. She stuffed it in her pocket and kept walking but hadn't gone far before the sensation of guilt became unbearable. She ran back to the house and left the watch on the back steps. Phil and Dave refused, often roughly, to let their sister play with them, and there were few girls close to Betty's age nearby.[12] When friends were available, she played "house" and other games with them. Otherwise she played alone or with her imaginary friend, Miss Dowd. Betty was praying for a sister, so she was pleased when her mother began knitting baby booties and gathering supplies to take care of a new baby. Virginia Anne Howard, called Ginny, was born in February 1934.

That was the beginning of two difficult years in the Howard family. First, as she did with all her children, Katharine had great difficulty with breastfeeding. It's not clear whether she was ever able to establish nursing. A private nurse, recovering from a major illness and wanting light work, came in to help. Then in short order, Philip got sick with his frequent and worrisome chest congestion, Betty got tonsillitis, and Phil got the measles, then the mumps. Just as he was recovering, Betty came down with mumps, and just as she was getting over them, Dave got them. Finally, Katharine had them as well. They had a quarantine sign on their door for five long months, meaning that only the primary wage earner could go in or out. After the mumps, Phil, Betty, and Dave had to have their tonsils out, and Dave had to have surgery on his inner ear. Then in November, Katharine got pregnant again. Thomas Trumbull Howard was born on a scorching late July day in 1935. Again Katharine struggled to breastfeed but was unable to. About the same time, Philip was ordered to half days of bed rest by his doctor in an attempt to ward off tuberculosis. He went to the office in the mornings, then worked at a lap desk in bed at home in the afternoons.

———

By 1936 family finances must have begun to improve. Philip and Katharine bought their first car, a used Plymouth, and sold the little house. With each new baby the house had felt smaller and smaller, and they were glad to move into a rental in a quiet neighborhood in Moorestown, New Jersey. The new house had seventeen rooms—though still only one bathroom!—and a big porch on two sides where the babies could play in the sun, and a large yard with mature trees and a sandbox.

The Howard household revolved around books and writing. There were bookcases in almost every room, even in the halls. The Bible was the book of books, and each child was given his or her own at age ten. Even as babies they were given picture books, and their mother read aloud to them from an early age. The dressed animals of Beatrix Potter gave Betty a "delicious feeling of order and comfort."[13] She identified the animals of A. A. Milne with members of the family: Katharine was Kanga, Phil was Pooh, Dave was Piglet, and she herself was Eeyore—a little apart from the others, seeing things differently from her own corner of the Hundred Acre Wood. Philip also read aloud to the children: Jonathan Edwards, George Whitefield, English travel writer George Borrow, to give them an ear for good writing, and Henry A. Shute's *Diary of a Real Boy*, which made them all roar with laughter. He kept a dictionary by the dinner table to settle any points of difficulty over the correct use of language. The children were aware that they came from a family of writers—their father, their great-uncle Charley, their great-great-aunt Annie Trumbull Slosson, and her brother, their great-grandfather H. Clay Trumbull.[14]

Betty's earliest surviving foray into publishing was a short book entitled *Party*, about a little girl's party for her doll. Philip ran a family newspaper for a while, and involuntary contributions were solicited from each of the children. Young Betty kept a diary, written with a chronically dull pencil in a large, round hand and labeled in all caps as being entirely off-limits to boys. It chronicled the happenings of a child's existence: playing at friends' houses; Sunday with its routine; school and its woes; playing Sorry and Tiddlywinks with friends; her father coming down with one of his worrisome colds; her little brother spilling her mother's coffee all over the good tablecloth; hide-and-seek and tag with her younger siblings when it was too chilly to go out; a real party at Aunt Annie's with games and favors.

In addition to the steady emphasis on tidiness, household chores were assigned to the children. They learned to make their beds, do the dishes, set the table, help with laundry, take out the trash, dust, sweep, and shake out the rugs. Betty helped to care for each of her three youngest siblings as they arrived. Katharine also had a series of live-in "mother's helps," who must have seemed more like a burden than a help at times. Some were

Bible school students, gone the better part of the day. One woman would lean over the banister in the morning and call down that she hadn't slept all night and couldn't possibly work that day; then Katharine had to bring her breakfast in addition to her other work. Another took the chickens Katharine had stewed for a company dinner, poured the good broth down the drain, and stuffed the chickens into the quart jars meant for the broth, mangling the dinner.

In the summer the Howard family adjourned to the White Mountains of New Hampshire, to the cavernous old house where Philip had vacationed as a boy and where Katharine and Philip had honeymooned. The house was lighted with kerosene lamps, heated with a huge fireplace, and filled with all manner of strange and wonderful things—fishing rods and guns, old furniture, stuffed animal heads, glass cases of pinned moths and butterflies, a stereopticon, paintings of distant and forbidding ancestors. Gale Cottage was a repository for a whole raft of eclectic reading material: Civil War field manuals; law books; Mrs. Oliphant; the unabridged *Arabian Nights*; Robert Louis Stevenson; *Hell on Ice*. The children read, swam, hiked, fished, played, hosted hymn-sings, made friends with the mice and chipmunks who crept into the house at night, watched birds, played charades, and learned botany from making pressed-flower books. Betty developed a love for nature that lasted the rest of her life.

In junior high, she began a scrapbook: snapshots with friends from summer camp; a report card that said she talked too much; a letter from author L. M. Montgomery in response to Betty's fan mail; brochures about nursing, a profession she was interested in pursuing. She kept souvenirs from a seemingly endless stream of plays, choir and orchestra concerts, variety shows, talent shows, and missionary meetings; a week with a friend at the friend's family summer home; the World's Fair; her second-place finish in the Moorestown Grange Spelling Bee.

During this period Betty put a good deal of time into art: drawing elegant fashions for paper-dolls, entering a coloring contest at Christmastime, and turning in several nicely illustrated school projects. She did a lot of writing, both in and out of school: stories of the Howard family dog, Tuck; an ending of her own to "The Lady or the Tiger?," a story about a young man's first date; a novella by "Elisabeth Howard, the Great."[15] As a freshman she won a contest sponsored by the American Legion with her essay on Americanism. Like much of her work at this time, it shows a tendency toward melodrama that would do credit to a young Anne Shirley. Betty had a penchant for writing stories featuring young women named Annie in hair-raising blood-and-thunder plots with impossibly starry-eyed endings.

One winter day, thirteen-year-old Betty came home from school and went into the kitchen to see her mother, who was fixing dinner. When Katharine looked up and asked, "Which would you like to have—another brother or another sister?" Betty's heart sank. She felt she had "helped to raise" the last two babies and didn't want to do it again.[16] The youngest Howard baby was born in 1940 on another hot July night and christened James Nash. The arrival of each new sibling provided Katharine with a natural opportunity to teach her elder daughter about human reproduction. Before Ginny was born, Katharine explained the way a baby grew inside its mother; this time she talked about a father's role in the process. Not long after, she took Betty for a drive and a more detailed discussion of menstruation and sex.

It was an important coming-of-age moment, but certainly not the first— nor the most pivotal—for Betty. The gift of a nicely bound Bible for her tenth birthday had been emblematic of other changes in her life. Betty had believed her parents' teaching about God as a young child of four or five. But it was the year she was ten that she had heard a preacher talk about Jesus's teaching that "no one can see the kingdom of God without being born again" (John 3:3 GNT). She wanted to be sure that she was in a position to "see the kingdom of God," so when the preacher gave an altar call, she had gone forward. As her understanding of Christian teaching continued to deepen, she had come to the conclusion that if she was going to accept Jesus's offer of rescue, she would need to let him be the one in charge of her life. She was twelve when she made a commitment to follow Jesus, praying: "Lord, I want you to do anything you want with me."[17]

2

Be, Not Seem

AT HALF-PAST FOUR in the morning on September 1, 1939, the ominous rumblings echoing across Europe distilled into the thunder of tank tread and the roar of radial engines as Germany invaded Poland. Great Britain and France had stood by while Germany violated the Treaty of Versailles again and again—amassing a huge military force, annexing first Austria and then the Sudetenland of Czechoslovakia—but with the fall of Poland they reluctantly declared war on Germany. World War II had officially begun. Although many Americans were strongly isolationist and the United States clung to official neutrality, the nation continued to sell arms to Allied combatants, protect the shipping of Allied nations from Axis navies, and otherwise become increasingly entangled in European affairs. The autumn of 1940 saw the institution of the first peacetime draft in US history, highlighting America's continued movement toward war.

Against this backdrop of upheaval and uncertainty, far-reaching changes occurred in the Howard family's ordered sphere. In January 1941, when Betty was fourteen, Uncle Charley died suddenly of a heart attack. Philip, who had been sick for several days with one of his frequent bouts with the flu, was still bedridden when he heard the news. He was not only grieved by the loss of his uncle but deeply discouraged and overwhelmed by having the full editorial responsibility for the *Sunday School Times* fall on his shoulders. Katharine's father had died just the month before, apparently of spinal cancer, and been buried beside his first wife, Katharine's mother. His widow, Katharine's Aunt Lizzie, had moved in with her daughter's family but was unhappy there. After several months, Lizzie approached Katharine with a proposal: she would provide the down payment for a house if the Howards would allow her to live in it with them. Katharine and Philip readily agreed.

That September the family moved into a big house with plenty of bedrooms, a fireplace, a big front porch covered in wisteria vines, and a large lawn shaded by trees. They hung a bird feeder outside the kitchen window and named the new house Birdsong. Nana, as the Howard children called Lizzie, moved into the master suite. She was convinced, apparently without foundation, that she had breast cancer and would die in a few weeks. Despite Katharine's repeated attempts to draw her into their family life, Lizzie kept to her rocking chair and her room. For the eight remaining years of her life, the family bore with her with a determined cheerfulness.

Katharine's father had left her a portion of his investment income, and with Philip's increased salary as editor, this allowed the Howards a financial leeway they hadn't had before. Seventeen-year-old Phil had graduated from high school in the spring, and now his parents would be able to send him to Canada's Prairie Bible Institute (PBI) in the fall—the beginning of the fulfillment of a lifelong dream for Phil, who had spent his childhood reading everything he could find about the Arctic. PBI required twelve hours a week "gratis work" from its students, and Phil would supplement his ninety-dollar annual tuition by shoveling coal. Betty had "longed" to attend Hampden DuBose Academy (HDA) in Florida ever since Uncle Charley had brought back a copy of the school's yearbook from a speaking trip. The pictures of beautifully dressed students against a backdrop of trimmed green grass, palm trees, beds of flowers, and white buildings bright in the sun had captured her imagination. And the idea of a Christian school appealed strongly to Betty, who knew no other Christians at Moorestown High and felt "very much left out." Now the three hundred dollars a year for room, board, and tuition at HDA would be possible.[1]

Phil and Betty left New Jersey by train in the fall of 1941, Phil heading northwest to chilly Alberta and Betty south to Orlando. She was thrilled right up until the train left the station. As she lost sight of her family, the bottom dropped out from under her heart, and she was flooded with affection for home and the homefolks. She knew she would not see them again for almost a year. The family's added income allowed for the tuition at PBI and HDA, but only just—there was no question of traveling home for Christmas. Betty wore her good northeastern autumn traveling clothes, "a beige *felt* hat . . . blue *wool* dress, and brown *suede* pumps," which she quickly realized were not quite the thing as the train rocked south into the damp heat of a Florida September. A teacher dressed in cool white met her with the school's station wagon and drove her to the old mission-style hotel building that was to be her home for the next nine months.[2]

———

Hampden DuBose Academy was begun by Pierre Wilds DuBose and Gwynn Ewell DuBose in 1934. The school, named after Mr. DuBose's father, was initially housed in what had been the Francis Marion Hotel. In 1943, two years after Betty started attending, the DuBoses bought Sydonie, a forty-one-room lakefront mansion on two hundred acres that had originally belonged to James Laughlin Jr., a steel tycoon on the magnitude of Rockefeller or Carnegie. A series of postcards from just after the move show various beauty spots on the Zellwood, Florida, campus with the accompanying note: "A Christ-centered interdenominational college preparatory high school on a picturesque two-hundred-acre campus. Here boys and girls enjoy the culture and refinement of the Old South along with the health of Florida sunshine and citrus groves. The cultivation of spiritual life, sound education, cultural awareness and athletic competition all combine to fulfill the purpose of the school—'Educating for Eternity.'"[3]

HDA was run along lines similar to those of Amy Carmichael's Dohnavur Fellowship: the DuBoses asked God for money rather than soliciting funds directly from people and provided employees with food and housing but not a wage or salary. They aimed "to train Christian leadership," and to that end they operated what they called a fivefold program of training, focused on "spiritual, intellectual, physical, cultural and social advantages," and "the disciplines of the work program which aid in developing Christian character."[4] The school offered basic courses—four science classes; three English classes; three math classes; US and world history; a choice of Spanish, French, or Latin; Bible, where freshmen and sophomores read the Pentateuch and the Gospels, while juniors and seniors studied Acts and Daniel; a handful of electives; and mandatory study hall, where students were to spend any portion of the school day when they were not in class. In addition to Bible class, students were given Bible teaching in church, chapel, vespers, Bible conferences, dorm prayer times, and devotions at the beginning of every class period, and were encouraged to pursue private devotions. Although it was a small student body, with eighteen juniors and just nine seniors during Betty's senior year, there was also a dizzying array of extracurricular activities advertised, including swimming, boating, volleyball, speedball, basketball, track and field, football, baseball, softball, tennis, table tennis, archery, badminton, bowling, and horseback riding.

If Betty Howard had not been interested in clothes before, she would have become so at HDA out of self-defense. Before the school year started, students received a six-page list of required clothing for weekdays, Sundays, and formal occasions in each season (summer, winter, and the elusory "between seasons"). Public school students of the time had their own strict, self-imposed dress code, but it was nothing like this. Headed "Definite Needs," the list spelled out students' wardrobes in exhaustive detail. For female students this included "two suits, slacks, pedal-pushers, three pairs of cotton pajamas, two pairs of flannel pajamas (not shorties), rain gear . . . plastic boots," as well as hats, stockings, white gloves, and two evening dresses. "Every evening dress must have straps and a net stole or cape of dress material." The specific fabrics required for many of the items were mentioned, along with acceptable colors and accessories for each season. HDA students were to wear "'appropriate travel clothing'—suits and heels for the girls and ties and jackets for the boys"—on their way to and from the school. On campus, they dressed for dinner in the evenings. The cost of this type of wardrobe could be a real burden for families, and Betty clearly worried over the strain on her family. But wearing what Mrs. DuBose considered the correct clothing for every occasion was part of the culture and refinement the school promised to instill.[5]

The available record of Betty's first two years at HDA is sparse. Katharine's memoirs provide a few details about what was happening in the family during those years, and school yearbooks and memories of other alumni provide background. A fuller picture emerges in Betty's letters home during her senior year of high school. As was common before the advent of cheap long-distance telephone calls, the Howard family corresponded weekly.

Each Sunday the absent family members would write a letter to the home folks, and Katharine (and sometimes Philip) would write to each of the absent children. These letters were passed around so that Katharine enclosed Phil's letters from PBI with her own and sent them on to Betty, and vice versa. At the beginning of her senior year, Betty asked, "Mother—would you mind keeping my letters—I have no diary this year & would like a record."[6]

As an adult, Betty would write of herself and her siblings, "We never were teenagers. I can't help being very thankful that the term had not been thought of in my day."[7] Actually, the word *teenager* came into widespread use in 1944, just as seventeen-year-old Betty was finishing high school, and was coined as a needed descriptor for a group that had already been recognized by American society in one form or another for more than seventy years. The fact of puberty is unchanged by societal trends, and "youth," with its emotional intensity and volatility, its dreams for the future and "concentration on the instant," its potential for greatness and for trouble, had been recognized as distinct from both childhood and adulthood for decades before Betty reached her teens.[8]

The cultural conversation about "youth" as a discrete group focused, then as now, on adult concerns about young delinquents, rebels, and hedonists. This must be what the adult Betty was thinking of when she disclaimed the label "teenager." "We were not taught," she wrote, "to expect a stage of chaos and rebellion."[9] But the young woman who lives again on the faded pages of the letters sounds very much like a teenager. She is breezy and cheerful, full of enthusiasms. Her handwriting has matured to a slender, adult script, but her letters are full of slang and sentences beginning with the word *well*. She spells *thanks* as *thanx*, and writes her mother's name and address on the envelope in bubble letters. The front of her Bible is filled with snappy aphorisms: "Let Go and Let God," "Sin will keep you from this book, or this book will keep you from sin," "God said it; Jesus did it; I believe it; That settles it." She dislikes the way she looks in pictures and carries herself with the slouch of a tall girl who wishes she were shorter.[10] She is concerned about whether her mother is working too hard, is outraged by her mother's interference in her life, and abases herself in the proverbial sackcloth and ashes when she makes a mistake. She works hard herself, but much of her work goes to make play. She is thinking about her future, dreaming of greatness, and wanting to find the right life path.[11]

By September 12, Betty and Dave—Betty returning for her senior year and Dave a rising junior starting his first year at HDA—were settled in at school. Betty was ensconced in a two-bedroom suite with bathroom, dressing room, and "darling window seat," which she shared with a junior, a sophomore, and a freshman. She wrote home:

> Here I am again in grand old H.D.A! You can't possibly imagine how wonderful it is to be back! Everyone is so swell, and the place is so lovely and cool and I'm _so_ happy! I can't really believe I won't be coming back next year. Honestly, I'll just die. I'm hanging on to each day as it passes. Well, praise the Lord He's made it possible for you to send me here for three _perfect_ years. . . . Please pray for my year here—my _last_ one—that it will be _all_ that the Lord wants for me, because truly I want to give Him my best, trusting implicitly in Him to make the year _count_.[12]

HDA students were expected to dive right into the work program, the fifth pillar of the school's educational platform. Not only did it add to their education; it provided much of the labor that kept the school functioning. By the time she wrote her first letter home Betty had already spent a good deal of time cleaning various campus buildings, helping prepare meals, and serving coffee to adults and guests after dinner. Various Christian speakers came to the school to address the students, and people who lived within driving distance came to hear them, so that there were often groups of adult guests until late at night. Work-program jobs were assigned among all the students and rotated biweekly. Boys' jobs included waiting tables, blowing the rising and lights-out bugle, burning trash, and "lock-up," where a student armed with a billy club patrolled the grounds. Girls were assigned gardening, housework, and waiting on Mrs. DuBose. Betty's various jobs appear regularly in her letters home: "I'm sort of tired—kitchen for four consecutive hours sort of wears on you, but I love it! The joy of _the Lord_ is my strength!"[13] She was also washing linens by hand, scrubbing the large outdoor porch (with a horrifying succession of cleansers including bleach, ammonia, and kerosene), arranging flowers ("that means 9 vases and an Italian bowl as big as a bird bath, without any exaggeration"), putting down rugs and hanging drapes and curtains in preparation for winter, washing windows, cleaning woodwork, and polishing silver.[14]

Hard work and cheerfulness were not the only things Betty was practicing. Whether or not she was thinking of herself as a writer by now, she was certainly writing. In addition to school assignments, she was in demand among her schoolmates as a poet and regularly composed original poems for a variety of social events, the school paper, the yearbook, and just because. At HDA, she later wrote, "I was encouraged to write. . . . I began to try to think things through, to clarify alternatives and to shape ideas into words."[15] Her weekly letters to her family and a variety of friends gave her plenty of opportunity to practice narration and description, although they showed the uneven quality one would expect from a high-schooler, ranging from the poetic to the inane.

In late September, Betty wrote to thank her mother for a package of food and to ask for some stamps and some things she had left behind: notebook paper, stationery, some poetry and a story she had written ("DON'T READ THE TRASH, PLEASE!!" she begged), and a folder of bits of other writers' work that she had filed away for future reference.[16] These saved bits—both one's own work, however inadequate it seems, and tidbits by others which have resonated for some reason—are tools of the writer's trade that can serve as catalysts for new work. Betty would save clippings related to things she might want to write about for the rest of her life.

She not only expressed insecurities about her writing; she also voiced her ambitions. She was studying the Romantics in English, and quoted a few lines from Wordsworth: "The Poets, who on earth have made us heirs / Of truth and pure delight by heavenly lays! / Oh! Might my name be numbered among theirs, / Then gladly would I end my mortal days."[17] "Of course I realize that there are lots of things of far greater eternal value than poetry," she mused, "but how I long to write one really good poem, or compose one piece, or write a book good enough to be published! Well, whatever will honor the Lord is what I want, after all. 'No purpose, no aim, no cause, but His!'"[18]

———

For her senior year, Betty was taking English 4, general science, American history, and a one-semester course in civics, and she had three study hall periods, which she used for practicing music and speech. She felt competitive about her schoolwork, writing, "I'm going to get that speech award this year if it kills me and also retain music award. Well—I can do <u>all</u> things through Christ which strengtheneth me. My motto for the year is 'Not overwork, but overflow.'"[19] But her extracurricular activities occupy the most space in her letters home. In the first class meeting of the year—an outdoor affair involving snacks and made particularly exciting by an interruption from a nearby alligator—Betty was elected senior class president. She was also elected president of the literary society, made captain of one of the two girls' sports teams, and elected editor of the *Esse* (the yearbook). There were game nights, bowling, snacks hosted in the teachers' quarters, late-night sessions playing around in the kitchen, and afternoons when "Doc," as students called Mr. DuBose, would play home movies.[20] Betty loved riding the school's horses, donated by the father of an alumna. And in the bits of spare time left between everything else, she listened to the radio—the New York Philharmonic; the Blondie show, based on the comic strip—and she read. "I'm reading 'Jane Eyre' and it certainly is one of the most extraordinarily well-written books I ever read. A marvelous vocabulary and diction."[21]

———

The first plank in the platform of education at Hampden DuBose was religious teaching, a major part of the school's attraction for Betty. She found the community of other people from similar backgrounds and belief systems encouraging, and she loved the opportunity to do things like gather around the piano after church with a group of friends and sing hymns. She was working to consistently pursue a personal spiritual practice as well, and finding personal connections to God. "He really means a lot to me—more each day."[22]

For Betty, faith meant more than following a set of rules for behavior. The school motto was "Esse Quam Videri," "to be, rather than to seem," and she took it seriously. She wanted her actions to line up with God's will, but she wanted to experience inner transformation as well—to have her visible self and her inner person be consistent. She worked to discipline her thoughts and feelings and change her attitude as well as her behavior, describing one such incident in a letter home. The students waiting on guests had served a multicourse meal and had just finished

BE, NOT SEEM 31

cleaning up when another group arrived, and they had to prepare fresh food and start again. "I could have cussed, almost, I was so mad, and about that time Bruce came into the pantry singing 'Thank you, Lord' and it certainly was a rebuke to me. Well, I began to thank the Lord for another opportunity to serve Him and I finished up the evening with real joy."[23] When she discovered that one of her roommates didn't think she could do anything wrong in a place with rules for behavior such as HDA had, Betty was concerned about the younger girl. "She doesn't think much about unselfishness, and doesn't seem to realize that there is any sin besides movies, dancing, etc.," she wrote to her mother. "Please pray that I may in some way be a testimony to her. You know how hard it is when you're rooming with someone, because they know everything about you, and the least thing counts, but He is able to keep me from falling, and I'm banking on that."[24]

Betty also worked to make Bible reading a priority, believing God would communicate with her in its pages: "I am reading through the Bible consecutively, something I haven't done before, and my what blessings God has given me! I'm up to Deut 12. I usually have to get up early to read, but it's worth it!!"[25] She felt that her effort was rewarded. "The Lord is certainly good to me—now I have my quiet time at 6 since I have to go in kitchen [sic] at 7 and He has spoken very clearly to me through His word every morning."[26]

———

The student body at HDA was often described as being made up in equal parts of MKs (missionary kids), PKs (preachers' kids), and OKs (ordinary kids). It was the usual procedure in the 1940s for missionaries to send their children away to boarding school for their education, often as soon as they were school-aged. Mr. DuBose had himself been an MK—his parents had been missionaries in China—and one of his goals in starting HDA was apparently to provide a home away from home for children and teens like the one he had once been. His attempt to create a home-like atmosphere is apparent in the school's traditions, which went beyond standard US holiday celebrations.

The first such event in Betty's senior year was the "Senior Sneak," a class trip that she looked forward to with great anticipation. Three-quarters of the fun was getting off the campus without the junior class noticing. The rest seems to have come from food. After much plotting and planning, the nine seniors crept out of English class and piled into Mr. DuBose's car, ducking down in the back seat so no one could see them go. He drove them to the station, where they caught the train for Orlando. There they had lunch, called HDA to tell the juniors they were gone, wandered around town, had supper, played miniature golf, and ate barbecue. In the morning, they had breakfast, walked over to the former Academy buildings, ate a large brunch, walked around town again, bought gifts for the DuBoses, walked some more, and ate supper, finishing their fling with popcorn on the train ride back to Zellwood.

Halloween was the next big event on the HDA calendar, and pictures of the party always merited a big spread in the *Esse*. In 1943 it consisted of a parade, a costume contest—the senior class had a group costume as a war-bond parade float, with Betty as the Statue of Liberty—lawn games, a "perfectly terrible Poe story" retold in the dark at the edge of the lake by a teacher, and all the "ice cream, doughnuts, punch, popcorn and apples" they could hold. "We . . . ate till we popped," Betty reported cheerfully.[27]

World War II, which the US had officially entered almost two years before, had its effect on the school. Betty wrote home about how sheltered they were from the war, but they were certainly aware of it, as evidenced by the war-bond costumes. They practiced blackouts. Their access to goods was affected, and Betty bought her baccalaureate dress early to get it before clothing rationing began. The DuBoses started what they called Victory Club, a combination Bible class and social hour in town for service members in training or waiting to ship out. "Doc" would teach and the high-school girls provided conversation and square-dance partners; from this larger group Mrs. DuBose would invite soldiers she felt were respectable to many of the school's club meetings and holiday celebrations. Former students, and family members of students and faculty, were enlisting or being drafted.

But with all this, the war must have seemed a bit remote. It hit closer to home in November, when Betty's science teacher learned that his twenty-five-year-old brother had died of a pulmonary embolism they believed to be connected to his Army Air Corps training. "It was a great shock," she wrote to her family, "but the Lord has a perfect plan, and we never know what He may have been saving him from. Mr. and Mrs. Glat took it beautifully—they left on Friday afternoon for Illinois where the funeral will be."[28] Although it's hard to tell with no context from tone of voice or body language, Betty's response to her teacher's loss sounds almost pat. While it would be unsurprising for a teenager with little personal experience of bereavement to lack imaginative empathy, her comment suggests an underlying belief that calm, stoic acceptance is the best way to handle grief.

———

The next big event of the year was Thanksgiving. Betty started the day by playing in a basketball game, then washed the tablecloths and other linens and decorated the dining area. Decorating for formal events was always elaborate at HDA, and she helped make place cards and programs, create massive centerpieces of candles, greenery, flowers, and fruit, and set up sprays of flowers and greenery throughout the dining room. Finally she could dress for dinner. Her date for the evening, Pete DuBose, brought her a corsage of red roses, which must have looked striking against her rustling blue taffeta formal and blonde hair. Dinner was roast chicken with lots of trimmings, and there were ice cream sundaes for dessert. Various students played music, delivered toasts and readings, and gave testimonies, and Betty recited an original poem. "Oh, how wonderful the Lord is to us!" she wrote afterward. "Imagine a perfect banquet like that, with a war on in Europe and practically everywhere else but here. The Lord truly 'hath done great things for us, whereof we are glad!'"[29]

Pete, a junior, was Pierre Wilds DuBose Jr., the son of Mr. and Mrs. DuBose, and Betty's regular date to school events her senior year. Dating was allowed at Hampden DuBose, and dates for formal occasions were assigned as part of the "social events . . . to train them in Christ-honoring poise and etiquette." Pete was apparently interested in Betty beyond the call of duty, judging by the regularity with which he gave her presents and his persistence in spending time with her. So were several other HDA students and alumni. Betty's letters are littered with references to dinner dates, corsages, correspondence, and birthday and Valentine's Day gifts from a variety of young men.

Years later, Betty would describe her younger self as a painfully shy "wallflower" who was "not . . . what the young men that I knew seemed to be looking for,"[30] quite different from the young woman who emerges from the letters. The difference may be caused by her natural insecurity. More than thirty years later, during a Howard sibling reunion, Dave was startled when his siblings "talked about the terrific inferiority complex they've had all their lives." Betty told him, "You wouldn't believe how inferior I feel."[31] Tom would later describe her as "terribly unsure inside herself."[32] Perhaps she didn't think the boys who kept writing and sending gifts and asking her out to dinner were actually seriously interested. In any event, it's clear that the boys who were interested in her were generally not interesting to her. She summed up one date to her mother: "Good dinner, good time! Good kid—(but who likes kids?)"[33]

———

Like many religious educational institutions, HDA had a pledge which its students were required to sign. Students agreed to abstain from certain behaviors, including "movies at theaters . . . dancing, drinking, card-playing, or smoking," and the administration expelled students who violated the terms.[34] The pledge was presumably intended to delineate what it looked like to live according to the standards for Christian behavior set out in the Bible. Unfortunately, this approach to guiding spiritual practice often seems to degenerate into an attempt to control people's spiritual condition by controlling their actions, and HDA did not escape this hazard. Students' spiritual state was judged by external behavior and external pressures applied to bring their spiritual selves into line. In early December, Betty wrote to mournfully inquire about the weather and the Christmas preparations at home, lamenting that Florida's heat and humidity didn't seem like winter at all and that she wouldn't be able to send home presents for her family; Mr. DuBose had revoked their privileges because students were not demonstrating spiritual fervor.

Disciplining people for a thing so thoroughly in the eye of the beholder tends to break down sensitive spirits while hardening the tough-minded. Certainly the pledge and other attempts of the administration to control the spiritual atmosphere didn't stop students who were determined to do things differently. In a private note to her mother, Betty wrote of fellow students who were making out, some with several different partners. Another former student described being sent to school as an alternative to bad influences at home and finding another bad crowd ready-made and waiting at HDA.

———

December was a month of great excitement. Betty's birthday was the twenty-first, and of course Christmas at HDA was celebrated with grandeur. In her last Sunday letter before the holiday, Betty wrote a bit wistfully of how nice it would be if the whole family could be together. But she quickly reminded herself of the apostle Paul's words on finding contentment in all circumstances and finished by counting her blessings and looking forward to seeing her parents at graduation.

Her birthday itself coincided with the annual buffet supper. Betty played the piano and helped serve coffee for guests during supper, then was feted with a big birthday cake. The next evening she returned from bowling to find a surprise party waiting for her, with decorations, another huge cake, and a whole group of students gathered to sing "Happy Birthday" as she came into the room. She received gifts from several admirers, including Pete.

On Christmas Eve, Betty was part of the group that helped with the weekly Victory Club meeting off campus, then went out Christmas caroling. When they got back to campus in the early morning hours, she served coffee to guests, staff, and alumni who had come to spend Christmas, then helped finish the Christmas preparations—wrapping gifts, hanging dozens of stockings, and washing dishes. By then it was time for the rising bugle. Everyone sang Christmas carols around the tree and opened stockings. After a late breakfast, preparations for Christmas dinner kicked into high gear. And after dinner, there was a formal Christmas party for soldiers from Victory Club. Betty got home from the party around 1:00 a.m. on Boxing Day and collapsed into her bed, tired but happy.

———

January was quiet. Betty was down and out with an infected scrape on her knee that required a week of bed rest, and everything seemed to be in the post-holiday doldrums. In her family letter she wrote sadly of missing suppers around the fire on Sunday evenings at home and grumpily of the late-night gabfests and flighty girls she felt Dave was wasting his time on. But by the end of the month, with the annual Valentine's Day party to plan for and look forward to, she started to sound more chipper.

On Monday of party week, Betty cleaned, picked flowers, and packed dishes for a women's meeting associated with the school. She traveled to Orlando, cleaned the venue, set up for the meeting, prepared food, served guests, and cleaned up afterward, getting home after suppertime. On Tuesday she got up early to make charlotte russe (spending three-and-a-half hours whipping thirteen quarts of cream), went to one class, and spent the rest of the morning and afternoon setting up for another meeting. That evening she ran a buffet supper table for almost ninety women and cleaned up afterward, getting back to her room at 1:00 a.m. On Wednesday she went to her first-period class, then spent the rest of the day working on the Valentine's Day party, followed by a meeting of the student body in the evening. Thursday and Friday she spent the whole day working on the party, with Victory Club Friday evening.

The party was Saturday night. Students played organized games around the lavishly decorated campus, then provided formal entertainment by singing, playing, and reciting. Betty sang a duet with Pete's older sister, Peyton DuBose. The DuBoses took the opportunity afforded by the party to announce Peyton's engagement, handing out favors and having the older students serve cake and ice cream. Betty, who had missed supper because she was serving, finished up the night by taking down the decorations and cleaning up from the party and finally got a chance to eat some leftover cake and ice cream just before she went to bed at 3:00 a.m. She was up again early the next morning for church, spent the afternoon serving coffee and doing dishes until time for supper, and finished the exhausting week by singing with the choir at a nearby church's evening service. She snatched a few moments to write to her mother, warning her that she probably wouldn't be able to write again this week since she would be helping to put on the wedding.

Because her fiancé was shipping out for Europe soon, Peyton DuBose was married a week after the engagement was announced. The wedding was held on campus, and the students put a tremendous amount of work into the event. It seems unlikely that Betty attended any more classes in the week before the wedding than she had in the week before Valentine's Day. She wrote her mother the day after with a rapturously detailed description of the event—the altar decorated in white satin, the music, the dresses, the flowers, the supper, the guests. "It was absolutely the most gorgeous wedding anyone could dream of."[35]

The next big project of Betty's senior year was the yearbook. School was canceled for a day while a professional photographer took staged photos. Betty was responsible for acquiring the props—sports equipment, furniture, camping accessories, food and drink, articles of clothing, floral arrangements—and for writing a good deal of the content, including two poems. As editor, she was also in charge of layout. After it was over she began a family letter, writing a little giddily, "Another tremendously busy week has just flown by and again I take typewriter in hand to write you a letter in pen, because I couldn't find my pencil, so you'll have to excuse crayons."[36] She was ecstatic at having pulled it all off but told her family she was praying not to get caught up in her accomplishments but to bring glory to God.

———

By early May the class of 1944 had turned their attention to graduation, and preparations for the big event were in full swing. Betty ordered her invitations and wrote anxiously to her mother asking if she could have some money to pay for them. All year she had worried over how much it was costing to keep her in school and provide for her fun and her fancy clothes, and she hated asking for money again, particularly because it was still up in the air whether her mother would be able to afford to come to her graduation. Nevertheless, she told her parents, she was sure God would provide for them.

There was still plenty to do, but much of the workload was beginning to shift onto the shoulders of the junior class. Betty luxuriated in the chance to sit and enjoy coffee on the porch instead of having to serve it. She was overjoyed when her parents decided they could both come to see her graduate. The ceremony was held on May 23, with speeches, awards, music, flowers, and all the usual trappings of an HDA celebration. Betty graduated, as she would later say, "with most of the available honors," including that of valedictorian.[37]

Katharine also attended Phil's graduation from Prairie Bible Institute, where the speaker used Matthew 9:38 (KJV)—"Pray ye . . . the Lord of the harvest," Jesus tells his disciples, "that he will send forth labourers into his harvest"—to exhort his audience to pray for God to send out more missionaries. Katharine had an uncomfortable feeling, when she began to pray, that the Lord was asking her: "Whose children are you going to pray Him to send?"[38]

———

Betty's high school letters are peppered from beginning to end with gushing exclamations about HDA. She doesn't make a fuss about the work of the Christmas festivities keeping her up for almost forty-eight hours straight, or about missing class for days in a row before the Valentine's Day party, or about so often having to cobble together meals out of leftovers. The closest she gets to complaining is when she talks about Mrs. DuBose. Gwynn DuBose could be cordial and kind, but she could also be harsh. Betty's letters home describe one evening when the older woman gathered the high school girls for a warm, friendly conversation about etiquette, attire, and young men, and another where she chastised Betty harshly because younger students had spilled brass polish in the DuBose suite. These back-and-forth moods occurred regularly enough that Betty expected them, observing in one letter that although Mrs. DuBose had recently been encouraging her to spend time with Pete, she would probably change courses soon and lecture her for paying too much attention to him.

Other alumni remember troubling behavior from both Gwynn and Pierre DuBose. William F. Luck Sr. writes of impromptu compulsory meetings in the chapel when Mrs. DuBose would rant at the student body about their attitudes, then make them sit for hours until someone confessed—to something, anything, no matter how inoffensive. Mary Anne Phemister remembers Mr. DuBose saying repeatedly, "If I tell you the moon is made of green cheese, then I expect you to say, 'Yes sir! I believe it even smells like green cheese.'"[39] The couple also passed on racial prejudice, idealizing "the culture and refinement of the Old South" in the school's promotional materials, warning students on lock-up duty to watch out for black men "lurking" in the orange groves, and inviting at least one visiting speaker who taught that rock-and-roll was bad because "the rhythm . . . came straight from the jungles of Africa."[40]

While many alumni share negative experiences, many others report that their time at the school was, in the balance, a positive thing: "While it is true that there were a good many things not right at HDA, there were more that were right." "This was one of the happiest times of my life." "I have many wonderful memories." These different experiences are surely influenced, as one former student wrote, by differences in "personalities and backgrounds."[41] The upbeat persona and the inclination toward stoicism that appear in Betty's letters may have contributed to her positive description of the school.

The positive things she had to say about HDA may also be tied to inexperience. When it came to adult-child relationships, Betty had been raised to obey first and ask questions later. Uncle Charley had praised the school; her parents were sending her there; and she may not have realized, at least at first, that there was any other way for things to be. Then, too, she was strongly invested in pursuing a personal relationship with God, and the DuBoses functioned as arbiters of that relationship.

Betty's attitude toward HDA would change over the years. In 1957 she would write privately to her mother that she could no longer recommend the school when Peyton took over leadership. In 1965 she would worry over her niece Kay attending HDA. In a 1966 letter to her mother she would deliver a stinging assessment of the school: the DuBoses said that HDA epitomized Christian society, but their actions directly contradicted Christian teaching; they were manipulative and tyrannical; they used the school for their own gain. In 1967 she would name specific things that had happened while she was a high-schooler at HDA: Gwynn DuBose had spanked her and publicly called her a prostitute; Peyton had shouted repeatedly at another student that she was going to hell—for wearing the wrong set of gym clothes. As an adult, Betty believed that the administration at Hampden DuBose Academy had failed to live out their claims to represent Christ and had dangerously muddied the waters around the idea of what it meant to be Christian.

Just after her fortieth birthday, Betty would offer her mother an explanation for not speaking more openly during her time at HDA. Gwynn DuBose had made her promise not to tell, she had been afraid of what they would do to her if they found out she told, and she had felt a sense of loyalty to them and to the school. When she had made a few hesitant attempts to hint at what was going on, she had felt that no one believed her. It had not encouraged her to risk a clearer statement of the facts.

And the situation was complicated by the fact that she also felt there had been legitimately good things about attending HDA. Betty was not the only one of the Howard children to share negative experiences at the school later in life, and Katharine was understandably upset as she grasped more of their experience there. But, Betty told her—in the same letter in which she described spankings, public shaming, and threats of hell—Tom was right when he said the school had also been good for them. She said that good and bad were mixed up together in all human endeavors and told her mother not to worry about it any longer.

All this would take time. In her formative high school years, Hampden DuBose Academy was a strong influence on Betty. Whatever the atmosphere she had grown up in at home, the climate at HDA did not encourage critical thought about religious systems or Christian culture. Betty Howard was committed to pursuing a personal relationship with God. It's unsurprising that at seventeen, she seems to have absorbed her surrounding religious environment fairly uncritically—not only the good and the true, but also the platitudes and cultural views mistaken for biblical values. It's equally unsurprising that the unfolding events of her life would challenge every assumption.

For Christ and His Kingdom

BETTY'S FATHER HAD BEEN Phi Beta Kappa at an Ivy League school, and his love of learning stayed with him all his life. His children "just took it for granted" that they would go to college.[1] They knew their father hoped they would attend his alma mater, but they also knew they were ultimately free to make their own choice, and that money was an object. Wheaton College, where Philip was a trustee, was substantially cheaper than Penn. As an added incentive, children of trustees received a substantial scholarship, lowering the cost even more. So Betty chose Wheaton.

Although not a member of the Ivy League, Wheaton College had prestige of its own. By the time Betty arrived at the school, it was one of the oldest Christian colleges in the United States, with more than ninety years as an institution under its belt. The school had "a sterling reputation" in the close-knit evangelical community for sound theology and academic rigor.[2] The latter was a self-fulfilling prophecy. With far more applicants than places—about 25 percent of applicants were admitted in the fall of 1944—Wheaton could afford to pick and choose, and they chose the cream of the academic crop.

Theologically, Wheaton's origins were thoroughly entwined with those of American Christian social activism. As slave-holding became an increasingly divisive issue in the mid-1800s, the white American Methodist church, which had always been vocally antislavery, had decided to allow slaveholders to continue as members in good standing. A splinter group that abhorred this compromise withdrew and established the Wesleyan church. The new denomination emphasized not only abolition but pacifism, revivalism, temperance, health reform, coeducation, and the full personhood of women and children.

Over the course of the next decade, some Wesleyans became concerned that children raised in the denomination were abandoning abolitionist beliefs when they went away to college. In 1853 they founded Illinois Institute, a college which was, as historian Donald Worster says, "militantly abolitionist and moderately feminist," and "highly conservative on issues of personal morality."[3] By 1859 the school was badly in debt, and the Wesleyans turned for help to Jonathan Blanchard, a Congregationalist whose outspoken support for abolition and emphasis on personal holiness were similar to their own. In 1860 the school passed into his hands.

Jonathan Blanchard appointed a new board of trustees and renamed the school, calling it Wheaton College after donor Warren Wheaton. Blanchard was a "radical" who saw Christians as social-justice activists working to remove impediments to Christ's millennial reign.[4] He strove to make Wheaton a school that led students "both by precept and example . . . into a zeal for reformation," and heavily emphasized the school's motto, "Christo et Regno Ejus," "For Christ and His Kingdom."[5]

After twenty-two years in office, Jonathan Blanchard retired at the age of seventy-one and handed the reins of the school to his son Charles. The younger Blanchard would hold his position as president for forty-three years. In his writing and the descriptions of others, he comes across as a warm, kind person, better suited for giving pastoral care than for the managing and fundraising that the job required. Nevertheless, he was committed to upholding his father's legacy.

During Charles Blanchard's lifetime, a seismic shift occurred in the way Americans thought about Christianity. This change revolved around so-called higher criticism, which had originated in the seminaries of Europe before gaining prominence in the US. At its most fundamental level, higher criticism emphasizes placing the Bible in its original historical and cultural context and studying it as one would study any other ancient document. A debate arose over the ramifications of this approach, however, with modernists espousing higher criticism wholeheartedly and conservatives often seeing it as a challenge to the Christian faith—particularly "the authority of Scripture, its scientific accuracy, [and] the supernatural elements in Christ's person and work."[6]

As the debate expanded beyond seminary lecture halls and into local churches, white American Protestantism increasingly felt divided into two opposing camps, each side certain that it was the one "contending for the faith once delivered to the saints" (Jude 1:3 KJV). The Christian world in which Philip Howard and Katharine Gillingham Howard grew up, married, and became parents was shaped by this tension. Ironically, although the majority of conservatives were fairly moderate, the conflict effectively created hardline fundamentalism, as conservatives from a wide variety of denominational backgrounds and theological positions began to unite under attack from an aggressive modernism and to identify themselves as fundamentalists.

Charles Blanchard ensured that Wheaton College maintained its major doctrinal positions in the face of modernism. But at the same time, Blanchard and the school clearly shifted from an offensive position to a defensive position, and—because many modernists argued that social activism was the true test of Christian faith and that theology was irrelevant—from an emphasis on social activism to an emphasis on correct doctrine. Where the elder Blanchard had emphasized working *for* social reform in a "Christian" society, the younger began to be primarily concerned with holding ideological ground *against* an encroaching "secular" culture. By 1925, a year before Betty Howard was born, Wheaton found itself squarely under the umbrella of fundamentalism.

———

With Charles Blanchard's death in December 1925, Wheaton was left without a Blanchard at the helm for the first time in sixty-five years. Two months later, the trustees appointed a successor, J. Oliver Buswell, a Presbyterian pastor who had served as an Army chaplain during the Great War and been wounded in the Argonne. Buswell was chosen largely for his ability to keep Wheaton theologically the same in the face of the changing modern world. But the boisterous young man, just thirty-one when he assumed the presidency, must have seemed quite a change from his mild-mannered, dignified predecessor. One cannot imagine Charles Blanchard singing old Army songs at student-sponsored entertainments or wandering the campus in the fall wearing the freshman "dink"—the brightly striped beanie that was part of freshman hazing each year.

Buswell's dynamic style swept through Wheaton. He overhauled the curriculum, met and exceeded the requirements for academic accreditation, hired a slew of PhDs, and started a graduate program. A thoroughgoing antimodernist, Buswell "supported the trustees' decision to require all faculty members to assent to a nine-point fundamentalist doctrinal statement." But he wasn't afraid to foster a climate of intellectual openness and serious debate, and his classes included "books written from perspectives hostile to fundamentalist—and even Christian—viewpoints."[7] He intended to show the world that Christian faith and intellectual rigor could coexist—and that they did at Wheaton College.

Not all fundamentalists were comfortable with his open-door policy toward ideas. Then, as now, many people apparently saw willingness to understand and respond to a set of ideas as the first step on the slippery slope to adopting those ideas. Buswell believed ideas had to be understood in order to be effectively opposed. Ironically, when, after fourteen years, Buswell was fired, it was for being both too open (to ideas hardline fundamentalists were uncomfortable with) and too closed (for example, to a difference of opinions about what it meant to act as a good Presbyterian, or to understand the first chapters of Genesis). He had been unable to communicate his vision for an intellectually robust Christian faith to a wide enough swath of the fundamentalist coalition.

It was in this atmosphere of conflict that V. Raymond Edman became president of Wheaton in 1940, two years before Philip Howard became a trustee and four years before Betty Howard would arrive at the school as a student. A WWI veteran, former foreign missionary, and pastor, with a PhD in international relations, Edman had come to Wheaton as an associate professor three years before and had only recently been promoted to full professorship and head of his department. In many ways, Edman was "very nearly the photonegative" of Buswell.[8] Unlike the more scholarly Buswell, Edman's published work was primarily devotional. Buswell had focused on strengthening the school's academics; Edman concentrated on expanding enrollment and the physical plant. He spoke of chapel as "family devotions" and often led services himself, drawing on personal Bible study and experiences, particularly as a foreign missionary, for his talks. He was well-known for cheerful aphorisms such as, "It's always too soon to quit," "Never doubt in the dark what God has shown you in the light," and "Not somehow, but triumphantly."

Edman was a sentimental and kindly man "of prayer and great piety,"[9] and protecting and encouraging piety in Wheaton's students would be his highest priority throughout his presidency. He shut down the philosophy department that had been a major focus of Buswell's administration, placing all philosophy classes under the auspices of the Bible department and firing a professor who shared Buswell's philosophical approach. His attitude toward the relative merits of Christian belief and higher education is further exemplified by his quip that he'd been "demoted" from foreign missionary to college president.[10] Edman was far from alone in his views. He was part of a subculture in which foreign missions were seen as "this greatest of works," the apex of Christian life.[11] Then, as now, many churches had weeks and months of missions emphasis, with special offerings donated entirely to missions and slide shows and talks given by missionaries on furlough.

American Christians had always been interested in missionary work. By 1860, when Jonathan Blanchard became president of Wheaton, there were more than twenty American organizations actively sending missionaries to other countries, with hundreds more working to recruit and fund those missionaries. Interest in foreign missions continued to grow through the rest of the 1800s and early 1900s, with a surge after World War I, when high hopes for world peace and the spread of democracy seemed to align with missionary aims.

This surge was particularly strong in conservative circles, where doctrinal distinctives, particularly the spread of premillennialism, contributed to a sense of urgency about evangelism, and hence about missions. Premillennialists believed that Jesus's return was imminent, and time was short to help people hear about him before the opportunity was gone forever. This produced a particular emphasis on "unreached" people groups, based on Jesus's instructions to "make disciples of all nations" (see Matt. 28:19) and the apostle John's vision of every tribe, and tongue, and nation worshiping before the throne of God (Rev. 7:9). Some felt worldwide evangelism could hasten Jesus's return, because he had said in Matthew that "this gospel of the kingdom will be proclaimed throughout the whole world . . . and then the end will come" (Matt. 24:14). Missionaries and missions organizations issued calls to "proclaim the good tidings to every living soul in the short-est time,"[12] to pray "that the gospel may triumph, and the remaining few be gathered in; so that Jesus may come for his own."[13] The changing inter-national scene after WWI, with improved transportation and increasingly open borders, further contributed to a sense that the time to act in foreign missions was *now*.

Another thread running through the fabric of missionary zeal was the American Holiness movement. Holiness adherents emphasized a "higher" or "victorious" life, in which a Christian would not continually try, fail, and try again when it came to obedience to God but would be able to sustain a life free of sin. Although this teaching tended to find practical application in an emphasis on various codes of behavior as outward signs of victory over sin (including, at various times and in various sects, no alcohol, to-bacco, gambling, dancing, movies, makeup, etc.), the primary emphasis of Holiness teaching was on total commitment of the whole person to God, whatever the outcome. With total commitment would come the power to live a victorious Christian life.

As historian Joel A. Carpenter observes, this played a two-part role in attitudes toward foreign missions. First, the assurance that with total commitment comes power "offered faith missionaries the courage they needed" to commit to difficult, often dangerous work. Second, becoming a missionary became a way to demonstrate commitment. "More than any other, the missionary vocation was considered to demand the most radical self-denial and devotion."[14]

Betty Howard grew up immersed in this atmosphere of emphasis on per-sonal holiness and foreign missions—at home, at school, at church. In 1924 her great-uncle Charles Trumbull was a founding member of "American Keswick," a Holiness convention in New Jersey. After Philip and Katharine moved back to the US, Philip spoke regularly at Keswick meetings, and the whole family often went with him.

Betty would find the same emphasis on Wheaton's campus when she ar-rived four years into V. Raymond Edman's presidency. Edman had taken the reins at Wheaton at a time when external circumstances were particularly fitted to his warm pietism and missions enthusiasm. As World War II wound to an end and returning veterans began to transition back into civilian life, another surge in missionary zeal swept conservative American Christianity.

The destruction and loss of life and limb gave many a strong sense of the fragility of life and of the enormity of need around the world. They had been asked by their country to work and save and go without and give up loved ones and perhaps to die for a good greater than themselves, and once the war was over, their awakened valor was free to run in another channel. For many Wheaton students, that channel would be foreign missions.

———

In September 1944, as Allied troops in Europe began to tighten the net around Germany, Wheaton College was gearing up for a new school year. Seventeen-year-old Betty Howard had spent the summer at home in New Jersey. Now she and her trunks arrived at Wheaton Station, where she was met by "a pile of students," including her "big sister," an older student assigned to show the incoming freshman the ropes.[15]

After settling into her dorm room, she sat down at the pretty new maplewood desk she would share with her roommate to write to her parents. "Well, here I am at last! Wheaton is a really wonderful place and I'm so happy to be here." After her nine-person graduating class in high school, the five-hundred-member freshman class at Wheaton seemed enormous. Since college-age men were heavily involved in the war effort, four hundred of those students were women, making housing a bit tricky. Betty had been assigned a two-person room in brand-new North Hall. She reported that she was leaning toward a major in either philosophy or English, and that she had plans for both extracurriculars and a part-time job. "Meals are wonderful. Beds comfortable, etc. etc! In other words, everything's O.K."[16]

As she had been trained to do at Hampden DuBose Academy, Betty quickly filled her schedule with work and play. She had six classes—French 2, English literature, composition, survey of the Bible, history of North and South America, and gym—and by the end of the first month she had found a job helping with housework at the Edman residence across the road from her dorm. She was making about three dollars a week—decent pocket money, even if it often meant ironing, a chore she disliked.

The school had many formal events to welcome incoming freshman, including a concert and a faculty reception where Betty found herself a minor celebrity because of her family connections. She was "worn to a frazzle" by the time she had made her way through the receiving line. "But think of the teachers—they had to meet 500 of us!"[17]

Less formally, freshman hazing—which Betty declared to be "<u>awful!</u>"— was still a part of life at Wheaton. The sophomore class published a list of rules (titled "Squirm, Worm"), which included things such as wearing and doffing the freshman dink with the appropriate ceremony, wearing the student handbook on a string around one's neck, taking off socks and shoes to use the main campus thoroughfares, and walking backward up the steps to the student union building, affectionately called the "Stupe."[18]

In addition to the more or less mandatory activities, Betty attended a whole slew of optional extracurricular events—pep rallies, dinners at various people's houses, football games ("Yesterday was our big game with North Central! . . . Sue and I went together, and hollered and jumped and tore our hair for the Crusaders"), lectures, hikes, sing-alongs, walks, parties, concerts, recitals, dates, handball games, special prayer meetings, a prayer group that met regularly, and church multiple days a week.[19] She joined the debate team, the Foreign Missions Fellowship, one of the two women's literary societies, and the Oratorio Chorus (which performed Handel's <u>Messiah</u> at Christmastime each year), and signed up to write for the campus newspaper, *The Record*. By the end of November her schedule was full almost every night of the week.

Betty continued to do the private writing essential to most writers—letter writing, journaling, jotting down snatches of things that occurred to her while she was doing other work. Her journals were sprinkled with her own poetry. She was delighted when she met another woman in her dorm who shared this interest, and they spent hours together reading and discussing each other's work and favorite poets. This camaraderie whetted her creative faculties. "Last night as I was running my bath I suddenly was inspired and jotted down some lines on summer night! I get ideas at the most inopportune moments. Well, I hope someday to write a poem worth publishing, but there cannot be wheat without chaff!!"[20]

During her sophomore and junior years she attended the Pleiades Writers' Club, where students listened to talks related to writing ("a comparison between Christian and secular short story" was one night's topic[21]) and criticized each other's work. Betty had a poem and an essay included in the annual Pleiades anthology. And when Wheaton's new literary magazine, *Kodon*, published its first issue in the fall of 1946, she was startled to find one of her poems featured as a full-page spread with illustration, although she had not submitted it. *Kodon* published another of her poems the next year, but the second time it wasn't a surprise. She also continued to write for *The Record* at least through her sophomore year, though she felt increasingly that the paper showcased endless arguments over human standards while treating them as if they were the essentials of the faith.

Every writer is by default a reader, shaped by what she reads. In school Betty was reading Shakespeare, Bunyan, the Romantics, major American modernists, essayists, classics, and ancient philosophers, among others. She often noted in letters how many books she had to get through for her classes in a given week. She was also doing a good bit of extracurricular reading, especially in the subjects of Holiness theology and foreign missions: L. E. Maxwell's *Born Crucified* (emphasizing victory over sin through the cross); John Wesley's journals; J. Wesley Bready's *England: Before and after Wesley*; William Barclay's *Ambassador for Christ* (on the apostle Paul); C. S. Lewis's *Christian Behavior*; *Perelandra*; and *Screwtape Letters*; Norman Grubb's *The Price They Paid* (about Worldwide Evangelization for Christ missionaries in India); and Howard and Geraldine Taylor's *Hudson Taylor's Spiritual Secret*. In her sophomore year, her Bible teacher lent her a book by Lilias Trotter, the talented artist and writer—and protégée of famous art critic John Ruskin—who spent the last forty years of her life as a missionary in northern Africa. Betty would recommend Trotter's books for the rest of her life.

The author she mentions most frequently is Amy Wilson Carmichael. Carmichael, an Irish woman, moved to India in her twenties, started an organization called Dohnavur Fellowship to rescue children from temple prostitution, and lived there for the rest of her life. Gwynn DuBose had introduced Betty to Carmichael's writing, and Betty's college letters are peppered with quotations from Carmichael's book of poetry, *Toward Jerusalem*, a gift from her father. She also read *If*; *Windows*; *Ponnammal*; and *God's Missionary*. "Praise God," she wrote, "for such authors. Perhaps He will allow me to write some day about the mission field."[22]

And above all, she was reading her Bible, huge chunks of twenty and forty chapters at a time for school, with prolonged meditation over a chapter at a time for personal devotions. By the summer of 1947 she would be reading it in Greek as well as English.

———

Every aspect of life at Wheaton was affected by the war. In chapel, which was daily and mandatory, there were somber announcements when a former student had been killed. Whenever students left campus they were likely to meet traveling service members. Betty wrote after one such encounter, with a man who had been in the Battle of Guadalcanal, "Boy, we civilians don't know the half!"[23] Even social events and campus entertainment often related to the war in some way. Wheaton had a student war board that showed propaganda newsreels every Friday night. Betty entered a poetry contest at one of these events and won second prize: war stamps, which could be collected and put toward the purchase of war bonds.

Several of her friends and acquaintances from high school and the home neighborhood were serving in the Armed Forces, and she received regular letters from many of them telling of their wartime experiences. These personal connections brought events in the news closer to home.

> George Grieb wrote me two letters. He is with Gen. Patton's 3rd Army in Germany (now in Berlin, according to radio). Says he can hardly remember what clean clothes are like, they've been marching and taking towns for so long. . . . It seems so strange that he's over there now, since so much news has been coming in from there.[24]

George Griebenow, a fellow HDA alum, had some amazing stories to tell. He had been involved in the capture of SS General and Gestapo head Ernst Kaltenbrunner when his patrol had unexpectedly discovered Kaltenbrunner in a ski cabin in the mountains of Austria and sent him on to stand trial in Nuremberg. George had been awarded the Army Commendation Medal for his role in the capture, a Bronze Star for pulling a fellow soldier to safety under enemy fire, and a Purple Heart for wounds received in the invasion of Germany.

The end of the war in Europe in May 1945 came as a relief, but it was not unmixed with grief. Everyone mourned what had been lost, and everyone knew that troops from the European theater would soon move to the Pacific front. Betty took a radio to her morning French class and they listened to President Truman's address to the nation. She wrote to her family, "They rang the Tower bell but apart from that there was no celebration. We sang the Doxology, a Mighty Fortress is our God and the national anthem in chapel and most of us just sat there and cried."[25]

———

Betty's oldest brother, Phil, had graduated from Prairie Bible Institute in the spring of 1944 and gone on to study missionary medicine at the National Bible Institute in New York City. He had been drafted into the Army in the summer of 1945 and sent to Florida for training. Despite VE day, he would ship out for Italy at the end of the year. Dave, who had graduated from HDA in the spring, joined his older sister at Wheaton for the 1945–1946 school year.

Betty began her sophomore year as busy as ever. On top of classes (biology, general anthropology, psychology, English history, early church history, and PE), she was taking voice lessons, working a couple of hours a day, participating in a range of extracurriculars (adding to her list the honor society Pi Kappa Delta, of which she was secretary-treasurer), and occasionally leading the prayer meeting for her dorm floor. "I read them Amy Carmichael's poem 'Make Me Thy Fuel'. It's wonderful—answers a lot of arguments in the lines—'From all that dims Thy Calvary, O Lamb of God, deliver me!'"[26] She especially enjoyed her science class, which included field trips to the zoo, the conservatory, a museum, and the aquarium, and she marveled over the wonders of creation revealed at the other end of her microscope. She also loved debate. Although the topics were "the most crashingly boring subject[s] imaginable," things such as "compulsory arbitration and free trade," she enjoyed the challenge, and particularly the trips off campus to debate at other schools.[27] She made the varsity team her sophomore year, and the next year she and her partner would go on to win the Northwest championship.

In letters home, Betty comes across as strongly opinionated, in constant motion, and almost ruthlessly cheerful. Looking back over her journals and memories forty years later, the adult Elisabeth remembered a young woman who sounds quite different—uncertain, shy, lonely. At first this seems contradictory, perhaps even the deliberate creation of a persona. But everyone has a private self from which even our closest family and friends are necessarily at one remove. The public self that emerges in the company of those closest to us is not a false front but a facet of the whole person, which needs those particular personalities to draw it out. When the Howard family was together, they shared anecdotes and told jokes and laughed until they cried. And if Katharine Gillingham Howard's memoir, written for her family later in life, is any indication, Katharine's weekly letters to her children were chatty and cheerful. It's natural that Betty's letters were largely in a similar vein. Her brother Tom would later say that Betty was "not a person . . . who wears her heart on her sleeve, not only with the public but in the family."[28]

It is also possible that her buoyant, social persona was a result of her working on being who she thought she ought to be. In 1940s America, introversion was often seen as an unhealthy trait, even a personality disorder. This appears to have been what was taught at Wheaton while Betty was there.

In psychology class the other day we discussed the 13 characteristics of introverts. I find that 11 of them are very [underlined three times] true of me. It is rather discouraging to study psychology. I hope it doesn't make a worse introvert out of me. The Lord can change that in me, I know, for it certainly is a bad thing to be an introvert.[29]

Betty's belief that it's best to keep things close to one's chest and work them out privately is consonant with an introverted, internally processing nature. So is her relief over a night free from outside commitments or the rare solitude provided by an occasional babysitting job. She would not get a single room until her senior year at Wheaton. It must have been very difficult to spend six years, first in the frantic social atmosphere of HDA and then the busyness of college, with not even a room of her own. It would certainly explain the lines from an undated poem from her Wheaton days: "I am crushed with the din of words. / I am crowded with talking."[30]

However, believing that introversion is bad, she wouldn't have shied away from attempts to change. Betty was deeply impressed by what she would characterize as Carmichael's "awesome discipline," and though she found living by a schedule, for example, at odds with her natural inclinations, she began to work at it in her sophomore year as an opportunity for self-discipline and personal growth.[31] During her junior year, she rejoiced that others were seeing growth in this area of her life. "Truly the Lord wonderfully sustains, and helps me to organize my time. I thank him for a comment Miss C. made—she said I lived systematically and exhibit a solidity of character. You know how contrary to my nature is living by schedules! But the Lord truly gives grace to abide by a rigid and relentless self-discipline when necessary."[32]

Betty was capable of rigidly and relentlessly sticking to her guns on things besides self-discipline. Early in her freshman year she apologized to her mother for her behavior over the summer: "I do want to thank you again for all you've done—not only materially but spiritually and every other way. I am really sorry that my continual antagonism and argumentative spirit was such a sorrow to you this summer. I know I say that every year, and every summer I act the same way. But I do thank you for having such a sweet, forgiving spirit."[33] It is unfortunate that Katharine's side of their correspondence is lost. Again and again, one can only guess at what the mother may have said from the daughter's response. There is no way to know whether this was written in reply to something Katharine said or in response to the prickings of Betty's own conscience—or what behavior one or both of them considered to be antagonistic and argumentative.

But this remorse did not stop Betty from continuing to vigorously defend her own opinion. When her mother voiced some concerns about the kind of reading involved in an English major, Betty responded:

Mother—you seem to have been worrying about my English major. Well, may I straighten you out on the fact that the book on Franklin had positively no connection with English. It was a collateral for history. And all collaterals are matters of choice. We read what we like so long as it's on the list, which is widely varied. The only things we're required to read for English are Pilgrim's Progress and a Shakespeare Play. Anything wrong with them? And also—you suggested Bible major. There is one paramount difficulty there—it prepares you for nothing specific. Why go to college if you're going to come out with no preparation for earning your own living? If I were to study just Bible and relative courses, I should go to Bible school. Kids who are Bible Majors are planning for the mission field and nothing else. I believe that unless the Lord has definitely called a person for the mission field, we should be prepared to meet the <u>world</u> on its own grounds. But mainly—the Lord <u>definitely led me</u> to the choice of English—in fact it was the day before registration when I changed my mind from a zoology major to Eng. I know He wants me to. Perhaps <u>He</u> will change my mind again but until then I shall continue in the way He has pointed.[34]

When Betty's letters began to mention poor grades and getting up in the middle of the night to study, her mother again expressed concern, but Betty consistently resisted the idea of quitting any of her activities. She continued to struggle with the balance between grades and extracurriculars through-out her sophomore year, and she continued to rely on her own spiritual impressions rather than her mother's counsel in the matter. "Mother—you need not worry about my having too many irons in the fire. I have prayed very definitely about them."[35] Betty lived in a culture where the individual's obedience to God's private leading was emphasized preeminently, and she wanted very much to hear God's direction for herself and to be obedient.

———

The Holiness milieu in which Betty had grown up emphasized "the cross" as an important part of hearing and obeying God. This theme was drawn from passages like Matthew 16:24, where Jesus says, "If any man will come after me, let him deny himself, and take up his cross and follow me" (KJV) and Philippians 3:10–11, where the apostle Paul says that he wants to know Christ "and the power of his resurrection and the fellowship of his sufferings, being made conformable unto his death, if by any means I might attain unto the resurrection of the dead" (KJV). In Holiness terminology, "the cross" had become shorthand for taking up one's own difficult "cross," and—through personal experiences of "dying to sin and self"—sharing in Christ's sufferings.

Betty worried that there wasn't enough emphasis on the cross at Wheaton, and as she had been at HDA was concerned that her classmates were not fully understanding or applying the truths of Christian faith and personal holiness. "Few seem to know the Cross and the truth of Gal. 2:20," she wrote to her family.[36] Nevertheless, her letters mentioned sermons on these subjects several times, and she had no trouble surrounding herself with Holiness ideas. During her freshman year she had joined a women's discussion group focused on themes such as "the cross, death to sin, victorious life, etc."[37] Much of her personal reading was focused on the cross, and she wrote about it in her classwork when possible—a speech on the cross that received high marks from the teacher, a paper that considered Athenian political philosophy in light of the cross. In her journal she recorded her meditations and prayers connected to this theme. "My life is on Thy Altar, Lord—for Thee to consume. Set the fire, Father. Now I begin to know that song! Oh, how can I call it sacrifice, when Thou dost so richly repay—with song, with joy, with love. Bind me with cords of love to the Altar. Hold me there. Let me remember the Cross."[38]

This was more than high-flown rhetoric. Betty was aware that dying to self would involve sacrifice, and she tried to be alert to areas in her own life where God might be calling her to give. When part way through her freshman year her mother had gotten very sick, Betty had written offering to come home to take care of the younger children:

> I've been praying for you every time I think of you and I trust that the Lord is having His own way. I have been wondering if maybe He brought this illness on you to teach me some lessons. I just pray that I may be so close to Him that He will easily be able to show me His will so that you will once again be healed. I've been doing a lot of thinking lately and I realize more and more my selfishness toward you and utter indifference. I have faced out several issues before the Lord, one of them being the possibility of staying home next semester. At first all I could see was how much I'd lose out and how hard it would make things, but as I prayed about it, the Lord revealed to me the joy that there would be in it. . . . If that's His will, it's all right with me. He has shown me Himself, and truly, "the things of earth grow strangely dim!"[39]

This excerpt highlights Betty's youth and personal inexperience with suffering, as well, perhaps, as an aspect of her personality. She tries to "read the tea leaves" of events to try to discern God's will, and seems to imperfectly understand the Bible's image of God's role in suffering. Her response also emphasizes her commitment to the idea of the cross as she understood it, and her desire to be willing to do whatever it took to stay within God's will.

———

Betty's junior year classes included PE, voice lessons, a speech and debate class, introduction to philosophy, art of ancient cultures, the contemporary American novel, and first-year classical Greek. This last signaled an important decision: after a long period of thought and prayer, Betty had settled on a course of action to pursue after college. During the summer she had felt a call to missions—"pioneer" missions, she hoped, taking the story of Jesus to people who hadn't heard it yet. She had spent the intervening time praying about what type of work to do as a missionary, since she was interested in both medicine and linguistics. Then, while reading Isaiah, she had felt called to Bible translation.

Reaching this decision gave Betty a new sense of focus. She wrote to her family shortly after returning to school for her junior year:

> On Wednesday I came to the portion of Isaiah in my regular daily reading in which the Lord called me to translation work. Primarily Is. 42:6—and 48 different verses in the following chapters up to 50:7. It gave me a new thrill to realize that I am commissioned as an ambassador for the King of kings—and new seriousness of purpose here in school, for after all, we do not have tomorrow in which to serve Him—only today! As a young person, it is often hard to keep from living in the future, with the idea in mind that things haven't really started yet—we still have a lifetime ahead. Perhaps—but the Lord gives a moment at a time, and trusts us to invest it for eternity.[40]

She began to pursue classes she felt would help her as a missionary. One of these was an anthropology course, "which teaches an approach to the study of primitive peoples which is applicable to any field."[41] Another was Greek, the original language of the New Testament. Although she had been intimidated initially by the reported difficulty of the classes, she turned out to enjoy it tremendously. "It seems funny to suddenly, overnight, be able to <u>read</u> Greek words even if I can't translate them, for that's what I can do now, having learned the alphabet and sounds and pronunciation last night," she wrote early in the semester.[42] She apparently had an aptitude for the language; her grades in Greek were consistently the highest of any of her classes.

———

Betty's college letters record a steady string of dates. The young men who wrote regularly from overseas also sent cablegrams, called long-distance from Europe, traveled with her framed picture, and sent her flowers and gifts. (The latter were not always welcome: "I got my <u>sixth</u> (6th) bottle of perfume from him yesterday!" she told her mother. "Honestly, I can hardly thank him sincerely."[43]) A handful of these men were frequent visitors when they were in the Wheaton area and asked her out several times a week. However, in a student body of around 1,600 people, Betty must have had a pretty good sense of the dating life on campus, especially during her sophomore year when her dorm room offered two windows, "one affording a perfect view of the campus" and the other of "the front door, which makes it interesting just before 10 at night!"[44] Her own list of suitors apparently seemed insignificant in comparison to those of the women around her.

Since shortly after the turn of the century—certainly since Betty's mother was a child—dating, for high school and college students in the United States, had functioned less as a search for a mate and more as a popularity contest, with young women experiencing peer-group pressure to have as many different escorts as possible to as wide a variety of activities as possible. This paradigm must have made it very difficult to feel successful socially. Betty was thoroughly steeped in these cultural expectations—in fact, when she learned that her older brother Phil was seriously interested in a young woman he had met at the National Bible Institute, she wrote to her mother: "I am intensly [sic] interested in this Phil-Margaret deal. What's she like? I hope she's O.K. I wish he'd date other kids more so he'd have an idea of various types! Wait till he comes here—plenty of opportunity."[45]

But while Betty was writing blithely about her brother getting "an idea of various types," she was also unhappy when her regular dates also dated other women. This was likely due in part to the rapidly changing values of

American dating culture during the 1940s. During this decade, in response to the economic developments caused by the world war, the average age of marriage for women dropped sharply and dating became focused on having a steady partner with marriage as the end goal. Wheaton was the scene of fast-and-furious popularity-focused dating, but it was also peppered with couples getting engaged and married. Betty wrote home in the second semester of her freshman year, "There were 21 engagements announced over Christmas holidays and I know of at least 3 marriages."[46]

Not only was the transition from one model of dating to another putting conflicting pressures on all young people, but Betty had a strong desire for a serious partnership rooted in her personal views:

> I am very glad you are beginning to see the light when it comes to college education for women, Mother! After all—"unless we know geometry, we cannot be a good wife and mother!" I'm sorry Nana cannot understand, but I don't guess a college education would do her much good now anyhow. But she has a point there—women should be keepers of the home, and I think all this career business nowadays, to the extent of neglecting the highest calling of a woman—that of making a home—is tragic.[47]

Betty was looking for more than an escort to pass the time. She wanted someone who was serious about the same things as she. "I'm reading Hudson Taylor's Spiritual Secret—it certainly is wonderful. I wonder if there are any men like him now."[48] None of her dates seemed to fit the bill. "Honestly," she wrote to her mother, "I get so sick of the shallowness of most fellows. As soon as you begin talking sensibly they get confused and embarrassed. One guy told me outright that all a fellow wants on a date is a good-looking girl who can just shoot the breeze. If that isn't some admission to make!"[49]

George was Betty's most persistent suitor, taking her out three times a week shortly before he shipped out for Europe. He had written faithfully while overseas and even called her from Switzerland—for six minutes at the rate of about ten dollars per minute—an event which set the whole campus in an uproar. By the fall of Betty's junior year, he had been discharged and was at Wheaton, still pursuing her. He had even given her his war medals. Betty wasn't thrilled, complaining to her mother, "The trouble is he never tells me personally how he feels, (which I hate), so I have no opening to tell him what the score is. I don't want to crush him if he really likes me, but I sure wish I knew how to ditch him gracefully."[50] But she wouldn't stop accepting his invitations and continued to date him steadily through fall and winter and into spring. Katharine worried about Betty's treatment of George; Betty assured her he was fine.

Finally in April, Betty decided to formally break things off. George was deeply hurt. He had felt she was *the* woman for him and had longed for her companionship through the difficult passages in his life for the past few years. Betty wrote in her journal, "Now I feel terrible—hadn't realized it would hurt him."[51] It is difficult to imagine how a woman could have a man call her from Europe in 1946 and give her his war medals when he got home and *not* realize he was serious about her. Her sense of self-doubt and difficulty in reading others must have affected her understanding of his behavior.

For the next several days, she repeatedly noted in her journal feeling "positively miserable about George."[52] But a week later, after she saw him again to return his medals, Betty complained to her mother:

> He told me how hard it was for him to reconcile himself to it all, which was rather an awkward situation, because I guess it's just about as hard for me to. . . . No matter what a girl may think of a fellow, she always enjoys attention, and I admit I miss a lot of it. But I'm glad it's over—for some reasons. However, I'd like to have his friendship, but it doesn't seem as though it works that way. He can't talk to me naturally any more for some reason, and frequently won't speak to me. . . . Well, I did all I could to end things on a pleasant note, and if he doesn't want to take it that way there's not much more I can do.[53]

Her claim that the breakup is "about as hard" for her as for him—when she was missing the status his attention gave her and he was missing her—combined with her complaint that he can't behave normally around her indicates again a struggle to empathize. She had behaved so passively that she didn't communicate, then was annoyed with him for not taking her sudden rejection with a stiff upper lip.

Another major factor in Betty's response to George seems to be that she had been struggling for some time to break up not just with him but with romantic love in general. She had grown up in a culture and subculture that emphasized romantic love as the ultimate human fulfillment and full-time homemaking as the highest calling for women, but also in a subculture that treated foreign missions as the highest calling for Christians, and sacrifice, including the sacrifice of personal ties, as an important indicator of the validity of personal faith. After her decision to pursue Bible translation, Betty had written in her journal:

> Translation work is a full-time job. I cannot see how it would be possible from a purely human standpoint to do that and raise a family. Of course if God should one day reveal His will for me to be married, He would supply the needed strength and grace to do both. But as I see it now, He would have me for Himself alone, that I might "care for the things of the Lord" (1 Cor. 7:34).[54]

Nevertheless, there were times when she longed to love and be loved. She confided to her journal: "How subtle is the flesh! I think that my whole life is utterly lost in the Father's, and then comes a suggestion that perhaps He would lead this way, and immediately I rise up, almost unconsciously, in objection! . . . When I think that I am longing to know His will, I find that my own heart is choked with human desires."[55] The wrestling match in her heart may also have contributed to her treatment of George.

Betty believed that the will of God was a very particular thing. Both in the big decisions of her life and in the small choices, she was looking for specific direction from God. As she finished up her junior year, she wrote to her mother, "Also pray for the Lord's very definite guidance as to courses, room, room mate, and work for next year. I've run into several perplexities, and this being my last year, I feel the tremendous importance of knowing the Lord's will for every detail."[56]

After a short visit at home, Betty returned to Wheaton for summer school. Although she missed being at home, she believed she was being obedient to God's will for her life and worked to be content. Her weekly letters over the course of the summer chart her immersion in language study, a little outside work and play, and the evolution of her plans for the future. The summer Greek students—about sixty men and three women—had four hours of class time a day, and Betty was spending more than eight hours a day on homework outside of class. Although she found the classwork challenging, she was delighted to find Koine Greek easier than classical Greek. "After reading Xenophon's <u>Anabasis</u> the New Testament is like falling off a log!" she wrote to her family. She was thrilled to be reading some of the Bible in its original language. "What rich shades of meaning and connotation the Greek holds which the English is simply not equipped to express!"[57] By late July, she had decided to change her major to classical Greek. The chairman of the foreign languages department agreed to allow her to take the third- and fourth-year classes concurrently so that she could graduate on time.

After summer school ended, Betty spent a short time at home. Phil and Margaret, the young woman he had met at the National Bible Institute, had gotten married in May 1947, and Phil had decided to use his GI Bill to pay for a year at Wheaton. So when Betty returned to Wheaton for her senior year, there were three Howard siblings on campus.

As a senior, Betty was asked to give a welcoming speech to new students on the topic, "What I wish some senior had told me when I was a fresh-man." The copy she sent home to her parents shows her sense of humor. (It begins, "Undoubtedly there are a good many things by this time which you wish people would <u>stop</u> telling you. For example 'You are welcome at Wheaton,'—or—'Please read all directions at the top of your paper. Care-fully.'") It also sheds light on her frame of mind as she began her senior year. She emphasized the importance of individual obedience, noting that even at a Christian college, "there will always remain our own personal deci-sions of a moral nature which can only be made with the help of the Lord."

We need to examine our sense of values. We may glibly say, "God has brought me here for a purpose." Do we make it our business to aggres-sively seek to fulfill that purpose? Are we <u>convinced</u> that He has one? If so, we have a dynamic for the work that we do and a directive for the course of our lives. This year I have found it necessary to give up my favorite, though very time-consuming extracurricular activity, realizing that the Lord had something else for me to do in preparation for the future. We must live with eternities [sic] values in view.[58]

Debate, which had consumed huge portions of her time during her junior year, was the favorite activity she had given up. She closed the speech with Isaiah 50:7 (KJV), the final verse in the chapters that had constituted her call to missionary work. She had it committed to memory and so did not need to write it out in her notes: "For the Lord God will help me; therefore shall I not be confounded: therefore have I set my face like a flint, and I know that I shall not be ashamed."[59]

———

At the end of her junior year, Betty had requested a single room, and after some shuffling due to an administrative error, she was given a room in a three-room suite shared with two other senior women. At long last she had a place to herself. She was still wrestling with whether the call to missions was also a call to renounce marriage, and it was a help to have a place to be alone. By the middle of her senior year she wrote to her mother that she had reached a place of peace. "One other point—you mentioned your joy in my attitude toward marriage. The Lord has worked a real miracle there. The thought of marriage seldom if ever crosses my mind anymore, and I will confess that for the past two years my thoughts dwelt much on the subject. Oh, I am amazed, for the Lord is doing so many things of which I am only gradually becoming aware."[60]

She was still busy with classes, and despite the challenges of Greek, she was doing well in school and expected to graduate with honors. She had a job in the dining hall. She continued to sing in the glee club, to be interested in literature and writing, and to write for publication. But she had taken her own advice and was spending more of her time on fewer activities. She wrestled with the relationship between what she saw as spiritual and what she saw as earthly—concerned, for example, that her "intense . . . desire to graduate with high honor" was "unholy,"[61] and writing that "somehow I don't have very much interest in the entangling affairs of this world just now!"[62] In place of social engagements and extracurricular commitments, her letters increasingly focused on her thoughts about spiritual things.

Since the beginning of her time at Wheaton, Betty had attended the weekly Wednesday night meetings of the Foreign Missions Fellowship (FMF). During her senior year, she began to spend more of her time and energy on the group. She was not the only student increasingly drawn to a passion for missions and active involvement in the organization. During her freshman year, Wheaton's FMF chapter averaged about ninety-five students at a meeting; by Betty's junior year, there were more than three times the attendees. And by the second semester of her senior year, FMF members had embarked on an ambitious project: praying for one thousand students from Wheaton's current student body to go out as foreign missionaries.

Betty continued to search earnestly for direction from God as to where and when she should go. Various speakers, both to FMF and at other meetings she attended, spoke of the need for missionaries in various parts of Africa and China, and she considered whether these repeated requests might be the voice of God directly to her. "I have been thinking and praying much about next year," she wrote to her family. "I feel more and more anxious to get out to the field. Dr. Singer gave a lecture last Friday in which he stated that if we're going to the mission field, we better get out there, as the next war will take place within the next four years, and doors may be closed within 6 months from now. I am impressed with the urgency of the times." Nevertheless, she did not want to run ahead of God's direction:

> I know that God has much to teach me before I could even be usable on the mission fields. God forbid that I should rush out unprepared in spirit. May He make me pliable and broken at His feet. It is one thing to say that—but I have no idea how He may choose to accomplish it. Whatever it is, "Oh, give me grace to follow." I know that I shall never get to the field except it be by His grace.[63]

Another important influence on Betty's life at this time came from two speakers visiting on campus. One was Stephen Olford, a young British preacher whose parents were Plymouth Brethren missionaries. Betty wrote to her mother after a week of Olford's teaching, "I have been greatly challenged by the observation of a life wholly crucified and alive unto God." He encouraged the same system for daily devotions she had been using. "I read just one chapter a day. I read it over and over, praying as I read that God will show me a new meaning in each verse. Then I meditate upon it, and finally get on my knees and pray it all the way through, back to the Lord."[64] She decided to adopt his suggestion of keeping a spiritual diary, in which she would record what she felt she was hearing from the Lord during her quiet time. Betty also recorded in her journal Olford's teaching on a verse from Song of Solomon, which she copied down: "'I charge you, O daughters of Jerusalem, that ye stir not up, nor awake love until it please.'" She went on to explain, "He interpreted this to mean that no one, man or woman, should be agitated about the choice of a mate, but should be 'asleep' as it were, in the will of God, until it should please Him to 'awake' him."[65] This must have played a part in Betty's determination to put aside her wrestling over singleness and marriage. At the same time, the regular emphasis of speakers on the subject of romantic relationships, combined with circumstances and her own feelings, must have made it difficult to "sleep."

The other speaker was Hans Bürki, a young Swiss theologian pursuing a doctorate in the United States. "I have never been so impressed with a man's very presence!" Betty wrote to her family.[66] Bürki taught on personal interaction with the Bible and encouraged students to ask God to bring the Bible to life for them personally. "And I can truthfully say," Betty wrote, "that I've never before had such a longing to know Christ through His Word."[67] She took every opportunity to attend events where Bürki was speaking during his time at Wheaton, even canceling plans for a date to attend a Bible study he was holding. "It was really marvelous. We really got down to business and studied the word. Jim Elliot and I had mutually agreed to break our dorm party date to go. It sure was worth it."[68]

Jim Elliot was a classmate and good friend of Betty's brother Dave. He had made his first appearance in her journal back in the spring of her junior year: "Met Jim Elliot. Good talk. Wonderful guy."[69] Jim was considered unpinnable on the wrestling mat, made the honor roll regularly, and used his spare time to memorize Bible verses, and Betty was impressed by the commitment to excellence and the passion for the spiritual that these things suggested. By her senior year, Jim and Dave were living across the hall from each other, serving as resident assistants and class officers together, and generally spending most of their time together, as Dave later recalled. Betty couldn't help but run into Jim around Wheaton's little campus. They were both Greek majors, both FMF members, both on the student council, and both elected to the faculty-student committee tasked with handling student discipline. Jim's name started cropping up in Betty's letters home with increasing frequency.

But Jim was not the only interesting young man around. Over the course of her senior year Betty wrote to her mother about a few others. Bud Young was "a terrific language shark," with plans to go into Bible translation, who enjoyed music and painting.[70] Don Keeney was another fellow Greek major who loved to sing, played an instrument, wrote poetry, and was tall—always a bonus for a woman insecure about her height. These young men and a few others who asked her out over the course of the year were interested in more than shooting the breeze. Betty wrote happily after a late night of studying with Don, "Mother, I think it was about the most wonderful talk I've ever had with a fellow. Our friendship is platonic enough, and we have enough of an understanding, to be able to talk about all kinds of things. We discussed spiritual things, intellectual, and even got around to marriage and such. . . . It's so nice to be able to talk to a fellow without any of this stupid stuff of his thinking I'm making a play for him or vice-versa!"[71]

Katharine wrote back, concerned that it was impossible for a man and a woman to be "just friends," and that Betty was encouraging this young man to hope for a romantic relationship. In a measure of how she had changed since high school, Betty wrote back thanking her mother for her advice and agreeing that in general she was right. She also reassured her mother that Don dated other women, did not plan to be married at all, and knew she was not interested in a casual fling. "True, we do discuss very deep and personal things, but in quite an objective manner. So, I hope you won't be too concerned, thinking I'm on the verge of an 'affair'—far from it! He called me an 'ice box' one night, so you see he realizes my attitude!"[72]

While this comment leaves open the question of whether Betty was reading Don correctly, it highlights her own attitude toward dating, which was wholly in keeping with her mother's advice about how to deal with the other sex: "1. Never chase them. 2. Keep them at arm's length."[73] Betty had no intention of engaging in a physically romantic relationship until the right man had made a commitment to her. And Hans Bürki's teaching had strengthened her resolve.

On Friday night Mr. Burki [*sic*] spoke on the subject of love and friendship. It was the best I've heard him. He dwelt much on the love of David and

Jonathan, and pointed out very strongly that unless we can understand and fully enter into the meaning of real love for and fellowship with those of our own sex, we can never know the fullness of love for the opposite sex. . . . He showed that "love seeketh not her own"—and as soon as it does, it is lust. . . . It only makes me all the more thankful that the Lord has given me no opportunity to love any man yet, for I am not ready. If I have been "too fussy" heretofore, I guess I am now a hopeless case with regard to the general run of men from now on! For, if I cannot have someone who knows this pure love, I have no desire for anything less. May the Lord teach me to love Him in such an all-consuming way, that my love for those about me may be only the love of Christ.[74]

Betty was developing close friendships with women her senior year as well. One of these was Eleanor Vandevort, "Van," a junior and fellow Greek major. They met in gym class, and Betty said later, "I'd never been able to stand on my head or do a cartwheel and the only . . . P.E. class that fit my schedule that year was tumbling so I took that class. I think the reason the Lord let me do it was to meet [Van]." The two women quickly became friends. "She used to come up to my room in Williston before meals and we would read the Scriptures together and very often pray together and she [became] one of my closest friends."[75] Betty described her friend to her mother, "And what a wonderful week! Anything particular? Yes—the Lord! How He has blessed me! Just came home from a wonderful hour of fellowship with my good friend Van. She sure is one radiant Christian. And we shared so many things we had learned from the Word."[76]

Interpersonal relationships were not all smooth sailing for Betty, however, even with close friends and family. Vandevort later described "Bets," as she called her, as "standoffish. Off by herself. Didn't talk with people."[77] This is consistent with the idea that Betty was an introvert who believed she should behave as an extrovert. She was very socially active, but regularly putting oneself in social settings does not create the extrovert's social *joie de vivre*. Always outgoing, Vandevort found Betty's persona a stimulating challenge, but not everyone felt the same way.

Betty received repeated "exhortations" from other students about her behavior. In November 1947 she recorded in her journal, "On the way home Jim Elliott [*sic*] told me some of the reasons why I have such a bad reputation among the fellows. I am terribly sarcastic, for one."[78] And in January 1948, "I guess I'm in for another period of remonstrance and exhortation from Brother Jim (Elliot, of course.) . . . We're to meet at 2:00 p.m.—don't know what I am in for! But I do appreciate it, and realize that it is done in 'a spirit of meekness' as Paul says."[79] She later recounted that over a snack in the Stupe he had passed on criticisms of her that he had heard from others—presumably about her reserve—and "rebuked me as a 'sister in Christ,' urged me to be more open, more friendly. Christ could make me freer, if I'd let Him."[80] Don Keeney, too, "often mentioned" things "which he thought were not consistent" in Betty's life, and she in turn did the same for him.[81]

While some people found her too aloof, others found her overbearing. Betty repeatedly clashed with other people in her living situations. The argumentative spirit she mentioned as a freshman must have been something of a byword at home, for when she was installed as an officer of her literary society in her senior year, she wrote to her mother, "I am critic for the semester—no doubt you'll agree that I'm well suited to the task!"[82] She wanted to be an influence for good with her roommates, but her methods—repeated invitations or exhortations to church, Sunday school, and daily devotions, and even setting a roommate's alarm clock, without her knowledge or consent, to get her up in time for church—weren't particularly popular.

Jim and Don's freedom to criticize Betty in the spirit of helping her improve contrasts with the general failure of her attempts to do the same for others, suggesting that a person's right or duty to comment on others' behavior was sometimes accepted and sometimes not. In Betty's case, personality must have been a factor. She had always tended, as Tom would later remember, to cut straight to the chase: "She didn't have a lot of silly small talk. . . . She wasn't at home in all the little, somewhat frivolous exchanges that really make up . . . student life."[83] Despite her good intentions, this directness could be abrasive. And while Betty recognized that her personality wasn't always making things easier, recognizing that there is a problem doesn't mean one knows how to fix it.

Then too, although Betty felt her experiences deeply, in some ways she was thick-skinned. Tom would say that his sister was "never offended, you can't offend her. You might stump her, but you can't offend her."[84] Betty herself told her mother in the fall of 1947, "It takes a great deal to hurt my feelings—in fact I can't think of a time when I've really been hurt, and therefore it is very difficult for me to understand other people's being crushed by some of the sarcastic things I say, often unwittingly. . . . I realize it is a fault in one way, for I probably do hurt a lot of other people without so much as thinking about it."[85] She was hard on herself as well as on others, judging not only her behavior but also her emotions as good or bad. After several days of an overwhelming workload, illness, and homesickness, she wrote to her mother, "Miss you so much at times like this! But the Lord's grace is sufficient—it is wrong for me to even feel like this."[86]

But she was trying to improve. And the changes she saw the Lord making in her life were not all in her head. She continued to be more open to correction and advice. In response to a letter from her mother in the fall of her senior year, she wrote, "Yes, I realize I am much too preoccupied at times, and don't give other people's feelings any attention. It is selfishness—the old 'I' in sin. The Lord has been dealing with me along that and several other very important lines recently. How merciful and longsuffering He is!"[87] And when Katharine wrote again about Betty's future plans, the younger woman was able to listen:

> Your suggestion about staying home is a worthy one. No, it was not a bombshell at all, and quite plausible. I want very much to have some more time at home before I leave you for the field. But my driving self-discipline says I must go to Bible school. This could very easily be merely self, rather than self-discipline. Then, too, I would feel that despite all the suggestions for ways of occupying my time I would just be marking time. This, too, is very likely a product of the energy of the flesh. Christ was silent for 30 years, and the Father said, "This is my beloved Son, in whom I am well-pleased." Paul "went into Arabia." Perhaps I need to be "set aside" as it were, from the pounding pressure and rigid routine of school-life. . . . I am earnestly praying, Mother, that the Lord Jesus will lead me where he sees fit next year, not where I think I "ought to be." It is a joy to know that you are praying with me.[88]

In December, Dave invited Jim Elliot to come home with him to Birdsong for Christmas, and Jim accepted. The Plymouth Brethren church to which

Jim's family belonged did not celebrate religious holidays, believing it to be discouraged by Paul's frustration with the Galatians over "observing special days and months and seasons and years" (Gal. 4:10 NIV). But the Howard Christmas traditions don't seem to have fazed Jim. In his letters home to his own family he called them, "a fine family . . . particularly godly."[89] He joined in all the seasonal activities with a will. When there were no organized activities underway, he found the toolbox and wandered around the house singing and repairing the little things that accumulate over time, or presented himself in the kitchen to wash and dry dishes for Mrs. Kershaw, the elderly woman who was cooking for the Howard family at the time.

One night during the Christmas vacation, Dave woke up in the small hours of the morning to hear Jim coming into the room they were sharing. "And I sorta said, 'Elliot! Where in the world have you been?' and he just quietly said, "Well, talking to your sister.' And I thought, Talking to my sister? Till 2:00 in the morning?!"[90]

Betty and Jim talked late into the night about a wide range of topics, including pacifism and war, "New Testament principles of the conduct of the Church, women, poetry, and many other subjects on which his views were, I thought, out of the ordinary."[91] She later remembered, "The more Jim talked, the more I saw that he fitted the picture of what I hoped for in a husband. He loved to sing hymns, and he knew dozens by heart. He loved to read poetry, loved to read it aloud. He was . . . strong, broadchested, unaffected, friendly, and I thought, very handsome. He loved God. That was the supreme dynamic of his life."[92] Here, at last, was a man who was as serious about spiritual things as she.

For some time, Betty had been thinking and praying about "some form of specific Christian service,"[93] and when she got back to school, decided that "God wanted me to go to the railroad stations with the group that was going every Sunday."[94] For an introvert, spending an afternoon each week trying to talk about spiritual things with passersby was an intimidating task. But, "remembering Jim's admonitions in the Stupe, I determined not to be daunted."[95] After her first trip to the station she wrote to her mother, "There's joy in obedience! I talked with four girls."[96] There was also embarrassment. Arriving at the station she had realized for the first time that Jim was already part of the group; she was mortified, sure he would think she was chasing him. But obedience was its own reward; one week he sat by her on the train for the trip home and then walked her back to her dorm. He began to sit by her in Greek class too, even when "he had to trip over other people to get to the seat." In April he asked her out on a date—"to a missionary meeting at Moody Church."[97] She wrote in her journal afterward, "Jim is without exception the finest fellow I have ever met."[98] By May they were studying together three days a week.

When FMF sent a team of students to Taylor University in Indiana, Jim and Betty were thrown together again. She wrote a rapturous letter to her mother, describing the trip in detail and the wonderful sense of camaraderie and like-mindedness she had found with the rest of the team. They held a morning meeting, in which Jim preached on the importance of foreign missions, then spent the afternoon talking with students individually before holding another formal meeting after supper. "I've never heard three fellows preach like that. God poured out His Spirit upon us, I am sure. Thank Him for that. The trip home was a similar time of real communion. It was practically a brand new experience for me. I've never spent a day like it in my life."[99]

What she did not tell her mother was that Jim asked her to sit by him on the drive home and talk to him to help him stay awake. Their conversation included, among other things, Jim reciting "from memory twenty-one stanzas of Anne Ross Cousin's hymn, 'The Sands of Time Are Sinking,'" including the one which Betty had earlier copied out in her journal.[100] It was another indication to her of how much they had in common.

———

Every year, the women's glee club selected a group of singers to participate in the "Spring Tour," in which the students sang in various churches across the Midwest and Southeast. To her delight, in her senior year Betty was invited to participate in this trip. As they traveled through eleven different states, she sent postcards home from each stop, then settled down when she got back to Wheaton to write a more detailed account based on the record she had kept in her journal:

Our first night was spent on a hay farm out in the middle of a mostly submerged cornfield in Iowa! There was no running water, and they <u>asked</u>

us if we wanted sheets on the bed! But I think I received a greater blessing from being there than anywhere else. . . .

Out in Nebraska we stopped at one little town where the thermometer read 90° and right below it was a snowdrift! . . .

In Omaha we stayed with the Sawtells—he founded the Pioneer Bible Club movement, and thinks the S. S. T. is wonderful.[101]

The letter provides interesting glimpses of mostly small-town America in the late 1940s, as well as a window into the interests of the Howard family. Betty's observations about the places she visited deal with the things the home folks enjoyed hearing about—food, scenery, wildlife, and human beings. The Howards loved to observe people, their similarities and differences, and got a good deal of fun out of retelling for maximum effect stories of people whose behavior had struck them as funny.

Betty's recounting of her journey also provides a glimpse into a less appealing aspect of the cultural influences of her childhood. She was aware that there were things in her life that were at variance with Christian standards, and had once written to her mother, "I find myself so sinful, and with such beams in my own eye, that it is very hard to live consistently."[102] But in addition to those she recognized, she had cultural and theological faults she did not recognize. She described one stop in Mississippi:

Wide old entrance hall, stately columns, beautiful rosewood furniture, antique china and silver, four posters, trundle beds, and an old brick cook-house out beyond the garden. How I wish you all could see these things! Hostesses were dressed in hoop-skirts and lace caps. Negro Mammys like Aunt Jemima served wine in tiny glasses, which we refused![103]

Betty painted nostalgia for the Old South as something innocent and entertaining, with no awareness of, or lament for, the oppression undergirding it. In another anecdote, she described fishermen netting crawdads in the Louisiana bayous, casually using the n-word to describe them. Her family letters would continue to contain periodic expressions of racial stereotypes and racist language at least through the 1970s, when she was in her fifties.[104]

During this period, racist attitudes and language were rampant, and largely exhibited with impunity. Legal segregation was still in place in the

South, and in the rest of the country, racial segregation had been growing steadily worse since the start of the Great Depression. By and large, the white American church was no different. Other than the occasional missionary (Leland Wang, who stayed at the Howard house during Betty's childhood, was Chinese), Betty appears not to have been exposed to people of races or socioeconomic groups other than her own while she was growing up. At Hampden DuBose Academy, the atmosphere was at the very least casually racist. Wheaton, though founded by radical abolitionists who worked to make the school racially integrated, was effectively segregated by the time Betty enrolled. Her encounters with people of color during her time there were primarily as a member of the audience during on-campus entertainment, or as a "home missionary" to those who might need to be "saved." The theological fundamentals that evangelicals focused on defending did not emphasize Paul's declaration to the Galatians that in the church, "there is neither Jew nor Gentile, neither slave nor free, nor is there male and female, for you are all one in Christ Jesus" (Gal. 3:28 NIV).

———

Graduation for the class of 1948 was looming on the horizon when FMF had its end-of-the-year breakfast picnic on Memorial Day. Betty went back to her room at the end of the day and wrote to her mother. "It's been so long—I don't know how long—since I wrote. Where shall I begin? Your letters mean so much—it is wonderful to have such a mother. I am looking forward with great anticipation to your visit here, for there is so much that I want to talk with you about. My heart is full—the Lord has been so wonderful, and I want to share so many things that cannot be put on paper—hardly can be <u>told</u>."[105]

The news with which she was brimming over: Jim Elliot had walked her home from the picnic and told her he was in love with her.

Although she had tried hard to sleep "in the will of God," Betty found she was "very much awake" after all. She later called Jim's declaration of love "the revelation I'd been hoping for."[106] But the declaration was not, as she had been taught it should be, followed by a commitment. Jim's call from God, as he understood it, was to work as a pioneer missionary in the jungle, and older men had told him that was a job for a single man. He told her, "I can't ask you to marry me, and I can't ask you to commit yourself to anything whatever. I can't even ask you to wait."[107]

The next few days were a whirlwind. Katharine, who had sold her own mother's beautiful Rose Medallion punch bowl in order to pay for the trip to Betty's graduation, later wrote that it "was not a happy graduation for me—in spite of our pride in Betty's fine record at college—for she told me when we got out there that she and Jim had found out they loved each other but that they would not ever see each other after graduation, as he felt he must serve God as a single man!"[108]

Betty had a few short days remaining before she would leave Wheaton. She was torn between spending time with family and spending time with Jim. On June 3, he slipped her a little gift, a hymnal, in which he had marked the hymn beginning, "Have I an object, Lord, below / Which would divide my heart with Thee?" On the fourth she wrote in her journal, "I could not get to sleep last night, and then I woke at 2:30 a.m. and stayed awake! Could not eat much breakfast." On the seventh, they went for a walk together, discussing whether their mutual attraction and similar life plans were a sign from God or "a test of our stand with Him for a single life."[109] On June 9, they went for a long walk, ending up in a cemetery near the campus. As they talked, the moon rose and cast the shadow of a headstone, in the shape of a cross, between them. Almost sixty years later, Betty would still cry when she spoke of it.

———

A good deal of growing goes on in the years between seventeen and twenty-one. Betty would later say that she could remember "being aware . . . of the development of my intellect" over those four years at Wheaton, particularly during conversations with her father over meals in the dining hall when he was in town for trustee meetings.[110] There was spiritual development as well, visible less, perhaps, in her passionate words about stirring spiritual ideas and more in a gentle answer returned to her mother's advice, or her earnest attempts to replace fun with work that she felt would matter forever. During those years she had heard the words of the prophet Isaiah as though they were spoken directly to her: "I the LORD have called thee in righteousness, and will hold thine hand." And she had responded with words from the prophet: "For the Lord 2 will help me; therefore shall I not be confounded: therefore have I set my face like a flint" (Isa. 42:6; 50:7 KJV). What that would mean for the future, she did not know. But she wanted, she was determined, to obey.

I was just saying to my room mates on Saturday that I've certainly had every possible opportunity anyone could ever hope for—at home, church, and school. . . . Sometimes I am <u>afraid</u>—I've often felt that the Lord is perhaps preparing me for some extremely hard or difficult task, or some overwhelming crisis. I tremble to realize the price that we must be at least <u>willing</u> to pay. He requires of us abandonment—utter and aconditional. What may it mean when I pray for His whole will, for Him to <u>break</u> me? Oh, may He teach me to be faithful![111]

4

Red Mud and Hoar Frost

THE NIGHT AFTER her Wheaton graduation, Betty Howard slept fitfully in her seat as the Santa Fe Railway's Texas Chief raced south and west to Oklahoma. In the months leading up to this moment, she had prayed earnestly about her next step. She was anxious to get out into the mission field, but what did *God* want her to do? She had considered applying to join the Africa Inland Mission or Sudan Interior Mission, teaching for a year at Prairie Bible Institute or Philadelphia School of the Bible, pursuing further education or training, taking some time at home to rest and help her mother. Eventually she had decided that the Summer Institute of Linguistics, in Norman, Oklahoma—almost 900 miles southwest of Wheaton—was her next step. The 1948 session had started a week before, but she had been assured that it would be all right for Wheaton students to arrive late.

The program, founded by William Cameron Townsend in 1934 in an abandoned log house, had grown by 1948 into two entities—the Summer Institute of Linguistics (SIL) and Wycliffe Bible Translators (WBT). SIL was responsible for linguistic training and for dealing with the nonevangelical and non-American worlds. WBT existed to liaise with the evangelical world, primarily in the US, particularly in publicity and fundraising. SIL's training program was housed at the University of Oklahoma under the auspices of the Department of Modern Languages, offering classes in phonetics, phonemics, morphology, and syntax. These were designed to teach both theory and practice: the theory of how sounds are made, including pitch, "tone, intonation, stress, quantity and voice quality," and of how sounds function in units (words) and systems (languages); the practical techniques needed for "reducing a language to writing,"—by analyzing and recording sounds, word formation, and grammar—and for teaching single-language speakers to read the language for which writing has just been created.[1] During the final two weeks of the session, students were assigned to work with an "informant," a native speaker of a minority language, to practice all they had learned in a field environment.

As Betty dozed and woke on the rocking train en route to Oklahoma, she thought of Jim Elliot, back at his aunt's house in Glen Ellyn, Illinois, a small town near Wheaton. That afternoon he had driven her to the train station. He would spend the summer of 1948 at his parents' home in Portland, Oregon, then return to Wheaton for his senior year. Jim, who had been planning to enter the foreign mission field since he was a sophomore, felt that God had shown him during Bible study that he should not look for a wife: as Adam was asleep while God made Eve to be his partner, he should be "asleep" about romantic relationships unless God brought him an "Eve."[2] It's not clear why he hadn't seen Betty as his Eve, unless it was that he had also taken Matthew 19:12 (KJV), with its reference to those who "have made themselves eunuchs for the kingdom of heaven's sake," as a personal call to him to give up marriage. His feelings for Betty caused him to question whether he was hearing God properly, but he did not want to depart from the "word" he felt he had received without clear redirection. In their last days together, Betty had suggested that they not correspond, feeling, as she later wrote, that it would be hard to hear clearly from God if she was focused on hearing from Jim.

She quickly found, though, that not *hearing* from Jim was not at all the same thing as not *thinking* about Jim. On the Wednesday after she arrived in Norman, Oklahoma, she sat down to write her mother:

Our Lord is exceedingly tender and gracious. In an unspeakably wonderful way He has met me these last two days. (I can hardly believe it is only 48 hours since I was <u>with</u> Jim.) How He sustained and gave His strong hand to us we alone can understand. I could not write it or tell it. What passed between us during those last moments was not in <u>words</u>. (A. Carmichael says, "The dust of <u>words</u> would smother me . . .") The interflow of spirit was as a triangle, with Christ at the apex. Once again the words came "the Lord giveth—the Lord hath taken away—<u>blessed be the name of the Lord.</u>"

. . . He gave me grace to keep back any tears until I had passed the gate. Then, of course—the flood gates were opened. There is only an evidence of my humanity. The spirit truly <u>delights</u> to do the will of the Father. We only find it difficult in terms of our own hearts. It was a joy to be able to tell Margaret all about it that evening. She understood, a little. She and Phil had come to the place of the crucifixion, too, but in their case God, in His mysterious ways, gave them back to each other. With us, this is as final as the Cross.[3]

In her journal Betty wrote that she was "at peace, but when I pray for J. the tears must come." And the next day, "It is impossible for me to dismiss all thoughts of ever seeing him again. I find myself thinking of how I will talk with him. Each time the future comes to mind, he is there."[4] She would later say that "hope was always there that God's will would bring us together," but that even in her journals she was hesitant to write out all she felt, "afraid to articulate, even for myself, feelings I might have to get rid of."[5] Perhaps she was trying to spare her mother (and herself) disappointment, should their separation indeed turn out to be permanent. Certainly her experience of delight to do the will of the Father did not mean things were easy. Nevertheless, she was determined not to "give place to myself, my own moods and feelings. The Lord save me from belonging to the Order of the self-pitying. No man hath a velvet cross."[6]

In fact, Betty was so focused on this that she resisted any explanation for her current circumstances other than a call to self-sacrifice. Katharine had passed on a comment from Dave, drawing a parallel between Betty and Jim's separation and the story of Abraham's sacrifice of Isaac: he had suggested that as God had intervened to stop the sacrifice at the eleventh hour, so their sacrifice might not be final. Betty replied that they had thought of that, "but it is too <u>easy</u> for us to apply this to our situation. God moves in mysterious ways, and deals with His own very differently."[7] Betty and Jim were afraid that the easier or more comfortable path must be deceptive, second best—and that second best was the same thing as *wrong*. Although they were genuinely in love with each other, there was perhaps also a part of them that was in love with being in love, and with the idea of a glorious sacrifice, of giving up their one true love for Jesus. "We had so little time," she told her mother. "Now it seems almost as a dream. . . . It is blessed to look back upon this as another of God's stepping stones. One more thing—but O, what a <u>great</u> thing—to show me in a new way <u>Himself</u>."[8]

———

After the busyness of Wheaton, SIL was restful, even boring. At first Betty felt, with a sense of mingled anticipation and arrival, that she was at last directly preparing for the mission field. But by mid-July she was writing, "Never have I known time to drag so!"[9] Students had about four hours of classroom time a day, followed by two hours of assigned homework. She found the work easy and quickly caught up from her late arrival. The rest of her time was her own. There was no mandatory chapel, no mandatory dining hall, no mandatory class attendance, no curfew, no lights-out time, no prohibitions against behaviors like going to the movies. It was a strange feeling. She and a roommate were housed in an ugly and utilitarian dorm, empty for the summer, that had originally been built as a Navy barracks. At night it was almost too hot to sleep; daytime temperatures were around 100° F. The weather changed rapidly and regularly, and Betty frequently found herself soaked through by sudden rain. She gave up on curling her naturally straight hair and pinned it up out of the way instead, reporting with amusement that "the only way to get around" during these downpours was "in boats, hip-boots or barefoot. I have chosen the latter."[10] But the vast skies of Oklahoma—which she called "the land of red mud and straight horizons"—filled her with a sense of awe.[11]

The light schedule, the summer-quiet campus, the wide-open spaces, and Betty's loneliness for her family and for Jim combined to give her time at SIL a feeling of emptiness and stillness. She spent much of her time at the top of the deserted stadium or on the grass behind the campus buildings, reading, thinking, praying, working on her tan, and watching the ever-changing skies. She was still reading Amy Carmichael's *Gold Cord* and finding application in her own circumstances.

I quote lines which plumbed deep the other day:
"No, it is not by giving us back what He has taken that our God teaches us His deepest lessons, but by patiently waiting beside us until we can

say: I <u>accept</u> the will of my God as good and acceptable and perfect, for loss or for gain." (page iii, <u>Gold</u> <u>Cord</u>)

And my heart can only cry out the prayer of that hymn "O Teach me what it meaneth, that Cross uplifted high." Perhaps we have learned to apply that Cross in some measure, but little do we understand of all that it means.[12]

She also read Carmichael's *Kohila* (the life of a woman who grew up in Dohnavur); a book about David Brainerd ("His affections were literally <u>set</u> on things above, and his sole aim was to please God! What mediocrity we actually seem to <u>enjoy</u>! Oh, there are thousands of Christians, but where are the <u>disciples</u>?"[13]); *The Imitation of Christ* by Thomas à Kempis ("Chapter XI, book II . . . impressed me yesterday. . . . 'Jesus hath many lovers of His kingdom of heaven, but He hath few bearers of His cross'"[14]); F. J. Huegel's *Bone of His Bone* (on the cross and oneness with Christ); and the poetry of Edna St. Vincent Millay. And she found comfort in her Bible reading, particularly the Psalms.

Betty was writing a little, including a poem that she submitted anonymously to the *Sunday School Times*, but primarily journal entries and letters. Besides her family, she was corresponding regularly with Eleanor Vandevort, and in her loneliness found great value and encouragement in their friendship. Although she and Jim had agreed not to correspond, she thought of him often. She wrote to her mother:

I've had the most <u>blessed</u> letters from dear old Van! I'm saving them to show you when I come home. The things the Lord shows her are treasures—"precious things, put forth by the moon." And her letters fairly flow with her great, loving heart. Why should the Lord so bless me in such precious friends? Oh, the pure joy of Christian friendship! Truly one of earth's greatest blessings. And of course, in that category is Jim. I am continually amazed that the Lord should allow me even a glimpse of such a life—of one who has so well learned what it is to be a "good soldier of Jesus Christ." His very life impelled to the highest those whom he met. Many were the times when I was overwhelmed with shame at the low plane at which I was contented to dwell, when he was so obviously "living above." Oh, the Lord is kind![15]

She would later write that during this summer she found herself unable to "think, read, or pray except about Jim Elliot. He loomed in every thought, every line I read in the Bible or anywhere else. He got mixed up in the morphology, syntax, and phonetics I was stuffing into my head. He distracted my prayers." This worried her. She wrote in her journal, "Does the fact that I do not forget Jim indicate that God does not want me to, or is it my own unwillingness to forget that has kept God from answering my prayer to that end? Or does He want me to remember— to 'suffer me to hunger' so that I might the more fully learn to find all my satisfaction in Him? . . . Can it be that by a show of what Paul calls 'will worship' I should crush the bud of a flower of God's creation? I know no prayer other than Thy will be done."[16]

———

Phil and Margaret were also enrolled at SIL, and Betty saw a good deal of them. They went for walks, sat at the top of the stadium to catch the cool breezes at the end of the hot days, and went to church together. Near the end of her first week there, she met another student, Jim's brother, Bert Elliot. Like Betty, Bert loved to sing and play the piano, and he and Betty enjoyed singing and playing together and talking about the Bible. He often sat by her in class and made funny little asides that made it hard for her to keep a straight face. When he got a letter from Jim, he let her read it, so that even though she wasn't corresponding with him she could keep abreast of what he was up to. They spent so much time together that the gossips started speculating about them, which amused Betty.

The Elliot family were, as Betty would later say, "dyed in the wool" Plymouth Brethren, so Bert was attending the Brethren assembly—"the little group of Christians," he called it—in Oklahoma City, about 20 miles away.[17] The Brethren have their own vocabulary and avoid much common evangelical Christian jargon. Many people would call them a denomination; they call themselves part of a movement of the Holy Spirit, a group of believers in Jesus who eschew human-made religious forms and follow the example set for Christians in the Scriptures. Other Brethren distinctives include lay preaching, the absence of paid clergy and traditional denominational structures, celebrating Communion every Sunday, and forbidding women to speak, as well as requiring them to wear some kind of head covering during the formal portion of a gathering.

Betty had visited an assembly in the Wheaton area while she was in summer school between her junior and senior years. "It was a unique service," she had written at the time. "They serve real wine and literally break bread. There is no minister or instrumental music."[18] She had been wanting to go again, so she and Phil and Margaret took the opportunity to attend with Bert. Afterward she wrote to her parents, expressing her appreciation of what she found there. "I am more and more impressed with the wide and intimate knowledge those brethren have of the Word. . . . That deep grasp of the Scriptures is to me the strongest recommendation of any group. After all, <u>what</u> else counts?"[19] Eventually she decided to attend Brethren meetings full-time.

The SIL course lasted just eleven weeks, so by the beginning of August students were finishing didactic work and starting practice with informants. Betty, who seemed to have a natural talent for language learning, was bored and more than ready to move on. "Pardon the stationery, but I'm in Translation lecture. Dr. Nida (what a character!) is expounding the problems involved in Quichua, which I never expect to learn. We spend a lot of time around here in rather redundant lectures—they go over and over the same stuff till we can practically say it back to them."[20] Working with an informant was a little more interesting. Students were assigned to work in pairs—one hour spent eliciting information and the other hour observing their partner do the same—with the rest of the day to be spent analyzing their freshly acquired data and memorizing phrases in the informant's language for the next day. This took Betty about an hour. But although she was ready to be done with SIL, she was still uncertain about what to do next. "Mother, you asked about the fall. I can only say 'We know not what to do, but our eyes are upon Thee.'"[21]

———

On her way home from SIL, Betty stopped to visit Van. She knew that the family at home were anxious to see her, but as the women prepared for the mission field, she felt it might be their last chance to see each other "before we become 'like Him, for we shall see Him as He is.'"[22] She arrived home in Moorestown about August 25, still unsure of her next step. On August 30 she wrote in her journal, "It is the first time in my life when plans have not been laid out for me far in advance. I am cast only upon my Lord. Oh, that 'Christ, the wisdom of God' might have full charge. Never have I felt so completely helpless and ignorant of the way I should turn. I turn, O God, in faith and love, to Thee."[23] During the next four weeks she came to a decision: she would attend Prairie Bible Institute (PBI), and she would apply to the Sudan Interior Mission (SIM) as a missionary candidate for Africa.

This raised another difficult question. The train trip to PBI involved passing through Chicago, so Wheaton was essentially on the way. Should she—or shouldn't she—visit Jim? She agonized over the choice in her journal. Eventually she decided to go.

On September 22 she was back at Wheaton; on September 28 she would leave for Canada. Jim met her at the station. She had worried that a summer apart might have done away with his feelings for her, but when she saw him, she told her mother, she could "read in his eyes" that he was still in love with her. Jim had classes, sports, and other commitments (including serving as Foreign Missions Fellowship president), but they attended meetings together, took long walks arm in arm, talked for hours, and read each other's journals from the past several months. She wrote to her mother, "It was truly a glimpse into the inner sanctum of his soul. . . . The more I know of him, the more awed I stand at the vast reaches of his soul—the more I see the partial embodiment of the life to which I so long to attain. What can I offer to such a one? Truly, nothing but the love of God. And even there, I am such a clogged channel. O to be holy!"

Betty told Jim that she was in the process of applying to SIM. He responded, "Well amen! Go right ahead." Betty told her mother, "I must admit, in all honesty, it was no easy thing to apply in the first place. I hesitated, somehow, because of him. But the Lord seems now to give freedom to continue with my application."[24]

Although Betty had suggested that they not write at the beginning of the summer, she leapt at the chance when Jim told her that he now "felt that God had given the liberty to start a correspondence." Jim's liberty, however, did not extend beyond letter writing. He and Betty talked about marriage, "puzzling," as she would later write, "over the thought that for us it might amount to an admission that Christ was not sufficient."[25] She wrote in her journal that, "yes, God led us both separately to that decision" to write, but it is difficult not to see *their* puzzlement as *his* puzzlement, particularly when she explains that *their* idea that getting married might show Christ to be insufficient came from *Jim's* reading of 1 Corinthians 7:37. [26]

Betty saw Jim as a modern missionary hero in the making, the fulfillment of her ideal. And Jim's reading of the passage was informed by his belief that God had called him to "make himself a eunuch for the sake of the kingdom of heaven," and by the influence of his father, who, Betty would later tell her mother, hoped that Jim would be "a modern Paul—unmarried, sold out to the work of the Lord." Fred Elliot had made his views clear to his son, and Jim held his father in high regard. Despite all this, on the night before she left for PBI, Jim told Betty, "I love you," for the first time.[27]

———

The scattering of the Howard family, begun when Betty and Phil left for Hampden DuBose Academy and Prairie Bible Institute, had continued apace. In autumn 1948 only Tom and little Jim were still at home. Ginny was in Florida, attending HDA. Dave was starting his senior year at Wheaton. Phil and Margaret had gone from SIL to work for a church in northern Minnesota. And Betty was on the train, heading northwest across the prairies to Three Hills, Alberta.

Prairie Bible Institute was founded after World War I by Alberta farmer and lay preacher J. Fergus Kirk. Increasingly concerned about modernism, Kirk had looked for someone to help him start a small, conservative Bible school. He found Leslie Earl Maxwell, who was just graduating from Midland Bible Institute in Kansas. Together, the two men launched PBI in 1922 with eight students; they gradually added a farm to feed students and staff, a high school, and an elementary school for the children of staff, students, and local residents. Life in a farming community didn't provide much in the way of extras, especially during the Great Depression. Austerity was necessary for both staff and students. Kirk sold part of his farm to get the school off the ground and did manual labor to supply student needs; for the first three years, Maxwell was paid in food. The men were imbued with a sense of urgency about Jesus's return that made material things seem unimportant, and they believed with King David that they should not offer to God that which cost them nothing. These attitudes helped lay the groundwork for the school's attitude toward sacrifice and hardship.

When Betty arrived at PBI just after its twenty-fifth anniversary, Maxwell's strong personality was so influential at the school that, as scholar and alumnus Tim W. Callaway notes, "'L. E. Maxwell' and 'Prairie Bible Institute' were virtually synonymous terms."[28] Maxwell was a friend of Betty's father, and Betty was delighted to see him again. "What a character he is!" she wrote to her family. While Maxwell lectured he made faces, used funny voices, and even hid behind the lectern. He would ask a question in a soft, inquiring voice, then pound the pulpit with his fist and laugh uproariously. Not everyone appreciated his style, but to Betty he was "a refreshment."[29]

Since Phil was a PBI graduate, Betty had a pretty good idea of what the school was like before she got there, so she was not surprised by conditions—but neither was she impressed. Things were disorganized, and new students were corralled for hours in an empty classroom before being assigned rooms. The food was primarily starch; dinner was the same three meals on rotation, lunch was always boiled potatoes and gravy, and they only got milk to drink when it was beginning to turn. Using Howard family shorthand, she chalked it up to "GMT," good missionary training. Betty's roommate turned out to be Phyllis Gibson, a fellow Wheaton grad who had dated Dave steadily the preceding year, and the two women reveled in care packages of food—cookies, canned fruit juice, nuts, dried fruit, Spam, cheese, and date bread from Katharine, and "a loaf of delicious fudge" from Dave.[30]

In Oklahoma it had been hot, with "burning blue" skies.[31] In Alberta, with winter coming on, daytime temperatures sank more than twenty degrees below zero. In the early mornings, when Betty went out for gym class, stars were still visible in the "brooding blue of the winter sky," with "occasionally a faint gray-purple crack . . . just over the smooth horizon." Hoar frost came down from the north, "a white, thick mist, and in an hour or so [it] has coated literally every side of every branch, twig, & pine needle so the landscape is an absolutely solid white, with scarcely any lines of distinction or shadow." On long walks outdoors her breath froze on her face and hair, making the latter "look like spun sugar" and leaving "a film of frost" on her cheeks.[32]

At SIL everything had been optional; at PBI everything was mandatory—classes, meals, meetings, bedtimes. Ironically, the schedule was so minutely detailed that Betty could not even find time alone for personal devotions. The dress code, which included a prohibition against pants for women and girls, was never relaxed, even for (mandatory) gym class or in the coldest winter weather. After a Sunday walk with a friend, Betty wrote that "my legs were red and they began to swell as they thawed out. Now Mother—no suggestions please! We are not permitted to wear ski pants under any circumstance, which I must say I feel is a very foolish rule up here. You should see the poor little grade-school children, trying to keep warm with only cotton stockings. Of course all rules apply to grade school, high school & Bible school alike, including segregation of the sexes."[33]

This segregation was another PBI rule that provided Betty with opportunities to bear and forbear. When she first arrived, the women hauled their water up four floors from the basement in buckets (and heated it under steam jets) until the administration decided that standing in a line for water with the single men housed on the first floor of the building might cause "unnecessary conversations," and consigned the women to carry water from the laundry, two blocks away.[34] There were men's and women's steps and doors into each building—classrooms, dining hall, library, chapel, etc.—men's and women's lines in the cafeteria, and even men's and women's sides of the room when giving public testimonies. Not even married couples were allowed to sit together. Betty tried to be understanding, given "some of the things that go on in Wheaton," but observed that it created "a very unnatural environment," giving the impression "that to speak to a man under any but compelling or necessary circumstances would be moral sin."[35]

Scrupulously avoiding sin was heavily emphasized at PBI. Along with the administration's thorough management of students' time and behavior came the expectation that students would minutely scrutinize their own actions and attitudes. Sunday afternoons were set aside for the purpose, though the practice was not limited to one day. Betty wrote repeatedly, and often hilariously, of the kinds of things being confessed: "The other night a fellow got up in the dining hall & confessed having 'understanding looks' with girls. Another confessed having looked over the girls to see what type of a wife he'd like to have. . . . In choir yesterday a fellow confessed having told his room mate we had some pretty homely kids in the choir!"[36] Another week she wryly reported that several men had confessed to looking at women, "not even in an understanding way, so far as they mentioned."[37]

Betty sometimes found it difficult not to laugh, but she also found it confusing and discouraging. "I come away from such lengthy confessionals feeling very depressed in spirit, and oftentimes disdainful of the students. Please pray that the Lord Himself will rebuke their spirit, and also show me just what is _His_ will for _me_ along this line." The thought that she might be supposed to participate must have been miserable for a fastidious and reserved introvert. But because she did not want to do it, she was afraid it meant she should. She worried, "Perhaps my fear of becoming 'a typical P.B.I.-ite' is the devil's subtle trick to harden me."[38]

Her parents tried to encourage her. Her father sent an article cautioning against overscrupulous confession, particularly when more likely to cause offense than assuage it. Her mother suggested that there was room within obedience for different people's consciences to allow for different practices, as indicated in Romans 14. These, with her own Bible reading, helped Betty find peace of mind. By early December she reported, "My spirit is no longer pressed by such matters, but the Lord has taught me some lessons in love and the responsibility of each to his Lord."[39]

The public emotionalism of confessionals was always distasteful to Betty. She felt students were "always trying to work themselves up to some sort of crisis—as if every day were the turning point in a life supposedly long since given over to Him."[40] To Betty this suggested failure to mature. "For myself," she wrote, "I experienced conscious deepening and help for my soul, but no climactic revelations. . . . Must we leap from peak to peak in our Christian walk, rushing madly from 'revival' (?) to 'revival,' seeking to '_really get_ something' this time? O where is the man who _walks_ _with_ God? Not just _visits_ Him." [41]

As one would expect from an institution founded in concern about modernism, PBI fit neatly beneath the umbrella of fundamentalism, with an emphasis on Holiness teaching and foreign missions. The school held a fall Keswick conference and a spring missionary conference, and Maxwell forcefully promoted the idea that foreign missionary service was the ultimate sign of commitment to God. "Christianity is missionary," he wrote in 1948. "And the spiritual depth of any institution may be measured by the percentage of graduates who obey Christ's last command." For Maxwell this emphasis went hand in hand with antipathy toward academia and the intellect. Study of anything outside the Bible was viewed at PBI as a digression from the purpose of Christian life and a possible opening for modernism and worldliness. In 1945 Maxwell wrote of PBI students, "If we give them degrees, they will go into nursing, school teaching, commerce and various professions. We want them to stick to missions."[42]

The standards for women's dress, the emphasis on self-sacrifice, the separation of the sexes, the weight given to scrupulous personal holiness, and the exclusive prioritization of missions were all part of PBI's emphasis on living a "crucified life." Maxwell taught that this meant having "nothing to do with the world," which he defined as "the whole orbit and life of the natural man." "It is likely that many of my readers are, as a whole, unworldly," he wrote. "But let me ask, Are you the victim of a single worldliness? . . . The apostle does not say, 'Love [the world] not too much, or love it not so much'; he simply says, 'Love it not at all.'"[43] He also taught that God could not fulfill the divine purposes because not enough Christians were willing to "sink into a selfless, carefree contempt for their own lives, forgetting their reputation and position, their cause and kingdom, and . . . to expose themselves to every battery the devil can muster against them."[44]

———

The normal course of study at PBI lasted three or four years. Maxwell put together a one-year schedule for Betty: Bible III and IV; Doctrine I and III; Personal Work III; Leviticus; Psalms; Acts; and Hebrews. Maxwell and Kirk's mistrust of human reason led them to emphasize a didactic approach called the "search question" method, which Maxwell had learned during his time at Midland Bible Institute. Rather than reading books *about* the Bible (even commentaries were actively discouraged) students were expected to approach Scripture directly, using a given set of questions. Betty wrote, "The classes . . . are totally different from anything I'd had previously. I really feel that I'm learning something for myself. It is not a course in indoctrination, but individual investigation."[45]

Some students found that if the understanding they gleaned did not match the theological emphasis of the school, their grades suffered, leading them to feel that the emphasis on searching God's word for oneself was only lip service. Betty appears to have had no trouble with her discoveries falling outside the prescribed lines. "Maxwell's classes are a real thrill," she wrote. "I'm getting into Romans as I never did before."[46] She would later call Maxwell "the most significant teacher I ever had."[47] But she disagreed with many things about the school that, whether she knew it or not, were heavily influenced by Maxwell. She was unimpressed by the climate of anti-intellectualism. When asked to speak on SIL as part of a program, she complained to her mother:

> People ask me how college differs from [PBI] and one of the things I mention is outside activities. This calls for a long explanation, since such things are unheard of here. Then the question is, "Is Wheaton spiritual?" . . . I have to speak on "The Scope of Linguistic Training," giving a non-technical explanation of Phonetics, phonemics, morphology, and syntax. We have to be careful not to alienate the entire student body by sounding as if we are advocating education. One would hardly dare mention the fact that it is college level work, and accreditable![48]

And when faculty member Ruth Dearing preached one Sunday, Betty wrote home, "<u>Miss</u> <u>Dearing</u> brought the <u>Sunday</u> <u>morning</u> message! Wow! I'm afraid I'd make a good <u>P.B.</u> [Plymouth Brethren] when it comes to that—I can't see it."[49]

Maxwell was not a modern feminist. In addition to his abiding concern over the length of women's skirts, in the 1960s he wrote PBI's choir director, a woman, and asked for more "virility and masculinity and attack" in music selections, suggesting she achieve this by getting a man to lead the choir.[50] But, as he said, "I am teaching women to minister; I want them to be free to minister."[51] Maxwell consistently encouraged Dearing into public leadership roles, including preaching, from the time she arrived at PBI until his death in 1984. Maxwell's attitude toward women's dress framed women primarily as bodies that tempt men and placed the burden of preventing temptation on women, even when the "prevention" harmed them—for example, by causing frostbite. But his approach to women in the pulpit sharply contrasted this. Ted S. Rendell, president of PBI during the 1980s and 1990s, called Maxwell's position "ahead of his times," but as scholar Timothy Larsen points out, "It would be truer to say . . .

that he was one of the last living links to the old acceptance of women in public ministry from the fundamentalist Bible school culture of the first half of the twentieth century."[52] Larsen notes that even Betty's father and great-uncle were, at least at one point, in Maxwell's camp: during Betty's childhood, militant British suffragist Christabel Pankhurst preached in their home church in Moorestown, at their invitation.

———

The day before she left for PBI, Betty had written to her mother that her questions about her relationship with Jim were stilled when she remembered the love of God, expressed in Jesus's death on the cross. But as is the way with stillness, this was a tenuous and flickering achievement. On the train to Alberta, she had read the book of Colossians, with its "warnings about forced piety, self-mortification, severity to the body. How," she wondered, "could I tell if this was what I was guilty of?"[53] She was afraid of rejecting a gift from God, and she was afraid of giving too much weight to her feelings for Jim and stepping outside God's will. In an anguished letter to her mother she wrote:

> More than anything else in the world I fear myself. I can trust God to be unchangingly faithful—I could trust Him to keep me and guide me if I could honestly say I desire nothing save His own, complete will. But how do I know that that is all I desire? How can I know a heart that is deceitful above all things and DESPERATELY WICKED? God judges those who are disobedient. We must suffer. Oh, suppose I should, by allowing feeling to overcome faith, miss His direction?[54]

Betty was wrestling with uncertainty because of Jim, but her questions were bigger than Jim. They revolved around the character of God and the complexities of humanness.

The anxiety voiced in this letter stems from three interwoven ideas. First, Betty treats God's will as minutely specific, leaving little or no room for human freedom and personality. It is as if God were a mother sending her children outside to play in the fenced backyard. Ordinarily, in such a situation, the mother's will is that the children stay inside the fence, avoid the flowers, and not deliberately hurt each other. Given those parameters, she doesn't care whether they swing on the swing set, climb the trees, or dig in the sandbox. But Betty sees God following the children through the yard and telling them, in code, which toys they may play with, and how to conduct their play. Human free will is limited to the choice to obey—or disobey.

The idea that there is one right choice is very appealing. It creates the possibility that we can choose correctly and have everything turn out okay. But the other side of the coin, the second element of Betty's worry, is that with such a view of obedience, even an earnest seeker can miss the narrow path. Because she wants to do God's will *in the abstract*, but in the *particular* she also wants to be with Jim, she is afraid she might be deceived even about her desire to obey.

The third strand of the rope is belief that God's guidance and care are, to some extent, dependent on the perfection of our hearts. "I could trust Him to keep me and guide me," she says, "*if* I could honestly say I desire nothing save His own, complete will" (emphasis added). If there is one right choice, and if even trying hard to make the right choice is no guarantee because of the heart's deceitfulness, then it is possible to miss the right choice and step outside God's care.

———

In November, Jim's mother invited Betty to spend Christmas at the Elliot home in Portland. As much as she wanted to see the West Coast and spend time with Jim, however, she declined the invitation. It would have been difficult to manage due to both financial and time constraints, but more importantly, she explained to her mother, "Jim & I cannot allow ourselves to go ahead and do things ordinarily done only by those who plan to be married. One just doesn't go buzzing around the country, spending the weekend in the homes of young men!"[55] Instead, she would spend her first Christmas alone. On December 25 Betty wrote in her journal:

> I am alone, in the evening of a strange Christmas Day. My heart seems to be full of unnamed yearnings mingled with praise and at the same time an aching void. How to describe it? Someone in the opposite dormitory is playing "Jesus, Keep Me Near the Cross." It strikes home. For shadowing

that joy to the world which the incarnation brought was the inexorable, eternal purpose of Bethlehem—Calvary.[56]

As it turned out, Jim would not have been in Portland if she had gone. He spent the holiday with his aunt near Wheaton, then got special permission to take his finals early so that he could go home in January 1949 for his brother Bert's wedding. It was the last time all the Elliots would be together.

Back at Wheaton for his final semester, Jim was reading the book of Romans. He began to feel that he had been living by a pious "code of don'ts," and that chapter 14, especially, meant he was free to enjoy many things that he had previously seen as a waste of time. He called this new sense of freedom his "renaissance," and started to play in new ways: dressing up in silly costumes for junior-senior rivalry week, attending parties, buying a harmonica, going camping or to the lake with classmates, skipping class, dating.[57] He wrote of it to Betty, who felt on reading his letter as if he had become a completely different person. She wrote in her journal: "I had been faced with eternity today, reading Revelation 15 and 16 and A.C. *Things As They Are*—and could not but weep my heart out at the disappointment all this has been."[58] After everything he had said to her and others about wasting time on nonessential activities—after everything he had told her about sacrificing their love for higher things—she was afraid his behavior meant he was leaving the narrow path.

She wrote him to tell him how she felt and also wrote his close friend Bill Cathers, "asking him to pray and, if he deems wise, to exhort the brother along the line of Titus 2:6."[59] Then she waited—more than a week—for her letter to get to Jim and his to come back.

When it came, his reply was even more upsetting. He made a pretense of apologizing, but most of the letter was by turns defensive and flippant. Implying that she was overreacting, he told her she could like it or lump it in regard to him and his behavior. She had already been considering lumping it, writing in her journal even before his response came, "Should all be revoked?" Because Jim did not start saving Betty's letters until well into 1949, there is no record of what she wrote in reply. Her journal makes note of how she was working to restrain herself from making the "choice retorts" that came to mind. But his next two letters were equally painful, telling more stories of his dates with other women that directly contradicted his earlier professions of love to her and accusing her of craftiness and possessiveness in their relationship. She argued back in notes penciled in the margins of his letters and confided her lacerated feelings to her journal. "Last night, after receiving the first letter in three weeks from Jim, my soul was nearly torn apart. . . . Then I remembered. I had prayed, 'No matter how'—it is only for my Lord to choose my cross. Can He not give grace and enable me to go in peace? . . . 'Though He slay me, yet will I trust Him.'"[60]

———

Betty continued to pray over her next step. She had received no response to her application with SIM. After sending it she had learned that there were far more missionaries in Africa than in South America, and she was beginning to question whether SIM was the right organization for her after all. Then, too, there was the question of money. She had been praying all year for "the Lord to make it possible for me to be financially independent of the family in some way or other."[61] In early March, just before news of Jim's renaissance, Betty had spoken with her student counselor, explaining her perplexity "about Jim, the S.I.M., etc., . . . She advised me strongly to withdraw my application and go out in Canadian S.S. Mission this summer."[62]

The Canadian Sunday School Mission (CSSM) had begun in 1927 "to carry the Gospel to the 'otherwise unreached' in rural Western Canada, primarily by organizing and supervising Sunday schools."[63] The CSSM job Betty was considering would include traveling throughout a rural district, making home visits, recruiting students, organizing and facilitating Sunday schools, teaching Bible classes in the public schools until they let out for the summer, and then creating and running vacation Bible schools. She shrank from the prospect of so much personal contact with strangers. But it would solve the immediate problem of what to do after leaving PBI, and it would take care of her financial needs for the time being, since, as she cheerfully noted, the CSSM would pay her living expenses "plus 12.50 a month, if they have it."[64] And they would provide a coworker and a place to stay. She sent in her application.

The next order of business was to break the news to her family. In her journal she wrote that she "could not refrain from a few tears at the thought of having to tell Mother that I will not see her for at least six months,"[65] but in her letter she exhorted her family to "rejoice and be exceeding glad, for great is our reward in heaven. . . . Every day the Lord gives me greater joy in thinking of it, and I am amazed that He could make me want to do a thing like this!"[66] Three days later, when her formal acceptance letter arrived, she had cold feet again: "You can't imagine how I tremble at the prospect of this work. It will be so new to me, and if I fear this missionary experience, what kind of a foreign missionary would I ever make? So please pray that the Lord Himself will be my teacher during the short period I have before I am thrust out."[67]

———

The last two months at PBI went by quickly. The school allowed students going on to work for the CSSM to stay on campus until it was time for them to take up their positions, working half-time to earn their keep and making any necessary preparations, "such as flannelgraph making, etc."[68] Betty was assigned to chop and prepare vegetables and serve in the cafeteria, and she spent her free time for the first week doing laundry and mending so her wardrobe would be ready for the summer. After that, she used her afternoons to read. She had already ploughed through the school's collection of Carmichael books, so she started E. M. Bounds's *Power through Prayer*, then Jessie Penn-Lewis's *Thy Hidden Ones*, which examined Song of Solomon as an allegory for the Christian life. Her father sent her *The Life and Diary of David Brainerd*, a new edition of the eighteenth-century home missionary's journals, which had been heavily edited by Jonathan Edwards before their original publication; the introduction and a brief biography of Edwards were written by Philip himself. Betty wrote to thank her father for the gift, saying that "the sketch of Edwards is especially valuable to me," and noting of Brainerd, "He certainly burnt out for God, if any man ever did."[69]

Meanwhile, Katharine had written to remonstrate with Betty over how much she was apparently relying on Carmichael's ideas in her decision-making, particularly in her relationship with Jim, and to gently suggest she read other things. For months, Betty had been consuming a literary diet composed exclusively of writers who passionately exhorted their readers to self-sacrifice, backing it up with the strongest claims to spiritual authority.

She was not reading with an entirely uncritical eye; when she finished Hudson Taylor's biography, *Growth of a Soul*, for example, though she recommended the book highly she also noted that it was "probably like any other biography in glossing over some of the discrepancies in character . . . spiritualizing some things which perhaps are not very deserving of such treatment."[70] But her letters show that she was clearly being influenced by her reading. Her language had increasingly become the ornate language of those authors and was thick with quotations, from Carmichael in particular. Katharine was understandably concerned that Betty was going to be led by her admiration for Carmichael into unnecessary sacrifice and pain. Betty wrote back saying that she welcomed her mother's advice and always prayed about it, but that she was basing her decisions on a confluence of circumstance and Scripture and felt that her understanding of God's guidance was sound.

This was not the first time Katharine had voiced concern over Betty and Jim's relationship. A few weeks before, she had questioned whether Jim was right to disclose his feelings without making some kind of commitment. Then, too, Betty had responded by agreeing in principle but sticking to her guns:

> I know just exactly what you mean, and that is the way I have always looked upon it. No man should tell a woman he loves her and then leave it there, for her to wait and wonder, hope and plan her strategy to nail him. But in our case, Mother—(Oh yes, I know—everyone says "in our case . . .") but that is all I can say. How can I convey to you the assurance I have had from the very first moment of the Lord's direction?

She tried to reassure her mother that they had both received individual guidance from God pointing them in the same direction. "There was no period of 'courtship,' no dates and 'growing attachment,' none of the usual accoutrements of so-called romance. It seemed that we were separately led in the same ways." And she argued that although their separation might seem inexplicable to others, "there have been lessons learned which could not have been otherwise. Power to help others in a new way is ours. New understanding of the Cross, and its meaning when Paul said 'What things were <u>gain</u> to me, those I counted lost for Christ.'"[71]

While Betty and Jim had not followed the typical pattern of their peers in the sense of dates to entertainment events, it's not accurate to suggest that there was no "period of 'courtship'" or "growing attachment." They had been gradually becoming attached since her junior year at Wheaton, had talked long after the rest of the family had gone to bed over Christmas vacation, had studied together and been on weekly mission trips together for much of her senior year, had shared meals and walks and talks. Jim had deliberately pursued her—had been, as he said, "knocking himself out" to get to know her—and he later told her that by the end of that Christmas visit he had "grown very much into attachment" to her.[72]

From the beginning of his interest in Betty, Jim wrestled with an apparent conflict between that interest and the idea that Jesus should be all he needed. And Betty—both at the time and years afterward—repeatedly described their early relationship in terms of puzzlement and questions. But Jim did have times where he felt assured of God's leading, and in Betty's definite reply to her mother's concerns, there are again echoes of Jim, who had written to his parents, "What God's way is in bringing me [to the Howards' for Christmas] I cannot now say, but that He is leading and that His purpose shall not fail, I know without doubt."[73]

———

"Darkness is settling over the boscage behind my tiny home," Betty wrote to her family, "and I write by the coal oil lamp light. The peepers in a distant slough are tuning up for the evening concert, and an occasional barnyard animal makes a disinterested remark. I am alone. Yes, for the first time in my life, completely alone."[74] Her assigned coworker had a prior commitment until early June, so after convincing their supervisor that she wouldn't be afraid, Betty had gotten permission to head to her station by herself. Early in May, she had arrived at the little trailer on the edge of the Alberta farm that was to be her home for the summer. "It is a new and strange experience," she wrote in her journal, "and I feel keenly my need of the mighty Fortress."[75]

Betty had cleaned out the cigarette butts and empty whiskey bottles left by some unauthorized visitor who had used it after the last summer missionary left, dusted and swept, and unpacked the little box of canned beans, cheese, candy, fruit, honey, tea, instant coffee, homemade jam, and baked goods given her by some kind people at PBI. The C family, whose land she was staying on, brought over a quart of milk fresh from the cow and showed her the "fridge"—a hole in the ground "lined with boards & paper" in the woods nearby. Betty made herself a cup of tea on the smoking woodstove, then settled in to write a letter home. "It is hard for me to realize that I am actually here—in mission work!"[76]

"Here," was more or less Patience, Alberta, about 130 miles north of PBI. Patience was not an official town but a rural post office. The surrounding area was primarily populated with German immigrants, and most families were bilingual. Many were Lutheran, Seventh Day Adventist, or Jehovah's Witness. The area was considered difficult to evangelize by the CSSM. Travel was challenging, particularly when rain turned the gravel and dirt roads into sticky, sucking mud. And some people naturally resented attempts to convert them, while others just weren't interested. It was hard for summer missionaries, unable to develop relationships over time, to get much attendance at meetings. Betty got to work right away. "I intend to go tomorrow to secure permission from one school board to hold S. S. this Sunday. Visitation work begins immediately, of course." The CSSM had provided her with a bicycle, "with which to cover the some 10 mile radius, including 3 or 4 school districts," for which she was responsible.[77]

The work could be further complicated by the missionaries themselves. Betty discovered that her hosts, who were Adventists, had been off put by the previous summer worker's attempts to argue them into his way of thinking. Betty tried to take a more thoughtful approach. At the end of her first week she had bicycled about 17 miles and made eight different home visits, issuing invitations to children who had been absent when the Sunday school was announced, but had "felt it best to just try to become acquainted so far, and have had reading & prayer with only one lady, yesterday." Her biggest concern at first was that adults were asking for church services, which contradicted her beliefs about women preaching. But, trying to remain sensitive to God's direction, she did not discard the idea. "There are no able men here to preach, so it is a question in my mind whether, in such a case, it is our responsibility. . . . My heart & mind are open to the leading of the Spirit in this matter, & I do hope you will pray especially that I will have wisdom." Ultimately, she and her coworker would take it in turns to "bring the message" at services.[78]

Life in this rural community required some adjustments from Betty. There was no heat in the trailer overnight or in the mornings until she got out of bed and made a fire. Even at the end of May, fresh snow was falling, and she was sleeping in her sweater, with both of her coats piled on top of her blankets. She did her laundry by hand—and sometimes did it twice if Mrs. C's free-range pigs got into the basket of clean clothes—then ironed it with cast-iron sad irons, heated on the cookstove. To a city girl the small houses built by the farmers seemed primitive, and after the thorough orderliness of Birdsong, many seemed disorderly to the point of squalor.

Manners were not always what she was used to either. She was horrified while visiting to watch one family eat with their hands and throw the bones from their meal on the table itself. And after a lifetime in various consciously Christian communities where many things weren't done or were only done in secret, many of the things she was now exposed to were strange or upsetting. She was scandalized that the Lutheran church served beer at its twenty-fifth anniversary party, as well as by the gambling she saw. She wrote to her family of the "terrible sin which abounds in this place": profanity, adultery, alcoholism, domestic violence.[79] She learned that her landlord was running a still but decided as a safety precaution to ignore it until the summer was over.

Teaching was challenging. "I find it hard," she wrote, "to teach these same lessons over and over, and keep them living—'Spirit and Life' to me and to the children."[80] She felt unprepared and often discouraged.

> The enemy is sifting me, I can well perceive. . . . He comes to me with such remarks as, "What can _you_ do here where for at least three summers others have worked the same hard soil? . . . How can one with a personality like yours ever break thro' the barriers when meeting people with the gospel? How can you, whose own life so greatly lacks in spiritual things, ever hope to help others?"[81]

Home visiting, too, was uphill work. Some people were dismissive of her efforts, and those who took her more seriously were not necessarily in agreement with her.

Letters from home were a small bright spot. So was a letter from Jim, indicating that Bill Cathers had indeed "exhorted the brother," and he had begun to listen. He admitted that his "liberty became license in some things, and a stumbling block to some people."[82] And he said that she and Bill were not the only people who had taken him to task: "Others have come to me with such reports, and I have been tremendously helped by their frank tolerance and love. I have had to make several apologies about my overdoing this freedom. . . . Your prayers have done more than you now imagine."[83] This was not the end of her heartache over the situation, but she was comforted by his changing attitude.

———

When Betty's coworker finally arrived after three weeks, things became more difficult. The CSSM had been reluctant to place the two women together in the first place—not only because Fay Fredricksen had also attended college and could also ride a horse and drive a car, and they wanted to spread the talent between stations, but because, as Betty had told her mother, both women were "strong minded." Betty had looked forward to it as "a good test and trial of our faith, and grace," but the mission had been concerned that they would have trouble working together.[84] Those concerns turned out to be well-founded. The pair had their first conflict the day after Fay's arrival, with Fay objecting to the way Betty treated her, and Betty bewildered as to what she'd done. Two days later she wrote in her journal, "I honestly have no idea when she will take what I say as an affront. Oh, Lord—I beseech Thee to make me loving and lovable."[85] When Betty tried to share her struggles in the work and the spiritual lessons she felt she was learning, Fay's response seemed uninterested and unsympathetic to Betty.

If Fay did not see Betty's perspective, neither did Betty understand Fay's. One journal entry recorded, "This afternoon as we rode along, Fay began questioning whether or not the heathen were lost. I gave her a few scriptures to show that they were, and said I thought that such questions were dangerous. 'Oh, fiddle!' she said, 'Betty Howard, you act like I didn't have a brain in my head!'"[86] Betty worried that Fay was too frivolous, making it look as though both women were out for a good time rather than for spiritual gain.

One incident particularly illustrates the difficulties between the two women. About 2 miles into an 8-mile journey, Betty and Fay were caught in the rain. The road quickly turned to viscous, sucking mud. They got stuck and stuck again—and again—Fay more often than Betty because of the design of her bike. Finally Fay lost her temper. Betty tried to help, offering to trade bikes or to take turns pushing Fay's bike ("for I've had experience with such mud before and I don't get <u>mad</u> at it,"[87] she told her mother), but Fay ridiculed the suggestion and marched on angrily. Betty didn't respond directly to the sharp things Fay said to her, but she did wait for Fay to get ahead of her and then start singing a hymn. It's unclear whether Fay could hear her. Happily, before they had gone much farther a local man drove by and gave them and their bikes a ride the rest of the way in his Jeep. One can see how Betty was trying to have a good attitude in a difficult situation, to be helpful to her coworker, and to maintain a proper perspective. But one can also see how, particularly because of Betty's ongoing struggle to convey a warm mien and their history of disagreement, her vocal, determined cheerfulness could have irritated.

The women continued to have difficulties through their time together. Although Betty felt they "had some blessed times, and many victories have been won individually & collectively,"[88] their relationship was perhaps her biggest challenge. In this as in other circumstances, she tried to control not just her public behavior, but also her own thoughts and the way she spoke of Fay behind her back. She shared some of her difficulties with her mother, and asked her to pray for them, but worried that sharing too much of her struggle was unfair. "Oh, Mother—I cannot tell you more. Perhaps I should not have told you this much, for I do not wish to judge her, and I find my own soul so desperately in need."[89] Despite their struggles, however, the women managed to forge a cordial enough relationship that at the end of the summer, Fay invited Betty to visit her parents' vacation home with her, and Betty accepted.

———

Running in the background throughout the summer was the tension on the C farm. It was a difficult summer for farmers, with a drought followed by destructive hailstorms. Before Betty had been there two weeks,

Mr. C had spent the night in jail for public drunkenness. She reported to her mother that Mrs. C was seeing another man, while Mr. C was running around with multiple women and systematically selling off farm equipment to buy booze. Mrs. C was left to take care of the farm work, the housework, and their four young children by herself. "The barn is just about to fall over," Betty reported, "and Mrs. [C] is desperate to know where to keep her cows this winter."[90] But his absence was better than his presence, since he regularly physically abused his wife and had threatened to shoot her if she tried to leave him.

Betty originally resolved not to get involved but found herself increasingly drawn into the conflict. And after her first report on the dangerously abusive situation, her sympathies seemed increasingly to lie with the husband. When Mr. C went into town for a few hours and didn't come back for two days, Betty noted disapprovingly that when she questioned his wife, she seemed unconcerned about his absence. It is hard to know what else Mrs. C could have done, since she couldn't control her husband's behavior, couldn't very well leave the farm work and the children to try to find him, and barely knew this pious young woman who was asking questions about her marriage. In the same paragraph Betty happily reported watching Mr. C shoot gophers and remarked on his good aim, an anecdote that becomes macabre in light of his threats to shoot his wife.

Over the course of the summer, Betty repeatedly dismissed Mrs. C's experience as not worth making a fuss over, blamed her for provoking the abuse, and counseled her to stay in the dangerous situation. In July Betty and Fay came back from work to find that Mr. C had hit his wife so hard he had knocked her unconscious, and Mrs. C was selling her livestock in preparation for leaving him. But when Betty reported this to her mother, she noted that Mrs. C had slapped him first and thus invited the abuse, asserting that "all along, Mr. [C] has shown a far more tolerant spirit than has she."[91]

When Mr. C realized that his wife really meant to follow through on leaving him, he showed up on Betty and Fay's doorstep with a hard-luck story about his marriage. Fay was out and Betty was home with a cold, so she became literally his shoulder to cry on. For the next three hours, while the C children watched and listened, their father sobbed and bewailed "how great a sinner he was, & how he had tried so many times to do better, & failed," how he could never be saved, and how he had hoped his wife would help him but "instead . . . she curses him." Betty, clearly unaware of the cycles of abusive relationships and the manipulative behavior of abusers, was deeply moved and readily convinced of his sincerity. She alternately listened to him cry and repeat himself, and tried to convince him that he needed to turn to Jesus for forgiveness and salvation. He finally stumbled inside to bed, and one of the children reported to Betty in the morning "that after her daddy got into bed he said 'Kids, for the first time in my life I believe there is a God. And I feel as light as air.'" Betty wrote to her family, "Need I ask you to pray as you have never prayed before? God will surely have to do a miracle such as I have never seen. Oh, I pray that Mr. [C] may not be kept from salvation because my faith is too small!"[92]

The next day, Mrs. C came back to the farm. And for the next few weeks, Mr. C gave some evidence of change. When someone came by to purchase moonshine a week later, Mr. C refused to sell, saying he had quit drinking. A week after that, the C family attended one of the CSSM meetings for the first time, and Betty reported that "Mr. [C] had tears in his eyes as we sang 'Jesus, Savior, Pilot Me.'"[93] But by mid-August the couple were in conflict again. Although the Cs' difficulties were quite complex, with emotional, relational, psychological, physiological, cultural, socioeconomic, and spiritual components, the only tool Betty could offer was spiritual. Her inability to address the other aspects of the family's trouble is due in large part to the limitations of the time period and of her own youth and inexperience. From a twenty-first-century perspective, Betty's response to this abusive family situation is deeply flawed, but it was entirely in keeping with the cultural attitude of the time.

———

The other constant of the summer of 1949 was the great kindness the local people showed the two missionary women. Betty's letters continually report lavish gifts of food—home-canned jams, home-cured bacon, freshly caught fish, fruit from the orchards, vegetables from the gardens, even whole cooked meals. And this was despite the fact that drought and hail had destroyed most of both the gardens and the cash crops in the area. The Cs' also took Faye to the doctor when she was sick, sheltered the two women during the catastrophic hailstorm, and brought them along on fun family outings. Betty and Faye were invited to delicious meals at people's houses several times a week. People lent them books. Passing farmers stopped to give them rides. Given the hard work that these families did every day to survive and the hardships the summer had brought them, the care which the community provided for two sometimes-difficult strangers is remarkable.

Nevertheless, Betty was lonely. She missed her family, and long stretches of time went by with little news from Jim. He was living with his parents, working on the house his brother Bob was beginning to build, helping around his parents' house and at their church, studying the Bible as much as he could, and trying to discern God's will for his future.

In July Jim wrote to Betty that "these days seem strange ones of waiting, sort of marking time till all the red-tape gets time to pass, but I am sure I have not missed the Lord's mind. . . . I have had to reconcile myself to staying in the U.S. until I've proved myself in the work here. The brethren would have it no other way." A few days later he wrote in his journal, "Painted part of the [Brethren meeting] hall today. Restless to do other things more directly related to the Lord's work."[94] He was chafing under the sense that the *real* work was *out there* somewhere.

Jim's letters were often unsettling for Betty. In one, he reported a practical joke in which he had convinced many people that he was engaged to a local friend—then complained that he had heard a rumor that he and *Betty* were engaged, and spoke of this as evidence that their relationship had been "careless."[95] Another letter accused her of intentionally writing infrequently in order to manipulate him, leaving her at a loss as to how to respond.

In August Jim's mother extended another invitation for Betty to visit the Elliots in Portland. Betty was "full of misgivings," as she would later write, and initially told her family, "I can't see doing it unless the Lord works a miracle to provide the way."[96] But eventually she felt she had received assurance that she should go. The fact that spending a weekend in a young man's home was "ordinarily done only by those who plan to be married" was no longer a sufficient reason to decline.

Betty and Fay said goodbye to their little trailer on the last Thursday of August, heading for Poulsbo, Washington, a small farming and logging community where Fay's family had a vacation house. They stopped along the way to do a little shopping and sightseeing. Betty kept a careful tally of her expenses for the journey on the back of an envelope, including a ten-cent ice cream, and $5.15 to have her old coat dyed to smarten it up. After a couple of days with Fay's family, Betty took a Greyhound bus to Portland.

Jim met her at the bus station and drove her out to the Elliot family's rambling home on Mount Tabor in Southeast Portland. "I am actually in Portland, Oregon," Betty wrote in her journal that night, calling it a "name that has always sent chills up my spine."[97] The Elliot family was spending Labor Day weekend facilitating a Brethren conference, so her first night there was spent in a meeting (at which Jim spoke) and a hymn sing. There were three meetings a day on Saturday, Sunday, and Monday, but Betty and Jim squeezed in a little time alone by skipping meals.

Much of the rest of the ten-day visit was filled with sightseeing. The couple canoed out to an island on the Columbia River, where they read and discussed their letters from the last year, trying to smooth out some of the misunderstandings, and spent a day at the Oregon coast, where they swam in the ocean and sat talking by a driftwood fire while they watched the sunset. On their last day together, Betty and Jim went hiking on Mount Hood. Although Betty called it in her journal "one of the most wonderful days of my life! A *perfect* day," the trip ended "in silence and tears," at least in part because of a disagreement over physical contact.[98] Jim wanted more than Betty was willing to engage in. "Her uprightness makes it so hard," he wrote in his journal. "She loves, I know, but, oh, how bitter is love unexpressed. And she will not let me hold her, hardly touch her, for she says, 'I am not mine to give you.'"[99] They cried again as they said goodbye at the bus station.

———

From Portland Betty took the bus down the West Coast, past redwood forests, through San Francisco, over the Golden Gate Bridge, through Los Angeles (with a visit to friends at Fuller Theological Seminary in Pasadena) and the Painted Desert, to Albuquerque, Denver, St. Louis, and Philadelphia on her way to her parents' home in Moorestown. "It was only $9 more to come this way," she wrote to her mother, and it let her see parts of the country she had long wanted to visit.[100] She delighted in the beauty around her at each stage of the trip. But in Pasadena, she was upset by more detailed reports of Jim's renaissance. Previously she had had only Jim's description of his actions to go on, but after hearing the perspectives of friends there, she felt that his behavior had been even worse than it had originally seemed.[101]

And when she got home, more heartache was waiting for her. Jim had sent a mortifying letter: "What I am going to write now," he told her, "I do not know whether I should say. It seems almost like betraying my folks before an outsider, but I am going ahead—painfully for us both—trusting that this will eventually be for your good." The impression she had made on his family "could not have been worse." His mother thought she had seemed "obsessed" with Jim and chilly toward everyone else, making her "a poor prospective missionary." She had spoken of Betty as an "institution child" with "little domestic adaptability," making her a poor prospective homemaker as well. His father had said she was unattractive—"no face, no form . . . spindly"—and conniving. His sister "never saw you reading your Bible" or "taking any lead in spiritual converse," and formed an unfavorable impression of her faith. Only his aunt and his sister-in-law had seen something positive, saying, "These quiet people feel more deeply than those of us who say so much," and "I admire her for not putting on a show for us." Perhaps worst of all, Jim followed it with, "I don't write now as if they were all wrong." Betty was "utterly crushed."[102]

She waited almost a week to write back, uncertain as to how to respond and dreading the "3,000 miles of possibility for misunderstanding."[103] When she finally sat down to reply, she first addressed the renaissance, which had never really stopped bothering her. Among her concerns were the "kissing incidents" that had been reported in Pasadena:

> Jim, I must say these things because I feel them strongly, and am not yet at rest about your attitude toward the whole business. . . . To be *very* specific, for example, it confounded me how anyone who defines the significance of a kiss as you once did to me, could carry on in such an utterly frivolous vein, joking about it, a thing so sacred. . . . Jim, it doesn't hang together. You can't behave like that one minute, and turn around the next and say you love in purity. . . . It seems now, after what I've heard, that you acted contrary to scriptural principles. . . . Jim, my brother, (I call you that now, for it is the only basis on which I dare talk to you this way)—what think ye? Am I unfair, harsh, unduly concerned?[104]

When she had told him of her concerns in the spring, he had chided her for being possessive and manipulative. He had suggested that since he had made it clear from the beginning that he was not *committed* to her, she had no grounds to be upset. So in this letter at the end of the summer, she addressed him not as a lover but as a Christian brother. He had "acted contrary to scriptural principles" and dragged others down with him. Just as he had done many times for her, it was her duty to speak up when he was in need of course correction. Her bringing the issue up again was not manipulation, but sincere concern for his spiritual well-being.

But in his earlier accusations against Betty, Jim had been equivocating. He had made her no formal commitment, claiming that he was not free before God to commit. He had said that if he was ever free to do so, she was the woman he would marry. It was not unreasonable of her to expect him not to date and kiss other women, regardless of how the situation appeared to the rest of the world.

Next, she responded to the criticism of herself. Although she did try to explain what had happened in a few specific situations where she felt she had been misunderstood, she took the blame for "the awful 'flop' I made of my visit," saying that she knew she was "greatly in need of openness in meeting new friends," and that Jim's mother "was most gracious and thoughtful of me, especially in view of how she felt about me—I don't see how she could put herself out for me as she did." She was deeply discouraged because the Elliots' first impression of her was already formed. "I have sealed my image in their minds, even if I do improve, which by the grace of God I have purposed to do. Letters would accomplish nothing now—I am the faker who writes high-sounding letters and is a different person in actuality." Nevertheless, she accepted their criticism. "Pray for me, Jim—and continue to be devastatingly honest, even if it crushes me flatter than I am now! You are right that I cannot be excused, and the Lord alone is able to do anything with this mess." Then she sent the letter off and waited on pins and needles for his reply.[105]

When it came, two long weeks later, it softened some of the sting of the last. Jim responded to her unrest about his behavior with a real expression of remorse: "Your recent concern over the Renaissance I consider neither harsh, undue, nor unfair. My private regrets are more than I care to share with you—deeper than I am able to share, I think. . . . For the fact that it has blackened my conscience, hurt you, stumbled others, and brought dishonor to Christ, I now experience overwhelming sorrow."[106] This was a comfort. Then, too, the situation with his family did not sound quite as bad now as it had before. Much could be attributed, he suggested, to the difference in communication styles between their families. And their opinion of her was not set in stone, as she had feared. He had explained to his mother that she had misunderstood Betty's character, and she had replied, "Well, we must have her back again, I have misjudged."[107]

But to Betty's frustration, Jim also brought up the status of their relationship again. Dave, he said, had told him he ought to stop writing to her, to stop pursuing a relationship when he still had no plans to marry. Jim reiterated that his "answer from the Lord about marriage" was still no, and said that he would leave to her the decision about their correspondence.[108] His letter came on a Monday, and after thinking about it for the week, she sat down on Friday to respond. Dave might not have known all the facts of their relationship to date, but Jim did, and she was dismayed to find that he felt he had to ask again.

> Have we not hashed this out from start to finish? Have I not told you that the whole business, for my part, has undergone exhaustive examination several times in the past six months? Would I not long since have thrown in the sponge without waiting your "permission" had I any doubts as to its legality? You speak of *your* liberty, *your* choices . . . *your* decisions. Rest assured, Jim, my consent to correspond was based on the liberty the Lord gave *me*.[109]

Then, too, she wondered whether he was concerned about her, or whether Dave's letter had irked him because it suggested that she felt possessive of him or was trying to manipulate him into commitment—two things he had suggested were the case in the past.

> And I am not just sure whether your fears that I shall be hurt are fostered by a genuine tenderness and solicitude for my well-being, or are perhaps faintly tinged with the suspicion that things matter far more hugely to me than they do to you. If this latter is your thought (and I do not suggest it *accusingly*, for it may be true, I being of the "weaker sex"), I wouldn't

worry my head too much about it if I were you. . . . Did I consent to correspond with any illusions as to the outcome? I think not. We were very clear on this point.[110]

She knew and had spoken her own mind and was responsible for her own conscience before God. She was *not* trying to manipulate him into commitment. In fact, she was bending over backwards to keep her feelings for him to herself ("how I long to be with Jim sometimes," she wrote in her journal at about the same time) and behave toward him as she would toward her other good friends.[111]

But Jim wanted to have his cake and eat it too. Although when there was conflict between them, he repeatedly emphasized that she had no claim on him, he responded to this letter by complaining that she was too "nonchalant" about their relationship, "not taking me as seriously as I should like you to!" He even asked her to send a picture of herself as his Christmas present, saying it was a "necessity" to him.[112] And try as she might, she couldn't help the butterflies that came with these signs of his romantic feelings for her.

———

Betty spent the fall in Moorestown. With the exception of a short trip to the National Bible Institute in New York City, where she substitute-taught a Greek class for a friend of her parents', her days were full of sewing, "painting the porch and a room inside; baking bread, cleaning every Wednesday and Thursday, etc., besides regular household chores," teaching Sunday school, and studying the Bible.[113]

Guidance for her next step came in the form of a request from the DuBoses to work as a substitute teacher at HDA. Mr. and Mrs. DuBose were in increasingly poor health, Pete was away at college, and Peyton DuBose Cole, who had just taken over official management of the school in the summer, was pregnant with her first child and needed someone to assume some of her teaching duties. Betty accepted, though she was apprehensive about returning to HDA. She wrote to Jim not long before she left, "There are things involved which I cannot write, but will mean the necessity of keeping low before God."[114] Years later she would call it "a decision which I feared considerably."[115]

By the end of January 1950, she was in Florida. HDA was the same whirl of activity it had been in her student days, and Mrs. DuBose was as mercurial as ever. Betty was assigned to teach two sections of speech, coach declamations, give singing lessons, help with debate, entertain guests, supervise work groups, and do a fair amount of manual labor herself. She worked hard to have a good attitude, asking her mother to pray "that I may be true as steel and <u>faithful</u> in this which the Lord has given me to do. It is not easy in some ways, but I am glad to be here for this time. <u>The Lord is the strength of my life.</u>"[116]

At HDA, Ginny and Betty now saw each other on a daily basis for the first time in years. Their relationship since Betty had left home almost a decade before had not always been smooth, with Betty alternately teasing Ginny, getting irritated with her, and lecturing her from afar. But the opportunity to spend more time together left Betty impressed by her sister's talents and character, proudly reporting to her mother that "when someone shows a good spirit about something that ought to gripe them, they are said to be 'pulling a Ginny Howard.'"[117]

The sisters were also brought together by shared concern for their oldest brother. Phil, whose first child had just been born, was experiencing a spiritual crisis, and Betty and Ginny got together regularly to pray for him. He had quit pursuing missionary work entirely and was working as a truck driver. Although Betty did not fully understand what was wrong, she reported to her parents after visiting Phil en route to Zellwood that his struggle was "definitely about the justice of God." She felt that she had experienced similar doubts herself but had been able to set them aside as something not understood but accepted in faith. Wisely, she realized that arguing with her brother would make things worse. Instead she had encouraged him to commit to regular Bible reading and prayer even though he didn't feel like it. "If God is not true, you will discover this for yourself," she told him, "and at least you will have given Him a chance to prove Himself."[118]

By late April, the family saw signs that Phil had turned a corner. Betty found this encouraging in regard to her own situation, telling her mother that if God could "do that for him, He also can lead me."[119] She still did not have a plan for her next step after HDA, and although throughout the semester she had written that she was not worried about it, the frequency with which she mentioned it belies her words. "Still I have not been given light on what I should do this summer, and so I ask you all to continue to pray that I will know."[120] She was struggling with loneliness and a sense of emptiness in her daily life as she waited for guidance. Like Jim, she viewed this as a time of preparation for her real work. She told her family:

> I can see that God could not have let me go to the mission field when I thought I would be going, and through these two years since college He has taught me things, which if I had not learned before going out to the field, might have meant my downfall, and the downfall of others. But it is easy to be impatient. I like the part in [Carmichael's book] "His Thoughts" [*sic*] about "The time of preparation is longer than I had expected." How true! . . . I love each one of you, and love to hear from you all.[121]

But the time of preparation was also a time of *being*, in and of itself, a time of being with God and learning to enjoy God. In another letter Betty wrote, "I was reading this morning in Deuteronomy how that the Lord's people are His inheritance. I had realized before that the Lord is our inheritance, but I had never before seen the interrelation, and oneness with Him. To think of it, that the King of Kings and Lord of Lords, the One who owns the cattle on a thousand hills and who could have anything He desired, should choose me as His Inheritance! 'O Love of loves, I love, I worship, Thee.' as Amy C. says."[122] And in her journal: "'The beloved of the Lord shall dwell in safety by Him, and the Lord shall cover him all day long, and he shall dwell between His shoulders.' Deut. 33:12. Oh, the joy, first of all in simply *being* 'the beloved of the Lord,' then in the assurance of dwelling *safely by Him*."[123]

———

The Gospels record that when Jesus sent his disciples out to talk about God's kingdom, he split them up into groups of two. Jim saw this as a pattern for missionaries to follow, and he had been praying for a partner since he was at Wheaton—specifically for another man committed to singleness. Dave recalled later that during their time at Wheaton, "Jim had always expressed himself very strongly on campus, in general, that he believed God's highest calling to any man was celibacy. If you're really gonna be sold out for the Lord, don't waste your time on the women, don't waste your time on parties, you know, just give yourself totally to the Lord."[124] Once Jim decided that God was calling him to Ecuador, he tried to convince Dave to be that single partner. But although Dave felt called to missions, he believed God was directing him to a different approach than Jim was pursuing. Jim remained unconvinced.

When Phyllis and Betty had lived together at PBI, Betty had observed that Phyllis stopped writing to Dave, and had assumed that they were no longer an item. Then while visiting the Elliots in September 1949, she had received a letter from her mother containing news about Dave and Phyllis that startled her. In her reply Betty assured her mother that she and Jim were praying seriously for the couple. In her memoirs, Katharine Howard would recall how she had learned that the type of work Dave felt called to was thought to be most suited for married couples, and while praying for a wife for him, had suddenly thought of Phyllis Gibson. When she casually asked Dave what had ever happened to Phyllis, Dave looked at her in shock. He had been thinking of Phyllis all summer, he said, and had prayed that if she was the woman he should marry, God would give him a sign. Then he had picked the most impossible sign he could think of: his mother would bring her up. This could certainly have been the startling news.

When Betty had gotten home after her visit in Portland, she had been "electrified" to learn that Dave and Phyllis were engaged. Betty had written to Jim: "No doubt Dave wrote you of his engagement. Were you as floored as I was? More so, probably, for it was you who said, 'Oh no, he'd never do that.' Tell me what you thought when you heard. They seem supremely happy, so I am glad."[125] Dave remembers:

> When Jim found this out, he still . . . had questions about whether I really oughta get married or not, and was Phyllis really the right one for me. And he wrote me a letter. . . . He said something spiritual like, "Well, we never know what God's gonna do. We just have to trust God, that he knows what he's doing." . . . And then the rest of the letter was okay, and he talked in a more normal way.[126]

Betty's job at HDA ended with the school year in early June, and on July 1, 1950, Dave and Phyllis were married at Wheaton. Jim was Dave's best man, and Betty one of Phyllis's bridesmaids. Betty and Jim had a few hours alone together after the wedding, then Betty went back to Birdsong, and Jim to Oklahoma where he was completing the SIL course.

———

Nine months before, Jim had heard from his older brother of a British Brethren couple, Wilfred and Gwendolyn Tidmarsh, who had been missionaries among the Kichwa people of Ecuador for some time. In December 1948, Gwen had broken both legs when the Mission Aviation Fellowship (MAF) plane she was riding in got caught in a downdraft and crashed on takeoff, and the couple had felt they could no longer sustain the rugged lifestyle required by their rural location. Wilfred had written that he was looking for someone to take their place, and Jim had begun to pray about whether this request was God's call to him personally.

Then, at SIL, Jim heard through Dave Cooper, a Kichwa-speaking missionary working as a language informant, of a neighboring tribe called "aucas," much feared by the Kichwa, who had never had peaceful contact with outsiders. Here was a chance to reach a brand-new people group with the good news about Jesus, a chance to achieve the greatness for God that Jim longed for.[127]

When he returned to SIL after Dave and Phyllis's wedding, Jim decided to spend a stretch of ten days praying for a "definite answer" as to whether this was God's call for him. On the tenth day, he found it, recording in his journal, "I was reading casually in Exodus 23 when verse 20 came out vividly. 'Behold I send an angel before thee to keep thee by the way and to bring thee into the place which I have prepared. Take heed before him.'"[128] Now all he was missing was a commission from the elders of his church and a partner to travel with him.

After the disappointment of Dave's marriage, Jim had high hopes that Bill Cathers would be his partner. Bill had gone to China as a missionary after their Wheaton graduation but had been expelled shortly afterward as part of the widespread ejection of foreign missionaries by the new Communist government. The two men worked together after Jim graduated from SIL, doing odd jobs to earn their keep and working as home missionaries whenever they could while they applied for passports and gathered supplies. Then Bill and his college sweetheart, Irene Deamantes, got engaged.

Around the time of Bill and Irene's engagement, Jim heard from Ed McCully, another Wheaton friend, who was dropping out of law school to pursue missionary work. Jim began to consider whether Ed was the man God had in mind to go with him, and he and Ed spent the next five months traveling together for home missions. But while they were speaking at a youth group, Ed met the church music director, Marilou Hobolth. In the spring, they became engaged.

And then that summer Jim attended a Brethren youth conference and reconnected with a family friend named Peter Fleming. Both men participated in a hiking trip on Mount Rainier, and Jim wrote that "Pete is a most engaging traveling partner, interested in all the things that I notice—geology, botany, history, and the sky and all the good things God has scattered through the west in such extravagant variation."[129] A year younger than Jim, Pete had just graduated with a MA in English. He had felt for some time that God was leading him to a career in teaching, but was increasingly concerned about spending his working life immersed in literature that he felt excluded Christian thought. He had debated teaching at a Christian institution or going to seminary, but neither felt right. Jim's forceful personality and vigorous exposition cut into Pete's uncertainty like a knife. Jim preached at the Brethren assembly that Pete attended on being a "eunuch" for the sake of Christ. Using his own life as an example, he issued a call for some young man to join him. Less than a month later, Pete decided that Jim's call was God's direction in his own life. He broke his private engagement to Olive Ainslie, the young woman he had been pursuing for the last three years, and committed himself as Jim's single partner to Ecuador.

———

There are no surviving family letters from the end of Betty's work at HDA in the summer of 1950 to the beginning of her job as a camp counselor in the summer of 1951. If her journals become available for scholarship at a later date, they may reveal more about her thoughts during this period, but the absence of family letters indicates that she spent this quiet year living with her parents at Birdsong. She had definitely ruled out Africa and the SIM and was praying about going to the Solomon Islands with the South Seas Evangelical Mission.[130] In September 1950 she was working a few days a week as a saleswoman in Blum's department store. She spent a year tutoring two children of missionary parents in or near Moorestown, and she joined a Brethren assembly in Haddonfield, New Jersey, about a twenty-minute drive from Birdsong, attending there long enough that she was able to go to the mission field under their auspices.

The journal excerpts that are available, with passages from Betty's infrequent letters to Jim, show a young woman who was still in "an almost agony of waiting—wondering what the Lord would have me do," but at the same time delighting in a deepening sense of a relationship with Jesus: "Oh, the marvelous, unspeakable interchange of joy—He my joy, I His joy."[131] When Jim wrote in the fall of 1950, rubbing yet again at what he called the "old sores" of their relationship, she could cheerfully reassure him that she felt no claim on him and wished him to pursue God's will for his life without worrying about her. As Valerie Elliot Shepard has pointed out, this seems to have been a time of particular discouragement for Jim, and Betty was able to offer him encouragement—the same encouragement she had gotten during her time in Bible reading and prayer over the preceding difficult months.

Betty would later write that in the fall of 1951, "several events," which she did not enumerate, "indicated that the door to the South Seas was closed to me," and she began instead to pray about going to South America, specifically to Ecuador. Jim strongly encouraged her:

> For a long time there had been no question in either of our minds as to whom we should marry should marriage be the will of God. Had He indicated that this was His will? For each of us, the answer was still No. Jim felt, however, that this was no reason to dismiss from our minds the possibility of God's leading me to South America. He asked me to consider this seriously before the Lord, fully realizing that such a course would lead to criticism and misunderstanding.

And "the answer given during the next four weeks of prayer . . . was that I should go to Ecuador."[132]

Again, it is difficult to know since Betty's journals for this period are largely unavailable, but it appears that the "several events" were actually a visit from Jim in September 1951. He was on his way to the East Coast, where he and Pete would raise financial support by speaking in a series of

Christian meetings, and he asked if he could stop at the Howards' house for a few days on the way. His journals indicate that when he arrived at Birdsong on September 20, Betty still felt led to the Solomon Islands. In what he called a "terribly upsetting" conversation the next day, Jim told her again that he loved her and that he still felt "that God wants him on the field as a single man."[133] It appears that he also asked her to consider going to Ecuador herself as a single woman. By September 27 Betty had formally decided not to go to the Solomon Islands. Although she later wrote that her "inquiries . . . had proved unfruitful," there is no available record of her conducting any inquiries in that seven-day period.[134] On September 29 she wrote in her own journal that "we spoke of the possibility of engagement before his going to the field, but it is not yet the Lord's time. Each of us feels, in our heart of hearts, that God will eventually lead us together."[135] Her course was finally set: she would go to Ecuador.

———

At this time, Jim's letters to Betty and journal entries about her become clearly sensual. Quoting poet James Whitcomb Riley, he wrote of "that *carven* mouth with all its deep intensity of longing . . . !" and how he imagined her "with your slender, white, and empty arms there in a warm bed." Later in November, "I'm glad that last is still ahead. Glad I'm not jaded by nights in bed with you. . . . I have you now unravished, and that is just how I need you now. . . . God knows it is a stay to purity, and He knows how many shakings to purity are ahead." In February, on shipboard, he wrote to her, "Last night in a dream you were more alive than ever—just your face, near and inviting. Oh, how did I resist kissing you before now."[136] From today's vantage point it is difficult to read Jim's writing without the mediating lens of purity culture—a movement that Elisabeth Elliot would later help to shape—and his behavior does not fit the standards of that movement. He seems to have had no problem dwelling on an imagined physical relationship and to have been frequently pushing, both in his letters when they were apart and in his actions when they were together, for more physical contact as well.

Betty had been developing her thinking on this subject for some time. At Wheaton, the teaching of Hans Bürki had influenced her thinking on the unselfishness in love that ought to exist for Christians even in their romantic relationships. In the summer of 1949, after her visit in Portland, she had exhaustively studied the Greek words for love and read widely on love and friendship—Goethe; Emerson; Aristotle; Oswald Chambers; a book by her own great-grandfather, Henry Clay Trumbull, called *Friendship the Master-Passion*. In her journal at the time she had written, "The Lord is wonderfully opening my eyes and showing me what I believe is the explanation of my confusions and perplexities re: the course of our relationship, its changes and anomalies, nature, and degree." She had written to Jim that November, trying to express the idea of "friendship love" that she had developed from her extensive reading.[137]

Although Betty was strongly attracted to Jim and longed for a commit-ted romantic relationship with him, she was disciplining her thoughts and feelings and working hard to make sure that her main concern was that Jim grow in his relationship with God. But, she had pointed out, if they were going to continue without romantic commitment, it would have to be on the grounds of the friendship love that she was outlining: "I believe that you and I, Jim, if we are to continue, must know this *true friendship*, apart from anything else, for it is this alone which continues without con-summation, for it is in itself and by its very nature a fulfillment."[138] In this thoughtful approach, Betty was aligning herself with historic Christian teaching and practice.

Jim was apparently able to conceptualize this kind of friendship in same-sex relationships. He records again and again in his journals his desire for a "David": "The love of David and Jonathan ([1 Samuel] 1:23–26)—felt again today for Bill C. [Cathers] upon receipt of a letter from him en route to China. . . . Oh, to spend eternity with such whose spirit quickens my own—makes me throb just to read his soul's surgings. . . . How I long for another like him—one whose 'love surpasses that of woman.' . . . Lord, give me a *David*, I pray."[139] But he was unable to grasp the idea in a relationship with a person of the other sex. When Betty wrote the November letter about friendship love, pointing out to him that he kept "insisting on claims and evidences" of her love for him, while she was "trying to maintain a relationship that is 'from feeble yearnings freed,'" and reminding him that "the love that is true friendship is selfless," he wrote in his journal, "I wish I understood what Betty wrote."[140] When he finally responded to her letter,

it was to say that he didn't understand and wasn't going to spend time trying to respond.

As Jim continued to push Betty for more sexual expression in their
relationship, he also wrote in his journal, "How many young men in the
church today procure—court and keep—their wives in purity, honor, and
not in lustful passion? The sex hungers of the generation are so intense that
seldom does an average woman arrive at marriage a virgin, and hardly ever
a man—while 'neck happy' Christians regard true courtship as going as far
as one can outside of marriage."[141] This disconnected thinking appears to
be linked to his beliefs about men and women. In the summer of 1950, he
wrote in response to 1 Corinthians 7:

> Man is but a symbol of what exists in the Godhead. God, the Head, Christ,
> the Body, doing what the Head directs is symbolized in man whose head
> directs his body (ideally). Woman is peculiarly more directed by her feel-
> ings, her body, her heart, than by her head. . . . Man, the image of God, is
> covered by nothing, controlling the woman. Woman, the glory of man,
> is covered, controlled by man, as man should be by Christ, as Christ *is* by
> God. Woman has her source in man and her existence on man's account.[142]

Jim's interpretation of Scripture reflects his culture's understanding of
the sexes. As Beth L. Bailey shows, both scientific experts and cultural authorities of the time were busily proclaiming that men and women innately
behaved in certain narrowly defined ways: "Masculine men are powerful,
dominant, aggressive, and ambitious; they are at home in the 'world' and
provide for their wives and children. Feminine women are dependent,
submissive, nurturing, and belong in the home." The experts also said that
the sexes needed to work hard to behave in these ways or society would fall
apart. This self-contradicting belief system saturated American culture right
down to the advertisements in the newspapers, and it carried into the realm
of sexual activity as well. Bailey points out that "the system took for granted
that men would naturally want some form of sexual activity" in a relationship, while placing the moral and actual burden of limiting that activity
not on "innately dominant" man but on "innately submissive" woman.[143]

Betty also accepted this idea that although the responsibility for leadership lay with men in every other area of life, it lay with women in the area

of sexual activity. Though she had not hesitated to reproach Jim when she believed he was out of line spiritually, there is no suggestion that she admonished him for persistently trying to push her past her comfort zone. Her statement that he was "insisting on claims and evidences" was charity itself: she pointed out that true friendship is selfless, not to take him to task for his behavior, but to explain that she did not always live up to her own ideals. "I am selfish, human. So I have fallen many times. But can you see any evidence of my goal, at least, in our past contacts?"[144]

Thirty-five years later, Betty would tell her and Jim's love story in *Passion and Purity*, interspersed with her advice on how to "bring your love life under Christ's control." She would write of "the knowledge that is deep in a woman that she holds the key to the situation where a man's passions are involved. He will be as much of a gentleman as she requires and, when the chips are down, probably no more, even if he has strict standards of his own. He will measure her reserve, always testing the limits, probing."[145] This sentiment mirrors general-market American dating etiquette books from the nineteen-teens onward, sometimes essentially word for word. Bailey records one such manual that counseled: "Remember that the average man will go as far as you let him go. A man is only as bad as the woman he is with."[146] Although *Passion and Purity* reaches toward a countercultural Christian perspective on romantic relationships, it repeatedly echoes general culture from Betty's youth and young adulthood.

Jim's conduct was repeatedly at odds with aspects of *Passion and Purity*'s teaching. He didn't have a job or a way to support a wife; he didn't know what his next step would be; he believed he was called to stay single for an undefined period of time. Despite all this he deliberately pursued a relationship with a woman and declared his love to her without offering commitment. The book lets him off the hook, claiming that things were different for them:

> Can I recommend Jim's plan of action to others? Never in a million years. I feel quite certain he would not have wanted anyone to build a doctrine on it. But the situation was unusual. Not that he was called to a lifetime of celibacy. He did not know whether it was for life. He did not need to know. He was called to stay single, unattached, uncommitted at least until he had missionary experience. He had reason to believe that he had

awakened love in a dedicated woman and that he could trust her with the information he wanted to give her.[147]

From the beginning of their relationship, Jim had acted as if, because he had made no formal commitment, he could keep his commitment to singleness and keep a relationship with a woman with whom he was in love. Arguably he had no business pursuing a relationship that might lead to "attachment," and to do so in the first place required a certain amount of self-delusion. But once he had formed an attachment, it was unrealistic, if not simply dishonest, to continue to proclaim himself unattached because he had made no formal commitment. And surely the point at which it ought to have become clear that he *had* formed an attachment was when he started writing to his beloved about his overtly sexual desire for her.

Jim's refusal either to commit himself or to deny himself might have been less problematic had he and Betty been the only people affected. But by continuing to publicly preach on marriage and singleness with apparent certainty, using his own life as illustration, he swept others along in his wake, including Pete Fleming and Olive Ainslie. In his book about Pete's life, Pete's brother Ken Fleming notes Jim's "magnetic personality" and sees Pete as one in a series of people "captivated" by Jim's vision for Ecuador—and singleness. Fleming also notes the difficulties that Pete and Olive experienced in the course of their relationship, though he says politely that "Olive was sensitive and supportive to Pete during this struggle. . . . They concluded that if marriage was God's plan for them He would work it out in His time."[148] Olive would later write more frankly about her hurt and frustration and her sense (shared by both her parents and Pete's) that Jim's larger-than-life personality was responsible for Pete's sudden change of course and poor treatment of Olive. Dave Howard confirms this:

> Their relationship was greatly affected by Pete going and being with Jim Elliot. And when I read Olive's book, I thought, yeah, yeah. I know exactly what's going on here, because I suffered through the same kind of thing with Jim, and he probably is making Pete feel like a second-class Christian because he's got a girlfriend and he's engaged and he's talking about being married, and Jim still has this celibacy idea and he had not

yet given in to the fact that he was in love with Elisabeth—he didn't really want to admit that.[149]

Olive would later recall that Jim "appeared to have settled the question of being single. Whenever he had spoken to churches or to his friends, he had communicated that he clearly knew God's will and was following it joyfully."[150] But in fact, by September 27, 1951, when Jim spent the evening at Birdsong after a full day of speaking, what Betty had characterized as his "hope that God meant marriage for us eventually" had coalesced in his journal into "our desire and intention, under God, of marriage."[151] On November 20, he was again expressing uncertainty:

> I began last night to consider engagement with Betty. Frightens me to think of finally leaping over all the old barriers I've raised against marriage. Is it to be, after all, the conventional life of rugs and appliances and babies? Is Paul's example of single intensity beyond me? Am I at last not one of those who make themselves eunuchs for the kingdom of heaven's sake? . . . No settlement in my mind one way or another though I feel strongly that for my own stability, for Betty's ease, and for most folks' tongues, I should buy a ring.[152]

Nevertheless, he did not propose.

———

Nor did he share his indecision with Pete. In mid-October, when Jim and Pete's fundraising tour was finished, Phil and Margaret took Betty and the two men on a trip to Gale Cottage in New Hampshire. Betty later remembered, "Winter had closed in for good, and the old house . . . was frigid without central heating. We spent the days hiking the White Mountains. . . . In the evenings we all huddled around the fire, toasting marshmallows, drinking hot chocolate, while Pete read poetry aloud. The others were gallant in going up early to the arctic bedrooms, leaving Jim and me to talk late and watch the embers die."[153] In her journal, she exulted in the chance to share her beloved Franconia with Jim, and in God's goodness in allowing them the time together. After another stop at Birdsong, where Betty and Jim had their picture taken under the apple tree in the yard—their first photo together—Jim left for Portland, where he would finish his arrangements for the journey to Ecuador. Betty took him to the train station. They stopped on the way "to pray and cry."[154]

Betty did not have time to mope after Jim's departure, even if she had been inclined that way. Her decision to go to Ecuador had raised a new set of questions about next steps. She needed another single woman to be her partner, she needed to raise funds, and she needed to start learning Spanish. She had possible leads for fulfilling each of these needs, but she waited for clear, specific direction from God. By the time Jim sailed, she felt she had received that direction and had begun moving forward. She was glad to be busy, writing to Jim, "I find that I welcome *any* activity, any social engagement, any place to go, not for the thing itself, but merely from an impatient, undisciplined desire to *kill time.* . . . Yet gently, quietly, the Shepherd leads me beside still waters, makes me to *lie down.* . . . He is teaching me to rest in his everlasting arms."[155] One of the ways she felt she was learning to rest was by exercising the faculty of thankfulness. She wrote in her journal, "I believe that perhaps the most effective 'balance wheel' in a believer's life is just this. In each event of life, we are to give thanks."[156] This tool is one Betty would use for the rest of her life.

Through Jim, Betty had connected with a possible partner—Dorothy Jones, a young Brethren woman from Texas who was also headed for Ecuador—and with a Brethren assembly in a Puerto Rican area of Brooklyn, New York. This group had offered the two women use of a fifth-floor apartment near their assembly hall so that they could learn Spanish by immersion. Betty's mother drove her up after Thanksgiving. Dorothy would arrive in January, but at first Betty had the place to herself. After a trip to the basement-level grocery store for cleaning supplies, Betty set out to scrub the apartment from top to bottom. That evening she had dinner with the Montalvo family, who, though she did not live with them, appear to have functioned more or less as her host family. She ended her day by attending a prayer meeting.

Betty would later remember that "there was heat in our apartment for a couple of hours a day, and we never knew which hours those would be. . . . The Rhinegold Brewery was right next door, and we smelled beer and listened to the noise of trucks all day and all night. There were rats—large black rats, big enough to dump over the garbage pail in the kitchen."[157] The hot water never really got hot, and the apartment building smelled of cooking and old radiators. She was lonely and homesick in the unfamiliar environment, "with not even a tree to relieve the oppression of filthy walls," as she wrote to Jim. "But the Lord has given many kinds of balm, not the least of which is your love."[158] In fact, her loneliness seems to have been increased by the change in her relationship with Jim, and as she drew nearer to leaving the country, she seemed to miss everyone more. "I think of dear Mother. . . . As I look forward to my departure for the field, it is very hard to think of what it will mean to her. The Lord alone can sustain us," she wrote in her journal.[159] But she turned to the Psalms for comfort. And when she sat at the table in her sunny kitchen to write to Katharine, she tried to put a cheerful face on things.

In the evenings, Betty attended meetings in the Spanish-speaking Brethren hall and in her halting Spanish helped Mrs. Montalvo teach children's Bible classes. During the day she worked as an assistant in the office of Voices from the Vineyard, which received and distributed donations to Brethren missionaries and reported news from missionaries to their supporters at home in an eponymous publication. There Betty met Katherine Morgan, a widowed Brethren missionary about fifteen years her senior, who with her four daughters was in the US on furlough. Morgan took Betty under her wing, sharing information she would need on the field and offering friendship and a family atmosphere to the lonely younger woman. Years later Betty would remember a "hat show" she and the five Morgans put on together for their own private amusement at the Morgan home using hats donated to missionaries: "We laughed so hard we choked!"[160]

Privately, Betty was struggling with the feeling that she should be doing more—specifically, visiting her neighbors "with the gospel." She wrote in her journal, "I am afraid. . . . Of what, I hardly know. Is this direct, deliberate disobedience? Am I defeated, Lord? . . . Give me power or love or both, or whatever it is I need. . . . And here I am, a prospective MISSIONARY."[161]

Betty spent Christmas in Moorestown. When she returned to Brooklyn in the new year, she and Dorothy began the time-consuming process of managing paperwork, travel arrangements, and supplies in preparation for their departure for Ecuador. Betty also had the chance to meet another missionary on furlough, this time from Ecuador. Doreen Clifford, a Britisher who had spent some years in the same area of the country where Betty and Dorothy hoped to live, was a fount of useful information.

> Well, you can imagine I had a thousand questions to ask, and it was surely satisfying to get so much info really first hand. She described the sort of house I will have, split bamboo with thatched roof; the kind of clothes to bring and the food to expect; Indian life, trekking through the jungle, etc. etc. There are some thrilling things to pray about which I don't feel I can tell you all now, but I would like you to pray very definitely about who I am to work with. If it is Doreen, then that means some terrific things (in the good slang sense of that word) and I hardly dare think the Lord may be leading that way.[162]

In her journal, Betty recorded the details she had not shared in her family letters for fear that she would seem too "visionary": Doreen had told her "of the burden she has for the yet untouched Auca tribe of Indians on the Napo River." They were a dangerous group. "Humanly, it would be impossible for women to do such work. Men have tried, and been killed." But Doreen felt God had "given her this concern for some purpose" and asked Betty "to pray about whether He might want me to go with her."[163] This was high adventure indeed and a potential route for fulfilling her call to pioneering linguistic work. As she kept on trying to work out the details of how she would get to Ecuador, she began to pray about these "aucas."

———

February found Betty still in the States. Phil and Margaret and their little daughter had recently gone as missionaries to a remote area of northern Canada. Jim had finished his packing, seen his equipment and supplies loaded onto the ship, called long-distance from California to say goodbye, and sailed. Betty had embarked on her own round of fundraising, and since women were not allowed to speak at mixed-sex Brethren gatherings, she was speaking to women's groups, worn out by the steady round of "meetings, teas, contacts, letter-writing."[164] Her time in Brooklyn was up at the end of the month, and she went back to Moorestown for a final few weeks with her parents.

At last, in April, everything was in order. Betty's passage was booked on the *Santa Margarita*, a combination passenger-cargo ship with room for fifty-two passengers and amenities including air-conditioning and a swimming pool. On Saturday, April 5, 1952, it was finally her turn to go. In her mother's blurred photograph, taken as the family said goodbye, Betty stands smiling on the ship's deck, turned a little away from the camera. She is dressed formally in a suit and pumps with her heavy coat thrown over her shoulders.

After the ship was underway she sat down to write to her "Beloved family":

Now I can attempt to say all the things I didn't <u>dare</u> say two hours ago—I knew it would bring tears. I picture you all now, perhaps just getting back to a dark, quiet house on this rainy afternoon. Perhaps it has cleared there by now—we had flashes of sunlight as we steamed by the Statue, but it is now quite foggy again. We have been sounding off frequently. I just wrote in my journal, and have been asking God to be your Rock and Fortress. It is very easy to trust for oneself—I have had very little experience in trusting for others. Now God is giving me this new lesson. It is not an easy one—but <u>He</u> is my teacher! I have no tears for myself. I let go only when the great door clashed down, shutting off the last possible glimpse of you dear ones. And then the tears were more for what it meant to you all, for I have learned, as I've said, to trust God absolutely for myself. . . .

   I feel like two people—and it is best to think on the second! First, I am not without longings for you all—although I appear quite calloused, I know. Mother, you remember how we spoke in the car the other day of the possibility of <u>miraculous</u> sustenance at such a time as this. God has done this for me, I know. But home is very dear to me—the States are dear to me—though I never knew it before. I cannot let myself, just now, think of all the happiness and blessing of such a home. "I <u>am</u> but a child, and know not how to go out or to come in"—I can feel myself the little girl once more, and sense a longing to stay right at home, in the comfort of Mother's and Daddy's taken-for-granted love, to be rid of all sense of adult responsibility, to run back to you, and forget all this wild dream of going to a far country. In this person, Jim has no part. But I feel myself another—"God's missionary"—Yes, I—actually going to "the field." And there is the thought of Jim ahead—of all the possibility of the future. . . . <u>God knows it all</u>.[165]

PART 2

———————

1952–1963

In a Different Time, in a Different Place

THE *SANTA MARGARITA* was a world apart. For the ten-day voyage, Betty Howard lived in a style to which most people would like to become accustomed. In addition to the swimming pool, where she spent a good deal of her time, and the air-conditioning, there were organized games, tours of the ship, sightseeing expeditions in ports along the way, and a piano available for her use in the lounge. And the food! Dinner consisted of several courses and included dishes like lobster or oyster cocktail, roast beef, frog legs, roast gosling, and duckling with figs. "I never dreamed it could be such a wonderful trip!" Betty wrote to her family.[1]

The other passengers at her table, mostly on vacation, were "dumbfounded" to find she was a missionary: "They have been plying me with questions all evening—asked me to go up to the lounge with them and talk after dinner. . . . Had some chance to witness, but I plan to give them both barrels. Just breaking them in with the 'interesting adventure' part now!"[2] More than a decade later, describing the voyage through the protagonist of her novel, *No Graven Image*, she would call it "a world I had never known and would not know again, a world of luxuries," writing, "I wanted to prolong, not just indefinitely but forever, those timeless days . . . when I was no longer preparing to be a missionary nor had yet become one. The irresponsibility was intoxicating."[3]

When the *Santa Margarita* reached the Gulf of Guayaquil on the southwest coast of Ecuador, Betty boarded a seventy-five-passenger yacht, the *Santa Rosita*, for the four-hour trip up the Guayas River in the sweltering heat. On disembarking in Guayaquil she was met by a couple she had known at Prairie Bible Institute. They had only been in the city two weeks themselves, but they took her to a rundown hotel where she could stay while she waited for her possessions to clear customs. She wrote to her family, "I . . . had to sort of pinch myself to realize that I am in Ecuador—my home from now on."[4]

When Betty awoke the next morning, she was swept with a wave of "that nameless depression which comes to me when alone and in new circumstances."[5] By lunchtime, feeling out of place and alone, she decided to go down to the lobby to sit and read her *Time* magazine in an attempt to lift her spirits. A man reading a newspaper struck up a conversation, introduced himself as an American living and working in Ecuador and Colombia, and offered to take her on a tour of the city. She agreed, and the hour-long taxi ride enabled her to see more of the city than she would have otherwise done.

In Guayaquil she found a city of contrasts, and she wrote to her family of the modern, American-style houses built cheek-by-jowl with split-bamboo and corrugated-metal buildings whose overhanging second stories felt almost medieval. Houses and businesses crowded right up to the edge of the streets, many of which were unpaved and seemed to be full of children and animals—goats, cows, burros, mules, pigs, even vultures—and garbage. In a letter to her family, she commented naively, "I couldn't get over the squalor in which nearly all are content to live, when they can look right across the street and see a nice, clean home (undoubtedly American!) It's one thing when people know nothing else, but here—honestly! All the big American companies have concerns here, Goodrich, Coca-Cola, General Electric, General Motors, etc. and put up some fine buildings—but not in a 'nice section'—there are none! Right next to dreadful little hovels!"[6]

What Betty did not mention in letters was the sexual harassment she experienced wherever she went. In her journal she wrote, "Surely this is no place for a single woman. Men here do not know the meaning of the 'cold shoulder,' and ogle and whoop at me." She was also taken aback by public nudity, linked again to poverty and her judgments about poverty. "Such misery written on faces, I've never seen before. Such rags of clothing, such utter lack of industry or desire for improvement. The street by the river is by far the most popular thoroughfare, yet by the shore were some nude men, bathing and washing clothes. My whole being recoils at such sights—not that I am shocked, in the sense of 'surprised' or horrified, but it is a shock to my nature. I cannot express just how it affects me."[7]

When her luggage still had not been unloaded the next day, the PBI couple invited her to stay with them. This gave Betty a chance to stop spending money on the hotel—a welcome change since she did not have a salary but lived "in faith" on whatever donations Brethren in the US felt moved to send. It also gave her more English-speaking company. "It was so good to get out of the hotel and have a little fellowship!"[8] But she was impatient to get to the next stage of her journey. Language study—and Jim—were waiting in Quito.

Finally the barges arrived from Panama, her seven pieces of luggage were cleared through customs, and on day ten Betty caught the daily Panagra flight to Quito, where Jim met her at the airport. Jim and Pete had made the same journey two months before and been bouncing from place to place since their arrival. They wanted to live in a Spanish-speaking home so they could be immersed in the language but had not been able to find a place. Instead, they lived primarily at the Tidmarsh home in Quito, with periodic visits to another family, Marie and Norbourne "Dee" Short and their children, in Santo Domingo, and to British missionaries Doreen Clifford and Barbara Edwards in San Miguel. A week later, Dorothy Jones arrived as well, and she and Betty found lodging in the home of a Christian Ecuadorian couple, Señor and Señora Arias. A month later, Jim and Pete finally found a Spanish-speaking household where they could rent space, the home of Señor and Señora Cevallas, right across the street from Betty and Dorothy.

The four new arrivals quickly found themselves with a busy social schedule. There were numerous missions with a presence in or near the city, and the newcomers found themselves inundated with invitations. There were dinners, suppers, get-togethers over coffee or chocolate con queso,[9] a women's tea, day trips, mountain climbing, hiking, even a wedding and a bullfight, all with four or six or eight or more missionaries from various organizations. Jim contrasted their current lifestyle with the idea of the self-sacrificing missionary, noting in his journals after a waffle-and-banana-split party: "Nobody here suffering much lack!"[10] Pete also commented in his journal, "It is good, but it is not the sort of thing I came to Ecuador for; life at home was too full of it. And it is increasingly obvious that a missionary could spend practically all his time in this type of nicety. I trust

God preserves me from it."[11] Betty's letters don't record any concern over all the play. As with the voyage to Guayaquil, she seems to have been able to enjoy it as a pleasant interlude, imitating the apostle Paul's contentment in plenty as well as in need.

Quito was, after all, only a waypoint for the four new missionaries. They were there to learn Spanish, Ecuador's national language, before moving out to rural stations where they hoped to live and work long-term. In the chilly mornings, Betty, Dorothy, Pete, and Jim had classes most weekdays with a Señorita Balereso. Then over lunch each day, Señor Arias would drill them on what they had learned in class that morning. Wilfred Tidmarsh gave them a course in homeopathic medicine. And they followed it all up with Spanish textbook study on their own and as much conversation with native speakers as they could manage.

Jim and Pete often went to street meetings or handed out tracts with Wilfred in the warm, sunny afternoons, or traveled with Dee Short as he worked. Dee introduced Betty to a college student who invited her to her home for language practice. "She is studying Latin, French, and Eng. in the University, and suggested that I could help her with those, as well as get some good practice on my Spanish," Betty wrote. "Of course we will talk about the Bible, too," though this was easier said than done between the language barrier and the Ecuadorian woman's gradually waning interest.[12] Betty also accepted a request to teach an hour-long religion class twice a week in the American School, "really a wonderful opportunity; they are kids of diplomats, government missions, company representatives, etc., who know <u>nothing</u> about the Bible."[13] And, like most missionaries staying in Quito, she was regularly recruited to help with programs for HCJB radio. She also contributed to the monthly "Greetings" segment, which gave missionaries from around Ecuador the chance to make personal contact with their families in the States, even if only one-way.

———

Guayaquil, at only 13 feet above sea level, had been sweltering even in early April. Quito, seated at 9,350 feet in the arms of the mountain chain that bisects the country, could be positively chilly, with daytime highs between 50°F and 70°F and nighttime temperatures of about 40°F. And since there wasn't much seasonal fluctuation in temperatures, it would remain cool throughout Betty's time there. "Your talk of sleeping with an electric fan made me shiver!" she wrote to her family in late June. "I go to bed every night of my life with a hot water bottle and two heavy blankets."[14] The substantial temperature difference in cities an hour's flight apart was another of the contrasts Betty saw everywhere she looked. She was enthralled by the natural beauty of the area. A few blocks from the house where she was staying was "a sort of meadow" that appeared from a distance "to rise into a beautiful mountain beyond—but as we approached, behold a magnificent green gorge of a valley dropped between the meadow and the mountain! It was one of the most breathtakingly lovely sights I've ever seen."[15] A short walk in the other direction took her into the lovely, bustling old city.

But not every contraposition was beautiful. Sometimes the magnificent landscape served to emphasize the horrors of history, as when Betty and Jim hiked Panecillo, where the stunning scenery made an eerie counterpoint to the area's history of human sacrifice. Sometimes it accentuated present suffering. When Betty sent home scenic photographs, she wrote:

> Soon I want to get some of the seamy slum ("seamy" is the understatement of the year—where beauty abounded filth and sorrow did much more abound). O it makes me want to cry to see constantly about us poor, tiny, filthy (I wish there were a stronger word), rag-clad Indian children, so often crying. I never saw so many children crying—with no one paying any attention, much less helping them—as I've seen in Ecuador. . . . Oh, if I could describe things as they really are!

This heart's cry of the writer was a recurrent theme for Betty: the desire to catch every detail, to portray with accuracy, to make the reader *see*. So was the desire to view the suffering around her through the eyes of Jesus. She wrote that the people of the city were "scattered, as sheep without a Shepherd, many of them homeless—it was this that aroused compassion in our Lord Jesus. Oh, that I may learn in this something of the fellowship of His suffering!"[16]

Despite the heartbreaking poverty around her, Betty's delight in her new adventure kept bubbling over. The Howards had always stored up the things that happened during the day to share around the dinner table, and now that they were largely scattered, they transferred their storytelling to writing. Though too busy to write much in her journal, Betty still wrote long letters to her family, trying to paint in words all the things she was seeing and doing.

Jim loved to mountain climb and Betty often joined him. In May they made the sixteen-hour trip to the summit of Pichincha volcano with a group including Pete, Bill Cathers, the Tidmarsh's teenage son, and Abdón Villarreal, an Ecuadorian man who had been spending a good deal of time with Jim. Sunrise from the trail was "such glory as one could scarcely dream of. Below us the city of Quito was completely shrouded in clouds. Beyond, the mighty pyramid of Antisona seemed on fire. The opposite side of the great valley we were skirting . . . was shining with moonlight, and our side was lit with the rising sun! Oh, for words to describe it! We just stood, dumb with praise."[17] Betty had pictured life on the mission field as an exercise in sacrifice set against a harsh environment, but now she reveled in the breathtaking beauty God had made.

Another group trip took her overnight to Otavalo, colder even than Quito, though the elevation was 1,100 feet lower.

> I really felt as if I was in one of those paper-backed novels up in the cottage [in Franconia]. As one looked up the street, nothing was visible except the dim white walls of the adobe houses, no windows, only wooden doors. The cobblestones lent an Old-world charm to the scene, and at each corner a lamp burned feebly. Once a horse with Indian rider clattered past us. It was the first time I had ever heard galloping hoofs on cobblestones.

The empty streets and impassive walls of the sleeping town made a striking backdrop for the jewel-toned bustle and hubbub of the densely packed market when they visited it early the next morning. "How can I make you see it? There was a huge plaza, filled with thousands of Indians, the women dressed in long skirts and colorful shawls, with strings of gold beads and earrings, and huge sombreros of pure pressed wool, heavy as lead (Jim and I tried some on that were for sale)." After breakfast the group hired a taxi for sightseeing and drove out into the mountains where they saw "a beautiful, dark lake . . . surrounded by great rock cliffs," "great flocks of what looked to me very much like egrets," and many little towns. They got back to Quito that evening so coated in dust from head to toe that they were the same color as the roads.[18]

———

Just as in high school and college, Betty's letters from Quito were primarily filled with the details of daily life and the things she was enjoying, along with periodic requests for her mother to mail her things like toothpaste and rainboots. She continued to hold the things she felt "most deeply" in reserve for private writing and prayer, at least until she had worked them into a manageable form that she felt comfortable sharing with others. Her journals were an essential outlet for her to process and record those important thoughts and feelings. "I wrote things there," she later said, "that I could not say to people or write in letters to Jim."[19] The journals from this period are largely unavailable, but comparing excerpts from Jim's and Pete's journals during this period with Betty's letters home gives some insight into thoughts and feelings she was not yet ready to share with others, and how she worked through them privately.

Jim's journal shows that his and Betty's first chance to spend time alone after she arrived in Quito had come on April 28, not long after her arrival. Afterward he wrote: "She came to [the Tidmarshes' house] at 8:05 for the med course at 9:00—med course: heart disease. Then, 11:00–12:30 behind the American school. 'Good of the Lord to stop the rain.' 'I wouldn't mind sitting down.' 'How many years.' 'I don't think you know what being alone means.'"[20] The sentences he quoted appear to be things Betty said during their time together. *Passion and Purity* records how Betty would hold her breath at each meeting with Jim after a long separation, hoping he would finally have the go-ahead from God to get engaged—only to be disappointed. "How many years?" must have been her question when she heard again that Jim's plans still included singleness for the foreseeable future. He recorded her response: "quiet sobbing."[21]

Three days later, Betty wrote of Jim's plans to her family, explaining that he and Pete planned to move to the eastern jungle, reopen the school Wilfred had abandoned, and learn Kichwa, a task which they expected to take two years. Then they wanted to hand that station over to someone else and move into an area where there had never been a missionary presence, working as single pioneer missionaries for at least three years. Betty wrote:

> I confess quite freely that my heart sank when I realized what this may mean. But now I am at peace and in 100% accord with their aim, as God leads them. I believe, with Jim, that our <u>prime</u> is to be given wholly to this particular work. . . . We have bargained for nothing less—for we have <u>asked</u> for God's will, at any cost. And He has taken us at our word. So, anew, I take <u>His</u> promise, and I am happy.[22]

In the time between Betty and Jim's meeting and the writing of the letter, she appears to have done at least some grieving of the hoped-for commitment. "Sobbing" has been mitigated to "my heart sank." She found renewed encouragement and comfort in reviewing the promises recorded in the Bible, particularly those she felt God had given specifically to her.

Feeling settled and at peace in the midst of a difficult and ongoing situation is a hard-won thing, and usually requires refighting the same ground again and again to stay there—or perhaps more accurately, to get back there. Jim's journals repeatedly note Betty's ongoing struggle and sadness as she worked to reconcile herself to their relationship. He enjoyed the opportunity for "just loving, giving and taking, waiting and holding" that living closer gave them, but also recorded that Betty "notes constantly" that "there is a pain in it, being unable to consummate now as we are. . . . I pity her as I see she worries over the future—loving and losing. God, let me be faithful to her. And let me live to love if it please."[23]

One night after walking home from the Inter-Mission Fellowship Conference, Jim wrote in his journal that Betty had been "unusually quiet." He had tried to start a conversation, telling her, "I'm afraid it's going to be a long, hard road for you . . . waiting for me." She had replied, "I'm not waiting for you."

> That started it. Her wise unwillingness to be syrupy now, struggling with her desire to really be nice, often results in a negative tone that nettles me. Somehow tears explain things that words never can, so when she cried and explained in the fields above Arias's place, it came clearly to me how she really felt. Her restraint from speaking of her love—to me or to anyone—is a hard thing for her.[24]

And the nearer Jim's departure, the harder it became.

Her grief was compounded by family news. Early in August she received family letters rejoicing over Dave and Phyllis's new baby and announcing that Ginny, part way through her freshman year at Wheaton, was engaged. Jim wrote in his journal that Betty was "broken up through the whole day" and "crying when I came over to ask her for a walk in the evening. . . . It was more tears than talk tonight."[25] By the time Betty wrote back to her family, she was able to cheerfully rejoice with her siblings, looking forward to pictures of the baby, complimenting Ginny's engagement photographs, and sharing her sister's excitement over her ring. But it was not without effort.

———

In 1952 the evangelical missionary community in Ecuador was a small world, where social and work circles heavily overlapped. There were around two hundred evangelical missionaries in the country, but as Betty had told her family in June, their numbers paled in comparison to the size of the country itself.

> The other day I saw a huge map of the Oriente [eastern lowland jungles] which Jim is making, with vast jungle regions in which there is neither town nor road. Scattered throughout such areas are the semi-nomadic tribes of the Aucas, Cofanis, Yumbos, and others, as yet wholly untouched with the gospel. It is such virgin territory that the gov't has no census of the population, not even any idea where the Indians live (the other day there was a little item in the paper saying that another settlement of the Aucas had been seen from the air, which had hitherto been unknown to exist). . . . And of all the missionaries in this tiny country, not one of them has yet succeeded in touching some of these tribes, and actually very few are trying to—most of them have centers in the cities, to which the vast majority of Indians never come.[26]

Ecuador is about 1,158 square miles (3,000 sq. km.) smaller than the US state of Nevada, but the population at the time was nearly twenty times that of Nevada—and as Betty said, that estimate had no good way to account for most indigenous groups. Although almost half of the two hundred evangelical missionaries in the country attended the 1952 Inter-Mission Fellowship Conference, missionaries generally moved in smaller circles defined by mission organization and by the type of work they were trying to do. Betty's companions going forward would be, for the most part, the handful of other Brethren missionaries who worked or hoped to work in rural Ecuador.

The Tidmarshes were the senior Brethren missionaries in the country and functioned in something of a supervisory capacity for the newcomers. Britisher Wilfred Tidmarsh had been there since 1939 and had spent much of his time in the eastern jungles, working to translate parts of the Bible into Kichwa, with trips to the western foothills of the Andes to try to lay groundwork for a missionary presence.[27] In 1946 the Shorts had arrived from the US, and after spending some time at San Miguel, a tiny village in the eastern foothills, had moved north to the town of Santo Domingo. Another American Brethren missionary, Gwendolyn Gill, had come at the same time as the Shorts, and she and Wilfred had married shortly thereafter. Doreen Clifford and Barbara Edwards had arrived from Great Britain a handful of years before Jim and Pete, and had taken up residence in San Miguel. These six, plus the six new arrivals (the Catherses arrived less than a month after Jim and Pete), made up the Brethren team in the summer of 1952.

When a group of people spends a good deal of time together, interpersonal conflict is unavoidable. Betty soon discovered that missionaries were no exception to the rule. Jim was thankful for the chance to learn from the Tidmarshes' experience, but the relationship also had its challenges; after more than a decade virtually alone on the field, Wilfred seems to have struggled with giving up control. His behavior concerned Bill Cathers so much that Bill tried to avoid working with Wilfred, afraid he would be unable to do so without what Pete called "an open clash" over how to handle the work.[28]

Dee Short's attempts at starting a trucking business also caused apprehension. Betty later noted that "as time went on, it appeared that [he] had a great many things going besides his missionary work. In fact, there seemed to be less of the missionary business than met the eye."[29] Jim wrote in his journal, "He insists his trucking takes no time, but it took this whole morning and will kill this afternoon. I am suspicious of this business, but he hopes to make the mission self-supporting. Seems like a hard thing to do with the work so new and the outreach so vast."[30] The apostle Paul was a tentmaker to earn his keep while he taught about Jesus, so there was good biblical precedent for Dee's plan. But the apostle Peter also emphasized that Jesus's followers should submit to human authority "for the Lord's sake" (1 Pet. 2:13)—and as is common practice, the requirements for receiving a missionary visa in Ecuador included an agreement not to engage in business.

The four new missionaries had difficulties among themselves as well. Their close association in language learning could be frustrating, at least for Jim and Pete. Betty later wrote that "the competition got hot at times as we raced to master the language, all of us eager to get to the jungle."[31] Her apparent enjoyment of their competition may have been due, at least in part, to the fact that she was usually winning. She wrote to her family expressing frustration with her language progress—"I have gotten now so that I can understand just about everything said to me, but Oh, the maddening frustration of being understandable! I am impatient to be able to say what I mean!"—but she quickly demonstrated a good deal of proficiency, shopping alone, talking for hours with Angelita Arias, the daughter of her landlords, and even helping Señor Arias, a professor of psychology, grade papers.[32] Pete found himself having to guard against a desire to "hoard" his "insights into Spanish idioms" rather than share them with the others, as if "by their weight the balance to test intelligence would tip in my favor."[33] Jim was downright depressed by being surpassed: "When Betty first arrived and saw Pete and I were studying at the same level, she said, 'How did you get so far behind?'—that Pete should be up with me. And now she is competing with us both, right along in the same material! . . . Felt weepy and useless yesterday at noon, swept with waves of envy and defeated wonderings about such things."[34]

Another conflict arose when Dorothy, Jim, and Pete were invited to a fiesta. Encouraged by the Ariases, they went. Although, as Pete wrote afterward in his journal, they "tried in Spanish to explain why evangelicals didn't," eventually they gave in to social pressure to dance and have a cocktail. On the way home they talked it over, wondering "if we had acted wisely and at the same time thinking that it was just into such situations that Christ went, though without defiling himself." Betty did not see things the same way, Pete recorded, and "cried and was moody all day over it." After much discussion, they were unable to reach a consensus.[35]

Pete and Betty were well-matched Scrabble opponents, but they appear to have disagreed over more than alcohol and dancing. Pete's published journal entries featuring Betty sound sympathetic and understanding, but more than sixty years after their time in Ecuador, Olive Fleming Liefeld would remember, "He and Betty didn't get along, really. Pete stood up to her, I guess."[36] One disagreement was over what it meant to be in the will of God. Pete wrote in his journal, "Betty and I had a good talk about guidance and the 'PBI' approach to spirituality," characterizing his own point of view of the human person as "an entity led now in this moment by God Himself," and the PBI understanding of a human being (which apparently Betty was defending) as "a vacuum and a bad-smelling one at that—or a vessel which ought to be a vacuum and needs to be emptied of self in order to be filled with the Spirit."[37]

The relationship between Betty and Dorothy was another source of friction. Jim wrote in his journal in early June:

> Betty doesn't seem to really want intimacy with D.J.—something my personality will never understand. . . . Her natural reserve is strong; she only gets intimate with those who "happen to fit"—or, as she says, "with those friendships that are outright gifts from God." Although she recognizes that some friendships must be made, I think she is not willing to expend the effort to make one with D.J.—mainly because she doesn't really believe that they are a pair, she doesn't think D. will really be capable of being "made" a comrade.[38]

As Liefeld notes, Betty's lack of interest or ability in making friends with Dorothy changed things for all the missionaries. Betty and Jim were, as Pete had told Olive not long after Betty arrived in Quito, trying to maintain a public pose as just coworkers. But rumors flew in the small community, and the news of their interest in each other had gotten to Quito before Betty. Jim wrote in his journal that they were treated as a unit, that when one was invited to a social event, the other was expected as a matter of course. It seems impossible that Dorothy failed to notice or to feel like a third wheel. Certainly Liefeld suggests that Pete believed Dorothy to be lonely and felt responsible for picking up the slack. And of course, it left Pete on his own as well.

Betty and Jim, though, were wrapped up in their own concerns. Jim's journal entry continues:

> I agree. D. doesn't look like the right kind of stuff. But, oh, how I want to see Bett happy these waiting years without each other, and an intimate with whom she could share things would be such a boon. Still, she says as I said when D. was en route to New York, they have nothing in common. . . . But, Father, they have Christ in common, and I want You to teach them *how to share Him.* I can't expect D. to be for Betty what Pete has been for me, but at least she can be some sort of outlet to confer with, some sort of balance to stabilize all Betty's inwardness.[39]

As an introvert and internal processor, it's unlikely that, even in the best of circumstances, Betty would have found someone so different from her an "outlet to confer with" or a "balance to her inwardness." It would have been an effort, an act of self-giving, in the best of times for Betty to recognize Dorothy's loneliness and reach out in friendship despite the lack of natural connection. And these were hardly the best of times; Betty had her hands full with her up-and-down love affair with Jim.

———

At the beginning of June, Betty wrote to her family: "Jim and I were out for a little paseo [a walk] last night, talking of how the Lord had done for us what we could not have <u>chosen</u> to do for ourselves. Imagine living right across the street from one another!"[40] It was wonderful to live so near to each other, to be able to see each other almost daily. But proximity heightened their desire for closeness. And Jim, while continuing to seek out time alone together and increased physical affection from Betty, also continued to put on the brakes when it came to commitment. Three days later, he wrote in his diary:

> Living right across the street, eating a meal a day together, on the bus, walking puts me on an entirely different basis than I have ever known with her before. Not only is the problem "how far should I go?" (she usually has that set, thank God), but "how often?" Fighting between two opinions.

Should I take all of her I can get now and live on the memory, feeding love full every opportunity that comes? Or should I go cautious, keeping it the rare occasion so as not to overdo it—and possibly tire too soon? (So far I've been surprised that I do not tire of holding her; it doesn't get old, but more real, like getting used to a strange place. The shyness goes, and a little of the surprise, but none of the niceness, none of the real joy of being there.)[41]

Jim was able to worry less about "how far to go" and even about "how often," because he was relying on Betty to set and enforce a standard for their behavior. But it must have increased the strain on Betty to have to be constantly on her guard against his importunity, constantly saying no when she wanted to say yes.

Jim's writing about his and Betty's physical relationship is vague enough that it's unclear how much physical intimacy they shared. Their behavior seems to have been restrained by the standards of the day. But *Passion and Purity* implies that until engagement their premarital physical relationship was limited to walking arm in arm, sitting with their shoulders touching, and "on one occasion as we sat on a park bench his suddenly stretching out on his back with his head in my lap," during her visit to Wheaton in autumn 1948. After describing this contact, the book says they regretted even that, and does not mention this aspect of their relationship again—except to describe a time when, alone on the Oregon coast, they were tempted to physical intimacy but resisted. In contrast, Jim's journals make it clear that they engaged in romantic touch over the course of their time in Quito:

May 8
This much I know, we were made for each other—if I for "comfort," then she for "speed"—though I have not found her incómodo [uncomfortable] in the least! My arms are for her "homing," a place to rest, shelter, shield, and strength. What having her there means to me cannot be said.

May 19, 20
Afternoons with Abdón and then Betty over at the *bodega* [storeroom]. Feels like the hungry time of the month for me, and I can't keep my hands off her. . . . Praying that God will make me wise enough to treat her right, love her well, and control our playing.

June 15

She suits me fine in public, and in private . . . ! Stars afterward above the house here in the soft, wet grass; the sound of her breathing, the weight of her body, the billow of her hair under her head—seems like she gets nicer every time. Still, we haven't kissed. I can't believe it sometimes, but it's so. Who ever heard of people in love like we are in love sporting as fondly as we do, and as often, who have never met at the lips? Can it really be there will be *more* thrill than now?

July 10

3:00 a.m. to 8:00 p.m. with Betty alone. Circled Rucu in hopes of getting to Guagua but were slowed by a valley we didn't know of before. . . . Slept in each other's arms for a few minutes in the big valley floor behind Rucu. Love is developing to a solid thing with me. A touch is more than sexually arousing. It is a conveyor of meaning now.[42]

So why does *Passion and Purity* give a different impression? *The Journals of Jim Elliot* were published in 1978 and *Passion and Purity* in 1984, so it is unlikely that the latter was an attempt to hide the extent of their physical relationship. The difference may arise simply from the way books are written. A book, no matter how autobiographical, must be built around a framework. The author must include the details that flesh out that framework and exclude those that blur its shape. Elliot's mail was full of letters asking how Christians should handle their love lives, and *Passion and Purity* was her attempt to answer those questions at greater length than she could afford in individual letters. The details she included about her and Jim's relationship would necessarily have been those which fleshed out the beliefs of a woman three decades older and three marriages more experienced than the woman who dated Jim Elliot. Perhaps the convictions of a sixty-year-old woman didn't always match the conduct of her twenty-five-year-old self. Perhaps her deep affection for Jim, her reverence for his spiritual status, and her beliefs about the nature of male-female relationships continued to blind her to the reality of his impetuous behavior.

In early August 1952, Jim wrote of Betty in his journal, "Sense great moving of heart wanting to be fair to her, wanting to marry her, wanting, wanting. But now I feel no guiding from God, not even for engagement.... We talk of it freely together, she and I, and my reasoning must be making it worse for her, but I know—reason or not—that now is not the time."[43] His sense that repeatedly talking through his thoughts "must be making it worse" for Betty highlights an important difference in their personalities. Betty was an internal processor. On subjects that seemed important to her, she thought about them, wrote them through in her journal, prayed about them, and reached her position on them before she voiced her thoughts and feelings about them. Jim had all the hallmarks of an external processor, formulating his opinions and reaching decisions by verbalizing his ideas.[44]

Jim had described this difference in his journal back in May, writing, "She often sees clearer than I, and faster, to the end of things, and moves ruthlessly and rapidly to state what she sees," and again in July when he had written, "She is settled in her thinking about things (she knows that it is inherently wrong to possess a book of nude photographs; I have to puzzle it slowly through making blunders and contradictions). I haven't thought about them seriously."[45] Betty had thought about the subjects they discussed and already had a reasoned argument to marshal in support of her position; Jim would begin to formulate his position in the course of their discussion. This might not have mattered much in discussions about where to go for dinner, but it made a big difference when it came to conversations about the state of their relationship.[46]

Because Jim fashioned his ideas by trying them on for size and seeing how they felt, emotion seems to have been a major part of his decision-making. Although on paper he believed women to be more emotionally driven than men, he repeatedly describes himself as making decisions and discerning the will of God based on how things feel and speaks of Betty as having reasoned things through to reach her positions. In May he had written:

Tried to explain to her something of what I wrote about Uriah on May 5 while we were walking downtown today. I don't know why, but it seemed unreasonable to her, and she laughed at me. Flaring back at first, I soon lapsed into silence, and by the time we reached her bus stop downtown, I was seeing only sidewalk and biting my lip. And then I cried, and we walked. I couldn't understand why I was unable to explain sensibly just *why* it was not time for engagement.

I suppose I couldn't say it, because I don't *know* it in words. The knowledge is inward, and it may be that there are no reasons to be given. . . . So, as for not being engaged, I simply know it is not for now—that knowledge is inward, God given, and to be obeyed at whatever cost. . . .

Then, too, I learned something about Betty today. She makes me feel "on the defensive" in arguments (in the kindest sense of the word). . . . From her point of view we ought to be engaged—though she is not trying to force me to it. (This I know, first, because she says so, and I trust her; she fears breaching the will of God for the work; I think she knows how impossible it would be to make me do such a thing with arguments.) When I couldn't explain well why we shouldn't be and I choked up, she immediately changed her attitude and went on the defensive herself, saying she understood, that she was sorry that she had said anything, that she hoped I didn't think I would have to produce "reasons" for staying apart. I was sorry I couldn't control myself, because I fear to make her less expressive than she is in these matters. I want her answers, suggestions, outlook—no honest man could fear them—and today I may have been too sensitive to them so that she thinks it hurts me to hear her "debate." But I swear it was not against her that I cried, rather against myself—that I could not say what I know.[47]

Jim apparently wanted Betty's "answers, suggestions, outlook" because he was trying to put his feelings into thoughts and words, and the back and forth of discussion would have helped him to do that. Betty seems to have assumed that he had already articulated his position to himself. It evidently hadn't occurred to her that he literally couldn't put it into words.

Later in May, Jim had written that God was "answering my prayers for wisdom to treat her properly—not through my understanding of how far to go or just how to love her—but through her attitudes, restraints, and liberties." He went on to say that Betty "is a marvel for having the right 'feeling' for things, and after I try to figure out her feelings, I find that they are often the best *reasons* for doing or refraining from any given thing."[48] But as Betty had made clear in her letter on "true friendship" in the fall of 1949, her "attitudes" were not based on "feeling." She had carefully thought out her position with study and prayer, and in fact, she held that position despite the fact that it went directly *against* many of her strongest feelings.

Meanwhile Jim regularly describes his own overwhelming emotion in his journals, maintaining his belief that women are emotional and men are logical by labeling his emotional response as woman's behavior: "I don't understand what there is about loving her that makes me such a damned woman. I can hardly begin to describe it; I only know that I feel it strong and that I can't talk of it without twists coming to my mouth. Lips get dry and tears seem to brim at my eyes, and there is a crushing sense in my chest."[49]

Recognizing this sharp difference in their personalities helps to clarify their relationship. Jim had noted that spring that Betty "thinks I'm inconsistent, Lord, seeming to be self-contradictory so often in speaking plainly of marriage and then seeming to be so unsure about it all."[50] She was not the only one. Dave, who still speaks of Jim as his best friend, would later say bluntly that during their premarital relationship, Jim "played her like a yo-yo."[51] This up and down is apparent in Jim's journals. He conveyed certainty of purpose in his conversations with others and in his public speaking but sounds much less certain in his private writing. During their time together in the fall of 1948 he lamented, "Oh, that I could understand my heart toward her." After Betty left for PBI: "I fear that the excitement of her presence roused me to an aggressiveness in my ardor that I do not really feel." His thoughts and feelings about celibacy strengthened as their time together faded in his memory, and he would tell Betty again of his inclination toward celibacy, apparently not having considered how it sounded in contrast with his previous expressions of affection. When he realized he had hurt her, he was remorseful. In January 1949, he recorded, "Stung with a regret that almost brings me to sobbing as I received Betty's letter of the twelfth. I wrote carelessly that I felt God was leading me singly to the field, and it has touched her far more deeply than I supposed."[52]

While they were apart, he continued to be unsure of his feelings. During his renaissance, while she was considering ending their relationship, he felt the "little rift" between them was "tremendously inconsequential."[53] On June 25, he wrote in his journal, "Letter from Betty here today makes me feel strange; I cannot tell whether or not I love her, and I tremble to write how shallow a prayer comrade I've been."[54] On August 1, he accused her of writing infrequently in order to conduct a "'war of nerves' to feel me out or something."[55] On August 23, he recorded again the difference between her certainty and his uncertainty about the relationship. "Learned yesterday that Betty is coming next week. I will need Thee much, Lord Jesus, to deal justly and kindly by her. It is hard for me to admit that I am wholly unworthy of such a girl. My care for her is so shallow, but her love seems unflagging."[56]

Then Betty arrived in Portland in autumn 1949, and Jim seems to have found himself carried along, somewhat unwillingly, in the current of her certainty. On September 6 he wrote, "Startled to find ourselves talking about marriage so offhandedly last eve. I noticed that she was pained in hearing of some of the social aspects of this Spring's renaissance. I felt sorry for myself for much of it." His self-pity seems to have been because Betty was expecting him to act like a committed man, and he didn't want to think of himself that way. But over the course of her visit, he again found himself swept up in his attraction: "She has been gone just one hour. What thunders of feeling I have known in that short time. . . . How terrible I sound sobbing. . . . Leaving her is terrible."[57]

There are very few entries about Betty during 1950. Jim briefly recorded their time together for Dave's wedding in July, in an entry that highlights his tendency to get carried away by his feelings and say and do things he wouldn't otherwise: "Warned of the Lord by Genesis 49 concerning Reuben's loss of prestige because of his volatile nature. 'Boiling over as water thou shall not have the preeminence' (49:4). My own volatility was manifest after the wedding and my loss of spiritual potency as well. Warned, I did not watch and fell into folly." The next series of entries about Betty was made in September 1951: "Arrived in Moorestown, New Jersey. Came to settled rest about Betty. I love her. The problem from now on is not 'whom should I marry?' but 'should I marry?'"[58] Though he wrote of this as a new decision, he had already said these words to Betty before her Wheaton graduation three-and-a-half years before.

Four days later he wrote in his journal, "Went to Moorestown. Sat close, very close, as we neared there. She had told her parents the news of our desire and intention, under God, of marriage." Although Jim's "settled rest" was a return to a former position, it appears to have led Betty, unaware of his intervening vacillations, to think he had made a more definite commitment. Not only did she tell her parents that they intended to be married but she allowed him to touch her more than she had before. On October 18 he wrote:

> I am discovering Betty all over again these days. She has taken on a new meaning and power—and purity. Last two nights on top of Shelton delightful. Her body, once the thing that disturbed my thoughts of marrying her, seems now to fit the picture well. Thank God for her! Pure and warm and relaxed in my arms—I never guessed it could be.

A month later, he hesitated again:

> I began last night to consider engagement with Betty. Frightens me to think of finally leaping over all the old barriers I've raised against marriage. Is it to be, after all, the conventional life of rugs and appliances and babies? Is Paul's example of single intensity beyond me? . . . No settlement in my mind one way or another. . . . Lord, which way?[59]

Jim's blowing hot and cold makes sense in light of the idea that, as an external processor, he was thinking out loud about their relationship in his conversations with Betty, and often carried away by his emotions in the moment to say things that he was less sure about when his feelings had cooled.[60]

———

Before leaving the US, Jim and Pete had committed to reopening Shandia, the station on the Napo River where the Tidmarshes had once lived. By mid-August 1952, with more than five months of study under their belts, they had decided their Spanish was as good as it was going to get, and it was time to get to work. They left Quito early on a Friday morning by bus, heading east and south toward Shell Mera, a little town begun as a base camp for exploration by the Dutch- and British-owned Shell Oil in 1937. Shell had moved out in 1948 after deciding that the Middle East would be a more profitable place to develop for oil. As they were shutting down operations, Mission Aviation Fellowship had moved in—the electricity, running water, and runway left behind by Shell made the place a perfect base of operations for their work in the eastern jungles. MAF had invited the

Gospel Missionary Union (GMU) to join them, and the two organizations had bought land, buildings, and supplies from the oil company.

MAF missionaries Marj and Nate Saint, a nurse and a pilot, respectively, had set to work constructing a house large enough to shelter the travelers they expected to flow through Shell Mera, and a hangar just big enough for the little Piper PA-14 Family Cruiser that Nate would fly to supply rural stations. The GMU had begun work on a Bible school. Here on the western edge of the jungle, in what Betty would call "an unpretentious huddle of dilapidated wooden buildings: houses, a hotel, and stores on one side of the road, and an army base and mission-sponsored Bible school on the other,"[61] Jim and Pete would work as camp counselors at a boys' camp run by the Bible school for two weeks before heading north and farther east to Shandia.

Betty and Jim said a painful goodbye, knowing they would be separated by all the immensity of the Andes, not knowing how long it would be before they saw each other again. But they resumed their correspondence on a new footing. Jim called their time together—the longest they'd ever known—"a get-acquainted period," which "we needed . . . more than we know."[62] His freshly fanned attraction to her had grown strong enough that this time it did not begin to dissipate with absence. And although they were not engaged, and so Betty was still not comfortable sharing all of her feelings for him, she did now freely admit that she was attached to him and that she missed him and thought of him often. This regular reciprocation of his feelings must have continued to fan the flames for Jim.

Betty's days were full of trips with the Shorts, street meetings with the Tidmarshes, various social functions, and endless errands: "Every day I have a dozen things to do—money changers, post office, visits to make, photos to get developed for various people, etc.—official papers, red tape, bodega, etc., etc."[63] She had come to Ecuador with no firmer plans than a hope to use her linguistic training somewhere in the jungle, and as she continued her Spanish study, which included reading Spanish novels and the Spanish Bible in addition to lessons with Señorita Balereso, she prayed for guidance as to how to proceed.

She was also reading in English in her spare time—W. E. Cule's 1926 allegory, *Sir Knight of the Splendid Way*, and Geraldine Taylor's *Behind the Ranges*, a biography of missionary James Outram Fraser.[64] "Last night [I] came across a passage which _precisely_ fitted my thinking—about how he was no more doing the work of the Lord in bringing the Word of Life to China than you are, for example, in tying up a package to send to the tailor's. How absolutely <u>true</u>."[65] Jim had written similarly to his parents back in May: "A well-made piece of furniture and a healed blind man represented the same thing to the Father—a job well done; mission accomplished. So with us here. Nothing great, but what is that to Him with whom there is no great or small?"[66] This differs from the implicit understanding of foreign missions as the greatest work that they had absorbed growing up; perhaps this new understanding stemmed from increased exposure to the day-to-day mundanities of life on the foreign mission field. Certainly Betty was disturbed by much of what she was seeing of missionary life, both in her own experience and in letters from friends, such as Eleanor Vandevort, who were missionaries in other parts of the world. Betty wrote about this time lamenting the many dishonest "missionary reports" that were circulated and the "crooked patterns" by which many missionaries appeared to her to be operating. "It has been shattering to realize the things that have gone on in the name of Jesus Christ."[67]

By late September, she thought she finally had a clue to her next step. She and Dorothy had visited Doreen Clifford and Barbara Edwards in San Miguel, a tiny settlement southwest of Quito in territory that had historically belonged to the Tsáchila people. Afterward, Betty wrote to her mother:

> I'm beginning to wonder if God would have me go down to San Miguel for a few months to help with the organization & analysis of the Colorado language. I had a <u>wonderful</u> talk with [Doreen], and felt a unity I've not felt with anyone for so long—don't know if I've <u>ever</u> felt it so. Last week she had told me that God had provided a teacher & she felt she should begin studying the language, but hardly knows how to begin. . . . I couldn't get the idea out of my mind, since I've had linguistic training & she hasn't.[68]

Here was the "fit" missing from her relationship with Dorothy. Here, too, was the language work opportunity she had been hoping for. By the sixth of October, it was settled: she would go to San Miguel. "Pray," she wrote to her mother, "that I shall be able to <u>remember</u> what I learned at Wycliffe! It's been over four years!"[69]

Discouragement came in many forms during this time. The Shorts had been gone on furlough only a month, but in their absence the other missionaries were making some embarrassing discoveries, including Dee's 50,000 sucres of debt. When the Catherses arrived in Santo Domingo to fill in for the Shorts, they "found there was practically nothing to 'carry on,'" Betty wrote. "And every day they hear more tales from the people, so that now they say they can hardly look anyone in the face. May God guard us from such devastating failure—think what it means to the work!"[70] Philip Howard was having ongoing health problems for which they could not identify a cause. Ginny and Bud were dealing with something difficult, though the letters do not say what. And then there was Jim. "Had a 7-pager from Jim last night, in which he relates some of the things which threaten on every side to dishearten and innervate [sic] him spiritually. I felt like bawling when I finished his letter."[71] Everything they owned had mildewed, none of their carefully selected plants were growing well, they were struggling with starting over in language learning for the second time in a year, Pete had been sick for weeks, Jim was missing Betty badly, and Jim and Wilfred were clashing over design and construction of the new buildings needed in Shandia.

But nothing could entirely dampen for Betty the excitement of the thought that now, at last, she was about to embark on real missionary work, the thing she had come to Ecuador to do, her life's calling. There was a flurry of activity as she made her preparations. After a few days of laundry, sorting equipment for Jim and Pete, and packing—most of her belongings for storage and the rest "in small wooden boxes which can be carried on mule back"—topped off with a trip to the dentist and a last round of social visits, Betty was ready to go. As a parting gift she had a lovely compliment from Angelita Arias: "[She] told me . . . that I spoke better Spanish than any other gringa she knows! And she knows everyone at HCJB—Thanks be to God for his help."[72]

———

Betty left Quito on the back of a banana truck on October 28, following the same route that she and Dorothy had taken when they had visited Doreen and Barbara in early July. With her rode Marj Jones, the twenty-four-year-old daughter of the founder of HCJB, who worked for the radio station and had decided to spend her vacation in San Miguel. The road they had to travel was a "chain road": too narrow for two-way traffic and blocked at each end by a chain and a man with a radio whose job was to count vehicles. Two or three times a day, when all the cars that had entered at one end had been counted leaving at the other, the direction of the road was changed and the cars waiting at that chain were allowed to enter. Pichincha volcano towers 6,346 feet above Quito on its eastern side, so the road climbed "up over a shoulder of Pichincha" before starting down toward the valley.[73] The truck left Quito at about noon, working its way up to make the 2:00 p.m. chain. Since leaving the States Betty had felt as if she was in a sort of limbo, between worlds, first on shipboard and then in Quito with Jim. Now, at last, she was on her way.

After cresting Pichincha, the heavy truck plunged down and down, deeper and deeper into the jungle. Betty had written to her family after her first trip on this road of "the incredible descent. . . . 9,000 ft in about 60 miles! I had some idea of counting the horseshoe curves, but then realized there was nothing else to the journey."[74] The road was dangerous and frequently closed by landslides; Sheila Leech, a British Brethren missionary who has been living in Ecuador since the early 1980s, calls the road from Quito to Santo Domingo "the most spectacular and most terrifying in the world."[75] The countryside had a lonely, wild feeling to Betty. Long after, she would remember the drive from Quito as "a journey into a strange dreamland— from the bright and colorful city of Quito where the sun shone every day of the year and the gardens were bright with flowers and the white houses dazzled your eyes in the equatorial light—into this deep canyon of grotesqueries, wetness, and increasing gloom."[76]

After about eight hours on the banana truck, Betty and Marj reached Santo Domingo, "a hole if I ever saw one," as Betty had written in July. Built around a mud plaza, it resembled a stereotypical American "Old West" town. A vacant lot constituted the town bathroom. She had been horrified by the Shorts' house when she visited in the summer—black with mold, unlit, filthy, and overcrowded by an assortment of people whose names she never learned. In the damp environment, the Catherses hadn't been able to improve the situation much, and she had noted that summer that "in three days, any book left lying on a table is covered with mould (how do you spell that?). . . . And this is the dry season!"[77] Now, in late October, it was no longer the dry season. But Santo Domingo was the end of the road for automobile travel. San Miguel, 6 miles away, would have to be reached by horseback. This, Betty warned her family before she left Quito, would mean slower and more erratic mail, since mail would come in or out only when someone was already making the trip for another reason.

Betty and Marj spent the night with the Cathers family, waiting for Wilfred to get back with the Brethren's one horse so they would have fewer to rent. Finally on Thursday morning the two women set out, arriving in time for lunch, which consisted of "rice, beans, eggs, soup, and pineapple—the main stays here," followed by swimming in the river.[78] Betty spent the rest of the afternoon unpacking and arranging her belongings. She was to live above the school with Dorothy, Marta (the white Ecuadorian schoolteacher), and two students who helped around the house in exchange for board. Doreen lived next door above a clinic and the girls' dorm for the school, and Barbara in another house nearby.

The next day, Betty sat down at her typewriter to describe her surroundings for her family. "Dearest Folks: The day has come. I sit at a little table in a bamboo and thatch house, while the thick wetness of the jungle drifts in through the wide screened windows, making me feel mildewed already! . . . Numerous little birds twitter indistinguishably in the lush herbage around the house, and I am also interrupted by the mumbling of the school children in the room below."[79] Her bedroom was on a corner of the house, with big windows on both exterior walls which were always open, sheltered from the rain by the deep overhang of the roof. The heavy wooden double bed built by Dee looked odd with its single mattress, and the stacked wooden packing boxes and plastic garment bag hung in a corner made a poor substitute for a dresser and closet, but it was a room of her own and she was happy.

A few years later, Betty would write that "Jim and Pete became full-fledged missionaries for the first time" when they reached Shandia.[80] The same thought must have been in her mind for herself when she wrote, "The day has come." At each step along the way—learning Greek at Wheaton, studying linguistics in the vastness of Oklahoma, lugging pails of cold water from the laundry at Prairie Bible Institute, bicycling through rural Alberta for the Canadian Sunday School Mission, teaching and polishing brass at Hampden DuBose Academy, tutoring her pair of students in New Jersey,

shaking her head over the messiness of her charges at Pioneer Camp, working in the Vineyard office in Brooklyn, swimming on the *Santa Margarita*
en route to Ecuador, practicing her Spanish with shopkeepers in Quito—she
had felt herself to be in preparation, always looking ahead to the day when
she would be a *real* missionary, the kind that spoke at church and came for
dinner when she was growing up, the kind she had read about in biography
after biography. Now she had arrived.

———

Tucked into the folder in the Billy Graham Center Archives that contains
Betty's letters home from Ecuador is a sheet of cheap paper, browning with
age, with a note scrawled across the top in her handwriting: "All San Miguel
letters except these destroyed by EHL [Elisabeth Howard Leitch], Nov.
1971—after copying all interesting passages, in preparation for a book."[81]

Gaps in the record of a life are unavoidable. Even if someone wanted to
leave an account of every detail of her time on earth, it wouldn't be possible. Biography has to assume that we won't know, can't know, everything.
Even if every letter were still in existence, these letters would show only
the parts of life that Betty felt comfortable sharing with her family, or occasionally just with her mother. But the intentional destruction of existing
documentation raises questions.

Betty was in San Miguel from October 30, 1952, until June 18, 1953—
not quite eight months. From November 1952, her first full month in San
Miguel, there are six surviving letters. In contrast, there is one letter from
early December, none from January, one from February, and one from
March. There are no letters from April or May, and no letters from June
until a letter written on the twenty-seventh from Dos Rios, her next place
of residence. Three letters remain from a period of seven months. Yet the
"interesting passages" she typed up to save come to barely more than two
double-spaced typewritten pages.

Although she does not record which book she was working on when she
destroyed the letters, it was almost certainly *These Strange Ashes*. Published
in 1975 and built on the framework of her not quite eight months in San
Miguel, the book shares the questions spurred by her early missionary
experiences and the spiritual lessons she took away. In the book's first

chapters, she describes the journey from Quito into the western jungle in evocative detail, then goes on to explain the work the missionaries were trying to accomplish in San Miguel. There was a Brethren assembly, a school for the children of white Ecuadorians (since they were struggling to attract the Tsáchila students they had originally hoped for), a medical clinic, and an ongoing attempt to reach out to the Tsáchila. Doreen ran the women's meeting, Sunday school, and clinic; Dorothy and Marta ran the school; Barbara worked on establishing contacts among the Tsáchila,[82] who lived dispersed throughout the forest; and Betty's job was to reduce Tsafiki, the Tsáchila language, to writing, so that the Tsáchila could learn to read and the Bible could be translated into their language. Whoever was available dealt with medical emergencies.

Elliot wrote with humor of the difficulties of rural life for city-bred transplants: the time spent hauling water; the struggle to sterilize the water, which came from a river that doubled as an outhouse, and to cook food over an open fire that kept going out; problems of food safety (they were supposed to boil everything to kill bacteria but drew the line when it came to butter); the impossibility of keeping anything really dry. She wrote with awe of the beauty of the jungle and her sense that she had entered not just a different place but "a different aeon in time."[83] The work of the church and school were made more difficult by a rivalry with the priest and the nun who ran the Catholic school across the street. The language work was made more difficult because the Tsáchila were so spread out—it was time-consuming to go to them, and they very rarely came to the clearing where the missionaries lived. But a member of the Brethren assembly, Don Macario, who was fluent in both Spanish and Tsafiki, agreed to give her an hour or two of time each day, which produced all the linguistic information she could get sorted and filed before the next day's session. Many of these details from *These Strange Ashes* appear in some form in the few remaining letters.

The book also describes two major events from Betty's time in San Miguel that are not mentioned at all in the surviving letters. The first was the death in childbirth of a woman named Maruja. Betty and Barbara were called out to help, but by the time they arrived Maruja was dying from blood loss and a prolapsed uterus. After her death, her baby starved to death over a period of days. To make Betty's inner turmoil worse, it went against her every understanding of how God had promised to behave.

The second crisis was the murder of Macario. He was shot in the head while working to clear a field and brought into town on a blanket, grotesque with rigor mortis. The sheriff's deputies who came to investigate said there must be an autopsy if they were to prosecute the murderer, so "a missionary named Bill who had come in with the authorities" used a meat saw to retrieve the bullet.[84] The skull "had been cracked by the blast" and "fell into several pieces." No investigation was ever made. This, too, was appalling. And with Macario's death, Betty lost her sense of purpose. "I could do nothing, be nothing," Elliot wrote in *These Strange Ashes*. "Without an informant, I was not a 'linguist' or a translator. I could only wait." Again she felt as if God had failed to behave as promised. "I felt like a son who had asked for a fish and been given a scorpion."[85] Elliot's scrawled note from 1971 suggests that when she destroyed letters from San Miguel, she kept the interesting, important material. But these events are more than interesting. They are gripping, riveting. They were formative in Betty's life.

Unless the journals become available for scholarship in the future, *These Strange Ashes* is the only available record of these deaths and virtually the only record of Betty's time in San Miguel. But the remaining documentation suggests that the book's narrative is not always reliable. The first four chapters describe the parting from Jim, the sense of adventure, the rough ride on the tailgate of Dee's pickup truck, a stay of at least thirty-six hours with the Shorts in Santo Domingo, a side trip with Dee while he did some preaching in various locations, and the muddy ride from Santo Domingo into San Miguel on horseback with Dorothy Jones. But by the time Betty moved in late October, Dorothy Jones had already been living in San Miguel for two months, and the Short family had been out of the country on furlough just as long. Although Betty and Marj Jones took the same route on their banana truck as Betty and Dorothy Jones (no relation) had taken with Dee, the first trip into the jungle described in *These Strange Ashes* actually occurred and was documented in detail in Betty's letters home in early July, while she was still living in Quito. The book repeatedly interweaves, without comment and over a span of almost twenty-five pages, thoughts and feelings from Betty's move in October with passages describing events that actually occurred in July, presenting them as one journey.

As with the differences between *Passion and Purity* and Jim's diaries, the likeliest explanation for this discrepancy seems to be that Elliot wrote the book around a central idea—this time about the nature of missionary work and of obedience to God—and included the details from her life that supported that framework. The July journey was an important part of the paradigm shift that the book tries to describe, though it did not fit neatly in the bounds of her first year as a jungle missionary. The October journey fit the book's timeline but was lacking both the shock of first impressions and the social interactions that had been so unsettling on the first trip. And the explanations necessary to include them both would have made the narrative more clunky and fragmented. So, for the sake of the story, she conflated the two.

The decision makes sense from a purely literary standpoint. *These Strange Ashes* tells a compelling story in spare and lyrical prose. The additional exposition needed to explain what really happened would likely have destroyed some of the book's plangency. And Elliot's use of her material seems to fall well within industry standards of the time for acceptable artistic license. Indeed, it seems more factually precise than that of many other writers of the era, ranging from Jane Dolinger to Joan Didion: Elliot rearranged events but she did not, as far as one can see, invent them.

Nevertheless, the elision of the two journeys compounds the questions raised by the destruction of the letters. Although each little set of details is true in itself, the first portion of the book tells a story that didn't quite happen; with nothing to measure the rest of the book against, there's no way of knowing what else may not have happened quite as it's told. And the sheer volume of letters that were apparently destroyed makes it impossible not to speculate that, while Elliot was reluctant to erase the entire record of her time in San Miguel, there were things in some of the letters that she wanted to remain unknown.

This raises the question of how to respond both to the book and to the remaining letters. The picture they present may not be much different from what happened. Perhaps the letters contained things which seemed to be primarily someone else's story, which Elliot felt were not her place to make public, and which seemed to her to make no difference in the telling of her own story. It's unclear what audience Elliot had in mind for the note or the remaining letters in 1971. She may have been thinking only of family reading them after she was dead, although given her experience with posthumous interest in Jim's story, it seems likely that she already had posterity in mind. She did not donate papers to the Billy Graham Center Archives for the first time until 1985, and when she did, she placed them under restriction; documents from 1973 onward were sealed until forty years after the date of the most recent document in each folder. In 1971 she may not have been aware that such a procedure existed; destroying the record could have seemed the best way to protect the privacy of the living.

On the other hand, she may really have been thinking only of a family audience: she may have been seized with a fit of tidiness and thinned out her file folder after she made her notes for the book, only keeping the comparatively cheerful personal details she thought would be of most interest to those she left behind. If this was the case, perhaps she did not thin the letters from other periods simply because she didn't have them at the time; the notes at the archives indicate that a good number of the letters now in the archives may have been in the possession of Elliot's mother until Katharine's death in 1987. Or she may have experienced a feeling of revulsion on revisiting a difficult period in her life and wanted to get rid of letters that brought it back viscerally and immediately, preferring to confine the story to the more manageable form she would reduce it to for the book. There is simply no way to know why Elliot both destroyed the letters, and, at the same time, left a clear record that she had done so. What is evident is that the events of these seven months began a process of change in Betty Howard.

———

In San Miguel, Dorothy Jones volunteered to manage most of the cooking and cleaning for their household so Betty would have more time for language work. Betty was happy to agree. In addition to her regular work with Macario, she gathered linguistic data wherever and however she could—following the Tsáchila cook over the trails when she went home, tagging along on group fishing trips, and spending time with any Tsáchila who happened to come into town. After an afternoon collecting language data from two women who had come to do some shopping and had agreed to talk with her, she wrote to her family:

> Sometimes I can hardly believe that this is I in this situation—that this is IT! That I am actually doing that to which I have looked forward for

six—no seven—years! I praise God that He has fulfilled His word to me at that time, and I rest on one of the special promises given to me very forcefully in 1944—Is. 50:7 "For the Lord God will help me. Therefore have I set my face like a flint, and I know that I shall not be ashamed."[86]

Life was not all roses, however, even as an actual missionary doing real linguistic work in a genuine jungle. To Jim she wrote:

> I enjoy tearing around in jeans on horseback, walking with one of the girls in the jungle. . . . I love that sort of thing. I also love the linguistic work. But always, and underneath, I try to imagine you there, working alongside, coming "home" to the house, riding the trails with me, struggling over some phoneme or allomorph. And such a thought is always better than *this*, no matter how much fun I may be having.[87]

And by the end of the second week, the chaos and monotony of daily life were beginning to reassert themselves. The difficulties in cooking and cleaning ceased to be amusing and became merely annoying. Interruptions and distractions began to eat away at her time. Doreen would ask her to take her teaching session for a morning so she could go to Santo Domingo, or Macario would go out of town for the day to visit his mother, or she would have to interrupt desk work to grind peanut butter because they were out again.

There were bigger problems, such as an ongoing feud with the Catholic clergy and religious in San Miguel. The stepfather of a young Tsáchila boy called Vicente had asked the missionaries to board him, and allowed him to attend their school. Doreen, who had so far been unable to recruit any Tsáchila students, was delighted. But it seemed to the Brethren missionaries that the priest was jealous of them and tried to disrupt their work. In this instance, they believed he had accused them of kidnapping Vicente and was attempting to have him removed from their custody.

Although the Catholic-Protestant situation in Ecuador was comparatively peaceful, the missionary grapevine would have kept Betty apprised of greater conflict in other parts of South America. In Colombia, where Dave would soon become the field director for Latin America Mission (LAM), the political tug-of-war between conservatives and liberals led to a prolonged period of violent conflict that was particularly intense from the early 1940s to the late 1950s. Over two hundred thousand people were killed during this period. And as historians Justo L. González and Ondina E. González have noted, "the difference between political violence and religious persecution was difficult to determine," particularly to those experiencing violence. In Colombia "between 1948 and 1955, more than 165 Protestant schools were closed, 42 churches destroyed, and 112 people murdered—4 of whom were children."[88] Regular reports on the situation were circulated by the Evangelical Confederation of Colombia to missionary organizations and major news organs in the US and internationally, so Betty would have been well aware of what was happening.

During her time in Quito, Betty had written repeatedly of her distaste for priests: "It makes me sick to see the priests gliding around the school grounds."[89] She felt the Catholic clergy and religious had disrupted Brethren street meetings, and when she heard that the priest in Shandia was paying workers a sucre a day more than Jim and Pete had offered, it seemed like another attempt to thwart their work, particularly when he followed it up by telling the Kichwa that the evangelicals were demons. In late September, Betty had written passionately:

> This morning I was reading Saul's reply to Elymas the sorcerer—"O full of all subtlety and mischief thou child of the devil, thou enemy of all righteousness—will thou not cease to pervert the right ways of the Lord?" How perfectly it fits the priests. Really, it makes me cringe every time I see the filthy creatures board a bus in their long shirts, flat hats, sickly weak faces, and pot bellies. Many's the time I've seen a woman stand up and give one her seat. I could knock his face in. Children of the devil—enemies of all righteousness. I just read again God's Missionary (A.C.). O we must be pure to be powerful—and nothing short of the resurrection power of Christ, dwelling in us, suffices in this battle. As yet I still feel as though I'm just in the bleachers, so to speak, but soon to be in the thick of it.[90]

Now she was living on what she saw as the front lines. In mid-November she wrote to her family that she was trying to hide her linguistic work, even locking it up when not in use, because the Catholics were already competing with the evangelicals over the school and the visitation work and she didn't want them horning in on translation as well.

Betty had been developing her thoughts on missiology through a variety of avenues over a period of years, but perhaps the single biggest influence on her thinking had been her extensive reading in Carmichael's work. Betty's attitude toward Catholic clergy is reminiscent of Carmichael's toward Hindu priests: "Half animal, half demon, not man at all, he sat, a coiled mass of naked flesh, in a huge armchair, watching us with snakelike eyes."[91]

Betty's thoughts reflected Carmichael's in other ways as well. Carmichael had been deeply troubled by missionaries who had come to India only to live in their own compounds, wear their own clothes, carry on their own cultural behaviors, and expect Christian converts to become culturally British. She had tried as much as she knew how to adapt herself to Indian culture and to raise the children she cared for in Indian culture.[92] Though she was far from perfect, much of her missiology sounds remarkably relevant in the twenty-first century, and Betty's own writing on missionary aims and techniques often reflects this:

> I read again the other day *God's Missionary* by A.C.. . . . We must recognize that as foreign missionaries we are not called to transplant an American culture pattern to another people. This is IMPERATIVE. We are called to leave home and kinfolk and all that our former life involved, and live Christ in another context than that to which we are accustomed. Already I see the sad failure of the attempt to superimpose an American culture (I use the word in the ethnological sense only) upon another people.

She recognized that this was easier said than done, but she was trying: "I find it a constant effort to project my mind into the Latin mind, to understand them, to appreciate them, to think from another point of view. And always, when I speak English, or read TIME or something, I have the sense of settling down in an easy chair, 'at home' once more. But I believe God to give me the spirit of understanding that I may at least appreciate (in the true sense of the word) the Latin mind."[93]

Her ideas were also developed in conversation with Jim, who had been thinking of the necessity for a Kichwa church—rather than an American church in Kichwa territory—since at least the summer of 1950. Less than two weeks into his time in Quito, he had written to his parents, "It becomes increasingly obvious that our job here is to train Ecuadorians. We will never be able to speak as they speak nor get next to their own people in the way they are next to them."[94]

The difficulties involved in putting theory into practice became more apparent with time in the field, continuing to challenge the idea of missionary work as the highest form of Christian service. Betty wrote to her family, "The more I experience of this missionary business, the more convinced I am that it is not any different from any other calling. I am on no different level than the simplest believer here in San Miguel, in the sight of God, and we do all in our power to make them understand that."[95] But no matter how hard she tried, there were ineradicable differences. Leaving behind *all* that her former life involved began to seem impossible. *These Strange Ashes* records the sense of being unable to participate fully, either in the life around them, or in the cultures they had come from:

> We had to eat. We had to live in reasonable cleanliness. We had to maintain some standards. Or were we wrong? What we ate, what we called clean, what standards we maintained, would have offended our neighbors here as well as our relatives back home—too good for the one group, too poor for the other.[96]

Then there was Vicente. They had welcomed him, hoping that his presence would encourage other Tsáchila children to come to their school, but though they were soon delighted with the child for his own sake, his presence did not bring the results they had hoped for. In fact, it seemed that instead the Tsáchila began to see him as an outsider. *These Strange Ashes* records:

> He lived a new life, in a class by himself, neither a foreigner, nor an Ecuadorian, nor an Indian. This raised the question we struggled with all the time we were missionaries: how to make *Indian* (not American or British) Christians. How were we to live among them and not change a thing except their attitude toward God? We did not see what was happening to Vicente at the time. He was only a little boy, and instead of

his providing us with the Colorado viewpoint, we, willy-nilly, quickly gave him ours.[97]

———

Sometime after Betty's letter of December 2, she was called out into the dark night to attend a birth, only to find the mother, Maruja, thrashing wildly in pools of her own blood, to hear her final words, to watch her die. A week later, she watched the baby die as well.

Twenty years later, Elisabeth Elliot wrote that Maruja's death "produced a tremor in the foundations" of her faith. "It was a life-and-death matter, and if God had spared Maruja's life, the whole Quiñones tribe might have been delivered from spiritual death. In my heart I could not escape the thought that it was God who had failed. Surely He knew how much was at stake. Surely He could have done better by all of us. To my inner cries and questionings no answer came. There was no explaining any of it. I looked into the abyss . . . there was nothing there but darkness and silence."[98] She wanted to run away, to escape the situation entirely.

Then, on the morning of January 26, 1953, Macario was brought into the plaza, "gray in the face, stiffened, and with that gaping cave in his temple." His head was sawn open on a poncho in the plaza. He was waked overnight, and buried in the morning, in the rain:

It had been, I wrote to my parents, "the most nightmarish day of my life." As we walked home in the rain from the graveyard, it seemed to me that everything was over. . . . I went over and over in my mind how it had come to be that I was here at all, that Macario had been my colleague. The work we did together was the work to which each had been clearly called. We had been called, had we not? I went back to the night in New Jersey when I had knelt in my room, asking for assurance that the call was God's voice and not a figment of my own mind. It seemed that He answered me through a Bible verse, "I the Lord have called thee and will hold thine hand." I thought of those who had prayed for me and encouraged me in so many ways, I thought of all the sermons I had cringed under about the coldness of the churches and their disobedience to Christ's commission, "Go ye." . . . How was I to reconcile His permitting such a thing with my own understanding of the missionary task? . . . I came to nothing, to emptiness.

Elliot has written that she began her work as a missionary with "a deep conviction that God will bless those who obey Him and work things out in beautiful, demonstrable ways for those who have given themselves to do His work." These days of crisis began to strip away that sentimentality.[99]

———

Jarringly, Betty's next surviving family letter bursts onto the scene with a flurry of underlining and exclamation points. Written from Quito on February 1 it begins:

Dearest Folks,

I'd just like to pick a bone or two with Ginny. In August she made the categorical assertion that she had the most wonderful man and the most beautiful ring in the world. She should see mine!!! (Yes—man and ring.) The first is the same one I've loved more than he or anyone else knew, for nearly five years. The second is white gold with a single diamond set in a raised square. . . .

He is all, absolutely all, I could ever desire, and God alone knows my need of him. God has tried us in the fire and has waited, that He might be gracious unto us. We have sought as earnestly as two human beings can seek, we believe, to be obedient to the Lord in this matter [that] is of paramount importance. He has not let us make a mistake. We are grateful, beyond all words or thoughts.

On a Thursday night three days after Macario's death, Bill Cathers had ridden into San Miguel in the dark to deliver a telegram that read "Jim will come to Quito Friday come."[100] Betty left in the morning for the twelve-hour trip. When she arrived on January 31, she and Jim went downtown for supper, then spent the evening together in front of the fire in the house they were renting as a bodega. Jim proposed, she accepted, and they shared their first kiss. *These Strange Ashes* records a pause between Jim's proposal and Betty's acceptance, while she thought of all the good reasons that had been sufficient in the past to keep them from marriage, reasons that had not changed. "But I loved him. I had loved him for a long, long time, and I had tried to keep that love in a tight rein. . . . And so I asked Jim if he believed God had given His permission for us to marry. He did, and that was enough for me."[101] Afterward in her journal Betty wrote, "The relief of being able to tell him my love, of feeling free for the first time, is simply unspeakable. I literally ache with love for him and long now for the day when he will be my husband. O, I want to be *possessed*. I desire him, and his desire is toward me—Oh, perfect love, all human thought transcending."[102]

The newly engaged couple spent the next two weeks making the social rounds in Quito, doing the tourist scene, drawing plans and buying supplies for the houses Jim had promised to build for the Cathers and McCully families, and reading each other's diaries from the past year. Betty felt too happy for her own good, writing, "I fear the future—that something will happen to make me lose Jim. 'It's too good to be,' I think, 'That which I feared is come upon me.' I am sure everyone experiences this, but I've never known it to be so strong, and at times I sink under it. Pray that I may exercise faith and refuse the imaginations of a doubting heart. 'He cannot have taught us to trust in His name and thus far have brought us to put us to shame.'"[103]

The idea that she would be required to suffer at some point in the future because of the blessings she had received crops up repeatedly in Betty's letters. She had mentioned it in college, and again during her summer in Quito: "I read the other day the familiar verse, 'For to whomever much is given, of him shall much be required,' and it smote me. To whom could more have been given than to me, and to each of us six? Then how much will be required? It is a solemn charge."[104] In her journal in late 1952 she had written, "At times the thought comes to me that it can't be again that we should see one another, that surely something will happen to one of us. 'But the Lord is kind.'"[105] Jim had noted a similar fear not long before they got engaged. "Still I do, Betty, I do fear sometimes, like a worrying mother, that something will happen to you and I will lose you, and then what would I do?"[106]

Disaster struck at the end of the two weeks when Betty's routine chest X-ray showed tuberculosis. For most of human history, tuberculosis had essentially been a death sentence. There was essentially no effective treatment, no cure, and the vast majority of those infected died. A single-antibiotic treatment for TB, which was somewhat effective, had been available for less than a decade, and the modern triple-antibiotic response to TB, which would turn out to have high efficacy rates, had just been discovered in 1952 and was still something of an unknown quantity.

Betty cried and cried when she received the diagnosis. "I have never been so crushed by anything in my life," she wrote in her journal. "It may mean going back to the States, for three months of absolute rest in bed. How can I leave Jim? I cannot be a hindrance to him."[107] But Jim was confident— confident that God had led them to engagement, and so confident that God would make a way for them to get married. He went back to Shandia, apparently the day after Betty received her diagnosis, and Betty went to the TB clinic in Quito for further testing. The list of "interesting passages" typed up from the letters destroyed in 1971 says: "x-rays, stomach pump ('the worst physical torture I've ever been through[']), choking, gagging, retching, gasping, tears streaming. Blood test—the nurses couldn't find a vein, kept jabbing and fishing around under the skin. Then a call to the doctor's office after several days, no findings whatever. The cause of the lesion, unknown, but it had completely disappeared."[108] It never came back.

———

Jim's proposal of marriage came with two conditions: Betty had to be willing to tolerate a long engagement, perhaps years long, since his prior commitments such as house building would have to be fulfilled before he could set a date. And she had to learn to speak Kichwa. "I've seen enough of missionary wives who come out all starry-eyed expecting to work alongside their husbands, and then get bogged down taking care of a household and having babies so that they never get around to learning the language," he told her. "That won't happen to you. You'll learn it first."[109] So Betty went back to San Miguel to get her work into a shape that Doreen and Barbara could go on with so that she could move to a place where Kichwa was spoken.

In April the Cathers family moved back to the US because of health problems. That scratched building their house off Jim's to-do list, and Katharine, who was praying that God would make a way for Betty and Jim to be married that summer, was encouraged.

In early May, the couple met again in Quito. Jim's journal entry for May 11 records that she was asleep when he arrived at the Tidmarshes' house, and after trying and failing to wake her up by rattling the door handle, he went in and woke her with a kiss: "It was the beginning of two most intense weeks of embracing." The couple attended the Inter-Mission Fellowship conference, visited with other missionaries, bought a rug for their future home, and spent evenings at the bodega in front of the fire. "If there was before anything tentative in our loving," Jim wrote, "it is since then destroyed."[110] At the end of the two weeks Jim went with Betty to San Miguel for the weekend. *These Strange Ashes* speaks of "pleasant evenings sitting on the railing of our back porch together, watching an apricot moon float above the mystic trees of the *plaza* where the old white ox munched softly."[111] Jim's journal entry says merely, "San Miguel. The peasant blouse, the thin blue dress, and the plaid blouse, and jeans. The shoulder, the leg, and the naked waist."[112] Then Jim went back to Shandia.

Betty had a few more desultory linguistic contacts—an hour's visit with a Tsáchila woman sitting by her fire, lunch with the chief's brother, an hour on the porch with another man, a few words picked up on a visit to an old man with malaria. She spent the next four weeks finishing the alphabet and teaching Barbara how to use the linguistic materials so she "could take it up where I left off."[113] It was a struggle to keep her mind on the job, and her letters to Jim often contained requests that he would pray about her "inability to concentrate, the lack of any real will or desire to get anything accomplished."[114] Years later, in *These Strange Ashes*, she would write that she had been eager to leave, to get away from "the births, the deaths, struggles, failures, losses, and all the days and weeks of common, ordinary missionary life when I accomplished nothing visible or tangible, when I often wasted time and wished I were elsewhere and allowed my thoughts to go off in all directions except where they belonged. . . . My language files and notebooks would provide a foundation for the future translation work which I felt sure someone would do, and I was glad to go."[115] She finished her Tsafiki alphabet on June 16 or 17.[116] On the eighteenth she packed her things back into their wooden cracker boxes and a lone saddle bag, and rode out of San Miguel.

———

Betty was headed for Dos Rios, a Christian and Missionary Alliance station about 15 miles northeast of Shandia on the Misahuallí River, a tributary of the Napo. The missionaries at that station, Carol and Jerry

Conn and their three children, were leaving in August on vacation, and it had been arranged that Doreen and Betty would hold down the fort while the family were gone. Doreen was waiting in San Miguel for the arrival of a new Brethren missionary, American Emma Guikema, who planned to take over the medical clinic, but Betty had gone on ahead, anxious to begin learning Kichwa. Carol Conn spoke the language well, which would give her a jump start.

Between washed-out roads and flights canceled by bad weather, the trip took almost a week, and Betty was delighted to arrive at the Dos Rios station, which felt beautifully clean and well-tended after the mold-darkened buildings in Santo Domingo and San Miguel. It was, she said, "brand new, all board, painted white, and with aluminum roof. Such luxury I never anticipated in the jungle! I have a room on the second floor, with a spring bed, and even a closet." There were Kichwa staff, so the missionaries did not have to do the cooking and housekeeping. If linguistic work in San Miguel had been a bit of a disappointment, had turned out not to be so different from ordinary life and had yielded little in the way of visible results, here was a chance to move the marker for having arrived a bit farther down the road. "As I sit at my wide set of windows, I look out over a very green stretch of jungle grass, breadfruit trees and palms to a beautiful river, the Misihualui [sic]. Beyond the river is a high cliff, backed by jungle, and then lovely blue mountains which give the same appearance, from here, as those of Franconia! Yes, I am at last in the great, wonderful Oriente, my home!" And Jim was just on the other side of those mountains, "only six hours by trail."[117]

Betty tackled the language with enthusiasm. After the first day and a half she had fifty expressions written in her notebook, and by the end of her first month "quite an extensive file of morphemes."[118] She also took over the job of running the radio contact with the other jungle missionary stations, which freed up an hour for the Conns to work on other things and also gave her a chance to hear Jim's voice every day. He came for a visit a week after Betty arrived, and they spent three days working in the mission school, drawing house plans, studying Kichwa, sitting on the porch, and swimming in the river. "We . . . are praying definitely that the Lord will let us be married within a year," Betty wrote to her mother. "It seems a long time, but we are both busy, and the Lord will give us grace until His time."[119]

She continued to make observations and adjust her missions theory as well. A couple of weeks after Jim's visit, the government examiner came to conduct oral examination at the mission school, a major community event involving military drills and free food for all. The Conns provided a meal of local staples—plantains and manioc—and 83 pounds of fresh meat. But it seemed to fall flat, compared unfavorably with more lavish spreads given by other missionaries in the past. Betty noted that both in Dos Rios and in Shandia, the first missionaries to arrive had seen their new neighbors as lacking good things and had tried to give them those things as much as possible: "food, clothes, money, etc." Although such gifts were well-intentioned, dumping goods from an industrial society into a preindustrial economic system caused conflicts both between missionaries and permanent residents and between members of the indigenous community. "I do not think it's good ever to give anything away," Betty decided now, "no matter how ridiculously small a sum you may charge for a thing, just the principal [sic] that they must work or pay for what they get is healthy."[120]

Seeing beyond a Western-centric cultural lens was easier said than done. Her own difficulty in adopting a new way of seeing was highlighted in the way she described the Kichwa and some of their practices to her family. "The Indians are very attractive, physically, even though they don't paint like the Colorados. They are handsomer, with very distinctly sculptured faces, like bronze statues. Their build is very stocky and at times grotesquely proportioned, with very short legs and a long trunk."[121] When she told of being present for the delivery of a baby, she wrote, "When the women here give birth, they kneel by the wall and yank on a cord which is tied above their head. It is most barbarous."[122] It was one thing to try to understand "the Latin mind" in order to live among white Ecuadorians whose culture had some similarities to her own, and another thing entirely to try to see things from the point of view of people whose culture seemed different from anything Betty had known.

———

Summer 1953 was unusually rainy, even for a rainforest. In June, five days and nights of continuous rain turned the Napo River near Shandia into a torrent. It began to eat away its banks, first downriver from the station, then close enough that one of the trails leading into the station crumbled away, then at the station itself, washing out the runway. Before the river subsided, it had consumed 15 yards of land—half the distance between the water and the house Jim and Pete had just finished for the McCullys—and the building that had housed their generator. They had managed to save the generator only by roping it to a tree farther inland. It had been decades since the area had seen this kind of rain. It continued to rain, and the missionaries decided that the only thing to do was take the house apart and build it again farther from the new cliff's edge.

In mid-July rain fell so hard that it filled the 400-gallon Dos Rios water tanks "in ten minutes or so."[123] Betty had planned to catch an MAF flight to Shandia at the end of the month to see Jim's home and then hike back with him to Dos Rios so they could spend the weekend together, but it would not stop raining. "So the plane could not come in, and Jim had to walk over alone."[124] The couple spent a happy few days on language study and house planning, finding time alone in the field outside the house after everyone else had gone to bed. They discussed wedding dates, although there were still impediments everywhere they looked. Over the weekend they "tentatively planned a Nov. wedding."[125]

Then Jim went back to Shandia and talked things over with Pete. Pete had renewed his engagement to Olive Ainslie in March, and the men agreed that they should stagger their weddings so one could remain at Shandia while the other was honeymooning, and that they should get in some travel before either of them got married. In the course of their conversation, Jim apparently decided that January would be better after all. On Thursday, July 30, he wrote in his journal, "It is raining hard and the river is very high again, so there will be no work outside. I feel happy at settling on January for a wedding."[126]

He never had a chance to tell Betty about his change of mind. After writing in his journal, he and Pete had put in some time on the Kichwa dictionary they were making, then, as Pete recorded, "had an early lunch and watched anxiously as the water rose."[127] Soon the ground had begun to crumble into the river again. That night, Betty's letter to her family reported that during the afternoon's radio contact Jim had alerted her that the house and other buildings were now only 15 feet from the cliff's edge with the bank still crumbling, "and if he did not come on the contact again at 2:30, we'd know that they'd abandoned the house!" She had not heard from him since. "Tonight's DL says, 'God has not given us the spirit of fear, but of power, of love, and of a sound mind.' I surely need that now. I feel as though I won't get much sleep tonight."[128]

In the morning she added to the letter. "Friday a.m. Not a sound out of anyone on the network this morning. That's the way it is sometimes, and today, of all days!" There was no word all day. Betty was sure the house must be gone and wrote to her parents, "Oh my, I just don't know what this flood is going to mean to our getting married. Instead of finishing McCully's house soon, they'll have to put up some sort of shelter for themselves. It may mean that Shandia is no longer a suitable site for a station, which means opening a whole new station, and a whole year's work gone. Well, I do not believe it is in vain. The Lord has His purposes, which will surely 'ripen fast.'"[129] Saturday morning again there was no word.

Finally, Saturday afternoon, a letter came from Jim by a courier. The "cataclysmic event" that, back in March, he had half hoped would come and disrupt his plans had happened.[130] Jim and Pete and a group of Kichwa volunteers had worked thirty-six hours without pause, saving the large equipment and most of the McCullys' belongings, but the Shandia station was gone—not just Jim and Pete's house, but every building belonging to the missionaries and several Kichwa houses—washed away with the roaring river.

Betty walked to Shandia with a handful of Kichwa companions as soon as she heard the news, arriving late Sunday morning. She cried when she saw the extent of the destruction. Then she got to work, spending the next two days "arranging their tent for them . . . drying clothes, cleaning the refrigerator, spreading out books and stuff in the sun, fixing up decent beds for them, and showing the cook some tricks like serving the hot food hot."[131] Ed came out to help Jim and Pete decide what to do next. The ruin was so complete that the men could not really wrap their minds around starting again. Finally they decided that they would have a better idea of how to proceed if they took a trip to see what else was available in the way of potential stations—places where there were both an interested community and a feasible building site. Betty would return to guard their supplies lest the Catholic priest hire people to steal them in the men's absence.

Before the flood, Jim had been planning to go to Quito for a week in August to help with a youth camp, and Wilfred had planned to hold down the fort at Shandia during that time. Emma Guikema was recovering from jaundice, so Wilfred had planned to drop her off at Dos Rios on his way, to rest and visit with Betty. The Conns had gone on vacation at the end of the first week of August, and Doreen had apparently not arrived, so Betty was manning Dos Rios alone for the time being, leading the church meetings in Kichwa and even preaching—through an interpreter—in Spanish. Although Jim was no longer going to Quito, Wilfred arrived in Shandia anyway, "insisting" that the station "be immediately rebuilt," and stayed several days, much to the chagrin of Jim, who was coming down with malaria and felt terrible. "I am persuaded that that esteemed brother has one grave fault," Jim wrote in his journal during this time, "he talks—too fast, too precipitously, and too much."[132]

In the middle of the night on August 15, just after the worst of the malarial symptoms passed, Jim decided that he and Betty should get married in October "and wrote her so right after breakfast."[133] Apparently the fact that she still couldn't speak much Kichwa was no longer a problem. Four days later he radioed to tell her he'd built a shack for her to sleep in. Two days after that, she was on her way back to Shandia, leaving behind "a rather apprehensive" Emma, who did not even speak Spanish, let alone Kichwa, as the only English speaker in Dos Rios. Betty and Jim had four days together, then he left to meet up with Pete and Ed, who had gone to get supplies, and she settled down—without a radio but with a revolver—to wait. "I <u>ought</u> to learn Quichua!! . . . Don't worry, Mother—by the time you get this the men will probably be back!"[134]

They were gone three-and-a-half weeks, flying back into Shandia on September 19. On the twenty-second, Betty wrote to her family to announce that they had returned "much impressed with the need, and convinced that they must branch out." A community called Puyupungu had invited them to open a school, and Jim, Pete, and Ed had all agreed "that the ones to man the new station are the Elliots. So on October 8, 1953, in Quito, Ecuador, South America, I expect to become Mrs. Philip James Elliot. Don't all faint."[135]

Betty and her mother had been writing back and forth discussing wedding plans for most of the summer—sending and receiving bridal magazines and pattern books and sketches of dresses, and trying to figure out if there was a way for the Howards to come to Ecuador for the ceremony. The flood changed all that. Though she had written to Jim that "I cannot help thinking of the disappointment to our folks . . . [,]"¹³⁶ she tried to encourage them when she wrote to explain: "We expect to have nothing but a civil ceremony. . . . No reception or anything. Are you disappointed? We both are as one on the matter. The Lord has shown us clearly that this way is the appropriate way for <u>us</u>. No one else will understand, except you all and I think you will." She would have enjoyed the chance to have a more traditional American wedding, "with all the lovely hymns I've had picked out for years," if she had been able to have her family there, but was uninterested in waiting any longer just to "put on a show" for the other missionaries she had not known long or well. "I would very much like to have you all near to share, but the Lord knows all about that."¹³⁷

A week later, Nate Saint flew Betty and Jim from Shandia to Shell Mera, where they caught a truck for the long drive to Quito, made longer by landslides across the road, which they had to be lifted across "on a board platform hung on a cable." They had a week in Quito, which they spent "shopping, having dentists & doctors check-ups, T.B. x-ray (all o.k.) etc." Jim made honeymoon reservations, Gwen Tidmarsh threw a shower for Betty ("I got a gorgeous cotton denim tablecloth with 12 napkins, a pitcher & set of glasses, a small embroidered tea linen set, a lovely Van Raalte gown & slip to match & other lingerie. It was surely lovely."), and Betty and Jim went to a jeweler and ordered her wedding ring, "made exactly as I'd wanted it."¹³⁸

Their wedding day, October 8, was Jim's twenty-sixth birthday, and "a beautiful day."

Tidmarshes & Jim called for me in the car (I was staying at the bodega) & we went down to the Registro Civil. McCully's [sic] met us there (at 9:30) & we were ushered into a huge, dingy, and rather tawdry elegant room where sat this ancient judge. Gwen & the Dr., as official witnesses, were asked to swear that we were single, & then the secretary rattled off a page or so of baloney, ending with "son legalemente casados." (Are legally married). We had to sign 3 or 4 things, & that was that. It took about 7 minutes—wonderfully simple.¹³⁹

After almost five-and-a-half years of uncertainty and waiting, Jim Elliot and Betty Howard were man and wife.

Ed snapped some pictures, and the new family and their witnesses went out for "coffee & cake at the Colon Hotel." After praying for them, Wilfred drove them to the airport, where they departed for their honeymoon in a shower of rice thrown by HCJB staff. They spent six days in Panama, four days in a surprise visit with Dave and Phyllis in Costa Rica (Dave had not even known they were married, Betty wrote to her parents: "Wish you could have seen his face! He could hardly speak.") and two more days in Panama on their way back to Ecuador. They reveled in luxury at the El Panamá hotel—a long-distance phone call to each set of parents, all the modern luxuries in their room, a private balcony with French doors and an ocean view, an orchestra in the dining room and fancy meals ("everything from Colorado brook trout to broiled lobster and raspberry parfait"), movies (they watched Disney's *Peter Pan*), a swimming pool, boutiques. On their wedding night, "after dinner . . . when we came up to our room, we had our own little 'wedding'—thanking the Lord for all the way of His leading, singing together on the balcony our 'special' hymns, & finally Jim put the ring on for keeps. It was so sweet—just what I'd wanted, <u>all</u> I'd wanted in the way of a wedding."[140]

———

Back in Quito, the newlyweds sorted yet again through their stored possessions and packed what they would need at their new station into rubber bags and plastic-lined boxes for the canoe trip. "I'm so thankful for the equipment I've brought for really primitive living, now that we'll be in a tent for a time. (Washing plunger, hand wringer, gas iron, lamps, poncho, etc. And all those cans for storing food in.)"[141] Betty was reveling in her marriage, writing to her family:

My, it's a wonderful state, this married one, isn't it, those of you who know??!! I just can hardly believe, sometimes, that the Lord has actually done all the things I dreamed about for so long, in giving me Jim. Somehow time means nothing to me anymore. Always I used to be looking forward to his coming, or dreading his leaving, and wishing my life away. I hated to see birthdays approach, marking one more year of single life, gone. Now I don't care how soon I reach 30! It used to seem so ominous to me! He is all I wished and hoped for, and absolutely a model husband, thoughtful in every way and still a real "man's man."[142]

Although it meant waiting for four days for a flight with room for them, the couple were glad for an opportunity to move themselves, their new puppy, Ushpalito, and 1,000 pounds of gear to Shell Mera for free by tagging along on an Ecuadorian Army flight. There they spent a weekend waiting for some Kichwa men to take them by canoe down the Puyo River.

Puyupungu, their destination, was a settlement of five houses plus two traditional Kichwa-style buildings constructed for the Catholic priest as a house and a church building (these last were generally vacant since the priest visited once a year). The five families had eighteen children among them and were "most eager for a school," so Betty and Jim planned to build a house and an airstrip, start a school, and try to "get the Gospel down the Puyu," as Jim wrote in his diary.[143] High on a cliff, their building site looked across the Pastaza River and the forest to two huge active volcanoes, Sangay and Tungurahua. Sangay smoked all day, and at night "huge red hot boulders" could be seen rolling down its sides. "I doubt if Puyupungu is excelled in Ecuador" for the view, Betty wrote, and "sunsets, over the river, behind the mountains, are something indescribable."[144]

She and Jim spent their first night in Puyupungu in the empty priest's house, but as "the cockroaches were legion, and the roof leaked" they moved into their tent as soon as they could. Jim put up an aluminum roof with no walls for a kitchen, but he was so sick with jaundice that he went to bed afterward and stayed there for much of the next few weeks. It continued to rain, heavily and frequently, turning the ground into squelching, sucking mud, and spattering mud all over the contents of the kitchen. One night it rained so hard for so long, "we thought our bed was going to float away. . . . Jim dropped his pillow off the bed and it fell into a mud puddle!"[145] She would later remember this as the occasion of their first fight. Jim, having used up the batteries in his own flashlight, took hers; she lost her temper; he yelled back; and they both ended up laughing hysterically over the impossibility of the situation.

On the first of December, Jim wrote in his journal:

It is not raining at the moment but the fresh-cut bamboo slats are chunked with fresh mud, and the other half of the tent, not yet floored, is slippery gum from an all-night rain on Saturday. . . . Perhaps we will be fully floored this week. Betty took matters in her own hands this afternoon while I rested (I am supposed to have had jaundice—almost since the day we arrived, November 11—and am still a part-time bed patient) and put down sticks between the tent and the eight-by-ten mud-floored kitchen, as yet only half walled. She is there cooking now while I sit at the card table, decked with an aster-flowered tea cloth with a centerpiece of white candle and a graceful-leafed little forest flower set off beautifully in a tin can.

But despite sickness and mud, the couple seemed to be enjoying themselves. Jim went on to describe the ease with which they felt they were settling in together (noting Betty's inherited tendency toward dramatic turns of speech):

She is just what I always knew her to be, all woman, with her habit of being surprised and shocked at things I do and say (an amusing habit to me, and an incentive to keep saying shocking things), her tendency to use exaggerated words ("horrible," "awful" in tones of utter disgust), and to feel things strongly and with a love for me that I can neither understand nor appreciate, let alone be worthy of. We have had nothing but harmony, from our wedding night in El Panama to the last time we spoke—about the men bringing bamboo to the plaza just now. The "marriage adjustment" is something—if it exists at all—that I am going through effortlessly, unconsciously, even.[146]

Gradually they added more comforts to their home, finishing the bamboo floor in the tent so that they no longer had to "sort of wade around inside when it rained," and adding walls to the kitchen "so my dishes aren't always muddy."[147]

Simultaneously they tried to work on the things they had come to Puyupungu for: a church and a school. On the first Sunday they held a "gospel meeting," and not long after they arrived a Kichwa man named Lucas came from Shandia as a teacher for the school they were starting.[148] At last, more than six years after that night when the shadow of the cross fell between them in the cemetery in Wheaton, they were embarked on their life's work, together.

6

Through the Waters

ON APRIL 7, 1952, while Betty Howard was two days out to sea on her way to Ecuador, *Life* magazine ran a cover story on Marilyn Monroe, "The Talk of Hollywood." In October, while Betty was moving from Quito to San Miguel, Dwight Eisenhower's presidential campaign was airing the first ever political television ads in the US. In January 1953, a week before the murder of Macario, more Americans watched an episode of "I Love Lucy" than the inauguration of President Eisenhower. In May, while evangelical missionaries were gathering in Quito for the annual Inter-Mission Conference, moviegoers in America were attending showings of the very first 3D movie, *It Came from Outer Space*. On December 17, 1953, the FCC rubber-stamped color television, and Betty Elliot sat at the table in her tiny kitchen in Puyupungu to reply to the mail the Mission Aviation Fellowship plane had dropped the day before. While she wrote, Jim was telling the story of the Nativity in Kichwa for the school Christmas program. It was the first time, they believed, that some of those present would hear "why the whites celebrate Christmas."[1]

Betty and Jim spent their first Christmas as a married couple in Shandia, celebrating the holiday with the McCullys, Pete Fleming, and Emma Guikema. The Elliots stayed on at the northern station afterward so Jim and Pete could put on a five-day Bible conference for young men the following week. The two Americans did most of the speaking, but, Betty told her folks, one or two Kichwa Christians also taught. And Jim had the opportunity to baptize two new Kichwa Christians, the first baptism in Shandia. This time away from Puyupungu gave Betty and Jim the opportunity to be part of a church of more than two people again. It provided Betty, now sick herself, with a chance to rest more than she might have allowed herself to do at home, since Marilou was there to do the housework. And Betty wrote to her family of the "happy breaking of bread meeting" they had the Sunday after Christmas, "the first in a long time for us."[2]

The Elliots were back in Puyupungu by the end of the first week of January. Jim spent a good deal of each day supervising the men he had hired to clear a runway—a mammoth job done entirely with machetes, crowbars, and muscle. The tent they had been living in since October was rotting in the constant damp and sprouting leaks at an increasing rate, so he also started work on a house. Much of Betty's time was taken up with the exigencies of trying to keep up some semblance of suburban American housekeeping in a decidedly nonsuburban environment. She hired some Kichwa women to help with dishes, cooking, cleaning, and laundry, and in the bits of time that gave her, she continued to work on learning to speak Kichwa. Both she and Jim were working on reducing the language to writing, running the school (and sometimes teaching), and holding meetings to try to explain Christianity.

Each of them wrote during this time of the slowness and uncertain results of their work, in both building projects and attempts to talk about Jesus. They had different cultural expectations about employment than their employees and were frustrated when rainy days and agricultural rhythms repeatedly stopped the work they were focused on. They struggled to understand and to know whether they were understood. And they were not immune to the irritations of daily life: wet firewood, mildewed laundry, fourteen consecutive days of heavy rain. But there were simple pleasures— letters from the home folks, making candy with freshly harvested peanuts, reading A Tale of Two Cities aloud, collecting orchids, gifts of armadillo and capybara meat from their neighbors. And there were little glimpses of what felt like progress as well: the baptism at Shandia, gradual progress on the runway and house, rapid headway for two teen boys Jim was teaching to read in Spanish.

At the end of February, the Kichwa held a feast day. Fifty-one people, "counting babies and children," came to the Christian meeting. Betty sent home an account of the party to which they were invited afterward, with a teasing description of chicha, the centerpiece of the festivities. "Mother, you'd love it. It's made of manioc root, thoroughly chewed and spit and fermented. Just as they hand you the half-gourd from which it is drunk, the Indian woman puts her hand in it and gives the wad of manioc pulp a squishy squeeze, and then puts it to your lips. It is a milky fluid, with lumps and strings in it, a very sour taste."[3] Although it took some getting used to for American palates, it was a nourishing and hydrating dietary staple for people who spent much of their day in manual labor. Chicha was mildly alcoholic, though in Betty's experience it was only consumed to the point of drunkenness in a stronger version used on feast days. As a mainstay of the local diet, chicha was part of the hospitality the missionaries were offered whenever they visited in people's homes. Noting that her family might have concerns, she reassured them that she and Jim (and Pete, Ed, and Wilfred) felt liberty to accept it when offered.

Betty's thinking on this subject had changed since she was upset by Jim, Pete, and Dorothy drinking cocktails at the fiesta in 1952. Jim had recorded in his journal just after they got engaged that he and Betty had bought wine together, and Betty's brother Tom would later say that Jim "taught her to drink wine."[4] It would be interesting to know whether she arrived at this new position prior to her engagement to Jim, perhaps as a result of the conversations around the 1952 fiesta, or whether she felt in this case as she clearly felt in many others: that Jim's liberty gave her liberty, or that she was to follow Jim's lead regardless of what she would have done if she were single.

Before engagement, Betty had made a point of seeking God's will for *herself*, following where she felt God was leading *her*. She had argued back, told Jim where she thought he was wrong. Once engaged, her response had changed. In the summer of 1953, Jim had written her:

Frankly, I was not satisfied with your attitude toward [Pete] in the few remarks you made in Dos Rios. It is not sufficient to say that "there is something about him that just *gets* you." All the more reason why you should make an effort toward true compatibility and understanding. I threaten to make it hard for you, if you are going to be continually criticizing him—regardless of how he "gets" you. And I'm afraid I'll be adamant on that point, darling, as I regard it a development of Christian grace in you, and will be happy with nothing less than a spirit of sweet reasonableness in such matters when you are my wife.

Although Betty had been startled by his letter, feeling that his response was more severe than her passing comment had warranted, she had not questioned his basic assumptions. Her response shows how she understood her role in relation to him, even in engagement: "But immediately I realized that I must begin now to be subject to you, Jim, and take your correction with a true womanly spirit. It is a role I must learn, for my first impulse was to argue. . . . I ask your forgiveness for criticizing the one whom God has sent you to work with, for I know he has many fine qualities."[5]

In March, Betty and Jim had finished *A Tale of Two Cities* and were reading aloud a new biography of Amy Carmichael. The Irish missionary's story seemed to take on new life for Betty now that she, too, was on the field. She wrote to her family, "There are always difficulties and discouragements, but it is a great comfort to read how God met her."[6] Difficulties and discouragements continued to arise. The little dog Ushpalito disappeared, apparently stolen. Work on the runway was achingly slow.

And the young missionaries continued to struggle with cross-cultural interaction. When the schoolteacher's extended family came to visit from another community where other missionaries had given away goods, they began asking the Elliots to give them things as well, "medicine, soap, bullets, food, etc. etc." Betty believed they also encouraged the Puyupungans to ask her and Jim for more pay. The young couple did not know how to handle the situation. "They see all our luxuries, our rolls of bills when we pay the workmen, our food, and then when I say I will not pay more than three sucres for the week's wash, what will they think? But we want to teach them that our primary purpose is not material benefit here."[7] The problem of colonialism was too big for Betty and Jim to escape, though they kept trying to see beyond their own cultural context. They consistently and vehemently rejected, for example, the received wisdom that said indigenous adults were beyond conversion. But adult converts were slower to appear than they wanted them to be. Jim, who had longed to get to Ecuador so that he could preach in "a place where the Scriptures have not been twisted," must have been doubly frustrated to find himself still embroiled in so many complicating factors.[8]

By the end of March, the new house was finished enough to live in. To keep out the rain, its overhanging roof was much larger than the floor space, and it was built on stilts, leaving a six-foot-high dry space beneath "for working, hanging clothes, hanging up our heads of bananas, etc." [9] This also increased their privacy, as it made the house too high off the ground for passersby to look in the windows whenever they felt like it. Betty could stand up straight again, anywhere in the house, and she no longer had to worry about falling through a rotting floor. "One learns to live that way, and not mind, but it's just that I appreciate so much more what a house means now!" [10]

The Puyupungu runway finally became a reality at the beginning of April. After a test landing to pick up some mail, Nate Saint came in on the first Saturday of the month and ate lunch with Betty and Jim. They spent the afternoon making movies. "Jim took some of him dropping a parachute, of us hauling it out of the top of the lemon tree in which it landed, of me opening the sack of vegetables, of Jim and me talking on the radio, of the house, the strip, etc. etc. It is to be used as a seven-minute sequence by MAF, I think." [11] The parachute delivery system was Nate's invention. He had turned an oil drum into a "bomb bay," and by pulling a release cord, could hit a one-hundred-square-foot target with whatever goods rural missionaries needed. This was how he had been delivering mail and supplies since they arrived in Puyupungu. He had just worked out a method to pick up mail as well, by dropping a bucket on a long tether, flying in a circle so the bucket would remain stationary while mail was put in, and then reeling it back in with a fishing reel. Since the other mission stations in the area had runways, the Elliots had been the first to benefit from the technique, making Puyupungu a good location for footage about MAF's role in pioneer missions.

Not long after this, Ushpalito unexpectedly reappeared, much to their delight. He had been found starving on a trail and brought back by a neighbor, kept alive on a diet of bananas. His return and the completion of the runway were encouragements; another discouragement came in a letter from Barbara Edwards, letting Betty know that much of the Tsafiki language material she had created during her months in San Miguel was lost, "all my Colorado file . . . stolen, along with Barbara's luggage which was on Dee Short's truck, on the way to Quito." But Betty responded philosophically, telling her family, "Poor Barbara was just sick about it, but said she'd managed to make up most of it again, having memorized it almost from end to end! I'm not too worried about it, though it represented a tremendous amount of work. She still has all my notebooks intact."[12] Betty wrote in her journal about this time, "Life can be very routine—rise at 6:00; breakfast 6:30; clean the house; devotions at 8:00; read, write, or study; cook dinner; radio at 1:30; dinner at 5:30; bed at 8:30. Lord, cause me to remember continually the reason I am here. Cause me to look at the things which are not seen. And one more prayer I bring—O Lord, give us a son."[13]

About this time, Atanasio, the influential Kichwa who had invited the missionaries to Puyupungu, had them over for soft drinks. He thanked them heartily for coming and offered Jim a leadership role in the community. Betty recorded that he told them, "Hearing your teaching, it is like waking up. Before, the priest used to come for just three days a year. He'd make a few masses, say a few prayers, charge me forty sucres, and—zas! Away he'd go, back to Puyo. I didn't learn anything. How can anyone learn anything in three days a year? We want you to stay for always." She said, "It impressed us anew with his unusual spirit and desire for improvement. Pray that it may really develop into a genuine spiritual hunger."[14]

Jim declined the position of responsibility, feeling that he could not add it to all the other things he was already doing. It's not clear why Betty did not understand Atanasio's words as a legitimate profession of faith, particularly as they seem to have believed his gratitude was sincere. But several years later, Betty would write, after watching members of another indigenous group repeat a prayer, that this might be either "a sign of the new birth," or evidence of a "sociable desire to please" the original speaker of the prayer. "It is not nearly so important that a man learns the forms of prayer as it is that he pray, conscious of his own need of prayer."[15] These musings on the difference between forms of religion and faith itself may shed some light on her response to Atanasio. In any event, his request is poignant. The Brethren missionaries had decided not to give up the Shandia station after all, and the Elliots now planned to establish Puyupungu as an outpost and live in Shandia the majority of the time. They would be leaving at the end of the school year.

For months, Jim had been hoping his father would come to Ecuador to help him with building projects. After much difficulty with government permits, Fred Elliot arrived in late April 1954 with a good deal of equipment (including a mattress, a table, and two refrigerators!) for various missionaries. Betty and Jim met him in Guayaquil and helped him navigate customs, then took him to Quito, where they spent several days shopping, visiting the dentist, and attending the Inter-Missions Fellowship Conference. They returned to Puyupungu in mid-May, with Jim and his father stopping in Shandia on the way to choose a building site.

In Puyupungu, the men worked on projects around the house for a handful of days, such as building a bedframe to hold the new mattress, then headed back to Shandia so Jim could baptize some new Christians. He had planned just a weekend trip but decided once he got there that he would stay on and help with the rebuilding, asking Betty by radio if that would be okay. "Of course it will not," she said in a letter to her family, "but what can a wife say to her husband over the radio? Or anywhere for that matter, if we are to be submissive and obedient!"[16] Jim had said more than once during their engagement that he wanted her ideas, her perspectives, her "counsel"—that when she was upset about something, he wanted her to be "willing to tell me. It would disturb me, Betts, if we came to such an impasse and you refused to complain—just shut up and wouldn't be plied. . . . However small, I want to know what is troubling you." But she had a definite understanding of what submission meant. In 1952, before their engagement, she had written in her journal:

> He goes ahead building, actually thinking in his own mind that I shall someday be in Shandia, but not so much as asking me how I feel about it or what sort of house I might like. I have no desire to go to Shandia, actually, and much less to live in a house planned and built by someone else. What is there for me to do in Shandia, anyway?
>
> But this morning the word of the Lord quieted anew. "I would seek unto God, and unto God (not 'unto Jim') would I commit my cause." . . .
>
> There are times when I feel I should let go and "tell Jim off"—tell him how I feel about the way he is handling me. There are other times, when I think of his love for me, and my own unspeakable desire and love for him, that the former thoughts are overwhelmed and lost. It is God that maketh my way perfect. In Him do I trust, and I will not be afraid.[17]

So now, in the summer of 1954, she kept her thoughts to herself and waited on God to take care of her.

In June, Betty and Jim acquired a record player and Bible recordings in Kichwa and Spanish, which they played when the neighbors got together for a community workday. In their free time they were reading *Kon Tiki*, Thor Heyerdahl's 1948 account of his voyage by raft from Peru to the Tuamotu Archipelago, working on plans for their new house in Shandia, and daydreaming about how they would decorate it. "Jim & I have been poring over Marilou's copies of Better Homes & Gardens, getting loads of ideas."[18] Jim made another building trip to Shandia, and Carolyn Orr, a missionary at a nearby Summer Institite of Linguistics station, came to stay with Betty and discuss linguistic challenges. With Orr's help, Betty said, "I think I've about got the alphabet decided on now, and am anxious to get started on the morphology (structure of words), which will be far more interesting."[19]

As the school year drew to a close, the Elliots began the process of moving back to Shandia. They invited Orr to live in the Puyupungu house, leaving Ushpalito to keep her company, "tho' Jim misses him a lot."[20] Puyupungu was, Betty felt, a better location for learning Kichwa than the SIL station where Orr had been living, and having the house inhabited would help protect it from falling into disrepair. It seemed a mutually beneficial arrangement. But Betty was becoming increasingly disenchanted with SIL. She was frustrated because Orr had only been able to obtain permission because there was "no established church" at Puyupungu.[21]

Although Betty continued to refer to the organization as "Wycliffe," WBT was actually the US-based fundraising arm of Cam Townsend's brainchild, and SIL the arm operating in the field. The SIL policy was to enter countries as a linguistic rather than a missionary organization, and to avoid activities that could lay it open to charges of proselytizing. Townsend felt that members were invited into host countries as guests, and he wanted them to be good guests. In June 1952, when SIL was preparing to sign a contract with the Ecuadorian government, Townsend had told SIL national director Bob Schneider to emphasize to officials:

We are anxious to find ways of serving in each country [where] we work. That's where literacy and medical help come in. While we are evangelical in faith, we are not fighting anybody, not even the witchdoctors [*sic*]. If people are in need we will serve them, be they Catholic, Protestant or pagan. They in turn will serve us. All we want is an opportunity to give the Word of God to the Indians.[22]

Townsend hoped this approach would help SIL translators avoid controversy while still fulfilling the Great Commission, since, as he had long argued, the Bible in a group's native language was the best missionary there could be. Meanwhile, WBT could appeal to its evangelical financial base in the US as an openly evangelistic organization.

To others, including Betty, the approach seemed to achieve neither goal. Some felt SIL was abandoning "Christian work" for "secular involvements."[23] Some viewed the organization's claim to be purely linguistic as dishonest, since they were not merely reducing unwritten languages to writing but also translating the Christian holy book. Betty seems to have felt that SIL's efforts toward avoiding the appearance of evangelizing were hampering attempts at collaboration among missionaries. She had invited Orr to stay with her before, in the summer of 1953, but SIL had rejected the request. Neither, Betty complained in a family letter, were SIL workers allowed to attend the annual Inter-Mission Fellowship conference.

Betty was not the only missionary in Ecuador frustrated by the situation. In January 1954 she had written to discourage her brother Phil from joining SIL, citing a conversation with an SIL doctor in Ecuador who had told her Phil would be better off on his own. Then, too, Nate Saint, whose older sister Rachel Saint had been with SIL since 1949, told Betty he didn't understand how his sister could justify working for the organization. He had concerns about lack of cooperation between SIL and other missions organizations and shared the frustration of many evangelical missionaries over SIL's willingness to work with Catholic priests.

———

Back in Shandia, Betty and Jim slept in Pete's little two-room shack, since he was in the US for his wedding, and had their meals with the McCullys. The aluminum-roofed buildings, set well back from the river, were sweltering, especially after the thatch-roofed stilt house near the water at Puyupungu. A few days after they arrived, Betty woke in the night to find the kitchen on fire, just a few feet from the storage shed filled with their belongings. While she ran to wake the McCullys and find water, Jim pulled the roof apart with his hands, putting out the fire. All the buildings were saved.

In the second week of July, Betty wrote to her family announcing that the McCullys were leaving on vacation, and she and Jim would be living in the big house while they were gone. She added mischievously, "Marilou is expecting next January, Cathers in the fall, Marge [*sic*] Saint in December, etc., etc. ad inf.—to say nothing of my sister & in-laws! Ho hum!"[24] Katharine apparently interpreted this to mean that Betty was worried because she was not pregnant yet, and wrote to reassure her daughter. But Betty must have been beginning to suspect that she herself was pregnant as well. She and Jim had used contraception for the first few months of their marriage, and then in February had begun to track her menstrual cycle and try for a baby. She must have been about two weeks late for starting a new cycle, and since they had been trying to conceive, she was almost certainly aware that it was late. There was no such thing as a home-pregnancy test, but on July 23, not even two weeks after writing the letter to her family, Betty recorded in her journal: "Praise, praise to Him from whom comes every good and perfect gift. I am quite certain that I am pregnant. Jim and I are so happy about it."[25]

Happily, Betty was experiencing none of the typical side-effects of early pregnancy. Shandia was a much busier station than Puyupungu, and taking over management must have been challenging enough as it was. For missionary women in the jungles, meals were one of the most difficult aspects of daily life. They were almost wholly dependent on MAF flights for their food supply, and the steady flow of visitors—who tended to announce they were coming rather than ask—complicated things further. "We were informed this a.m. by radio that two ladies from Ocean City (no idea who they are) are coming here today to visit 'the jungle'—don't know how long they'll stay, but that's the way it goes here!" she wrote to her mother in late July. "Your remark about dashing up town to buy some food for supper makes me a bit envious today—here I am with two guests coming and practically nothing on hand but a few carrots and beets, one small piece of meat, and some lettuce."[26]

Servants were an expected part of missionary households on many mission fields, allowing the wife in a missionary couple to spend her time on more than household tasks and contributing some wealth to the local economy. A bright spot for Betty at this time was Carmela Shiwango, one of the women baptized in January, who was working for the missionaries. "What a joy she is!" Betty wrote.

> She is very eager to learn, and each time I correct her, she thanks me and says, "Teach me" ("Make me know" literally). She can now iron very nicely, make delicious bread, and wash dishes the way I want them washed! Today she said to me, "I have a great desire to know God's word. Please teach me, every little moment you have." What an encouragement! Do pray for her.[27]

And although mixing and pouring concrete by hand was backbreaking work, the new house continued to show progress. When it rained, the men picked up projects they could do under cover. Fred Elliot built a dresser for Betty, and she was delighted to have drawers again. Jim was making a coffee table out of a huge stump that had been dug out of the runway.

In August, Betty and Carmela planted seeds—carrots, lettuce, tangerines, and tomatoes—at the building site to complement the existing pineapple patch and the banana plants that lined the path to the runway. They planned to add avocados and papayas as well, and Jim had begun laying a rock path from the house to the nearest stream. He was deeply discouraged during this time because young men who had made professions of faith kept leaving to find work in more populated areas. He wrote in his journal, "But, Lord, is this why we have trained them, that they should leave the forest for white man's culture? Was it not that they should go reaching their own people with the Word? Wherein have we missed in setting before them the wrong ideal that they should regard money as of more worth to seek after than souls? Lead us out of it, Lord, and back to a simple principle of operation. School is a chore; house building, a heaviness now as I see little of what I aimed at accomplished."[28]

In late August, Betty spent a week in Puyupungu packing and working on Kichwa morphology with Orr. At about the same time, Ed traveled to Arajuno, another former Shell Oil outpost northeast of Shandia, to begin the process of building a station there. He cleared the overgrown runway in an afternoon and built a two-room house, a process made much easier because he could cannibalize Shell buildings for lumber rather than having to hand-cut boards or wait for supplies to be flown in. Although the Elliots had hoped the McCullys would treat Arajuno as an outstation and keep Shandia their home base, Marilou and Ed decided to make it their home indefinitely. Not only would such a move give them access to a Kichwa community that as yet had no school or church; it would position them to approach an even more untouched group.

Arajuno was inside the boundaries of land belonging to the mysterious "aucas" that both Betty and Jim had been intrigued by while still in the US. The group had an almost fantastic reputation as ferocious killers. As far back as anyone knew, they had rigorously defended their borders with nine-foot-long spears made from the hardwood chonta palm. Their first documented conflicts with incomers appear to have occurred in the 1800s, when they guarded their place and their people against rubber hunters who stole from them, trafficked them, and murdered them outright. There were clashes scattered through the first half of the twentieth century, particularly with plantation owners who took over tribal land and tried to draw the people into their own economic system. "Aucas" had killed Shell Oil employees at Arajuno in 1942 and 1943, and some felt that these deaths had been a key factor in the company's withdrawal from Ecuador. Most recently, in the summer of 1954 "aucas" had attacked Kichwa living at Villano, a former Ecuadorian Army post just outside the borders of their land to the south of Arajuno, perhaps in revenge for a Kichwa raid two generations old. The missionaries were well aware of this: Nate and Marj Saint had helped care for two survivors of that attack. When the McCullys began living in Arajuno, Betty wrote to her mother that Nate "insists we send Ushpalito down to act as watch-dog" for the McCullys, "since the Aucas have been known to appear in Arajuno and bump off Indians now and then."[29] Nate also rigged an electric fence with a burglar alarm, creating a perimeter around the McCullys' house out of spear range.[30]

———

Creature from the Black Lagoon had hit US theaters in February while Betty and Jim were reading *A Tale of Two Cities* in Puyupungu. The Mc-Carthy hearings had begun in June as the couple were moving to Shandia. It was the golden age of television, and while Betty was trying to figure out how to feed a planeload of guests with "a few carrots and beets, one small piece of meat, and some lettuce," Swanson had begun marketing a new product called "TV dinners."[31] In September, the first episode of *Lassie* aired, and in Shandia Jim and his father wore the skin off their fingertips building a rock fireplace in the new house. Betty drafted lesson plans for the women's class she planned to start soon and felt the baby move for the first time. She and Jim were praying for a boy: "an older brother, the firstborn, the heir," as she would later write.[32] Dr. Paul Roberts came down from the HCJB clinic to run a free medical clinic in Shandia for a day, and "Jim or I acted as assistant and interpreter all day, and got into some interesting cases. . . . Everything from terrible worm-cases to sore fingers, tropical ulcers, schizophrenia, abortion, malaria, and a micro-cystalic baby."[33] Betty wrote to her family about these cases, noting that sometimes they created situations where she and Jim could try to talk about God—situations that seemed few and far between outside the formal classes they were teaching.

In October the couple marked their first wedding anniversary. Jim spent the day teaching school, and Nate and Marj flew in to have lunch with him and his dad. Betty was in Quito, trying to hire a new teacher and doing the shopping for the jungle mission stations. "I've been tearing around like mad since I got to Quito, buying plumbing supplies, (groan! I don't know any of the stuff even in English, let alone Spanish!) food for McCullys & Elliots et al. for six months, (cases of everything) draperies, and, above all, searching for an American made wood stove."[34] Emma Guikema had been in charge of purchasing supplies for the jungle missionaries but had gone home in August to see her elderly father, who was not expected to live much longer. While there she had been hospitalized for "nervous collapse" and other health problems, and her doctors had recommended that she not return to the field. This left the families on the rural stations with not only the time-consuming shopping expeditions but a bit of an albatross in the guest house. With the air of one throwing up her hands, Betty wrote, "What we will do with the Quito house, contracted for 2-1/2 more years, we just don't know. That makes the 25th missionary to leave the field permanently since I came to Ecuador! Imagine! One trembles to think who might be next."[35]

While in Quito, Betty went to visit Doreen Clifford Villarreal, who had married Abdón Villarreal and whose first child had been born in mid-September. Betty had known for some time that the child had been conceived before the couple were married, because Doreen, following the instruction from the book of James to "confess your sins to one another and pray for one another" (James 5:16), had told the Tidmarshes, and Wilfred had consulted the other Brethren men, "asking what discipline should be exercised on the part of the church."[36] Privately, Betty laid the blame for the situation on Doreen, writing to her mother, "She was very unwise in her handling of Abdón. I often noticed it and told her so. So did Marie Short. She has no one to blame but herself. She has a bodega here in Quito with Abdón, which they got long before they were married, if you can imagine such a thing." There is not enough information to show why Betty saw this differently from the afternoons and evenings she and Jim spent alone in the bodega in Quito before their own marriage. Nevertheless, she believed that a Christian who had confessed and repented of sin should be treated by the church "like any other blood-washed sinner."[37] Before her trip to Quito, she had written to Doreen, "telling her that I wanted her to know I knew about it. . . . I told her I had heard she confessed it to T's and I believed she was restored to the Lord's fellowship, so I did not want to have any difference in our fellowship."[38] Betty was deeply upset to find that the Tidmarshes were not allowing Doreen to participate in the Communion service during church gatherings.

Betty found a new schoolteacher in Angelita Arias, the daughter of her former landlord. She rearranged the things in storage, had some maternity clothes made, and read Bess Streeter Aldrich's historical novel *A Lantern in Her Hand*. She wrote a chatty letter to the Howards, responding to various family notes, reporting that she had finished her shopping, noting that two more missionaries were leaving the country because of illness, and in the last sentence casually announcing: "I am pregnant—till around February 28. Please send me one or 2 maternity dress patterns—skirts & tops, Mother, if you could—size 14. Much love to each, Betty."[39]

———

By the last week of October, the McCullys were living in Shandia during the week and spending weekends in Arajuno so Ed could hold Christian meetings there. Fred Elliot had gone on to Peru to visit Jim's older brother Bert and his wife, Colleen, and Betty and Jim moved into their new house, a huge relief for Betty. During their engagement she had written to Jim,

"I am looking forward to being in Shandia, but, oh, darling, how I hope it will be the last place either of us has to live 'in someone else's house.' I am so tired of knocking around, living on other people's stuff."[40] After years of dormitory living and staying in a spare corner of someone else's space, it was wonderful to have a place of her own which she could order as she wished. She and Jim continued to eat the main meal of the day with the McCullys, since the stovepipe they ordered had not yet arrived. "But Mother and Ginny, I wish you could see my kitchen! What a dream!" Betty wrote:

> All built in cupboards with green vinyl-topped counters, a stainless steel sink, my new white stove, a special lower and wider counter for kneading bread, a very clever vegetable storage space, with screen bottomed drawers, and plenty of shelf space. . . . On the other [side] will be cupboards for storage of china, with doors opening on both dining room and kitchen side, and when we set the table, they are taken out from the other side. There will also be a built-in ironing board which swings down on hinges, a file for pot lids, and a cupboard with shelves built especially for each size can which I always have on hand (namely, powdered milk, catsup, tomato paste, sardines, gallon-size cooking oil cans, and oatmeal.)

They even had a kerosene-powered refrigerator, cut in half, flown in by MAF in two trips, and reassembled. "Our bedroom is lovely, with the dark rose chenille spread the Philadelphia sisters gave me, a rose and white goat's hair rug which Ginny and I had in our room, and drapes which Jim brought to the field—gray background, large tropical leaf pattern in dubonnet, rose, and chartreuse."[41] The tree root coffee table was finished, and they decorated the living room with a gray couch and red and white curtains and throw pillows, using wooden candlesticks and bookends, a bright-green Kichwa feather crown, and a colorful Tsáchila skirt as accent pieces. Betty finally had a place for the organ that Jim had bought as a gift to her just before she left the States.

Despite the example of missionaries like Amy Carmichael and Hudson Taylor, who had lived as much as possible like the people they wanted to convert, Betty and Jim intentionally chose to build very differently from the Shandians. They had received criticism, she explained to her family, but felt they had good reasons for their decision. Hygiene and disease prevention were a major consideration. They felt the concrete floor would be easier to clean thoroughly and the aluminum roof would cut down on insect problems and provide a way to collect clean water. Another factor was durability and cost-effectiveness. Split-palm houses with thatched roofs typically had to be torn down and replaced every few years, as nothing lasted well in the damp climate; a more permanent dwelling would save time and money in the long run. And she was beginning to think that total identification was neither possible nor, from an indigenous perspective, desirable. "Whenever we use an Indian implement, put on Indian dress, or do a thing in an especially characteristically Indian way, it brings forth much laughter and comment. In my experience, limited to be sure, it seems to be laughter of ridicule, rather than of appreciation. The Indian has his own culture, he expects the Ecuadorian white man to have his, and certainly the gringo to have his."[42]

Betty also wrote two letters to her mother in early November, answering questions about her pregnancy and sharing her growing excitement. She had realized that Katharine had been hurt by her decision to wait more than five months to share the news, and she was sorry. She tried to share as many details as possible to make up for both the geographical distance and her earlier silence: she hadn't seen a doctor yet, but she was reading pregnancy books and felt things were progressing normally. To avoid spending six weeks in Quito around her due date, they would go to Shell Mera—where a hospital was reported to be under construction and the Saint home was available as a backup—for the birth. She planned to breastfeed—"A formula would be so expensive and complicated here in the jungle, for one thing. But above all, I believe a mother has an almost moral obligation to let her baby have what was meant for it!"—and to keep baby equipment to a minimum—"We have agreed the baby is not going to run the house. . . . Don't we sound just like expectant parents who haven't had any children yet??!!"[43]

Still saddened that she had hurt her mother, Betty wrote again two days later, trying to explain why she had waited so long to share the news, and assuring her mother that she was the first person to know. "I can't tell you how badly I feel, Mother dear, for not having told you sooner about the baby. I realize now that I should have. Somehow it didn't seem very real till I was sure, and then too I thought the nine months would seem shorter if

I didn't mention it sooner. But I know how you long to enter into all the joys of your children, and that is one thing you should have been allowed to enter into sooner." It had all seemed surreal at first, but she was starting to get excited, and increasingly wished she was nearer to her mother.

> I long to be able to talk to you about it all. I've been reading some of the Spock book, and he says new mothers sometimes go through times of feeling blue, so I guess that's what I've had occasionally lately. I have felt just a plain honest homesickness, and loneliness for you. In fact, the day your letters and all the packages came it came over me, and I had a "weepy" spell. Haven't done that for ages. But I am very happy, and Jim is too. Says he thinks about our baby all the time, and can hardly believe he's going to be a father. Oh Mother, thank you <u>so</u> much for the packages. . . . Just having the little blankets to look at makes the prospects seem more real, and I try to visualize <u>my</u> (!) baby in them.[44]

———

November was abnormally hot. Pete and Olive Fleming, who had arrived in Ecuador at the beginning of the month, had planned to live at the Quito house while Olive studied Spanish. Since Emma Guikema would, they thought, be running the household, Olive would be able to concentrate on language study, and Pete, who knew that Jim was discouraged by having to spend all his time building, would be available for regular trips to Shandia to help him. But with Emma's departure, the Flemings found themselves responsible for running the house, hosting guests, and supplying the Brethren jungle stations, which made language study extremely difficult. To make matters worse, Olive seemed to be struggling to adjust to the altitude and was often ill. The Flemings planned to visit the jungle missionaries shortly after they arrived, but poor health repeatedly delayed their trip.

Then Señor Arias suddenly asked Angelita to give up the teaching job. Betty ascribed this first to his Catholic mother's interference and then to downright dishonesty—a desire to get a jungle trip for his daughter at low cost—but whatever the reason they were unable to talk him out of it, and Angelita left in the second week of November. Pete had to add finding a teacher to his to-do list. Betty had also lost Carmela's companionship and help when she and Jim moved into the new house, as Carmela had originally been hired by the McCullys and continued to work at their house. In her place the Elliots hired Eugenia and Camilo, a pair of children who had asked to come and work for them. "They are both baptized believers, he is in the school, and she is in my school. Just one oddity—she is about 17, he about 11 or 12! They have been married at least <u>three years</u>! His sister is about 9, and has been married for two years to [Eugenia's] brother, a boy of about 18. It is really sad. . . . Pray that we may be a help to them spiritually."[45]

This was a difficult situation for Betty and Jim. They wanted to see change in the cultural practice of child marriage, which they believed to be harmful. But they did not want to impose it from without, but rather to introduce the Shandians to Jesus so that the Holy Spirit could make any needed changes in the culture. This may have made them reluctant to interfere—and even if they had wanted to, it is difficult to know what they could have done in the face of community-wide acceptance and reliance on the custom. In 1956 Betty would write to her family: "There must be some basic changes in the way of life here. Child marriage is one of them."[46]

Twenty years later, Elisabeth Elliot would write about these two couples in her book *Let Me Be a Woman*. In a chapter called "What Makes a Marriage Work," she explains that the mother of the two younger children had died, and "the father had decided that the easiest way to see that they were properly taken care of was to give them to their respective promised spouses." She also confirms that the couples were sexually active, writing, "I asked one of the Indian women if these couples actually slept together. She whooped with laughter and said (her colloquialism loses a lot in translation), 'No wife sleeps closer to her husband than Carmela!' [the 9-year-old]." The passage is written in such a way that Elliot seems to invite the reader to share in the older indigenous woman's amusement. Elliot did not have access, either in 1954 or in 1975 when she was writing the book, to much of the research now available on the lifelong health risks to children, particularly girls, who are married before fifteen, which are even higher if they are married before twelve. But she had understood instinctively at the time that it wasn't good, compassionately observing that the situation was "really sad." In the book, Elliot's only comment is that "both marriages seemed completely successful."[47]

In late November, Shandia marked another feast day. Betty and Jim were invited and warmly welcomed when they arrived. But things quickly turned sour as the revelers became increasingly drunk. "I can't describe all the mess and sickening scenes. Mothers so drunk they could hardly stagger across the floor, trying to balance themselves with their babies hanging in a cloth around their shoulders." There were various fights, and Jim intervened in one instance where a man was beating his pregnant wife. At one point Jim was asked to break up a brawl: "It took an hour or more to get them all apart. . . . Dogs barking, children screaming, women shrieking and tugging on the arms and legs of the fighters, men cursing and roaring at each other, and so on. It made me feel as though Satan himself were in the midst, as indeed he must have been."[48]

As a result of this miserable day, the Elliots decided to try to create a gathering for Christians as an alternative to these feasts where drunkenness was so prevalent. They hosted the first event the next week, inviting the believers to their house and giving everyone who came a notebook in which they could create their own copies of "the Quichua choruses we've written, and when that's done, some scriptures. About ten came, including most of my school girls." Betty ended the letter that described these events with a quotation from Amy Carmichael's book, *Gold by Moonlight*, which gave her "great comfort": "The enemy will contest our confidence at every point; he will remind us of the human cause of our trouble. But faith looks above the human. . . . The only thing that matters when trouble is appointed is our attitude towards that trouble."[49]

In mid-December, Pete and Olive finally made it down to Shandia. For the next five days, the three American couples divided their time between the McCullys' house and the Elliots'. Betty wrote: "How thankful we were for the fireplace during the past two days! It was so nice for us all to be able to sit around the fire, while the jungle rain poured down steadily. And we were <u>very</u> thankful for a big house! . . . You know how you get on one another's nerves on a rainy day if you're cooped up in too small a space. As it was, everyone was comfortable."[50]

Not everything was as smooth. Betty and Olive had been corresponding since Betty's departure for Ecuador but had never met in person. Olive came to Shandia expecting to find in Betty the warm personality that had come through in letters. Instead, the older woman seemed cool and aloof with a tendency to say things that hurt Olive's feelings. To make matters worse, Olive was feeling poorly when she arrived. She went to bed early on her first night in Shandia with warning signs of what she later realized was a miscarriage. She later said, "My first impression of her was not a good impression. . . . Betty always seemed to say things that—I'm sure she never realized how she sounded."[51] Betty didn't seem to feel comfortable around Olive either, and while she told her family afterward that Olive was "very nice," "sweet, and quite attractive," she also noted that she "seems quite young, and it was strange to be around someone like that for a change."[52] The two women had not gotten off on a good foot.

Because letters and packages traveled so slowly, Katharine had already planned out Christmas gifts for her children who were overseas and wrote to let Betty know what to look for in the mail. Betty responded, "I think it's wonderful of you to send us books for Christmas—I assure you there's nothing either Jim or I could appreciate more. So don't be apologetic, saying you're 'just sending books.' We need them."[53] Both Betty and Jim felt a strong desire for things to enjoy during leisure time. Jim wrote in his journal, "Everything is so half-done and left-to-be done that it makes me feel the need of a really nice piece of work, something fine."[54] Betty had asked for records so they could listen to music, and Tom, now at Wheaton, had picked out several—among them Vladimir Horowitz's performance of Mendelssohn's "Wedding March"—for their parents to send her.

Despite the eight-and-a-half years between them, Betty and Tom were very close. Jim wrote that there was "something strong between them, something so like about them that they are closer than any of the other members of the family."[55] Even when Betty was at Wheaton herself and Tom was a preteen and young teenager, they had discussed books and ideas with what Tom later called "an undefined, unmistakable affinity."[56] For some time now, they had been exchanging letters: what Jim characterized as "Latin phrases, or hymn quotes, or tidbits from some author I've never read," what Tom would call, "keeping abreast of each other."[57] The younger brother often suggested books to his sister.

In Betty's response to her mother's letter about Christmas presents, she went on to ask her parents to send her books by specific authors who it seems likely had been suggested to her by Tom. Her current read-aloud was Paul Blanshard's *Communism, Democracy, and Catholic Power*, which compared the Kremlin and the Vatican at several points and rejected both as authoritarian regimes threatening American democracy. But she asked for a long list of Catholic writers from the 1200s through the 1700s. "Dad, do you know where you could get me any of the works of Tersteegen or Tauler? Three friends of God? Or Madame Guyon? Or Raymond Lull? [*sic*] Would Leary's have them, or that place in England? I'd surely like to have anything you could dig up sometime along that line—the medieval mystics, etc."[58] Gerhard Tersteegen was the only Protestant in the bunch, and in addition to his own writing, he was known for his translation of the works of several Catholic mystics. In a few more years, Tom would go on to join the Anglican Church, and his journey to a more high-church view must have been well underway by this point. He would later say that his sister as well had been "greatly influenced" by these writers.[59]

When the Flemings left Shandia on December 17, the McCullys went too. Marilou's due date was drawing near, and she planned to have the baby in Quito. The Elliots closed both schools for a two-week Christmas vacation, and the new schoolteacher went home for the break. They had invited several different people to celebrate Christmas with them, but no one was able to come, and things were quiet around the station. Betty was thinking of home and family. Phil was in Canada's Northwest Territories, working on the language of the Dene people. Dave was running LAM's seminary in Costa Rica. Ginny was working as a missionary in the Philippines. But Tom and Jim would be at Birdsong, home from Wheaton and Hampden DuBose Academy. In a family letter dated three days before Christmas, Betty wrote a bit wistfully:

> It's hard to imagine that in the States everyone is in the midst of the Christmas festivity, and that 3 West Maple is probably blossoming with greens and holly. Things are exactly as usual here in the jungle, except perhaps a bit quieter.... Pete and Olive kindly sent in a bag full of brightly wrapped gifts for Jim and me, which we're saving to open Christmas eve. That will be the extent of our celebration, I guess, except that I plan to open a can of chicken for dinner on the 25th. It will be wash day as usual on Saturday, and we will have our regular Sat. afternoon children's

meeting. But I'll surely be thinking of you all at home, and of the others in their respective places.[60]

———

Just after Christmas, Betty received a letter containing "BIG NEWS": her parents were coming to visit.[61] Philip had been feeling ill for some time, and the *Sunday School Times* board had offered to pay for him to travel, hoping it would help. The Howards had decided to take their vacation in Central and South America, to visit Dave and Phyllis and their two young sons in Costa Rica, see good friends in Panama, and time their arrival in Ecuador so that they could spend about nine days visiting their elder daughter and see the new baby.

Amongst all the busyness of daily life, Betty was working on more literacy materials, including a second volume of a Kichwa primer. She was reading "a little book of sermons (more like essays, really) by C. S. Lewis—TRANSPOSITION. Very incisive. Tom if you can find it in the library at Wheaton, read the one on 'Learning In War Time.' Also, if you have time, 'The Weight of Glory.' I found them most helpful and stimu-lating. He has a delightful way of illustrating his points, and some quite humorous touches as well."[62]

Jim continued to struggle with discouragement. "Cast down on this Lord's day morning," he wrote in mid-January. Attendance at their Christian meetings was increasing, but it did not feel like success to him since it was "mostly schoolboys and young women." He worried that his preaching was ineffective, that he was spending too much time building and not enough time in Bible study. The thing he had feared seemed to have happened: "Marriage has been a hindrance," he wrote. "Betty doesn't like me to get out of bed amorning without some little loving," and he seems to have believed she was prioritizing their homelife over the work of the gospel. "House and furnishings *must* take second place now. Getting the Indians out to meet-ings and individual witness to them has got to be my foremost concern."[63]

But he could not get away from the things that felt like distractions and hindrances. His parents and sister arrived in the second week of February. Betty wrote that Jim's mother was "sewing and mending everything she can get her hands on. (Not that I had let things go—but there were a few socks, etc.)"[64] Clara Elliot made diapers for the baby, curtains for various

rooms in the house, and clothes for Betty. On February 24 the whole family moved to Shell Mera to wait for the birth. Jim promptly got roped into
helping two missionary doctors with the hospital they were trying to build.

Other than suffering from the heat, "even at night, when Jim would be
snuggling under a wool blanket!" the last trimester of pregnancy had been
fairly uneventful for Betty.[65] On the twenty-fifth she wrote, "I've had quite
a few strong contractions, but no pain, so I'm not very hopeful of an early
delivery."[66] The next morning she went into labor. Philip and Katharine were
in Costa Rica when they got Jim's cablegram: Valerie Elliot was born in the
early morning hours of February 27, weighing seven pounds, ten ounces,
and measuring twenty-and-one-half inches long.

A week later Betty wrote in her journal, "Jim was with me every minute,
which meant more to me than he will ever know."[67] Years afterward she
told her daughter, "I could see his face when the doctor said, 'It's a girl.' He
smiled at me and said at once, 'Her name is Valerie.' . . . He was perfectly
contented, I could see, to be the father of a daughter instead of a son. So
I was content. It was God who had given you to us, God to whom our
prayers for a son had been made, and God who knew reasons we did not
then know that made His choice far better."[68]

Jim's parents and sister had to go home early because Fred Elliot was not
feeling well, but they were able to meet Valerie before they went. Philip
Howard was continuing to feel poorly as well. He had spent part of his
time in Costa Rica and in Panama in the hospital, although no one was
able to determine the cause of his illness. But he and Katharine made it to
Ecuador, and Jim and Betty and little Val were there to meet them at the
airport in Quito. Wilfred drove them down to Shell Mera in his station
wagon, and Nate flew them to Shandia. After their visit ended, Betty wrote
to her parents:

> It seems impossible to be writing you at 3 West Maple, when it was only
> a few days ago that dear mother was sitting right at this very desk! Your
> visit was so brief I find it hard to believe you were really here. But how
> wonderful it was to see you again. . . . I feel as though you're closer, now,
> in a sense, in that you can better share in the work by your first-hand
> knowledge. And I'm sure we don't seem so far away now, as places seem
> nearer and less romantic when you have been there.[69]

In April Jim made the trip to Quito for some dental work. He was home for a day before he and Betty left for Dos Rios, where he was teaching in a Christian conference. They made the journey on foot, with Eugenia carrying six-week-old Valerie because Betty felt the Kichwa woman was less likely to fall with the baby. Traveling together made "for an excellent opportunity to learn the language." Betty and Jim had repeatedly been disturbed by how poor a command of Ecuadorian languages many long-term missionaries had acquired, and they were working for mastery. Betty lamented after the conference that one speaker, who had been on the field for two-and-a-half terms, "gave a whole sermon on the Holy Spirit, in which one of his main points was based on the use of personal pronouns, which was supposed to prove that the Holy Spirit is a person. In Quichua the personal pronoun is the only one there is—that is, there is no word for 'it', so of course it was completely untranslatable." Wilfred and Jim were more intelligible, and several people made professions of faith. Although there had been Western missionaries in Dos Rios for a quarter of a century, Betty wrote, "it is only in the past year that they have seen really significant results." So they were encouraged. Not even coming home from the conference to find a mass of termites eating huge holes in the desk in their bedroom could completely damp their spirits.[70]

During this time, Betty received news over the radio that her father had been diagnosed with a brain tumor and rushed into surgery.

> Well, I was floored, as I'm sure you all were. . . . The Lord did not leave me to myself, however. As soon as I got home I opened my Daily Light to the words, "The Lord was my stay." And, "The eternal God is Thy refuge and underneath are the everlasting arms." The Lord gave me peace which really did pass understanding, and I asked especially for the same for Mother, as I'm sure it was hardest for her.[71]

She later wrote to her mother, "Poor Dad! It made me, too, feel weepy to hear how badly he felt before the operation. I'm sure we should all be far more tolerant and loving toward our fellow men, (let alone toward our intimates), if we only knew and understood half of the cause of their troubles and seeming peculiarities."[72] With her mother involved in caring for her father, home news was hard to come by for some time.

At the end of April Betty came down with her first bout of malaria, and for twenty-four hours was miserable with fever and chills and exhaustion. She recovered quickly, which she attributed to Camoquin, the latest malaria drug. There were signs of progress in their missionary work. "About ten young Indians have recently expressed a desire to be baptized. It seems to be a real work of the Holy Spirit, and we stand humbled and amazed. There were 21 out to the believer's [sic] meeting on Monday even though Jim was not here, and yesterday 17 came to prayer meeting. Pray for them."[73] Betty was beginning to feel that people were really understanding what they were trying to teach. Not only were the men responding to Jim's teaching, but the women attending her school were making progress as well. "I'm sure it must be the answer to many prayers."[74]

In mid-May, attendance at the "believers' prayer meeting" that they held each week was so high that they split into two groups so that everyone would have a chance to pray. "Jim had the men down at the school house, and I had the women here. Twenty came! Imagine. Only a few months ago we were doing well to have six to ten all told, men and women! We do thank God for this. Pray that they will come to a true understanding of the Way."[75] Betty continued her language work, including developing literacy materials in Kichwa, which she could not create fast enough to meet the demand. "The kids are thrilled to death with anything we turn out, and eagerly read it. How will we keep up with them? Pray for us in this, will you?"[76]

The days continued to be full of a wide range of events and activities. Betty was still breastfeeding. She treated a woman recovering from a late miscarriage. Eugenia was bitten by a snake, but thanks to quick action from Jim and Betty she made a full recovery. Jim kept on working on their house little by little—installing plumbing, tiling a shower stall, building bathroom cupboards, landscaping—and started work on a new house for the schoolteacher. Valerie had her first cold. Betty read Christiana Tsai's 1953 autobiography, *Queen of the Dark Chamber*, and Raymond Murray Patterson's *The Dangerous River*, which described the part of Canada's Northwest Territories where Phil and his family were now living.

June found her dealing with yet another time-consuming difficulty. "I guess before I'm through with this missionary business I'll have run the gamut of horrid ailments," she wrote to her family, "my latest—head lice!"[77] There was a smallpox outbreak in Puyupungu, and when Jim went down for the end-of-year ceremonies at the school, Betty stayed home because Valerie was not vaccinated. The Salk vaccine disaster, in which forty thousand children got polio from faulty inoculations, had made headlines just two months before, and Betty had read about it in *Time*. The Elliots were waiting to vaccinate their four-month-old baby until they were sure of a safe batch of vaccines. Knowing this would worry her mother, Betty wrote, "Guess we'll just have to trust the Lord until some good vaccine is available. 'Pretty risky business, ain't it?' someone has said! (Trusting the Lord, that is!)"[78]

The steady stream of visitors to Shandia continued—a two-week visit from Bert and Colleen Elliot, who were Brethren missionaries in Peru, and various missionaries from within Ecuador. In the middle of the month, while Jim was away at Puyupungu for the end of the school year and a series of Christian meetings, Betty had a visit from Rachel Saint and her coworker, Catherine Peeke. With them came two Ecuadorian men, sons of Carlos Sevilla who owned the Hacienda Ila where the SIL workers were living. Although Betty enjoyed her time with the two missionary women, hitting it off especially well with Rachel Saint, whom she called a "grand girl," she struggled with her natural reaction to the other guests. After they left she wrote to her mother, "Well, I know your feeling about 'dirty old colored men,' but between you and me, I think I would rather entertain a dozen good old American colored men than two Ecuadorians! They were the typical greasy, slick, sweaty, Latin type, the kind that just take over wherever they go." She disciplined herself to provide hospitality though, "I confess I did it without much grace, and I am sure there will be no reward in heaven for me because of it. They smelled up the whole house with their cheap Ecuadorian cigarettes and hair tonic, muddied up the bathroom, and lounged with their greasy hair on the back of my pretty light gray sofa!" Writing to her mother after the men had gone, Betty described her frustration over the situation and over her own inconsistency. "Oh my, why do things like that bother me so? I wish I could just take them in my stride, as some do."[79]

This awareness of her difficulty in obeying the biblical injunction to hospitality and love for those outside her own circle affected her thinking about her work in Shandia as well. In the same letter she wrote:

> How I long to teach my school girls some of the principals [*sic*] so vital to
> the Christian walk, and yet there are just no <u>words</u> in which to express even

the simplest of them. How to get them across? And the answer came—
there is only one way. It is not in telling, but in showing. And perhaps
that is why God sent me to this kind of a language. You know what a one
I am for talking or writing differently than I behave, and the question of
the Hindu, put to one of the Dohnavur fellowship, is pertinent, "Can you
show us the life of your Lord Jesus?" I have a long way to go before I will
be able to express these things to the Indians, but you will pray, won't you,
that I shall be enabled?[80]

Jim's time continued to be filled with manual labor and social events. July
included a trip to visit the McCullys with Bert and Colleen, the six-month
shopping trip in Quito, an inter-mission Kichwa-language symposium, and
a Brethren missions conference. In the middle of the month Jim examined
and baptized fourteen new baptismal candidates with help from one of
the Kichwa believers. He felt he was seeing "evidence of real discernment"
among many of the new Christians, but despite that he sounded discouraged. There were no other missionary men to help him with the examination, and he felt "lonely," and concerned about whether he was making the
right call in allowing them to be baptized. "My flesh often lacks the deep
feeling that I should experience at such times," he wrote in his journal, "and
there was a certain dryness to the form this morning, but I cannot stay for
feeling. . . . I am most always operating on the basis of pure commandments, forcing myself to do what I do not always feel simply because I am
a servant under orders."[81]

Valerie was a delight, and Betty would sometimes sit and just watch
her little girl. Her letters during this time were regularly punctuated by
news about Val, particularly letters to Katharine, who delighted in updates
about her granddaughter. "She has discovered her hands and feet now,
and lies watching them for long periods. She has the loveliest little hands,
already expressive, and so dainty and feminine." Betty had typical worries about whether all was well—whether Valerie was growing properly,
whether she should be sleeping longer stretches at night—and wrote
back and forth with her mother asking for and discussing suggestions.
Betty told her mother, "I love you so much, and the more I learn to love
Valerie, and realize what raising a child means, the more I appreciate
what you've done for me."[82]

While in Quito, Betty took Val to see one of the HCJB doctors and was much relieved when he declared her to be "a model of health, happiness and vigor." She wrote to her mother, "[He says] she is getting plenty to eat, and it is foolish to expect a baby of five months to give up her night feeding if she doesn't want to. His daughter had one for a year. I talked to three different mothers in Shell Mera who said their babies had night feedings at least for seven months and several for a year. So, mother, just calm your nerves! Valerie is fine."[83] Katharine continued to be concerned about Valerie's health—and Jim's and Betty's—and encouraged her daughter to consider taking a furlough to get a real vacation. But Betty gently reminded her mother that God was able to keep them. "Amy Carmichael had no such change. I don't claim to be anything like her, and I suppose probably we will take a furlough sometime, but we have the same Lord who gave her grace to continue and kept her on an even keel. . . . Wish I could have a good long talk with you. I love you, and appreciate your concern for us and all your advice, but I don't want you to worry."[84]

———

In August, another SIL worker arrived in Shandia to spend ten days making a Kichwa dictionary. Betty's letters do not name the worker, but her assessment of the woman's linguistic approach was scathing. At first she was annoyed that the woman thought she could complete a dictionary in a few days, when the Brethren team had been working on a dictionary for almost three years and still felt it was not complete enough to publish. Then she was horrified by the woman's lack of facility with the language, noting that she frequently made important mistakes in speaking and often appeared not to understand her informant's answers. But the final straw seems to have come when the other woman asked Betty to edit her dictionary, correcting any errors and adding missing words. This would have been an immensely time-consuming job if done properly, and Betty declined, telling her bluntly that it was not possible to do an adequate job in such a short time, and that if SIL was going to publish the dictionary under their imprimatur, their workers ought to be the ones doing the work. "I don't in the least object to their doing [translation], too," she wrote, "provided they do it right, they share their material, and they <u>don't</u> make it look as though no one else had ever touched the Quichua tribe—Tidmarsh worked here for twelve years before we got here, and we were here two years before they ever got here."[85]

It appears that this woman also visited Puyupungu to ask Pete for the same kind of help. Olive would later describe how difficult she found it as a new Kichwa learner to have more experienced missionaries arguing over the best approach to the language, noting that "Betty's strong opinions about the subject" made it particularly challenging for her. Although she does not address the specifics of the disagreement between Betty and the SIL worker (whom she identifies only as Betsy), she does note that "at about this time, Pete remarked to me how he was impressed that Betty's gifts tended more toward intellectual pursuits than to personal ministry," and that he was beginning to pray for a "writing ministry" for Betty.[86] This sheds an interesting sidelight on the situation, suggesting that perhaps Pete felt Betty was in the right over the linguistic aspect of the disagreement but that she could also have handled the situation more tactfully.

By the end of August, the garden at Shandia was beginning to produce fruit. The coffee trees, citrus trees, and corn were growing well, gladiolus were blooming, and they had pineapples, tomatoes, papayas, and bananas almost ready for eating. Valerie was now six months old and fourteen pounds and drinking out of a cup. Betty was starting to wean her, hoping to have breathing space before they tried to conceive again. "Jim is very anxious for another baby just as soon as possible. Did you ever hear of a man who wanted them one after another?? . . . I feel especially that it would be nice for Valerie to have a little playmate just as soon as possible, here in the jungle, since there would be no other English speaking playmate about. I don't want her to have time to get an 'only child' complex. I trust the Lord has other children for us. We're getting old, you know. I shall soon be 29."[87]

At the beginning of September, Pete and Olive arrived in Shandia for a weekend visit, and then they and Jim went on to Dos Rios, where Jim and Pete would teach at a three-week Bible school. Valerie got her first tooth. Betty was working on Kichwa morphology and hoping to accomplish more Bible translation and create additional literacy materials for the women's school, which would resume in October. In her free time she was rereading a biography of missionary J. O. Fraser. When Katharine wrote offering to send some Beatrix Potter stories, she replied, "Yes, we would be very grateful for

Potter books for Valerie. We would, in fact, be very grateful for any books for any of us! I have read every book in the house, and am starved for more reading matter." She requested Dickens, poetry, *The Wind in the Willows*, books on Amazonian plants and animals, and "biographies of anybody—I love biography. . . . Thanks so much for thinking of books—nothing is more welcome here, where reading is our only diversion (and always has been my preferred diversion!)."[88]

On September 29, Jim left on another trip, flying east to Arajuno, then south to Villano with Ed and Pete. From there they had a three-hour hike to Huito, a settlement they had not visited before. It was a good trip, Betty reported to her mother when he got home a week later; they had found a sizable community, held Christian meetings, and been invited to come again. Most exciting of all, "On the way over, they sighted some Auca houses. This is <u>strictly</u> secret—don't spread it at all. They're not telling any of the other missionaries, <u>least</u> of all Wycliffe, as they would publish it, get the government informed, etc. which is the last thing we want. The fellows have various ideas in mind about how they may be reached—you could be praying about it." Betty closed her letter with another prayer request:

> Pray, Mother, that we may be shown God's whole will for us here—we feel that perhaps we should be reaching out more to other areas. It may mean weeks or even months away from this house, camping, travelling, or living in Indian style. The flesh shrinks, frankly, with a baby to think of, but if that is what the Lord wants, it's no good singing "Where He leads me I will follow" unless I'm willing for that, too. Just coming to Ecuador is <u>not</u> following all the way. Oh that we may <u>do His will</u>—nothing else is worth while.[89]

———

By September 1955, Nate Saint had been flying in Ecuador for seven years, and as a general rule he flew around—*not* over—"auca" land so that if he had to make a forced landing, he wouldn't have to walk out through their territory. When the McCullys had moved to Arajuno in the spring, however, Ed had asked him to overfly the land and look for signs of people. Nate had seen nothing but the breathtaking immensity of the great, green ocean of trees. They had tried again on September 19, and to their delight had found houses and fields about 50 miles northeast of the McCullys' house. They had shared their discovery only with Nate's fellow MAF pilot Johnny Keenan and with their wives. They wanted "to keep the 'find' in the family," as Nate later wrote, "until we were sure it was okay to spill it. . . . It seemed providential that we had investigated that tiny spot that turned into the first Auca clearing we had ever laid eyes on."[90] The "family" seems to have quickly grown to include the Elliots; Betty would note later that they learned of the sighting sometime in the remaining days of September. "From that moment on," she would write, "Jim had, as the Spanish say, 'one foot in the stirrup.'"[91]

When Nate ferried Jim and Pete on the twenty-ninth, he took new routes so that he could search again. Just fifteen minutes out from Arajuno, with Pete in the plane, he had spotted a second settlement, apparently larger than the first. After the flight Pete had written of "the thrill of seeing my first Auca houses. . . . This gave us a real spurt toward making some plans for the Aucas."[92] "The family" grew to include five families—the Saints, McCullys, Keenans, Elliots, and Flemings. Nate also noted the thrill of the sighting and mentioned again the sense of providence: "To some of us the most significant thing was not the information gained but the fact that after so much fruitless searching we had located the first group of Aucas and then in a couple of weeks had stumbled over the other group. It seemed to mean that now was the Lord's time to do something about them."[93]

Jim, Nate, and Ed were planning another trip to Huito for the end of the month, though their minds seem to have been more than half on the "aucas." Jim, at least, could think of little else. He had first heard of the people from his informant at SIL in July 1950. Hopes for an opportunity to contact them had contributed to his hesitation to engage himself to Betty. Now his innate love of adventure, his long-felt desire for "pioneer work" in "a place where the Scriptures have not been twisted," and his discouragement over the Shandian church and endless building projects contributed to an almost overwhelming excitement about the possibility of being part of the team that would reach the tribe at last.[94] He had lived in Shandia for just over two years: a year building with Pete, a month away for his wedding and honeymoon and eight months in Puyupungu, and a year and three months in Shandia again with Betty. In the fifteen months that he had lived in Shandia since his marriage, he had still been heavily engaged in construction, and he or Betty or both had traveled out of the area in all but six of those months and been gone for an entire month at least twice. But although he had hardly had a chance to establish meaningful relationships in Shandia, he decided that the Shandian Kichwa had had their chance to hear the gospel. As Betty would write a few months later, he felt that "their blood was now upon their own hands."[95] Perhaps he would have seen things differently had he been another decade down the road of life and seen how slowly most good things grow, but he was just twenty-eight, vigorous and full of enthusiasm. He was going to the "auca."

The five families had known for some time that there was an "auca" woman living on Hacienda Ila, where Rachel Saint and Catherine Peeke were doing linguistic work. The woman, Dayomæ, had run away from her tribe after her father was killed almost a decade before and had become one of the many indigenous people enslaved to work Sevilla's fields.[96] Now, in preparation for the trip to Huito, which would provide another opportunity to overfly "auca" territory, Jim volunteered to travel to Ila and meet with Dayomæ. Since they both spoke Kichwa, he was able to ask for several phrases in her mother tongue—the equivalents of "I like you; I want to be your friend," "I want to approach you," "What is your name?"[97]

———

Rachel Saint had learned of the existence of the "aucas" from her brother Nate in 1949, when she visited him on her way to Peru. She would later say that God had spoken to her in a vision when she was seventeen, calling her to live with brown people in a green jungle, and that when Nate told her of the group she knew this was her tribe. When Ecuador had opened its doors to SIL in 1953, Rachel had requested a transfer. Somehow she had learned of Sevilla, who had four "auca" women working for him. When he heard of her interest in the tribe, Sevilla had invited Rachel and Catherine to live in his house and undertake linguistic work with these women.

In February 1955 the two SIL workers had settled into a second-story guest room at Hacienda Ila.[98] Sevilla's generosity only extended so far, however. The indigenous women still had to work sixteen-hour days in the fields, and while the missionaries were waited on at Sevilla's table and served meals cooked by indigenous servants, the indigenous field workers were responsible for preparing their own food. They must have been exhausted by the time they finally sat down with the missionaries at night, which can't have increased their helpfulness as linguistic informants. The SIL workers had quickly realized that the women, who had not spoken their mother tongue in years, had essentially forgotten it. Dayomæ remembered more than the others, but what she remembered had become blended in her mind with Kichwa.[99] And although she was an interested and willing informant, she was often unavailable. Then in June, Rachel had gotten sick and had to leave.[100] In the three months of fractured time they had spent with Dayomæ, the two SIL workers could barely have scratched the surface of the language. Nevertheless, they had accumulated a larger linguistic file than anyone had managed before.

This file would have been useful to the group preparing to approach the tribe, but there was no way they could get access to it without piquing Rachel's curiosity, and they had agreed to keep their plans secret. In a record Nate had begun at the beginning of October, which he planned to share with prayer partners after the time for secrecy was past, he explained that the group had adopted the policy because they wanted "to avoid arousing other non-missionary groups to competitive efforts." These groups, he wrote, "would undoubtedly employ a heavily-armed invasion party going in overland," which they feared "might set back for decades the missionary effort."[101]

To the other couples, Nate had also made it clear that he did not want Rachel, in particular, to know about their plans. Although Betty mistrusted the SIL organization and did not want it involved, she would later remember remonstrating with him about this: "I said, 'Nate, you can't do that to your sister!' He said, 'You don't know my sister.'"[102] Nate had not minded Rachel knowing in general terms that one of the McCullys' aims in moving to Arajuno was to achieve "friendly contact with the Aucas" at some unspecified point in time.[103] But when it came to an immediate, material plan, he was a key influence in the group decision to keep his sister from becoming involved.

From childhood, Rachel had charmed when she wanted to, and when charm failed, had stubbornly ignored those who disagreed with her. Nate had good reason to know that she was perfectly capable of spiking their plans if she didn't like them. After the group came to their decision, he had written Rachel a letter, labeled "to be held until further notice" and kept among his papers, explaining that it had been a difficult choice, but that the group was including her in the general injunction to secrecy, because "as we see it, you might feel obligated to divulge this information to save me the risks involved."[104]

It seems that he may also have felt that his sister would be possessive of the group, not wanting to share her special tribe with other missionaries. The letter gently reminded her that she was not the only one with a call. "As you know, the reaching of the Aucas has been on our hearts for a long time. It has been heartening to know that the Lord has laid a specific burden on your heart also and that you are currently engaged in work on their language.... Our efforts will be directed toward inspiring confidence in Ed McCully who is, as you know, living within easy reach of the Aucas in two days overland."[105] Although Rachel wasn't there when Jim went to Hacienda Ila, he tried hard not to arouse even Dayomæ's curiosity about why he wanted the phrases. More than twenty years later, author Rosemary Kingsland wrote in her biography of Rachel Saint that if Rachel had been there at the time, "she would have guessed the reason and, in her determined way, would have caused the fur to fly."[106]

The phrases that Jim collected from Dayomæ were to be an important part of the charm offensive the men had agreed upon. The first stage was to drop gifts weekly at the settlement, using a version of the same technique that Nate had used to pick up mail from Puyupungu. The Saints and Keenans had immediately begun running tests of the drop apparatus, and on October 6, Nate and Ed had made the first gift drop: an aluminum kettle containing salt—which Dayomæ had said her people had never used—and buttons. On the fourteenth, the men had dropped a machete, and were delighted to see a group of people run eagerly to get it. Afterward Nate had written, "Several things seem evident: They got our first gift. They aren't afraid of us in this type of approach. They are as animated, in one way or another, about this thing as we are." This had seemed to the missionaries to indicate that things were moving quickly. "We had not hoped to see this for perhaps months."[107] A third flight, on

October 21, brought Ed and Nate close enough to see the faces of those on the ground.

On the fourth flight, at the end of the second trip to Huito, Jim finally got the chance to ride along. Using a battery-powered loudspeaker and the phrases he had gotten from Dayomæ, he called again and again his best approximation of the sentence, "You will be given a machete to exchange." That night he wrote in his journal, "First time I ever saw an Auca—fifteen hundred feet is a long ways if you're looking out of an airplane."[108] Betty would later say that "coming back from an Auca flight . . . Jim was so excited he could hardly eat—I am sure that if I had fed him hay he would not have given it a thought."[109] Just as he had done with his Bible memory verses when he was in college, he began to carry notecards with the "auca" phrases on them in his pocket so that he could study them in spare moments.

As the campaign to create friendly relations continued, the missionaries struggled to agree on a plan for attempting contact. From the beginning, Nate had proposed taking a team of men. Betty believed that it would be much safer if she and Jim and Val went in by canoe instead, traveling downriver to a landing point as close as possible to the houses. She pointed out that the tribe "certainly would not feel threatened by a man with his wife and baby." And, she reasoned, if something did go wrong and Jim was killed, she would rather die with him than be left behind. Jim agreed, calling it "a *great* idea," but when she explained it to Nate, she said later, "he listened very intently and very politely. And then he said no."[110] Olive later remembered that all the other men had reacted negatively to Betty's idea. There is no indication as to why they disregarded her suggestion, apparently out of hand. They decided they would enter the tribe's territory themselves, travel downriver by canoe (which would require two Kichwa rivermen to agree to take them), and use flybys to attract attention to their location once they had set up camp.

Nate, however, was endlessly inventive, and he was enamored of the idea that the airplane—"the modern missionary mule," he called it—was going to solve many of the problems of missionary life in rural areas.[111] In late October, the dry season was well advanced, and as the water level in the rivers dropped, he noticed that there were more exposed beaches and sandbars than usual. He began to look for one that might work as a runway, and even considered the possibility of buying special landing gear for soft, rough surfaces. After the October 29 flight, Nate, Jim, and Ed talked things over again and agreed that the response to the gift drops was so uniformly positive that they would plan a ground contact to coincide with the next full moon, which would fall on December 14. When Pete heard this he wrote to the other men that it seemed premature to assume that this historically hostile people were ready to welcome them, arguing that they would be better prepared if they spent more time acquiring a working knowledge of the language from Dayomæ. The others agreed to postpone the attempt, but only until after Christmas.

———

In the first week of November, Nate and Ed made a fifth gift drop. There were no signs of fear or anger, Ed reported, and "if there were a ladder down from the plane to them it would seem a good and safe thing to go among them."[112] In Shandia, Jim was planing boards for the new school building and building a "Christopher Robin" bed for Valerie. At almost eight months old, Val was crawling and had just begun pulling herself to stand and cruising around the edge of her playpen. Jim described her to his parents as "a regular giggling doll. . . . She laughs an awful lot, looks like an Elliot."[113] On November 12, the sixth gift flight, Nate's line came back up with a return gift attached, a green feathered headband. Betty was still wrestling with her Kichwa morphology. "Every time I look at it, it seems I think of another morpheme not accounted for."[114] And she and Jim were working on completing their translation of Luke's Gospel. Jim felt a sense of urgency about getting it done before the contact trip.

The week before Thanksgiving, Jim and Nate made a seventh gift drop, flying low in hopes that the people on the ground would be able to see their faces. They dropped some of the gifts, attached to toilet-paper streamers, in the tops of the tallest trees, hoping they would be cut down so the plane could fly even lower on future visits. Back in Arajuno, the Kichwa already knew that the Americans had seen "auca" houses in September, but the missionaries realized that they had also figured out the flights were gift drops when someone asked them, "Why do you crazy fellows give all that good stuff to Aucas?"[115] This appears to have heightened the American men's sense of urgency; it must have seemed only a matter of time before their activities were widely known.

Nate began to be concerned about whether they had enough team members. Pete was involved in planning, praying, and paying for the gift flights, but he was still trying to discern whether he should make part of the contact team. Johnny Keenan had agreed to act as a backup pilot in case they got into difficulties with the plane, but he would not be on the ground. Nate was uneasy about Jim and Ed staying alone overnight, but if they were in fact able to go in by plane, he did not want to stay overnight himself and leave the Piper unguarded on the beach. It was during this time that, with the permission of the other men, Nate invited Roger Youderian to join them. As a GMU missionary who had spent the last three years pioneering among the Shuar tribe in the southeastern forest and as a former US Army paratrooper who had survived the Battle of the Bulge, Roger had a skill set that Nate felt would serve the team well. Roger, who like Jim was discouraged by a lack of converts at his present station, had been planning to give up mission work and move back to the US. He quickly agreed to join the group.

———

The Elliots celebrated Thanksgiving with the Conns, the family Betty had lived with in Dos Rios, and two days later Nate and Jim made the eighth gift flight. Jim was exhilarated to see a man outside one of the houses wave "with both his arms as if to signal us to come down! Aucas waving at me to come!"[116] The ninth drop took place on December 3. Again the "aucas" sent up a gift, and Nate and Ed found that the trees marked on the previous flight had indeed been downed. Someone had also built a model plane and affixed it to the roof of one of the houses. Nate felt sure this was an indication of goodwill, and Ed, who had previously wanted to delay contact and build a runway first, wrote a letter to Jim afterward, urging ground contact and even advocating hiking to the settlement if the people didn't come to them at their landing site within a few days.

In Shandia, Betty and Jim got new books for Christmas: *Les Miserables* and Kenneth Roberts's 1937 historical novel *Northwest Passage*.[117] Jim was spending a good deal of his time trying to teach the Shandian Christians how to lead the church themselves so that he would be free to spend his time elsewhere if contact were successful. They had begun children's meetings "managed entirely by the Indians," Betty explained to her family, and

Jim was teaching just one Bible class a week, devoting the rest of his time to teaching "an older believer, who in turn teaches it in the school. This of course takes more time than it would for Jim to do it himself—sometimes he spends two hours a day with the ones who are going to teach, but it is the road to indigenous work, and is working out quite well. For the last two Sundays Indians have done the preaching, too, in the regular meeting." They got good news from Puyupungu as well. Twelve people had made public profession of faith, "confessing specific sins and asking forgiveness. These are the first in Puyupungu, and you know how happy we are to hear of it."[118]

During the first full week of December, the missionaries continued to iron out the specifics of their plan. They pored over the scanty accounts of the 1943 deaths of missionaries Dave Bacon, Bob Dye, Cecil Dye, George Hosbach, and Eldon Hunter in Bolivia, hoping to learn from those men's mistakes. They discussed precautionary measures, and because it seemed that accounts of encounters indicated that the people would be afraid of guns, they planned to carry them in case they were threatened, but to keep them carefully hidden. Nate noted that "the first shot fired signals the failure of the entire project and the scuttling of any hopes in the near future."[119] He also wrote of the desirability of bringing a raft in case they needed to leave quickly. And they settled on a new date: January 2, 1956.

The tenth gift drop came on December 10. Again, the people had cut down trees that the missionaries had marked with streamers. They saw a young man run out of a house carrying a lance but when they came around for a second pass, he had put it away. Along with the gifts they dropped pictures, "four 6 by 9-inch portraits of the team-members, tinted and bearing the insignia of the operation, a drawing of the little yellow airplane."[120] Again they got a return gift, this time a live parrot tied in a basket, with a banana to keep it happy during the flight.

After the drop, Nate flew along the Curaray River looking again for possible landing strips. By dropping carefully weighed packages of powdered paint pigment at timed intervals, he could mark off two-hundred-yard lengths. In this way he found a low, gravelly beach with a fairly open approach that would be long enough to land on. Afterward he wrote, "This finding brings into focus the possibility of landing the team right there with a prefabricated tree house. . . . It would mean that no Indians need to be in on the deal at all, and barring flood it would mean that I'd be able to fly them all out following a contact or whenever they should be ready to come." He felt that finding this sandbar seemed to be "another indication of His leading and care."[121]

On the same day that Ed and Nate were discovering a possible runway, Betty left Valerie and Jim at home and made a covert trip to get more language data from Dayomæ. When she got home three days later, she sat down to write a note to her mother. Along with updates on Valerie, their flock of ducks, and the fresh peanut butter she was making (peanuts were in season) she told Katharine about her trip, the first hint since the houses had been sighted in October that she and Jim were doing more than praying about reaching the "auca." She concluded:

> Must stop now—Jim is likely to come in and want to read this, and I haven't told him that I've told you about my working on the Auca, so you had better not mention it or my trip to Ila in any return letters. It really would be disastrous if this got out to anyone. . . . I don't think it will be too long before I can tell the family of the plans and all the details, but till then, suffice it that you know we are interested in reaching them, and praying for God's guidance. That is the most important thing—it would be folly to attempt anything with a tribe like the Aucas, without clear guidance.[122]

The next day, Jim left for Puyupungu. Pete and Olive had been planning a Christmas fiesta for the fifteenth through the eighteenth of December, and both Jim and Ed were teaching. This seemed quite successful, though there was unexpected excitement when Ed had to leave early because a man with a lance had been seen just 150 feet from the McCullys' house. Marilou, who was home with Stevie and Mikey, had managed to keep any of the men in the community from going out with a gun to chase the warrior and had gone out herself to offer a machete as a gift, calling out the friendly phrases gleaned from Dayomæ. When Ed and Nate arrived, they did the same but received no reply. The fact that the visitor, though armed, had not offered violence seemed positive, but to emphasize their continued friendly intentions, the two men decided to move up the eleventh gift drop, originally scheduled for the next day. After a brief landing on the chosen sandbar, Nate wrote, they flew over the houses and delivered a package: "beef, chocolate, manioc, cookies, candy, and some beads." In return, the people on the ground tied on a "basket cage," containing another live bird and "a spinner's distaff loaded with cotton yarn."[123]

On December 22, the Elliots, Flemings, and McCullys gathered in Arajuno to celebrate Christmas. They enjoyed the chance to be together and to have a vacation from much of their usual work. The adults rested, visited, and played games, and Mikey McCully and Valerie, who were just two months apart, had fun playing together. Jim and Ed, who had a long history of carryings-on together, were particularly full of fun and mischief. Olive remembered how they teased Betty. "One evening, Jim and Ed started telling stories. And they went on, and on, and they were *so. funny*. But in the way they were telling them, they really were making fun of Betty, and the more upset she got the more everybody laughed, because, she was the serious one. When you got Jim and Ed together, it was just—hilarious."[124] Years later Betty would chuckle remembering one of Ed's pranks.

> I guess all of us were either sitting around, or some of the others were having naps, and after an hour or so, we heard rustling in the room where Ed was, and he came to the door, and he just looked like a *zombie*. I mean he was just *cross-eyed*, standing there, this tall, huge guy, and without any warning whatsoever he just fell *headlong* on the floor, just *flat*. And Marilou just *jumped*, you know, and all of us just were aghast! But then Marilou, she just sat back in her chair and she started to laugh, and laugh, and laugh, and she said, "*Get* up off the floor, will you?" and he gets up and just laughs his head off![125]

The McCullys had made a special shopping trip to Quito for the occasion, and Betty wrote rapturously to her family of the food they had, "stuff such as one doesn't dream of in the jungle—pop corn, Spam, pickles, olives, packaged puddings and jello, candy, vacuum packed nuts, etc. etc."[126] But the plan for contact was never far from anyone's mind.

Although the Youderians were unable to be there, Nate and Marj flew in for the day on December 23, and four of the families were together for the first time to discuss strategy in person. Roger had drawn up and sent over a detailed plan, including emergency signals and maps. He would put together first-aid supplies. Ed would buy more gifts. Jim, with his building experience, would prefabricate a treehouse and be in charge of weapons.

Nate would be responsible for transportation and radio communication. Pete still felt he had no clear answer about what God wanted him to do, but Ed and Nate both said they felt he would be a helpful addition. So Pete agreed to go, and was assigned to assist Nate with the flights. Barbara and Marilou would supply the men's meals, and Marj, as always, would run the radio traffic. Olive still wasn't well, so she would stay with Marj in Shell Mera. And Betty's job would be to host Rachel in Shandia and pretend that nothing was happening.[127] They set their start date for Tuesday, January 3. It was a little past the full moon, but they were already committed to hold a conference on the Gospel of John in Shandia through January 1, so it would have to do.

On the same day, Nate and Jim made a twelfth gift drop, flying lower than they ever had before. Both men noted that one man was obviously terrified. But others seemed pleased to see them, and they received another gift—pottery, assorted foods, and another parrot. Nate called it "by far the most all-out effort at a fair-trade arrangement," and they didn't give the man's fear much thought. Months later, Betty would write that everything—the apparent success of the gift flights, the increasing talk among the Kichwa about the flights, the sighting of an "auca" at Arajuno, and the oncoming rainy season, which would obliterate their landing strip—"seemed to be catapulting them toward their D-day with now-or-never exigency."[128]

Marilou had made a mock Christmas tree out of bamboo, tinsel, and Christmas lights, and on Christmas Eve, the families exchanged gifts. Jim gave Betty "a lovely new watch, white gold to match my rings." Christmas Day was a Sunday, and the missionaries held a Christian meeting for the Kichwa in the morning as usual. Betty had brought a duck from the Shandia flock, and they had that for Christmas dinner, "roasted with orange dressing." The cherry on top of the celebration was a baptism, "the first . . . in Arajuno."[129] In the afternoon, the men quizzed each other on the phrases gleaned from Dayumæ. For the next two days, while they worked on their preparations with what Olive later remembered as "an air of anticipation," their wives had conversations about what they would do if they were widowed.[130]

Back in Shandia, Betty wrote a cheerful note to her family, describing their happy Christmas and her preparations for the conference. They were hosting ten missionaries, and she was making up beds all over the house. People came from the areas around Arajuno, Dos Rios, and Panos in addition to Shandia, and both missionaries and Shandian men taught. "The most gratifying result of the meetings," Betty told her family, "was the profession of faith of two <u>older</u> Indians. . . . As you all know, we have had hitherto . . . no believers over 25 years of age."[131]

During the conference, Betty asked Olive how she was feeling about the contact plan, and the younger woman admitted that she was unhappy about the risk. Nevertheless, she was trying to put a brave face on things for Pete, not wanting to hold him back. Ed and Marilou went for a walk, and Marilou told Ed, "It doesn't sound to *me* like Jim, or Pete, and maybe even Nate, are as sure as you are that everything's going to be safe." Barbara Youderian was not at the conference, but she spoke later of feeling afraid, and of minimizing her feelings to herself and pushing them aside: "I thought, 'I can't keep my husband home just because I have a fear.'"[132] Betty herself was anguished over whether Jim was supposed to go, but as she had done so many times before, she thrust her own opinions and emotions down and submitted to Jim's feeling of certainty. The women seem to have been experiencing what many evangelical Christians would call "a check in the spirit"—a persistent sense of disquiet and uneasiness—but for a variety of cultural and personal reasons, they voiced it hesitantly or not at all.

Sometime during the week of the conference, Betty wrote to her parents, briefly outlining their plans and reminding them to keep the news private. She concluded: "There are so many more things to tell, but Nate is writing up all the details of the operation, including the flights made every week for the past ten or 11 weeks, and when we feel it is safe, it will be made known. Until then, no one has been told. Pray hard. . . . And don't breath [*sic*] it to a soul. Nate's parents do not know—nor does Rachel. Much love, Betty."[133] Betty may not have known it, but this was not true. Not only had Nate already mentioned it to a couple of friends in letters, but he and Marj had written a letter much like Betty's and sent it to both sets of their parents, asking for prayer and urging complete secrecy. Jim had also written to his parents, concluding, "I know you will pray. Our orders are 'the gospel to every creature.'"[134] The McCullys had told their parents as well. Perhaps each one reasoned that by the time the letters made it to the States, it would be too late to give away the secret to anyone close enough to interfere.

———

On Monday, January 2, 1956, as the other missionaries were getting ready to return to their respective stations after the conference and the five men were getting ready to meet in Arajuno for their final preparations, Betty sat down at the typewriter to rattle off a short letter to her mother. Marked "Top Secret," it began, "Just a wee note this morning before the plane takes off," and concluded, "I am at perfect peace about Jim's going. I hope you will not worry. The Lord has given direction, and confidence. We are in His keeping, and want Him to be glorified."[135]

A little later in the morning, as she helped Jim get ready to leave, she kept thinking, "Will this be the last time I'll help him pack? Will this be the last lunch he'll eat in Shandia?"[136] She bit her tongue as they left the house to walk down to the airstrip to keep from saying to an exuberant Jim, "Do you realize you may never open that door again?"[137] And as she watched the little yellow plane disappear toward Arajuno, she felt a strong desire to run away. All she could think was, "Chances are, I'm not going to see him again."[138]

———

On Wednesday, January 4, a mail drop brought Betty a note, letting her know that the beach landing had worked and the men had successfully established their little camp. She typed out a brief but cheerful letter to the Howards, describing the successful conference, telling of her ongoing visit with Rachel Saint, and sharing a few details from a letter from Eleanor Vandevort about her life among the Nuer tribe in the Sudan.

———

On Friday, January 6, Betty wrote another short note to her mother. "I know that if you have gotten my other letters about Jim's trip, you are on pins and needles to know what is going on." What little Marj knew couldn't be passed along the radio because of Rachel so there wasn't much news to share, but "I have been quite at peace since Jim left."[139] She had taken Valerie to play at the river the day before and was teaching her to float.

———

On the afternoon of Sunday, January 8, Betty took Val down to play at the river again and got some cute snapshots to send home to her parents.[140]

———

Monday morning, at 8:00 a.m., Marj Saint contacted Betty via the radio. "We haven't heard from the fellows since yesterday noon." She had gotten in touch with Johnny Keenan, and he was out overflying the area where the men were camped. She asked Betty to "stand by at ten o'clock" for a report. Betty went upstairs to finish teaching her women's class.[141]

At ten o'clock, Marj reported that Johnny had spotted the plane on the beach, visibly damaged. There was no sign of the men. Rachel, who was sitting nearby, jumped up, asking excitedly if the men were in "auca" territory, and whether the plane had been burned.[142] The usually unflappable Marj replied, with a catch in her voice, "We don't know, but I don't care any more about the old airplane. Just about the fellows."[143] She ended transmission without signing off.

Something was wrong. "When thou passest through the waters, I will be with thee; and through the rivers, they shall not overflow thee. . . ." Isaiah 42 came unbidden to Betty's mind. She began praying silently, "Lord, let not the waters overflow."[144]

———

Time became a torrent. A US Air Force reservist who was in Shell Mera got hold of Howard family friend General William K. Harrison Jr., who had oversight of the US Air Rescue Service unit stationed in Panama. Someone contacted HCJB, and the news that the men were missing began to make its way around the world. Barbara and Marilou, who had been together in Arajuno, were flown to Shell Mera to be with Olive and Marj, then Marilou was flown back again because if the men managed to hike out, she wanted someone to be there to receive them. A group of Kichwa men from Arajuno set out by canoe to look for the men along the river. Marj asked GMU missionary Frank Drown to put together a ground search party.

On Tuesday morning, Johnny picked up Frank and brought him to Shell Mera. Someone flew Rachel and Betty in from Shandia. By the time they arrived, there were so many people at Shell Mera that Frank could not get from the airfield to the Saints' house. The Ecuadorian Army and the US Air Force were represented. Commercial airline pilots who knew Nate had come to offer their services. Missionaries from Quito and the surrounding areas were there to volunteer for the search party.

Some of the pilots began cruising over the jungle. Radio traffic skyrocketed, and the five women were kept running all day long. Providing meals for dozens of people. Washing the endless flow of dishes by hand. Tending the babies, all suddenly sick. Caring for the older children. Doing laundry, including four sets of diapers. Hoping the diapers on the line would dry in the damp air. In spare moments, Betty searched her Bible for promises that Jim would come back. She grabbed onto a sentence from Jeremiah: "Jacob shall return, and shall be in rest, and be quiet."[145] Something to pin her hopes to. The busy days were better than the stillness of the nights.

Wednesday, Betty was upstairs taking care of Valerie, when Marj shouted her name. Running down, she saw Marj with her forehead resting on the radio. Johnny had found a body. Facedown in the water. Near the camp. Flying as low as he could, he had been unable to identify it. They knew then that the most likely outcome was that all five were dead. But until they *knew*, it was impossible not to hope.

That night, Betty scrawled a letter to her parents. "I want you to know that your prayers are being answered moment by moment as regards me—I am ever so conscious of the Everlasting Arms. As yet we know only that two bodies have been sighted from the air but not identified." She briefly described the search effort, and concluded:

Remember that the Lord emphasized to me a long time ago—<u>When</u> (not if) thou passest thro' the waters. . . . And He is fulfilling His word.

Jim was confident, as was I, of God's leading. THERE ARE NO REGRETS.

Nothing was more burning in his heart than that Christ should be named among the Aucas. By life or death . . . O may God get glory to Himself!

Pray that whatever the outcome, I may learn the lessons needful—oh, I want to serve the Lord in the future, so pray for His continued grace & guidance. I have no idea what I will do if Jim is dead, but the Lord knows, and I am at rest. . . .

We hope for final word tomorrow and trust our loving Father who <u>never</u> <u>wastes</u> <u>anything</u>.[146]

On Thursday morning, with searching aircraft circling overhead, the ground party making its slow way downriver through the forest met the Kichwa men in their canoes coming back upriver. They had found Ed's body and brought back his watch and one of his enormous shoes to confirm identification. At Shell Mera, the waiting women listened to the guarded radio chatter and tried to guess what was happening. When they heard Ed's name they knew that his body must have been identified. Ed, who had been such a clown at Christmas just a couple of weeks before. Betty wrote in her journal: "I feel sick at my stomach."[147] They listened as the USAF helicopter moved slowly down the river, then stopped to hover for several minutes in one location. When it moved two hundred yards and hovered again—and again, and again—they realized that more bodies must have been found.

Late that afternoon Johnny flew Marilou back to Shell Mera again, and the five women listened to the helicopter's copilot give identifying information on the bodies he had seen. Pete and Roger were identified. Ed's body had been washed off the beach. The other two bodies were unrecognizable from the helicopter. It was still possible that either Nate or Jim was still alive, somewhere in the forest.

But on Friday, the report came: the ground search party had identified the bodies of Nate and Jim. All five men were dead. The four bodies had been buried in a common grave. Frank Drown had reluctantly vetoed a further search for Ed's body, not wanting to put members of the search party in greater danger. The helicopter brought back the men's wedding rings and watches.

———

Saturday morning, a US Navy pilot flew the widows over the beach where the men had died. Betty wrote later, "The Curaray lay like a brown snake in the undulating green. Pressing our faces close to the windows as we knelt on the floor of the plane, we could see the slice of white sand where the Piper stood. . . . As the plane veered away, Marj Saint said: 'That is the most beautiful little cemetery in the world.'"[148]

Sunday morning the last returning members of the ground party were flown back into Shell Mera. Through tears, Frank Drown told of the simple graveside service he had conducted, "entrusting them to God's watchful care until the resurrection."[149] As they sat around Marj and Nate's dining table, HCJB doctor Art Johnson, who had been part of the ground search party, answered the women's questions about how their husbands had died. Lances, as big around as a man's thumb, broken off in heads and bodies. Faces hacked by machetes. The submerged portions of the bodies had been eaten away, sometimes to the bone, by fish, so identification had been made by articles of clothing: Pete's belt, Roger's blue jeans, the nametape in Jim's T-shirt, the way Nate wore his watch pushed up above his elbow when he wanted to remember something. "We urged him to give us all the facts," Betty said later.[150] Imagining was worse than knowing.

———

There was a small memorial service for the men at the GMU Bible school in Shell Mera where Jim and Pete had been camp counselors in the summer of 1952. Various missionaries, friends, acquaintances, and relatives streamed in and out of the mission compound, hoping to be of help to the bereaved women, creating an enormous amount of housework, cooking, and dishes. In the midst of it all was a photographer from *Life* magazine taking hundreds of pictures. Betty's brother Dave came in from Costa Rica, and her parents sent a cablegram. She wrote a brief note to reassure them:

> Forgive me for not writing sooner. You understand. . . .
>
> The Lord keeps me in peace. Oh the joy of thinking of dear Jim, without fault, before the Lord he so passionately loved! I can't get over it. The glory and the triumph! What must it be!
>
> Have no fear for me. Isaiah 43:2 <u>wonderfully</u> <u>fulfilled</u>.[151]

———

On Thursday, January 19, a week and a half after Jim had walked out their door without a backward glance, Betty and Valerie returned to Shandia. With them went Dave Howard, Olive Fleming, two men from the Brethren organization, and Katherine Morgan, who had driven almost forty-eight hours from Colombia to be with Betty. The two Brethren men stayed a few hours and left again. Dave and Katherine, who were among the few who had come to help that were actually helpful, would stay over the weekend; Olive indefinitely while she dealt with her belongings and decided on her next step. Betty knew what her next step would be: she would stay in Ecuador and continue the work she and Jim had been doing in Shandia. Though she felt again the strong desire to run away, she squared her shoulders and turned to the tasks at hand.

One of the first things she did after getting home was to sit down at her typewriter and write a family letter, the first since Jim's death.

> I know you all are wondering how I am getting along. I can only say that the peace I have literally passes all possible understanding. There is no human reason for the utter satisfaction I find, and the almost exuberant spirit which is mine today.... "The Lord Jehovah is my strength and song." I find it gives me joy to look at pictures of Jim, read over his diaries, look at this lovely home which he built with his own hands, and handle his things. I am filled with Thanksgiving for the two years and three months when he was my husband—I still feel that I didn't deserve even that much, and can only bless Him whose hand guided, whose heart planned it all. Of course, the second I start thinking about <u>myself</u> and how in the world I am going to carry on, etc., I am immediately let down. That is fatal. But thinking of the glory and triumph of Jim's death, the unsullied joy which is his before the face of Him he so passionately loved, and the challenge of his life, totally sold out for God, fills me with unspeakable happiness. ... And I know only praise, praise, praise in my heart. I can truthfully say that I have shed not one single tear over the fact that Jim has been killed.... I have learned, I believe, the lesson which A.C. speaks of in her poem—"In acceptance lieth peace." How true. I accept, gratefully, from the hand of God, this experience—I suppose many would call it a trial. I hardly think of it that way. It is just one more of the blessed experiences which God uses to bring us to Himself.... I believe that he and the other men now have a special fellowship with Christ, in that they, like Him, died for the salvation of that benighted tribe. I feel confident that the door to the Aucas, far from being closed, is now open. I have said nothing to anyone else of this, but my longing now is to reach them.... Pray that he will teach me <u>all</u> that He wanted me to learn through this, and oh, that I might be prepared to fulfil all the good pleasure of His will—if it be to go to the Aucas, I should be loaded down with what A.C. called "over-

weights of joy." Nothing would thrill me more. For the present, it is clear to me that I am to carry on the work here in Shandia. When I asked Jim, before he left, what I should do should he fail to return, he said, "Teach the believers, darling. We've <u>got</u> to teach the believers. And by all means, close the school." . . . I must stop now—I wanted to just let you all know that I am fine, that Is. 43:2 has been literally fulfilled. Rejoice with me!"[152]

Later that day, she sat at the desk in her bedroom, the desk Jim had made, and wrote in her journal. The little book she had started using when she and Jim were married was full, so she fished out an old notebook she had used after college that still had some space in it.

Life begins a new chapter—this time without Jim. . . . I have been reading over some of the first part of this book—it is almost prophetic. They were days when God was teaching me to find satisfaction in Himself, without Jim. But always there was the hope that someday He would give us to one another. He did, on October 8, 1953. Two years and three months together.

"If Thy dear Home be fuller, Lord,
For that a little emptier
My house on earth, what rich reward
That guerdon were."
AMY CARMICHAEL

These words come to me over and over. The peace which I have received is certainly beyond all understanding.[153]

An Alien, a Stranger

THE GREAT WAVE OF DEATH had crashed against Betty Elliot, and it had not washed her away. The days flowed on. Buoyed by her faith in God and her desire to live up to Jim's example, she felt she had been raised above temporal things. "I am thankful," she wrote, "that the things of earth mean <u>nothing</u> to me now, and I pray that I may never fall back into that rut."[1] But composed as we are of body as well as soul, it is impossible to disentangle the earthly and the spiritual. Betty still had to care for Valerie, manage their home, host guests, and do her own part of the thousand and one jobs needed to run the mission station. Now, too, she had to sort out which of Jim's tasks to address herself and which would have to go undone.

Although Jim had said she should close the school if he were killed, Betty kept it open, feeling that the students ought to be allowed to finish the year. Venancio Tapui, the assistant schoolteacher, had taken over most of the Christian meetings, so she spent hours going over the text with him ahead of time, as Jim had been doing. She resumed coaching teachers for the children's Bible classes. The church had thoroughly studied all the Scripture portions she and Jim had translated, and there was an urgent need for more. Even answering the mail had become a mountainous task. She drafted a circular letter to be mimeographed and sent to as many people as possible, but she was still typing more than one hundred letters a week to those she felt deserved a personal response, and her pile of unanswered mail kept growing.

Then there was the question of what to do about the other Brethren stations. Marilou, almost nine months pregnant, had already gone to the

US to be near family for the baby's birth, so the house at Arajuno was vacant. Olive felt she did not speak Kichwa well enough to run the station at Puyupungu; she, too, decided to go back to the US. Although Betty planned to travel to Arajuno periodically to visit the Christians there, she could not oversee maintenance on other stations in addition to her own. Arajuno could survive some neglect thanks to the infrastructure left behind by Shell, but the unpaved strip at Puyupungu that had taken so long to clear would be reclaimed by the jungle almost immediately. Without it, it appeared the station where she and Jim had started married life would have to be abandoned.

But though the enormity of the task at hand was daunting, Betty would have preferred handling it alone to coping with the steady stream of well-meaning attempts at help. A wide range of people sent advice, came to visit or to help, and embarked on courses of action that affected her future, often without talking to her first. Just as when the crowd of "well-wishers and curiosity seekers" had descended on Shell Mera while the men were missing, these people added hours of extra work to her days—more letters, more time-consuming radio contacts, more meal-planning and cooking and laundry, more travel, more decisions, more of the surface-level socializing that can be so tiring for introverts.[2] To make matters worse, it seemed that most people felt sorry for her—an attitude she found almost unbearable—or seemed not to want to talk or think about Jim at all. Betty appreciated help on projects such as the completion of the schoolteacher's house, but at the same time, she wanted to be left in peace to remember Jim, to enjoy Jim's house and Jim's things, and to carry on her work in the way she felt God was showing her.

But the stream could not be diverted. What had been quiet work in an undistinguished corner of the world was now the focus of widespread attention. The private plan to reach the "aucas" had become public knowledge—and public property, many felt. HCJB's Abe Van Der Puy had already started writing a book about the five men, apparently at the request of the widows, and he wanted to interview Betty and see Jim's diaries. Despite her workload, her fresh bereavement, the day on each end that it took to prepare the house to be left empty and then get everything running again, the difficulties of travel, and the fact that she had to take an eleven-month-old with her wherever she went, he asked her to travel back to the city again to meet him. Dee Short announced before the end of January that he planned to move to Arajuno, despite the fact that he did not speak Kichwa.

Betty wrote to the Elliots and Howards to explain what Marj Saint had not been able to tell her back in January with Rachel listening. After two days and three nights of fishing, swimming, reading, slapping bugs, and shouting cheerfully into the woods, the five men had been delighted to see three "aucas"—two women and a man—appear on the bank across the river and wade across to them. The visitors had spent the day, eaten hamburgers, been introduced to insect repellant, and looked at a *Time* magazine. The man had even agreed to ride in the Piper. The missionaries had taken pictures and videos and done their best to invite them to return with friends. Then the trio had peacefully disappeared back into the trees, first the younger woman, then the man, and sometime later, the older woman. The contrast between the apparent friendliness of this group and the subsequent killing led to much speculation in the missionary community.[3] "Some feel that perhaps there was a friendly group . . . represented by the three whom the fellows contacted on the beach, and another group who were hostile," that there might therefore be intratribal violence after the killing, and that the group interested in contact might come to Arajuno for safety. "For this reason, many feel it is vital that someone be in Arajuno to receive them, regardless of whether they know Quichua or not." She added dryly, "Marilou and I both feel that this is a little visionary."[4]

Betty felt that if missionaries were to come into the area, they should start by learning the predominant language, and she offered to host the Shorts and act as their language teacher. Her concerns about Dee's missiological approach, formed by his business practices during 1952 and 1953, were reinforced when he declined her offer. It is ironic that Olive, who had been studying Kichwa for months, felt she was not qualified to run a station in a Kichwa-speaking area because she did not speak the language well enough, while Dee, who had never studied Kichwa, was apparently confident he was the man for the job at a station that had the added complexity of potential contact with yet another linguistic group and the looming possibility of violence. Betty was relieved when he decided not to move after all.

It was important to Betty that God's guidance shape whatever came next. She declined offers from Jim's parents and from Bert and Colleen to come and stay with her long-term, writing, "I want you to know that I appreciate more than I can say your offer . . . but I am sure that that will not be necessary at present." She did not want to pursue any course merely because it seemed easiest or most logical to her or to others. Instead she badly wanted to rely on God, both to provide for her and to give her direction. "True, the burden of responsibility is great," the letter went on, "and I realize every minute what a gap Jim has left. . . . But I do not feel that anyone should come down now. Oh, I hope you all will pray that no one will come rushing in here, feeling that the 'gap must be filled,' unless they are clearly led of God."[5]

At about the same time, Betty received a letter from Jim's Wheaton buddy Bill Cathers. Bill and Irene Cathers had come to Ecuador at about the same time as Jim and Pete, and had lived in Santo Domingo for several months before leaving because of their health. The Elliots hadn't heard much from them in the intervening years, but now Bill wrote that they wanted to come to Shandia and learn Kichwa so they could work as missionaries in the eastern jungles. Though she would have preferred to live alone, Betty believed this approach to be consistent with God's leading, and agreed to host and teach them.

A letter from Wilfred, announcing that he was cutting short his furlough and coming back to the jungles, was harder to accept. Betty was afraid he would assume she wanted him to take over the Shandia station, and she shrank from the thought of having to work with him, though she told her mother she was *not* worrying. "If I should start fretting over such a matter after what happened Jan. 6, God's lessons would be in vain. Just pray that His will be again accomplished, will you?"[6] But her instinct proved correct. Not long after, Wilfred wrote (to Dee, not to Betty) announcing that he would make Shandia his base.

The two Brethren men seem to have thought of the jungle stations as belonging, not to the Elliots, the McCullys, and the Flemings, but to Jim, Ed, and Pete. Although single women had worked alone in difficult environments for as long as Americans had been sending foreign missionaries, and although "faith mission" missionaries had been overwhelmingly female for longer than he had been alive, Wilfred in particular seemed oblivious to Betty as a missionary in her own right. Meanwhile, Puyupungu, which had seen the least consecutive missionary presence and had the most fragile infrastructure, was going both unvisited and unmaintained. But neither of the men volunteered to move into that community: it was neither at the center of things like Shandia nor close to the "aucas" like Arajuno.

And everyone wanted a piece of the excitement surrounding the fabled tribe. While those who had already been involved continued their slow efforts—Johnny Keenan making gift flights, Rachel Saint working on the language, Betty gleaning information from Kichwa who had experience with the tribe—rumors swirled about other attempts: two Canadians making plans with local priests for a trip onto the tribe's land, "a scientific expedition" from California, "Hollywood" preparing "to build a fort" in the area, a husband and wife from Florida come "to take pictures" with the wife "going in alone first."[7] The people living at the mouth of the Arajuno River later reported that this couple had somehow bullied or cajoled a Kichwa woman into posing naked for photographs, holding a chonta-palm lance. It appeared to Betty that the Americans planned to pass the photos off in the US as evidence of contact with the fabled tribe.[8]

"I am asking the Lord to show me my part in reaching the Aucas," Betty wrote to her family. "The urgency is upon me . . . ," an urgency that stemmed in part from these rumors.[9] She was deeply concerned that these efforts might harm the evangelical attempt to share the story of Jesus with the tribe. Because this goal was so closely tied to the loss of Jim, the possibility of interference was particularly painful to Betty. Her own desire to be one of the people bringing that story felt stronger and stronger as the days went by. Nevertheless, the thing she wanted to want most of all was God's will. She wrote to her family, "Pray that God will thwart all plans which are not of Him, mine included."[10]

———

After a lifetime of keeping her own counsel, Betty had found in Jim someone with whom she could share the details of her life, "not only the many things we have in common," as she had written him in the fall of 1952, "but now also the little things we don't have in common: my family, your family; my daily happenings, yours."[11] Now his absence was woven through all these things. When she did a new bit of translation, Jim wasn't there to cross-check it. When Valerie smiled, her wide grin and dimples looked like Jim's. Even a care package from her mother was bittersweet because Jim wasn't there to see her pretty new clothes and fancy soap.

"The early morning hours are hardest for me," she told Katharine wistfully at the end of January, "for then is when I often lay with my head on Jim's strong shoulder and we talked of all sorts of things. It was always especially meaningfull [sic]."[12] She dreamed of him at night, but even in her dreams he refused to speak to her.

Then, too, Betty kept thinking about Jim's death, pondering the scanty evidence gathered by the search party, trying to understand what had happened. Before he died Pete had theorized in his journal (in what historian Kathryn T. Long aptly describes as "a statement loaded with cultural assumptions") that the younger "auca" woman had been offered as a gift to the missionaries.[13] Betty questioned, "Were they miffed, perhaps, because their gifts were not accepted?" When the group that killed the men was on their way to the beach, Nate had overflown them and had not seen any spears: "Had they planned to have him see them without lances? . . . Well, it is all a matter of speculation now."[14] Two weeks later she wrote, "I keep trying to picture it. Which ones saw the others go down? When did they first realize what was taking place?"[15] After the film from Nate's camera finally came back from the developer: "Those pictures are just tremendous, aren't they? Oh, to see those dear Indians, so relaxed, so animated, so perfectly at home with the fellows—there is not the slightest doubt in my mind now that they were not sent as a decoy. There must have been a faction in the tribe. . . . And then, to see those dear men, Jim's dear face and strong body, broad smile—how can I believe he is gone?"[16] While she wrote confidently in her circular letter that "there is no way in the world [Jim] would rather have died," that did not change the fact that his sudden, violent death was traumatic.[17]

As she had done for years when things were hard, Betty intentionally managed her thoughts and feelings. She welcomed the fullness of her days because work demanded her attention, taking her mind off Jim. She prioritized daily Bible reading, noting in her journal things that stood out, questions she had, passages where she felt she had gotten insight. She prayed the Psalms. She found comfort in the theology expressed in hymns and sang as she worked. And she tried to direct her thoughts. In mid-February she explained to her mother: "The Lord is helping me wonderfully, and I keep so busy now . . . that I just don't have time to weep or think about myself. Valerie is still waking four and five times a night. . . . So of course when

I am awake so much at night, I do have time to miss Jim. But I have shed no tears. I just go over and over all the happiness we knew together, all the way the Lord led us . . . and the privilege that has been mine in having him. I try not to think about the future."[18]

This echoes the letter written just after her return to Shandia, in which she had explained that she was not crying over Jim's death, but thinking of "the glory and triumph" he was experiencing.[19] In another letter to her mother, she wrote:

> At times the hunger for Jim is so huge I wonder how long I will be able to stand it, but years ago I asked the Lord to choose my inheritance for me. This is His choice. So it is right, and best for me. Hence, I have no fears for the future, but trust Him to lead me on, to satisfy every need, and help me to discipline myself to draw from the Source. Oh how I loved him. Did ever woman love man as I loved him?[20]

In her anguish, reminding herself that God is loving and good and in control, that Jim had died for something important and was now with God—in other words, that there was more to reality than the pain of her loss—gave Betty comfort.

The valuation of calm acceptance as *good* grief that had been evident in Betty's life at least since high school also affected her approach to loss. Her recurrent declaration that she was not crying over Jim's death, offered as evidence that she was doing well and experiencing God's peace, suggests that at this time she saw tears as a sign of doing poorly, of failure to rest in God. In another family letter she wrote:

> I find that no human <u>event</u> can change the soul. It is in our response to any given situation that we are changed. The Indians, for example, though many of them are deeply moved by the death of all their "gringo fathers," are the same people, feeling sorry for themselves, pestering me every minute to sell them medicine, ammunition, etc., lazy (I have a hard time persuading any men to work), etc. . . . I find it in myself, too, that I am the same hopeless wretched sinner, but I can see that God is teaching me, and I am constantly asking Him not to let me miss a single lesson. . . . God intends to consume our dross and refine our gold—oh, may we let Him.[21]

Less than three weeks after the violent death of her husband and four of her friends, Betty judged herself harshly for the physical and psychological effects of grief.[22]

The centrality in Betty's thinking of the idea of learning spiritual lessons, of not standing in the way of God's refining process, also highlights how important she felt it was to respond well to her pain and loss. She felt that if she could get her response right, her obedience would facilitate the good things God planned to bring out of the situation; if she got it wrong, it would prevent those good things and waste Jim's death. "Pray," she told her family, "that He will teach me all that He wanted me to learn through this." And, "Oh, how I pray that I miss nothing that He has for me in this!"[23]

In the week of Jim's death, Betty had noted gladly the reaction of the US Air Force rescue crew to the outward calm of the widows. "That particular crew had 108 rescue missions in 1955, and of course they are used to having to break terrible news to people. They said they'd never seen anything like the way the wives held up and remained calm. Said usually they got hysterical and berserk. I only tell you this so you will know what your prayers were doing for us all. . . . I lost eight pounds from Monday to Thursday, but I never broke down, and in my heart there was a peace all the time."[24]

Betty was also encouraged by the response of *Life* photographer Cornell Capa. Capa had lost his beloved older brother to a violent death not quite two years before. Perhaps because of his own loss he was sensitive to the human longing for spiritual connection, and he was intrigued by the "totally unfamiliar world" the missionaries represented.[25] He was also impressed by the apparent calm of the widows, noting their lack of "complaints" or "self-pity."[26] He had asked many questions during his time in Shell Mera and had seemed moved by the portions of Jim's diary that Betty had shared in an attempt to answer his questions, telling her repeatedly that they were, "fantastic," "tremendous." The pair had struck up a friendship, and Betty told her family afterward, "Someone gave him a Christian book before he left, and he said, 'You could never convert me with this, but you could with the diaries of those men.' . . . Pray that the right impression may be given in the publicity."[27] Although Jim had not directly succeeded in his attempt to tell an unreached group about Jesus, visible signs that others might hear the story because of his death helped create a sense of meaning in her suffering.

Ironically, the stoicism Betty admired as a sign of trust in God was offensive to many Kichwa. Later that summer, when a rumor started that
Shandian men working away at the coast had been killed, Betty reassured their worried relatives that the rumors were false, "and even [if] it
were true the Lord could comfort [them] as He had comforted me." One
woman replied, "Huh! You sure forgot fast. You being a 'senora', nothing
makes any difference to you. You aren't even sad about your husband. But
we—we feel things. We love our relatives." Betty concluded, "Talk about
being a 'testimony to the Indians,' etc. means nothing in this case. One must
leave the results to the Lord."[28] She would later argue that Christians have
a responsibility to understand the culture in which they find themselves
and learn to communicate in a way that makes sense in that culture. But in
1956, doing her best to keep her head above the water, it's understandable
that Betty couldn't transcend these preexisting cultural barriers.

Valerie had started babbling the word for "father" in Kichwa just before
Jim left. She had lost progress developmentally during the ten days he was
missing and even stopped eating solids or drinking from a cup for a time.
She was up every two hours all night long. Betty had tried everything she
could think of—rocking her, feeding her, going in to comfort her, leaving
her alone—and for a while nothing seemed to help. But by her first birthday,
the little girl was sleeping and eating more regularly and playing happily
with visiting children during the day. Betty was hosting eight guests but
made time to throw a little party. "Had the teacher's and assistant teacher's
kids up, with the Short kids, a pink cake with one blue candle, put . . . the
little white nylon dress with blue flowers on Valerie, a blue ribbon in her
wisp of straw colored hair, and took pix of the children standing around
the coffee table outside in the sunshine, with the cake in the middle. Hope
they come out. If only Jim could see her now! She is a little doll."[29]

Growth in the church in Shandia was an encouragement. Eleven people
whom she had not made any attempt to evangelize professed faith in response to interactions with fellow Shandians who were Christians. "So the
indigenous church is already fulfilling the great responsibility for which
Jim prayed, that they should reach their own people. I am thrilled with this

work of the Spirit, for that's purely all it is. . . . They have all come since the death of the five men, and I believe this is the firstfruits here in Shandia of their martyrdom."[30]

In mid-March, Mrs. DuBose gathered up Betty's mother and swept into Shandia for a short visit, giving Katharine a chance to see her daughter and granddaughter for the first time in a year. When her mother left, Betty traveled north beyond Quito to the mountain village of Calderon for a conference for Kichwa speakers at which she had been asked to teach. Co-incidentally, on the day she had received the invitation, her daily reading had included the passage in 1 Corinthians 14 concerning women talking in church, which she described as being "about women keeping silence, and asking their husbands at home what to do."[31]

English translations universally render this passage as instructing women to ask their husbands for *information* rather than direction. But as she thought about what to do, Betty focused not on whether women may speak when the church gathers but on the idea that she would have to make her own decision. Oddly, since one of the major issues facing the early Christian church was the care of widows, she decided that the apostle Paul had failed to envision a scenario such as hers when he wrote his letter. "I feel just completely left out of Paul's considerations—he never thought of there being no men, no husbands to ask. I'll have to ask the Lord."[32] After praying about it for a day or two, she had agreed to speak. She enjoyed her time at the conference and felt that she did well at both understanding and being understandable.

The invitations did not end there. After her time in Calderon, Betty stopped in Quito to sort her belongings, giving away Jim's clothes and re-ducing her own stored effects to just one trunkful so she would no longer have to rent a bodega. While she was there, she spoke at a women's tea as-sociated with the American embassy "about the Aucas, God's dealings with me in this time of sorrow, and the work in Shandia."[33] She was also asked to address a women's Bible class and to tape a talk for a radio broadcast. The community attitude toward the deaths of the five men less than three months before is like something out of a Flannery O'Connor story. *Grotesque* is the only word for asking a woman to talk about her husband's violent death over tea and cucumber sandwiches. But perhaps because of her desire to give a good testimony, Betty does not seem to have been bothered by this ghoulishness at the time.

Back in Shandia, Betty was looking forward to the coming of Bert and Colleen and of Tom. "They will be so interested to talk about Jim, something no one (or I should say almost no one, for Mother was) seems interested in doing, and that is the thing I'm starved for!"[34] But she was worn out with hosting comparative strangers. "<u>Please</u> stop worrying about my being alone," Betty wrote her mother, "—I <u>wish</u> people would 'leave me <u>be</u>!'"[35] At the end of May, she wrote, "If Cathers come in June, I will be hung. I have about 15 people planning to visit me in June or July, and I <u>would</u> like some time alone with Tom."[36] She was relieved when the couple decided they would stay in the US until their baby was born and come in the fall.

Bert and Colleen arrived in early June, six months after Jim's death. Their sixteen-day visit was an "untold help and blessing" to Betty. "Bert is like Jim in his grasp of the word, and has been able to help me with a lot of questions I had. Also, he is fixing everything in sight around the house. . . . Colleen is a gem—I love to talk to her, and she is doing most of the housework."[37] With their help she was able to get on top of the mail, make progress on her "auca" language files, and complete a good deal of Kichwa translation work.

But it was bittersweet. Bert was like Jim in other ways as well—facial expressions, the way he moved—and a constant reminder of Jim's absence. Little Valerie was enchanted with this uncle who was so like her father, and Betty wrote to Katharine, "When I see them together, I just wish that he could have her, and that she could have a father. It seems to me that the best thing that could happen would be for me to die, so they could have her. Now don't say that's 'an awful thing to say.' I am quite serious, and I don't think it is an awful thing to say at all!"[38] The week after Bert and Colleen left, she dreamed of Jim almost every night, dreams that emphasized their separation: "Still he says nothing to me. And still, when I wake in the morning, it is just as utterly incredible to me that he is dead as it was in January."[39]

Tom arrived partway through the Elliots' visit for a two-month stay, and being able to pick up right where they left off in the particular affinity and comfort of their relationship was another gift. He fit right into Betty's routine, taking care of Valerie "for hours on end" and accompanying his sister on medical visits and other trips. They went to the mouth of the Arajuno at the end of May to find out if a Kichwa woman who had been captured by "aucas" and later escaped could provide any linguistic information (she could not). A month later they traveled to Riobamba for another translation conference, this one a gathering of Kichwa-speaking missionaries. Betty found the chance to consult Ellen Ross of the American Bible Society immensely helpful. "She gave me even more freedom in translation than I had felt warranted in taking."[40] In the week after Betty returned to Shandia, she translated the first three chapters of 1 Timothy: "Words like bishop, church, unholy, law, patience, profane, and unjust pose real problems, but it is good to get down to radicals again [the basic forms of words] and find out what the word meant to those simple unsophisticated Christians to whom it was written."[41]

———

Even before Jim's death, Betty's dream of becoming a published writer, her enjoyment of reading biographies, and her feeling that Jim particularly exemplified the Christian ideal had coalesced into the desire to write her husband's biography. Looking over his journals in November 1955 she had told him, "I'm glad I have these. I'm going to need them when I write your biography."[42] After his death, she began reading the journals again almost immediately, with an eye toward writing his story. As she read, she typed out passages for Abe to use in his book, which he was calling *Through Gates of Splendor*, a line from the hymn which the five men had sung together as they set out on their contact attempt.

By late June Betty was working on an outline. At first it had given her "joy" to read the diaries, but as time went on, she told her family, "to saturate myself for an afternoon in his thoughts remembering how God led him (and me) leaves me spent, and heavy in spirit. But the Lord has fulfilled His wonderful Word once more and given the 'garment of praise'. I find nothing more 'balancing' to my vacillating soul than praise, acknowledgement [*sic*] of God's eternal love, wisdom, and faithfulness."[43] Two months later, she had finished working her way through the diaries and wrote to her mother that she was "thrilled with the possibilities" for the book. "Pray that I may do a job which will glorify Christ."[44] She turned next to Jim's letters, beginning with his letters to her. This was even more difficult than the diaries: "The hardest part so far—reliving all the events and emotions again, I nearly hit bottom, but 'there is a lifting up.'"[45]

Betty hoped to use Jim's journals and letters to tell his story primarily in his own words. By mid-September she had culled "direct quotations sufficient to cover several months of Jim's life" and was trying to decide how to connect them.[46] She had seen enough of Abe's manuscript by this time that she knew what she did not want to do: stuff the book with "morals and little personal evaluations."[47] Clarence Hall, the *Reader's Digest* editor who was hoping to condense *Through Gates of Splendor* in the magazine, agreed with her evaluation of Abe's writing, wryly observing to Betty, "A cat is a cat. You don't need to say, 'It's a cat.'"[48] Although Abe had virtually finished his manuscript less than two months after the five men died, he was unable to get it into the form *Reader's Digest* wanted in the time frame the magazine needed; when they published the condensation in August, it was ghostwritten by Hall.

Abe continued to work on the manuscript through the summer. Through Capa he had gotten in touch with a researcher, Jozefa "Zef" Stuart, who came to Ecuador apparently to help with the rewriting process. In early October, Stuart traveled to Shandia to consult with Betty. "I talked to her for hours, of course," Betty reported to her family, "and she read all my manuscript of the biography, looking for information."[49] But the time with Stuart had an unexpected outcome.

"You'd better sit down to read this," Betty wrote to Katharine a few days later.[50] She was coming to New York in less than three weeks. Harper & Brothers, the publisher that held the contract for Abe's book, was getting down to the wire on publication, and they wanted someone, apparently, to come to the city as a consultant. Abe felt unable to leave HCJB, and since Betty had been fairly involved in the project already, she was a logical choice.

With three hours to decide, Betty consulted Marj, who encouraged her to accept. Stuart would pay for Betty's travel through her expense account. Though the invitation at first had felt like "a stunning blow," once she had agreed to go she began to anticipate seeing her mother again. "I look forward with longing to fellowship and sharing with you—perhaps in less than two weeks from today! God is good. He knew the longing which I have felt keenly (I don't know why) since about August or so. His lovingkindness is better than <u>life</u>!"[51]

Betty planned to leave Val with her parents at Birdsong during the workweek while she was in New York and spend weekends in Moorestown with them. She intended to stay only a month—three weeks in New York and one with the Elliots in Portland—and she asked her mother not to share the news. She was not even going to tell the Elliots until she was in the country. "It will just be impossible for me to come if I am to feel that I 'must' see this one & that, & of course speaking engagements are out of the question. Cathers will be here—but I must return immediately, before Christmas, I trust, to help them."[52]

Because she was seeing her parents regularly, there are no surviving family letters from the first part of this trip. But during her time on the East Coast, Betty received another shock. Harper's editor Mel Arnold told her that they wanted her to write the book.

If it had been a "blow" to be asked to leave Shandia, her home, her translation work, her teaching, the school, and her work on Jim's biography for a month, this must have knocked the wind out of Betty. But it was a breathtaking opportunity. She had prayed that "the right impression . . . be given in the publicity" surrounding Jim's death. Here was her chance to have a hand in telling the story. Capa had said that he could never be converted by a Christian book but might be persuaded to believe by the journals of the five men. Here was her chance to give him, and the world, a book sharing the convictions of the men in their own words. She agreed to Harper's terms. The book, when it came out, would not be by Abe Van Der Puy but by Elisabeth Elliot.

So Valerie stayed with the Howards, and Elliot spent November and the first week of December in a fancy hotel suite, writing feverishly. Although the time frame seemed daunting, she found as she worked that the story was so "clear" in her mind that it was not as difficult as might have been expected. She would later remember this as the time when she realized that she was a writer.[53] Capa visited her almost daily, read her work, encouraged her, and appointed himself her cheerleader with Harper's. Because not every voice was as enthusiastic, Mel Arnold began taking Elliot to dinner regularly and checking what she had written in the last few days, and he was also very positive about the quality of her work. And though both Arnold and Harper's author Marguerite Harmon Bro, who had apparently been asked by the publisher to give her opinion on the manuscript, seemed to want to tone down the evangelical specificity of her writing, Arnold backed her up when Elliot insisted that she tell the story in her own way. Arnold and his wife, Valerie, and Cornell and Edie Capa also went out of their way to make sure Elliot had a chance to enjoy the city during her stay. The Arnolds took her out to dinner, and the Capas took her to plays and movies and invited her into their home.

The manuscript was unfinished when Elliot and Valerie left to spend Christmas with Jim's family in Portland. There they were met by a crowd of Elliots, a picture-postcard blanketing of snow, and a whirl of family dinners. Everyone was warm and welcoming, but, she told her mother, "to be in the home Jim loved, where he grew up and played—does things to me."[54] She and Jim had not spent time together in the US as an acknowl-edged couple, and their pre-engagement relationship had taken many ups and downs. Elliot "had looked forward so very much to furlough, when I would be able to meet his friends and relatives, and have the great joy of presenting him to mine. We . . . had so many happy plans."[55] Now she was meeting them without him.

In and amongst family visits, looking through family photos, getting mother-daughter studio pictures with Valerie, and even speaking at a Brethren assembly (to both women and men, which ruffled a few feath-ers—but not enough that the Brethren prevented her from speaking), Elliot spent the rest of her stay in Portland finishing a draft of the book. On December 31 she wrote to her mother, "I finished up the MS. Friday and am having it typed now (at a cost of $55!!) They'll probably send it back to me in Quito for further rewrite—they've moved the publication date up to May now."[56]

Elliot spent the first week of 1957 making the journey back to Ecuador—first a flight across the US, with a layover in Miami where she saw Dave and Peyton DuBose Cole for a few hours, then an international flight. The next week was spent in Quito, taking care of all the things that time in Quito usually entailed. She and Val stayed with Marilou, who had come back to Ecuador after all, and was running a home for missionary children. Olive was also in the country taking care of the last of her possessions, and the five widows managed a brief reunion.

On the first anniversary of Jim's death, Elliot wrote a letter to the How-ards and Elliots:

> A year ago tonight I was a widow, and knew nothing of it. Jim has known the glories of heaven for a whole year—but for him there is no passage of time. If only I could even imagine what it is for him and the others. But

it is as impossible for me as it would be for a fish to imagine the world of air. Only I know that when I get there, I shall be <u>at home</u>. . . .

On the Back Home Hour on Sunday night, the HCJB choir sang, "For all the saints," "We Rest on Thee," and others. Marj gave a testimony, speaking for all of us widows. For those who listened, I suppose they imagine that we have "gotten over it" by now. Nothing could be further from the truth. Quite the contrary, it seems harder for all of us now than it was a year ago. It is harder to face the public composed. Tonight as Marilou and I were putting our babies to bed, she started to cry, thinking how Ed and Jim would have loved their little ones, how proud they would have been. . . .

This past year has brought me to know Christ in a way which would have been impossible had I not "suffered the loss of all things." If I may but win Christ, the price is not too great. But oh, it is not worth any of it if I do not learn to trust Him. How worthy He is to be trusted—for He is my strong Tower. How worthy to be loved—His is an Everlasting Love. His the beauty of the Morning Star. What will it be to see Him? Perhaps 1957 holds that for us![57]

———

In 1957 Elisabeth Kübler-Ross's five stages of loss were still more than a decade in the future. But in reading Elliot's letters and journals, it seems apparent that in returning from the US to Ecuador, and especially to Shandia, she was also moving from a period of grief in which shock and numbness had played a dominant role, to a stage that Kübler-Ross would later label "depression," marked by deep sadness and feelings of emptiness and futility. The year 1956 had been a blurred succession of arrangements and adjustments, conferences and guests, translation and childcare, whizzing by like electric poles out the windows of a speeding car. Now, in the second mid-January with no Jim in it, something was shifting in Elliot. A week after arriving in Shandia she wrote, "Since returning, the reality of what has happened has begun to settle in on me, and sometimes I wonder how I can possibly go on without Jim. The future seems a complete blank to me, and I long either for the appearance of the Lord or of the Aucas."[58]

The passage of time and the vagaries of grief were part of the reason for this shift. So was the living situation she returned to. The Catherses had arrived in Shandia in mid-October, just before Elliot left for New York. Three days after their arrival, she had written cheerfully to Katharine, "I am thankful to God for this further step in His leading for me. I am confident that He sent them here, and it is good to have their fellowship. They are both working on the language already, as they can find minutes between caring for the children. Bill has the work on his heart, and we agree 100% on everything we've discussed so far as policies, methods, etc. are concerned."[59]

But while the two families had the most important things in life in common, it quickly became apparent that they differed in their approach to workaday things, including personal habits, laundry, cooking, childcare, and household management. And while disagreements on big ideas can often be set on the back burner and worked around, daily, repetitive friction intrudes insistently on our attention. Elliot wrote in her journal that she *knew* the things that were bothering her were small things but that they felt harder to deal with than big things. Even in the few days the two families were together before Elliot left for the US, the living situation had challenged her. Coming back to it was difficult.

On the day after her return, she noted in her journal that this was an opportunity to live out the exhortation from James 1:2: "Consider it all joy . . . when you meet trials of various kinds." But it was painful. Though she rarely spoke of it in family letters, journal entries for days afterward contained lists of the things she was continually finding damaged or ruined—dishes, linens, furniture, appliances, plumbing, tools, generator, lawn mower, landscaping. The noise level in the house was difficult as well. The Cathers children were four, three, two, and four months old, and with five children in the house it seemed someone was always crying or shouting. And it was difficult to know how to raise Valerie when the two families had different rules and expectations for behavior. Before the Catherses' arrival, the house at Shandia had been a haven for Elliot. Now it felt like a madhouse. She longed to be alone.

Both Elliot and Valerie, now almost two, got sick almost as soon as they returned. Valerie contracted chicken pox and spent the days fussing and wailing. Elliot had recurring diarrhea, which left her "weak and depressed."[60] She struggled to concentrate through the fog of grief, the exhaustion caused by sickness, the constant noise. But she viewed her struggle not as the result of a physiological response to events but as a failure of self-discipline. She tried hard to rule herself, praying fervently for the grace to live up to what she believed. At the same time, she was casting around desperately for a way to lessen her acute discomfort.

She immediately began to think about leaving Shandia entirely, since to stay and watch the destruction of Jim's handiwork felt unbearable. But none of the alternatives seemed workable. Arajuno seemed too remote and primitive to manage by herself with a toddler, and the priest there had been hostile to evangelicals. Another Brethren missionary, Jean Richards, was already planning to move to Puyupungu. Starting a new station would have at least as many problems as Arajuno. She longed to go to the "auca," but that seemed the least practical of all.

After hashing it all over in her journal for two weeks, she decided she *had* to have someplace to be alone. She had a tiny stilt-house built with one room for Valerie's bedroom and one for her own use, and named it "The Aerie." She asked Katharine to keep the news private: "Please don't spread this far and wide—it makes Cathers feel kinda bad, of course, that they 'forced poor Jim's widow out of her own house which he had built for her with his own hands, etc.' This is their idea—such doesn't bother me. This is the only solution, for the present at least." She closed the letter by saying, "The Lord has given me perfect peace about the future, whatever it is to hold. I love you Mother, and you can't know how much I count on your prayers."[61]

At the same time, her journal records a deepening struggle against despair. Ten days before she wrote to her mother, she made an entry questioning the reality of God's comfort and the meaning of biblical promises. Six days after that she told God she was ready to die for the "auca," quoted Mark 9:24 (KJV), "Lord, I believe, help Thou mine unbelief," and noted the bitter irony of having to put time into caring for her body when she wanted to leave it behind so she could go to Jim. The next day she pondered whether, if she were to be bitten by a poisonous snake, she would seek treatment or accept the opportunity to die. Waking and sleeping she longed for Jim. It seemed impossible, she wrote, that any resurrection could ever come from her living death.

After just three weeks in Shandia, Elliot traveled to Quito for a last review of the edited manuscript for *Through Gates of Splendor*. She stayed with Marj, who, along with Ruth Jordan and Marilou, helped care for Valerie so Elliot could hole up in the attic to write. But when the manuscript arrived she was dismayed. The revised version, she wrote to her parents, "is a change in style, it is non-evangelical in terminology, it is very inaccurate, it is obviously written by someone who has never been in Ecuador, and in all, IT IS NOT MY BOOK." Marj, Marilou, and Olive all saw the manuscript, and, Elliot wrote, all agreed it was "impossible."[62] But she dreaded the thought of yet another rewrite. To make matters worse, the manuscript had arrived with a letter telling her that Harper's had printed galley proofs of this "impossible" version of the book and were already sending them out as advance reading copies.

In response to all of this, Sam Saint, Nate and Rachel's brother, who was acting as US representative for the widows, sent a cablegram to Betty, following it with a letter copied to Harper's and all five women. He agreed that Harper's proposed manuscript was unacceptable, effectively silencing the voices of the men themselves. And he hinted that if Harper's didn't play ball, the families would take their story to another publisher. In the cablegram, which arrived first, he said that he would undertake alternative revisions himself. "I am wondering what he meant by a 'revision,'" Elliot wrote to her parents. "My heart sinks. . . . I hope Sam has nothing extensive in mind. I think we must give Harper an ultimatum—mine, or nothing."[63] She waited uncomfortably for more than two weeks for Sam's revisions to arrive. Not long after they came, Sam telephoned, asking for her approval of his changes: Harper's wanted to print what they hoped would be a final edition the next day. Elliot gave it.

It's unclear what changes Sam ended up making to Elliot's original manuscript. She did have the opportunity to read the final edition and respond to it, but she left no record of her impressions. Whatever the changes to her manuscript that Elliot approved by long-distance call, they must have been minor.

The account that was published bore the clear imprint of Elliot's mind. As Sam had noted in his letter, extensive quotations from the five men were a key part of Elliot's vision for the collective biography from the beginning, and they are the backbone of the published book. This was in keeping with the fact that even before tackling *Through Gates of Splendor*, Elliot had planned to write Jim's biography using his own words. The importance of this technique must have been pressed home by Capa's statement that nothing could express the men's spiritual fervor and commitment so well as their own writings. Only one chapter of the book, as Long points out—the apposite "Silence"—does *not* contain quotations from the five men.[64] Both the first and last words of the book are Jim's.

In telling the men's story to the world, Elliot framed the narrative in terms of the beliefs that had provided her own comfort and sense of meaning during the ten chaotic months between her loss and her decision to write the book: the men had not acted on their own initiative but in obedience to the specific direction of God for their lives. The particular will of God is first mentioned just three short paragraphs into the book, and language emphasizing God's step-by-step leading—over the whole course of the missionaries' lives and in the planning of "Operation Auca"—recurs almost constantly. Two-thirds of the way through, as she described the last few days before the men's departure, Elliot made the remarkable assertion that "God's leading was unmistakable up to this point." A few pages from the end of the book, she stated plainly that the deaths of the five were "what God had planned."[65] Long has emphasized that this "providential focus" is an important difference between the Van Der Puy/Hall version and Elliot's book.[66] It was also a direct reflection of Elliot's long-held understanding of the particular, detailed will and guidance of God.

Throughout the book, Elliot persistently underlines the idea that "once sure of God's leading," Jim and the others were not deterred from obedience by distractions—the opinions of others, talents that might lead in a different direction, family obligations, previous plans or commitments, even their own fear. As she describes the days leading up to contact, Elliot does briefly acknowledge the "devastatingly meaningful" possibility of death, writing of the missionaries' "soul searching" and "counting the possible cost." But just as she always followed admissions of sadness in her family letters with a reminder of God's help, she turns immediately to mention again their "peace of heart," their "confidence," and their obedience. Even her own poignant thoughts as she helped Jim gather his things for departure—"Will this be the last time I'll help him pack? Will this be the last lunch he'll eat in Shandia?"—serve to emphasize the idea of *confident* obedience: "Jim did not look back." The picture that emerges is of a group of people who clearly understood God's guidance for each step and obeyed it joyfully and without hesitation.[67]

Years before, at Wheaton, Elliot had observed—and disapproved of—a tendency in Christian biographies toward sentimentalism. She thought writers tended toward "glossing over . . . discrepancies in character" and "spiritualizing . . . things which perhaps are not very deserving of such treatment."[68] She worked to resist this tendency in the multibiography, including, for example, Roger Youderian's depression and decision to leave the mission field. But as Long notes, in Elliot's eagerness to show the watching world "the genuine and exceptional spirituality" of Jim and his friends, she made narrative choices that also "tended to downplay aspects of their humanity, including any weaknesses they might have had."[69] She essentially left out Wilfred Tidmarsh and Rachel Saint, whose inclusion might have required awkward explanations of personality differences and relational difficulties. She minimized the fear and ambivalence that had touched each family in the days leading up to "Operation Auca" almost to the point of erasing it. She made no mention of the month of "wretchedness" Jim had recorded in his journal just before he left.[70] Elliot was not immune to the pressures that lead writers to make the narrative choices that gloss over and spiritualize their subjects.

In making these choices, the constraints of time and space must have been a factor. Harper's was in a hurry to get the book to the public, and telling a more detailed story would have taken more time. The desire to create a good impression of Christianity, to extend the public testimony of the five men, must have been an influence. And in a very real sense, the book belonged to the other widows as well—they were her friends, and she would have wanted to write a book they would be happy with. But perhaps the most fundamental thing affecting Elliot's treatment of the story was timing. Given the enduring appeal of *Through Gates of Splendor*, and its profound influence on how American Christians have understood the events it describes for over sixty years, it can't be emphasized enough that Elisabeth Elliot wrote the book in just eight weeks, only ten months after the violent death of her adored husband. She had the project dropped in her lap unexpectedly just after she marked her first wedding anniversary without him. She wrote her second draft in his childhood home while celebrating her first Christmas without him. She submitted the manuscript with the first anniversary of his death looming just a week away. Had she written it even a year later, it might have been a markedly different book.

———

When Elliot returned to Shandia on March 8, she brought Capa with her. He was working on a follow-up story for *Life*, timed to coincide with the release of *Through Gates of Splendor*, and he planned to interview the four widows still in Ecuador, along with other missionaries. For the next two-and-a-half weeks, Capa was in and out of Shandia, following Elliot as she worked and taking "roll after roll" of photographs—Valerie playing at her mother's feet as Elliot, dressed in neatly ironed pleated skirt, print blouse, and stylish wedges, teaches barefoot Kichwa schoolboys; Valerie holding on to her mother's skirt while Elliot, in practical tennis shoes, makes the daily radio contact; Elliot, barefoot and in pearls, praying in church with her head covered.[71]

As Capa snapped away, he and Elliot talked. Capa asked questions, still trying to understand the beliefs that impelled the missionaries. Elliot felt he was thinking deeply about spiritual things and responding positively to Christianity. She told her family, "He is too keen an observer to be impressed by the talk of most Christians. He will have to be shown, as an Indian once asked A.C., 'the life of your Lord Jesus.'"[72]

Capa's respectful attitude did not necessarily mean he was a convert. He would later say only that he left Shandia at the end of that visit "a bit shaken."[73] Elliot asked her family not to discuss him with their friends in order to protect his privacy. But, she wrote, "I expect to see him in heaven."[74] Capa's questions, in turn, caused Elliot to think more deeply about her beliefs. Years later, she would say that Capa "hadn't met very many Christians" and "had hardly *heard* of missionaries. He did not know *why* we were there or what it was we were trying to tell these Indians. . . . And in my *desperate* attempts to tell him what Christianity was about, he would stop me, again and again, and say, 'Wait a minute. What does that mean? What are you talking about?'"[75]

Elliot discovered that the vocabulary she had used all her life—growing up in a Christian home, going to church regularly, attending a Christian high school and a Christian college–couldn't convey the things she believed to this talented, intelligent man. It must have been tempting, in communication breakdown between her and the Shandians, whose culture sometimes seemed to her uneducated and superstitious, to assume in the back of her mind that the blame lay more in their failure to understand than in her failure to explain. But with Capa—almost a decade older than she, cosmopolitan, sophisticated, multilingual, successful in a way she could recognize—it began to dawn on her that the root of the problem might lie at her doorstep. After Capa left, Elliot wrote to her family, "I am disturbed about the lack of impact which the Church makes on the world. It is no wonder we are incomprehensible to them. Granted, the preaching of the Cross is foolishness, but there is no need to create our own foolishness [sic] by employing the goobledygook which most of us use so thoughtlessly."[76]

———

Although Elliot had largely kept to herself her desire to try again to reach the tribe whose warriors had killed Jim, she had continued to pray and look for ways to pursue her goal. From the beginning she had wanted to participate in the ongoing gift flights, but the Mission Aviation Fellowship hierarchy had rejected her requests.[77] She had also continued to put out feelers among the Kichwa, looking for any additional information about the "aucas" or their language, but nothing had come of these efforts. Finally in February 1957, during her stay in Quito, she discussed her desire with the other widows. She did not record their response, but it seems to have further strengthened her longing to go; she described in her journal her inability to focus on anything else.

Elliot was well aware that there continued to be many obstacles. Wilfred Tidmarsh had moved his family to Arajuno in the summer of 1956, and this made the Tidmarshes the missionaries closest to the tribe. But Elliot continued to struggle to know how to work with Wilfred. She also had responsibilities to the Cathers family, to the Shandian church, and most importantly, to her daughter, and she was not sure how to reconcile these with her desire for another contact attempt. Then there was the complication of others interested in the same goals, including Rachel Saint, who had access to the only available linguistic source in Dayomæ. And what else might be going on that she was unaware of? Elliot wrote in her journal that the challenges seemed insuperable.

In late March, with Capa tagging along, Elliot set out for Shell Mera, hoping to resolve at least one of these questions by meeting with Rachel. On paper, it made perfect sense for Saint and Elliot to work together. They had much in common, having grown up within 20 miles of each other in devoutly religious families centered around the Bible, church attendance, missionary stories, and enjoyment of nature. When Elliot had visited the American Keswick as a child, Saint, twelve years older, was there working in the dining hall. Each had felt called to missionary work in her teens. Each felt a strong personal call to this specific group. Each had been trained at the Summer Institute of Linguistics, and while Elliot was the stronger linguist, Saint had an established relationship with Dayomæ and knew more about the culture than anyone outside the tribe. But the reality was more complicated.

Although the women had started their relationship on a cordial footing, differences of opinion between them—over SIL policies, for example—had been fraught with potential for conflict from the beginning. Then Saint had been understandably hurt by the decision to exclude her from "Operation Auca," a decision Elliot hadn't liked but had nevertheless been instrumental in facilitating. In March 1956, Elliot had been involved in an episode in which Dayomæ was brought to Shandia in an attempt to gather more linguistic information to use during the ongoing gift flights. It appears to have been something of a nonevent to Elliot, who only made passing reference to it in a family letter, but whoever planned the meeting did not discuss it with Saint, waiting until she was away to carry it out. To make matters worse, a rumor began to circulate afterward that Elliot had accomplished as much in three days as Saint had in three months.[78] In January 1957, Saint was upset again when she read parts of *Through Gates of Splendor* in manuscript and saw little mention of Dayomæ.

In Shell Mera, Saint and Elliot met on more or less neutral ground. Elliot was hoping to collaborate on the language in the short term and perhaps initiate contact together in the long term. She had been wanting to move *now* for months and was actively looking for a way to take immediate steps forward. Saint knew better than anyone outside the tribe the extent of violence in the culture because of her time with Dayomæ, and she knew she wanted to take things slowly in regard to contact. After the meeting, Saint sounded positive but vague publicly, telling SIL's Kenneth L. Pike that the two women had been able to "air out a lot of misunderstandings," and that "the up-shot was she [Elliot] hoped we could have fellowship with each other even if we do not agree about mission policies."[79] Elliot received a less positive impression. She wrote in her journal afterward that Saint had given no indication that she would consider working together, that the sticking point seemed to be Elliot's own concerns about SIL. Airing previous misunderstandings did not fully resolve their differences. Nor did it prevent ongoing miscommunication.

But this did not deter Elliot. Unlike Saint, who was under the direction of a board and in regular consultation with Cam Townsend, Elliot was essentially answerable only to God. Uncomfortable in her current living situation, she restlessly looked to the future, questioning again and again what her next step should be, making list after list in her journal in an attempt to clarify her thinking: Should she keep doing what she was doing? Should she pursue a writing career? Should she pursue the "aucas"? She was sure God intended to reach them, she believed he could work a miracle to make it happen, she was willing that she and Valerie be part of God's plan, she felt she was seeing God's general leading to the tribe in her Bible reading and her ever-growing desire to go. But, she concluded, she needed to wait for specific direction.

A note to her brother Jim as he tried to decide what to do after high school makes explicit Elliot's understanding of God's guidance. "No one can tell another what God wants him to do. Remember that the guidance of God will come to you as you wait in His presence. He will cause circumstances, the witness of the Word, and your own peace of mind to coincide. The decision will be obvious when the time to make it comes (and very likely not before)."[80] A few days later, she would address the idea again in a family letter, saying that God's will, "that hackneyed, nebulous idea we toss about so casually," really comes under two headings, the revealed will for everyone, which is "set forth in the Gospels, in the Sermon on the Mount, specifically," and the specific will in a given situation: "We waste time futilely trying to 'discern' the Will of God in [the latter] without bothering our heads about giving to him that asks, or bearing false witness against our neighbor."[81] Elliot was trying to act in obedience to gospel principles one day at a time in the place where she was, while waiting for circumstances, Scripture, and intuition to make clear her next step. She had tried to move forward through collaboration with Saint and felt that avenue had failed. But that did not outweigh her sense that God was directing her to keep trying for the same goal.

Neither did the ongoing difficulty in her relationship with Wilfred. In early March she had learned through the grapevine that he planned to move again, building a house and runway a few miles from where the five men had died. Although she recognized that the older missionary, who had been on the field a decade longer than any of the families involved in first contact, had likely been hurt when they excluded him from a plan that was, broadly speaking, his invention, she was not particularly sympathetic.[82] After several years of interaction she did not have confidence in his linguistic abilities, his approach to missions, or his decision-making. And though she believed he had formed this plan at least partially in response to pressure from the public and from MAF, who felt obligated to pick up where Nate had left off, she was frustrated with what seemed to her a rash idea. She must have felt he was a danger to himself and others, that he could jeopardize the whole objective. But as a fellow Brethren missionary, he too was essentially responsible only to himself. There was nothing she could do.

From an outside perspective the two missionaries were doing the same thing: pursuing an inherently dangerous course of action in response to guidance that no one else could recognize. Their relationship provides a case study of the difficulty inherent in deciding whose understanding of God will be prioritized and treated as authoritative. Later in the year Elliot would write, "What can you say when a person assures you that this is the <u>Will</u> of <u>God</u>? If it really is, then all difficulties and objections fade. If it is not, it is not up to me to say that it is not."[83]

While she waited for a clear word from God, Elliot continued to put one foot in front of the other. She oversaw the baptism of seven more people, bringing membership in the Shandian church up to fifty-one. She hosted the continual assortment of visitors, supervised station maintenance, and started writing a pedagogical grammar textbook. The variety of her reading—helpful for both her mental health and her development as a writer—was greatly increased when Harper's began sending her "books by the ton."[84] During this time she read Billy Graham; Katherine Mansfield; W. Somerset

Maugham; the "reprobate" Gustave Flaubert;[85] Edna St. Vincent Millay; Amy Carmichael; missionaries J. O. Fraser and Isobel Kuhn; a *Geography of the Bible*; *New Testament Words*; a biography of Mansfield;[86] Herbert Read's *English Prose Style*; a book on Catholic missionaries in Africa called *The White Fathers*; Jim Bishop's *The Day Christ Died*; and Morey Bernstein's account of an American woman who came to believe she was a reincarnated nineteenth-century Irish woman, *The Search for Bridey Murphy*.

Elliot spent much of April traveling, with a week in Quito taking care of all the usual business, and a final meeting with Capa, who sold her one of his cameras and told her "to send him my first six rolls and he'll tell me what I do wrong."[87] He was as good as his word, and she learned a good deal about capturing a meaningful photograph—much harder then than now. From there she drove south through the mountains to Riobamba for another conference for Kichwa-speaking missionaries and then on to Colta for a Bible conference. Ellen Ross, the American Bible Society representative, came back to Shandia with her afterward and spent the next two weeks helping with the existing jungle-dialect Kichwa Scripture translations. With Ross's assistance, Elliot finished translating Titus and made progress on the pedagogical grammar.

As she waited for direction, Elliot continued to remind herself that God had a plan that would become evident when she needed it to. That faith was a choice she was making, not a feeling. After a phone call from Bert underlined again her longing for and distance from Jim, she wrote in her journal that even her hope of heaven seemed foolish to her, and that clinging to it was at this point an exercise in stubbornness. In a family letter a week later she reemphasized the beliefs she repeatedly rehearsed: "The knowledge that this is His place for me, that the state of widowhood is <u>His</u> choice, that this is what I asked when I asked for His will, is stabilizing. The very difficulties are cause for rejoicing in themselves, as the soil in which the fruits of the Spirit may grow."[88]

"Things are quiet in Shandia," Elliot wrote to her family at the beginning of May. The Cathers family had gone to Arajuno to housesit for the Tidmarshes, and it was "a relief to be alone for a while." While Eugenia cared for Valerie, Elliot spent the day at her typewriter. After cranking out "three <u>badly</u> written pages," she turned to study other biographers: "two different biogs of Wm. Carey (who translated the Bible, incidentally into <u>40</u> languages) the new one of Bill Graham, one of McCheyne, and one of Fraser, trying to see how they treated their subjects. No ideas so far as to how to treat mine."[89] Her contract with Harper's had given the publisher first refusal for her next book, but she was not sure they were the right fit for Jim's biography. While *Through Gates of Splendor* had been her attempt to tell the men's story to the world at large, she felt this book should be aimed at the church.

As time went on, it became clear that having the place more or less to herself didn't necessarily make it easier to write. And although she had a tremendous amount on her plate and was attempting creative work under challenging circumstances, she experienced constant guilt over this difficulty. "I find that in some of these long days alone, with nothing to push me, no one to whom I'm responsible on earth (who will 'find me out' if I waste my time, that is, tho' I am aware of terrific responsibility to the Indians and to the folks at home), I can waste time at a terrible rate."[90] Although it had mattered so much that the story of the five men be told well, she could not muster much interest in the apparent success of *Through Gates of Splendor*. When she received her first copy of the book, along with celebratory mail from Harper's cheering the book's high sales and good publicity, she wrote in her journal that she could feel nothing. In fact, the letters and journals describe many of the symptoms of clinical depression: feelings of tiredness, guilt, social isolation, and hopelessness; difficulty concentrating; repetitive thoughts; loss of interest in activities; and a generalized feeling of discomfort.

A brief bright spot came mid-month, when Elliot got permission to accompany Johnny Keenan on a gift flight. She had her first sight of the people she longed to meet and afterward typed up a description of the flight for her father to run in the *Sunday School Times*: the foggy morning, gradually clearing to sunshine; the breathtaking speed of the little plane with its doors off; shouted communication over the roar of engine and wind; a glimpse of the "beloved spot" where Jim was buried; her tears when she recognized a warrior from the five men's snapshots.[91] Four days earlier she had written to the four parents asking them to pray:

They are a constant weight to me. Who is to go, and when? Should I go? What am I waiting for? Sometimes the temptation is strong to pick up Valerie, a Bible, pencil and paper, and start walking. I don't do it. Why? Either because I am afraid of them, afraid of public opinion, or afraid I'd be disobeying the Lord. I don't know my own heart well enough to tell which it is. But I am praying "Here am I, Lord. SEND ME."[92]

After the excitement of the flight came the inevitable letdown. It felt harder than ever to sit at her desk all day, and guilt and loneliness stalked her. She longed for the writing environment she had experienced in New York, then thought with shame of all the books Carmichael had written without ever leaving her mission station. Her family letters continued to share chatty details—errors and misquotations in Capa's *Life* article; her plan to close the school; anecdotes about Valerie, guests, and neighbors; book recommendations. She kept her struggles in her journal. Now that Jim was gone she felt there was no one else who cared to know the kinds of things she recorded there.

Another respite came in June, when Marilou and her boys came to Shandia for a ten-day visit. But when they left, Betty was faced again with her loneliness. She ached for Jim and for everything his presence had meant. Not only had she lost the one person whom she felt cared to know her intimately; she had lost a father for her daughter, a role that had been important in her own childhood. After weaning Valerie so that she could get pregnant again, she had lost the chance to have another child. Sometimes she dreamed at night that she was borrowing babies to nurse. She had lost her sexual partner, and the ache of unfulfilled desire was so strong that she felt overwhelmed by it. She dreamed of that too. Even her identity seemed lost as she was excluded from what she felt was her role as a woman. She was trapped in a liminal space between a past and a future both equally desired and equally unattainable.

After almost two months away, the Cathers family came back to Shandia in the last week of June. At first they said little about the results of their scouting trip, and Elliot concluded that they had not reached a decision. Then one evening about a week after their return, Bill announced that they felt led to make Shandia their permanent home. Elliot had anticipated this possibility and had told them it would be fine with her, writing to her mother at the beginning of the month, "If <u>God</u> wants them here, He'll show them. I frankly don't know what <u>I</u> want. There are advantages and disadvantages both ways."[93] Still, when the decision came, it hurt.

Over the course of July, Elliot used her journal to work out her thoughts and feelings. She accepted Bill and Irene's decision as part of God's guidance for both their lives and her own. But when she read the story of the twelve tribes' refusal to enter Canaan in her morning devotions, she began to feel that it was directed at her and that there was something rebellious in her pain at the idea of leaving the house she had shared with Jim. "Why am I made thus? Intense, sensitive, possessive—why should I care so deeply? Oh that Thy Will should be <u>all</u> I care for!"[94] Five days later she recorded a sense of great joy in her morning time with God, and gladness in obedience. The next day she felt she had received clear direction from God to give the house to the Cathers family, and was at peace. But by evening she was disheartened again—a pattern that she had begun to notice. She wanted a rest, someone to lift her burden of responsibility if only for a while, but she felt that to give in to her desire would be to run away.

The days dragged monotonously on. Elliot and Eugenia had been in conflict off and on for months, and finally Eugenia quit, leaving Elliot with no help with the housework. Although surrounded by people and desperate for time alone, Elliot was emotionally and intellectually isolated. At one point she wrote in her journal that she couldn't think of another person in the entire country with whom she could talk about her writing. She longed for conversation on deeper things. When a University of Tulsa botanist passed through on a specimen-collecting trip, Elliot thoroughly enjoyed the chance to talk to someone with a thorough grasp of a subject—any subject. After Sputnik launched in early October she would write to her family a bit wistfully, "Have any of you seen [it]? Can it be seen with the naked eye? How fast does it cross the sky (as fast as a plane, for example, or faster?) The thought that it is whirling around right over our heads strikes me as quite fantastic. Do you suppose anyone <u>will</u> get to the moon?"[95]

Immersing herself in Jim's writing as she worked on the biography was difficult. Though she was committed to thanking God for each memory as it came, Elliot found she had to take regular breaks from the material, leaving her desk to read her Bible or go for a walk to relax the emotional strain. Even so, she could only manage the task in the mornings. By afternoon or evening, when the morning's encouragement had faded, the pain felt unbearable. "My God!" she wrote in her journal, "How can this go on? This desperate wanting, aching desire, only to be with him, to share every single thought, to touch his forehead, to know his love as I once had it."[96]

In family letters written at the same time, she alluded to her feelings only obliquely, always ending on an upbeat note. "There are times when I feel 'shut up,' with all water withheld—but . . . I am 'dumb, because Thou didst it.' So there is excellent ground for the operation of faith. There is certainly room for nothing else!"[97] Her journal records anxiety and a repeated wish to escape her suffering by dying. Her worst nightmare had happened, and she couldn't wake up.

Despite the pressure of grief, Elliot was actually making steady progress in her writing. By mid-August 1957, she had finished what she called a fourth first draft of the biography and had set it aside in order to polish a final version of the grammar text. She had struggled for months to work out how much of her own writing was "absolutely necessary" to tie together Jim's words, studying biographies, reading reviews "to discover what it is that people do wrong," asking friends for advice and feedback.[98] In the fourth draft she had cut even more of her own words, writing to her family, "In spite of all anyone says, I feel quite sure that I want Jim's writings and nothing more except where absolutely necessary. I feel that these are facts (letters, diaries) and my job is to select them and arrange them in order that the facts themselves interpret the man."[99] The first several pages of the grammar text were already in use by several people who had asked for it, including Gwen Tidmarsh.

But Elliot continued to berate herself for laziness. In mid-September, after a day in which she had been the sole caretaker for Valerie and the four Cathers children, baked bread from scratch, cleaned the big house, and made a medical visit, she wrote in her journal that people said she was working too hard but that she knew she was undisciplined. Her sense of guilt was constant, and she began to be afraid that she would face God with nothing to show for her life. Part of her frustration was tied to her strong desire to finish the biography, a milestone that appears to have been connected in her mind with finally getting permission from God to escape Shandia.

Then with Jim's birthday and their wedding anniversary looming just a week ahead—Jim would have been thirty, and they would have been married for four years—Elliot's hopes for the "aucas" were chilled again when members of the tribe pillaged the little sleeping house at the new station on the Curaray. Wilfred had been in Arajuno nursing a dislocated shoulder, an inconvenience that may have saved his life. The hut was damaged, many of his possessions taken, and the doorway barred with spears. Any hope that the ongoing gift flights had smoothed the way to future contact was dashed.

Elliot continued to work doggedly at the biography. By late October she had the main body of the book finished and had begun on the front and end matter. She kept gnawing and worrying at herself over her pace. She recorded the events of a day: a morning of writing, lunch, a bath for her and Valerie, Kichwa lessons with Irene, the rest of the afternoon spent caring for Val. Then she berated herself for frittering her time away and achieving nothing. On paper she believed homemaking and childrearing were the most important work for women; in practice she seems to have been unable to value the time she spent on these kinds of necessary quotidian tasks.

Elliot's journal also reveals some of her thoughts on prayer. Again and again they record short prayers, sometimes just one or two words—prayers to keep quiet at the right time, prayers simply acknowledging God's presence, prayers for help. On a Sunday night in late October, Elliot wrote that she had spent some time singing hymns and praying, asking God to make her holy and to let her help the "auca"—though she didn't really have any tips for how that could be done—but in any event to send someone to help them. In a letter to her mother, Elliot explained how she believed effective prayer should be directed: "We are beyond their reach, to give the Word yet, and we cannot ask for faith for them as yet, but we can pray for spiritual preparation 1) in the unseen realm behind the Aucas, 2) in the hearts of the Aucas themselves, that they may be prepared to receive the messengers and the message, and 3) in the messengers whom God has chosen. (And I think He probably has them chosen now)."[100]

———

November 1957 seemed to bring a breath of fresh air. Elliot was still not satisfied with the biography, but she did feel she was nearing the end. And an opportunity had come up to get away from Shandia for a few days. Wilfred's response to the ransacking of his hut had been to put barbed wire

over the windows and go on building, but the Tidmarshes had asked Elliot to come to Arajuno and keep Gwen company while Wilfred was at the
building site. After time spent praying to discern whether this was within
God's will, she agreed to go.

Not long after she arrived in Arajuno, Wilfred received a letter from
Cam Townsend about his construction project. Elliot had not been the only
person concerned that Wilfred's perseverance could do more harm than
good. The broader missionary community, particularly MAF and SIL, had
seen the latest raid as a clear warning from the tribe and had been gravely
concerned by his plan to keep pressing forward. But while MAF had sent
circumspect intraorganizational mail urging its missionaries to exercise
caution, Townsend wrote directly to Wilfred, imploring him to stop what
he was doing and wait until Rachel Saint had mastered the language and
translated the Bible for the tribe. He added that he would end any SIL
participation on the project if Wilfred did not cooperate.

Elliot, who saw the letter and sent a copy to her parents, fumed over it in
her journal, seeing it as a continuation of the institutional approach that had
frustrated her for so long. She was particularly annoyed by the suggestion
that SIL would have a Scripture translation soon. Knowing probably better
than Townsend just how far Saint had gotten with the language, she must
have found the assertion ludicrous. Shared outrage seems to have caused
the Brethren missionaries to close ranks, at least for a while: the next day
Wilfred asked Elliot to consider working more closely with him and Gwen,
both in the Kichwa church in Arajuno and on the "auca" language if they
could find an informant. Still uncertain about her long-term plans, Elliot
agreed to extend her stay at least long enough that he could make a second
trip, this time to Quito.

On Wednesday morning at the beginning of her second week in Arajuno,
Elliot had finished teaching for the day and was writing letters when she
heard Gwen calling her urgently. She set aside the chatty family dispatch
she had just finished and went to see what was happening. Two men from
a Kichwa settlement on the Curaray River, about 15 miles into "auca" territory, had come to tell the missionaries that three women from the tribe
had emerged from the forest near their houses.[101]

This seemed the clear instruction she had been waiting for. She felt strongly
and immediately that she should go back with the men and try to arrange to

bring the women out to Arajuno as linguistic informants. Gwen agreed to this and helped her quickly pack a few essentials in a Kichwa carrying net. Elliot threaded another sheet of paper into the typewriter with shaking hands and dashed off a note to let her family know what was happening. Since there seemed to be no good way of carrying two-and-a-half-year-old Val over the rough trail for the six- or seven-hour journey, she was leaving her with Gwen. Knowing that she could be going to her death, she wrote, in the words of Queen Esther, "If I perish I perish, but I am convinced of God's timing. I was not brought here to Arajuno for nothing. I am sure this is what I am supposed to do, and go gladly and with great anticipation of what God is able to do for us. . . . I love you all so much, Betty."[102]

The journey must have seemed to last forever, but in reality they made good time, reaching the settlement an hour earlier than Elliot expected. The youngest of the three women had disappeared again into the forest not long after the men had left for Arajuno, but two were still there, dressed in borrowed clothes. When they saw Elliot, one of the women smiled a Mona Lisa smile. Elliot recognized the other from Nate's photographs. It was the younger woman who had been on the beach with Jim.

Aware that the women might decide to return home at any time, Elliot pulled paper from her bag and began feverishly recording her impressions, hoping to create as complete a record as possible for linguistic and cultural study. She invented names for the women, calling them after ancient queens: "Hepzibah," for the one who had met Jim, and "Hatshepsut." In true Howard form, Elliot immediately shortened these to "Hep" and "Hat."[103] She wrote down everything the women said and did; when there was a lull in the action, she recorded her own thoughts as well. She now identified her strong desire to leave Shandia as having been a sort of premonition and itemized her reasons for being certain she was within God's specific will: her presence in (and Wilfred's absence from) Arajuno at just the right time, her sense that there was an obvious right choice both in regard to going herself and in regard to whether to bring Val, and the fact that she had her camera with her. She was sure this was the miracle she had prayed for and felt she was experiencing the same sense of calm certainty that Jim had evidenced on his last departure from Shandia.

Everything about her present situation made her think of Jim. She was doing what Jim had done, meeting someone Jim had met. It was like being able to reach out and touch a wall with Jim just on the other side. How far the parallels between their situations would run was an ever-present question. She had no illusions about her safety and made a list of things that made it seem death might be coming for her soon, noting that she was caught up on her mail, that she had essentially finished the biography, that Valerie would go to live with Bert and Colleen and have a father figure again. Elliot wrote that she would welcome death as evidence of God's love for her, although if she were seeking it she would already have walked out into the jungle.

For the next four hours, as evening wore into night and the air filled with the sounds of insects and frogs, Elliot continued to note all the women's little behaviors and characteristics. They were carefully groomed, eyebrows completely plucked and hair carefully trimmed. They wore the clothes they'd been given but clearly didn't think of them as a cover for their genitals, re-peatedly exposing themselves with no appearance of either embarrassment or attention-seeking. They responded to cigarettes with disgust and to salt with disinterest. They were familiar with guns but not with whistling. Dogs barked, and one of the newcomers pointed into the trees, talking; Elliot recognized one word, "Muipa," the name of the man responsible for the deaths of Dayomæ's family. A man named Dario and his family had wel-comed Elliot into their home and offered the use of their kitchen. She made herself a cup of instant coffee, bringing her meals since leaving Arajuno to the coffee, two papayas, and half a cheese sandwich. She wrapped up her journal entry for the day by the light of a kerosene lamp, then, while the men of the community sat up with spears, she stretched her aching back out on the bamboo bed and went to sleep.

———

In the small hours of Thursday morning, Elliot was awakened by Hat singing a one-note song. It sounded sad to her, and she wondered whether it was crying rather than singing. With her limited vocabulary she began asking simple questions about their home and their families and trying to tell them about her own family—to explain where her own child was and what had happened to her husband. Sometimes she believed from their response that they understood her, but generally she could not understand even a word of anything they said in reply. The language seemed nothing like Kichwa. Hep was quiet, but Hat told a story with gestures and sound effects that Elliot was sure showed spearing, weeping, and dying. It was tantalizing to be with people who might be able to explain "what happened to Jim and <u>WHY</u>!" and to be fundamentally unable to communicate.[104]

By about 9:30 a.m., the day felt uncomfortably long and empty. In the absence of a radio, Johnny Keenan flew over for a wellness check. While Elliot stood in the open, waving her arms so he could see she was okay, he cut the engine and shouted that Wilfred was on his way. But he didn't arrive. The day dragged on, a day spent surrounded by people, crouched on a small piece of wood in the smoke of a burning termites' nest that did little to deter the massive swarms of biting flies. Finally in late afternoon Wilfred appeared; the two missionaries spent the evening demonstrating the tape recorder and making an audiotape with the women.

On Friday it poured down rain, bringing temporary relief from the biting flies and filling the rivers to the point of impassibility. Wilfred was stranded. The mutual observation society continued, and Hep seemed particularly interested when Elliot hummed or sang. Meanwhile, the host community had been discussing the missionaries' plan to move the women to Arajuno. Concerned that there would be retaliation if the pair left the settlement, they offered instead to let the missionaries build a house in the community.

Elliot felt she should "do <u>anything</u> to take full advantage of this miracle for which we've prayed," but she agonized over the decision.[105] She felt very strongly about not being separated from Valerie for a long period, but she was troubled over whether it was right to subject Val to the hardships involved in joining her, particularly the biting flies, which she herself could scarcely tolerate. And the possibility of another attack was ever-present in her mind. She knew viscerally that the apparent peace of their situation could change at any moment and wrote Arnold at Harper's to explain her situation and reassure him that she had made arrangements for the manuscript to get to him in the event of her death. However, she felt that she did not fear death for herself, and she resolutely reaffirmed her belief in God's providence for her daughter. She felt she could hear her Shepherd speaking. Obedience was the most important thing. She would stay.

The decision was made, but it was not easy to live with. Elliot felt she should not leave even long enough to go back for Valerie, lest the women go back into the forest while she was gone. She suggested that Wilfred stay while she went back to pack and get Val but believed that he had rejected her suggestion, offering instead to send the little girl as soon as possible. But this would mean waiting for either his airstrip to be completed or his house in order to free up Kichwa men to carry the little girl over the rough trail, and Elliot knew how unreliable construction timelines were. By evening, the first shine of excitement was gone, her fastidious personality was worn down by the unfamiliar environment, and she cried with homesickness for Valerie, worried about whether the little girl was feeling loved and cared for. Then she berated herself for weakness and self-pity.

The next day Wilfred went back to Arajuno. Johnny flew over at noon and delivered a telephone by bucket drop so that they could have a conversation—a welcome relief in the intellectual monotony of the day; later he made a second flight to drop mail, her language notebook, and some odds and ends. Otherwise it was another long day sitting in the smoke. On Sunday morning, by popular request, Elliot held a Christian meeting, and virtually the whole community showed up. Afterward she noted that it was the first time she had ever shared the whole story of Jesus's life, from birth to resurrection, with people who had never heard of him before.

On Sunday evening Wilfred reappeared. He had after all approved of Elliot's suggestion that he stay with the two women so that she could go and get Valerie. They spent Monday making another tape—showing the two women photographs from *Through Gates of Splendor* and recording their response. They hoped Townsend would change his mind and allow Rachel Saint to work with them on transcribing and translating the tapes. Elliot wrote to her family, "If the Aucas should leave today, or I should be killed, I would still feel that the greatest longing of my heart had been fulfilled—to have <u>some part</u> in reaching them."[106]

The next day, Tuesday, November 19, she walked out to Arajuno. On the twentieth she was in Shandia, where Marilou and Barbara met her to help her pack her belongings for storage or transport. To her family she wrote of the lovely time she was having with her friends; in her journal, of the sadness she felt at spending her last nights in the home she had shared with Jim. On the twenty-second, waiting for the plane to arrive, she typed a family letter asking for prayer: "I feel my weakness very, very keenly just now—people will I suppose think this is all a great lark for me, big thrill etc. I feel now as though that part is over—and the real battle is about to begin, and I confess to you (just to you all!) that were it not for the certainty that my Shepherd is leading, and I know that the rewards of obedience are far greater than anything I can imagine here, I would not be able to face it. But I go in faith."[107]

———

Elliot left most of her luggage with the Tidmarshes until more men were available to carry it in since the "barest minimum" for a long-term stay had amounted to an alarmingly bulky "three kerosene boxes, three canvas pack sacks, and an aluminum table and two chairs roped together, plus a can of gasoline, machete, carrying net and typewriter."[108] With two men helping her—one to carry Valerie on his back in a wooden carrying chair he had built for the purpose, and one to carry a bag of truly essential supplies—she pressed on again to the settlement. They arrived at about 5:00 p.m., soaked to the skin from fording waist-deep rivers in a drenching rain. The two women were still there, and some men had cleared a site for her house. Dario and his family again welcomed Elliot into their home.

Wilfred left first thing Saturday, and the rest of the day passed quietly. On Sunday, most of the men in the community set out to hunt or fish, and the women went to work in the fields. Honorio and Maruja, Dario's next-door neighbors, went out fishing in their canoe. Elliot took Valerie down to the river to play and bathe with Hat, Hep, and the children of the community. It was still early when Elliot finished her bath. Standing in the river in her skirt and bra, she had just begun to wash her blouse when the forest became pandemonium. On both sides of the river women began shouting and running. Someone yelled: "aucas."

Elliot was flooded with adrenaline. Snatching up Valerie, she ran out of the river, water pouring from her hair and clothes. Dario ran past with his gun. Hat ran after him. As they disappeared from view, Hep, who to all appearances was quite calm, sat down quietly on a rock. Gradually the women of the settlement began to gather around her, and the group, Elliot included, huddled together, "waiting their fate."[109] After a while, when nothing happened, Elliot dressed her little daughter, put on dry clothes, put up her hair, and gathered her camera and notes.

Bit by bit, the community pieced together what had happened. A woman walking home from her fieldwork had noticed a "pile of sticks," then blood on the ground.[110] Looking more closely, she realized the sticks were spears—eighteen spears—in the body of Honorio. Most of the men were still out hunting and had no idea what had happened, but Dario organized a search. It turned up the speared body of the couple's dog. Maruja was nowhere to be found.

Elliot considered following Dario in order to document the killing *in situ* but decided that neither leaving Valerie behind nor taking her were acceptable choices and stayed where she was. (She later wrote privately to Katharine, "I guess my courage just <u>failed</u> at the thought of seeing a duplicate of what Jim must have looked like."[111]) Before noon Honorio's body had been brought home, and the community was gradually gathering at his house as they returned from the day's work. The women were keening, and as more and more returned from the fields the wailing grew louder and louder, making the situation more and more nightmarish for Elliot. Hat was shaking and obviously upset, talking loudly. Elliot thought she could pick out the words for "killing" and "lance." Valerie was hungry, but none of their hosts had any attention to spare to the idea of food. Elliot fought for composure.

It was difficult to think or pray in all the chaos. It seemed crazy to stay, but she could think of examples of God calling people to do crazy things. She turned to her Bible. Jeremiah 42, with its exhortation to the people of Israel to trust God for protection and not to flee for safety to another place, seemed to suggest she should stay; Psalm 32, with its warning against acting like a mule that won't heed direction, seemed to suggest she should leave. She thought about sending a message to the Tidmarshes, but she was afraid she would be pressured to come out and felt strongly that she had to follow God, not people.

As more men returned over the course of the afternoon, people began to argue about the cause of the killing. Many, including Dario, seemed to think the presence of the missionaries had caused the trouble and wanted her to go. Elliot argued back and forth with herself in her journal. She wanted desperately to leave, especially when she looked at her little girl. She wrote down Psalm 73:26 (KJV): "My flesh and my heart faileth: but God is the Strength of my heart, and my portion forever."

After a sleepless night for the whole community, Elliot decided to go. The bulk of her supplies had not arrived—and would not, once the carriers learned the news—and Valerie was almost out of powdered milk. Many community members continued to feel that her presence was dangerous. And the men from Arajuno who had agreed to build her new house had decided to go home because of the attack. If she went with them, they could carry Val. They set out at 6:30 a.m., taking Hat, who seemed suddenly eager to go, and leaving Hep, who seemed uninterested in accompanying them, with Dario's family.

Back in Arajuno after just two days, Elliot stayed with the Tidmarshes, and Hat with the family of Venancio Tapui, who had moved to Arajuno to teach in the school there. Though the other woman seemed happy enough, Elliot had no way of knowing what she really thought of the arrangement. As for herself, she was already having misgivings about her choice to leave the Curaray, even questioning in her journal whether the apparent lack of guidance now was punishment for missing God's direction. Problems that had seemed endurable when she thought of her stay in Arajuno as temporary loomed large when she envisioned staying long-term. Not least among these was communication with Wilfred. She thought at first he was giving her mixed signals: wanting to work together, urging her to leave Arajuno, disapproving strongly of her desire to go back to the settlement. Only gradually did she realize that he wanted to get Hat farther from the Curaray, not closer. He suggested Shandia, but going back seemed almost unbearable.

The three-part framework Elliot used to make decisions—"circumstances, the witness of the Word, and . . . peace of mind"[112]—seemed divided against itself. Her own strong sense was that she should go back to the Curaray. Much of her Bible reading seemed to encourage this as well—"Verses . . . about not fearing, about God's giving me possession of the land, etc."[113] But circumstances, in the form of Wilfred's adamant opinion, were against it. Although she was determined to follow God's leading in the face of any opposition, and although she could easily have set aside the older missionary's opinion as less important than her own intuition and "the witness of the Word," she did not decide that two out of three was good enough and go ahead with what she wanted to do. She could not bring herself to think that she should return to Shandia, but she set about pursuing any possibility for the future that might satisfy both Wilfred and herself.

She wrote to Rachel Saint immediately, hoping that they could get Hat and Dayomæ together for more effective language study. Though she believed that Saint had declined to work with her at their last contact, she hoped that the presence of an additional informant would change that. She still wanted to work with Saint as long as she herself was not expected to abide by SIL's rules or participate in what she privately called "publicity stunts."[114] It must have seemed that Saint, who had traveled to the US with Dayomæ almost nine months before after months of pressure from Townsend, was stuck in a never-ending publicity stunt. Townsend had designed the trip partly to raise money and awareness and partly to get Dayomæ away from the increasingly unpredictable Carlos Sevilla.[115] It had been supposed to last no more than the twelve weeks of Dayomæ's initial visa. Elliot could not know that Saint had been trying for eight months to stop the publicity tour so she and Dayomæ could get back to linguistic work—or that when Saint learned that two women from Dayomæ's tribe had come out of the jungle, she had begun trying even harder to get out of the US so the three women could meet.

Just as Elliot and Tidmarsh had made tape recordings of the two women in hopes that Saint and Dayomæ might help to translate them, Saint and Dayomæ immediately made a recording to be played for the women. And at virtually the same time that Elliot was writing Saint, Saint was composing a letter to share information that might be of use to Elliot and Tidmarsh. But Townsend and Wycliffe Bible Translators vetoed Saint's request to go back to Ecuador, apparently fearing it would compromise the attempt to free Dayomæ and her young son from Sevilla's patronage, and that it would look to the missionary community as if they were trying to horn in on Brethren territory. It appeared that door was closed, for both the missionaries.

In early December, a messenger arrived from the Curaray Kichwa community to announce that they were abandoning their settlement and moving north out of the other tribe's territory. This seemed the solution to all Elliot's problems. If she moved with them, she could live in the same house with Hat. She could get the indigenous woman farther from Catholic priests and gawkers who might approach them in more heavily populated areas. She herself could have some relief from the pressure of other missionaries' personalities. And it would satisfy Tidmarsh's desire to get Hat farther from her dangerous tribe. But when Elliot made the extraordinarily difficult journey to the new location to see if this was a possibility, the community made it clear that they did not want her or Hat with them. In fact, they put Hep in Elliot's care as well, charging the missionary two hundred sucres for the women's room and board. During this period Elliot finally learned the women's real names. Her companion for the past several days was Mæncamo; the woman who had met Jim was Mintaca.

Another disappointment followed close behind. Members of the Kichwa community asked the missionaries to fly over their abandoned settlement and check for signs of life, as the group had become separated in the course of the move. Hobey Lowrance took Elliot and Tidmarsh over the houses, which still looked deserted, then flew over the area where they had been dropping gifts to see whether the "auca" had burned their houses and moved after the killing of Honorio as they had after the killing of the five missionaries. There, though they could do nothing to rescue her, they saw Maruja, the kidnapped woman. And there, apparently wearing Ed McCully's old sweatshirt, was "George," the man who had been on the beach with the five men. He threatened the plane with his spear.

This was a heavy blow. The missionaries had filtered their understanding of the tribe's behavior through their own hierarchical and consensus-driven cultural paradigm. Against an expectation of consensus and conformity, a peaceful contact followed by violence had been puzzling. The idea of factions within the tribe had been a way to make sense of the facts—perhaps one group, represented by "George," was receiving the gifts and wishing for contact, while another, represented by Muipa, whom Dayomæ so feared, was doing the killing. Even after Honorio's death, the missionaries had hoped they would soon be able to successfully contact the peaceful group. Now behavior that had appeared friendly seemed a mask for ongoing hostility, apparently motivated only by fear or greed. Lowrance and Tidmarsh both came away from the flight convinced that the risk of attack made it too dangerous for everyone involved for Mæncamo and Mintaca to remain any longer in Arajuno.

"So the only way open to me now is to return to Shandia," Elliot wrote resignedly.[116] By December 10, she was living in the house of Kuwa, Eugenia's father, right by the river, a brisk walk from the house Jim had built. The location provided familiar food, familiar occupation, and access to running water for Mæncamo and Mintaca, and allowed Elliot to stay right with them. She was surprised to notice how much more she could learn about Kichwa culture too, when living with a Kichwa family. She had a tiny kitchen room built on to the bedroom Eugenia's family had provided, with enough space for a small writing table; it would enable her to work on Jim's biography and give her a place to set down utensils when she mixed Valerie's milk. But the repeated high-stakes decision-making and long, difficult hikes with scanty access to food of the past weeks, the second anniversary of Jim's death looming less than a month away, and the unpredictability, disorganization, and absence of privacy in her new life made this, as she wrote in her journal, one of the most difficult periods of her life so far.

Her new home reminded her constantly of early married life in Puyupungu, and hence of Jim. As she adjusted to living and eating in a Kichwa environment she developed a sore mouth and for a while could hardly eat at all. And the prolonged upheaval and frequent separations had unsettled Valerie. When she was with her mother, she was scared of the farm animals, upset by the biting insects, fussed for food Elliot couldn't provide, and wanted to go play with the Cathers children. When she stayed with the Catherses, Elliot missed her and worried about her training. And the little girl came down with one ailment after another—worms, mites, parasitic amoebas, bacterial infection, athlete's foot, pink eye, and ringworm, which, as fungal infections do, seemed to take forever to eradicate. Sometimes it felt to her harassed mother as though Valerie cried all day long. There was no way Elliot could make progress on her language work. But she realized the situation must be very difficult for the little girl, and she worked hard to set aside her other tasks and give her daughter as much snuggling and affection as she wanted, praying all the while for God to fulfill the promise of Psalm 68:5 and be a father to the fatherless. As they gradually settled in things began to get easier, and when several weeks later Valerie was treated for parasites, her mood greatly improved again.

Elliot, Wilfred Tidmarsh, and Rachel Saint, who was still in the US, continued to correspond, and Saint sent them the grammar material she had gathered so far. But the relationship between the missionaries continued to be stilted. Although Elliot realized working from a tape would be slower than working with an informant, she could not understand why it was taking so long for Saint to share information from the tapes of Mintaca and Mæncamo. After all, she had more than a year with the language under her belt. Elliot was impatient to learn whether the tapes contained news of Jim. She began to wonder whether Saint did not understand the language as well as it had appeared—or whether the other woman might be withholding information.

Then, too, Elliot and Tidmarsh were wrangling over just how to interact with Saint and SIL. Unlike Tidmarsh, Elliot was hesitant to communicate candidly, worried about being expected to abide by SIL's policies. Though she wanted Saint to return to Ecuador and come to Shandia, she deliberately did not make a formal or direct request, believing SIL would take such an invitation as a concession, or feel that it somehow gave them the upper hand. She hoped the other woman's own self-interest would be strong enough to bring her without an invitation. Meanwhile, unbeknownst to the Brethren missionaries, Townsend had explicitly directed Saint not to work with Elliot unless she received just such a clear invitation.

Nevertheless, life began to settle into a routine again. In the mornings Elliot did language work. In the afternoons she made a fair copy of the biography, committing to plow through ten pages a day. She also set herself a schedule for responding to mail—seven letters a day—to deal with the continuous flow of letters, mostly from strangers. Some were encouraging; many were odd, frustrating, or downright funny—invitations to dental school, requests to send a talk to be given at a large meeting in Singapore, a chatty letter from a family who had named their cows after the five widows. Many praised her, or *Through Gates of Splendor*, but these increased her sense of loneliness, making her feel that no one really knew her.

Her books she kept at the Cathers house, bringing down just a few at a time to her riverside room. She was reading Carmichael's *Walker of Tinnevelly* and more George MacDonald. She wrote to her family that she was greatly helped by MacDonald's depiction of "simple men and women in whom the image of Christ is clear because it shines through simple <u>deeds</u>. . . . The life of Jesus, as we find it in the gospels, is the pattern given us to follow. We have swung too far on the matter of 'reckoning ourselves dead,' 'taking it by faith,' the victorious life, etc. 'Faith without works is dead,' and for me, in these days, I have found a need of simple <u>doing</u>."[117] She continued to puzzle over how to put this into practice, pondering what in her days was necessary and what was getting in the way of showing "the image of Christ."[118]

Elliot and Valerie celebrated Christmas with the Cathers family, and Elliot was moved by the thoughtful gifts sent by other busy missionary families, though she worried guiltily that people were pitying her. On New Year's Eve she wrote wistfully in her journal of how much help Jim would be in the language work but reminded herself that God had good reasons for her loneliness. A week later she briefly noted the anniversary of Jim's death in her journal. She helped deliver several babies during this time, including a first successful breech delivery and Eugenia's first baby, Philip. Eugenia, who had worked for Elliot off and on since 1954, had helped Elliot in her own postpartum time with Valerie, and it was "a real joy" for Elliot to be able to care for Eugenia and little Philip in the same way, though at the same time it made her heart ache for Jim and the children she would never bear.[119] She continued to find hope and comfort in the Bible. When she learned that a family friend's baby had died, she wrote, in a poignant letter that is strikingly different from her response to others' sufferings years before:

> If one's faith were not founded on the Rock, one could echo the bitter words of Caitlin Thomas (wife of poet Dylan)—"One thing I have irrefutably proved, that however immune you may think yourself to be, to the bag of tricks in store, you need not worry, He will get at you, thro' some faultily cemented crevasse, and twist the needle."
>
> But I just read that wonderful story of Lazarus. It is an answer. So far as Mary and Martha were concerned, things could not have been worse. And the worst, most difficult part to bear, was that if only—Jesus could have prevented the death. . . . Even when He arrived, and gave the command, they knew better than He—didn't he realize that things were hopeless? Why, decay had set in. No. There was no chance now. What good could possibly come from this? And His great words: "If thou shouldst believe, thou shouldst see the glory." So faith is the ONLY answer. It is a question of simply believing, or denying oneself peace.[120]

———

After six weeks in Kuwa's home, Valerie was speaking Kichwa fluently, right down to "the proper noises which put babies to sleep."[121] But Elliot's progress in Mæncamo and Mintaca's language was agonizingly slow. Her initial hope that Saint's materials would lead to faster headway had quickly vanished, and she could still pick out only a handful of words. Aside from regular work in Eugenia's family manioc field and frequent baths in the river, Mæncamo and Mintaca had little to do, and Elliot spent long hours listening to Mæncamo talk, often peering into her mouth to see how she was forming sounds, but she could catch so little. She ached to be able to have a real conversation with the women. "I know exactly what Rachel meant," she wrote to her family, "by saying 'I'm worn out with not understanding.'"[122]

Adding to this frustration, she still had no clear sense of direction beyond the present moment. She began to have niggling doubts about the fact that not one, but two missionaries were pouring all their time and energy into a language spoken only by a dwindling handful of people. Although she was relieved to learn that Saint was apparently collaborating with Pike on her analysis, she was unsettled by letters from both Saint and Townsend that seemed to obfuscate more about their own plans than they made clear. Rather than trying to clear things up with the other missionaries through direct communication, she tried to follow the exhortation of Hudson Taylor to "move man, through God, by prayer alone."[123] She reminded herself that just as Mary and Martha had not needed to understand what Jesus was doing to obey, so she too could leave the reasons with God and simply follow orders.

The long-awaited translation of the language tapes arrived at the end of January 1958. It was extremely difficult to follow, but Elliot hastened to share what little there was with her and Jim's parents and the other widows. She typed up a slightly abridged version, leaving out only the most repetitive and unintelligible portions. A few themes emerged with stark clarity. Spearing, fear, crying, death, orphaned children, bereaved parents, kidnapping, running away, spearing, burial, killing, death, spearing, weeping, blood. The words appear again and again until the reader feels battered by horror and grief. Elliot concluded her letter:

> You, probably, like me, are disappointed that there is not more about the five fellows. It is almost impossible to tell where the scene is and who are the characters in most of this, as you see. . . . But it certainly gives us a picture of the Auca life, doesn't it? Life means one thing: death.[124]

As far as Elliot could tell from the transcript, it appeared that Mintaca and Mæncamo had fully expected when they came out to the Kichwa settlement that they might be killed and eaten, but the life they were leaving seemed to carry just as much risk. "I could cry," Elliot wrote. "How I thank God for the love those Curaray Indians showed them, and I pray that I may be given wisdom to know <u>how</u> to show mine when I cannot communicate."[125]

In February Elliot mailed the manuscript for Jim's biography to Harper's. She still wasn't happy with it but felt "entirely too immersed" in language study "to know which end is up as far as the book goes."[126] She hoped that Mel Arnold, who was in charge of seeing it to press, would be able to "tell me what's wrong."[127] And she began to have occasional glimmers of hope about the language. Although always afterward she would go back to feeling that "progress is still unnoticeable,"[128] her letters home were littered with little tidbits of new information. She was able to identify a few more words and even suffixes—although it was almost more frustrating to know what the women were talking about but not what they were saying about it. The translated tapes also revealed that Mintaca and Mæncamo were Dayomæ's aunts; as Elliot began to piece together more of their family tree, she was able to fit in the others who had been on the beach with the five men.

Although Elliot's little house gave barely enough room to turn around, she continued to have a steady stream of visitors. Townsend and Tidmarsh both made short visits during this time, and Dave and Jean Richards Cooper, Mardelle Senseney—a missionary with the Gospel Missionary Union who had a long-standing interest in the Waorani—and Marilou McCully with her boys and Ed's parents came severally for longer stays. At the end of February, Elliot threw a third-birthday party for Valerie "with a pink cake and candles, pink lemonade, and some gifts the Mc's had brought."[129] She worked to balance her desk work and linguistic work with parenting work, describing in a letter to her mother how she tried "to take every opportunity to show Val the Lord's beautiful world." "We go outside in the starlight, sit and sing hymns. She asks about the different jungle sounds, learns names of toads and things (in Quichua, since I don't know the English for most of them), brings me flowers, etc. As for what you could send that would help—books, books, and books!"[130] Children have little concept of a "workday," and Valerie ran in and out of her mother's working space, sharing whatever was on her mind. Elliot sometimes stopped what she was doing for a moment to write down something cute that Valerie said or did, and the little girl loved to take advantage of the pause to work her way up into her mother's lap, "write" in her notebook, and enjoy her undivided attention.

By mid-March, Elliot had memorized all the verb forms shared by Saint and was beginning to tease out some forms for herself with Mæncamo's help. She also began making her own transcription of the tape of Mæncamo speaking that they had made on the Curaray. Saint had supplied a tape of Dayomæ repeating Mæncamo's words that was apparently what her own transcription and translation were made from, and Elliot had worked from that first. Now as she tackled the original recording, she did a side-by-side comparison of her transcription with Saint's. Working from the tapes was difficult at best, but Dayomæ at least enunciated in a way that came through better on tape. Mæncamo's voice was a "muffled, throaty mumble."[131] Nevertheless, as Elliot's ability to understand gradually increased, she began to wonder if she was hearing things that did not appear in Saint's transcript. She was careful to remind her family that any bits of information she shared with them were still only guesswork.

Although Saint's materials had not contributed to a major step forward in her own progress after all, Elliot continued to hope that eventually she and Saint would be able to get the three informants in one place. She believed most of the difficulty in their relationship lay with Townsend, and that if and when he gave permission, their collaboration would provide a breakthrough in the language. So she was pleased to learn that Townsend had finally managed to bring Dayomæ's son to the US, effectively removing them both from Sevilla's patronage and clearing a major obstacle to Saint's return to Ecuador. Elliot reported with satisfaction that she was expecting the women in early summer. But she was bewildered by a rumor that had begun to circulate, that she was resistant to cooperating with Saint. On the contrary, she told her mother, she desperately wanted Saint's help and was trying hard not to write her too often out of deference to what she understood to be Townsend's request to leave her alone to work on Bible translation without distraction.

In mid-April, Elliot received word that Mel Arnold would be in Shell Mera before the end of the month to work with her on the biography. In a few days, she and Valerie, with Mæncamo and Mintaca, were on their way to meet him. Elliot had heard that *Reader's Digest*'s Clarence Hall had read her manuscript and suggested major changes, and that just as with

Through Gates of Splendor, voices within Harper's—such as Marguerite Harmon Bro's—were arguing for considerable revision. She worried that she would have to fight to tell Jim's story the way she wanted to. But to her relief, Arnold seemed prepared to back her decisions. After working steadily for a week and a half, she wrote to the Howards and Elliots, "I have tried very hard to put in the personal descriptions which everyone seemed to want, but I have not changed the purpose, or my basic policy of letting Jim do all the talking."[132]

Just before leaving Shandia to meet with Arnold, Elliot had a gripping conversation with Mæncamo. She understood the older woman to say that she and Mintaca wanted to go home and that Elliot could go with them. Preparing for this possibility became a top priority for Elliot.

———

The final version of Jim's biography was indeed much as she had sketched it in her letters from the beginning. Bookended with a preface, prologue, and epilogue, it broke the twenty-eight years and three months of Jim's life into four parts: family history and childhood, college, the almost three-year period between graduation and sailing, and the not quite four years in Ecuador. It relied heavily on quotations, primarily from Jim but also from his friends and family, with several pages at a time held together with just a few words—"From the journal," or "To me, he wrote."[133] Often stretches of two and three pages were Jim's words alone. The epilogue was, as Elliot had envisioned, primarily a repository of Jim's words that had not fit into the narrative. But the book was more than a collection of Jim's writing. Both through the selection and arrangement of quotations, and through her own words in the front and end material, the book is unmistakably shaped by Elliot's mind.

Shadow of the Almighty opens with a passage from J. B. Phillips's translation of 1 John, emphasizing practical obedience as the hallmark of Christian faith. Here is the idea that had stood out so sharply to Elliot in her reading over the past months, especially in MacDonald's work. She explicitly repudiates the idea that the men were martyrs, a term that had been plastered over the promotional materials for *Through Gates of Splendor*, and that she herself had used in the earlier book's acknowledgments and in her letters.

Instead she tries to remove the halo of especial holiness from Jim's life and death, claiming for him the kind of basic obedience John describes and offering a scathing indictment of a "Christendom" that would see such obedience as "extraordinary."[134]

In the prologue, Elliot gave a fictionalized account of the events leading immediately to her husband's death, embellishing the available facts with thoughts and motives—guessed at from her own cultural perspective but ascribed to indigenous actors—far beyond what she had any way of knowing. She began and ended this section with what have become the best-known words Jim ever wrote, his paraphrase of seventeenth-century nonconformist minister Philip Henry: "He is no fool who gives what he cannot keep to gain what he cannot lose."[135] (She also used this quotation chronologically in the main body of the book and a fourth time in the epilogue.) With this she argued that Jim's death was no extraordinary sacrifice: he had only lost a life bound to end someday, one way or another, and in so doing had gained the unending "weight of glory" spoken of by the apostle Paul (2 Cor. 4:17).

Elliot sketched Jim's family history with a few deft strokes, establishing him as a descendant of pioneers and good, plain Christians. Jim's natural confidence and outspoken personality quickly emerge, encouraged by parents who took a hands-off approach to raising him from the time he turned fourteen, and friends who cheerfully followed in his wake. In college, with letters home to his parents, Jim's own voice begins to fill the page, heavily supplemented by excerpts from the journal he began keeping in his junior year. The greater part of his well-known sayings comes from this time of youthful zeal. Jim's boldness, enthusiasm, and certainty that he recognized God's specific leading correctly—even despite his inability to articulate reasons for his conviction—are recurring themes. One can see why this self-assurance would have been attractive to the often-diffident Betty Howard.

Source material from Jim became more sparse in the period after their marriage, and Elliot's voice necessarily more prominent in explaining his thoughts and actions. She emphasized that his choices were made through the application of principles he had learned in study and prayer and highlighted the decision-making rubric she believed in: "Scriptural principles, God-directed circumstances, and Jim's own inward assurance were consonant."[136] She mentioned the struggle and discouragement of the last month of Jim's life and characterized it as spiritual warfare, through which he had persevered.

Elliot made clear that she had consciously tried to avoid the hagiography so common in Christian biographies, to show instead a real human being with strengths, weaknesses, and flaws. She chose quotations that show a range of emotions from ecstasy to deep discouragement, and of thoughts from sublime to foolish. She even included the story of the renaissance that had given her so much heartache. But painting a full picture of someone she loved and revered was hard to do—not because she wasn't honestly trying, but because it was hard for her to see her subject from any perspective other than her own.

In writing of the renaissance, Elliot spoke of Jim's behavior vaguely. Of the most questionable activities—the "kissing incidents," for example—she said nothing, so that the "license" that Jim condemns himself for ends up sounding like nothing more than a relaxing of overscrupulous standards in order to enjoy some good old-fashioned fun. In fact, because the section begins with a Bible verse that appears to support Jim's decisions and ends with his description of the spiritual growth he felt he experienced during the renaissance, the general tenor of the chapter comes across as positive, despite the fact that Elliot and others had been deeply grieved and concerned by his behavior at the time, and he himself had heartily repented of much of it. Other passages that are supposed to show the full picture of his humanity—discouragement, or strong sexual desire, or feelings of guilt and self-condemnation—ultimately serve to emphasize his exemplary spirituality. When he is discouraged, it is over not being passionate enough about God. When he experiences sexual desire, he does not let it derail his commitment to wait for God's direction. When he examines and condemns his behavior, it shows the sensitivity of his conscience. And so on.

Meanwhile, aspects of Jim's behavior that might justifiably give the reader pause are displayed positively. When Jim pursued a romantic relationship despite feeling called to celibacy, for example, Elliot saw a commitment to moment-by-moment obedience rather than inconsistency. When Jim decided that the Shandians had gotten enough opportunities to learn about Jesus, that "their blood was now upon their own hands" and he was going to a new tribe, Elliot saw dedication to the Bible verses known as the Great Commission rather than the youthful immaturity suggested by his impatience for visible progress during the brief, interrupted two-and-a-half years he had worked in Shandia.

So Elliot's understanding of Jim, which frames the terms in which the reader comes to Jim's thoughts and actions, emphasizes his status as a role model. The Bible verses she chose as epigraphs to each chapter do the same, suggesting that Jim's life during the period in question exemplifies or is described by Scripture. And the epilogue, which ends with two-and-a-third pages of unbroken excerpts from Jim's writing, drives the point home. The quotations are what one would expect to find in the journals of a young, enthusiastic person, raised in a Holiness milieu, who had spent most of his life in an essentially religious peer group. In other circumstances, sprinkled through the five years of writing they were compiled from, they would be unremarkable. But crammed together cheek-by-jowl and taken in light of his death, his writings about sacrificing everything for Christ sound prescient, fey, "fraught with new meaning," as Elliot put it.[137] Although she argues at the beginning of the book that dying for Christ was really no different from taking up your cross daily and that Jim's life and death were an example of basic obedience, the relentless pounding of his words about blood, fire, altars, and death—untempered by, for example, his prayer that God would let him live to love Betty—make him sound very different.

The framework that Elliot used to tell the story of the five men's deaths in *Through Gates of Splendor* remains the same in *Shadow of the Almighty*, emphasizing God's guidance, asserting unambiguously that Jim died because he obeyed God's clear direction. But within that structure there are hints of movement in her understanding. In the last chapter of *Through Gates of Splendor* she had written definitely of "lives . . . changed" by the deaths of the five men, the certainty that the people they had died to reach would someday "join us in Christian praise." In the biography's epilogue, which opens with a quotation from British writer W. Somerset Maugham, she pondered her late husband's legacy with more diffidence, deciding that Jim's legacy is the story of his life, a life committed to obedience to God. She wrote, "The interest which accrues from this legacy is yet to be realized," only "hinted at" in those affected by hearing his story. In *Through Gates of Splendor* she had stated confidently that "this was not a tragedy" because "this was what God had planned." Now she included a quotation from Jim that seemed to suggest that tragedy and God's plan could coexist.

Granted, fate and tragedy, aimlessness and just-missing-by-a-hair are part of human experience, but they are not all, and I'm not sure they are a major part, even in the lives of men who know no Designer or design. For me, I have seen a Keener Force yet, the force of Ultimate Good working through seeming ill. Not that there is rosiness, ever; there is genuine ill, struggle, dark-handed, unreasoning fate, mistakes, "if-onlys" and all the Hardyisms you can muster. But in them I am beginning to discover a Plan greater than any could imagine.[138]

———

After just over two weeks of revision work on the biography, Elliot, Valerie, Mintaca, and Mæncamo set out on the first leg of a sightseeing tour that would take them west and south through three different cities in the mountain region of Ecuador on their way to the bustling modern seaport of Guayaquil in the coastal zone. As far as Elliot knew, none of them were particularly excited about more travel, but it seemed important for the indigenous women to be able to tell the rest of their community "something of the outside world" should they decide to return home.[139]

This trip also helped to cement Elliot's opinion, erroneously, on an aspect of Mintaca and Mæncamo's language. Elliot had apparently known for some time that the people she was calling "aucas" referred to themselves as "Wao" (singular) or "Waorani" (plural). But she had shrugged it off. "It simply means 'person,'" she told her mother, noting that Mæncamo had seen small houses made of grass in the mountains and asked if "Waorani" lived in them.[140] To Elliot this made it seem that the word was not a proper name, since it was unlikely Mæncamo believed any of her own tribe might live in mountains she had never seen before. This assessment oversimplified the situation. As anthropologist James Yost has pointed out, throughout history and around the world groups have tended to have one term for themselves, meaning, roughly, "the people," and another for everyone else, "the outsiders."[141] In fact, though Elliot may not have known it, "auca" appears to have been just such a word, used originally by Ecuadorian Kichwa speakers to refer to any group that was not themselves.

By the eighth of May, the group was back in Shandia after more than two weeks of travel. A whole pile of mail was waiting for Elliot, everything from

an invitation from Capa to participate in a *Life* feature on Dayomæ, to another request to make a dramatized movie from *Through Gates of Splendor*,
to a letter from Marj, who was trying to decide whom to have write Nate's
biography. There was also a letter from Rachel Saint, urging Elliot strongly
not to ask Mintaca and Mæncamo for more information about the deaths
of the five men. Elliot did not speculate in her family letter over why Saint
might have asked, seeming mildly annoyed over what may have felt like an
attempt to control something that wasn't hers to control. Saint was finally
making travel arrangements to return to Ecuador, and although Elliot still
believed Townsend was getting between her and Rachel, she kept hoping
he would agree to Rachel bringing Dayomæ to see her relatives. In fact,
Elliot had relented and issued a direct invitation, sending multiple letters
to that effect. She had received no answer. But now there was a letter (*not*
from Rachel, although Elliot did not record whom it *was* from) saying that
Saint would *not* come to Shandia after all.

Elliot continued to struggle with an overwhelming sense of her own
sinfulness; with exhaustion; with longing for Jim. She kept dreaming about
him, and waking was agony. In her journal she wrote of his death as God's
punishment for her inadequacy. Nevertheless, she continued to work on
the Waorani language using all available sources, including the phonemics
paper put together by Saint and Pike. And Mintaca and Mæncamo's conversation seemed to her to have changed. It had seemed that they talked
of almost nothing but who had been killed and how. Now it appeared that
they talked mostly of going home and what they would say to their family
members when they returned. As far as she could understand, the women
continued to talk about taking her with them, and to reassure her she would
be perfectly safe.

On May 15, Elliot noted the six-month anniversary of meeting Mintaca
and Mæncamo in her journal. The combined force of her own desires,
Bible reading, and circumstances—such as the women's interest in going
home—seemed to indicate clearly that God was going to grant her prayer
and allow her to be an instrument for the realization of her and Jim's
dreams for the Waorani. God's voice in Scripture was one of the essential
parts of her three-legged decision-making stool, and she often recorded
in her journal the verses that seemed to be part of her direction. During
this time she was reading the book of Nehemiah. She made a special note

of Nehemiah 9:24 (RSV), in which a group of Levites, praying aloud the history of their nation during a public gathering after the rebuilding of the city wall, recounted the story of God bringing them into the land of Canaan: "Thou didst subdue before them the inhabitants of the land." She followed it with a prayer claiming this passage as a promise to her and a statement of already accomplished fact.

Elliot typed up a prayer letter to the four parents, the four widows, Doreen Villarreal, and Mardelle Senseney telling them she had been apparently invited several times to go home with the women. "It is crystal clear to me that this is the thing God wants me to pray for, and prepare for. I expect there will be testings and difficulties before its realization, so I ask you all to pray with me in the meantime. . . . For now I am being tested in the matter of patience!"[142] She found it harder than ever to settle to her work and began making lists of things to take with her. She wrote to her mother asking for things like food concentrate, a portable tape recorder, and small gifts for her hoped-for hosts: paring knives, colored rubber bands big enough to wear as arm- and leg-bands, and wide elastic to use for penis straps.[143] When Elliot's neighbors heard of her plans, they were dismayed. They appeared to go out of their way to try to scare Valerie, telling her horror stories of what the Waorani would do to the two of them, and upbraiding Elliot for exposing her child to such risks.

—

The next step, Elliot felt, was clearly to meet with Rachel and Dayomæ. They were due to arrive in Ecuador in two days and would be living in Limoncocha, a new SIL base about four hours northeast from Shandia. Saint had sent word that she wanted Elliot to bring Mæncamo and Mintaca and meet her there, and Elliot was eager to accept.

Finally the long-hoped-for day came. With Capa to take pictures of the reunion and Tidmarsh to make a tape recording of whatever was said, Elliot and Valerie, Mæncamo, and Mintaca made the journey to Limoncocha. They would spend four days with Saint and Dayomæ. At the end of their visit, Elliot wrote of what a help it had been. "Seemed I learned more in three days than I have in the past three months."[144] Elliot and Saint believed they had been able to confirm that the Wao man who had been on the beach with the five missionaries had been responsible for the decision to kill the Americans, and that Ed's body, assumed by the burial party to have been lost to the river, had been recovered and buried by Mintaca and some other women. They understood the Waorani women to say that their houses were only a half-day's walk from the site of the Kichwa settlement where Mæncamo and Mintaca had come out of the forest. Best of all, it seemed to Elliot that the three indigenous women were in agreement about going home soon and taking the missionaries with them.

She was disappointed to find that Saint would not commit herself one way or another regarding such a trip. The older woman reiterated that she would make decisions in concert with her sending organization and reminded Elliot that going to live with the tribe had been her goal for much longer than it had been Elliot's. Elliot tried again, inviting Saint to move to Shandia so the five women could stay together. When Saint declined, Elliot invited herself to Limoncocha but again got a noncommittal answer.

Back in Shandia, Elliot began to lay plans for the two women to stay in Limoncocha while she went to Quito to see the dentist and purchase supplies. Capa came back with her and stayed for two weeks, taking thousands of pictures. She appreciated the chance to talk about things that were meaningful to her, noting that he was thoughtful, both in looking out for her comfort and in terms of thinking deeply about life. He read a good deal of her Phillips's translation of Paul's letters while he was there, and they discussed it. She shared her plans to go to the Waorani, asking him to keep it private, afraid that gossip might suggest she was doing it for the publicity. He asked her to consider writing an article for *Life* when she was ready.

When the plane came on June 5 to take Capa away, it brought her brother Tom. Having been drafted into the Army a year after his graduation from Wheaton, he had planned a surprise visit before reporting for basic training. Elliot was flabbergasted but delighted. "I needn't tell you what a great time Tom and I are having," she wrote to their parents, adding that he was learning Kichwa quickly and everyone was delighted with him.[145] His visit was a refreshment, and Elliot felt he understood her and her situation as no one else did.

Although she was cheerful in her family letters about her decision to go, Elliot was waking up in the small hours of the night gripped by fear and had to discipline herself to trust God's guidance. A week later, she wrote of her decision to take Valerie with her, "I have the Lord's clear word for this . . . too, and nothing gives such peace as the knowledge that we are in His hand. It makes no difference to me if I am killed or not killed—it is the knowledge that He will do the RIGHT thing that gives peace."[146]

Not quite two weeks later, brother and sister traveled to Quito so that Tom could fly back to the US and Elliot could discuss her plans with Marj and Marilou. Although the busyness of Quito was always frustrating to Elliot, this would be a happy time for her, a rest from language work and another opportunity to spend time with friends with whom she felt a real connection. The siblings went first to Limoncocha to drop off Mintaca and Mæncamo. Elliot asked Saint directly whether Dayomæ would be allowed to travel with her and the other women, even if Saint did not want to go herself. In response, she understood Saint to say that Elliot should not go, period: that it was not in keeping with God's plan, and that it would be dangerous to the indigenous women for the missionary to go with them. Elliot recorded her recollection of Saint's words in her journal, then wrote out a list of passages from the book of Job, chapters 13 and 16, that she felt the Lord gave her as reassurance that she was on the right path.

Again it seems that the two missionaries were not communicating effectively either with each other or with the Waorani women. While Elliot believed Mintaca and Mæncamo had invited her to go with them on a now-or-never journey, Saint believed Dayomæ had told *her* that the three indigenous women should go home by themselves "first," which seemed to imply that there might be a later trip on which the missionaries would be welcome.[147] They seem to some extent to have been talking at cross purposes. Nevertheless, after Elliot left for Quito, Saint wrote her a letter inviting her to move to Limoncocha.

Elliot was deeply frustrated during this time by letters from her mother and Jim's, voicing concerns about her decision to go to the Waorani, and particularly her decision to take Valerie. She recorded some of the more strongly worded phrases in her journal. It felt like they were saying she did not know how to recognize God's voice, and coming on the heels of Saint's declaration that she was wrong about God's guidance, it stung badly. But unlike the situation in November when Wilfred Tidmarsh had strongly opposed her plans, she did not appear to see these objections as "circumstances" that should cause her to pause or to question her understanding of her own heart or of scriptural guidance.

For a week she thought and prayed about the situation. Then, in a letter addressed to "Dearest Folks," she asked them to read Acts 21:12–15, quoting the portion in which Paul tells his friends to stop crying and begging him not to travel to Jerusalem, because he is prepared to die there for Jesus's sake. She then pleaded vehemently with them to stop trying to change her mind: "May I emphasize again that I would NEVER GO . . . BECAUSE I THOUGHT IT WAS A SAFE THING TO DO. MY ONE REASON WOULD BE BECAUSE I BELIEVED IT WAS THE APPOINTED THING. Trust God to show me if I am mistaken in this. I cannot be moved by your tears, arguments, questions, and pleadings. . . . For me, nothing convinces but the settled Word."[148] The "circumstances" of what Elliot believed the indigenous women had told her outweighed the "circumstances" of opposition from her and Jim's parents, Saint, and SIL.

In many ways, Saint's invitation to Limoncocha was a fulfillment of Elliot's hopes. But already discouraged and upset by the opposition she felt, at first she experienced only deeper dejection. She had always hated the disorder and rootlessness of moving, and accepting would mean her ninth move in six years. Worse still was moving to a place she knew was impermanent, where she could not really settle in, where she would have to do without most of her belongings, where there would be the constant irritant of not having the right tool at the right time for the job at hand. Sharing her living space with other adults was exhausting for her, and living with Saint seemed likely to be more so than usual. The other woman seemed like a storm cloud blocking her path and the Waorani a refuge in comparison. To her family she wrote, "I don't know whether I need to explain how difficult this decision has been for me to make."[149] Nevertheless, she felt she should take advantage of every opportunity for language study. She hoped that it would be a very short-term arrangement, since the three indigenous women seemed increasingly impatient to go home.

When she returned to Limoncocha to pick up Mæncamo and Mintaca, Saint met Elliot with the news that the two women had been unhappy in Shandia. They had told Dayomæ that they didn't have enough fish, that people were stealing their food when Elliot wasn't around. That clinched her decision. She would not drag them away from their niece and back to a place they didn't want to live. She made a quick trip to Shandia to move out of Kuwa's house, storing everything she couldn't take with her in the Aerie. Although Saint had initially invited Elliot into her own home, a pair of SIL workers leaving Limoncocha for two months asked if Elliot would house-sit for them while they were gone instead. Elliot leapt at the offer. Mæncamo and Mintaca would sleep with Elliot and Valerie and spend the days with Dayomæ at Saint's house so that the three indigenous women could share a fire. By mid-July, mother and daughter were established in their new home.

Elliot spent her days caring for Val and working on the language, sometimes by herself, sometimes with Saint or one or more of the indigenous women. In her spare time she was reading two new Katherine Mansfield books someone had sent her. To her family she wrote, "I don't suppose I'll ever find another author who speaks to me as does KM. She also speaks for me. It is a pure delight, a continual joyful surprise to find that she has seen what I see, thought what I think. . . . I owe her a great debt."[150] But they were also bittersweet. Feeling that Mansfield's work spoke so eloquently of something in her own soul made her wish Jim could have read it too. She was still dreaming of him often, dreams where she implored him to come back and live with her but he would not even speak, dreams where she ached for sex and couldn't figure out why he wouldn't make love to her, only to realize again in the course of the dream that they were separated by death.

The barriers to effective communication that had plagued Elliot and Saint for years were not ameliorated by proximity. By July 18 the women were at odds again. The three indigenous women seemed to Elliot to be impatient to leave. She believed they wanted her to go with them and was eager to start; her journals and letters suggest that she did not understand at all the roots of Saint's reluctance. In turn, she must have seemed to Saint like the same type of loose cannon that Tidmarsh often seemed to Elliot herself. Saint understood Mæncamo and Mintaca to be talking about going home only because conditions in Shandia had been uncomfortable. She thought Elliot had misunderstood and had not been invited. It seemed to her dangerous, for everyone involved, for an outsider to go back with the women. Saint felt Elliot was badgering the three women into taking her, while Elliot felt Saint was trying to badger them out of it. Nevertheless, Elliot reminded herself that she might be wrong and Saint right about the best course. She would continue to ask God to change hearts and minds—Rachel's, her own, and any others that needed changing—so that the divine purposes would be fulfilled, whatever they were. This principle would see her through the days ahead.

The two women struggled to communicate effectively about the language as well. Elliot did not always understand Saint's reasons for translating the way she did, or her choices as they worked to reduce the language to writing. When she asked for clarification, Saint's explanations didn't make sense to her. The two women would laboriously translate one word at a time from one of the tapes, then discover that their newly translated paragraph was gibberish; Elliot was alarmed that Saint did not seem to see this as a problem. She wrote down snatches of their conversations in her journal, trying to puzzle through what was going wrong, asking for God's perspective. She asked for forgiveness in case she was in the wrong. And she did her best to keep her frustration to herself. In family letters she asked for prayer without going into detail. To Saint, she said nothing of her feelings or concerns whenever she thought it possible to avoid them honestly, and Saint seemed happy to do the same.

But events would not let the women leave aside the issues that divided them. After trying repeatedly to meet Elliot and the two Waorani women at various locations, and just missing them each time, the Canadian Robert Tremblay (one of the interested outsiders that had made the missionaries nervous in 1956) had indeed gone into Waorani territory in early June 1958. Now in late July Elliot received letters from both Hobey Lowrance and Wilfred Tidmarsh notifying her that Tremblay's house had been destroyed and the Waorani had again burned their own houses. This brought the issue of approaching the tribe to the forefront again. The three Waorani women were upset by the destruction of their homes. It seemed to intensify their desire to leave as soon as they could get ready.

During this time, Elliot received a letter from Townsend that she understood to say that Dayomæ was not allowed to go home until she had learned to read and had a portion of the Bible in her language to take back with her. In fact, Wycliffe newsletters and Townsend's own writing indicate that, despite Saint's efforts to set the record straight, he may have believed Dayomæ could already read (which presumed that the language was successfully reduced to writing) and that Bible translation was underway. Elliot believed it would be at *least* another year before Dayomæ could meet Townsend's stipulations. She did not think Mæncamo and Mintaca would wait that long.

Elliot also understood Saint to say that Townsend would consider letting Dayomæ go if she went *instead* of, rather than in addition to, Elliot. This was confusing and frustrating. Surely if literacy and Bible translation were that important, her absence would not make up for their lack. But when she tried to clarify her understanding of SIL's position, Saint, perhaps seeing her questions as an attempt to argue, apparently told her that she didn't want to talk about it. In the stress of this difficult situation, Elliot lost her appetite and started losing weight, then berated herself for failure to trust God fully. Nevertheless, when she asked her mother to keep praying for her relationship with Saint, she told her, "There has been NO real strain."[151]

By early August, it was clear that though working with Dayomæ had been helpful, the hoped-for leap forward in the language was not going to materialize. Elliot had observed for some time that she could understand Dayomæ talking to Saint but that when Dayomæ spoke to her aunts, or when Mintaca or Mæncamo were talking, her comprehension was more limited. At first she seems to have noticed only the implications for her own progress. But gradually it dawned on her that this must mean Dayomæ was speaking a different version of the language than the older women, at least when speaking to the missionaries. Concern began to grow in her mind about the integrity of a translation made with Dayomæ as informant.

Both because she felt a responsibility to the integrity of the work and because she expected to be asked for her opinion and did not want to talk behind Saint's back, Elliot felt obligated to share her concerns with the older woman. To Katharine, Elliot explained that she had told Saint she believed Dayomæ had serious shortcomings as an informant: her grasp of her mother tongue was so affected by her long years away from her home community that she spoke a simplified version, fairly different from the speech of Mæncamo and Mintaca. Saint's report of the conversation to Townsend suggests that Elliot's words came with a sting. Elliot, she said, had compared Dayomæ's speech to a toddler's, or to one of those stilted books for early readers, and had said any texts created with Dayomæ as an informant would be so muddled up with Kichwa as to be "valueless."[152] Saint seems to have acknowledged the truth of the basic facts that Elliot had marshalled but to have disagreed with the conclusion drawn from them. She argued that Dayomæ's command of the language was improving as she spent time with her aunts, that the older women understood her well enough to get by with, and that even if her speech was not perfect, she was still a helpful informant.

With the tension between Elliot and Saint sometimes in the foreground and sometimes in the background, daily life went on. Elliot and Valerie got the flu. Valerie absorbed the Waorani language apparently by osmosis, and played a good deal with Dayomæ's eight-year-old son, "Sammy." Elliot accepted another invitation to speak at a mixed-sex Kichwa-language Christian meeting, this one run at Limoncocha by a Christian from Dos Rios. Elliot decided the meeting did not count as a gathering of the local church because not everyone attending it lived in the same community. And since it was not a church and there were no male missionaries available, she felt there was no reason for her not to accept. In her family letter she closed this explanation with the conversation-ending pronouncement that Jim would have thought as she did. Her reasoning appears to have amused at least Dave, who commented on it in his next letter; Elliot wrote back demanding to know what was funny.

As time went by, it gradually got harder to find times when one of the indigenous women was willing to do informant work, and Elliot began to wonder how much longer she should stay in Limoncocha. She wrote a ten-thousand-word article for *Life* at Capa's urging, which they cut to three thousand words and weren't sure they'd use after all. She continued her voluminous correspondence. Letters from Eleanor Vandevort were an encouragement. Elliot shared an excerpt from one of them with her family, an approach to her decision about whether to go to the Waorani that had helped her: "Somehow I feel that if you did go in faith that He was leading, and it turned out that He wasn't, He would hinder you. I don't think that walking with the Lord is walking a tight rope—that if we fail to discern His will while living in obedience as we know it, we immediately fall into disaster. His promises don't indicate this."[153]

By the beginning of September, Elliot had been two months in Limoncocha. She had gathered enough language material that she would have plenty to occupy her "for a long time to come," with or without an informant: "tapes, material to memorize, filing to do, etc."[154] She had continued to make periodic attempts to plan with Saint but felt the older woman had steadily resisted, asking only to be informed when Elliot had decided what she would do. Regardless of Townsend's declarations about what Dayomæ could or couldn't do, the three indigenous women had continued to discuss their own plans and had announced that they were going home, now, just the three of them. It is unclear whether Elliot had, in fact, misunderstood, or whether events had changed the indigenous women's mind, but now they arranged for Elliot to wait in Arajuno and for Saint to care for Sammy. To her family, Elliot wrote, "Just what secondary causes may have brought about this change it is not for us to fret over. There are many factors involved, but I know one thing—far from upsetting any 'plans' I had, the Lord has simply led one more step."[155]

She accepted the Tidmarshes' offer of the use of the teacher's house—a tiny building a stone's throw from their home—for the rest of the summer and arranged with the three indigenous women that the missionaries would fly over after the women had a chance to get home. Early on September 3, Mæn-camo, Mintaca, Dayomæ, Elliot and Valerie, and Eugenia and little Philip left Limoncocha for Arajuno in an SIL plane with "three dogs, one cat, one parrot, and two hundred pounds of cargo." By 9:30 a.m., the three Waorani women had taken gifts for their families, photos of the missionaries, food for the trail, and the dogs, and headed into the jungle for the three-day hike home. Even beyond the regular dangers of the trail, there was the possibility of a hostile reception from their relatives, and the possibility—also disastrous from the missionaries' perspective—that once the women were home they would not be interested in maintaining a relationship with outsiders. Elliot knew there was a real possibility that she would never see them again. "But I know they are in the Lord's hands, and that's a pretty secure spot. He has not brought us this far for nothing."[156] She settled in to pray and wait.

Five days later, MAF's Dan Derr took Elliot on the prearranged flight. She thought she saw Mæncamo but couldn't be sure, and there was no sign of the others. They dropped some of Mæncamo's possessions from the plane just in case. Three days later and six days later they flew over again but saw no evidence of any of the women. Elliot, who had to be out of the teacher's house in less than a month, acknowledged to her family the possibility that the women were dead or had decided to break off their relationship with the missionaries, and asked them to pray about her next step. As news of the women's nonappearance spread through the evangelical world, a rumor that they were known to be dead began to circulate. But there was nothing anyone could do but wait. Elliot woke in the mornings thinking about Mæncamo, Mintaca, and Dayomæ. She took Valerie swimming every day, reread Carmichael's *Things as They Are*, and reminded herself of God's promises.

In late September, the women had been gone three weeks. The Tidmarshes arranged a trip to Quito for dental work, leaving on a Tuesday. Marj Saint and little Philip came in to stay while they were gone—a bright spot for Elliot—arriving Wednesday. That evening Elliot asked God to send the women back during Marj's visit if they were alive. The next day, as she was setting out laundry to dry in the late morning sun, Dario and two other men arrived from Curaray Kichwa settlement. After going through the usual greetings, Dario casually announced that the women had returned and had brought with them four more women and three children. Maruja, the kidnapped woman, had come out with them, and they had dropped her off on their way to Arajuno. The rest of the group were taking a bath in the river nearby, and the Kichwa men had come on ahead to announce the news. Grabbing the camera and Valerie, Elliot and Marj started out to meet them. As they reached the end of the cleared land near the runway, they heard Dayomæ singing "Jesus Loves Me," and the whole group came out of the undergrowth. Mæncamo, Mintaca, and Dayomæ were back, and they came with an invitation for Rachel Saint and Elisabeth Elliot to come and live with them.

8

Where Is Rehoboth?

NEWS OF TEN WAORANI in Arajuno spread like grassfire, and soon the little clearing was crowded with onlookers. Elisabeth Elliot and Marj Saint were both busy with prearranged tasks all afternoon—Elliot teaching and Marj with the radio—so they asked the newcomers to stay inside, hoping to keep them away from the priests. After work they got down to the business of catching up and making plans. It *had* been Mæncamo they saw from the plane; the others had merely been at a different site, not visible from the air. Their message about the outsiders had been well received. The men had only killed because they felt threatened. Now that they knew the missionaries were friendly, they would be glad to see them. As she sat with her guests, watching their kindness to each other and to her and Valerie, Elliot grappled with what she was seeing. "They come into my house, sit on the bed, look at my things, touch me, talk to me—it is quite impossible to fully apprehend that these are the wives, sisters, brothers, of the men who killed the five men." There was no question in her mind about whether to accept the invitation. She would go "to try to show them that Love which made the men do what they did, and which made Jesus do what He did."[1]

Rachel Saint, who had been checking in by radio daily, immediately sent an appeal for direction to Cam Townsend and set out for Arajuno, arriving the day after the invitation committee. Elliot dove into preparations. She wrote her family, asking for prayer. She wrote her supporters, acknowledging that although "the evidence at present points to a successful entrance," there had been other cases where all looked well, even for years, and then missionaries had been killed.[2] She contacted *Life* to stop publication of her article on Mæncamo and Mintaca, desperate to avoid further publicity. She hired carriers, packed and weighed and repacked her bag and box. She would carry very little: toiletries, a change of clothing, a blanket and waterproof sheet, first-aid supplies, camera and language materials, a Bible and a calendar, some shelf-stable food—"salt, sugar, oatmeal, coffee, tea, cocoa, milk, rice, lollipops (!)"—three spoons, and one each pot, plate, cup, and shaker to mix Valerie's milk.[3] The box contained things such as her language file and tape recorder that she hoped to have Mission Aviation Fellowship drop later if her hosts were comfortable with it.

There were many moving pieces to nail down. Should the two missionaries travel separately so Saint would not be annoyed by having to wait for Valerie, and Elliot would not be obligated to turn back if the trail proved too difficult for Saint? Or would being responsible for each other during the difficult journey finally provide the glue that was needed to mend their relationship? Various people offered to care for Valerie, and each time Elliot prayerfully reconsidered her plans. The Tidmarshes came back from Quito. Marj went home. Rachel left for a staff meeting to decide her course of action.

The next day, Elliot and Wilfred Tidmarsh met with Dan Derr and Johnny Keenan to discuss air support. There was some concern over whether MAF should cooperate with the Summer Institute of Linguistics because of their practice of conveying Catholic priests on their planes. Despite her long-standing irritation with SIL and with Ecuador's priests, Elliot wrote in her journal that she could see nowhere in the Bible that said the practice was wrong. Perhaps her experience with people refusing to grant legitimacy to her own sense of God's leading was increasing her ability to empathize, to imagine that SIL's policies might be due to their own understanding of God's leading. She told the others that she did not feel it would be at all helpful to query SIL's motivation or to try and argue them out of a decision made in sincerity of heart; God could take care of any problems that might arise from working together.

And then all the preparations and plans were complete. Saint came back with permission to go. They would travel together, and Elliot would bring Valerie. Dayomæ's son Sammy would stay behind to be homeschooled at Limoncocha. MAF would take the lead on air support with SIL providing backup. A date was set. Elliot's feelings roiled. Here was the thing that had thrilled her since Brooklyn, the thing she had wanted desperately for almost three years now. She *still* wanted it—and she was afraid. She was not, as far as she knew, afraid to die, but she knew that even if everything went well, the days ahead would be painful in many mundane ways. She looked around her tiny house and savored the conveniences even of such a simple space and thought of Gwen's kindness and the comfort of having her nearby. She felt she could grasp how Jesus could have delighted to do the will of the Father and still beg to have the cup taken away.

On the last night in Arajuno, she wrote to the Howards and Elliots:

"My flesh and my heart may fail, but God is the strength of my heart and my portion forever." I fully expect the first clause to be my case—if my days on the Curaray were any foretaste of what these next weeks may be. But I just as fully expect the next clause to be realized, as it was then.

Don't forget that I can receive mail all right—they'll be dropping it to us. But just how we'll get anything out of there for a while we do not know. So don't worry. Perhaps I can get Ruth Keenan to drop you a line whenever Johnny goes over, just to let you know that things are o.k. But then, if she forgot it, you'd be sure I was dead! Well—start trusting the Lord. Not trusting Him that I'll live, or that things will go well, just <u>trusting</u> Him.[4]

————

On October 6, a flurried week-and-a-half after the Waorani arrived in Arajuno, the group set out: eight Waorani, three Americans, and five or six Kichwa men hired to carry Valerie and the baggage and later to pilot the canoes. The first day's journey brought them to the repopulated settlement on the Curaray where Elliot had first met Mintaca and Mæncamo. Ever on the lookout for more information, Elliot questioned Maruja about the tribe. But her report filled Elliot with the same sinking feeling and desire to run away that she had experienced in San Miguel and at Jim's death. The women had been nice enough, Maruja said, but the men were "fierce," "no good."[5] She told a grim story of how the group had battered Tremblay's body and left it for the vultures: the ultimate horror to a group in which the dying would often ask to be buried alive rather than risk being left unburied after death. The missionaries, she said firmly, would shortly meet the same fate. Again Elliot reevaluated her decision. Again she reaffirmed her understanding of God's leading.

The next day the group pressed on, taking to the river in three canoes. The men took it easy, fishing as they went. In mid-afternoon they stopped, and the women and children swam while the men quickly made shelters for the night from towering wild grasses. That night after settling Valerie on her bed of banana leaves, Elliot sat by the fire with her journal, musing over the day and her traveling companions. She was impressed by their skill and ability: the grace of their movements as they leapt from the canoes to spear fish; the way they knew where and how to set out fishing lines as soon as they stopped for the night, so that half an hour later, when they had built shelters for the whole group, a table for the missionaries' radio, a pole for the radio antenna, and a cooking platform, they had enough fish to feed everyone. Again and again during the day Elliot had felt a sense of awe at her situation. It seemed surreal—the way the Kichwa and the Waorani laughed together, the way men who had known Honorio cared for women and children from the group responsible for his death. Her heart swelled with affection for them all.

After another morning on the river, they set out on foot after lunch Wednesday. The Kichwa men had planned to turn back at this point, but Dayomæ talked them into coming the rest of the way. Concerned about safety, Saint had initially suggested the whole trip should be canceled rather than take men into the tribe, but to Elliot's relief, the older woman allowed herself to be persuaded by Dayomæ. For another three and a half hours they hiked northward, Valerie falling asleep in the carrying cloth. Finally they emerged into a clearing near the bank of the Tewæno River. It was Jim and Elisabeth Elliot's fifth wedding anniversary, Jim's thirty-first birthday.

Waiting for them amidst a few small, open-walled houses were Mæncamo's brother Kimö, his wife Dawa, and Dayomæ's sister Guiimadi, who had met Jim. Despite the unplanned arrival of several armed men, the three Waorani rose from their seats to greet the newcomers with apparent calm. They were the only ones there at the moment, they explained, but the others would arrive in the morning. Valerie, awake now and released from the carrying cloth, plunked herself down on a log to watch Kimö. Eventually she said to her mother, "He looks like a daddy. Is that *my* daddy?"[6] Elliot had not spoken to Valerie of how Jim had died or of her belief that Kimö had helped to kill him, but perhaps the little girl had heard others talking and had somehow connected Kimö's people with her father. Or perhaps, with his wide grin, broad nose, and the crinkles at the corners of his eyes, Kimö simply reminded her of the portrait of Jim that Elliot kept in their home. Whatever their source, Valerie's words must have moved Elliot deeply. Everywhere she turned, something reminded her of Jim and emphasized again their surreal situation. It was a comfort when the Christians among the Kichwa men initiated a time of group singing and prayer before bed, thanking God for a safe journey and their new friends. That night Elliot and Valerie slept on a split-bamboo bed in their very own Waorani-style house.

Early the next morning, Kimö set out to let the rest of the group know of the newcomers' arrival, and Elliot began the task of observing, recording, and trying to understand. Her housekeeping work was the lightest it had ever been—daily radio contact, feeding herself and Valerie whatever was at hand, and periodically cleaning themselves, their one set of clothes, and their minimal dishes. The rest of her time went to taking pictures, making notes on anthropology and linguistics, and keeping an eye on Val. Elliot's journal records an assortment of impressions: A teenage girl's mother died of a bad cold; no one seemed concerned by the news that her sister planned to kill the girl as a result. Mæncamo was an expert at creating both furniture and firewood with a machete. The Kichwa and Waorani men fished together in the day and sang together in the evenings. Again and again as the days went by, Elliot marveled to find herself in *this* community, marveled that these extremely ordinary people were fabled killers. "After all these months of living on tenter-hooks, wondering, wondering—here I am. Here they are. And we live in peace."[7]

The Waorani were not the single homogenous tribe the missionaries seem to have imagined at first, but three or four largely separate kinship groups, maintained through endogamous marriage practices, speaking the same language and usually in conflict with each other. In 1958 they comprised about six hundred people total and cared for about five million acres of land nestled in the arms of the Curaray and Napo Rivers. There they practiced a semisedentary approach to hunting, fishing, and rotational farming beautifully adapted to local environmental conditions: extended families lived together in a longhouse, maintaining two or more houses in various locations and moving from clearing to clearing based on what crops were in season, whether a fishing or hunting area needed to rest, and how safe they felt from attack.[8] The community that had welcomed Elliot and Saint, the Guequitaidi, were the southwestern-most of these groups. Called after Guequita, the oldest man in the group, they numbered about fifty people, seven of whom were adult males.

In fact, virtually everything about the Waorani was more complex than outsiders, with their erroneous assumptions about "stone-age tribes" and "savages," had expected. This included the cultural patterns that led to violence. Later, anthropologists would record a long list of triggers for killing. Although these could be grouped under the general headings of anger, gain, revenge, and perceived threat, ultimately triggers were events that threatened the foundation of the Waorani worldview: a sense of human autonomy and control. Because loss of control was so contrary to the implicit understanding of how the world should work, it often caused overwhelming emotion. Killing was, as James S. Boster, James Yost, and Catherine Peeke describe, a way "to make graphically explicit the extreme to which [a] negative emotion has reached," and also perhaps a way of regaining a sense of agency.[9] This way of expressing emotion and exerting control can act as a deterrent to violence in the short term—causing outsiders to fear the group enough to stay away, for example—but in the long term, trap community members in a cycle of killing.

Oral records reveal that by the time Elliot arrived in the clearing by the Tewæno River, the Waorani had been caught up in unbroken revenge killing for more than forty years, with more than 60 percent of deaths intentionally inflicted. They felt that violence was beginning to threaten their existence as a people, and they had tried many ways to stop, including intermarriage, gift giving, running away (as Dayomæ, Mæncamo, and Mintaca had all done), and trying to eradicate hostile groups. Nothing had worked. When Mæncamo and Dayomæ arrived with news of outsiders who had a plan to stop the spearing, at least two people cried.

But much of this information would take years for outsiders to accumulate and interpret. Elliot and Saint were not trained anthropologists; they were barely trained linguists and still had limited proficiency in the language. Elliot had felt an outsider before—in San Miguel, Puyupungu, Shandia, Arajuno, on the Curaray—but whether she had realized it or not, had still existed to some extent within systems she knew how to navigate. She had been a white woman among people with experience of Ecuador's racialized class system. She had enjoyed comparative wealth among people who used money. She had spoken the language well enough to feel, rightly or wrongly, that she understood and was understood. There had been a social structure in place through which she could exert some influence over what happened. In Tewæno, she lost that sense of understanding and control.

Before, Elliot had run an essentially Western-style household, with servants to help with much of the manual labor and comparatively reliable food sources. Now she found she was not good at, or just could not do, most of the things a Waorani woman was responsible for—growing food, getting firewood, making pottery, and so on. Her struggles were underlined by the ease with which three-year-old Valerie gained facility in these things. Val quickly became an expert fire starter, even in wet weather; learned to find and cook various foods, wrapped in leaves; to roll fiber for weaving; clear weeds, dig holes, and peel food with the big knife that served her as a child-sized machete. Elliot could not devote her time to learning these skills because the language occupied all her attention. But despite almost total immersion and hours of intentional effort every day, she was often accused by native speakers of having ears without holes because she was so slow to understand. Meanwhile, Val soon spoke so idiomatically that her mother decided she "not only spoke Auca but thought in Auca."[10]

Being able to think like a Wao—this was the depth of understanding Elliot longed for. Nine months before, living with Mæncamo, Mintaca, and Eugenia's family in Shandia, she had told her family it was not her job to create understanding of her own point of view but to do her best to understand enough of her host culture that the people she was living with could understand *Jesus*. Her desire to see contextualization rather than acculturation, however imperfect, was light-years ahead of many other public Christians at the time. *Reader's Digest*'s Clarence W. Hall and *Harper's* Mel Arnold, for example, explicitly and positively connected missionary work with American cultural values, seeing missions as an excellent vehicle for spreading democracy and winning the Cold War. For Elliot, this missed the point entirely. It was not American culture for which she had risked losing Jim. It was not American culture she was risking her life and Valerie's to spread. It was the love of God for people, expressed in Jesus Christ. She wanted to present Christ in context, and it was to that end that she sought to understand both the language and the culture of the Waorani. Ironically, her growing understanding of how little she really knew probably made her much more perceptive than she had been in the Kichwa communities where she had spent the last several years.

———

When Dayomæ and her aunts left Arajuno back in September, Dayomæ had never gone all the way to the houses where the missionaries had been making gift drops. Instead, the women had made a new clearing about a third of the way there, and Dayomæ had sent a message by Mæncamo asking the rest of her family-group to come to her there. As Kathryn T. Long points out, it appears that multiple factors influenced Dayomæ's decision. Since leaving Carlos Sevilla's plantation, she had led a fairly sedentary lifestyle, and her feet had hurt too much to go farther. She also seems to have been nervous about exactly how she would be received, so the decision to have Mæncamo go on ahead may have been a safety measure, like Jacob sending gifts and messengers ahead to Esau in Genesis. And although it's unclear whether, with her Waorani childhood and her adult experience with sedentary cultures, Dayomæ originally thought of the creation of the new clearing as a permanent settlement or as another in a round of semisedentary locations, she may have been beginning a long-term attempt to transition the group to a more sedentary lifestyle and give them greater access to the outside cultures she had come to know.

The rest of the family-group had agreed to the new clearing—though again their long-term expectations for the location are unclear—and had built a few small houses there. But it would take time for fields to be cleared and crops to be established, and most people continued to spend most of their time at the northeasterly clearing, where a succession of plantings were coming ripe. When Kimö announced the arrival of the missionaries, three or four people came down the first afternoon, and six more the next day. Three days later, everyone but Dayomæ, Kimö, and Dawa had gone back again. Many days the missionaries were essentially alone. For the Waorani this was business as usual, but Elliot, expecting some kind of permanent resettlement, was worried.

She wished she could get to the other location and went as far as asking Dayomæ why they couldn't move there but received a diplomatically vague answer. People continued to come and go, but no one invited her along. A similar problem arose over food. Elliot had understood Mæncamo to say the missionaries would be well-fed if they came to Tewæno, and had brought dry goods only as a backup, but soon found she was depending on her backup regularly. Not only were the community's crops in one place and Elliot in another, but the absence of people meant a lack of protein as well. Women did fish in addition to farming, but generally men provided both fish and game, and frequently there were no men in the clearing at all. Even when food was available, it was not always offered to the Americans, in keeping with the foundational Waorani understanding that family came first when it came to sharing goods. At least once someone told Elliot to ask for food if she wanted it, but she was hesitant to do so, not wanting to wear out her welcome. This created another conflict between the American women. Saint wanted to obviate the problem by arranging regular food drops, while Elliot, fearing recreating the patterns of dependence she had deplored elsewhere, wanted to wait and see how God would provide. She offered to share dry goods with Saint whenever there was no other food available, but the older woman declined, saying she did not want to take food from Valerie.

Elliot's reluctance to ask for food or invite herself on journeys made sense in the context of her own cultural background, but not in her host culture. Anthropologists Clayton and Carole Robarchek have described the foundational belief of the Waorani worldview as the idea that people "are, and should be, in control of their own experiences" in the world.[11] One of the effects of this belief was the pattern of violence; another was that Waorani society was both ideologically and practically egalitarian. Each member of society was expected to be self-sufficient and autonomous. While much of American culture shares the assumption of human ability and responsibility, it was even more pronounced in Waorani communities. There was none of Elliot's idea that wives should submit to husbands, or Saint's expectation that employees follow the dictates of their employer. From the Waorani perspective, if Elliot wanted something to eat that wasn't being offered, she should ask for it; if she wanted to go to the other settlement, she should go.

But Elliot didn't know this. Nor did she realize just how much Dayomæ was changing things around her. The Waorani woman had spent half her life in other cultures—first in the Ecuadorian patronage system and then in SIL's little corner of American evangelicalism—environments where hierarchy was a fact of life. From her early egalitarian experiences, she had adapted to the role of one who took direction from leaders. Then Saint had encouraged Dayomæ to envision *herself* in a leadership role so that she could act as a missionary to her people. The younger woman seems to have embraced the idea, with a blend of traditionally Waorani self-agency and very non-Waorani assumption of authority over others. But although the missionaries didn't fully realize how countercultural Dayomæ's behavior often was, from Elliot's perspective it was bad enough. On her second full day in Tewæno, Elliot was already lamenting the younger woman's conflation of Christianity and outside culture and her determination to create change.

As Long points out, Dayomæ was well aware that the Waorani were considered "savages" by outsiders, and it seems likely that from the beginning her goals were not perfectly aligned with Elliot's or Saint's. As soon as she got back to Tewæno, Dayomæ started organizing Sunday meetings, where she gathered together everyone who was in the clearing at the time to listen to the Bible stories she had learned from Saint. As far as Elliot could tell, this kind of public meeting with one speaker was entirely foreign, and she noted with amusement that Dayomæ kept stopping her story to tell everyone else to "shut up" and listen.[12]

It was hard to complain about Dayomæ's willingness to introduce changes and everyone else's willingness to go along with them when it came to the Bible or, indeed, with her instruction that people stop defecating in the river where they got their drinking water. Other changes were more ambiguous. In September, she had cut everyone's hair, theoretically in an attempt to clear up lice, but perhaps also to make them look less like "savages" and more like Kichwa. Now she began handing out clothes, even sewing clothing for the babies. Within a few days everyone in the clearing was somewhat dressed. Doing away with nakedness eradicated a key marker of "savageness" from an outsider's point of view, and at the same time was in keeping with the foundational Waorani belief that good things ought to be experienced equally by everyone in the family-group. Elliot lamented the loss of traditional hairstyles and the substitution of ill-made, wrinkled, dirty clothing for the beauty of God's handiwork in the human form.

The big question for Elliot was not how to preserve an idealized "original" culture but whether a given change was useful or morally necessary. Here again the American women disagreed. To Saint, the adoption of clothing seemed sensible; she felt it would help prevent bug bites. Elliot also understood her to say that clothing was biblical, and that the Waorani were self-conscious without clothing now that they knew about it. To Elliot, who noticed that people took off their new clothes whenever they wanted to do something active, the latter idea seemed ludicrous. And though she gave serious consideration to the biblical justification, she decided clothing was legitimately a matter that could vary from culture to culture.

Meanwhile, the introduction of clothing clearly introduced new problems. The clothes Dayomæ was making fit badly, which not only made them a dubious form of bug-protection (in fact they seemed to increase the potential for bugs like lice) but meant that they were in the way. Clothes got dirty immediately, and washing required soap, something the tribe did not make. For menstruating women, the problems were more acute, requiring not just more frequent laundering but also the addition of another entire set of clothing—underwear, cloth pads, and sanitary belt, as Elliot had already discovered while hosting Mintaca and Mæncamo—and introducing new health risks. Then, too, fabric rotted quickly in the damp environment, raising questions of how clothes would be replaced. Elliot did not want to create the expectation that missionaries would always provide free clothing and soap. However, she did not try to stop Dayomæ.

Dayomæ also quickly started to broker marriages between Waorani women and Kichwa men. This, too, Elliot saw as creating new challenges. But here she thought the potential benefits might outweigh the problems. As she had gradually learned names and relationships from Mæncamo over the past year, she had realized the group was highly interrelated. She had seen this as evidence that spearing was decreasing the population and limiting marriage partners, and she felt men from outside the group might be what they needed to turn their population decline around. She had no way of knowing that while violence did affect their situation, the group would have been highly interrelated by custom regardless, or that the children of such marriages would traditionally not be considered Waorani.

Here, too, Elliot and Saint found themselves in conflict. While Elliot recognized the potential for trouble, she continued to take a hands-off approach. This was in keeping with her desire to observe and understand and reflected her belief that, ultimately, decisions about tradition and change were up to the Waorani. It's not clear whether Saint also saw potential for positive effects from intermarriage, but certainly the potential problems loomed largest in her mind. She had not wanted Kichwa men to come in the first place. She did not like it when they continued to visit or when Waorani went out to visit the Kichwa, as they soon began to do. She was not afraid to argue and try to stop such intermingling. But the Waorani had their own opinions. Now that they knew there were outsiders who were not hostile, they were interested in making new friends and connections, and not just with the missionaries.

———

Elliot's first stint in Tewæno lasted seven-and-a-half weeks. By early November, she and Saint were making plans for their first trip out. Elliot felt they should alternate any journeys so one of them could always be available to offer medical care. Contact sickness was beginning to move through the community. One woman, Mimaa, had died between the return of the three Waorani women in September and the arrival of the two missionaries in October, apparently from a bad cold exacerbated by malnutrition. Here again, however, was a point of conflict. Elliot wanted to go out in February so she could see Jim's parents, who would be in South America then. Saint planned to take Dayomæ to Quito for Christmas and to stay through the end of February, and she either would not or could not adjust her plans. Elliot was discouraged by this, and by her sense that even after weeks of immersion she could still understand only about 10 percent of what was being said around her or to her. The initial excitement of the long-prayed-for entrance into the tribe was past, and the frets and rubs of daily life were reasserting themselves. In her journal she wrote of a sense of spiritual attack and of her awareness that both fatigue and letdown after a long period of emotional tension were probably factors. She was able to give herself more compassion than she could a year before, recognizing that her emotions were not signs of sin or failure.

Time and circumstances were working many changes in Elliot, causing her to consider carefully things she had never had to think much about before. In her role as an observer of Waorani culture she came up against her own knee-jerk reactions almost daily, and often several times a day. In each case she tried to evaluate her response based on the Bible rather than her expectations as an American. She discovered that her own skills were largely useless, while the people outsiders thought of as "primitive" had highly developed skill sets that made them very good at their work. The kind of housekeeping she had spent so much time and energy on in other environments was irrelevant here. Even the building style, which she had seen as bug-ridden and impermanent, now seemed perfectly adapted to the needs of the people. Normative nakedness, she decided, was not only morally permissible but actually helpful, freeing people from temptation to sins such as vanity and prurience. She was repeatedly taken aback by how openly sex and menstruation were acknowledged and discussed publicly in Waorani culture, even by children, but she reminded herself that Americans did the same thing with different bodily functions, giving children dolls designed to drink and urinate. This type of conversation with herself—noting her initial sense that something was inappropriate, then reminding herself that the response was conditioned and that there was really no reason that it should be frowned on—occurs again and again in her journals.

Not only did her new circumstances cause her to reexamine her cultural assumptions in light of spiritual reality, but she was also seeing the Bible with fresh eyes. In the days before entering Tewæno she had pondered Jesus's words from Matthew: "He that receiveth you receiveth me" (Matt. 10:40 KJV). She had wondered aloud in letters to family and supporters about what this might mean for the Waorani, who were receiving followers of Jesus. Though she clearly did not think that physical reception of the missionaries translated to automatic spiritual reception of Jesus, she had asked her supporters to pray that the former would lead to the latter. To her family she had written that Jesus's words led her to hope that accepting the missionaries meant accepting Christ in the now-and-not-yet way that is so commonly described in the Bible. "May we not hope that it means they also receive Christ, though it may take a long time for them to realize it?"[13]

Now at the beginning of November 1958 she was pondering another aspect of what it meant to accept Jesus: was it really possible to tell people about Jesus in any meaningful way without also telling them about his instructions? Dayomæ seemed to be introducing a message that focused solely on passages of Scripture such as Acts 16:31, "Believe in the Lord Jesus, and you will be saved," but Elliot was pondering verses including John 14:15, "If you love me, you will keep my commandments." She wondered whether Dayomæ's teaching was adequate. But, she ruefully acknowledged, not only was she incapable of doing better; she was incapable of doing anything at all—she simply didn't speak the language well enough. She could only keep praying and relying on God to change the hearts and minds of people.

In mid-November, Elliot and Saint began meeting daily for Bible reading and prayer. Elliot hoped that this time together would strengthen their relationship, as they focused on shared faith and goals and the God they both loved. At first, though she realized that Saint was uneasy about some of her questions, she felt their time together was helpful. But it seems Saint was not able to approach their differences with the same equanimity. The kinds of questions Scripture raised for Elliot, the way she thought about the world, deeply concerned the older woman. It was Saint, after all, who had taught Dayomæ the approach that gave Elliot pause. After just seven-and-a-half weeks together, Saint began writing to Townsend that Elliot's faith was in "shaky territory."[14] Realizing that her attempts to build their relationship seemed to cause further friction, the younger woman redoubled her efforts to avoid voicing disagreement. As she saw it, it wasn't her job to control the Waorani *or* her coworker. But she was discouraged.

As the days passed, Elliot recorded the roller coaster of her relationship with Saint in her journal. One day she would feel her prayers for connection were being answered; the next day things would be more difficult than ever. With a remarkable commitment to setting a guard over her mouth (as the psalmist prays in Psalm 141) she often avoided recording any details of what was wrong, noting only her own sense of hopelessness and her repeated recommittal of the situation to God. She quoted 1 Corinthians 10:13, passages from Hebrews 12, and the letters of James and Peter (all of which she was reading from the Phillips translation) as passages that were giving her strength and encouragement, and prayed for God to help her live out what she was seeing in the Scriptures.

More encouragement came in the mail. A letter from Katharine seemed to indicate that despite her daughter's reticence, she understood and sympathized with her difficulties with Saint and was praying. A letter from Eleanor Vandevort, who was visiting Amy Carmichael's Dohnavur Fellowship, mentioned that *Shadow of the Almighty* was being read there. A recording of the choir at Hampden DuBose Academy singing hymns made her cry happy tears. She was thankful for the encouragement of the church militant, spread around the globe. There was also a letter from her brother Phil, who was praying about whether he should leave his current post. As she asked for wisdom to know how to pray for him, she wondered about her own situation as well, questioning again whether it was a good use of resources for two missionaries to work on the language of one small tribe, whether it was right for her to raise Valerie in their present circumstances.

One of the difficult things about living in the jungle was how different Valerie's childhood had been so far from what she would have planned, left to her own devices. She wished the little girl was not always dirty and afflicted with various ailments caused by being dirty, wished she could have party shoes and go to museums and zoos. Now Marj Saint and Marilou McCully had invited them to spend Christmas with them, and Elliot wanted very much to take her to experience a more typical American cultural Christmas celebration. At the same time, not only did she feel someone ought to stay to provide medical care to the Waorani, but she believed—a belief first explicitly revealed in her writing at this time—that when faced with two otherwise acceptable paths, the follower of Jesus is obligated to choose the more difficult. And in this case, the harder path was to stay in Tewæno.

So Elliot decided to go out in early December and come back in time to be there when Saint and Dayomæ left for Quito. She wanted to accomplish some of the paperwork that was difficult in Tewæno. She needed to meet with Mel Arnold, who wanted her to write a book about her experiences with the Waorani. And everyone else in Tewæno would be traveling to the northerly clearing for the peanut harvest about then, so it seemed like good timing. In making her plans, she failed to factor in the Waorani as agents on their own behalf. When Dabu learned of Elliot's plans, he decided to go along. Then, she reported to her family with amusement, "Mankamu decided she'd go along to cook for her brother. Kumi, her son, had to go along to 'see how the foreigners live.' Kinta is Kumi's shadow, so he said he'd go." At this point, "Watu would have been the only one left in the community where we were, so obviously there was no point in Rachel's and Dayuma's staying there by themselves," and they decided that they would go too.[15] Then, although she had planned to leave Tewæno on December 2, Dabu showed up several days early, ready to go and bringing a guest. On the second, the whole group was in Arajuno.

From there, Saint and Dayomæ flew to Quito, and the rest of the group settled in for a visit. "They are a great bunch," Elliot wrote to her family of her traveling companions, "and it is surely fun to be with them. Munga is getting over his shyness. Dabu never had a bit—he is the most outgoing individual you ever saw. The Quichuas are awed to see full grown Auca men out here, but it is moving to see them shake hands, play ball together, share their chicha—when you think what fear each had for the other a few months ago."[16] While they got to know their hosts, Elliot worked steadily at her desk, writing ninety-four letters in a three-day period. She saw Valerie off to Quito; the three-and-a-half-year-old traveled the first leg of the trip to Ambato with Gwen Tidmarsh and the second leg by bus under the care of another missionary. She would split her visit between the Saints and the McCullys. Elliot also agreed to a contract with Harper's for a book about life with the Waorani and encouraged Arnold to request a book from Saint about Dayomæ.

Although Elliot had hoped all along to go back to Tewæno, she never assumed automatically she would go. On her last planned night in Arajuno, she was still praying for a clear indication from God if she was to change her plans. Neither, when she decided she would return, did she believe she was guaranteed safe reentry. She noted in her journal that her arrangements had necessarily been so hectic that she had been forced to forego her usual ritual of preparing "as though for death,"[17] and that with her luck, it would mean this was the time she was killed.

The Waorani had stayed in Arajuno long enough that Elliot could travel with them on the return journey, and the trip felt idyllic. She was excited to try her language skills without Dayomæ there to interpret in a pinch, and it was cozy to sit around the fire in hammocks at the end of the travel day, looking forward to supper, tea, and a cozy evening. Her heart was filled with affection for her companions, and she wrote in her journal that although she still had times when she wished this period of her life was over, she now had times where she realized she was going to miss it when it was gone. In some ways, she had more camaraderie with the Waorani than with her fellow missionaries; Wilfred Tidmarsh had not asked her even one question about the Waorani during her time there.

On December 12, 1958, Elliot was back in Tewæno. She missed her little daughter and often thought of Jim, but her present lifestyle felt like the fulfillment of a long-held desire, like something out of the missionary tales of her youth. The sense of camaraderie she had felt on the trail persisted. She tried to share whatever of her own life was of interest with whoever was there. Her mail was a group pleasure, and after one drop she wrote to her family, "I have just spent an hour trying to explain everything in the <u>Life</u> magazine . . . from the car and liquor ads to the airview of this settlement. (The nude paintings don't even give them pause, let alone require explanation in this culture!) Fine exercise for my language study, but I hate to think what sort of ideas the Aucas end up with."[18] She felt that she connected particularly with Minkaye, and he seems to have felt the same way, giving her his own beautiful dart case, calling her his sister, and confiding his anxiety over the possibility of attack from another Waorani group downriver. In turn, she tried to communicate a little of her foundation for peace in the face of danger: her ability to communicate with God, her expectation that even if she died, it would mean a new life with God. She prayed that the Holy Spirit would enable him to understand.

About ten days after her return, Elliot finally had the chance to go to the older clearing. "This seemed the real climax to my dreams—to stand in the houses I had seen from the air."[19] Traveling with Mæncamo, Kimö, and a few others, she visited three separate Waorani clearings over a period of days and finally got to see a more established neighborhood, with one house boasting "18 hammocks around 8 fires," and "a great sheaf of spears . . . in the center of the house."[20] She had brought back little outside food and was essentially dependent on the Waorani, something she felt free to do since she was not responsible for Valerie's meals. She now found that chicha, which had long made her a bit squeamish, was perfectly adapted for jungle living and very refreshing on the trail.

This was not her only changing impression. When she tested the load Mæncamo was carrying for hours on the trail, Elliot found she couldn't even lift it off the ground. By the end of the trip she had recanted her earlier position (though she seems to have forgotten she had personally espoused it) that indigenous people were lazy and shiftless. She described in her journal the steady twenty-four hours of work Mæncamo put in at the end of their three-day hike: cooking, feeding all the men, sweeping out the house, splitting more firewood, walking a mile to the river and cutting stairs into the high, steep bank so she could fish, walking back, building a smoking platform, and staying up all night preserving fish. Almost daily she was impressed afresh with the talent, skill, work ethic, and stoicism of the people around her, particularly in contrast with her own inability to live up to their example.

Elliot's increasing respect for the Waorani was not idealized. She continued to note instances of cruelty that sometimes verged on sadism. They would band together to shame adults who made mistakes, refuse to feed the sick or injured, and terrify children by threatening to kill them. One day she recorded in her journal how Minkaye pinched a baby's sensitive parts with partially opened peanut shells. The little boy sobbed and sobbed, while the adults, even his mother, laughed. Elliot continued to be puzzled, too, by what her attitude should be toward their treatment of sex and sexuality. She reminded herself again and again that her own cultural expectations were not the same as Scripture, but she was uncertain of just what a scriptural attitude was in this context. Parts she was used to thinking of as private were open for public touching and discussion from an early age—a child putting her hand between an older girl's legs to check her menstrual status, an adult pushing back a child's foreskin to demonstrate something (Elliot couldn't understand what), people discussing the various sizes of vaginas and inquiring about hers. Group entertainment could include holding the female dog so everyone could watch the male dog mount her, or manually manipulating the male dog to an erection. There was little privacy other than darkness for sex acts. The unavoidable sight of men and women going to bed together made her ache for Jim.

In many ways Elliot's days during this time were leisurely. But she had plenty to think about. The Howards, the Elliots, her fellow widows, and her supporters all wanted news. The *Sunday School Times*, HCJB radio, *Life*, and Harper's all wanted pieces to publish. She puzzled over what to say to them all and how to balance their competing claims. She puzzled over why so many people were so focused on this tiny group in the jungles of Ecuador, when missionaries were working around the world, and in situations that seemed much more important or difficult than her own. She puzzled over her slow progress in the language. She puzzled over how to understand Waorani culture in the light of Scripture. And most of all, she puzzled over her relationship with Rachel Saint.

The women had parted on a note of disagreement. Saint had vehemently opposed Elliot's decision to go back to Tewæno without her. Though the older woman would soon spend long stretches as the only outsider in the community herself, for now she appeared to think missionaries should not stay singly in the community. Elliot could not understand why the situation between them was not improving. She felt that if both of them had "the mind of Christ," as Paul had encouraged the Philippians to do, then it would surely be impossible for their relationship to remain fractured.[21] She was doing the best she could to live at peace, and she also tried hard not to shift the blame for their conflict onto Saint, writing to her mother and in her journals that Saint, too, must feel she was doing the best she could.

———

After just three weeks, Elliot left Tewæno again on January 1, 1959. More Waorani accompanied her. "They don't consult me on this, or wait for an invitation," she wrote to her family. "They simply announce that they are going. This is fine with me, as it makes the trip twice as fun." Perhaps remembering Saint's objections, she added, "There was little we could have done to stop them anyway, so recognizing that there would be advantages . . . as well as disadvantages, I simply asked the Lord to do what was best."[22] They reached Arajuno on the third, and Elliot went on to Quito to pick up Valerie and meet Jim's parents. From there the four Elliots went to Peru to stay with Bert and Colleen, arriving in Lima on the twelfth. Their visit was busy, filled with shopping, trips to the dentist, touring the countryside, and taking three-year-old Valerie to see the ocean for the first time, but there was also time for rest and encouragement.

Elliot had determined not to talk publicly about her difficulties with Saint. So it was heartening to discover that, although she hadn't said a word, Jim's mother had been taken aback by Saint's behavior toward Elliot during a brief visit in Quito. It helped to know she wasn't imagining things. Then, too, Bert told of difficult relationships between several other missionaries he knew, suggesting that it was part of spiritual warfare—Satan's strategy to derail the work of God's kingdom. Whatever the cause, knowing that she and Saint were not the only people on the mission field having this sort of problem also helped her feel less like she was missing something or doing something wrong. She felt reminded that God saw her pain and her sincere desire to do the right thing in a difficult situation.

Elliot got back to Quito by February 10. There she met with Townsend, who was trying to arrange for Elliot and Saint to go back to the tribe together. Elliot had a good deal of correspondence to catch up on, so Saint, who had been waiting for Elliot at Townsend's request, went by herself after all. This rubbed salt in the wounds with which the two women had parted in December. From Quito, Elliot went to Shandia for a week, where she gave away even more of her possessions, leaving "nothing but books and kitchen utensils."[23] On the sixteenth she was back in Arajuno, where she spent a few more days dealing with mail.

With Saint's approval, Elliot had arranged for Marilou to come to Tewæno for a visit. After a grueling journey, with torturous insects, heat, pouring rain, and little to eat, they arrived about February 21. Saint and three Waorani were there to welcome them. Elliot enjoyed the chance to spend time with Marilou and show her something of life with the Waorani. But as soon as Marilou left, Saint seemed to turn on Elliot, criticizing her with language that felt harsh and hurtful. Elliot tried hard not to defend herself. She kept on looking for good in her coworker, writing in her journal that Saint was "strong, faithful," that she consistently worked long hours on the language, that she faithfully taught Dayomæ from the Bible, that she was dedicated to prayer, and that she seemed to excel in the simple faith encouraged by Jesus in the book of Matthew.[24]

By the end of the first week of March, Elliot was writing in her journal that she found encouragement in knowing that nineteenth-century Scottish missionaries David Livingston, Mary Slessor, and John Gibson Paton had all felt they would have gone insane on the field if it were not for the comfort of the Holy Spirit—she was not alone in feeling that she was losing her mind. By mid-March she could not muster enough interest to write, to watch the Waorani, or even to do much toward keeping up her journal. Her next family letter, dated March 21, the first since she had written from Arajuno a month before, explained the long gap in correspondence by saying that since her return she had "had no heart to write anything—even journal entries have been brief and superficial. I haven't any explanation."[25]

When not mired in the middle of the situation, the explanation seems clear enough. Loss of interest in things that once brought pleasure is a classic symptom of depression. The monotony of daily life, the regression in her command of Wao tededo that had occurred in the two months she was away, and the ongoing tension and loneliness resulting from a difficult relationship with the only other adult who spoke a language she was fluent in were all factors.

Reading continued to be among her few comforts. She read Catherine Marshall's *To Live Again*, a memoir of Marshall's experiences as a young widow, and was looking forward to a copy of a book by Lilias Trotter that someone had promised to send. Tom, now a chaplain's assistant at Fort Benning, continued to write regularly about his reading; Elliot responded in kind, and they discussed the questions they were pondering. Nevertheless, with her desire to exercise iron self-discipline and her belief that, given two otherwise equal options, the person seeking to follow in the footsteps of the suffering Savior should choose the more difficult path, she worried over whether reading was an acceptable use of her time or whether she should be spending every possible moment on language work.

The next week Elliot wrote home again, making carbon copies for the Elliots and Mardelle Senseney. This time there was news to report, though she asked them to keep it quiet. The Waorani had shared what seemed to be new information about the killing of the five men. Though she still could not understand enough to know who was who in the account, she gathered a picture of a frantic last few minutes on the beach. One of the five had run to the plane and climbed or leaned in, then gotten back out. Another had fired his gun, and a stray shot grazed the head of a Wao man. The Waorani attacked the shooter, and two other missionaries had come to his aid, until they were speared in turn. At least one American ran out into the water, and the Waorani would have let him go, but in the end he came back to the beach and they killed him too. This news seems to have started her dreaming more often of Jim again, and she recorded one dream in which she was alone in a huge assembly room while someone on stage panegyrized her. When Jim came quietly up next to her and reached out for her hand, she cried from relief at having someone with her who cared.

Elliot spent April struggling for contentment. The tension between her and Saint simmered and occasionally boiled over, leaving Elliot devastated. Dayomæ, rather than either Saint or Elliot, continued to function as the primary religious teacher, and Elliot worried that her approach to retelling the stories from the Hebrew Scriptures she had learned from Saint encouraged her listeners to trust God only in order to get good things. Nevertheless, she recorded again Saint's faithfulness and persistence, noting that she seemed better at the lifestyle they were living than Elliot herself. She was afraid that own her unhappiness meant she was rebelling against God's will. Another disappointment came when the Catherses wrote that they were moving permanently to Quito, asking what she wanted them to do about the house. Her sacrifice to help them settle in at Shandia seemed wasted.

But about this time Elliot also felt like she had a breakthrough in something she had been praying about and pondering for months. Since moving to Tewæno, she had been questioning her assumptions about missionary work: she could not talk about Jesus in any meaningful way, could not offer any physical help to speak of, could not do any of the things missionaries were typically supposed to do. What *was* she to be doing? Why *did* God want her here anyway? Reading her Bible in the evenings by candlelight, she gradually came to the conclusion that the word *missionary* did not appear in the Bible, that instead, the Scriptures talked about *witnesses*.[26] Now a passage from her special chapter in Isaiah came alive in a new way, and she wrote it in her journal. "'You are my witnesses,' declares the LORD, 'and my servant whom I have chosen, that you may know and believe me and understand that I am he. Before me no god was formed, nor shall there be any after me'" (Isa. 43:10). Perhaps to be a missionary was ultimately to be a witness to the nature and character of God. A witness observes and reports. This she could try to do. The discovery of this verse in this context produced a lifelong paradigm shift for her.

After ten weeks in Tewæno, Elliot left again on April 30, 1959. She would see Jim's parents again on their way home, attend a missionary conference, spend time with her sister, Ginny, and work on her "hopeless mountain" of mail.[27] Not only did she have a large personal correspondence and a good deal of business mail, but as a now-public figure she was inundated with letters from strangers. Occasionally one was so bizarre that she threw it away unanswered, but for the most part she conscientiously replied. "I feel it a terrific responsibility," she wrote, "especially the letters from young people making life decisions, writing me for advice. I fear they may take what I say as the oracle of God, and I have to pray that I may be that or else it would be better that I not write them."[28]

By May 7 she was in Quito, waiting for Ginny and her family to arrive. One perk of being in the city was a chance to talk to her mother by long-distance telephone. But given the cost, they kept it short, so the next day Elliot sat down to write Katharine. Philip's health had never been the same since his 1955 brain surgery. Katharine, who had also been suffering from life-threatening health episodes of her own, had shared the situation with her daughter. Elliot responded compassionately, acknowledging that in many ways her mother must feel she had lost her husband while he was still alive, "a much more difficult thing than death. I feel therefore that I can only sympathize in a weak and detached way. And yet for you the source of strength will be the same. The same Rock will steady you which steadied me."[29]

She also offered to pay for her parents to get a good long rest: "I would very much like to take care of any and all expenses involved in getting you and Dad away for a vacation of several months. Please don't go to any little cheap places with no conveniences. I would be much happier if you'd go where you could get services, and have no responsibilities of any kind, including cooking or housekeeping."[30] It is difficult to pinpoint exactly what this might have cost, since travel brochures often don't include prices, and seasonal specials listed in ads don't give a perfect picture of the cost of a prolonged vacation at regular rates. But even conservative estimates suggest that Elliot was far from necessitous. A 1959 advertisement offered a week-long Atlantic City hotel stay, including breakfast, dinner, and activities for $83.50 per person. For two people staying three months, that would be just over $2,000. A winter vacation in the Poconos with three meals a day and free equipment rentals was advertised for a daily special of $13 per person, about $2,200 for three months. A Hollywood Beach resort announced free golf, swimming, social programs, and parking, plus three meals a day, for $23 per person; a three-months' stay would have been $3,864. The median American family income that year was $5,400.

In *Shadow of the Almighty*, Elliot had touched briefly on her and Jim's financial principles. Quoting 2 Corinthians 8:14–15, she explained that they had not purchased life insurance, preferring to rely directly on God to meet their needs. Thus, she said, Jim left behind "little of value, as the world regards values," just "a home in the jungle, a few well-worn clothes, books, and tools."[31] No records seem to have survived to indicate how much Jim had in the bank when he died, and little documentation to show how much Elliot began receiving in donations after his death. Periodic mentions of finances in her letters and journals give some clues.

On February 5, 1956, less than a month after Jim's death, Elliot wrote to her mother, "As I said to Ginny in a letter yesterday, the Lord chooses the trials each of us needs. Financial ones have never been Jim's and mine here in Ecuador (or Jim's anywhere, for that matter!) though I know they have been well-known to everyone else in our family. Right now I really feel burdened to know just what to do with the funds which are flooding in. To say nothing of Jim's bank accounts in Quito and U.S."[32] When she asked her mother to send her things, she usually sent more money than was needed and encouraged Katharine to use the extra for herself. In August 1956 she sent money to pay for her brother Jim's fishing license, plus enough extra to buy Katharine a blouse. In October 1956 she wrote to Wheaton College, requesting that all Tom's bills—room and board, tuition, books—be sent to her so that she could take over those costs from her parents. Then she started making money as a writer. In March 1957 she asked Katharine to let her pay for boat tickets for Phil's family, saying that she did not want to be repaid. "I am already getting scared by the prospect of more money pouring in from Life [*sic*], with the new story, and possibly royalties on the book in a few more months."[33]

Elliot's own financial needs were small. She lived simply. Her only regular expenses were her MAF bill for food drops and, less often, travel expenses. And as she briefly explained in *Shadow of the Almighty*, she believed saving money *now* in case she needed it *later* was not trustful. She enlarged on the idea in family letters.

> As Tom says, "What's money for?" . . . It is meant to meet <u>today's</u> needs. If we insist on putting it by for tomorrow, we'll have "nothing over," as with manna. But if we spend it or give it away today, we'll have no lack. Now, I ask you all, which is the more excellent way? Do we feel "safer" if we've got a little nest egg tucked away? Then we are lovers of mammon. And for those of you who may reply with "common sense" arguments, God-given wisdom, or providence, my reply will only be the teaching of the Sermon on the Mount. Did Jesus mean that, or was He being cruelly impractical?[34]

A month later she emphasized that she thought "<u>saving</u> money—savings accounts, bonds, investments, insurance," was counter to the Bible's teaching.[35] "Extra" money was to be given away.

By October 1958, just before going to Tewæno for the first time, Elliot appears to have given away not only most of the possessions and equipment she and Jim had purchased before going to Ecuador but also a substantial amount of money. "O.K. on the checks you took from my account, Mother," she wrote. "I can't be quite so reckless at this point, as I've disposed of most of my funds now. . . . Reminds me of a Satevepost [*Saturday Evening Post*] joke: The relatives sit with bated breath while the lawyer reads out the will: 'I, John Smith, being of sound mind, have spent every damn cent I ever made.'"[36] She was not only, or even primarily, spending it on her family. But since the Sermon on the Mount seems to instruct Christians to do their financial giving privately, gifts to her family were generally the only kind she discussed in family letters. In December, she wrote in her journal that she had given away $3,800 while in Arajuno.

There seems to be no surviving record of where she sent these donations, but it's likely they went to other missionaries and mission organizations: one letter mentions a request for funds from the founder of InterVarsity Christian Fellowship in a way that suggests she had made a large gift in the past. In any event, the amount she gave away in Arajuno is toward the high end of possible costs for a long vacation for her parents. In 1958, when she donated it, it was 75 percent of the median American family income.

By the time Elliot urged her parents to take a rest on her dime just over six months later, she was back to feeling flush. Not only, she explained, had she rediscovered a savings account she had forgotten, but royalties from Jim's biography were starting to come in, and donors continued to send money. "One man who sends me a hundred dollars faithfully every month wrote recently to tell me he had already written me into his will for $10,000, but he had another $10,000 to dispose of immediately—did I want it?!!"[37] This gives some idea of the donations she was receiving. And although many other gifts likely came in amounts of $1.00 here and $5.00 there, the name recognition associated with a best-selling book and a handful of *Life* articles seems to have meant that even small donations piled up.

Elliot was acutely aware that most missionaries did not share her financial status. She knew something of the challenges of her fellow widows. Her own siblings on the mission field were sometimes out of money entirely. And she was aware that her parents had scrimped and gone without for years in their effort to live in obedience to God's direction in their lives—first in Belgium and then at the *SST* rather than at one of the many more lucrative positions her father could have filled with distinction. She also knew that no one's finances are more scrupulously examined by outsiders than the poor and those living on charity. So although she worried that people would get the wrong impression if they knew donations went into a joint account to which her parents also had access, her offer to send her aging and ailing parents on a long vacation did not seem to her to be frivoling with other people's hard-earned money. Instead she felt it would be giving money to the Lord's servants, just as if she were making a donation to another missionary on the field. "I would consider doing anything I could for you and Dad as money well spent, and spent for eternity," she told Katharine. "Please accept it in this spirit, and don't ever mention 'taking' my money."[38] There's nothing in subsequent letters to show whether the Howards took Elliot up on her offer.

In late May 1959, just a few weeks after she offered to pay for their vacation, she sent home a check to be deposited in her US account, with a note that explains something of her financial arrangements. "The check is royalty from <u>Shadow</u>. (I signed a contract which provides for no more than $2000 per year to be paid to me—this avoids having to pay income tax! The book has already earned over $22,000 in the first six months of publication, so I'll be getting these checks for some years to come.)"[39] It's unclear whether Elliot was also receiving money from *Through Gates of Splendor* at this time. The book, which retailed for $3.75, made *a lot* of money, selling over 175,000 copies in the first eight months. There seems to have been some misunderstanding about the contract, however, and though Elliot had intended for Sam Saint, as agent for the widows, to disperse the monies from the book, she had ended up the recipient of all royalties. Elliot prayed about how to manage this and ultimately made a trip to Quito to sign a deed of gift in front of a notary at the American consul, transferring the royalties to the Auca Missionary Foundation, Inc., a registered charitable organization the widows created to receive royalties from projects related to the five men.

The Auca Missionary Foundation is not to be confused with the Five Missionary Martyrs Fund. The fund, which Elliot referred to as the "Trust Fund," the "Martyr's [sic] Fund," or the "Washington Fund," had been created within days of the men's deaths, apparently at the instigation of HCJB's Clarence Jones. It was announced publicly on January 15, 1956, during a memorial service broadcast to the US during HCJB's *Back Home Hour*, and Philip publicized it in the January 28 *SST*. Financial donations earmarked for the families had already begun to arrive in large numbers at a variety of mission organizations, and the creation of the fund was an attempt to bring order out of chaos. It was deluged with donations. Money came from single people, married couples, anonymous contributors, junior missionary societies, Sunday school classes, Bible study groups, organizations such as Wycliffe Bible Translators and Christian Youth Crusade, churches ranging from Baptist to Episcopal, and from five continents. Occasionally there would be a donation of over a hundred dollars, and once in a great while one over a thousand dollars. But most were for one or two dollars, sometimes five or ten. This makes the eventual total of the fund—over $56,000 in the first few months; over $65,000 by May 1957 when the deluge slowed to a trickle; and eventually, with earned interest, over $92,000 in all—even more impressive.

To avoid having to jump through the legal hoops required to establish a trust, the fund was established under the auspices of the Evangelical Foreign Missions Association, with EFMA secretary Clyde Taylor, Wheaton's V. Raymond Edman, and Howard family friend General William K. Harrison Jr. as administrators. Someone printed receipt forms bearing the title of the

fund and a notation explaining that donors' money would be "administered
. . . in behalf of the immediate needs of the widows and the educational
needs of the children"; Edman's wife and daughter donated their spare time
to recording donations and sending receipts; and the committee set about
investing donations to best effect.[40]

Unfortunately, the terms of the fund were drawn up without formally
consulting the widows as to how they wanted to use donations, and the
details of administration of the monies were left to the administrators' dis-
cretion—as the women discovered when they started trying to use them in
January 1957. As the three men repeatedly changed the rules of the game
and threw up roadblock after roadblock to attempts to access the donations,
it became clear that they thought of themselves not as helping to manage
paperwork so the women could have the money without the hassle but as
acting *in loco parentis* for the widows. Just as when male missionaries had
laid plans for staffing the jungle mission stations without considering Elliot's presence, the administrators treated the women as though they were
not legitimate actors on their own behalf, not capable of knowing what
they needed or of making valid short- and long-term financial decisions
for their families.[41] By May 1959 the women had only successfully accessed
the donated money once, to help pay off a small portion of Marilou's house
in Quito, and there had been talk among the administrators of making that
disbursement a loan to be repaid.

Elliot didn't need money from the fund at present; she wasn't even trying
to save the money she had. As she had told her mother in the summer of
1957, "No, I don't intend to put anything 'away' for myself or Valerie. Val will
be taken care of by the Martyr's Fund, as far as education needs go. And the
Lord will take care of the rest. I keep thinking of Rockefeller's words 'He who
dies a rich man is disgraced,' or something to that effect. I have gotten rid
of a good proportion of what I had this past year, but still feel it a burden."[42]

But she was privy to the struggles of the other women, who were going
to great lengths to avoid asking for money from the fund after the way they
had been treated by the administrators.[43] And she was frustrated by the
way the whole situation was being managed. The widows were regularly
asked by donors about the money and were embarrassed to know how
to respond. To make matters worse, the fact that the public believed they
had tens of thousands of dollars at their fingertips made it difficult to raise

money for projects, such as a documentary film to increase the reach of the five men's story.

It was with all of this in the background that the women had decided to create a different kind of legal vehicle for the royalties from *Through Gates of Splendor*. They believed they would be able to make their own decisions about how to use this money.

———

While she waited in Quito in late May 1959 for Ginny to arrive, Elliot worked on her never-ending correspondence. Though her Spanish had gotten rusty, she also accepted speaking invitations, giving talks to groups of young people, to the philosophy faculty at the university, and to missionaries at HCJB. Elliot sent her parents a copy of her talk, which gives insight into her changing understanding of missionary work.

It is clear throughout the entire N.T. that the life which is offered to us in the Lord Jesus is not limited to certain places or times. It is a daily, down-to-earth, walk—whether we walk dusty roads of Galilee, as did Jesus, or cement sidewalks, or muddy jungle trails. Jesus never told us that to serve Him meant only to preach, or to be a missionary, or to pray. He <u>showed</u> us what He meant when He Himself lived and walked with ordinary men, shared in their wedding feasts, sat down with them in the jumbled mob of the market place, cooked breakfast for some fishermen on a seashore—these things were also the "things which pleased the Father"—as well as His Sermon on the Mount, His healing of the sick, His preaching to sinners.

I have thought much about Paul's word, "that the life also of Jesus might be manifest in my mortal flesh." I live among a people whose entire culture pattern is the antithesis of anything I had ever known before. I can hardly speak their language at all as yet. What am I supposed to be doing? I am supposed to be manifesting to them the life of Jesus, even before I can speak His <u>words</u> to them.[44]

Shortly after this, she wrote in a family letter, "Tom's statement, 'we set about doing His will and He takes care of the metaphysics of the thing' expresses my thought exactly." In her teens and twenties, Elliot had sincerely and enthusiastically embraced the Holiness teaching of both the Keswick Convention and Prairie Bible Institute's L. E. Maxwell. Now she wrote, "Keswick teaching was always 'too deep for me,' and not very practical. Maxwell, too. I find the words of the Lord Jesus, and Paul's lists of instructions much simpler to understand."[45]

Ginny and her family finally arrived, and the sisters spent a week together. Elliot was glad for the opportunity to see her sister and get to know her brother-in-law and nephews a bit, although Quito was always so busy she felt that she and Ginny never really got time alone for conversation. The chance to sit quietly after supper and talk, perhaps by a crackling fire, was, she said wistfully, "my favorite way to spend an evening."[46]

As soon as the DeVrieses left, Elliot and Valerie started the multistage journey back to Tewæno. After checking with Rachel, she invited Marj Saint and Mardelle Senseney to come for a visit. By June 16 they were in Tewaeno. Rachel and Dayomæ were not there; the groups had passed each other on the trail. The Waorani, who continued their usual semisedentary migratory behavior, were largely back in the older clearing. The presence of her friends helped Elliot with the transition. Having company that she could easily talk to and get along with was a balm, and she enjoyed seeing her friends' enjoyment.

On journeys, Valerie had graduated from riding in a carrying cloth or wooden chair to walking the trails herself. She was slow, but less from fatigue than from typical four-year-old distraction. After one trip Elliot wrote proudly, "Considering how many times she stopped to pick flowers, spot a bird, examine a snail shell or get herself a new blow gun, I don't think her time was too bad—fifteen miles in less than nine hours, through pretty rugged terrain. . . . To say nothing of its being the third day of a rather taxing three days!"[47]

Mother and daughter were spending daily "story time" together, and Elliot was considering homeschooling in the fall. She felt it would be good for Valerie, who usually did whatever she wanted all day with the other children, to have some scheduled time. Val was quite good at the standard activities of her environment, but she was also absorbing some things that concerned Elliot—like the time she carefully caught a tin can full of tadpoles, then cooked them alive. Another time, as Elliot was telling her the story of

Abraham and the angels in Genesis 18, she said "that Abraham had three angels for lunch. Val looked horrified and said, 'Did he kill them first?'" Given the cultural context, Elliot pointed out, "It was an obvious question."[48]

Although Saint had criticized her for not talking enough about God, Elliot was on the lookout for opportunities to discuss Christian beliefs whenever possible. Occasionally people seemed interested, but usually they acted bored or changed the subject. She mused a good deal over what would be an indicator that the Waorani were understanding and accepting the Christian God. Then in late July, during family devotions, as Elliot was singing a little song from the Victorious Life Hymnal, "Give your heart to Jesus, He is calling you," Valerie interrupted to say, "'I want to give Him my heart right now.'" The next day Elliot told the story in a family letter, adding that Val had prayed "and told Him just that. At breakfast she looked up suddenly from her oatmeal and said 'Is Jesus living in my heart now?'" Elliot, still meditating on just what constituted salvation, did not record her answer to her daughter's question, noting instead, "I was reading in Acts, noting how it was those who gladly received the Word who were counted converts. It seems a simple definition. Certainly there are those among the Aucas who have gladly received all they have heard."[49]

During this period, Elliot was reading Habakkuk, Acts, 2 Corinthians, Ephesians, and 1 John. She pondered how giving the Waorani were. Gikita speared a fish, only one, and gave it to Elliot. Someone else who speared a pig walked hours to share the meat with others. She felt that this behavior, so matter-of-fact among the Waorani, would be seen as a huge sacrifice in her own culture and wrote in her journal that the Waorani seemed to meet the criteria of "children of God" listed in 1 John 3 better than many professing Christians. On another occasion, Guiimadi, seeing Elliot struggle to cut firewood, intervened and deftly resupplied her. But when Elliot tried to share wood with Guiimadi in return, the whole community turned on her with scorn. She struggled to understand what had happened and to respond graciously to their mockery, which increased her sense of loneliness and isolation.

At the end of the first week of August, Saint and Dayomæ arrived for a six-week stay, with Sammy and six Kichwa carriers. Four days later, Elliot wrote in her journal that since Saint's return, everything she had suggested had been rejected, everything she had done had been questioned, and every offer of help she had made had been dismissed. It seemed she could neither work alone nor offer help to Saint, either as a Bible teacher or as a linguist, without causing conflict. She had often felt sick with guilt over her inability to mend things; now she felt she had done the very best she knew how and was at rest. She increasingly saw that she and Saint had two very different ways of understanding and responding to the world. Later in the month she recorded a conversation in which she had asked Saint whether she ever questioned her own thinking, and Saint had replied, "No, I'm not very analytical, I guess. Don't have <u>time</u> to be really. That's the whole thing." Elliot wrote that perhaps that was indeed "the whole thing" when it came to their relationship.[50]

This realization eased her. But it didn't solve the problem of what to do about the situation. Elliot began to ponder whether, since there was no work she could profitably do as a linguist, God wanted her to leave Tewæno. There was still Kichwa language work needed in Shandia and in the Sierra; perhaps she should take up one of those tasks. But it seemed that whatever she put her hand to turned to dust and ashes—her work on Tsafiki, her sacrifices for the Cathers family, her work on Wao tededo. She pondered the story from Genesis of the Philistines filling in Isaac's wells as fast as his servants could dig them, noting that finally, at a place called Rehoboth, he had been able to dig a well and stay there. Where, she asked God in her journal, would she find a place where she could *stay?* Ten days later she wrote that she was beginning to feel strongly that it was time for a furlough soon.

Elliot left Tewæno again on September 10. Saint and Dayomæ followed a few days later, en route to Limoncocha, where they would work with SIL writer Ethel Emily Wallis to complete the manuscript about Dayomæ that Saint had promised Harper's. Elliot told her family, "I plan to stay out as long as she does this time. I have enough language work to do to keep me busy for a long time, to say nothing of the heaps of mail to answer. It is good to be in civilization once more after thirteen weeks of bare feet and dirty fingernails."[51] It had been eleven months since the Waorani welcomed Elliot and Saint into their community. Saint had spent roughly seven months and Elliot roughly nine living in the little clearing in Tewæno. In that time the two missionaries had been together less than five months.

Within days of leaving Tewæno, Elliot made the decision to take her first furlough. There was "no special reason," she explained to her supporters in a letter written from Arajuno, "unless the Lord's clear word of direction may be called 'special.'"[52] The trip would give her the rest that comes from a change of scene and occupation, would give her and Valerie a chance to spend time with family, and would provide her with a prolonged period to work on the book she owed Harper's—a task that had begun to seem virtually impossible in Ecuador.

A gap in the family letters and in the journals available for scholarship means a bit of detective work is necessary to figure out what Elliot was up to during her first three months in the States. Three things help sketch a picture. She gave her parents' address as her mailing address for the duration of her furlough and wrote a circular letter addressed from Moorestown early on, attempting to stem a flood of speaking invitations. A long gap in family letters is always a strong indication that Elliot was seeing her parents regularly enough that there was no point in writing them. And a January 4, 1960 *Christianity Today* article based on a recent interview with Elliot noted that she was staying in "an ocean-side apartment in Ventnor, New Jersey," and working on a book.[53] Valerie was with her, and she was settled enough that she had not only her typewriter, notes, and language materials at the apartment but a framed picture of Jim. Furnished apartments run by the Society for Foreign Mission Welfare were available in Ventnor rent-free to missionaries on furlough and open to people from a wide range of denominations and faith-mission organizations. It seems likely from other indicators in the letters that these are where Elliot stayed. So from October through much of December 1959, while she wrote the majority of her third book, she and Valerie were most likely dividing their time between one of these apartments and Birdsong, though there is little to indicate how much time they spent in either place.

After Christmas, Katharine and Philip—now in their early sixties—left for a two-month vacation in Florida, where they would visit HDA and spend some time with their friends the Harrisons and the Buckinghams. It appears that during this vacation, Walter and Elvira Buckingham gave the Howards a generous gift: a little four-room house on half an acre of land bordering their orange orchard. The Howards would name the cottage Little Birdsong. Ginny and her family, who had apparently been at Birdsong for Christmas, went to Ventnor themselves, and Elliot and Valerie went to Birdsong.

After a few days by themselves in the quiet house, mother and daughter traveled through North Carolina, Georgia, and Florida to visit Ruth and Billy Graham, Tom, and Mrs. DuBose ("Doc" had just died). In the Grahams' big, beautiful house in the mountains, Elliot had the chance to do one of her favorite things—just sit quietly and talk of interesting things. Her time with her brother was packed virtually every minute with social engagements, and she spoke three times in the two days she was there, but she enjoyed the chance to meet many of Tom's friends and to tour Fort Benning, where he was stationed. For the six days spent at HDA, students waited on Elliot hand and foot, bringing her breakfast in bed, doing her laundry, and taking Valerie everywhere with them. Val enjoyed it so much that she asked if they couldn't move to Florida. Elliot spoke to the students nightly and to visitors from the local area on Sunday after church.

Back at Birdsong on January 11, Elliot took up her writing. "Please keep praying, or start praying again for help in this job," she wrote in a general letter to Howards, Elliots, and Marj and Marilou. For the moment, life was ordinary, filled with "writing, thinking, living . . . trips to the post office, supermarket, dry cleaners, etc."[54] By the twenty-first, she had three chapters of the book polished enough to send them to the *SST* "for advance publication."[55]

At the beginning of February Valerie went to stay with her Aunt Ginny, and Elliot went to New York to work on the Waorani book with Capa. She arrived in time to attend a photography exhibition to which he had invited her, where she met again several people she had become acquainted with while writing *Through Gates of Splendor*. She wrote her family a humorous account of the gathering. "I amused myself greatly watching the women with silvered eyelids and dyed hair, the crew-cut men with the black-rimmed glasses and London suits, the frantic waiters who served out forty bottles of liquor, Cornell told me next day. Several told me they recognized my nose, from Cornell's pictures."[56] She stayed in the same Park Avenue hotel where she had written *Through Gates of Splendor* and spent her days on the book, discussing it by phone and over lunch with Arnold and over various meals with Capa. At some point during her furlough she and Capa also recorded the narrative voice-over for *Through the Gates of Splendor*, a short documentary-style film telling the story of missionary contact with the Waorani. And they discussed "the meaning of faith." Capa was, she wrote to her family, "gay and witty on the outside" but "intensely serious underneath," "earnest about knowing people and why they do what they do. He contemplates life with far greater sympathy and understanding than most of my acquaintances. Keep asking God to give him faith, to give him the will to believe. He simply cannot see the kingdom of God. He just can't see it. He'll have to be born again, which means by the wind of the Spirit."[57]

But despite the fun of the hustle and bustle of New York City, the chance to do a little window shopping and buy some new clothes, Elliot was finding the process of getting the new book ready for press "a disappointment." "Or rather, I should not be disappointed, knowing that books are terribly painful processes, and there's no sense thinking you can do one without paying dearly for it." She lamented to her family:

> I seem to spend a lot of time here just as I did in Ecuador—alone, reading, thinking, wanting to talk, finding no one to listen, eager to get to libraries and museums and concerts and finding that the days slip by without opportunity. I might as well be in Tiwaenu for all the culture I absorb, except for the very notable exceptions of trips to N.Y., for which I am deeply grateful to the Lord. . . . Today I have done nothing but business correspondence and errands, till this letter, and it's 4:30. All is vanity and VEXATION OF SPIRIT.[58]

The change of circumstances did not alter Elliot's fundamental loneliness.

———

Elliot wrapped up work on the book, ultimately titled *The Savage My Kinsman*, in late March 1960. Both in size and structure, the finished product would be almost a coffee-table book. It was large—nine by eleven inches—and featured full-color photographic endpapers, fifteen full, two-page, black-and-white photographs and more than two dozen whole-page photos, plus almost a hundred additional pictures. The sheer size of many of them is arresting; one, a candid closeup of Mintaca and Elliot, is life-size. The pictures were taken by a smattering of photographers, including Capa,

Nate Saint, and Guiimadi, the older of the two Waorani women who had met Jim on the beach. The rest—the majority—were Elliot's own. Capa also wrote the foreword, offering readers a lens through which to understand Elliot's photographs, explaining her as a gifted amateur whose success came from her love of her subjects and her gift for truly seeing them.

But while Elliot engages in documentary-style photography here, she is primarily a writer. The book differs from a typical coffee-table book in that the extensive text is of equal importance with the pictures. Elliot seems at first to frame *Kinsman* in terms of answering questions about the Waorani and her work. But she also couches the book in terms of *un*knowing and ignorance, suggesting that even accompanied by text, pictures cannot provide as much knowledge as we want them to. There are only echoes here of the certainty that permeated *Through Gates of Splendor*. Instead, Elliot emphasizes how little time she has spent with the group, how little of the language and culture she knows. She highlights the fact that her guesses and suppositions about the Waorani have "proved to be quite wrong."[59] In fact, she casts the whole project not as primarily a way for readers to know the Waorani but as a springboard for considering their own culture, turning the assessing gaze back on itself.

Elliot's emphasis on limited knowledge echoes a letter sent to supporters just before her furlough. Looking back over the events of her life in Ecuador, she had written:

> Things which I knew before, I no longer know. Conclusions which I had drawn have proved to be quite inconclusive. Questions which a few years ago I could have answered quite easily are now unanswerable. One thing I know: As God said to Moses (four times in the first eight verses of Exodus 6) "I AM THE LORD." What, after all, is the whole purpose of all that life brings us, if not to bring us to Him? . . . Missionary work is generally supposed to bring men to Christ. Only God knows what part of my missionary career has contributed to this end. But much in that career has brought <u>me</u> to Christ. And for this no words suffice to express the thanksgiving in my heart.[60]

In the letter, Elliot presented her loss of knowledge and certainty not as loss of faith but as a stripping away of false knowledge to reveal the living heart of faith. She carries that theme into the book.

Drawn primarily from the record in her journals, *Kinsman* broadly follows the chronology of the past four years. Capa's foreword summarizes in the simplest possible way (for, he suggests, anyone who has been living under a rock since 1956) the story of the five men's contact attempt. Picking up the threads from Capa, Elliot begins her account with the return of the search party, describing how, "the crusading spirit, the thrill of reaching an unreached tribe, the passion for souls which is supposed to motivate some—all these faded out completely."[61] Bombarded with questions about the meaning of Jim's death and of life without him, she had found purpose in the idea of practical, step-by-step obedience, which she sees as the key to knowing God. In the first half of the book she describes the arrival of Mintaca and Mæncamo, the death of Honorio, the nine months of language study in Shandia and Limoncocha, the departure and return of the Waorani women, and her first journey to Tewæno.

Although the polished text lacks some of the emotional immediacy of the journals, Elliot was clearly trying to avoid writing a stereotypical inspirational missionary story and to instead present an honest and accurate picture. She describes the occasional small encouragements in language study but also the "agony" of the "painfully slow" process.[62] She talks of the Waorani women's patience and kindness but also the times they refused to speak to her or slapped Valerie in frustration. While she still believes she can understand God's specific guidance, she emphasizes that she has had no sense of assurance that God will keep her safe, and describes the challenges she has faced in making decisions and in her efforts to find guidance in the Bible. She is open, too, about her ambivalent emotions, her longing to go to the Waorani and her dread of going. Here is no gung-ho missionary striding eagerly into the unknown, confident of God's protection. Instead, we see a woman trying painstakingly to discern and do the will of God.

In a narrative choice that resists sensationalizing either missionary work or the Waorani, we are halfway through the book before Elliot gets to Tewæno. Rather than heightening excitement by plunging on in fast-paced narrative, she stops altogether, backing out of the story itself to talk again about ideas, principles. She emphasizes that she takes risks not for the sake of "adventure" or even "scientific study," but out of her desire to know God—a knowledge which requires practical obedience. And lest it sound as though missionaries are more naturally holy than run-of-the-mill

Christians—an idea she had come to abhor—she insists that in going to live with the Waorani, she and Saint were "not . . . any more doing our duty at that moment than at any other."[63]

Returning to the story, Elliot attempts to describe the material and moral realities of the Waorani. The people themselves are neither poor nor savage but dignified, often beautiful, mostly healthy and strong. She describes her dawning realization that what she had assumed to be a bare-subsistence lifestyle is actually well-adapted to the environment, constructed by people of knowledge and skill. The Waorani lack most of the things she had considered important to leisure and fun, but they aren't jaded or bored. Instead, they have an admirable ability to find interest and enjoyment in their surroundings. In a nicely drawn analogy, she describes how they watch birds "as Americans watch cars or planes, identifying the species as we identify makes and describing their flight in excited speeches like a sports announcer."[64]

She addresses and dismisses a handful of stereotypes. The jungle, called a "Green Hell" by outsiders, is both muddy and beautiful and safer in many ways than suburban America. The lifestyle is sometimes harder than in "civilization," sometimes easier. The people themselves are just people, worse in some ways than those of the world she grew up in, better in others. They aren't lazy; she chronicles with respect how long and hard they work without rest or complaint. They don't somehow suffer less than white people (though, she says, they do whine less—a real zinger coming from Elliot, to whom self-pity is anathema). They could sometimes be said to behave cruelly; so is American culture often cruel. Even killing, the thing the Waorani are famous for, is acceptable in some circumstances and not in others, just as in the US. And Elliot points out a range of ways in which Waorani culture surpasses American culture: no drunkenness or cutting gossip; "almost no vanity or personal pride, no covetousness, avarice, or stinginess"; remarkable patience and hospitality.[65]

Elliot makes clear that she and Saint cannot help the Waorani practically, in fact are reliant on them. "I realized that I had thought of the Auca as being particularly needy," she writes. "I was faced with the fact that socially I had nothing whatever to offer."[66] And spiritually? Elliot emphasizes how little she and Saint understand, how much less they can make themselves understood, the difficulty of communicating or understanding abstract

Elisabeth Howard, circa 1932

Peter

By Elisabeth Howard, the Great.

Title page of story signed "Elisabeth Howard the Great"

Hampden DuBose Academy
Zellwood, Florida
September 12, 1943

Dear Folks:

Here I am again in grand old H. D. A.! You can't possibly imagine how wonderful it is to be back! Everyone is so swell, and the place is so lovely and cool and I'm so happy! I can't really believe I won't be coming back next year. Honestly, I'll just die. I'm hanging on to each day as it passes. Well, praise the Lord He's made it possible for you to send me here for three perfect years. I certainly am looking forward to this year. We've a grand class— seven girls, two boys. No new ones !!! Some rivalry with the juniors — 18 kid — 12 boys, 6 girls! But will really have fun. Please pray for my year here — my last one — that it will be all that the Lord wants for me, because truly I want to give Him my best, trusting implicitly in Him to make the year count.

First page of a letter home, September 12, 1943. "Here I am again in grand old H. D. A.!"

<u>Home</u>

September 22 '52
Quito

Dearest Mother:

This will have to be a short one. Thanks so much for your personal letter of Sept. 16. I was so glad you and Dad & Jim were able to get to the Poconos. I hope the house was nice when you stayed. Also much interested — and thankful to God for His guidance of Phil & Margaret. I'm trusting Him to work out all the good pleasure of His will in them. Wasn't it good about the 2 ladies from Ft. Dix coming to see you? This is a great opportunity.

The main purpose of this is to tell you — and for the present please do not let it go beyond the family — that last night Doreen spent the night with me & I'm beginning to wonder if God would have me go down to San Miguel for a few months to help her with the organization & analysis of the Colorado language. I had a wonderful talk with her, and felt a unity I've not felt with anyone for so long — don't know if I've ever felt it so. Last week she had told me that God had provided a teacher, & she felt she should begin

Letter to mother, September 22, 1952. "I'm beginning to wonder if God would have me go down to San Miguel for a few months to help . . . with the organization & analysis of the Colorado language." Side A

studying the language, but hardly knew
how to begin. The teacher is an Ecuadorian - Christian — and the only
white man in the world who knows is.
I couldn't get the idea out of my
mind, since I've had linguistic
training & she hasn't. Well, when I
mentioned it to her, I could practically
see goose flesh — she was so thrilled, &
said she'd been thinking of the same
thing but hardly dared suggest it. Then,
perhaps, later God may lead us together
to the Oriente. Will _you_ pray that
this step may become perfectly clear one
way or the other, & especially that I
may know _when_ I ought to go. I don't
feel that I know Spanish well yet, but
God knows.

Had my first word from Jim since
he got into Shandia. The doctor is here
in Quito now for 10 days. Says the fellows are
thrilled with the place.

It's so good to be able to share these
things with you, Mother dear, just as you
were saying in your letter — letters, & prayer - what
blessings! Now I must trot downtown with
this. I love you so much — I look at your
picture, stuck in my mirror, _so_ often! Your own
Betty

Elisabeth Howard and Jim Elliot after their engagement, Quito, February 1953

Marilou McCully, Barbara Youderian, Olive Fleming, Elisabeth Elliot, Marj Saint,
and seven of their nine children, Quito, January 1957

Shandia, Ecuador
Jan. 6, 1956

Dearest Mother:

I kn ow that if you have gotten my other letters about Jim's
trip, you are on pins and needles to know what is going on. I
don't know very much myself, because Rachel is here and they
can't tell me much on the radio, but the plane came in Wed. and
brought me a note saying that the landing beach they had picked
out for the fellows was fine, Nate too k them all in on Tues.
and all the stuff, without any mishaps. The tree they picked out
to build a house in was just perfect, and everything was going
fine. On Wed., when everything was set up for "receiving visitors"/
Nate flew over the Auca houses with Pete, who spoke to them in a
loud speaker from the plane, inviting them to go over to the beach .
Later in the day they flew over again, and few Aucas were to be
seen, so they assumed some of them must have set out for the beach.
However, as of this morning no one had showed up yet (Friday), so
I haven't heard what the next step will be. It may be that they
will decide the Aucas are not ready for contact yet, and will simply return. On the other hand, if Jim can persuade them, I am sure
they will go on over on foot to the Auca houses. Nate was dead
set against this idea, as he says he is "yellow." Ed was on the
fence, having a baby arriving in a couple of weeks, plus two kids
and a wife in Arajuno, but Jim was all for going all the way, as
is typical of his spirit, and of course, I am with him in this.
If God leads that way, I think they should definitely go too.
But I suppose they are just sitting in the tree house, hour after
hour, studying their Auca vocabulary, etc., waiting "for something
to turn up." That is all I know up to now.

I have told Jim, incidentally, that you know about this venture,
so if you want to mention it in letters to us from now on it will
be o.k. He has not told his folks, however, so don't write them.
McCully's folks both know, but Saints do not, mainly because of the
danger of Rachel's finding out, I guess. So you are really on the
inside!   By all means, tell no one else yet, even the family.

I have been quite at peace since Jim left, more so even than
on some other occasions, not nearly so "dangerous" from the human
standpoint.

Valerie has learned to climb stairs now, all the way to the top,
which is a hazard. I picture her falling her from the balcony of
the stairs straight down onto the cement floor. I have barracaded
the stairway, but twice she has crawled over or through the barrier .
So I have to watch her constantly, as she has the run of the whole
house these days. I took her to the Talac River yesterday, with
Stevie Saint, who has been here for two days. She had the time of
her life, crawling along on the sand in shallow water, and she nearly
floated twice, with me holding her head. She ate quantities of sand
and pebbles, but seems to be none the worse today. My, she is cute!!,

Got to stop now -- have only three girls in school today because of bean planting season, but I've got to keep them busy.

Much much love,

Betty

Carmela Chimbu who is here in school asks me to salute you in her name
"She is my beloved old mother. Happily I salute you, praying to God for you."

Letter to mother, January 6, 1956. "I know that if you have gotten my other letters about
Jim's trip, you are on pins and needles to know what is going on."

Cornell Capa and Valerie Elliot

Elisabeth Elliot teaching with Valerie clinging to her skirts, Shandia, Spring 1957

Eleanor Vandevort and Elisabeth Elliot, 1965

The view from Indinyawi—Elisabeth Elliot's beloved White Mountains

Valerie Elliot and Eleanor Vandevort

Addison Leitch and Elisabeth Elliot, circa 1970

The house near Gordon-Conwell

Tom Howard and his son Charles

Elisabeth Elliot speaking outside Urbana, 1979

Elisabeth Elliot and Lars Gren, circa mid-1980s

The Haven

Elisabeth Elliot in her office overlooking the ever-changing sea, Massachusetts, 1986

Elisabeth Elliot and Lars Gren, circa early-2000s

Elisabeth Elliot at home

ideas. "We had come to offer something which, apparently, the Auca was not even looking for," she admits, "a Hope, an anchor for the soul, the person of Jesus Christ."[67] Dayomæ is teaching Bible stories she has learned from Saint, but it is hard for the missionaries to know what is understood, and whether, for example, repeating prayers after Dayomæ indicates belief, or merely sociability. What did this mean for her role as missionary? "We must get this straight," she writes. "We have come, not to be benefactors, but to be *servants*. 'Slaves' is the word Jesus often used."[68] The missionaries' very poverty in the Waorani context, she argues, makes it particularly important to disentangle American culture from the message of the Christian missionary. "Was I bringing them a foreigner's message, or had I something to offer which would mean Life to *them*, the very Life of All Ages, as John refers to Christ in his first epistle? If He is the Life of All Ages, He is the Life of All Cultures."[69]

The final chapter of the book draws its title, "Neither Foreigner Nor Savage," from the Phillips translation of Colossians 3:11, which says that in the "new man of God's design there is no distinction between Greek and Hebrew, Jew or Gentile, foreigner or savage, slave or free man. Christ is all that matters for Christ lives in them all." This passage had leapt out at Elliot near the end of her second short stay in Tewæno. She was a foreigner, living among those who had been called savages. There were insurmountable differences between them. How could the Scripture be true? Over the course of the book, she approaches the question with what ethicist William C. Spohn calls "analogical imagination," essentially employing a three-part analogy to compare Waorani culture, her own culture of origin, and the standard of human behavior laid out in first-century Roman and Jewish cultural terms in the Bible.[70] In so doing, she finds ways in which the two cultures she inhabits, though materially quite different, share a good deal of moral and spiritual common ground. "Human clay is not closer to porcelain in certain places, certain cultures, certain ages, than in others. Man has one desperate need. It is God. . . . One man, by his own efforts, or by whatever we may call progress, is not in any wise capable of making himself *less* needy of Christ than another man."[71] The Wao, the missionary, the successful American, she concludes, are all alike in their need of Jesus.

In one sense, *Kinsman* is a fleshed-out version of *Life* magazine's 1958 article on and by Elliot, describing life with the Waorani. It shares many of the same facts and contains many of the same pictures. But the book differs from *Life*'s presentation of Elliot's story in important ways. Henry Luce, head of *Life*'s parent company, Time, Inc., liked his publications to "tell a story" about events—not just reporting the news but helping busy readers to place it within an interpretive framework. The son of Presbyterian missionaries, who lived in China until he was fifteen, Luce seems to have thought in terms of American exceptionalism. He was a firm believer in Kipling's white man's burden, seeing a uniquely American duty to promote "progress"—which he defined as free enterprise, democracy, and a somewhat vaguely defined morality/spirituality—"throughout the world." With the added subvalues of "adventure," "self-reliance and independence and also co-operation," these made up the framework through which *Life* magazine interpreted America to itself and the world to America.[72]

Luce's trifecta of capitalism, democracy, and morality is neatly presented in the table of contents from the January 1956 edition of *Life* that announced the deaths of the five missionaries. The four stories big enough to merit their own descriptive paragraph and a picture are the deaths of the five; Ford Motors' record-breaking stock sale; an analysis of American presidential campaigns in new memoirs by former President Truman; and the new body style in American automobile manufacturing—morality, capitalism, democracy, and capitalism. The 1957 follow-up article on the widows emphasizes the special blend of "independence and cooperation." And the 1959 piece on Elliot and the Waorani came with an editorial note that fit Elliot into *Life*'s "story" by emphasizing adventure and self-reliance, describing her as a representative of that "irresistible quality of man, . . . his zest for life," and claiming, "She is full of eagerness about every detail of her new, and dangerous, life."[73] Never mind that her own emphasis was on obedience to God's leading as directly *opposed* to love of adventure.

As a long-time reader of Time, Inc. publications, Elliot had had plenty of time to absorb the story they told of America as good Samaritan to the world. In the nine months she had lived in Tewæno, she'd had plenty of time to contemplate that story in light of the civilization around her. At first *Kinsman* feels like an expanded version of the 1959 *Life* article, but it's clear on a closer reading that Elliot is pushing back, hard, against Luce's guiding ethos. *Life* seemed to want to use Christianity as an example of the wholesome morality America had to offer the world alongside capitalism and democracy. Elliot portrays faith in Jesus as a direct challenge to American exceptionalism.

———

In the spring of 1960, Dave had to travel to the US as part of his work for Latin America Mission. Since Elliot and Ginny were both in New Jersey on furlough, he suggested a family reunion. So at the end of March, Jim came home from Wheaton, Tom got a few days' leave from the Army, and Phil and Margaret and their children came from Canada. For three days and part of two more, Katharine and Philip basked in having all their children together, plus as many as possible of the "in-loves"—as the Howards called their in-laws—and grandchildren. They had professional family pictures taken in the living room of Birdsong, played charades, sang around the piano, looked at old photos, wrestled, ate, laughed, and talked. Philip was feeling poorly again, and just a few days later he had another brain tumor removed. Katharine was grateful that Ginny and Betty were still in the area.

Elliot and Valerie left for Portland in early April, stopping briefly in Wheaton on the way. They spent two months with the Elliot family, months stuffed to bursting with family get-togethers, social engagements, and church events. "There are meetings constantly around here, it seems," Elliot wrote wryly to the Howards, "and like Mt. Everest, if it's there, you climb it—or attend, as the case may be."[74] She did some shopping and made some clothes. Valerie had the mumps, then the measles. They took day trips— to Mount Hood to play in the snow, to the Oregon coast to play in the surf, out to a working farm in Troutdale—weekend trips, and even a train trip to Alberta for the week-long spring conference at PBI.

Elliot did not need to do any fundraising during her time in the US, and she had made a conscious decision before furlough to limit speaking engagements. But although she had declined advance invitations, she was asked to speak everywhere she went and often felt she could not refuse. Occasionally she even ended up presenting more than once a day. "Oh dear," she wrote after one such event. "Speaking is just not my calling."[75] Then too, Jim's parents seem not to have been oriented toward advance planning, and Elliot was sometimes bemused to find herself late at night the day before a planned event or trip without enough information to get herself and Valerie ready for the next day. "I'm learning not to stew," she wrote to her parents.[76]

More difficult was the lack of quiet time for relational connection caused by the busyness and disorganization. She lamented the almost total lack "of long quiet evenings to simply <u>converse</u> (the thing I get hungriest for in Ecuador)."[77] In mid- or late June she returned to Moorestown, where she spent her last two months with her parents.

As her time stateside drew to a close, Elliot wrote a letter sharing some of her experiences with supporters. Just as Waorani culture was different from US culture, so the New York art and publishing world was different from the evangelical world, and she had found much to ponder as she moved back and forth between her native milieu and the America "outside the missionary circuit."[78] In *Kinsman*, Elliot had tried to show the Waorani as fully human, made in the image of God, having things to offer rather than merely needing to receive. Now, quoting the same passage by MacDonald she had included in the book's conclusion, she tried to show her supporters, briefly, "the intellectuals of New York."[79] They, too, were made in the image of God; they, too, had gifts to offer the church. In the book Elliot had argued against the conflation of Christianity and American culture in foreign missions; now she suggested that the US church was conflating "the genuine life of the Spirit springing up to godliness" and evangelical culture.[80] The people she had met outside her subculture had important questions about existence, and she believed Christian faith held meaningful answers. But she questioned whether Christians knew any non-Christians well enough to know what those questions were, let alone to be in a position to offer an answer. "Is there any rapport whatever between the Christian and the world?" she asked. "Have we anything to say to them? Have we tried to say it?"[81] Elliot had tried to hold space for such a rapport, and when opportunities came, to say what Christianity had to offer in the big questions of life. She was about to go back to Tewæno, where she would keep trying to establish a rapport that would enable her to address big questions in Waorani culture. In the meantime, she was trying to encourage her fellow Western Christians to ask some big questions of their own.

———

Elliot and Valerie sailed for Ecuador on Grace Line's *Santa Cecilia* in late August 1960. The voyage was much like that of 1952—a fairy-tale interlude in real life, filled with shipboard acquaintances, poolside sunbathing, and elaborate meals elegantly served. Conversation with fellow passengers seemed less daunting to the thirty-three-year-old Elliot—who had seen birth and death, had lived among isolated blow-gun hunters and New York literati—than it had to the sheltered twenty-five-year-old of the first voyage, and she had "some wonderful talks with some who had sincere questions about the meaning of faith and the reason for missionary work."[82] Valerie had a wonderful time swimming and playing with the other children on board. "I'm enjoying all this to the fullest, trying to store it all up for the next months or years," Elliot wrote to her family.[83] There was an ache that came from remembering that earlier trip, when the country and her work had been unknowns, and Jim and hope for a future with Jim had been waiting for her. Now the place and the task at hand were, to some extent, known quantities, and there seemed nothing but loneliness ahead. Nevertheless, she felt a sense of assurance. She wrote to Katharine from aboard ship, "I go back wondering what the next eight years will hold but without any misgivings, for I know that He keeps His word."[84]

Guayaquil was the usual scene of chaos and confusion. There was someone to meet her at the docks only by accident, she and Valerie stayed with missionaries she'd never met since there had been no previous arrangements made, and the baggage took days to clear customs. Quito seemed hardly better, as most of the families she had known were gone, and construction had changed the city a good deal. Mother and daughter stayed with Marilou while they waited for the luggage to arrive, and Elliot went on "the first date I've had since Jim died."[85] She had hit it off aboard ship with a Catholic Costa-Rican American working as a language instructor in Quito's US embassy. In Guayaquil they had gone for a walk and talked about translation, language-learning, and faith. In Quito he took her out to dinner. It was "very nice," she told her parents and Ginny, "but don't get excited. I just felt that I wanted a man's company for a change, and he had more questions he wanted to talk over about faith and the Bible. Keep this to yourselves, please."[86]

Elliot also enjoyed the opportunity to spend time with Marilou and Marj. They spent some frustrating time working on the long-distance struggle with the Martyrs Fund administrators. But they had a relationship of mutual help and encouragement, and Elliot felt herself strengthened for the work ahead by their time together.[87] She was able, too, to see Rachel, who had come to Quito to drop Sammy off at school. But the older woman seemed uncommunicative, volunteering no news and saying little in answer to questions. Elliot had brought her a gift, a suit of clothes, and was disappointed to find it was too small. The meeting was a letdown.

Elliot and Valerie made the multistage journey to Arajuno with the help of a new Brethren missionary, Britisher Mary Skinner, who went along "just for the ride, and [to] help me, which she certainly did, by buying tickets, helping me with baggage and generally cheering our spirits. She is a great girl and I have wondered . . . if we might ever work together."[88] In Arajuno, Elliot found more changes—the Tidmarshes had moved to Quito, and the station was occupied by Dick and Jane Farstad, Brethren who had come to Ecuador in response to the deaths of the five men.

But nothing quite prepared her for the change she found on the last leg of her journey. First was the trip itself. The Tewæno runway, the beginnings of which had been pictured in the book, was now complete. After spending a few days in Arajuno to unpack, sort, and repack their household goods, Elliot and Valerie traveled to Tewæno on September 21, 1960, in an SIL plane, "a ten-minute trip which left me completely disoriented, when I'd formerly had three days to condition myself to the 'rugged' life!"[89] Already the world of *Kinsman* had passed away forever.

Instead of arriving in a nearly empty settlement, Elliot found a clearing full of houses, and "nearly all" the extended family-group present. Saint and a few Waorani were in Limoncocha for a language conference with SIL's Kenneth L. Pike and Catherine Peeke. Elliot's own house was unchanged apart from a nice new hammock provided by Saint, but the new houses had walls—an ambiguous addition since "I still get all the noise but none of the interest that went with being able to see all that went on inside."[90] There had been time to establish crops, and there was increased availability of staple foods. Clothing had become universal for teens and adults, although Elliot noted with dismayed amusement how often holes, missing buttons, and poor fit, combined with a complete lack of concern about genital exposure, tended to emphasize rather than obscure the existence of sex organs. Despite having forgotten some things about the language in the year she had been away, she quickly found herself able to converse again due to the growing ability of her friends to figure out what she was trying to say and help her along, and happily reported a "good long talk" with some of the women.[91]

Elliot also noticed changes in the Christian meetings, writing, "It cannot help but touch one to realize what these people have learned in two years."[92] At the first such gathering after her return, she taught the story of the conversion of Paul using flannelgraphs, the group sang a song about heaven (written by Saint to a Wao tune), and Guiimadi and Ipa, a young woman with a son about three years younger than Valerie, prayed aloud. People were also retelling and discussing stories from the Hebrew Scriptures—the life of Moses, say, or of David—as they sat around the fire in the evenings, and Elliot was impressed by their extensive, detailed knowledge of the particulars of the stories. "I cannot, however, be sure what it all means," she wrote.[93] As far as she could tell, the same word was used for *believe, remember,* and *think about,* and she wondered whether people were defining their belief based on how many Bible stories they could retell. She still did not know how much they understood of the life of Jesus or of the implications of trying to live in obedience to him.

As the days went by, Elliot resumed her daily language work, "trying to pick up what I'd forgotten."[94] Ipa began coming to work as an informant, recounting oral history for Elliot to record and then helping transcribe the tapes. Elliot started Valerie on formal schoolwork, allotting an hour of time a day to the first-grade curriculum from Calvert School, which provided everything needed to homeschool, even in a clearing in the Amazon jungle.[95] Three Kichwa men who had married into the tribe in her absence asked her to teach them about God, so she started regular evening classes for them. Johnny Keenan and Dan Derr landed on the new runway to deliver food and mail. Marilou and little Mike came to Tewæno for a six-day visit.

Rachel came back from Limoncocha early in November on the flight that took the McCullys out. Any hope that time apart would have mended fences was immediately dashed. A disheartened Elliot wrote tersely in her journal a few days later that nothing had changed. Though she recorded no details, she noted that she had put a foot wrong several times already.

The first point of conflict Elliot recorded lay in their different attitudes toward outside influence and Wao agency. In the six-and-a-half weeks she had been back in Tewæno, Elliot had weighed the pros and cons and decided she would like a more Western-style house, with walls, window screens, and private bedrooms. The culture was changing, had changed even in her absence, and she hoped that the potential for increased efficiency in language work would offset the potential disadvantages of introducing more changes. It would mean bringing in a crew of Kichwa men to do the building, but the Waorani she spoke with about it had, she believed, agreed to this gladly. The men looked forward with anticipation to male guests, and Dayomæ appears to have been interested in increasing the pool of potential marriage partners. But when Elliot raised the question with Saint, the older woman was adamantly opposed, apparently concerned about increasing the likelihood of immoral sexual behavior and the potential for violence. Elliot recognized these possibilities but felt the degree of outside influence in the community ought to be decided by the Waorani. She did not share these details with her family, however, reporting only that she was going to have a new house. Saint had agreed to it as long as Dayomæ was the one who put the process in motion.

Neither did Elliot share that on Saint's return the older woman had criticized her Wao tededo, nor that whenever she tried to share her language data it started another conflict. To the Howards, she wrote only that she didn't have much information yet as to the results of Saint's conference with Pike and Peeke and hoped to learn more after the older woman had gotten a chance to review her materials. Elliot continued doing her best not to gossip about her difficulties with her coworker. Even in the privacy of her journal she still tended to record her emotions—guilt over her inability to solve the problem, her yearning to connect, the way she lay awake at night with her mind racing—rather than the events that triggered them. As the days went on, Elliot began to feel that she *had* to find a way to stop trying to figure out what was wrong and how to fix it, to trust that God would make it okay somehow, even if nothing ever changed. If she didn't, she wrote in her journal, she was going to lose her mind.[96]

She turned to the Bible for a way to marshal her gnawing thoughts, looking for passages that provided instruction or reassurance for her situation. A letter to her family explains something of her thought processes, making no mention of Saint:

Am learning fresh lessons in waiting in quietness before God, to be still and do ONE THING, i.e. know that He is God. One prayer I often pray is Paul's of Col. 1, "that you may see things, as it were, from God's point of view." I feel acutely the danger of becoming warped & distorted in my thinking when I have no one with whom to confer & share all that I think, and I pray for light & correction where my vision is near-sighted or blurred. God has promised us "power, love, and a sound mind."[97]

This practice of turning her mind to God instead of the problem, praying, and remembering Scripture seemed to help her regain her equilibrium.

When Katharine wrote asking directly how things were going with Saint, Elliot admitted that things had been rocky initially but said that she was working "to try to keep a clear conscience before God, to ask Him to set a watch on the door of my lips, and to go on in peace and love." She had been praying that God would enable her to put their conflicts right out of her mind and now felt free from the compulsion to revisit what had been said and done and try to figure out where she had gone wrong. She was hopeful that Saint had all along been troubled less by their clashes than she—Sam had told her his sister was constructed of "cast iron"—and although she acknowledged that she couldn't know Saint's heart and mind, things seemed more peaceful for both of them. By early December the two women had been able to agree over the inadvisability of adopting Spanish orthography for Wao tededo.[98]

Elliot's little house was quickly finished, and she wrote happily to her family of the "immense psychological effect which four walls have had on me."[99] Screened windows cut insects down by about two-thirds, and walls meant things stayed dry. Now she could have a stove and oven so she could cook more than one thing at a time and even bake, and a table, so she could use dishes again. Her mother sent her teacups for her birthday, and she was delighted. "It is lovely to drink tea from a china cup, Mother!"[100] She enjoyed adding creative touches, coordinating Valerie's bedding in pink candy stripe and her own room with blue and aqua curtains and coverlet. She could even assign Val chores; it was the little girl's job to fill the new wood box every day. But best of all was the desk, which meant "I have been able to get all my papers, files, letters, financial business, etc. etc. in one place again, organized and neat and workable. Oh joy, oh delight."[101] Elliot had hoped to be able to offer hospitality to Saint in her new house, but Saint declined dinner invitations for herself and Dayomæ and refused to accept bread Elliot baked for her, saying she didn't want to take up any of Elliot's time.

The two women took turns leaving Tewæno at Christmastime. Elliot, Valerie, and Ipa, who had asked to go with them, left in mid-December and came back just after the holiday, and Saint and Dayomæ left a few hours before they returned and stayed in Quito until late January. Elliot's trip was another whirlwind, with company meals every night, visiting with Marj and Marilou, another date with the embassy employee, and sight-seeing with Ipa. On her way back to Tewæno, she left Valerie overnight in Shell Mera, and she and Mary Skinner attended a Boxing Day Kichwa-language conference in Shandia; she was pleased to learn that Skinner planned to move into the vacant station at Shandia. Despite her busyness, Elliot missed her family. She wrote wistfully, "It seems years since I saw any of you. The sense of time is distorted here. I heard about the big snowfall on the radio, but it seems incredible that it could be snowing anywhere, or that it is Christmas in the U.S. Merry Christmas to all, and to all very much love."[102]

Loneliness, the passing of another birthday, the turn of the year, and the approach of the fifth anniversary of Jim's death put Elliot in a meditative frame of mind, and she wrote to her mother, sharing some of her ponderings. She was increasingly aware of the march of time and its effects on her, noting the appearance of "distinct crow's feet and sagging jowls, loose neck and deep forehead furrows." "It is the fading of the brightness, of which the hymn speaks, that seems unbearable to me, and yet how often have I reminded myself that if God could be with me through losing Jim, there is certainly nothing to fear from whatever else life may hold." Then, too, she was pondering whether she was really doing anything worthwhile with her life. The new house required more housework than before, and she was discovering that she "could make a full-time job out of things which would be wholly unnecessary if I were not in Ecuador. Val would be in school, people would not be writing to me, and housework would be simpler. . . . Does the little bit of time I actually put into language work (and even that is not really constructive so far) or talking to Indians justify my being here, posing as a 'missionary'??? Oh dear, this missionary image disturbs me no end anyway."[103]

Though she rarely saw people with whom she could discuss the things she pondered, she continued to put her questions and thoughts and arguments into family letters. From Moorestown (Philip and Katharine), Canada (Phil and Margaret), Colombia (Dave and Phyllis), the Philippines (Ginny and Bud), England (Tom), and Wheaton (Jim), the rest of the family did the same, not only sharing news and jokes but talking over ideas from afar. They discussed several overlapping themes over a period of months, and Elliot's contributions to the conversation shed some light on her thinking during this time. In response to Dave, she wrote:

> I think you know my answer to the dramatics question: unquestionably a gift, and therefore as functional as any other gift in glorifying God. How does one glorify God through music? Is there something celestial about a tune (e.g. "Climb climb up sunshine mountain") above another tune ("A Capital Ship"), or is it the person, again, who glorifies God and not the thing in itself? . . . Does God give gifts only that they may be employed in some public form of "service"? Or are they simply a part of the fullness of life?

She went on to describe being moved by the movie *Ben-Hur*. "It did what you said MacD. does for you, Mother (and I am sure it's what MacD. does for me)—made me love Him more. In Thess. Paul prayed that their hearts might be directed into the love of God. Whatever contributes to this is to be sought." And then returning to Dave's letter: "You mentioned objecting to the Tenebrae service as an attempt to effect spirituality through emotion, or some such words. Is this always a mistake? What about the breaking of bread? A remembrance feast, but we do try to make ourselves 'feel' the meaning."[104] Later, "You mention that most dramatics appeal to the 'fleshly' side of our nature. To which side do sex and food appeal? This does not make them wrong. Again, it is the use of these things that determines their value, not the thing per se."[105]

Elliot was trying to let God use what she was learning to shape the way she lived. "Perhaps another man does in faith a thing which is deplorable to me. If it is deplorable to me, obviously I cannot do it in faith, so for me it is sin. God knows the love of a man's heart, and accepts us where we are. . . . I have been asking the Lord to help me in this, for I am well aware that my nature is to question <u>and to condemn</u>. The Word, and the Spirit of that Word, must guide me as an individual. There my faith can rest, and I must go in faith. For me, there's no other way to go on."[106] This played into her response to a letter from her sister-in-law as well:

> Margaret, your points are all well-taken, and in principle I am sure all of us are in complete agreement. It is the application of the principle which I still firmly believe is RELATIVE. It is different for each individual . . . and it is different in different times in the life of each individual, and in different places. . . . I have constantly sought out the meaning of worldliness for me, and the answers keep changing. . . .
>
> I keep going back to Jesus' own example—He conformed to His society & culture in matters of dress and activities (Imagine the Son of God at a village wedding, and then imagine Him supplying the seconds on wine, and even outdoing the host's wine in quality!) He did not thereby love either the world or the things in it. They were His. . . . We are Christ's & Christ is God's, and therefore all things are ours. It is in the giving of thanks that the thing is sanctified. If we cannot be thankful, we had best abstain. It is precisely because I belong to Christ that all that I do, even eating or drinking (be it steak and wine or chicken and monkey meat), may be done to His glory. How grateful I am for this liberation![107]

Replying to family mail in January 1961, Elliot addressed Katharine's meditations on whether "there may be much more in redemption than anyone ever conceived":

> There can be no question about that. And for some eye openers, try Phillips translation of Ephesians 1 (for example, "Everything that exists in Heaven or earth shall find its perfection and fulfilment in Him.") and Colossians 1 ("It was in Him that the full nature of God chose to live, and through Him God planned to reconcile in His own person as it were, everything on earth and everything in Heaven by virtue of the sacrifice of the Cross.") Will He perform what He has set out to perform? As in Adam all die, even so in Christ shall all be made alive. What do these Scriptures mean???? To me, there isn't much room for equivocation. (Plenty of room for suspended judgment on things we can't reconcile in the Scripture—I can't explain them by any means, but I've found a great liberating truth.)[108]

Although it did not make up for the lack of sympathetic conversation in daily life, the chance to tussle with ideas with her family long-distance brought her comfort and helped her sharpen her own thinking.

———

The usual business of missionary life went on: hosting guests, answering mail—everything from marriage proposals from Kichwa men to unsigned requests for jungle souvenirs with no return address—running her household with Ipa's help, doing school with Valerie, teaching the tiny faith formation classes, and working on the language at her new desk. "I hope to be able to make some sense out of Auca syntax soon—it is still very difficult for me to know when, who, and where an incident takes place. Often I follow the action well, but have no idea whom they're talking about, etc."[109] In her spare time she read everything she could get her hands on—*Anne Frank: The Diary of a Young Girl*, which she called "exquisitely perceptive"; the *New Yorker* magazine, to which Tom had given her a subscription; Thomas Belt's "fascinating" nineteenth-century *The Naturalist in Nicaragua*; Clarence W. Hall's *Portrait of a Prophet*, a biography of Holiness exponent and Salvation Army officer Samuel Logan Brengle; and, with Valerie, A. A. Milne's *Now We Are Six*.[110]

In February, Saint and Dayomæ decided to have a Western-style house built as well, and the project seemed to provide an opportunity for Saint and Elliot to connect. Elliot wrote Katharine, "I have enjoyed so much sharing in little decisions about her house and helping her fix up the stove from Arajuno (the old one I had) etc."[111] Valerie turned six, and Saint threw her a party in her new home, with gifts, a scavenger hunt, and other games. Elliot baked a birthday cake and gave Valerie a dress and some other small gifts she'd been saving for the occasion. Valerie's enjoyment of life brought sunshine into Elliot's days. She loved watching Val hike the trails like a veteran, enjoy impromptu camping trips, develop her woodcraft and command of Wao tededo, talk and sing to herself or with her friends. She tried to include anecdotes about Valerie in letters to the grandparents as often as possible. "You should have seen her this morning," she wrote near the end of the month, "shigra [carrying net] full of doll clothes on her head, some burning sticks in her hands to make a fire with, Taemanta [a friend] in tow, pushing a baby buggy full of dolls down the airstrip!"[112]

March was full of language work. Elliot tackled her existing statement of suffix order hoping to reduce it to the simplest possible form. Catherine Peeke came to work with Saint for a few days, and Elliot enjoyed the chance to get to know her a bit and learn from her about approaching the language. At the end of the month Elliot and one of the Kichwa men who had married into the Guequitaidi traveled to Dos Rios for a large Kichwa-language Christian conference.

The month also brought the publication of *Kinsman*, with an initial print run of forty thousand copies. Though her parents each wrote with praise and encouraging words, Elliot was disappointed. She had not realized just how big the endpaper photographs of naked women fishing in the river would turn out and worried that the pictures would distract from the message. Her concerns were well-founded; within weeks she would begin to receive mail notifying her that the book had been banned from some Christian bookstores and churches because of the pictures. She was also frustrated to discover that the book had lost valuable publicity because rumors were circulating in New York that it had been ghostwritten. *Through Gates of Splendor* continued to sell around 775 copies a month, however, and she received word that Harper's had granted translation rights yet again, this time into Urdu. Arnold wrote to her, "The continuing strength of this book is one of the phenomena of the publishing world."[113]

While Elliot was in Dos Rios, she was approached by the head of the government committee tasked with spraying DDT to reduce malaria about adding Tewæno to the rotation. She had felt she could not make a unilateral decision and had promised to discuss it with Saint on her return. Saint, however, was no more comfortable with visitors from outside than she had been in November and rejected the idea. On this occasion Elliot departed from her usual practice of avoiding disagreement. It's unclear why; perhaps she felt that more than her own opinion was at stake in the possible prevention of malaria or in the maintenance of a good relationship with the government. In any event, she pushed back, suggesting that the scenario might be less clear cut than Saint believed, less negative than she seemed to fear. But Elliot was not the only one who had been keeping her own counsel in an attempt to avoid open conflict. Her pushback seems to have blown the lid off for Saint, who responded by expressing long-standing concerns about Elliot's theology and behavior.

After their conversation, a heartsick Elliot sat down at her typewriter to write privately to her mother. She opened by quoting Psalm 73:21–26: "When my soul was embittered, when I was pricked in heart, I was brutish and ignorant; I was like a beast toward you. Nevertheless, I am continually with you; you hold my right hand. You guide me with your counsel, and afterward you will receive me to glory. Whom have I in heaven but you? And there is nothing on earth that I desire besides you. My flesh and my heart may fail, but God is the strength of my heart and my portion forever." "This is all true just now," she wrote. "Especially the last part. It is my song. I <u>know</u> that God is the strength of my heart and my portion forever."[114]

Then she explained Saint's concerns as she understood them. The older woman was deeply troubled over Elliot's spiritual state, believing her to hold dangerous doctrinal positions. These Saint had not enumerated, saying that she believed Elliot already knew what they were; perhaps she feared being drawn aside into secondary arguments. She felt Elliot had persisted in courses of action she knew Saint believed to be dangerous. She had been mortified to have a visiting SIL colleague see the books—including those by Sigmund Freud and Christian philosopher and theologian Paul Tillich—on Elliot's shelves. Saint had long prayed that either she or Elliot would be able to recognize their error and change but saw no sign of change in Elliot, no indication that she herself was wrong, and no guidance as to what to do about it. For all these reasons she had been avoiding as much as possible both social interaction and collaboration, whether on language work or in telling the story of Jesus. She did not expect that to change. And she did not want to talk about it anymore.

Elliot had been troubled, even before her furlough, by what had seemed a deliberate refusal to work together or even converse, so in one sense it was a relief not to have to worry anymore that it was all in her head. She tried to understand Saint's concerns, rather than defend herself, so that they could work through them. But by the end of the conversation, it felt as though Saint had shut the door on that possibility with a bang, and with it, the door to Elliot's life in Tewæno. The language could not be properly analyzed by either of them without all the available data, and the Christian message of reconciliation must seem a farce when delivered by two people who could not work together even for a cause that both of them considered the most important thing in the world.

If she and Saint could not collaborate, it seemed foolish for her to stay. And yet she had no sense of guidance toward a new job or a new home and did not see how she could go without that guidance. Then, too, she dreaded the questions that were sure to come from all sides if she left and had no idea how she would truthfully answer them. Nevertheless, Elliot reassured her mother (and herself) of God's faithfulness. "In short," she wrote, "from a human standpoint, my labor has turned to dust. . . . I stand with no clue as to the direction He will lead, but utterly at peace in the knowledge that He <u>will</u>, and that His leading thus far has not been in vain. God never wastes His servants' time. This is a good thing for me to remember when I think of the long time I've spent on my files and tapes, etc. I know that when I see Him I will sing with all of my heart that He led me all the way."[115] She asked Katharine to keep the matter entirely to herself and to keep praying for them.

Saint planned to leave in a week to spend a month and a half in Limoncocha for another workshop with Pike, and Elliot was relieved to look ahead to a good stretch of time to think and try to hear from God without needing to worry about interacting with Saint. But the intermediary time was painful. Saint raised the subject of their relationship again a few days later. This time she explained, as Elliot understood it, that she had avoided interaction because Elliot refused to take no for an answer, trying to strong-arm her into agreement and making things uncomfortable if she refused. The older woman did not feel she had the energy to deal with the emotional fallout. This puzzled Elliot because she had tried so hard *not* to insist on continuing conversations in which they disagreed. But much worse was that Saint seemed to have understood their previous conversation so differently than Elliot that the younger woman could not even recognize much of it as the same conversation she had participated in. Saint repudiated statements that were burned into Elliot's brain and ascribed to Elliot statements that the younger woman could not imagine ever saying in a million years. Elliot felt stunned and bewildered.

Still she worked not to assume she was right and Saint wrong. In a second letter to Katharine, Elliot pointed out that Saint must be as disoriented as she, and that though she sometimes wondered if Saint was crazy, it must appear to Saint that *she* was crazy. In fact, she herself had begun to wonder if she *was* crazy. She ruefully noted that talking things through—her default response to disagreement—was obviously not going to fix their problem. But, she pointed out, neither was the Christian fallback, prayer. That was what was so crazy-making. She had *been* praying, for years, and so had Saint, and so had Katharine—and things were *worse*. Even her practice of meditating on the promises of God was an irritant in itself now. She could not rely on the promises (she quoted Isaiah 30:21, "Your ears shall hear a word behind you, saying, 'This is the way, walk in it,' when you turn to the right or when you turn to the left") as reassurance that she was right, when they were promises to Saint as much as to her. She felt trapped, "shut up . . . at the end of the world," "wretched." As she had done when Jim died, she made the conscious choice to view this loss of comforts, even spiritual ones, as an exercise in trust, "a new opportunity to say 'I love Thee, trust Thee, praise Thee. Do with me what Thou wilt.'"[116]

———

At the end of April, Elliot composed her first letter to supporters since returning to Ecuador eight months before, ascribing the delay to a lack of "thrilling progress to report" or any "new request for prayer." She had been "at a loss to know what to write." The missionary letters Elliot was familiar with seemed like clear-cut stories of steady spiritual advance; her life lent itself less and less to that kind of narrative. But a letter of some kind had to be written. She did her best to give an honest report: there had been changes in Tewæno, incremental, ambiguous. Some seemed purely material: Kimö had developed an interest in Western-style carpentry and built himself a bed and a chicken pen. Other changes had implications for the Christian message: Saint was doing a trial run with simple literacy materials, though they still didn't have a finished alphabet. People were repeating Bible stories and prayers. Elliot was unsure what that meant for their understanding of the Christian faith. She closed by asking for prayer for the downriver group, for the language work, for "evidence . . . of the Life of the Spirit in these who say they believe," for "the fruits of repentance," and most of all for Dayomæ, the primary Bible teacher, and Saint, Dayomæ's constant companion and teacher. Come what might in her own future, she wanted the Waorani to learn to walk with Jesus.[117]

Saint returned from Limoncocha in late May. Until Elliot could learn whether Saint and Pike had altered the typography during their workshop, she could not make more early readers, but she kept plugging away at what she could do. "I've been transcribing and translating tapes lately," she reported to her family.

> I'm reading Proverbs now, and appreciate especially the several verses which say that although men may plan and devise, it's the Lord who actually directs steps and brings things to pass. I cannot avoid speculating and conjecturing as to just what in the world He wants me to do here in this tiny corner of the earth, but until the cloud lifts here is where I remain, trusting Him to give me faithfulness in the work I do have to do, which is not insufficient to keep me busy, to be sure, but the ultimate usefulness of which cannot but be questioned.[118]

Elliot could not help speculating and conjecturing, either, about the events of her life so far. She had discerned a call to missionary linguistics, but it was beginning to seem that she could not accomplish anything in the field. In the last nine years she had worked in three distinct languages, Tsafiki, Kichwa, and Wao tededo. There is no record that she knew anything about the current status of the Tsafiki language work, which she had left to marry Jim. Since the Catherses had left Shandia, no one was using her Kichwa materials. And Saint's refusal to collaborate seemed to indicate that the work she had done on Wao tededo would be useless. She wrote to her mother:

> It sort of makes me chilled when I think that possibly I've been here just to write a book and get my name identified with this heroic effort! God knows that was not my motive, but I shrink from that sort of judgment, which is bound to come if I leave here soon. Well, another chance to "die"! (Quote L.E.M.) It does seem strange that I've really done almost nothing else but write books, when I'm supposed to be a missionary.[119]

Her inability to make measurable progress in linguistics made her wonder if she was in fact being pointed in a new direction entirely.

I was reading this morning in Eph. about the different gifts, and feel that perhaps I am meant to stick to writing. I have always felt that even more than writing God had given me a gift for language, but I see no means of stirring up that gift. Daily the exercise in Auca is interesting to me, and I confess I enjoy it, but to what end? Well, some of us are meant to be "hands" in the Body of Christ—get things done. Some of the rest of us are meant, perhaps, to be "eyes." To contemplate, observe, perceive. Does it sound preposterous? Maybe it is.[120]

One of the tapes Elliot spent the month of May transcribing and translating was a detailed firsthand account of the killing of the five men, told by Minkaye, who had participated. She sent copies to Wilfred, the other widows, and Katharine, explaining, "I have remembered how desperately, in Jan., 1956, we wished we could talk to someone who saw what happened. Now I've done that, and felt compelled to put it down on paper, regardless of the feelings awakened by so doing."[121] Those feelings must have been deeply painful. Minkaye described a scene of horror, men backed against a wall of forest, shouting and firing warning shots, the first thrust of a spear, the dying man "jerking around" on the sand, another speared, and another, groaning and crying, fighting back, spears torn out and plunged in again, cries of anguish, falling face-first into the river, unable to get out, dragged to shore and speared again and again, chased down the beach, spears broken to pieces so the warriors could stab again and again, bleeding slowly to death, taken by the current, drowning, hit with rocks, crying, speared and speared, slashed with machetes. At the end it still wasn't clear who had died at what point in the proceedings or just what each man had suffered, only that the Waorani had believed the five were cannibals, luring them with gifts in order to eat them. Elliot made no other comment on the account.

About a month later, Elliot and Valerie made an overnight trip by foot and canoe to the place where Jim had died, traveling with a group that included Dayomæ, Kimö, Guiimadi, and Benito, one of the Kichwa men who had married into the group. Afterward she wrote to her family describing the trip. In early afternoon they had reached their destination. There was debris from the treehouse on the beach, and Benito had found part of Nate's plane mostly buried in the sand. Elliot took a small piece for Marj. The Waorani had pointed out the location of the grave, and Guiimadi had indicated the spot where she and the others had come out of the forest when they met the five, the same place the Waorani men had hidden before their attack. Valerie had asked "where her Daddy was."

I looked at the beach and trees around, and marveled again at Nate's skill in landing there. I looked at that immense forest giant which lay right in the middle of the sand—far higher than my head on its side, probably ten feet in diameter anyway, which the river had deposited there during a flood. I thought again how easily the Lord could have put an obstacle there so that a landing would have been impossible. . . . I looked at the waters of the Curaray, flowing silently as ever, and the forest around, apparently lifeless and imperturbable, and it seemed a dream that anything of any import could have happened there. But there was the plane, there was the grave, there was the aluminum. And Kimu walked around quietly, with a spear on his shoulder, smiling mildly as is his wont. . . . I couldn't help thinking of Wordsworth's poem which Jim used to quote, and of which he used to say that Wordsworth had said one of the few meaningful things that could be said on paper about love:

"But [he] is in his grave, and, oh,
The difference to me!"[122]

Life went on. Elliot made plans for a second reading primer, which she would begin as soon as Saint finished her feedback on the first one. Saint threw a birthday party for Dayomæ, and Elliot and Valerie attended. Sammy and young Steve Saint arrived to spend their school break. Elliot ordered second-grade coursework for Valerie. Guequita gave his own account of the death of the five men, essentially consistent with Minkaye's. Elliot was reading Beatrix Potter with Valerie, and in her free time, Catholic priest Lorenzo Scupoli's *The Spiritual Combat*; the New English Bible ("don't find it much better or worse than the RSV which I've been using regularly for a long time"); *Anna Karenina* ("I can't remember reading a greater book. It is Truth, with a capital T, and superbly distilled. If Jesus is Truth, if His Spirit is the Spirit of Truth, surely He is the source of all Truth, and that which is True originates in Him, and glorifies Him."); and Camus's *The Fall* ("It is a demolishing piece of work, which had something of the same effect

... as A.C.'s 'If.' [*sic*] No man can escape judgment. . . . Of course the man's solution is mere acceptance of this guilt, once it is recognized, while the Christian knows a better answer. I wish all of you would read the book.").[123]

She continued to pray for guidance as to where she should go if she left Tewæno. Mary Skinner was in Shandia, so she felt her presence would be extraneous. Arajuno had the Farstads. Puyupungu was home to one of the Kichwa men who had proposed to her, so that seemed out. And she had no sense that she should try to launch yet another new station. In fact, she began to wonder if the lack of a sense of leading meant she should stay in Tewæno after all. "I am grateful for the quiet and freedom I have here. I have done a lot of thinking lately about possibilities for writing. This is an ideal place to write, and maybe God wants me to stay here a little longer and think some more."[124]

Elliot's ideas about the clear and unmistakable leading of God, expressed so often in *Through Gates of Splendor*, were undergoing changes. She returned repeatedly to Vandevort's picture of obedience: "Following Him is not like walking a tight-rope." This seemed to suggest room for more than one right answer. Over the past months she had argued that "worldliness" was determined by a person's attitude more than by a set of specific behaviors; now she appears to have applied that standard to understanding God's direction. In mid-July she responded to Tom's thoughts on God's leading: "I particularly take issue with the school of thought which insists that one must 'reach the place where he had no will of his own before he can discern God's will.' No. Jesus had a will of His own, and it must have been contrary to God's, if He could pray 'Not my will but Thine.' This is the prayer to pray, and God knows it's the deepest desire of our hearts." Elliot wrote to Katharine of her ongoing inability to understand what God wanted her to do and her growing sense that she could trust God to make it okay even if she didn't know what God's will was, even if she was mistaken—even if she was not within that will:

Yesterday as I was praying, and puzzling again over what the Lord is doing with me here, I felt like saying (and when I feel like saying, I say, to God, for He knows the thought anyway, and He's my Father . . .). "Why did you bring me in here if there's nothing for me to do, and if you're not going to give me the faith necessary to see these Aucas delivered and changed?"

And suddenly I thought of the verse, "I brought thee out so that I might bring thee in," and I wondered if it's possible that He brought me in that He might bring me out! It seems absurd, but I guess He knows what He's doing, and I can only trust Him. If I'm way off the beam, badly mistaken and negligent to my duty, off on a tangent or thinking crookedly, wresting the Scriptures to my own destruction, or whatever, I <u>trust</u> Him. He has promised to guide and teach. He'll have to do it. "Fear thou not, for I am with Thee." I believe this.[125]

On July 21 Dave arrived for a week's visit. He taught in Spanish at the Sunday meeting, with Dayomæ translating, and Valerie thoroughly enjoyed showing her uncle around, although she kept forgetting she had to speak English to him. When he left a week later, Elliot and Valerie went out to Quito with him. Elliot received "invitations galore" for social events and speaking engagements, spoke several times, and went sightseeing with friends. But she appreciated most the opportunity to talk face-to-face in her mother tongue, especially a few hours of conversation with Capa, who was in South America on assignment. And Elliot was beginning to recognize some of her prejudices. After describing one of her hostesses as "Jewish, of course, but such a lovely, sympathetic person," she immediately went on, "Forgive me. I certainly should not have put that 'but' in that sentence. Just shows one's subconcious [sic] prejudices, and the inexcusable arrogance of the Gentile race. (of the 'Christian'!)"[126]

From Quito, Elliot and Valerie traveled to Shandia, where Elliot spent two weeks teaching Kichwa-language classes to Mary Skinner and three other missionaries. She used the language materials she had created in 1957, "supplemented by informant work, tape transcription, conversation, and story-telling, with each one giving a sentence of a fairy story or Bible story, going round the circle in turn. I have enjoyed the time very much, and I hope it has been helpful." It seemed "very strange indeed" to be back in Shandia, but it was comforting to see the once-abandoned station given new life, and to discover that the church was still in existence.[127]

They got back to Tewæno on September 8. Coming home to a house in the jungle was a labor-intensive proposition—everything was covered with mildew, often things were ruined by insects or trespassers, once Elliot even found a rotting rabbit in the house—but Dayomæ (who with Saint was gone on an eight-week trip to the US) had asked someone to sweep the dead bugs out of Elliot's house before her return, which was a pleasant surprise. Mother and daughter started second grade, and Valerie was delighted with it. Elliot taught at the Sunday morning meeting on God as our shepherd. The weather was growing hotter and buggier, and she enjoyed the screened house and the shade it provided. "It is a most pleasurable, peaceful life, and for all one's human perversity of feeling which looks at its disadvantages and at the advantages of some other life, one is frequently aware that one would miss the jungle and its beauties, the Indians and their attractions and foibles." And although she still struggled with the fast pace of conversation, she told her family, "Have done some work on certain morphemes which have been bothering me for years, and feel that light has really begun to break through. I went back to some old taped texts and found that I could actually make some sense out of them, which is hopeful, as usually I get a conglommeration [sic] of ideas with no idea how they are connected."[128]

In early October there was news of another Waorani spear killing, raising again the question of whether there was any way to contact the downriver group. Elliot asked whether a deputation of women might be successful, but the general consensus was that the downriver group would assume the women were decoys for an ambush such as they themselves had used when they attacked the five missionaries. Mary Skinner came for a visit, and Elliot made plans with Barbara and Marilou for visits in November. Elliot kept reading—J. D. Salinger's "To Esmé, with Love and Squalor," ("I was enchanted"); an account of Francisco de Orellana's yearlong exploration of the Amazon jungle ("an absorbing tale, to say the least"); Leon Uris's *Exodus* ("Can't figure out what all the shouting is about. Found it eminently boring"); and J. B. Phillips's *God Our Contemporary* ("am delighted with it"). She reassured her mother, who had expressed concern over her isolation, that she felt the opportunity to spend time reading and thinking was "part of God's purpose for me now." Writing seemed increasingly like it might be her job, and "surely if God wants me to write I must read rather widely in order to know my own contemporaries, those to whom I must speak, as well as to increase my own ability to express myself on paper."[129]

Saint and Dayomæ returned on Halloween, bringing with them three weeks' worth of mail, including a letter from Philip asking permission to print Elliot's letter describing her trip to "Palm Beach." When she had sent that letter in late June, she had asked her father not to print any more excerpts from her letters. The visit to Jim's grave was "too sentimental for publication," and she felt people were getting tired of her updates.[130] She herself was tired of the intense public interest and wished people would stop fixating on one tiny tribe and two struggling missionaries and focus on their own responsibilities. Even now, four months later, she felt that not only were her graveside meditations personal but also that since she had not written them for publication, they were not as polished as she would like. Nevertheless, in a letter dated November 2, she reluctantly agreed to her father's request.

———

Ten days later, on November 13, 1961, Elliot announced her departure from Tewæno. To her family and Jim's parents she sent a personal letter, enclosing a formal statement of resignation. She sent copies of the latter to the bare minimum of people she felt needed to know: Rachel Saint, SIL's Ecuador director Don Johnson, MAF, Marj, Marilou, Wilfred, and Jim's siblings. In the formal statement, Elliot explained that she and Saint had differences of opinion (she did not elaborate), and that although she considered them nonessential and was happy to work together toward shared goals, Saint considered them insurmountable. Because of this, Saint was unwilling to have her teach the Waorani or to work together on the language and had suggested that she continue independent linguistic work. However, it was impossible to properly complete analysis of the language when there were two sets of linguistic data. The decision to leave had been difficult to make, and she had been considering it for months, but she believed that she was following God's leading in leaving, just as she had been when she moved to Tewæno in 1958. She did not say that in many cases she did not know what their differences were, or that she and Saint had never, in over three years, been able to work or even to live together without conflict for any length of time.

Elliot never did explain in family letters exactly what happened during those ten days. But a few things can be pieced together. She had told her parents on November 2 that she still had not even "a glimmer of light," but that she was thinking of asking Saint for a clear yes or no on whether they could ever work together. A no might be her sign to go. Whether consciously or unconsciously, she had relinquished the idea that she had to know where God was leading her next before she left Tewæno. She must have asked the question almost immediately, because the November 13 letter describes the preceding two weeks as "pretty difficult." Clearly the answer had been no.[131]

On November 6, Elliot typed up the formal letter and gave Saint a copy, asking the older woman to let her know if it was just. She got no response. The next day, the guests Elliot had made plans with a month before arrived in an SIL plane—Barbara Youderian and Marilou McCully with little Mike and Ed's father. The McCullys were there a few hours; Youderian stayed a week. While everyone was there, Elliot invited Saint, Dayomæ, and the SIL pilot to her house for a meal. Saint did not appear. Elliot was comforted by the chance to see her friends and especially by her time with Youderian, to whom she confided her decision. The younger woman read her 1 Corinthians 15:58 in the Phillips translation: "And so brothers of mine, stand firm! Let nothing move you as you busy yourselves in the Lord's work. Be sure that nothing you do for him is ever lost or wasted."

Elliot waited a week and a day for Saint to acknowledge her letter. Finally, though she dreaded the repercussions, she felt she had no other option than to send it. But although Saint never responded to the letter, the women must have had at least one conversation about the *why* of the matter, because Elliot shared a few more details about the conflict in her family letter. At least some of Saint's concerns regarding Elliot's theology came from her writing. Although one reviewer had said *Kinsman* should be mandatory reading for Peace Corps candidates, Saint told her it was unfit for prospective missionaries. And she said the *SST* version of Elliot's letter about the trip to Jim's grave had caused her to question Elliot's belief in the bodily resurrection of Jesus.

But these snippets of information only kicked the questions farther down the road: Saint still refused to explain what elements of the book worried her or why the letter seemed to her to dismiss the resurrection, asserting again that Elliot already knew what she was talking about. This was intensely frustrating to Elliot, who was kept up at night by fear that she might be unable to see her own spiritual error.

Although Elliot's public statement is cool and collected, grief and bewilderment come through strongly in her family letter. She could not understand how two of the most prayed-for missionaries in history could be so utterly alienated. She was heartsick to think of telling the Waorani goodbye. She was struggling to eat or sleep. She could not even begin to imagine how God could bring anything good out of this. There was no way to put a triumphal spin on it. But she had done the best that she knew how to do. "How I have prayed and sought God's face in this thing, only He knows," she wrote, "and if I am dead wrong in the whole thing, if I am making a mistake to leave here now, I still say He is my Refuge, and He will just have to show me. I have no other arm to lean upon."[132]

Elliot still had no sense of leading about where to go next, but she planned to tell the Waorani of her plans, pack immediately, and leave as soon as possible. In the short term she would attend a Christian conference in the Dos Rios area, and then, since she had a standing invitation from Mary Skinner, she would go to Shandia, "to be quiet for a while and seek the next step."[133] Her plans were interrupted by a request from Don Johnson for Elliot and Saint to come to Quito for a meeting. Both women felt that nothing could be said that would make a difference, and both dreaded what seemed likely to be a miserable, confrontational gathering, but they agreed to Johnson's request. On November 17 they made the series of flights to Quito together. Marilou met Elliot at the airport, while someone from SIL picked up Saint. Marilou, Marj, and SIL's John Lindskoog were also present at the meeting. Saint continued to be uncommunicative, and Elliot felt Johnson and Lindskoog were more worried about publicity than resolution. Nothing changed.

There were only four days left before the conference Elliot had agreed to help with, so she asked Saint to keep the situation private so she could break the news of her departure to the Waorani herself, and stayed on in Quito over the weekend before going on to Dos Rios. But when she got back to Tewæno on November 28, ten days after she had left, Elliot quickly realized that Saint had not honored her wishes. The Waorani were treating her differently and seemed standoffish. Elliot asked Saint what she had told them. Saint replied that she had given a plain account: Elliot was leaving because she was angry with Saint.

Elliot felt sick. Not only had she been denied the chance to break the news to her friends herself, not only were they avoiding her, but worst of all, she felt this explanation introduced a kind of offense to the Waorani that they had not known before. "We have brought them the Gospel, yes," she mourned, "and we have brought them the most deplorable of sins."[134] Elliot felt powerless. She could only tell the Waorani that she was not angry, but was leaving because God had told her to. Letters from her mother and from Dave gave her strength to get through the next few days.

Elliot still felt nauseated when she thought of Saint's words to the Waorani, and she struggled with her attitude toward the older woman. She was sad too, because no one seemed to mind her going. An older woman named Dyuiku cried when she said goodbye, and the Kichwa men from her Bible class said they would miss her teaching and brought her a lavishly generous farewell gift, a rooster. Otherwise she was largely ignored. It hurt especially that Ipa seemed to deliberately avoid her. But she felt God was giving her peace in spite of it all, and when Saint came for their regular prayer time, Elliot found she was able to pray with her. She wrote that she was "trusting God to effect His own desires in both of us through this situation. . . . I have to <u>hope</u>, without any evidence seen, that things will come right in the end—not merely that we shall receive compensation, but that we and all creation will be <u>redeemed</u>. This means infinitely more than that the good will eventually outweigh the evil."[135]

On Friday, December 1, 1961, the story that had begun for Elliot with the purring buzz of Nate Saint's little Piper Cruiser, bringing news of Waorani houses, ended in the treble roar of SIL's Helio-Courier, lifting her above the thatched roofs of Tewæno, no longer her home. She had prayed about life with the Waorani since she first learned of the people almost a decade before, had longed for that life since Jim's death nearly six years ago. Though she had been present in the community for a scattered year and nine months, the clearing in the jungle had been her home base for the last three years.[136] Now her prayers, her hopes, the countless hours poured into language learning, the hard days on the trail, the linguistic material painstakingly compiled, the friendships formed, the painful effort to get along, all seemed to have gone up in smoke. By any framework she had previously used to understand life, the unresolved conflict made no sense. She had not even a guess as to how to assign meaning in these circumstances. What had happened? Why? More than half a century later, the same questions remain.

Any number of things may have contributed. Despite their many similarities, the two women also had personality differences and different backgrounds. Though Elliot often came across as assured, her self-experience was more tentative; Saint seems to have felt more inner certainty and confidence. Elliot had basked in the glamour of her voyages to Ecuador; Saint had found life aboard ship "vapid."[137] The Howard household had been one of deliberate structure; the Saint home one of artistic chaos. The Howards' halls were lined with books of all kinds; the Saints seem to have read only the Bible. The Howards did without a clothes washer or a car during the Depression; the Saints often did without enough to eat. The effect of these kinds of things is difficult to pin down, but they can play a bigger role than many more obvious influences.

Friction can occur in any situation where people live or work closely together, and Elliot and Saint had a difficult history even before they lived together. Although Elliot had warm relationships with several close friends, her demeanor was often received as abrasive by others; perhaps Saint was among those with whose personalities Elliot's did not naturally mesh. If Saint felt a sense of ownership of the effort to convert the Waorani—and her ongoing difficulty in working with others over the years to come seems to indicate she did—then she may have felt from the beginning that Elliot was an intruder.[138] Both women felt impelled to follow their own understanding of God's guidance against all odds. As Long has pointed out, "The very qualities that brought Elliot and Saint to Tewæno made it hard for them to work together there."[139]

Elliot's and Saint's areas of disagreement included SIL's approach to missions; whether to try to influence Waorani behavior directly; how much contact the Waorani should have with outsiders; whether to discourage exogamy; how to present the story of Jesus; how much spiritual weight to assign to external behavior; how to interpret changes taking place in the Guequitaidi community; what constitutes appropriate reading material; and whether Christians may use wine to celebrate Communion.[140] But although these were important questions, and the various possible courses of action carried serious implications, none of them center around foundational tenets of the Christian faith as expressed in the historic creeds of the church. Nor, despite Saint's unexplained concerns, do they come under the purview of the "five fundamentals" hammered out in the modernist-fundamentalist controversies: the inspiration and inerrancy of the Bible; the virgin birth; the deity of Jesus; the bodily resurrection of Jesus; or the historicity of the miracles described in the Bible.

Nevertheless, at least as early as the end of their first seven-and-a-half weeks together, Saint was seriously concerned that Elliot was leaving Christianity. This seems initially to have centered around the questions Elliot expressed in their daily prayer times. One question seems to have bothered Saint particularly: that of what might be required for salvation and how that worked out practically for the Waorani. Elliot had been pondering this since before they moved. In her last prayer letter from Arajuno she had expressed awareness that an invitation to the missionaries was not the same as an invitation to Jesus, but that she was encouraged by Jesus's words from Matthew 10:40 (KJV): "He that receiveth you receiveth me," and was praying that this would prove true for the Waorani; Elliot shared these thoughts with Saint in relation to the death of Nænquiwi ("George"), the Wao man Jim had met who had been spear killed before she and Saint arrived. He had never heard of Jesus, but he had, as far as Elliot knew at the time, received the five men peacefully. How literally could Jesus's words be applied? Might Nænquiwi be in heaven? There seems to be little difference between these ponderings and Saint's own hope that perhaps Mimaa, who had also died before their arrival, was in heaven because she had heard the little Dayomæ had to say about God on her first brief visit. Elliot based her tentative hope on the words of Jesus, Saint apparently on belief in the power of hearing of the Christian God's existence, and both women seemed to rely on the merciful character of God. But Saint was upset by Elliot's questions.

Saint also had concerns over the *SST* account of the visit to Jim's grave. Elliot's description recounted very simply what happened on the trip, reflected on how easily God could have prevented the men from landing on the beach, and closed with the last two lines of a Wordsworth poem, a favorite of Jim's: "But she is in her grave, and, oh, / The difference to me!"[141] Saint could perhaps have taken the declaration that God could have stopped the deaths of the men as criticism (though everything else Elliot had written on the subject had affirmed her belief that God had orchestrated Jim's death in wisdom and love and would use it to fulfill God's good purposes). Or Saint could perhaps have interpreted Wordsworth's poetic description of the lover being *in* the grave as applying spiritually as well as physically (though to castigate Elliot for it would indicate a misunderstanding of how literature functions). But neither of these possible scenarios touches on either the future resurrection of the Christian or the bodily resurrection of Jesus.

Perhaps Saint's discomfort with Elliot's writing ultimately stemmed not from what it said but from what it didn't say. She worried that the younger woman's questions and opinions that did not accord with her own indicated unsound beliefs about the essentials. Perhaps, against the background of six years of difficult interaction, the fact that Elliot did not explicitly affirm the resurrection in the *SST* or share Billy Graham's four steps to peace with God in *Kinsman* was enough to confirm Saint's suspicions.

Elliot's journals and letters show that she *was* moving away from the certainty on secondary issues evident in her earlier writing, certainty that Saint still seemed to hold. But there is no indication that this loss of certainty extended to the essentials of the Christian faith. She still believed in the creeds, in the fundamentals, in an all-powerful God of love involved in the details of human life, in obedience as the path to knowing that God. This faith was the foundation of her life. She still believed that God speaks through the Bible and pored over it daily, reading large portions at a time, meditating on smaller passages, searching for both principles and specific guidance. She also recognized that Christian faith didn't make every choice or situation crystal clear and that the importance of the Bible did not mean the Scriptures were always easy to understand or spoke clearly on every subject.

A case in point lies in Elliot's response when her mother raised the question of what happens to the soul at death in a letter. Elliot felt unable to take a defined position, noting that some passages of Scripture seemed to clearly support the idea that the soul "sleeps" until the final resurrection and others just as clearly to support the idea that the conscious soul is immediately with Jesus. To take a settled position seemed to require discarding some of the evidence. "This is the difficulty I find with so many fundamentalist doctrines," she explained. "They are willing to pin their hopes on what they call a 'clear' passage, and explain away the others, while I might bring up a verse which proved, apparently, the opposite, and the answer they would give is 'Oh, but you can't take a single verse, you have to take the whole tenor of the Scripture.' So—there we are."[142] In many instances her loss of certainty actually came from her commitment to Scripture.

Elliot had become painfully aware that there was more than one side to most questions, that often there were so many sides, she could not even see them all. Though still adamant that she would follow at any cost wherever God led, "I cannot help remembering that right is never entirely on one side, nor wrong entirely on the other, and some of the worst atrocities in history have been committed in the name of God, by dedicated, God-fearing people, who thought they did God service by killing, either literally or figuratively, those who were not on 'their side.'" She longed "for the Day when we shall see issues unclouded!"[143] The triumphal tone of *Through Gates of Splendor* had been replaced by a more subdued acknowledgment of complexity.

Perhaps her attitude can best be summed up in a prayer written by a nineteenth-century Anglican bishop, which she quoted in a family letter: "In times of doubts and questionings, when our belief is perplexed by new learning, new thought, when our faith is strained by creeds, by doctrines, by mysteries beyond our understanding, give us the faithfulness of learners and the courage of believers in Thee; alike from rejection of new revelations, and from hasty assurance that we are wiser than our fathers, save us and help us, we humbly beseech Thee, O Lord."[144] She was a different person than she had been when writing so emphatically in 1956 about her correct understanding and execution of God's direction.

To say that grief had changed Elliot seems to be to state the obvious, and it raises the question of why grief does not seem to have changed Saint as well. But if *Through Gates of Splendor* is any indication, the loss of Jim didn't alter Elliot's certainty and triumphalism—at least not right away. It was not until after the first anniversary of his death that she seems to have begun to feel uncomfortable in her assumptions about faith and the world around her. (What had Jim died for, after all? Surely not the endless round of missionary social events in Quito?) Then, as her friendship with Capa blossomed, their discussions caused her to begin to think carefully about what she believed and why. At about the same time, Elliot had become a Harper's author, and her publisher had begun sending her books by the dozen.

From early childhood she had been exposed to a wide variety of reading material, but since college at least, her reading had been weighted toward religious writing, and within that, had been heavily Holiness-oriented. Now it contained a higher proportion of general-market books, while the religious books came from a wider sampling of the Christian tradition.

Tom, undergoing a theological and ideological shift of his own, also sent her books from a range of perspectives. Grief was a softening agent, but exposure to other points of view was part of her changing understanding.

Thanks to her parents' approach to literature and her liberal arts degree, Elliot had long exposure to the idea of critical reading—reading to understand and to grapple with ideas. She read these new books critically: to learn about reality, to understand the world beyond the evangelical subculture, to compare ideas against the Bible, to set aside the bad and gather up the good, to share the good with those around her. She saw it as part of her job as a witness. Saint's horror at Elliot owning books by Tillich and Freud seems to indicate that she considered reading a particular author or book tantamount to agreement.

By the time the two women moved to Tewæno they were already on divergent paths, not because of their approach to the fundamental doctrines of Christianity, but because of their approach to the relationship between that faith and the life of the intellect. Living among the Waorani, Saint continued to interpret events with the framework she had always used. Decades later, Elliot mused that for Saint, "everything was black or white, there was nothing in between." Meanwhile, Elliot found that living *with* indigenous people rather than separately caused "all kinds of things . . . to light up in my mind," and confirmed her growing sense that reality "is much more complicated than I thought it was."[145]

———

By December 3, 1961, Elliot was in Shandia. Mary Skinner had been living since May in the house Jim had built, so Elliot and Valerie settled in again at the Aerie. As she sat again at her desk, she remembered the fear, sadness, and uncertainty she had felt there before going to live with Mintaca and Mæncamo. Then she had gathered comfort from Psalm 118, with its assurance of God's love and help. Now—heartsore, grieving the loss of her life with the Waorani, unsure whether she had done right—she drew comfort from the same source.

There were additional consolations. After months in a culture where people did not greet one another, after the long slog under the weight of Saint's rejection, Elliot basked in a sense of welcome. A crowd met the plane when she arrived. People came from all around to tell her they were glad she was back, some walking more than an hour one way. Skinner seemed genuinely pleased to have her there. "It is relaxing and refreshing," Elliot wrote, "in a way I have hardly ever appreciated in just this way before, to be with those with whom I know a spiritual bond." "It is so lovely . . . to look over at the other house and see a light, and know that if I want to I can go over and chat, and even be given a cup of tea!"[146] It was restful, too, to understand what was being said around her, to make herself easily understood. Valerie quickly picked up Kichwa again and seemed happy.

Tewæno's isolation had decreased exponentially since 1958, but even so, Shandia was bustling and cosmopolitan in comparison. In the midst of all the hubbub, Elliot unpacked and resumed six-year-old Valerie's schoolwork. It was a relief not to have to sit on her hands to avoid unnecessarily changing Waorani culture or offending Saint, and she dove into helping Skinner reclaim the station from the predations of time and vacancy.

After just twelve days, Elliot and Valerie made the Shandia-Shell-Ambato-Quito trip to spend Christmas with Marj and Marilou. Then, back in Shandia, mother and daughter attended the annual New Year conference, inaugurated by Jim, Ed, and Pete just before their contact attempt with the Waorani. This seventh iteration was put on entirely by the Shandian church, "from inviting speakers and delegates to making out a roster for cooks and song leaders." Elliot was encouraged. "Over three hundred were in attendance at some of the meetings, and five were baptized today."[147] Things were not perfect, but people were coming to meetings, and a few Kichwa men were teaching insightfully from their own time in prayer and study.

Life settled into a loose routine. Elliot started her day with her own devotions, followed by breakfast, school, housework, and translation. She and Valerie ate the noon meal with Skinner. The two women took turns cooking and worked through a Kichwa language lesson together each day. In the afternoons, Elliot answered mail and checked the morning's translation with Venancio Tapui. After supper, she and Valerie would often work in the garden for a bit, then wash their feet, have family devotions, and read aloud from a storybook. Once Valerie was tucked in for the night, Elliot would either work at her desk or spend time with Skinner, perhaps ironing her clothes while they talked. The women ended most evenings with shared devotions.

Elliot was reading and thinking about what she read. She finished *Catcher in the Rye*, writing to her family that "the book ought to be a requisite for every adult who has to deal with young people of this generation. . . . But unfortunately many Christians would probably put the book down after a few pages, simply because the boy's language is 'dirty,' and thereby miss an enlightening book."[148] On another pass through Genesis, she was struck by the way the Bible recorded the reality of the human condition, "all the sins—deceit, chicanery of all kinds, casual moral standards, etc., which are simply <u>narrated</u>, with no mention whatsoever of their being sin."[149] She had been pondering what constituted Christian writing and the claims of those who said it ought not to handle sin. "This talk about morality in literature— usually those who argue about it say that at least the Bible calls it sin and refers as well to its punishment. This is just not true. The Old Testament is a pretty sad record of what man is like, but a wonderful picture of God in His different roles—Creator, Guide, Savior, Judge, Redeemer, Friend."[150]

Elliot reveled in Kate Douglas Wiggin's 1900 novel, *Penelope's English Experiences*, passing it on to Skinner and then her siblings. The published letters of Edna St. Vincent Millay were "marvelous,"[151] though not as good as Mansfield's. Skinner and Tom each gave her novels by Françoise Sagan. "What a contrast does the life she describes present to the life we lead here," Elliot wrote to her family, "and it is this contrast that makes books especially stimulating to me. The perspective that they provide forces me to think outside the mould in which I'm poured."[152] Someone sent her a copy of Andrew Murray's *Divine Healing*, which flummoxed her by arguing that all Christians should expect to live out the psalmist's entire "threescore years and ten" (Ps. 90:10 KJV), and that those who are right with God will not get sick. "Because of my respect for Murray's writings, I tried to read it with an open mind," she told her family, "but it does violence to the powers of reasoning which God gave me, and I cannot, at this point, believe it. Another way, perhaps more euphemistic, of saying this would be to say I haven't the faith for it."[153]

Elliot did not believe that such reliance on reason was problematic. When her brother Jim wrote seeming to suggest that his doubts suggested spiritual immaturity, she suggested that this was a misunderstanding of the nature of doubt. "I am sure that God allows us to have different kinds of doubts at different times in our lives, and just tonight Mary and I were discussing some of ours—elementary at most, but real, and just as necessary to commit. (Commit to God, I mean.) MacDonald says 'The man that feareth, Lord, to doubt, in that fear doubteth Thee!' You must read his long poem, 'The Disciple.'"[154]

Elliot's willingness to think outside the box soon caused a flap both in Shandia and in the Howard and Elliot families. Some members of the church had asked whether it was a sin to smoke or drink alcohol, and she had not given the expected missionary answer, explaining instead that the Bible forbade *drunkenness* but not alcohol, and did not address smoking as such. "I simply cannot bring myself to go beyond what we find in Scripture in teaching believers," she wrote when telling the story in a family letter. She had also tried to encourage confession "one to another," as the book of James describes, rather than public confession meetings, which often led to gossip and shaming instead of repentance. In each instance, she said, the important thing was the intention of the heart. Various family members took her to task for not being careful enough, while some members of the community began to spread rumors that she had said it was fine to get drunk and that confession wasn't needed at all. She tried again to explain "the truth as it is in the Bible; the responsibility of the individual before God; the true meaning of a holy life." There was nothing else she *could* do, except "pray that the Holy Spirit will teach." To her family she wrote in frustration, "I have searched my heart on these matters, and no matter what arguments may be presented from the standpoint of 'What will it lead to?' I must, I simply MUST, evaluate truth not by what it does but by what it IS. The former is the pragmatist's position, and is not Christian."[155]

In May 1962, Elliot attended an American Bible Society conference at Eugene Nida's invitation. Most of the week was devoted to translation workshops and daily lectures on "the question of communication with Latin America."[156] Watching Nida go over translation with missionaries working in other languages, Elliot realized that she needed to start over again on the translation she was currently making of 1 Corinthians. Translation meant much more than creating a literal equivalent of Greek words in Kichwa. First Corinthians 3:12–13 (KJV), for example, posed a problem when it encouraged Christians to build their lives on the foundation of Christ using "gold, silver, precious stones," rather than "wood, hay, stubble." In Shandia, of course, "there is no such thing as a 'precious' stone . . . and wood, hay, and stubble, are in effect the chosen materials of jungle Indians for building a good house!" "I have been very free in my work," she told her family, "but I understand now that I have not been nearly free enough."[157]

As for the lectures, she came away feeling that she, and virtually everyone else, was "all wrong" and "accomplishing nothing" with their efforts—that although there were "more missionaries per capita" in Latin America than anywhere else in the world, there was also "less being done."[158] This had to some extent been her own impression when she first arrived in Ecuador and realized how many missionaries lived in the cities and how few among indigenous people. In the excitement of marriage and the effort to keep going after Jim's death, this disparity had moved to a back burner in her mind. It was discouraging to have it brought forward again, this time with the added weight of a respected scholar's opinion behind it, and with enough experience in the trenches to realize how hard it would be to effect change.

Nida had invited Elliot to the conference because he wanted her to undertake translation of a new edition of the New Testament, one that would serve speakers of both highland and lowland Kichwa dialects. She pointed out to him that the consensus among translators in 1957 had been that such a translation would not work, but Nida seemed to believe she was skilled enough to pull it off.

The proposal brought Elliot's swirling thoughts about the future into focus. First, she realized, she would have to consider whether the push for everyone to have the Bible available in their mother tongue was as well-considered as she had once thought. Not only was the Ecuadorian government working to acculturate indigenous peoples and requiring government-run schools to be taught in Spanish, but it appeared to her that the Kichwa themselves preferred to learn Spanish. Just as Dayomæ had wanted to Kichwa-ize the Waorani to shed the "savage" stigma, so the Kichwa, aware of the socioeconomic stratification between themselves and native Spanish speakers, often seemed uninterested in becoming literate in their own language. Evangelical missionaries in some parts of the country had been "severely criticized for their attempt to 'hold back' the Indian—i.e. to teach him in his own language."[159] It seemed likely that by the time she could finish such a translation, there would be no one to read it.

This brought her up against the question of whether she still belonged in Ecuador at all. In the short term, the church in Shandia was using Kichwa materials, and she could continue her translation work for them. But without a concerted effort to promote indigenous-language literacy, it seemed less and less likely that they would be using them in the long term. And if she stayed in Shandia, dividing her time between homemaking, home-schooling, parenting, station maintenance, literacy classes, medical visits, Bible classes, supporting the local church, and translation, she wondered whether she would be able to do any one thing adequately. If she were to move to the Sierra, learn the mountain dialect, and embark on a translation for jungle and mountain dialects, she would have to send Valerie out to school and translation would still be a full-time job and there would still be a need for an accompanying effort in evangelization, church-planting, and indigenous-language literacy.

And Elliot was increasingly troubled by her inability to provide things like piano lessons, museum visits, and the kind of stability of routine and tradition that she herself had cherished as a child. Valerie had begun asking repeatedly why they could not live in the US, and though Elliot explained that she did not think God wanted them to leave Ecuador, she was unsettled. As she pondered her options after the conference, she considered the idea of spending a trial school year in the US, acknowledging for the first time the possibility of leaving Ecuador for good.

Elliot and Valerie spent late May and most of June in traveling—an overnight walking trip to visit a very isolated believer followed by two weeks sightseeing with Marj Saint and Mary Skinner. The four went south down the Andes through Riobamba, Colta, Azogues, Cuenca, and Loja. Wherever they stopped overnight Elliot gave showings of a movie about the Waorani. Then they went north again for a long stretch in Quito, finishing up with a visit with Marilou, who was getting ready to leave on furlough and seriously considering staying in the US. Back in Shandia, Elliot went on medical calls—even successfully treating a woman with a prolapsed uterus—and completed another edition of the first eight chapters of 1 Corinthians. And she prayed about whether to go back to the States for her brother Jim's wedding and an Elliot family reunion.

By mid-July, Elliot had decided to decline Nida's invitation. She would stay in Shandia for the coming school year to give seven-year-old Valerie, who had not lived in one place for more than a year at a time in the last six years, greater stability. Skinner felt running the busy station was interfering with her language acquisition and asked to trade houses with Elliot. This fit well into Elliot's plans. The added space meant Valerie could have her own bedroom, and they could have a discreet school room instead of making two tiny rooms do for everything. By July 24 she was writing again at the desk Jim had built for her and tackling a whole pile of projects—cleaning the house, organizing, decorating. She hired men to remodel the attic into two bedrooms, and two women, Antonia and Antuca, to live in and help with the housework.

Elliot also decided to attend the family events. When she thought of Carmichael, who never took a furlough, she worried that she was being too soft but ultimately came to believe "that since I have the money to do this sort of thing, and I only have it because Jim was killed, the Lord would perhaps have me use it to make up in a small way for what Val has missed in not having a family."[160] Two weeks after they moved into the big house, they left for the US. They spent a week in Quito while Elliot got a perm, had her skirts hemmed up to a more fashionable length, and acquired the necessary travel documents. Then they met Bert and Colleen, and the four of them flew to Portland for the family reunion. They arrived on August 14 and "were met by about 40 relatives."[161] Elliot and Valerie went on to Moorestown on August 30 for Jim's wedding. They were also able to see Dave and Tom and visit Franconia. On September 23 they left Moorestown and by September 27 were in Shandia again. "Really, it is hard to orient oneself when travel is so rapid,"[162] Elliot wrote. It was a different era than when she had first traveled to Ecuador by ship a decade before.

Back at home, mother and daughter tried again to establish a routine. Mary Skinner was staying in Puyupungu with an eye to moving there, and Elliot missed her. Wilfred Tidmarsh had done all the paperwork to register the Shandia school with the government, which meant the missionaries did not have to supply a teacher, but Elliot still had to manage enrollment, prepare a room in the school building for the teacher and his family in the short term, and supervise the construction of a house for them in the long term. She and Valerie started third grade, and school seemed to take all day, punctuated by tears on Valerie's part and doubt on Elliot's as to whether she had been right to stay. Val began telling her mother that God was telling *her* they should move to the US.

Some time before, Elliot had asked to have her status changed to "self-supporting" in *Voices from the Vineyard* so potential donors would know she was no longer in need of support—"a relief to my conscience."[163] But she had continued to have more money at her disposal than she could use. As she had prayed about how to understand "my responsibility as a steward of God's money," her position on saving had gradually changed, and for some months she had been looking for a prudent investment, explaining privately to Katharine, "I have to think of Val's future." In Franconia after her brother's wedding, Elliot had learned of three acres near Gale Cottage that might be coming up for sale and had "felt that [land] would be a wise and less risky kind of investment than stocks, for example."[164] Since this particular land was in a popular vacation area, the value would only increase over time. She had written to the owners, Martin and Martha Herbert, explaining her situation and expressing interest. Then in mid-October, Martin died unexpectedly. Martha wrote to Elliot that one of the last things he had told her was that he wanted to sell to Elliot. On October 25 Elliot wrote a check for the property.

By mid-November, Elliot had the first portion of 1 Corinthians ready for final review by various native speakers who had agreed to check it. In early December, she and Valerie went to Quito to visit the dentist and buy Christmas presents and food. She had hoped Bert and Colleen, who had been in the US since the family reunion, would be able to spend Christmas with them on the way back to Peru, but their sending congregation had developed concerns about their theology and would not recommission them until their concerns were resolved. To Elliot, this seemed a case of quibbling over secondary things in the face of the great primary need of the world. She wrote in frustration, "I note that when Paul refers to 'doctrine' in his letters to Timothy, he is speaking of <u>practical</u> instruction—e.g. the treatment of slaves, wives, elders; avoiding godless chatter; women's dress; pensions for widows, etc. Strange that he never gives an itemized list of the 'doctrines' that are essential if he is to be a true missionary! I mean doctrines, in the sense generally understood nowadays—inspiration, redemption, eschatology."[165]

Despite this disappointment, Christmas was festive. Mary Skinner came with a friend. So did John Munday, a Canadian Brethren missionary who ran a boys' home in Quito, and the Landers family from HCJB. Valerie had a wonderful time playing with the Landers children and was delighted by a new doll from her grandmother Howard and a doll bed from her mother made to match her own, complete with pink striped dust ruffle and coverlet. Just after Christmas more missionaries arrived for the eighth annual New Year's conference. About two hundred fifty Kichwa gathered to listen to the speakers.

———

"Things seem very quiet here after Christmas and conference," Elliot wrote to her family at the end of the first week in January.[166] She finished a fair copy of 1 Corinthians and sent it to Wilfred for printing. She was writing articles here and there, some for the *SST*, one for *Moody Monthly*, though she was not pleased with how much their editors changed what she had tried to say. Though she had no present plans for another book of her own, she had accepted a request from Revell to edit their new edition of Matthew Henry's 1712 book *The Secret of Daily Communion with God* and write an introduction for it, and now she began on that project.

As she worked, Elliot experienced misgivings, concerned that a two-hundred-fifty-year-old book originally written as sermons was not well suited to a 1960s audience. Eventually she decided to anchor the book in the present by contrasting the modern emphasis on *communication* with Henry's use of the word *communion*. "The most significant progress in communication between men can never alleviate the primeval loneliness of the individual," Elliot wrote. "I do not refer to superficial loneliness—that of merely being alone, or of missing a specific person," but "to the profound hunger for dialogue with another who is intimately concerned."[167] She had experienced each of these types of loneliness herself; had always been possessed of a fundamental loneliness, had been, as Tom would later say, "the cat that walks by itself."[168] But her reading of her contemporaries suggested that in the nuclear age, this "primeval loneliness" was particularly pressing: "Modern literature is characterized by despair and a fatalistic sense of impotence before the prospect of annihilation. Even Christians (who believe that God *is* vitally concerned) often cannot escape the feeling that certain people are especially privileged to commune with God, and that they themselves are not among them." Thus Elliot suggested that Henry's "practicable" suggestions for how to live in intimate dialogue with God were "eminently relevant to our times."[169]

In its focus on the human relationship to God and the concerns of "our generation," particularly as expressed in literature, Elliot's introduction to *The Secret of Communion with God* reflected months of thought about how Christian faith comes to bear on a writerly vocation. She had come to see her call to missions as a call to be a witness: to observe and report, to know God and tell about him. She believed God had given her a gift for writing, a task that seemed particularly suited to the witness's role. She had studied what the Bible said about spiritual gifts and discussed the "gifts and the calling of God" in family letters (Rom. 11:29). She had concluded that creative aptitude was a gift from God not to be lightly set aside. (When her brother Jim was thinking about becoming a missionary, she discouraged him from pioneer fields, saying he ought to be where his artistic talent would be utilized and appreciated.) For Elliot, making art—which included writing—was interwoven with communicating a Christian understanding of reality and a Christian experience of God.

This meant that it was important to do it well, to study the craft, to read good writing, in order to "increase my own ability to express myself on paper." She would have to learn "to know my own contemporaries, those to whom I must speak," in order to communicate in terms that could be understood.[170] She and Tom talked about the idea that art should deal with "the great themes" of human existence.[171] She corresponded with Leslie Thompson from Literatura Evangelica para America Latina, who pointed out that Christian writers seemed to write only to Christians, "and publishers, too, are interested only in the 'inside', as Cornell always calls it." Thus Elliot felt that most of "those we call 'Christian' authors . . . do not fall into the category of artists," neither addressing the great themes nor communicating effectively.[172] She was not interested in preaching comfortably to the choir.

Meanwhile, Elliot and Valerie were struggling with school after Christmas vacation. Val was failing spelling tests, frustrated with math, and in tears "almost daily."[173] Perhaps because they had spent time with two-parent families over Christmas, the little girl had also begun talking more about her father. At suppertime one night she asked, "'If my daddy were here, I would say 'please pass the sugar,' and he would pass it to me, wouldn't he?'" Playing in the living room after supper, she started crying and "said she wanted her daddy." Several days later, Antuca found Valerie in her bedroom crying over her father. Later in the month, Valerie asked what had happened to her father's clothes, and when Elliot explained that she had given them away, responded, "Even his shoes?"[174]

Elliot mentioned these things in family letters without comment, as if they were merely anecdotes like the funny things Valerie said or her progress in school. In the same way, she mentioned repeatedly that Val loved babies and regularly wished for siblings. She said again and again that Val was growing up "without a family," and described what she herself would do differently, "if I had a family."[175] She never directly addressed the emotional subtext of these anecdotes and asides. But she had long felt the loss of Jim not only as the loss of her lover and friend, but also as the loss of longed-for children and of an essential ingredient for what she considered a family. Although Elliot did not directly acknowledge that Valerie's growing awareness of her loss was affecting her, it clearly played into her thinking about the future. In a private letter to Katharine, Elliot wrote:

> I'm praying that if the Lord wants me to leave Shandia next year, He'll make it "easy" by sending someone to take my place. I am not sure Val ought to stay here indefinitely, I'm still not at all convinced that it would be the right thing to send her away to boarding school, and I hate the thought of leaving here! So you will pray, too, for clear leading, as you are praying for Jim and Tom, I'm sure, and maybe for some of the others.[176]

———

At the beginning of January 1963 Elliot had received a bittersweet letter from Eleanor Vandevort, her friend from Wheaton gym class, who had spent the last thirteen years in South Sudan among the Nuer people. The nation had been in political unrest the whole time, and now tensions were escalating and the government was evicting all foreign missionaries. Vandevort had been given a deadline; she had to leave the country by January 19 at the latest. Weeks before Elliot learned of the situation, she had invited Van to visit her on her next furlough. So when Vandevort learned she was being forced out, she wrote to accept. She would later say that Elliot's invitation "literally saved me out of a total darkness."[177] Elliot sent two hundred dollars to help cover her expenses. Vandevort arrived in Shandia on Wednesday, February 6.

For the first few days, the two women did virtually "nothing but sit and talk," barely even stopping for meals.[178] Though the friends had corresponded, they had not seen each other since just before Vandevort left the US in 1949. In the intervening years, each of them had been through the fire. The more they talked, the more similarity of experience they found. Each had poured herself into missionary work and seen little of the results she had been led to expect. Each had been cut adrift against her will from what she had hoped was her life's work and was struggling to find a new path. Each felt separated by her experiences from the rest of humanity. Each had found much of what she thought she knew replaced by questions but had come to believe "that the true meaning of life is simply to Know God—to know, and believe, and understand, that 'I am He.'"[179] To see each other again felt like a gift from God to their lonely hearts.

In Vandevort, Elliot found a mind to rival or surpass her own. "She is a truly remarkable person, and a true worshiper of God. . . . She has translated Genesis, Exodus, and Luke, John, I, II, III John, Jude, Peter, Timothy, & Titus (& wrote a pedagogical grammar) into what Nida calls the most difficult language in the world."[180] And Vandevort was not put off by Elliot's rough edges, realizing that, as she would later say:

> her judgment of herself is thorough and critical and as honest as possible . . . so that any serious judgment she makes has had its own test-run within her. She sounds terribly dogmatic at times and people . . . tend to bristle, but they do not realize how what appears to be dogmatism is simply the expression of a very economic mind. She brings things down to the lowest common denominator at <u>once</u>, eliminating the intermediate steps which make for "brotherhood," perhaps, but blur the issue. Hence she's not too good at making conversation around coffee cups or in sewing circles. . . . Keenly aware of the image she has (and has had practically all of her life) and wanting to improve upon it, [she] has tried and keeps on trying to be more gracious—or perhaps the word is approachable—but the truth of the matter is that this essence of her being is the vital factor to what she is. To know her then requires one's willingness to be sharpened with iron, consequently few they be who will ever truly know her.[181]

Here was someone who shared Elliot's interests, who understood the things she thought about, who valued intellectual honesty, who could meet her on her own ground. Their similar experiences, interests, and turn of mind made them better suited than anyone Elliot had ever known, except perhaps Tom, and she basked in the sense of deep connection. She even gave Vandevort her journals to read, something she had previously done only with Jim. "She knows me," Elliot wrote, "as no other friend knows me, so this in itself gives a freedom in dialogue which I have rarely known."[182]

Vandevort's ability to match her intellectually made her someone Elliot felt she could learn from. Van had encountered suffering, and instead of retreating into the safety of pat answers had gone out like Jacob to wrestle with God. This, Elliot felt, made her worth listening to:

> She has been through terrific things in the Sudan—has faced life, not denied it, and has known God in it. Therefore she speaks the Truth as clearly perceived and deeply experienced, and it cannot be gainsaid. I asked her the other day to go through the first part of Genesis as she would teach it to a Nuer. I have never heard anything like it. What a gift of teaching she has! She has opened my eyes to whole realms of truth I had been ignorant of.[183]

Like Elliot, Vandevort had seen little visible change from more than a decade of missionary work. But she fairly glowed with love for God. "It appears that the evangelization of the world (i.e. missionary work) really amounts to the sanctification of the Church (i.e. the missionary)," Elliot told her family. "Of results in the Nuer tribe, Van has seen almost nothing, but she has come to know God, and one cannot help knowing this in knowing her."[184]

Leaving South Sudan was a great grief to Vandevort. She did not know what her next step should be. There were some Nuer in Ethiopia, and she considered trying to move there. She considered resigning from the Presbyterian Mission Agency. As she had once told Elliot, she felt that "following God is not like walking a tightrope."[185] She believed that one discovered the will of God "simply by living," trusting that if a change became necessary, the Holy Spirit would make it clear.[186] In the meantime, she addressed herself to learning Kichwa, helping Elliot, and teaching Valerie. Val took to "Aunt Van" like a duck to water, happily announcing that she loved her best. Elliot was deeply glad. "As I said to [Van] last night I have hardly done much praying for the past three weeks—all I can think of to say to the Lord is thanks."[187]

———

Bert and Colleen had finally come to an agreement with their sending congregation and arrived in Shandia en route to Peru in time to celebrate Val's eighth birthday. Valerie, who had been "especially praying" that they'd be in time, was "beside herself."[188] Skinner came up from Puyupungu for the celebration, and then the whole group traveled to Pano for a conference. Elliot, Bert, and Van all taught, Bert helping to baptize those who asked. Back in Shandia, Valerie basked in time with Uncle Bert, and the five adults worked and rested and enjoyed each other's company. Skinner taught the women's literacy class. Vandevort taught Valerie. Bert repaired the generator, took Val swimming, and gave haircuts. In the evenings they sang hymns in harmony, prayed together, read aloud, and talked. "Discussions have ranged from head-covering to the meaning of worldliness, Christian liberty, eating things strangled (Bert and Colleen refuse to eat strangled chickens in Peru if they know about it—this is a common method of killing, but they teach against it)," and books, including Søren Kierkegaard's *Purity of Heart Is To Will One Thing*, and Albert Camus's *The Fall*. "I've hardly picked up a magazine or book to read for a month," Elliot crowed. It was good to talk with those who were not threatened by questions or afraid to look at things from a variety of angles and try ideas on for size, good "to be exchanging ideas instead of absorbing them."[189]

Mary Skinner went back to Puyupungu at the end of the first week of March, and Bert and Colleen left not quite two weeks later. Although she still did not know what her next long-term step would be, Vandevort was beginning to look ahead to getting back to the US and seeing her parents. She agreed to stay, however, until Valerie had finished the school year. Elliot was thrilled. "The joy of being with Van goes on and on, day after day, like a pure stream, and still it is hard for me to believe the love God had for us both in working this out."[190] They kept talking and talking, sharing experiences, discussing things that puzzled them, talking over possibilities for the future.

Vandevort would later remember that Elliot was feeling "helpless. She didn't know what to do."[191] Elliot increasingly doubted that she was doing any meaningful work in Shandia. She was troubled by the relationship with her neighbors brought about by their financial disparity. It seemed no one wanted Christian discipleship, and everyone wanted "my time, my medicine, my money, my tools, and my chonta fruit and bamboo."[192] In early April, after a morning of desk work constantly interrupted by those who wanted to buy and sell, she wrote, "Van said she felt only a stumbling block to the Nuers, and I know what she means. We could give them the moon, and it would accomplish precisely nothing. We cannot be one of them—much less can they be one of us. Nor do they want either thing. What does God intend to do with them, anyway, and why does He want me here?"[193] The women's literacy class had dwindled to two students, one who still could not tell the language's three vowels apart, and one who wrote only the first syllable of any word. The church in Shandia seemed to be floundering. No one would serve as an elder, and when Venancio Tapui was out of town, no one spoke in church. In late May Elliot wrote, "Just what is the 'missionary task'? When Jesus said to pray for laborers for the 'harvest,' does not the word imply that someone has planted something? And in order to plant, must not the ground have been prepared? How can we give people what they don't want?"[194]

Elliot felt stuck between two painful prospects. She could stick at her post—continue to struggle through school with Valerie and work in which she was no longer sure there was any point. Or she could leave—the place she had lived with Jim, the house Jim had built, the task Jim had entrusted to her, the very self she had been with Jim. In a sense, it would be like saying goodbye to Jim all over again. And what would she do instead? She had never lived as an adult in the US, had never had to support herself there. Could she manage to make a life for Valerie and herself?

Vandevort encouraged her to go. In her own uprootedness, even in her deep grief and shock, she had experienced a clear sense of being carried by her Shepherd—"I just knew, the Lord is my shepherd, I shall not want. . . . I remember saying that, and I knew"—and she tried to support her friend in that same confidence. "I can remember urging her, saying, 'You can write, I know.' Obviously. . . . That's the only time I ever saw her hesitate."[195] And then, like "a bolt of lightning," Elliot felt she could see a way forward. She described it to her family as direction from God: "I am to leave Shandia, go to Franconia, build a house on my lot . . . and make a home for Val where she can go to school."[196] Three decades later, she would describe the sudden feeling of enlightenment with a quotation from seventeenth-century Jesuit priest Jean-Pierre de Caussade: "You are going East, he will turn you to the West. You are set fair on a course, he turns the rudder and steers you back into harbour."[197]

Though Elliot was "so excited and thrilled" by this new sense of freedom that "I could hardly sleep," she waited a few days to say anything to anyone else.[198] She wanted to be *sure* before she got anyone's hopes up. But if she was going to be established in a new house before school started in the fall, she couldn't afford to wait long. For three days she thought and planned, then left Valerie with Vandevort and traveled to Quito to begin preparations in earnest. She bought plane tickets for June 27, exactly one month away, sent a telegram to her parents, broke the news to friends, and began the process of finding a builder.

That evening she tried to explain her thoughts in a family letter. She wanted to write, and it seemed perhaps she could make a career of it; in the last couple of years she had sold pieces to major publishing outlets including *Christianity Today* and had received *very* encouraging rejections—the kind that come with a request to submit again—from such exalted publications as that holy grail of American publishing, the *New Yorker*. She wanted to give Valerie a stable home environment, family traditions, and broader learning opportunities, things that increasingly seemed incompatible with running a mission station. And circumstances seemed to favor these desires. She had financial independence. She had land already in hand. Her last US visit had emphasized the importance of family connections for Valerie. These were the positives; although she did not mention them in her letter, her discouragement over the status of missions and Bible translation and her concern over Valerie's loss in not having a father must also have contributed to her desire.

But perhaps most important was a new sense of rest in God's love. "The Lord is my Shepherd. I know this now and do not melt and quake within, wondering if I'm making a huge mistake, worrying about the future, stewing over leaving the Indians, etc."[199] How different from the anguished decision-making, the fear of being led astray by her own wishes, described in letters and journals ever since Elliot's Wheaton days. How different from the sense of increasing frustration over the past five years as her sense of unknowing increased. Her conversations with Vandevort over the past sixteen weeks had encouraged her to trust that God was not a hard taskmaster; that where her desires were not proscribed in Scripture she could do what she wanted and still be within his will; that God could be trusted to see that she did not stray from the narrow path. Her prayer that the decision to leave Shandia would be made easy for her had been answered, not by the arrival of someone to take over the station, but by the arrival of someone who could speak truth in such a way that her heart could receive it.

> Above all, I have realized what Van says, that "we must not deny that God is what He <u>insists</u> He is—ie., faithful. He leads us to these desires, He knows our heart's need and our natural wants, He will do what He wants with us." ... I am learning that the Lord's ways are higher than ours—that is, better, and not in contrast to our natural desires by any means. As Jim wrote, of the verse "My heart speaks to me for God," "I have known this—my heart speaking to me for God." The heart is deceitful, but my heart is in the hand of the Lord, and I can trust Him to turn it whithersoever He will, since I have asked Him in the integrity of my heart, to do this.[200]

PART 3

———————

1963-2015

The Will of God Is Not a Tightrope

ON JUNE 1, 1963, "It's My Party (And I'll Cry If I Want To)" hit number one on the pop charts, and Governor George Wallace promised to fight desegregation at the University of Alabama. On the third, Pope John XXIII died. On the seventh, the Rolling Stones appeared on TV for the first time. On the ninth, Congress passed the Equal Pay Act. On the sixteenth, cosmonaut Valentina Tereshkova became the first woman in space; the next day, the US Supreme Court ruled that state-mandated Bible reading and recitation of the Lord's Prayer in public schools was unconstitutional. On the twentieth, the US and the USSR signed the hotline agreement in an attempt to prevent nuclear war. A few days later, Elisabeth Elliot left Ecuador. She was thirty-six years old.

When Elliot had written her last family letter from Shandia, many of her plans had still been up in the air. She was looking into importing a Volkswagen; she had put out feelers for a place to stay while her house was being built; she didn't yet know whether she would visit Hampden DuBose Academy. She was planning to make the drive north with Vandevort, who had gone on ahead to visit an uncle in Florida. There are no surviving family letters from the summer, but the broad outlines of this plan seem to have stayed the same. As the US Postal Service debuted zip codes, NASA launched the first geosynchronous satellite, and a new band called the Beatles began to make a splash, Elliot made her way back to the US and north to New Hampshire.

Even before learning of their elder daughter's decision to move, Katharine and Philip Howard had been planning to summer in Franconia. The decision may have been prompted by concerns for Philip's health. It had not improved after his second brain surgery in 1960, and he suffered increasingly from anxiety. He had retired at the end of 1961, as Elliot was leaving the Waorani. Katharine had felt more and more burdened by the demands of caring for her husband and for their big old house by herself. Just before Elliot had decided to leave Ecuador, her parents had decided that they would sell Birdsong in the fall and move to Little Birdsong in Florida. For the summer, they rented a vacation cottage across the road from Elliot's land, and Elliot and Valerie stayed with them. The new house was still in the early stages of building when Katharine and Philip went back to New Jersey at the end of the summer to start packing. Elliot, Valerie, and Vandevort moved into the Howard family's beloved Gale Cottage for the fall, just in time for eight-year-old Val to start school on September 9.

By the twenty-second, Elliot's new house was dried in and the interior walls almost finished. She was hiring out painting, flooring, and the all-important (and expensive) drilling of a well through the granite of the White Mountains. The beginning of October saw the exterior painting finished and the septic system installed. As with any construction project, there were hiccups, and Elliot wrote wryly to her family of the mason who had agreed to do the fireplace but then backed out, the plumbers who "come only when they feel led," and the water pump that turned out to cost eight times the quoted price. She borrowed a few thousand dollars from her parents for a couple of weeks to avoid taking out a construction loan.[1]

Meanwhile, the trio living in Gale Cottage basked in the beauty of a rural New England fall. Valerie found that if she sat very still on the porch, she could feed the chipmunks and field mice with crackers. Bubbly and outgoing like her father, she seemed delighted by her new school and made friends quickly. Elliot shopped for furniture and household goods, consulted a financial advisor, did all the paperwork associated with moving, and tried to keep the big, drafty old cottage clean. Although they were cooking on a hot plate, they entertained visitors periodically, including Mel Arnold, who talked Vandevort into a book for Harper's about her time in South Sudan. Neighbors gave gifts of firewood and homemade jam and invited them to teas, dinners, and game nights. On evenings when they were en famille, Val and Van would play a board game, or Elliot would read aloud from *Little House in the Big Woods*. Vandevort left on a road trip to Seattle to visit friends, but to Elliot's delight, agreed to come back for Christmas and stay for six months while she worked on the book she had promised Arnold.

The Matthew Henry book Elliot had edited appeared, and she had made hesitant attempts toward a new project, but she found that her creative energies were absorbed by the building process, and she was unable to make headway. She was accepting speaking engagements, and in late October she and Valerie made the two-hour drive south to Andover, Massachusetts, where she spoke to about four hundred women at a missions conference.

By Veteran's Day the new house was not finished but habitable. They started sleeping there, and Elliot began sewing curtains and bed ruffles to the scent of the tile-fitter's cigars as he worked on the bathrooms. A week later, things were finished enough that she gave the house a thorough cleaning and began unpacking. She had sold most of her belongings in Ecuador but had brought back her tea kettle, the rug she had bought with Jim, the little bed he had built for Valerie, the tree-stump coffee table, and a Waorani lance and hammock. She bought some more furniture at auctions and sales—a parlor-size pot-bellied stove, a desk, a bedroom suite for herself and a canopy bed for Valerie, and a beautiful blue velvet sofa. Katharine had sent her things from Birdsong: pillows, dishes, lamps, rugs, the piano, a marble-topped dresser, and some good mahogany highboy twin beds and dresser that Elliot put in the guest room; they brought with them warm memories and saved a lot of money.

Surrounded by pretty things chosen to her taste, in a house designed to her specifications, Elliot luxuriated in comforts. Reliable electricity meant instant hot water—no more starting the day by starting a fire, then trying to get water to really *boil* over open flame; no more ash and soot everywhere. It meant reliable refrigeration—no more food going bad overnight. It meant plug-in appliances—no more messy, smelly, gasoline-powered ironing. A weather-tight house meant things she had cleaned *stayed* clean—"no mold on the counter tops," no floor covered in dead bugs to sweep every time she came home. She was warm enough at night, snuggled under plenty of blankets on a real mattress. She had lots of storage and work surfaces, organizational helps that made household tasks simpler. "I find myself enjoying housework of all kinds, something I never did before."[2]

She had a beautiful setting for it. Seated in a clearing at the brow of a wooded hill about a mile south of town, the house faced southeast over the valley toward Mount Lafayette, and the morning light streamed through the big windows. Elliot named it "Indinyawi," Kichwa for "Eye of the Sun." On the main floor were the living room with stone fireplace and built-in bookshelves, the kitchen with the latest amenities, three bedrooms, and two bathrooms. Downstairs were a laundry room, bonus room, and garage. Elliot chose a totally different color palette from the one she had used in Shandia, all white and blue and purple and gold, with lots of natural wood. There was a large attic for storage and a balcony wrapping two sides of the house. They got a puppy, a white mutt with black and tan spots that they named Zippy. They went sledding and hiking and had friends over. Valerie started piano and ballet.

Mother and daughter spent Thanksgiving with the Yeaworth family. (Irvin "Shorty" Yeaworth, who had directed the 1958 cult classic *The Blob*, was the distributor for the documentary film *Through the Gates of Splendor*.) They watched part of the Macy's Thanksgiving Day parade and went to see the new Sidney Poitier film *Lilies of the Field*, and the adults endlessly discussed the assassination of President Kennedy, who had been so shockingly killed a week before. Elliot and Valerie were home again the first of December to revel in all the trappings of a New England Christmas: plenty of snow and sledding; decorations all over the little town; shopping for gifts; learning carols; a school Christmas play, dance, and class party; a community Christmas program with gifts for all the children, in which Valerie recited and Elliot sang a duet. "Val is so thrilled with Christmas," Elliot wrote to her family.[3] Vandevort would be back for the day itself, and they planned to spend it at Indinyawi, hosting a few friends and making traditions and memories like those Elliot cherished from her own childhood.

———

On Christmas morning, one month shy of his sixty-sixth birthday, Philip Howard died. He had begun to see something over his right shoulder—out of the "peripheral vision" of his glass eye—during breakfast, and when he and Katharine arrived at the Buckinghams' house to open presents, he collapsed in the doorway, seized, and vomited. He was admitted to the hospital, conscious, talking, and calm. His doctor said the event was likely caused by scar tissue from his brain surgeries and could be part of his new normal. Katharine went home to meet her brother and sister-in-law, who were coming to dinner. Not long after she left, Philip died. Later she wrote, "He had often said to me in recent years 'If I should die suddenly I want you to be THANKFUL.' . . . by God's grace I was."[4] She was relieved that he was spared further illness. But she missed him. They had been married forty-one years.

Elliot, Tom, and Jim traveled to Vero Beach to be with their mother. Katharine's brother Tom and his wife, Dot, who had come to celebrate Christmas, stayed to help. The Buckinghams fed everyone. Philip had been a widely known figure, and Katharine was inundated with visitors, flowers, telegrams, and mail. The funeral was December 27. Elliot stayed on at Little Birdsong for another week, then accompanied her mother to HDA, where Katharine was waited on hand and foot and finally had a chance to rest.

After she returned to Indinyawi, Elliot wrote to offer Katharine the encouragement she had gleaned in losing Jim. "I am glad I could be with you for that brief time, and was encouraged by your brave trust. I know that you loved Dad, and your life was happy together, and I know too that now that God's time has come for you to be alone, He will be your portion as He promised, and you will find a new kind of life with Him."[5] She made no public comment on her own grief, noting in a family letter only that "it gives me a start to hear the high call of the Chickadee (for you Elliots—that was Dad's bird-call to Mother, which they both used to attract the attention of the other, wherever they were). Dad was such a flawless imitator one could not possibly tell the difference."[6]

———

Back from Florida, Elliot tried again to get started writing. Sitting in a comfortable chair with a book open on her lap or at the desk in her bedroom with Zippy quietly chewing a wad of paper he had stolen from her wastebasket, she would read and think, think and read, "trying to get an angle for a book. Seems hopeless just now, but God must have some idea which will be revealed in time."[7] She did write a few articles for the *Sunday School Times*, one about her father, a few on walking in the guidance of the Holy Spirit rather than by a set of predecided standards. But for a book, words would not come.

Elliot knew that fallow periods were necessary for most writers, but this did not prevent anxiety about her lack of progress—anxiety inimical to the quietness and enrichment necessary for creative work. In late January, she described the questions that plagued her in a family letter:

> The day has been a very quiet one indeed, Van working in the living room, and I here in the bedroom—reading from Simone Weil, Deuteronomy, and Ecclesiastes, and then just thinking, trying to formulate a book. It's the thinking that is by far the most difficult part, and I go through the same deep misgivings with each book—e.g., how arrogant, how fatuous to think I am qualified to write at all. Weil is so enormously erudite (she died at 33, too) and I have so little educational background. I do have things to say, but how to say them? And who will listen? And have I the courage to say what I see to be true, without fear of opinion? Well, as in any other endeavor, one must simply <u>do</u> it. I'll be glad of your prayers.[8]

She was encouraged during this time by reading the minor prophets, and particularly by a passage from the second chapter of Habakkuk that describes the prophet waiting to receive God's words, God's assurance that a vision will come, and God's instruction to the prophet to write down what he sees so that others can read it. "The utter honesty of those writings speaks to me," she said. "So this is my role now. To take my stand, to watch, to wait. Then to write—without fear—what I see."[9]

To *do it* was not simple though. There was still household business to attend to, and caring for Valerie. Speaking invitations came two or three a day, and with each she had to spend precious mental and emotional energy weighing the pros and cons of accepting and declining. "I do not want to take too many," she explained, "for the first task is the writing (after Val, who comes first of all)."[10]

But it was not easy to know how many were too many. The "money angle," as she called it, "cannot be ignored. Some of these places would give me something which would be a real help."[11] Her bills were paid, and she had enough saved for about a year, but eventually she would need income. And for Valerie to have the kind of childhood Elliot had wanted for her when they were in the jungle, there had to be money, not only for food and clothing and shelter but for skiing and piano lessons and dog food and Valentine's Day treasure hunts and parties and Halloween costumes.

On the other hand, each acceptance further diverted time and energy from both Valerie—who usually stayed with Vandevort when Elliot traveled—and the book. Engagements tended to require multistage journeys, with Van dropping her off to catch a bus for a long ride to the nearest train station or airport or bus transfer station. And for each one Elliot had to write or adapt a speech instead of working on the book. Nevertheless, she spoke four to five times a month for the rest of the school year, often on trips where she was away more than one night. After one such engagement, she reported without comment that "Val had cried a bit the night before, valiantly trying to hide her face from Van under the blankets, finally admitting 'I want my Mommie.'"[12]

In mid-February, Elliot spoke twice in New York, visited several friends in the city, and consulted a lawyer about her taxes. It was a busy four days, filled with plays, shopping, and conversation, and provided much food for thought. On her first night in the city she stayed with the Capas, which gave her a "good long chance to talk" with Cornell. "None of you can know what an influence he has had on my writing of the first three books," she told her family afterward. "I find in him a very clear thinker, an outside observer of the things which so deeply disturb me from inside, a catalyst for my own thought processes, and as usual, though quite indefinably, he was a great help."[13] He helped her pin down her own swirling thoughts.

Although she rarely goes into detail, Elliot's family letters during this time make clear that though she was still "inside" Christian faith, she was disturbed by the way many Christians spoke about who God is, how God acts, and how the life of faith works. It did not match her experience, nor that of many other people she had talked with. Life was *not* straightforward. Tragedy was *not* explainable. Missionary work was *not* "inspirational." And yet many of those "inside" the church continued to speak and act as though they were.

She was upset by what seemed like lazy thinking and even intellectual dishonesty: Christian jargon, religious platitudes, packaging God into a neat box that could be taken out after luncheon and put away again before the spring hat show. She felt she was expected to "further the 'cause' of missions,"[14] even at the expense of telling the truth, that people wanted a hero to worship rather than a fellow pilgrim who would share what God was showing her on the journey. She had written after one Bible study at the church she was attending, "Fundamental—oh sure, but where is the life? Where is the honesty?"[15] After a speaking engagement she wrote, "It was dreadful. Just plain dreadful. The whole hollow mockery, the show, the missionary machine, the Gospel Business, the introduction of me, the total lack of comprehension of what I was saying, the sheer phoniness of everything about it. Van and I came away appalled."[16]

It seemed to Elliot that in many ways, those on the "outside" had a better grasp on "Christian values" than those on the "inside." Spending time with the Capas and their friends, she was impressed by how they embodied virtues like long-suffering and loving-kindness. But they, too, seemed to be missing important pieces of the puzzle. She caught a couple of live productions while she was in the city—John Osborne's *Luther*, on the life of Martin Luther, and Archibald MacLeish's *J.B.*, based on the book of Job. After the latter she was invited to stay for drinks with the cast.

> I had opportunity to talk with the leading lady, and to ask her how emotionally involved she becomes in a part—esp. such a part as Job's wife. Did it reflect her own attitude toward God? No. Essentially she doesn't react to God at all. A writer whom I met there also told me she does not consider questions of the origin of man's mind, or the existence of God as issues at all. They simply do not occur. I am baffled anew—these serious people, who can portray so convincingly the basic problems of life, seem unwilling to come to personal terms with them. Again—what can one say to them?

Although she appreciated the play itself, she found the final act disappointing. It seemed to be trying "to give a more satisfactory answer to Job's questions than he got out of God."[17] This was the same thing she was frustrated with the church for doing.

But there were others who shared her concerns. At one speaking engagement, Dan Derr sought her out because he was beginning to feel he could no longer sign Mission Aviation Fellowship's statement of faith. Having "heard by the grapevine that I felt quite strongly about the ultimate redemption of all creation," he felt she might be a good person with whom to discuss his changing beliefs.[18] They talked for several hours. Elliot felt that his willingness to risk his career in order to think honestly about his beliefs was "far more courageous than going to the Aucas, for instance." And she believed it was part of Christian obedience. "When Jesus said 'I am the Truth' this is what He meant. We must be prepared to follow him with the <u>mind</u>, a far more difficult thing than to follow him geographically."[19]

On her last evening in the city, Shorty Yeaworth asked Elliot to coffee to tell her that his own beliefs were changing; he felt she ought to know if they were to go on working together. "I told him that whenever I see honesty and the courage to face deep-seated doubts, I am encouraged. Far from losing confidence in him, I am more inclined to trust him, for I see integrity at work—a thing so sadly lacking in much that passes for 'Christian work.'" When yet another friend approached her to talk about "the new fields of thought into which she has been led lately," Elliot noted the sheer number of questioners with whom she kept crossing paths. "It is significant to me that these people, each so different in personality, each in such different circumstances, has been led of God to see Truth in a similar light—and brought to me, too, so that I am forced to consider the truth from their viewpoints. He does know what He is doing—and I feel that His hand is on me here, and that He will give me something to write."[20]

In the first week of March, Elliot spoke at Rhode Island's Barrington College, first on the missionary's task as "knowing God," using her key verse, Isaiah 43:10, and then on the book of Job, "using Job's honesty in what he said about God as a starting point, speaking of the dishonesty in mission representation, our false sense of what it means to believe God, our mistaken idea of what it means to serve God, our 'partiality for God,' of which Job spoke in condemnation, etc." She felt "the attitude of students and faculty alike was one of earnest seeking for truth, an openness and willingness to listen to something new which I simply have not found in churches." The questions asked were thoughtful ("Not," she quipped afterward, "the 'You're not a <u>widow</u>, are you?' kind"), and her listeners seemed to get what she was getting at. It was encouraging to find that even those who wanted to challenge her on some point seemed to be doing it in the spirit of continuing the conversation rather than refuting an argument.

"The people there treated me like a human being, instead of a commodity, which is the feeling I usually get."[21]

———

Elliot's journal entries in March record her ongoing agonies over her inability to get started on a book. There was no one trying to buy aspirin or sell manioc now, but still nothing came. She read Isak Dinesen's *Out of Africa* ("Such dignity and grace, and truthfulness & brilliant imagination"[22]); André Gide's *The Immoralist*; Ezekiel; *Time* magazine; and *Playboy* (because the decade-old magazine was publishing serious writers including Ray Bradbury, Roald Dahl, Shirley Jackson, and James Thurber, and because she was curious about what the Playmates looked like). She chased the same thoughts around and around: What kind of form should the book take—nonfiction or fiction? Could she really manage to write fiction? How on earth would she come up with names for characters? Many evangelicals frowned on novel-reading, and many people interested in literature frowned on missionaries—would *anyone* read a missionary novel?

Finally, near the end of the month, she was able to put words on paper. She wrote to her family:

> It is a great relief to be working at last. Pray for clarity of vision, for the ability to put it down, for truthfulness in the inward parts. This is always a hard thing for me as I write—I keep feeling my own inadequacy in perceiving the truth and in actually formulating it on paper. One wonders if one's soul is really big enough for the task. I keep thinking of old John, seeing that tremendous vision, and being told <u>Write what you see</u>. None of us can do anything else in honesty—we must write what we see, not what someone else sees, not what we may think we ought to see, not what we wish to see.[23]

Sometimes she could write a couple of pages in an evening, sometimes only a couple of vague notes in her whole writing time for a day. She found it particularly difficult to get back into writing after speaking trips. But she did not think she should refuse these trips, not only because of the financial benefits, but because she felt she had a unique and brief window of opportunity in which to speak to Christians as a sort of "insider outside" and thus fulfill her calling to be a witness.

In April, Elliot left Valerie with Vandevort for a five-day speaking trip into which she squeezed a visit with Katharine in Florida and dinner and a movie with the Yeaworths in New York. Valerie came on another speaking trip that covered four states and included visits with, among other people, Vandevort's parents; Olive Fleming and her new husband, Walter Liefeld; Ed McCully's mother; Jim's parents and sister; Tom; and Jim and his wife, Joyce, and their new baby. Nine-year-old Val stayed with her uncle Tom or her grandparents when Elliot was speaking. After a night at home Elliot was off again to speak in Quebec.

In May, she attended Valerie's ballet recital, bought a hide-a-bed sofa in anticipation of Phil's upcoming furlough, worked in the yard, traveled to New York for a lunch with a Harper's rep, packed the wool clothes away in mothballs for the summer, and went to the Boston Ballet. She spoke four times, trying, as she wrote afterward to her family, "to point out . . . some of the things which disturb me so deeply in the field of Christian literature, which is worthy of neither the first nor the second term."[24]

After the second event she ran into Joseph Tate Bayly, a fellow Wheaton alumnus who had been in the audience. Like Elliot, Bayly had gone into "Christian work" after graduation, helping to found InterVarsity Christian Fellowship and InterVarsity Press. And like Elliot, Bayly was no stranger to loss and grief. In 1957 Joe and Mary Lou Bayly's five-year-old son Danny had died of leukemia. Months later their infant son John had died of complications from cystic fibrosis. In 1960 another son, Nathan, had been born with cystic fibrosis. And in December 1963 their eldest, Joe, had fallen from his sled during his Christmas break from Swarthmore College, hemorrhaged from hemophilia, and died what Bayly later called a "violent, awful death."[25] When Elliot saw him, she didn't waste time in small talk:

> I asked him right off the bat, "What sort of view of God do you and Mary Lou have now?" He smiled, said, "Very simple. You can't try to justify Him. We don't look on Joe's death in terms of Swarthmore students saved or stirred up. It comes right down to God Himself. There is no other answer." I asked about his child who now has cystic fibrosis. Would he die? "Yes," said Joe, "He'll probably die. Of course, we could pray that he won't. But

you can imagine how I feel about praying that people won't die!" He smiled again. We had a really good talk, and I was encouraged by his faith, and by, incidentally, his expression of appreciation of what I had said in my talk at the EPA. Wish we had had longer.[26]

Looking on a believer's death in terms of others "saved or stirred up" was exactly what Elliot had done in the conclusion to *Through Gates of Splendor*. Her appreciation for Bayly's sentiment is an indicator of how much her views on what was entailed in Christian faith had changed in the last seven-and-a-half years.

———

Elliot traveled and spoke off and on throughout the summer of 1964—Boston in June; Nyack College in July; a weeklong conference on Cape Cod in August; Maine and Massachusetts in September—and kept working on her novel, but much of the season seems to have centered around entertaining. In early June Elliot and Vandevort had a several-days visit from Lovelace Oden, a close friend of Van's who was an HDA and Wheaton alumna and former China Inland Mission missionary to Japan. Oden had also been romantically involved with Elliot's brother Tom for some time, and the couple got engaged a couple of weeks later. Katharine came to spend the summer and early fall. There was a steady stream of other visitors, often a different set every day in a week. Phil and Margaret and their family arrived to spend part of their furlough, and Dave and Phyllis and their children, also on furlough, came to visit. Vandevort was away for the month of August and Elliot missed her.

It was not an easy summer for Elliot or her mother. It was Katharine's first time in Franconia since Philip's death. Memories of their honeymoon and of family vacations while the children were growing must have been everywhere she turned. Harder still, Indinyawi was surrounded by chickadees, nesting and calling from the trees all around the house. The sound of Philip's call to her was in her ears all day long. "I fear I was not a very happy sort of guest that summer," Katharine would write years later. "I was finding the adjustment of widowhood hard to make."[27]

To Elliot, her mother seemed anxious and controlling. Just as Elliot's diary had received the details of her frustrations when she lived with the Cathers family and with Rachel Saint, so now she poured into her little brown spiral-bound notebook lists of the things Katharine seemed to worry at, the things she could not stop bringing up, from the cleanliness of the refrigerator, to her own plans for the future, to Elliot's parenting and Valerie's behavior, to the question of Christians and alcohol. Philip had seemed to grow more scrupulous and rigid in the last years of his life, but Katharine had expressed a difference of opinion from him often enough that Elliot had hoped she would be more open in her own views after she was no longer constrained by wifely submission. Now she decided in exasperation that her mother was doubling down on her father's convictions out of reverence for his memory.

Both women were dealing with the added burden of grief. Elliot struggled not to take Katharine's behavior personally, particularly when her mother brought up ideas they had disagreed about in the past. Although Katharine felt she was simply sharing the things she was thinking about, Elliot felt her mother was trying to nag her into agreement. She responded much as she had to Rachel Saint, deciding that discussion was increasing the tension between them and trying to avoid subjects on which they did not agree. Katharine realized that there was constraint between them but was at a loss to know how to reconnect.

As they had periodically throughout Elliot's life, mother and daughter had disagreed during Elliot's visit to Little Birdsong in the spring, but Elliot had put a positive spin on it at the time. She had joked that perhaps "my far-out ideas" were the reason Katharine was having trouble sleeping and thanked her mother for her "openness and willingness to contemplate my thoughts . . . We'll have a good time this summer!"[28] But she was aware that her "far-out ideas" were not always understood—or shared—by her family. After her April visit with various Elliots and Howards, Elliot had observed ruefully, "I am afraid I disturbed some of them rather badly. One does not relish being a rebel, impressions given notwithstanding."[29] Perhaps the sense that she was seen as a rebel was influencing her response to Katharine now.

Tom was the exception, the family member with whom she did not feel she had to be on her guard. With him she repeatedly found that sort of *aha!* moment described by C. S. Lewis as the foundation for friendship, "that moment when one person says to another: 'What! You too? I thought I was the only one!'"[30] About the same time Elliot left Ecuador, Tom had returned from two years of teaching at a boys' school in England. He had been going through his own process of spiritual reevaluation. He had tried desperately to make Victorious Life teaching work for him and failed and had left America, as he would later write, "prepared to set God aside . . . if to pursue Him meant to miss the cakes and ale" experiences of life. He had come back feeling unable to try any longer to reconcile "the data of human experience" and the Christian claim of a loving God.[31] How much of this he had expressed in family letters is unclear, but it was enough that Katharine was concerned for him. When she appealed to her elder daughter for help in understanding his views, Elliot had made clear that she identified deeply with her brother. "I am very much surprised that you got any comfort out of me . . . or that you look to me for help now, knowing as you do how Tom and I think alike. I supposed myself to be at least as great an enigma and therefore grief to you."[32]

In the same letter Elliot had urged her mother not to share her feelings with Tom. She acknowledged that her mother did not mean to strong-arm her children into agreement but knew from experience, she said, that "it makes one unspeakably uneasy to be the object of deep concern, and it seems to me that when we feel such concern, we ought to keep it to ourselves and God, not share it with the person who is the cause. How can this help?"[33] Instead she encouraged Katharine to pray for Tom and trust God. It seems likely that this hands-off approach is what she wanted from her mother in regard to herself as well.

Elliot had also acknowledged that interpersonal communication was complicated and that the differences between them must be painful for her mother, closing her letter, "Love you, Mother, and wish communication were not so utterly hopeless!"[34] A few weeks later she had sent another letter expressing her appreciation for Katharine's willingness to continue in relationship with her despite the difficulties. "I do love you, Mother, and thank God for you, for your constancy of love, and for the humility of spirit which enables you to seek to understand your offbeat children, rather than condemning them and crossing them off. You are, and I say this with all my heart, a VERY REMARKABLE MOTHER."[35] Elliot's decision not to discuss potentially controversial subjects with her mother did not last forever, and eventually she was writing again to her mother about things she knew at least some of her brothers would disagree with and asking for Katharine's opinion.

Honesty had been a watchword for Elliot for months; another theme that begins to recur in this period is the importance of love. Someone whom Katharine cared about very much appears to have been living with same-sex attraction, and mother and daughter discussed the situation by letter over a period of several months. In one letter, Elliot emphasized the visible fruit of the Spirit in this person's life: "unselfishness, thoughtfulness, a deep desire to know & understand people, a great capacity for love."[36] In another, she encouraged Katharine to accept the individual and trust God, trying to help her see that to experience attraction was not outside obedience to God:

> To hope for victory over such a thing . . . is like hoping for victory over blindness or paralysis. I believe God could do it, He could have given Dad two eyes again. But the problem is far more complex than a simple matter of sin. It is not sin in any sense of the word though it is a frame of mind and attitude which presents its own particular kind of temptation. Sin only enters when the law of love is transgressed, if I understand Jesus' interpretation of the law.[37]

Elliot went on to remind her mother of the biblical account of the deep relationship between David and Jonathan, particularly noting 1 Samuel 20:41, "they kissed one another," and 2 Samuel 1:26, David's assertion that their love was "surpassing the love of women." "I'm not building a doctrine on this," Elliot wrote. "I only want to face up honestly to what we are told in Scripture, not ignoring or explaining away any facets of it. Perhaps the truth is that there are no such things as lines drawn, coincident with sex. Love is the great thing. Without love, where does any human relationship stand? For you, in acceptance lieth peace."[38]

Elliot had written these things in fall 1963 and spring 1964. Now, in the summer of 1964, she continued to develop her understanding of the primary place of love in Christian theology. The beliefs she had developed and expressed in letters over the course of 1960 and 1961 were foundational: that the attitude of a person's heart determines whether an action is "worldliness," that each sheep has to hear the Shepherd's voice for him- or herself. Foundational, too, was her frustration with what she saw as American evangelicalism's myopic focus on avoiding *things* (such as alcohol and movies) while letting pass unchallenged *actions* (such as lying and idolatry).

Finally, in a long, late-night conversation with Phil and Dave, she argued that there was no such thing as lines drawn coincident with *anything*, except love. Dave said years later:

> I remember one night my brother Phil and I . . . got into a long, long discussion with Betty, just the three of us together. And Phil and I were expressing a strong evangelical perspective on things. And we tried to pin her down with some things she was saying. And I'll never forget this, at one point she said to me—and I talked about certain things being absolute—she said, "I'm not even sure if there are any absolutes in life." And then she said, "Unless it be love, maybe love is an absolute. But everything else is not an absolute."[39]

Elliot wrote cheerfully in her family letters of her numerous social engagements and travel plans; her journals gave her space to process the stress of her hectic schedule and conflict with her mother. After one busy week in July she noted her total inability to focus on writing. Two weeks into August she lamented that she had made no progress for weeks. In late September she recorded that she seemed unable to write with Katharine there. It is difficult to know why she continued to extend and accept invitations when she was so overextended. Perhaps she was still trying to discipline herself to live up to the extroverted ideal. In any event, with her deadline less than three months away she continued to host, travel, and speak. In October she and Van left Valerie with Katharine, Phil, and Margaret for ten days and drove first to New York City and then to Wheaton, where Elliot spoke at the annual writers' conference and in chapel.

Her talks were drawn from the things she had been wrestling with in her own thinking. At the conference she spoke on "Writing as Personal Discovery," arguing that we can only write with integrity about what we have learned through experience. The writer's task is to faithfully portray the things she has seen. This requires a posture of uncertainty and active searching in order to be *able* to see. It requires openness to change—it will mean that "we don't think the same way that we thought last year"—and to messiness. The psalmist, she pointed out, says in Psalm 37 not to fret, and then writes other psalms that are "just one long fret." And it requires a commitment to excellence in the craft of writing: good writing can be trusted "to give form to . . . truth," but "bad writing is a lie."[40]

In contrast to this vision, Elliot said, much of what is called Christian writing begins from the assumption that the writer's job is to expound the right doctrine, win adherents to the cause, create certainty, prevent change, preserve tidiness. The result, she suggested, is not art but propaganda: "It is the search for truth which gives rise to creativity." "I believe one of the reasons for the lack of really true Christian art is first of all that we start with the answers. We begin with the cheerful assurance that we know the truth and so the search that is the basis of art is thwarted."[41]

In chapel, Elliot spoke on Job, apparently a reprise of the talk given at Barrington College in the spring. She began by saying that her missionary experience was incompatible with the narrative expected of her by most Christian audiences. "When I am asked to speak I take it for granted that people are interested in my work in Ecuador, and I think I have an idea of what they expect me to say. But in honesty I cannot say those things." She went on to talk about Job's much-vaunted faith, describing the Bible's portrayal of it as "poles apart" from the faith she had been taught to pursue. She used her experiences with the death of Macario and the theft of her language files, which she now described as irrecoverably lost, as a springboard to talk about what she had learned about faith in those experiences.

She had been led to believe, she said, by missionary biographies and missionary speakers, that God behaves in certain ways. When events clashed with this belief, she had turned to Scripture to try to understand the discrepancy. She had found that many of the things she had been taught were not in the Bible. "He has never promised to solve our problems. He has not promised to answer our questions. He has certainly not answered mine. He has promised to go with us in this life. He has revealed Himself in His Word to be a sovereign, and at the same time an inexorably loving God. I can testify this morning that He has been that to me. But time and again I have had to acknowledge that nothing I knew about Him was adequate to cover the things which in honesty I had to face."

Behind all this lay the pointed implication that the missionary stories she had been reared on in places like Wheaton's chapel were *not* looking honestly at the facts of life. "My experience certainly was poles apart from missionary experiences of which I had read and heard, and I simply had to bow in the knowledge that God is His own interpreter." The insistence of Christians on interpreting God's plan in human suffering and loss she called "arrogant," "childish," "fatuous." In fact, the speech suggests that in their own partiality to God, the evangelical church in America had created an idol and were worshiping it in God's place. [42]

———

Katharine went back to Florida the day after Elliot got home from Wheaton. Phil and Margaret set out on a two-week speaking trip, leaving their children at Indinyawi. Nine-year-old Val and her cousins made Halloween costumes and carved pumpkins and went trick-or-treating. Elliot hosted the neighbors for Vandevort's birthday, went out to dinner, sewed new clothes for herself, made mayonnaise from scratch, went ice skating with the kids, and submitted an essay to *Redbook* (it was rejected).

Sitting down to her writing again the day after her mother left, Elliot had felt her manuscript was worthless. But she did not know what to do other than continue "sitting and staring at a typewriter, chewing a pencil, reading somebody who knows how to write, thinking, or just sitting most of the time."[43] The more she read, the more she felt that her Christian-school and Sunday-school background had left her with gaping holes in her understanding of the world and a picture of reality that was a fantasy, populated by two-dimensional figures who were either sinners or saved, who either had nothing to offer or had everything figured out. She chided herself for having been so slow to seriously examine her worldview and prayed for God's mercy toward her foolishness.

December came and went. Finally at the end of January she took the still unfinished manuscript to New York to show it to Arnold, who reported himself "quite pleased."[44] Her trip was a social and professional whirlwind including room-service tea at the Plaza and dinner out with Tom's future in-laws, and a twenty-four-hour stay with Virginia Ramey Mollenkott, a fellow HDA alumna who was a professor at Nyack College with a PhD in literature from New York University, and who had written to Elliot complimenting her writing and offering professional feedback.[45] Back at Indinyawi she wrote to her family, "All this week has been spent trying to recover and collect my thoughts and write something, but I didn't get a word on paper till today. God help us all. I don't know why people ever try to write books."[46] But she was finally working on what she hoped would be the last chapter.

After two weeks at home—in which she apparently finished a complete draft—Elliot was off again for another week. Leaving Val with Van, she went first to New York City, where she spent a day with Mollenkott and stayed overnight with the Capas. She and Cornell worked late into the night and all the next morning on her manuscript. The next afternoon she left the manuscript with Mollenkott, who would "work it over" in her absence, and flew to Minneapolis for a series of speaking engagements: three hundred Billy Graham Crusade employees, 150 InterVarsity Christian Fellowship alumni, a women's meeting, a series of seminars at Bethel College, a book signing, and half a dozen media interviews.[47] She rounded out the trip with a thirty-six-hour stay with her brother Jim's family, during which she spoke and showed slides to all comers in the high school gym.

The day after Elliot got home, Mollenkott arrived to spend five days at Indinyawi, during which Elliot threw a birthday party and sleepover for Valerie's tenth birthday. This was followed almost immediately by a weekend trip to visit friends on Cape Cod, a speaking engagement in Boston, hiking, and an operatic concert, but somehow Elliot managed to finish her revisions and start typing a fair copy to send to Harper's. She mailed it off on April 2.

———

The book was called *No Graven Image*, from the King James Version of the second commandment, "Thou shalt not make unto thee any graven image" (Ex. 20:4). The first-person narrator, a young woman named Margaret Sparhawk, recounts her first years as a missionary in Ecuador, and Elliot's loving descriptions of Ecuador in Sparhawk's mouth bring the story to life. Many details from Sparhawk's story will sound familiar to readers of Elliot's life: the family history of missions support, the preparatory work in rural home missions and linguistics, the shock of the poverty and dirt in Guayaquil, and even the Bible verses that seem to the young missionary to be the specific voice of God to *her*. Sparhawk, too, is living among Kichwa people, but she is in the Sierra region, in Indi Urcu, "Hill of the Sun."

The first half of the book revolves around the evangelical vision of missions, as Sparhawk's experiences raise questions that were never addressed in the endless Christian meetings of her upbringing. She embarks on the task of "winning souls" as best she can but soon realizes that none of the missionary books and speakers whose messages she has absorbed ever explained in practical, concrete terms how to *do* that. She finds her time filled with mundane tasks that could be done anywhere in the world, then struggles to frame her activity in spiritual terms for prayer letters to financial supporters. Her efforts yield uneven results. And at Sparhawk's first missions conference, which for Elliot was a key portion of the book, the tension between the grand clichés repeated endlessly at the conference and Sparhawk's own experience in the field fills her with a sense "almost of panic." "They all seemed to belong," Sparhawk says of the other missionaries, "they knew the lines, and they wore—I must be imagining it—the same masks."[48]

It is at the conference that Sparhawk meets missionary doctor Lynn Anderson, who politely refuses to be pigeonholed. She refuses, too, the commonplace chatter of the majority and instead asks questions that cut to the heart of Sparhawk's unease. "You see such a need all around and it seems so hopeless to do anything about it, and then when you hear all these reports you're convinced it's not hopeless after all," Sparhawk says rather breathlessly after the first morning of meetings. And Anderson replies, "And suppose, after a few years' work, you found that it was? . . . What would happen to your idea of God, for instance, if you found that your work was useless?" And it is not only that the doctor asks uncomfortable questions of others. She refuses to wear a mask herself. "What *is* the missionary task, after all?" another character asks Anderson rhetorically, and she replies, "I am no longer as sure as I once was."[49]

Returning to Indi Urcu after the conference, Sparhawk muddles on as best she can. Direct evangelism doesn't seem to work for her. She hires Pedro Chimbu, the only person in the area who speaks both Kichwa and Spanish, to work for her as a linguistic informant, hoping that making disciples will be easier when she has God's word in the language of the people. But the coworkers she has been expecting are turned down by the mission board. Now there will be no school to teach people to read the Bible even if she translates it; she has to grapple with what to make of "a negative answer to so many people's prayers."[50]

Feeling that God has redirected her through circumstance, Sparhawk begins to carry supplies for simple medical care. She has some successes—

she helps a woman successfully deliver a breech baby, a thing previously unheard of in the area—but these do nothing to open the door to talk about Jesus. And when she is called out in the middle of the night to help a child who dies just before she arrives, she wrestles with how to understand it. She gradually comes to believe that "my task was far smaller in terms of the effect it was to produce" than she had expected when she arrived in Ecuador, and "far larger in terms of my own life involvement. If there were times when I must be willing to pay any price for what was called the 'advancement of the Kingdom' there were also times when I must be willing to let such a price . . . be paid in vain. This, too, was a place to glorify God."[51]

As her view of her work is changing, a visitor appears, a Mr. Harvey, making a survey of missionary efforts so that he can "challenge the folks back home." As Harvey follows her around for hours, talking and not listening, looking for showy things to photograph, Sparhawk begins to understand that he plans to use pictures of her—confused, uncertain, hesitant, unsuccessful—to create those stirring presentations about missions that she has listened to her whole life. "I had been 'challenged' by men like him, had believed what they told me as though they had been oracles. Today I saw the makings of such a challenge." Although Sparhawk does not make the connection explicit, it's clear that she has been exhorted onto the mission field under the belief that "what God is doing" through other missionaries is clear-cut and straightforward, when the reality is as ambiguous as her life in Indi Urcu.[52]

As Sparhawk and Chimbu work together on the language over "long months," there is some progress. Chimbu has been listening to the Bible stories she has to share and eventually declares that he believes the story of the crucifixion to be true. He becomes invested in getting the stories in writing, and they begin translation of the Gospel of Mark. His children love the stories too, and are learning to read.[53]

And then Chimbu dies. Worse still, it seems likely that he dies of an anaphylactic response to the sulfa powder Sparhawk uses to treat a wound on his leg. The young missionary literally runs away. She locks herself in her house, but she finds she cannot lock out God, who is both too present and too absent. "Where is the refuge from Him? . . . Where was He, anyway?" There can be no Bible translation now. The family hates her. She is finished. Elliot's treatment of Sparhawk's panic and confusion is masterful.[54]

In the days following Chimbu's death, Sparhawk is forced again to come to a new understanding of herself and of God. Two of Chimbu's children come to her door asking for candles for their father's wake, bringing an invitation from their mother to come and sit with the family. She attends the wake and later the burial. Life goes on. The community does not exclude her. People visit her or welcome her into their homes or ignore her, just as they did before. She has not been the benefactor she had thought she would be; neither has she been struck with fire from heaven or run out of town on a rail. "What would happen to your idea of God . . . if you found that your work was useless?" Anderson had asked her. Standing at Chimbu's grave weeks after his death, Sparhawk asks herself, "And God? What of Him? 'I am with thee,' He had said. With me in *this*? He had allowed Pedro to die or—and I could not then nor can I today deny the possibility—He had perhaps caused me to destroy him. And does He now . . . ask me to worship Him?" The book ends with this question hanging in the air.[55]

The first part of the book addresses the American evangelical vision of missions; the second deals with the American evangelical vision of God. The themes of the novel are those that had populated Elliot's letters and speeches for months: the dishonesty of "the Gospel Business" about God and about life; the church's attempt "to give a more satisfactory answer" to life's big questions than that offered by the Bible. Her study of the prophets—Ezekiel, Daniel, Habakkuk, John—had compelled her to write what she saw: that evangelicals had set up a false god and would go to great lengths to keep it on its pedestal, that the true God would go to any length to knock the idol down. As Sparhawk muses over what her future may hold, she says, "It seemed, on the night of Pedro's death, as though *Finis* were written below all I had done. Now, in the clear light of day, I see that I was in part correct. God, if He was merely my accomplice, had betrayed me. If, on the other hand, He was God, He had freed me."[56]

Sparhawk does not abandon belief in God after the destruction of her graven image. Nor does she abandon the missionary task. In the final chapter of the book, she still believes that God wants her in Indi Urcu, that God communicates with her, that God responds to prayer, that God "is indeed of great mercy."[57] As a writer, Elliot refuses false tidiness. Having painstakingly smashed one god that can be explained, she declines to build a new one with the pieces. But the last chapter of *No Graven Image* closely parallels the last paragraph of Elliot's speech on the book of Job:

> There was a time when Job in despair said that he couldn't even find God no matter where he went—backwards, forwards—"God isn't there." He still didn't throw over his belief that God existed. . . . Let us learn to trust Him for who He is. Let's not be afraid to face the facts of life, even to articulate them as plainly as Job did. Who of us would have had the courage to put down on paper what Job said about God? But Job took this risk because he knew in the depths of his heart who God was.[58]

Elliot had done her level best to follow God's instructions to the prophet Ezekiel, to look and listen and think about what she saw and heard, and then proclaim it to anyone who would listen. She was writing out of what she believed to be obedience to God—a God she worshiped because of God's character, not because of God's gifts.

———

The spring and summer of 1965 were busy. Elliot spoke eight times in April and May on trips of varying lengths, leaving Valerie with Vandevort four times and a babysitter once. She attended a prayer conference with Vandevort while Valerie stayed overnight with another sitter; hosted various guests; worked on the manuscript of *No Graven Image* with Harper's editor Elizabeth Lawrence; took Val to the zoo, the circus, the fair, and the ballet; and saw Tom in New York City and Dave in Nyack. In June, the three denizens of Indinyawi attended Tom and Lovelace's wedding, and then while the newlyweds honeymooned in Europe, borrowed their air-conditioned car for a five-week road trip through eleven states. They spent the first week of August in a cottage on Cape Cod as guests of Dorothy Collins, a seventy-two-year-old Presbyterian woman Elliot had met at a speaking engagement the summer before. The rest of the month was devoted to hosting a stream of guests, with a four-day New York trip to go over the manuscript one last time squeezed into the beginning of September. Valerie started school again on the eighth.

Somehow in the midst of all this, Elliot finished edits on the book. She typed up a final copy during the first week of school and mailed it to Harper's on September 15. "Publication date . . . is March, '66," she wrote to her family. "After that—another book, or what? I have a couple of requests for magazine articles in my drawer so I'll probably do them. Speaking engagements in Sept., Oct. and Nov."[59] The process of deciding what major project to tackle next continued for several months, but Elliot had already been approached about what would turn out to be her next book.

R. Kenneth Strachan, the second-generation director of Latin America Mission, had died of cancer in February at fifty-four. LAM wanted a biography done, and Strachan's eldest son, twenty-three-year-old Harry, had tackled the project, hoping to find some clues to the heart and mind of his beloved father and to make some meaning of his death. Elliot must have seemed a good person to ask for advice, and in April he had arrived at Indinyawi for an overnight visit. To Elliot, Harry had seemed full of "fundamental questionings." Her reception of those questions apparently made a favorable impression; he had written afterward to tell her that "his 'cell looks brighter' after being here."[60]

But after a spring and summer of sorting through his father's papers and interviewing his father's friends and coworkers, Harry had been "profoundly disappointed" to find little of his father's "inner journey" in the documents he left. The young man was deep in grief and struggling with his understanding of Christian faith. He had decided he could not write the book. Dave, who was one of LAM's two assistant general directors at the time, had suggested Elliot as a good choice to tackle the biography instead. Now in September, Elliot met with the other assistant general director of LAM, Harry's uncle, W. Dayton Roberts, about some writing projects, which must have included this proposed biography of Strachan. Elliot ultimately agreed to take on the project, with the understanding that she be given "complete freedom to write about [Strachan] *as I saw him*."[61] She wanted nothing to do with adding yet another hagiographic biography of a "great Christian leader" to the shelves in church libraries.[62] She would pitch the project to Harper's, successfully, in early spring.

Autumn spent itself in a succession of trips, speaking engagements, and social events both at home and away. December found Elliot, Vandevort, and Valerie gearing up for a third Christmas at Indinyawi. They put up a tree, made candy and cookies, and decorated the house. They watched a brand-new television special, *A Charlie Brown Christmas*, and Valerie learned to play Christmas carols on the piano. They celebrated Elliot's thirty-ninth birthday with a gift from Dorothy—a weekend at the Ritz-Carlton to see Eva Le Gallienne in *The Trojan Women*—and came home to host a community carol sing with eggnog and cookies.

In and amongst the festivities, the galleys for *No Graven Image* arrived. Harper's was in a tearing hurry for them, so Elliot worked right through them and put them back in the mail again the next day. "Oh, it's a terribly boring book," she lamented, "and my heart sinks as I read it over again after all these weeks. But as Tom would say, there we are."[63]

The year 1966 comprised the same merry-go-round of social engagements and speaking engagements, punctuated with meals and laundry—and, somehow, reading and writing—that had filled Elliot's days since she moved to New Hampshire. Clara and Fred Elliot came to visit in January, followed by Tom and Lovelace and her parents. Elliot took skiing lessons in February and received the first bound copy of *No Graven Image*. The book made its way into the hands of the public in March and was reviewed in newspapers across the country, from tiny local organs to big names like the *Chicago Tribune* and the *New York Times*.

Reviews were largely positive, and many seemed to "get" what Elliot was trying to do. A handful called it an important book, even required reading, while pointing out that it was likely to appeal most to readers who already had an interest in missions. However, the group that general-market reviewers thought would be most interested in the novel seems to have appreciated it least. *Christianity Today* ran a review by associate editor Harold Lindsell, praising the book as "a solid, well-written piece of fiction," "crackl[ing] with life." But although Lindsell acknowledged the reality of what he called Elliot's "often . . . unpretty picture of evangelical life," he smoothed it away as much as possible; while agreeing that some evangelicals are as the book describes, he characterized them as "the idiosyncratic," "a minority."[64]

Harold Ockenga, who had helped to found the National Association of Evangelicals, Fuller Theological Seminary, and *Christianity Today*, asked

Elliot out to lunch and specifically addressed the novel. He asked if she had changed since leaving for Ecuador ("God help us if we don't change between the ages of 25 and 40," Elliot wrote afterward) and told her he felt the book was a caricature exaggerated to the point of falsehood.[65] She was nonplussed.

Over fifty years later, it seems clear that these men were reacting to more than just the book. The decades-long argument arising from the modernist/fundamentalist controversy—should missionaries focus on personal evangelism or on influencing social systems through the tenets of Christianity?—had gained new life while Elliot was in Ecuador. Although Elliot was aware that these kinds of discussions existed, it's unclear how much of the historical context she recognized. She disclaimed any of the labels floating around in intra-evangelical conversation. "I only know what God seems to say to me, and if someone else wants to label my thinking he will soon find the label breaks down somewhere, that no pattern can be found. Jesus said I am the Truth, not 'This is the Truth.'"[66]

Elliot's reading during this period was primarily among the great writers of her era, as she tried to make up for what she now felt were the deficiencies of her Christian school education. She makes no mention of reading books that were part of the missions discourse, such as James A. Scherer's 1964 *Missionary, Go Home*. When *Evangelical Missions Quarterly* approached her directly with "an inquiry about her philosophy of missions," Elliot emphasized that her job as a novelist was not to further a systematic theology or philosophy of missions but to paint a true picture, to "say what is" "about a single person, in a single situation."[67] But whether she wanted it or not, *No Graven Image* was being read in the context of this larger discussion.

In the months after *No Graven Image* was published, Winning Women, Inc. (run by R. A. Torrey's granddaughter Jill Renich Meyers), disinvited Elliot from a speaking engagement that had been booked for almost a year, and new invitations decreased. Even Harper's informed her that although *No Graven Image* was their best-selling novel of the year, they were hesitant to advertise it more heavily because they did not want to alienate religious readers. Perhaps most alarming, she was accosted after one speaking engagement by an enraged man who told her, among other things, that she was headed for hell. She was left shaking.

Elliot's approach to critics was shaped by advice Billy Graham had given her, to avoid arguments and attempts to vindicate herself. She wrote back "as nicely as I can" to everyone who wrote to her and tried to approach their critiques with an open mind, evaluating whether there was "any truth" in what they were saying, while still remembering "that it is to God alone that I must give account."[68] But the constant barrage of criticism could be discouraging.

None of the hoopla, positive or negative, derailed Elliot's work on Strachan's biography. She and Valerie spent most of August 1966 traveling. They visited Dave and his family in Colombia and Mary Skinner and some others in Ecuador, but the primary purpose of the trip was to conduct interviews and do research in Costa Rica, where Strachan had lived and where his parents, Harry and Susan, had founded LAM. As always, the trip was cram-packed with dinners and luncheons and visits and speaking engagements. Elliot was moved by how kind all the missionaries were about her novel. Eleven-year-old Valerie was thrilled to be back in a tropical environment and flitted from task to task like a happy butterfly, "occupying herself with reading when there was nothing else to do, making copies of things on the Xerox for me, running errands for Eliz. [Strachan], sorting second class mail for Lois Theissen, ironing for Marie Strachan."[69] Like her father, Val was outgoing and wanted to help, and like her father, now that she was out of the language-acquisition stage of development, she was of a typical ability with languages. Elliot seemed surprised that Valerie wasn't picking up Spanish from her environment but noted that it wasn't slowing her down: She "even went shopping on her own. . . . Can you imagine me doing that at her age—or ANY age!!"[70]

They were home in time for Val to start school, and Elliot was immediately plunged into hosting, correspondence, speaking, short-form writing projects, putting up applesauce for the winter, and for a few days—because the tiny tourism bureau was desperate for a place to refer callers looking for somewhere to stay while they took in the fall color—housing tourists "at $3 a head."[71] But despite all this, by the end of September she was working steadily on Strachan's biography. Mary Anne Klein, with LAM's US headquarters, came for a few days to talk and deliver source materials. Elliot began doing intentional supportive reading, including Boswell's famous *Life of Samuel Johnson*, Jean-Paul Sartre's autobiography *The Words*, a biography of A. A. Milne, and Harry Blamires's *The Christian Mind*. And of course she was reading source material. "Am spending most of my time reading Strachan letters," she wrote in mid-October. She had never met Strachan and was finding him, "a very fearful, doubting, ambitious, hopeful, demanding visionary. Will I be able to make him come through?"[72]

In November all the speaking and traveling and shopping and writing were punctuated by a week's visit from Capa, and another, this time a working visit, from Strachan's widow, Elizabeth. In December Elliot made a multistate trip, visiting the Strachan children and family friends in various parts of California; speaking at a college in Tarkio, Missouri; and seeing her new literary agent, Robert Lescher (who also represented writers such as Robert Frost, Dr. Spock, Madeleine L'Engle, Dick Francis, and Georgia O'Keeffe) in New York. She celebrated her fortieth birthday on December 21 and spent another quiet Christmas at Indinyawi with Tom and Lovelace, Van, and Val.

———

"Have spent the day writing about Ken Strachan," Elliot wrote to the Howards and Elliots in late January 1967. "It is a warm, rainy day with snow melting all around and clouds heavy on the mountains. Van and I had tea this afternoon down in the den where she had a nice fire in the stove and her papers spread out on the table. She is hoping to finish her book by February. Val is at the moment on the telephone with a friend trying to figure out something about least common multiples of composite counting numbers."[73] The Five Missionary Martyrs Fund dispute had, through the intervention of an attorney hired by Elliot, finally been settled through disbursement of the money to individual trusts for the children. She had heard from Harper's that *No Graven Image* was to be translated into Finnish and German.

Elliot was flying through the biography. By mid-February she was at LAM's New Jersey headquarters with Elizabeth Strachan, who was reading the "first draft of the biography (minus last chapter)."[74] Elliot disliked this, finding it "depressing" to have people see her writing in process.[75] Vandevort was the only other person who had seen any of the book; Elliot had not even shown it to Tom. But letting Elizabeth—and Ken's sister Grace and her husband, Dayton—see the manuscript had been part of the arrangement when she agreed to write the biography.

Capa worked with Elliot on the pictures for the book, as well as taking the picture that would be her author photo. In mid-April she was still struggling with the biography, but by the second week of May, just seven months after she started writing, she had mailed the completed manuscript. The title, *Who Shall Ascend*, was taken from Psalm 24:3–5 (KJV): "Who shall ascend into the hill of the LORD? Or who shall stand in his holy place? He that hath clean hands, and a pure heart; who hath not lifted up his soul unto vanity, nor sworn deceitfully. He shall receive the blessing from the LORD, and righteousness from the God of his salvation."

Evaluations of Strachan as a public figure were already available, so Elliot had attempted to look more deeply. In the introduction she wrote, "Again and again I found myself tempted to ask what my readers would want this man to be, or what I wanted him to be, or what he himself thought he was—and I had to ignore all such questions in favor of the one relevant consideration: Is this true?"[76]

She did not look away from what she found. To a reader with little knowledge of Strachan's public role as a missionary statesman, the picture is almost unremittingly bleak: a childhood of financial insecurity, frequent ill health, longing for affection; the lasting sense that he could never live up to his loving but demanding and unsympathetic mother and his perpetually absent father; a deep and abiding loneliness; recurring "spiritual crises" and deep depressions; "dreams of a quiet life on a little farm"; a helpless slide into the same pattern of constant travel, financial insecurity, and family separation that had been so difficult in his own childhood; self-doubt; worry; overscrupulosity; grief; regret; and then, in his early fifties, an agonizing death from lymphoma. Nor did she look away from the aftermath of his life and death: the anguish and anger and grief, the uncertainty and unknowing, even, for some who had loved him, the end of Christian faith.

Elliot did not name anyone specifically, but neither did she pretend that everyone mourning Strachan's death found comfort in his beliefs. "Most of those who had loved Ken," she wrote, "were able to hold onto this hope [of the resurrection]." Harry Strachan would later describe the summer after his father's death as the end of his own Christianity and his belief system in his sixties as spiritually interested agnosticism. Elliot received a letter from one reader who summarized the theme of the book thusly: twentieth-century American missions focus on "saving the world" while "letting the family go to hell." To her family, Elliot wrote that although most readers had apparently not recognized this, "it's in the book, alright."[77]

In summing up Strachan's story, Elliot now said outright what she had tried to show through story in *No Graven Image*, that we are too small, our field of vision too limited to say for sure just what is happening in our lives. "In terms of God's story—the whole current of His thought regarding the world and the race of men He made—who was R. Kenneth Strachan? The answer is beyond us. Here are the data we can deal with. There is much more that we do not know."[78] *No Graven Image* ended with an unanswered question; the last two pages of *Who Shall Ascend* contained thirteen of them. And yet in the midst of the questions is a note of hope—hope because of the resurrection, hope because of the love of God, hope because of the promise of the ultimate redemption of all things.

When it came out the following spring, *Who Shall Ascend* made less of a splash than *No Graven Image*. *Kirkus Reviews* concluded that "there is little here to extend this beyond a Fundamentally involved readership."[79] The problems Elliot raised were vital for those trying to live out Christian faith, but here was no pioneer adventure story or firsthand look at a "prehistoric" people to appeal to a general audience. *Christianity Today* ran a thoughtful review by former coeditor Frank E. Gaebelein, drawing attention to Elliot's important introduction and her focus on the inner man. Although he felt the biography could have benefited from more attention to the way others saw Strachan, he praised Elliot for "integrity and sensitivity" in handling her material.[80]

Gaebelein may have put his finger on another reason for the book's limited reception when he acknowledged that "some aspects of the book will disturb those who think that Christian leaders are somehow exempt from personal tensions and uncertainties."[81] Dave Howard would later remember that "the old veterans of the Latin American Mission, who were older than Ken, they did not like to have him toppled off a pedestal. . . . He was a man who really loved the Lord and he had his own failures. So at her request, we let her write about that. And there were others who didn't like that. They wanted him to be put out to be just a wonderful man of God who never failed or anything like that." But the remaining directors of the mission "felt that it was very true and should be published exactly as it was, and it was."[82]

With the manuscript off her plate for the time being, Elliot picked up the pace on her correspondence. By typing fifteen letters a day she managed to get to the bottom of her in-basket by the end of May. She hosted guests, went hiking, worked in the yard, and visited Katharine at Little Birdsong. Valerie went away to Pioneer Camp, where Elliot had worked the summer of 1951, and Jim's brother Bob and his family came to stay. Vandevort and Elliot drove to the Vandevort family farm in Pennsylvania. After a short visit there, Elliot went on alone to Tarkio, Missouri, where she spoke on Job five times at a week-long seminar, then to the Bedford Center for Creative Study for a week as guest critic, and then to New York City for a whirlwind of visits and meetings. When she finally got back to New Hampshire, Katharine and Valerie—whom she had not seen in a month—met her at the airport.

The rest of the summer passed in a succession of houseguests, writing, hikes, and picnics. Katharine's long visit this year seems to have gone more smoothly for mother and daughter, though Elliot still found it challenging. September found Vandevort working various jobs in the local area and finishing up her book, a memoir of her time in the Sudan, tentatively titled *A Leopard Maimed*. Elliot wrote several articles under deadline, sold a short story to *Eternity* magazine ("Well, it's not the New Yorker, but it's something!" she joked to her family[83]), and attended to the galleys of *Who Shall Ascend*. She also wrote an introduction to Vandevort's book, describing it as an encouragement "to believe in the God who has taken to Himself the whole responsibility for the ultimate answers."[84]

———

Elliot had been considering for some time moving to New York City for the 1967–1968 school year. She did not explain why in her family letters, but between recreational visits and work trips she was already there a good deal, usually without Valerie. Perhaps she felt that such a move would cut down on time away from her daughter and time spent traveling. Then, too, Tom was there, and the idea of living nearby would have been very appealing.

All that had changed however, when over lunch with Cornell and Edie Capa during her August trip to the city, Cornell had proposed a new project. He had in mind a *Life* article and a book for Harper's about Jerusalem— just united under Israeli rule in the Six-Day War, which he had covered as a photojournalist—and he wanted Elliot to collaborate with him on the book, traveling to the city for research. Although her plans were up in the air until almost the last minute, Elliot ultimately agreed. She would be gone for two months.

Unable to get Valerie into school in Jerusalem, she arranged for the twelve-year-old to stay with Vandevort, who would have power of attorney for the occasion. By late September, Elliot was getting vaccines and starting to pack. On the twenty-fifth she bought plane tickets, on the twenty-seventh she and Vandevort hosted yet another set of overnight guests, on Friday the twenty-ninth she went to New York for a weekend with Tom and Lovelace, and on Monday, October 2, she embarked for London, Rome, Athens, Tel Aviv, and finally Jerusalem.

By the time Elliot arrived at her hotel after almost two days of travel, she was so exhausted she "could think of nothing but the horrendous risk I was taking in this experiment, and of how awful it would be if it turned out that I could do nothing at all in the way of writing." But after a good night's sleep she woke up "thrilled," and "eager" to tackle the project. The thrill was a surprise; she had never felt any particular desire to visit the holy land, and she was unexpectedly moved to find herself in Jerusalem, "Jerusalem, mind you, where the temple stood, where Jesus stood trial, where who knows what things will one day happen."[85] For the next two months she would tour the city and other locations in Israel, sometimes with Micha Bar-Am, an Israeli photojournalist and friend of Capa's, as a guide, sometimes attached to a tour group, sometimes on her own. She would observe, ask questions, take notes, try to make sense of the bombardment of images and experiences.

Elliot was in Israel for a whole string of Jewish holy days: Rosh Hashanah, Yom Kippur, Sukkot, and Simchat Torah. While people-watching, she saw Moshe Dayan, Malcolm Muggeridge, and Danny Kaye. She wandered through the markets and took Turkish coffee "in a tiny hovel in an alleyway" with some African women who invited her in as she passed, though "we couldn't speak a word to each other."[86] She browsed bookstores and bought a copy of James Michener's historical novel on the Jewish people, *The Source*. She attended endless luncheons, cocktail parties, and dinners. She had tea in homes, at women's meetings, with wives of archaeologists, with Catholic nuns, with a pasha, with a Russian Orthodox reverend mother. She had hors d'oeuvres in a cave, shared the Sukkot meal in a rabbi's home, celebrated an American Thanksgiving at the YMCA, and ate fresh fish from Lake Galilee.

She saw camels and was interviewed by a reporter. She spoke to various groups, including a Southern Baptist women's retreat held in a Catholic convent, a Sunday morning service, and several groups of missionaries.

Everywhere she went "the talk . . . was [of] politics."[87] Elliot had arrived six months almost to the day after the war. There were still "holes in my bathroom door from the shooting," and her view looked out over bombed-out houses.[88] When she drove out of the city she could see burned-out tanks rusting in the fields. Tension had not subsided with the end of the war. During her stay a mine exploded in the old no-man's-land near her hotel, there were sounds of shooting in the distance, and Egypt sank the Israeli destroyer *Eilat* in international waters, killing a fourth of the crew. It was another chapter in the history of a conflict nearing six decades of existence, and everyone had an opinion, including outsiders. Even Christian missionaries, she found, "endlessly discuss the Arab-Jew question, and their own relations to the two groups."[89]

Elliot seems to have had little understanding of the political situation when she arrived in Israel. Her letters up to that point contain no record of reading on the subject. A month after arriving in the country she summed up her background by describing herself as "a Christian who is saturated in the Book and has been for years blown by every wind of prophetic teaching about Israel."[90] Certainly Christian Zionism, the belief that the political reestablishment of a nation of Israel would fulfill biblical prophecy and pave the way for Jesus's return, had been a good stiff breeze in American evangelicalism for longer than Elliot had been alive. It often included the teaching that God would "gather" the Jewish people from around the world and return them to Israel and that the modern state of Israel had a biblically mandated right to all the territory described as the Promised Land: "from the river of Egypt to . . . the river Euphrates" (Gen. 15:18). Many American evangelicals had advocated for policies they felt would promote these goals since the late nineteenth century, and there had been a good deal of excitement among them when Israel declared statehood in 1948. Likewise, Israel's land gains in the subsequent Arab-Israeli war (despite the loss of east Jerusalem) and heavy Jewish immigration to Israel in its aftermath were celebrated by many as fulfillment of prophecy.

With this belief system as her primary exposure to the situation in Israel, Elliot was taken aback by the complex situation that confronted her. "I hardly know how to select what to tell you," she wrote to her family two weeks into her stay. "Arabs and Jews have said to me, 'We are living in a dream'—i.e. for the former, a nightmare. For the latter, a fond hope come true."[91] Everywhere she looked, things clashed with the picture she had formed by listening to American evangelicals. Religion, national defense, agriculture, immigration, the refugee situation, all were deeply complicated. After another two weeks she wrote, "It is a totally baffling, heart-rending, overwhelming situation. . . . What I have to say at this point is, as much as I can make it, a report of what I have heard. I cannot make a judgment."[92] By the end of her two-month stay, she was more than ready to put some distance between herself and the holy city with its unanswerable questions.

Elliot stopped on the way home to visit Hans Bürki in Switzerland and was back in time to celebrate another Indinyawi Christmas. In the new year, she sorted through the stack of 3 x 5 cards containing her notes and got to work on the Jerusalem book. She planned to call it *Furnace of the Lord*, after the prophet's description of the city in Isaiah 31:9. As always when writing, Elliot was reading—Dietrich Bonhoeffer, Francois Mauriac, Hannah Arendt, William F. Buckley, Mary McCarthy. She also wrote several other smaller projects on the side: short articles; the foreword, afterword, and connecting material for a little book of her *Sunday School Times* articles, to be published under the title, *The Liberty of Obedience*; and the beginnings of a book on HDA, tentatively titled *Memories of a Christian Boarding School*.

As usual there was a steady stream of other things going on. *Who Shall Ascend* was published. Elliot did some speaking, she and Vandevort went to hear Nixon when he came to town, and she attended the parent orientation meeting at the local high school. Vandevort's book came out, now titled *A Leopard Tamed*, and Vandevort went to visit her parents for a few weeks. Valerie flew by herself to visit her grandmother Howard in Florida over spring break. The Jerusalem book seemed to fly together. Elliot mailed her manuscript to Harper's almost two weeks before her deadline. It had taken her just three-and-a-half months to write. They called ten days later to say they were pleased with it.

———

Furnace of the Lord opens with two quotations from the prophets: One, from Jeremiah, is a pointed rebuke to the ancient nation of Israel for committing injustice and worshiping other gods, for trusting for their security to the presence of the temple when they weren't doing what the God of the temple said. The other, from Isaiah, says simply, "But He was wounded for our transgressions" (Isa. 53:5 KJV). These encapsulated Elliot's approach to her subject matter. She tried to view the world from the point of view of Christian faith. One aspect of that faith was the belief that God outlines clear expectations for human behavior and that flaunting these expectations causes human suffering. Another was that God steps in to rescue human beings despite collective failure to execute justice and worship rightly. Elliot would assess her experiences in Israel through this lens.

She had been encouraged, she explained, to visit Jerusalem to see for herself the way biblical prophecy was being fulfilled through current events, but her own interest had been devotional, a desire for "the spiritual experience of seeing the land where Jesus lived and taught and died and rose from the grave." She had found, however, that she could not separate the spiritual from the political, or the past from the present. The situation had seemed to her to be one "of chaos in which God alone could possibly see any pattern." In fact, it was so complicated that she had found herself "tempted to accuse both sides of exaggeration and to avoid making any further judgments for myself."[93]

Since her move to the US five years before, Elliot had focused on writing the truth as it looked from where she stood, regardless of any sacred cows she might threaten in the process. In the same way she tried to tell the truth about the complexity of what she had seen in Jerusalem, even though she felt it contradicted the majority view in the American evangelical community. But what she had noticed and how she had thought about it seem to have been heavily informed by reaction, perhaps only half-conscious, against this majority view.

Elliot had spent time during her visit with both Jews and Arabs; she wrote of her appreciation of and admiration for the people she had met. She had heard both in America and in Israel that the situation in Jerusalem was the straightforward fulfillment of biblical prophecy; she repeatedly emphasized the deep complexity of the connection between prophecy and current events. She had heard that Israeli Jews were categorically God's people; she told of the evident love of God's word and longing to know God among many Jews, of what seemed to her the blasphemous self-confidence of areligious Jews who gave credit for Israel's victory to the people and not to God, of Arab Christians—God's people too—struggling with their faith in the aftermath of the war. She had heard of wrongdoing against Jews; she described the harshness and intractability of some Arabs toward Jews and Israel, the desecration of Jewish cemeteries and holy places, Jordan's closure of the Temple Mount to Israelis, *and* the vengeful attitude of some Jews, the suffering of Arabs caused by Israeli military activity, the hopelessness of Arab refugees. She showed that it was often impossible to tease out the truth of what had happened and was happening from a tangle of rumors and lies.[94]

In this way, the text is much like *No Graven Image* and *Who Shall Ascend*, in which she had raised questions and resisted being hurried into too-easy answers. But *Furnace of the Lord* makes a subtle shift. The first seven chapters—essentially the first half of the book—offer the sort of open-handed presentation of what she saw that had characterized her writing over the past five years. The second half of the book builds toward judgment with gradually increasing emphasis. Zionism, Elliot wrote, had originally been "a purely political movement with no religious purpose."[95] Thus it did not in and of itself constitute the kind of turning to the God of the Bible which the biblical prophecies foretold. This turning would be recognizable, according to the prophets, by certain behavior. "When God chose the Hebrews as a people to bear His name, He charged them with the responsibilities of privilege—to look out for the welfare of the stranger within their gates, to do justice to the foreigner—and warned them that His promises were contingent upon their obedience."[96] If the nation-state of Israel wanted the privileges of God's people, she concluded, it would have to follow the rules of conduct laid down for God's people. The clear implication was that it was not always following them now.

This was a significant change in Elliot's thinking about her role as a writer. She did not just report what she had seen; she made a pronouncement about what other people ought to do about it. This change may have been facilitated by the subject matter. The difficult questions surrounding evangelical missions involved the whole trajectory of her own life, while no one, as she pointed out in both her letters and the book, had proposed taking over Connecticut and turning it into a Jewish homeland. And while she had read tangentially connected writers such as Dietrich Bonhoeffer and Hannah Arendt during her writing process, it's unclear whether or how much she engaged in specific research on the history of the region.

This apparent absence of detailed research on one of the thorniest topics of the modern era sheds light on how Elliot herself seems to have thought of the book. Although she had found herself unable to avoid addressing politics entirely, the epigraph and conclusion of the book suggest that she never stopped thinking of her subject in primarily spiritual terms. "We are judged by the phenomenon of Jerusalem," she wrote. "At every point we find ourselves. We meet a mirror at every corner. We sit in judgment on others, and we find ourselves judged. We are all 'penned together in the prison of disobedience,' as the Apostle Paul expressed it, so that if anywhere, for anyone, there is mercy, it is mercy for all."[97]

———

The weather in New Hampshire was beautiful in the spring and summer of 1968. Between speaking trips Elliot took Valerie camping, worked in the yard, and enjoyed "picnics, outdoor suppers, swimming, etc.," with various visitors.[98] But she was troubled again by her difficulty in getting along with her mother, who was making another long visit, and by how hard she found it to get any writing done with Katharine there. Elliot was also troubled by repeated rumors that she had turned her back on Christianity and by confrontations with both friends and strangers who claimed they had divine messages for her and exhorted her to various courses of action that did not match the way she felt God had been leading *her*. After one such meeting she wrote in her journal that she felt as though she had been beaten.

And she was troubled by lack of communication from Harper's about *Furnace of the Lord*. By the second week of July, she was writing that the situation was casting a pall over her whole summer. A few days later she had requested the return of her manuscript. The exact timing of what occurred is unclear, but at some point after the book had successfully gone through copy edits, Elliot had received a letter asking for substantial changes. After reviewing their "two long critiques," she had requested a meeting.[99] With Tom along for moral support she had met with Mel Arnold and Harper's senior editor Cass Canfield. They had parted with the understanding that Elliot would await Canfield's personal evaluation of the manuscript. After a long delay she had received instead a request to return to Jerusalem for further research. This she was not willing to do. Within a few days of receiving the manuscript back, Elliot's agent had sold it to Doubleday & Company with no further edits required. It would be published in the spring of 1969 rather than the fall of 1968, with photographs by Elisabeth Elliot rather than Cornell Capa.

What had happened? Perhaps wider access to Elliot's journals would shed more light. She never shared in family letters what changes Harper's had asked her to make, saying only that she felt she had been unable to pin the publisher down to a direct statement of the problem. Her unsettling explanation was "Jewish pressure. There are plenty of means of bringing this to bear."[100] She had been warned by Arabs in Israel that she would not be able to find an outlet in America that would let her share an Arab perspective. She had believed that authorities were censoring her letters written from Israel. Harper's reversal on the manuscript seemed to fit into this view of how things work (though Doubleday's immediate acceptance seems to contradict it). Years later, in her journal, Elliot would note in passing that she felt the blame for Harper's change of position lay with one Jew in particular, Cornell Capa, though the two would remain friends for the rest of his life.

Placing the manuscript with Doubleday allowed Elliot to compose herself mentally to try to think of another book. In the meantime, she wrote several short pieces, traveled, and spoke. She read Shakespeare, Susan Sontag, Flannery O'Connor, and a biography of Amy Carmichael. Of Carmichael, Elliot wrote:

> Was interested to find that she had difficulties with her publishers because she told it too straight. Couldn't she soften it a bit? Did she realize what she might do to the cause? It hadn't occurred to her to ask what the public wanted. She simply wanted to tell the truth. . . . Rather than change Things as They Are she left the ms. in a drawer until some visitors asked if they could take it to a publisher in England who would be willing to do it without revision.[101]

This she shared without comment, but it must have felt like her own situation.

As summer shaded into fall, Elliot's family letters dwindled to about one every other month, with a few short notes to Katharine in between. Gone were the long letters sharing her thoughts on her reading or theological questions. Increasingly they read like a cross between a travel itinerary and one of the old social columns that used to be featured in newspapers. "I know I've not been terribly conscientious about writing family letters," one begins, "but it seems sort of nugatory to sit down with eight carbons unless one has something to say, which I still haven't, but here I am."[102] They give the impression that there was not much going on. In September, Valerie started high school. Vandevort stained the house. The two women left Valerie with friends over the weekend and visited friends in Rhode Island and an art museum in Boston. In October they celebrated Vandevort's birthday with a fancy home-cooked meal. In November, the three of them joined the Christmas choir at the Episcopal church. Valerie stayed overnight with a friend, and the two women traveled together to a speaking engagement. Mother and daughter made it out to Portland for Fred and Clara Elliot's fiftieth wedding anniversary celebration.

And then at the beginning of December, Elliot wrote a private letter to her mother making an announcement: she was getting married.

10

Woman Was Made for Man

FOR YEARS ELLIOT had been adamant that she would never marry again. Intellectually, remarriage seemed second best from a biblical perspective, and being convinced of this herself, she had also tried to convince others. In conversation with Olive in 1956 and in a letter to Marilou in late 1957 she had urged them to stay single as well, pointing to Paul's words in 1 Corinthians about staying unmarried in order to focus on pleasing God. But beyond being an intellectual position for Elliot, this was a position of the heart. Despite her onetime anti-Catholic leanings, she had pasted in her journal a quotation from the then-current Pope, Pius XII, and quoted him to Marilou: he encouraged widows not to remarry, calling it "a means of continuing a union and perpetuating the graces of the sacrament of marriage."[1] This must have appealed deeply to Elliot, who felt as committed as ever to Jim. "When I married Jim," she had told her family in late 1958, "the commitment was absolute and irrevocable. One does not do this twice. *Love is stronger than death*."[2] Even her subconscious recoiled from the idea of "getting over" Jim; she had suffered repeated nightmares in which she found herself married again. Now her heart had changed its ground. She was, she told her mother in December of 1968, "wildly and irretrievably in love."[3]

Addison Hardie Leitch was a sixty-year-old theology professor and public speaker. Born and raised in Pennsylvania, he had celebrated his eighteenth birthday in the fall of his freshman year of college about a month before a little girl named Elisabeth Howard would be born in far-away Belgium. After graduation Leitch had spent a year as a Presbyterian missionary, teaching science at Egypt's Assiut College, then pursued a master's degree at the Presbyterian Pittsburgh-Xenia Theological Seminary. He had married another teacher, Margaret Brown Heslip, in 1936, partway through his time in seminary, and they had four children: Elizabeth, Marian, Helen, and Katherine. Marian died in 1943 at two months of age from complications of spina bifida. After his time in seminary, Leitch had gone on to earn a PhD at Cambridge University, then returned to the US to teach, spending two years at Pikeville College in Kentucky, five years at Grove City College in Pennsylvania, and fifteen years at Pittsburgh-Xenia, where he was appointed dean, then president. In 1961 Leitch had taken a job as assistant to the president and distinguished professor of philosophy and religion at Tarkio College in Tarkio, Missouri. He had published five books and was an editor-at-large and columnist for *Christianity Today*.

Elliot had met Leitch in December 1966 when she gave a series of talks at Tarkio College. She must have made a good impression, because he had immediately asked her to speak again the following summer. Elliot had accepted, and in July 1967 had spoken five times on the book of Job. Though Margaret Leitch, who had been diagnosed with cancer a decade before, was ill, Elliot visited repeatedly in the Leitch home during her weeklong stay. She wrote afterward in general terms of the "wonderful people" she had met, people "of a very different stripe from the Fundamentalist or brethren ilk, but genuine and apparently very hungry," calling her visit "most exhilarating and demanding, but very enjoyable."[4] A year later, on July 16, 1968, Margaret Leitch died at the age of fifty-nine. By the last week of August, Elisabeth Elliot and Addison Leitch were—privately—engaged.

Add, as Elliot called him, checked many of the same boxes that had attracted her to Jim. He was tall—6'2"—and a lifelong athlete. He memorized poetry and liked to sing. An extrovert and an external processor, he exuded the charisma and certitude she felt she lacked. He was a Christian, but as an old-school Presbyterian he was from a slightly different corner of Christendom than she had primarily experienced. He seemed to her to be beyond her spiritually, to have things to teach her as a thinker and a theologian. Then, too, he had the educational background she felt she was lacking. He made her think of "what Jim might have been with thirty-two years more of suffering and experience and learning."[5] And he seemed, inexplicably, to want *her*. After more than a decade of bearing the full weight of responsibility alone, of wrestling with all the ambiguities that presented themselves to her, of agonizing over each decision, it felt impossible to resist the allure of belonging again to someone who seemed bigger than herself, someone who would carry the burden for her.

The exact timing of the couple's courtship and engagement is uncertain. A few facts can be pieced together from surviving letters and a fragment of Elliot's journal from the period. The earliest available materials show that in early June 1968, more than a month before his wife's death, Leitch called Elliot three times in forty-eight hours. Elliot, at least, was apparently wrestling with what constituted appropriate boundaries for their relationship at the time. After noting these calls in her journal, she wrote rather vaguely that the situation brought home the fact that Christian faith prescribes limits to moral human behavior and that those limits require making difficult decisions.[6]

The next entry that obliquely mentions their relationship records only that Elliot learned of Margaret Leitch's death on July 22, a week after it occurred. The following entry, on July 29, tersely notes that Elliot was in Chicagoland to speak at a writers' workshop; Leitch flew in to spend three days with her; they had lunch and dinner together one day and went to dinner and a movie on another. On August 7 she recorded that she felt lovesick, could not sleep, eat, or work. Then, vaguely again, she mused about their relationship. She prayed that God would stop her somehow if she was making the wrong choice, but at the same time mused that their love must be from God—God must have directed her in the path that led to their meeting; God would not lead her into temptation; therefore there could be nothing wrong in the relationship. She went on to list what she felt were weighty considerations: God had led her to work as a writer—would she be able to find the necessary autonomy and seclusion as a wife? God had led her and Vandevort together—what would come of this change? What about Valerie? What about her house? What about the age difference between them? On the other side of the balance was the allure of having a lover with whom she could again share the parts of her life that she felt no one else cared to share.[7]

Leitch continued to call Elliot pet names, send letters, and telephone almost every day. On August 14—four weeks after Margaret Leitch's death— Elliot made another ambiguous journal entry. She was still lying awake at night pondering the same questions, but she and Leitch appear to have discussed plans for a formal engagement, deciding that they wanted it to occur in person rather than over the phone or by letter. They also spoke about when to share the news with her family. Leitch wanted to wait until Christmas. There the available journal excerpts end.

Ten days later—not quite six weeks after Margaret Leitch's death—Elliot unexpectedly received another proposal from a widowed Wheaton alumnus who had been two classes behind her. She turned it down because she was already engaged to Leitch.

These facts suggest that Leitch and Elliot were in love before Margaret Leitch's death. The frequency with which he was calling, her awareness that the situation called for difficult choices and restraint, and the speed with which they moved to commitment after he was widowed all point in that direction. The silences and ambiguities of Elliot's journal entries are suggestive as well. Fifteen years later she would write of her college journals, "I was very cautious about what I put in the journals. I don't think it was because I feared someone else would discover my secrets. I think I was afraid to articulate, even for myself, feelings I might have to get rid of. Better to stick with what God was saying to me than what my heart was saying. It seemed the safer course. I do not repudiate it now."[8] Here, too, it may have seemed to her that the voice of her heart was not a reliable guide, that the safer course was to muzzle it, even in private, until she was sure of the path.

There is nothing intrinsically wrong with falling in love. Attraction is a biochemical response, and right and wrong arise in the context of behavior. So the question becomes whether Elliot and Leitch put appropriate boundaries on their attitudes and actions toward each other and toward Margaret Leitch. This we may never know. Eating meat and celebrating holidays are wrong for some and right for others, the epistle to the Romans says, and God is the only one who sees clearly enough into the human heart to adjudicate the matter.

One indication that Elliot and Leitch may not have been entirely successful in setting appropriate boundaries comes from Vandevort, who was living with Elliot throughout this time and was in her confidence to some degree. In early December 1968, after the couple's wedding date was set, Vandevort wrote to welcome Leitch, writing warmly of her appreciation for his "gracious recognition of who Bet is" and his "deep respect for her and love."[9] She knew him by reputation in Presbyterian circles, and, she wrote, when Elliot "came home from Tarkio saying she had finally met the man she <u>could</u> marry I wasn't surprised to hear that it was you."[10] There is nothing in the letter to place this conversation in time, and neither Leitch nor Tarkio appear in Elliot's surviving family letters between her July 1967 visit and December 1968. So it is unclear whether this indicates that Elliot was thinking of Leitch in terms of marriage beginning with the 1967 trip or after a later Tarkio visit which she did not disclose to her family. But whether or not Elliot thought of Leitch as a prospective spouse before his wife's death, Vandevort would say years later that she believed Leitch had thought of Elliot that way—that he had begun actively pursuing Elliot while his wife was still alive.[11] This could explain Elliot's initial discomfort with the rightness of their relationship even after Leitch was a widower.

The couple were certainly aware that the timing of their relationship would raise eyebrows. Just as Elliot had used misdirection to avoid having to announce her pregnancy in the summer of 1954, she had used her letters describing "nothing going on" in the summer of 1968 to hide her growing relationship with Leitch from her family. Vandevort knew at least by mid-September and shared, as Elliot wrote, "fully and sympathetically, in my joy because of the man I love."[12] Tom knew at some point, because he and Lovelace were helping plan the ceremony and reception. Elliot wrote of her engagement to her mother and to Ginny at the beginning of December, more than three months after it occurred and less than a month before the wedding. She called her other brothers to tell them after her birthday on the twenty-first and told Jim's parents on Christmas Eve.

As soon as she felt free to share, Elliot was practically effervescent about her fiancé. She oohed and aahed over his degrees, his resume, his writing. He was "a marvelous, loving, gentle, sensitive, thoughtful, powerful, intelligent man," whose suffering—through Marian's death, Margaret's long illness, and his struggles within his denomination—seemed to parallel her own. She basked in his desire for her, his daily phone calls and "his masterpieces of love letters." And "this . . . doesn't touch on the really big things," she wrote to the Howards and Elliots near the end of December, "the things that astound and overwhelm and dazzle me. Ours is a God 'who only doeth wondrous things' and I am His worshipper at the feet."[13]

Elisabeth Elliot and Addison Leitch were married in New York City on New Year's Day, 1969. Her brothers Tom and Dave, Van, and Cornell

Capa were there, with a few other friends. Thirteen-year-old Valerie, the lone bridesmaid, wore a pink dress. Elliot wore blue silk, and Tom gave her away. After the reception Vandevort took Valerie back to Indinyawi, and Elliot and Leitch spent a honeymoon week in the city, visiting museums, watching movies, attending the ballet, and luxuriating in the anonymity afforded by a crowd. Leitch had quit his job at Tarkio College and the couple planned to live at Indinyawi until he found another teaching position, so at the end of the week they drove back to New Hampshire. They got home, Elliot noted in a family letter, at suppertime on the anniversary of Jim's death. Vandevort had a hot meal waiting for them.

———

The rest of January passed in a flash. Vandevort went to visit Tom and Lovelace. Elliot and Leitch tried to dig themselves out from under accumulated correspondence, with breaks now and again to dig out from under the heavy snowfall outside, watch basketball—one of Leitch's interests—on TV, and host various guests, including Add's eldest daughter, Elizabeth Bonkowsky, and her husband, Fred. Leitch had a speaking engagement in Atlanta, and Vandevort came back in time to stay with Valerie so Elliot could go with him. On the way they visited Katherine in Florida, her first chance to meet her new son-in-law. The couple got home at the beginning of February. "Since then," Elliot wrote the Howards and Elliots a week later, "we've done little except open wedding gifts, answer letters, read congratulatory cards and letters, and turn down speaking invitations!"[14] They began to turn their eyes to the future, praying for God's direction to a job for Leitch.

In the meantime, they settled into a temporary routine. Leitch spent his days reading, writing, and smoking, while Elliot, in and amongst meal preparation and housework, turned back to her own writing. She had decided that she would still use the name Elliot publicly, although in private life she would go by Elisabeth Leitch. As always when she was trying to write, she fed her intellect on the works of others, and now she was reading Carlos Baker's biography, *Ernest Hemingway: A Life Story*; Faulkner's *As I Lay Dying*; and various short stories "to try to get my mind back in shape."[15] She was working on a novel again, but it was heavy going. Something, perhaps an article in *Time*, would spark her creativity briefly, but then she would get bogged down again. Fiction drew from a particularly deep well for Elliot. *No Graven Image* had been the most difficult and time-consuming of her books to write so far.

But it was not just work on the novel that was giving her trouble. Just as she had been unable to write effectively while supervising the building of her house, now marriage seemed to divert her energies. She had received requests for work from a variety of periodicals, including *Christian Herald* and *Practical Anthropology*, but just couldn't seem to get anything down on paper. Even reading, usually the easy part of her writing process, seemed harder to manage just now. In her journal she recorded her frustration over this; to her family she wrote cheerfully, "Being terribly in love with a new husband can prove to be a real distraction, I find!"[16] After a while, with her agent's encouragement, she decided to set the novel aside to clear and to pick back up the book on Hampden DuBose Academy.

Elliot had been joking when she said the couple did nothing but turn down speaking engagements. But she did notice that her own invitations, which had fallen off after the flap over *No Graven Image* and the less than enthusiastic response to *Who Shall Ascend*, had suddenly and dramatically increased. Jim's sister Jane Hawthorne wrote to tell her that "the word around Wheaton is that 'Betty Elliot is now back in the fold,'" and Elliot asked in some irritation, "Is it marriage that gets one 'in'?"[17] It should have come as no surprise that her marriage would lend her legitimacy in the eyes of the evangelical community. While her own tendency to question and challenge the status quo had earned her a name as everything from an existentialist to a spiritualist, Leitch had quite a different reputation. He belonged to a branch of Presbyterianism known for its conservatism. His books—introductory-level surveys of their various subjects rather than new departures—tended to rely on explaining received theological ideas and to lay out various perspectives without choosing a side. He was a champion of the institutional structures of the church. His articles and columns in *Christianity Today* tended to argue for tradition, authority, and absolutes, and against questioning, existentialism, and modern behavioral standards. Marriage would naturally suggest a certain level of agreement between them.

And despite Elliot's annoyance with the assumption that she had suddenly moved from one category to another, her thinking was changing rapidly. Leitch was an institutionalist to the core and devoted a tremendous amount of time to various Christian organizations. Elliot, who had been disgusted by many of these institutions, suddenly became much less vocally critical—so suddenly and so much so that Vandevort was horrified.[18] Leitch disliked the current cultural emphasis on speaking one's mind and argued vociferously against it, believing it to be an excuse for sloppy thinking and irresponsibility. Elliot, who had been emphatic about telling the truth and letting the chips fall where they might, now began to echo his perspective, referring repeatedly to "the youth cult of 'honesty,' which is really so phoney and dishonest and selfish."[19] Leitch wrote in opposition to the idea that behavior could be judged on "the one general Absolute of Love."[20] Elliot, who had told her brothers that love might be the only absolute in human existence, began to argue for many absolutes.

By mid-March, Leitch had decided to take a position as professor of theology at Massachusetts' Gordon Divinity School. He disliked intradenominational wrangling over theological positions and hoped that at Gordon the administration would not "be breathing down his neck doctrinally."[21] By late April, he and Elliot had found a house, a split-level ranch on 2.5 acres about ten minutes from the school. It had mature landscaping, lots of trees, two fireplaces, picture windows, and, except for the pink kitchen range, was already decorated in a way Elliot liked. There were three bedrooms, a study for Leitch, and even a room in the basement that would serve as Elliot's own study—her desk had always been in her bedroom before. They would move the first week of June.

Elliot's letters from the spring of 1969 are breezy and chipper, updating her family on each member of the household and sharing her newfound happiness:

> Marriage is a truly marvelous institution, one of the best ideas God had ("<u>You</u>'d never have thought of sex!" said C.S. Lewis), and I could not begin to put down here how grateful and happy I am. Van continues with us, a big help in many ways (she's doing the laundry now, and made a jello salad earlier), and apparently content to be just that. Val is delighted to have a daddy who took her to a basketball game this week, drives her to the school bus each morning, gives her lunch money, etc![22]

Unsurprisingly, the available journal excerpts show a more checkered picture, recording a whole range of emotions—euphoria, despondency, contentment, hopelessness, pleasure, even terror (there was a brief time where she was afraid she was pregnant, despite the birth control pills she was taking). Over the years, the audience for family letters had grown beyond her parents and siblings to include her siblings' spouses, their growing children, Jim's parents, and sometimes his siblings and their spouses and children, as well as whatever visitors any of those people might think of showing her letters. Now she added various Leitch family members to the list. As a private, self-doubting person, she would hardly have been inclined to share her emotional ups and downs with all these people.

One of the "ups" seems to have been Valerie's happiness. Now fourteen, Val could not remember her father, but she felt his absence and had long wanted siblings. She seems to have been thrilled to acquire sisters ready-made and someone to fill a paternal role in her life. She happily addressed Leitch as "Daddy" and showed him off to her friends.

But combining the two families was not all sunshine. Leitch's daughters, Elizabeth, Helen, and Katherine, made a valiant effort to welcome the newcomers to their family, writing sweet, funny, congratulatory poems to the newlyweds, calling Valerie long-distance on her birthday, and sending thoughtful notes to Elliot. But they had just buried their mother. It cannot have been an easy time for them. This seems to have been particularly true for the youngest, Katherine. Elizabeth and Helen were both married and living in other states. Katherine, who was still working on her undergraduate degree and living at home during school breaks, had to adjust to living in her stepmother's household rather than her parents'. To make matters more challenging, she seems to have had a naturally reserved, quiet personality, not unlike Elliot's in some ways. Elliot was trying to be friendly, but throughout her life her attempts at friendliness were not always successful; it would be unsurprising if the younger woman was put off by Elliot's unintentional brusqueness. The two women would struggle to connect through at least the first year of their relationship.

Then there was the marriage itself. Elliot found that Leitch could be a considerate and attentive husband. He was vocal about his affection and would go out of his way to make her happy. He read her books with appreciation and initiated meaningful conversations and prayer times together. He was a skilled lover, and Elliot exulted in their sexual relationship, repeatedly recording her delight in her journals. But he could also be critical, controlling, and intensely jealous. A visit from Hans Bürki in early March stressed their marriage to its limits. Leitch was jealous of Bürki and reacted by arguing with their guest, deflecting the conversation to his own exploits, name-dropping various theologians with whom he was personally acquainted, monopolizing the conversation, and saying cutting things to Elliot when they were alone. Elliot was miserable. In May, Leitch was upset again, this time because she wrote a note to Cornell Capa acknowledging an invitation to a photography exhibit. He didn't voice his feelings in a straightforward manner but picked at her for days, refusing to tell her what was wrong, needling her with passive-aggressive statements.

Deeply discouraged, Elliot prayed that God would free Add from jealousy. Perhaps his insecurity arose from discomfort over blurred boundaries at the beginning of their own relationship. Or perhaps it was connected to Elliot's behavior toward men. "I enjoy men," she had written in her journal in 1960 after one of her dates with the embassy employee, and certainly all her life she seems to have connected better with men than with women.[23] Despite her own impressions, she was attractive to men, and the two marriage proposals of the summer of 1968 were merely the last in a long series. Her letters—particularly to Jim Elliot and to the man who proposed to her just after she accepted Leitch—suggest that she did behave differently to men than to women, and this difference may have seemed alluring.[24] This does not seem to have been intentional on Elliot's part. Just as in high school and college, most of the men who pursued her were not appealing to her, so she was hardly likely to have deliberately played up to them. Even when men were of interest to her, she would still have been trying to follow her mother's advice to "let them do the chasing and keep them at arm's length."[25] But just as she had not blamed Jim for his behavior when they were dating, Elliot does not seem to have blamed Leitch now. Instead she assumed she was at fault and was swept by discouragement.

Another source of pain during this time was a rift between herself and Vandevort. When Leitch had taken the Gordon job and he and Elliot had found a house, they had told Vandevort that she could not move with them. It is unclear what the communication between the friends in regard to their living situation had been up to that point. Elliot's last journal entry before the wedding suggests she was expecting Vandevort to move out on her own at some point, but wasn't in a hurry, praying for God to guide her friend and give her rest while she waited for direction. But Elliot would write in her journal later in 1969 that she recognized and lamented the fact that she was not good at direct communication, even with those who were dear to her, and it's not clear whether she had communicated her expectation to Vandevort. With the couple's purchase of the new house, Vandevort had suddenly found they were giving her six weeks to find a new place to live.

Vandevort was happy for Elliot but also grieved at the idea of leaving the family that she had been an integral part of for more than five years and the child she had helped to raise from age eight to fourteen. And no new opportunities immediately presented themselves to her; she had nothing to pull her forward. She could trust that Elliot was acting in accordance with God's leading, but she did not yet feel that she had received guidance as to a next step for herself. She was deeply hurt at being given an ultimatum, feeling that Elliot of all people ought to understand the idea of waiting for direction.

Something had certainly changed between January and May, and it appears that something was Leitch. His attitude toward Vandevort differed sharply from Elliot's. To Elliot, Vandevort was the person she knew best in all the world, the friend who had imitated Jesus and "laid down [her] life" (1 John 3:16) for Elliot day in and day out, the friend whom she missed "dreadfully" when they were apart, even after her marriage.[26] To Leitch she was a sponge, and he told Elliot so flatly. Over the last five-and-a-half years, Vandevort had written a book and made a start on another, done some speaking, and taken jobs around the Franconia area, but primarily she had worked creating a home for Elliot and for Valerie. She had done a wide range of maintenance projects on the house, both major and minor, landscaped the yard from scratch over a period of years, and cared for Valerie and Zippy, running the household during Elliot's frequent—and sometimes lengthy—absences. There's no indication that Elliot paid Vandevort for any of this labor other than by providing bed and board. Van had been the homemaker Elliot needed to have a successful career as a writer and speaker and home stability for Valerie. Leitch failed to appreciate this.

Elliot felt torn between her husband and her friend. But she believed in wifely obedience. She had told her mother before she and Leitch were married, "Let it be hereby known that I already love and honor, and plan after January 1 to obey!"[27] And Leitch didn't want to wait any longer for Vandevort to move out. Gradually Elliot's perspective began to change under his influence.[28] In mid-May she wrote in her journal that she was beginning to see Vandevort differently and could not now tell which view was accurate. But because Elliot believed Leitch was spiritually and intellectually beyond her, she decided in almost the same breath that his perspective must be right. In fact, she wrote, she now saw Leitch as her and Valerie's and Vandevort's redemption. It is hard to see how she could make such a statement—especially in the face of her own and Vandevort's suffering—unless she had come to view the situation from Leitch's perspective. Perhaps, as with Jim's decision to contact the Waorani, Elliot had to believe that her husband was in the right in order to live with the consequences of his decisions.

———

Elliot left Indinyawi for the last time on June 5, 1969. Leitch had gone ten days before to fulfill a speaking commitment and help his daughter Katherine move to the new house for the summer. Valerie stayed behind to finish out the last week of the school year, and Vandevort stayed to care for Val. Elliot arrived at the new house in time to meet the moving trucks and set about the process of merging two households. "I just could not believe another box would come out of that truck before they got to the furniture," she wrote after receiving the load from Tarkio, "but still they came: 54 boxes of books, and 54 (yes, fifty-four) cartons—most of them enormous ones, about four by three by three!!"[29] She and Leitch unpacked everything in rows in the basement so they could take inventory (eight desks between the two households!) and pare things down to a manageable level. Then came the work of getting rid of some, putting the rest away, and ironing out a chore schedule between Elliot, Valerie, and Katherine to take care of it all.

If Elliot's social pace had been hectic before, as Leitch's hostess it was frantic. Leitch began teaching at the start of the summer session, and in mid-June Elliot wrote, "We attended a luncheon following seminary graduation on Saturday, and it introduced me to a new life: Wife of a professor, in the social swing for the first time in my life."[30] It quickly became apparent that Leitch was used to a different standard of living than Elliot—to a world of silver and china, fur coats and new cars, country clubs and lavish entertaining. They attended coffee hours, polo matches, "at homes," parties, "investment club" evenings where they played the stock market with a group of friends, and dinners at the club with his colleagues, and hosted a constant stream of family, friends, acquaintances, missionaries, seminary personages, and students and their wives. By late August Leitch calculated that Elliot had served two hundred company meals over the last eleven weeks—and they had been out of town for two of those weeks while he spoke.

Somehow Elliot, who was still hanging pictures and slipcovering furniture, managed to speak a little, read a little, and write a little, setting aside the book on HDA and making a stab at a book on Christian writing. But it was very little. In her journal she wrote that she was like Martha in Luke 10:40 (KJV): "cumbered about much serving," galled by distractions. Two days after returning from their trip in August, she made a long list of all she had to do and asked rhetorically whether this was the to-do list of a writer.

As if this was not stressful enough, Leitch could be harshly critical of *how* she was executing her social tasks. After an outing with his students and their wives, he accused her of not even trying, saying that nothing she could do would make things more difficult for him than the way she had interacted with them. Again Elliot took the accusation to heart, berating herself for failing to be loving toward others and failing in her role as a wife. She began to dream that Margaret Leitch was scrutinizing her work and pronouncing it inadequate.

Things shifted gears when Valerie went back to school but did not slow down. The family acquired a puppy, "Muggeridge," who refused to be housebroken.[31] They continued to entertain copiously and attend numerous events associated with the seminary. Katherine Leitch went back to college in Ohio, and Katharine Howard came for her annual visit. Vandevort, who had gotten a job in a department store, moved out of the dorm room at Gordon where she had spent the summer and into an apartment, and Elliot helped her move.

On good days, Elliot managed to fit in two hours at her desk to work on writing-related tasks between morning housework and lunch prep, but she had been unable to actually write anything for more than a month. Afternoons went to housework and errands. She began praying that God would show her how to work from a place of peace and would help her rightly approach her roles as wife, mother, church member, faculty wife, neighbor, and writer.

Finally in mid-October came forty-eight hours when the last of the houseguests had taken their leave, Leitch had gone on a speaking trip, and Vandevort had taken Valerie to Franconia for the weekend. Elliot had, unsurprisingly, come down with a heavy cold; she ate a nourishing meal, soaked in a hot bath, slept for twelve hours straight, and spent a day basking in the chance to be alone in a quiet house. Although it was a brief pause, it would prove to be a momentous one. She was reading Genesis, having started again at the beginning because Van had given her a beautiful new red leather Bible as an early birthday present, and was struck by the depravity of those through whom God had chosen to establish his covenant people, and the hope that gives for the salvation of the world. She was also reading Thomas Merton's *Conjectures of a Guilty Bystander*, which struck her as providing further evidence that God lives with and communicates with human beings. But the book that was occupying most of her attention was Tom's newest, *An Antique Drum*.

Thomas Howard's first book, *Christ the Tiger*, was a memoir, a description of how he had taken his inherited faith apart to examine the works and decided that it was worth reassembling. *An Antique Drum* enlarges on themes mentioned in passing at the end of *Tiger*. Prior to the Enlightenment, it posits, the Western world operated under the idea that there is more to reality than can be seen, a visible world and an invisible. In this view, things in the visible world—rhythms of nature, hierarchy, sexuality—carry a deeper meaning beyond themselves, pointing to truths about the invisible world. Beginning in the Enlightenment, this was gradually replaced by the idea that reality consists only of that which can be explored scientifically. The things in the world around us can be observed and described but the fact that they exist is not imbued with any deeper meaning.

But, Howard argues, human beings are incapable of living without a meaning-making framework. The modern mind may be occupied with the new myth on the surface, but down in the murky depths it is unable to discard the old myth entirely. We cannot help making connections, using one thing to understand another, as when we use a metaphor to describe an experience to a friend. Thus various human activities—from shaking hands to setting the table to holding a funeral—are all ways we both assign meaning to and extract meaning from the events of our lives.

For Howard, this isn't because we haven't quite shaken our vestigial superstitions, but because the old myth was actually rooted in reality. The rhythms of death and new life in the natural world, the inevitability of hierarchy, the prohibitions and privacies that traditionally surrounded sexual behavior—these things and more really *do* convey important information about the invisible world.

In fact, he argues, this way of understanding the world "is configured most immediately and obviously . . . in the commonplaces of . . . life." Pain and joy are both found in the process of a baby's birth; one can deduce "that pain is somehow bound up in the whole process of joy." A nursing mother must give of herself in order for her baby to thrive; one can deduce "that growth and strength derive from nourishment, and that that nourishment issues from the self-giving of another life."[32]

This sort of baptized Neoplatonism—it is Plato who argues that the visible world is an imperfect shadow of an ideal invisible world and that the imperfect forms can teach us about the perfect—has weaknesses as well as strengths. If the things of this world are imperfect images of the Real, how are we to know which aspects of a thing reflect the Real and which are flaws? If an image of God as "the old man on the throne . . . suggests wisdom and authority and majesty and antiquity and paternity and personhood, good," Howard says. "If it suggests senility and pompousness, it has broken down." But he gives no clues as to how to judge which aspects of the image represent the Deity and which are flaws. And if, as Howard argues, human beings should use ritual and tradition to "handle our experience in a way that both *imposes upon* and *draws from* it significance," it is difficult to know how to avoid reimposing a flawed understanding and entrenching error.[33]

Elliot does not seem to have noticed this tendency in the book. Perhaps her sympathy with her brother made her a less critical reader than she might otherwise have been. Or perhaps they shared the same blind spot, the tendency to leap from "this is the way things are" to "this is the way things ought to be." In any event, when she finished reading *An Antique Drum*, Elliot felt that she had reached a viewpoint after a long climb. While she had never doubted the core of her faith, she had been wrestling for years with much of the worldview inherited from her evangelical tradition. Since returning to the US, she had in many ways seen her role as that of a critic, a raiser of uncomfortable questions. And for at least the last twelve months, her personal life had been undergoing major upheaval, with scarcely a moment in which to take stock. Now here she was, with finally a moment to catch her breath and look about her; and here was Tom, her fellow wrestler and questioner, weeks from defending his doctoral dissertation, suggesting that there was a way of viewing the world rooted in a tradition far older than their own that could provide a valid, intellectually satisfying framework for understanding existence. This way of looking at the world seemed to offer a chance to stop taking things apart and start putting them together. Elliot embraced it wholeheartedly.

She found immediate application for Tom's ideas in her own life. In Ecuador, Elliot had berated herself for accomplishing "nothing" after days in which she had worked all day on housework and childcare; not six weeks ago she had recorded her frustration when household tasks prevented her from writing. Now she mused in her journal about how daily chores that interrupted writing—dishes, cleaning, bed making—were to be embraced as emblems of eternal realities. Not only was this a change from the perspective she had demonstrated in the past; it allowed her to view the hindrances her marriage placed on her writing as part of the meaning of existence, rather than as a sign that she might have misjudged either her decision to marry or her understanding of marriage roles.

As she made a conscious effort to adapt her thinking to this perspective, the ideas sank deep, increasingly becoming an intrinsic part of her own worldview. Her writing began to contain words, phrases, and themes strongly reminiscent of *An Antique Drum*. She would go on to argue that to understand suffering we have to recognize "two different levels on which things are to be understood," a "visible world and an invisible kingdom,"[34] that a story of a shepherd and his sheep provides "living illustrations" for "truths that are changeless,"[35] that in human hierarchies "there is a total view of life and the world at stake . . . a view that understands true liberty as obedience to a divine order,"[36] that in the roles of the sexes one sees a "tremendous hierarchical vision of blessedness—often compared to a Dance in which initiation and response are the movements."[37] These themes would appear in Elliot's work for the rest of her life.

———

One result of—and influence on—Elliot's Neoplatonist focus on imagery and hierarchy was her involvement with the Episcopal Church. Tom had fallen in love with the Anglican Church during his time in England and had become a member. He and Elliot had discussed this, and she had read some of the books influencing his thinking, including Charles Williams's *The Descent of the Dove*. As a result, she had been thinking about church history and the significance of liturgical worship at least as early as January 1963. What had first stood out to her as "truly noteworthy and amazing" in Williams's book was that "God has allowed Himself to be represented in such widely diversified ways throughout history."[38]

On moving to New Hampshire, Elliot had at first attended the nearby community church. But although on paper this church was sound on the "fundamentals," in practice she had found it lifeless and artificial. Ultimately she decided that the main point of attending church was not for her to talk with other Christians over coffee, or to silently agree with another's prayer, or to sing with a congregation, or even to hear preaching, but to engage in what she was coming to see as the primary task of God's people: worship. The liturgical service—with its beautifully written prayers of praise and of petition in which the whole congregation participates, its collective confession and repentance, its congregational engagement in the reading aloud of the Bible, its regular recitation of the historic creeds with their reminder of the central tenets of the Christian faith, and its weekly celebration of Communion—seemed to her to facilitate the act of worship better than the structure of churches she had attended up to this point. By the end of her first year back in the US she had begun attending the Episcopal church in nearby Littleton instead.

In 1967, just before leaving for Jerusalem, Elliot had attended a high mass conducted by the Archbishop of Canterbury in the Church of Saint Mary the Virgin in New York City. She had felt the importance of the ancient liturgy in worship driven home to her in a new way. When she and Leitch were married, he began attending the Episcopal church with her and greatly enjoyed the liturgy. After they moved to Massachusetts, Valerie went with a group of friends to the youth group at a nearby Congregational church—which Elliot called "<u>very</u> fundamental"—but the family worshiped at Christ Church, the Episcopal church in Hamilton.[39] In January 1970, mother and daughter enrolled in confirmation classes in preparation for formally joining the Episcopal Church.

Elliot was not particularly impressed with the classes. Her fellow candidates seemed at least as wooly-minded and biblically illiterate as the congregants at any church she had ever attended. But Elliot had not made the decision to pursue confirmation because she thought she had found a church that would make her feel good. Instead her decision had centered around a two-part rephrasing of her earlier question about why one goes to church: What is the church? And what is worship? In this her thinking had again been formed in conversation with Tom, who had wrestled with these questions over many years.

The siblings had come to believe, as Tom would later express it, that the church is "the people of God" across time and space. In meeting together in local congregations, the church gathers for the task of worship: not "an experience" to be had by individual congregants, but "an act" to be performed communally, a confessing of the truth about God and reality.[40] Elliot would write, "Worship is not an experience. Worship is an act, and this takes discipline. We are to worship 'in spirit and in truth.' Never mind about the feelings. We are to worship in spite of them."[41]

"Never mind about the feelings" can sound harsh, but for Elliot and Howard it was liberating. The churches of their upbringing had emphasized, as Tom characterized it, "one's own spiritual life" rather than "the corporate nature of the Church." This focus on individual performance had encouraged them—sensitive, conscientious people who wanted earnestly to do God's will—toward an endless and overburdening examination of their own hearts before God. Focusing instead on the church and on worship, they were "delivered," as Tom put it, "from the small confines of our own breasts."[42] Elliot would write:

> Finding my thoughts scattered in all directions and in need of corralling like so many skittish calves, I kneel before the service begins and ask to be delivered from a vague preoccupation with myself and my own concerns, and to be turned, during this short hour, to God. . . . When I stand to say the creed I am lifted up to eternal verities, far past the trivialities of how I feel, what I must do after church, what so-and-so-said or did to me. I hang my soul on those strong pegs, those "I believes." And I am strengthened.[43]

In liturgical worship, Elliot and Howard felt freed from the burden of sole responsibility, freed from struggling along on their own, hoping to be fervent enough. Instead they were welcomed into practices that the church has found helpful and important down through long ages of time. Engaging in these practices carried them even when their feelings didn't cooperate. And because various portions of the liturgy had been in use for thousands of years, participating in the liturgy connected them to the faith of Christians across time and space, gathering them up into the encouragement of faithful Christians who had gone before them for centuries. Not wanting to worry Jim's parents, Elliot said nothing about her decision in family letters. She told her mother in a private note mailed a few days before the confirmation ceremony itself, which took place on March 22, 1970.

———

It was another frantically busy spring and summer for Elliot. Muggeridge had been hit by a car, and there was a new puppy to train, a Scottish terrier named MacPhearce. Katharine Howard made her annual visit. Katherine Leitch got married. Elliot, Valerie, and Leitch visited Ginny and her family in the Philippines. Their home was burglarized in their absence. Leitch was ill and underwent a prostatectomy but was healing well. Fred Elliot, Jim's father, died of complications from diabetes and old age.[44] That autumn, as Val and Add went back to their respective schools for the 1970–1971 academic year and Elliot began transitioning into her fall routine, several strands that had begun to run through her thinking over the years came together and were plied into a single skein with the arrival of a letter from a friend.

Letha Dawson Scanzoni, almost a decade younger than Elliot, had been a student at Moody Bible Institute when Jim was killed. She had followed Elliot's career with interest, reading everything by or about the older woman that she could get her hands on. "Like many women of my generation," Scanzoni would later write, "I considered her a role model."[45] The two women had started corresponding in the fall of 1966 when Scanzoni wrote to say how much she had appreciated *No Graven Image*. Since then they had carried out a long-distance friendship, writing every few months and discussing subjects including books, poetry, the Bible, missions, faith, writing, truth telling, current events, and the role of women in the church and society. Now, in September 1970, Scanzoni asked Elliot what she thought about the phrase "Christian feminist."

It was a question with a long history. The first wave of the feminist movement in the US had originated in the revivals of the Second Great Awakening. Many of the great revivalists had encouraged women's full participation in what they believed to be a movement of God, drawing on arguments from Scripture and utility. God had said through the prophet Joel that the Holy Spirit and the gift of prophecy would be given to men *and* women, this was being fulfilled as women were experiencing a call to speak in revivals, and the high rate of conversion under female preachers signified God's blessing. This "democratizing force," as religious historian Margaret Lamberts Bendroth calls it, had spilled over into the rest of American society as both sexes took up work in a variety of reform movements, including temperance, pacifism, business reform, abolition, and feminism.[46]

The 1848 Woman's Rights Convention, hosted by the Wesleyans who would go on to found Wheaton College just a few years later, had given rise to the Declaration of Rights and Sentiments. Modeled on the Declaration of Independence, it noted that women were barred from voting; that they were held to "a different code of morals" than men; that they were effectively barred from "thorough education," from the "profitable" and "honorable" professions, and from "the affairs of the Church;" and that married women were without legal existence, barred from owning money or property, and could be raped, detained against their will, and beaten by their husbands without redress. Women, the declaration concluded, ought to have "immediate admission to all the rights and privileges which belong to them as citizens of these United States."[47]

Immediate admission had not been forthcoming. But through long struggle, change did occur. Married women's property acts began to spring up here and there. Maryland became the first state to punish beating one's wife in 1882. More institutes of higher learning became accessible to women. Women's suffrage was finally won in 1920.

Changing laws does not automatically change hearts, of course, and many people still accepted as a matter of course that men were inherently leaders and providers, logical, "crude," "powerful, dominant, aggressive, and ambitious," while women were "best fitted" for "raising children and keeping house," emotional, "more fragile, daintier and smell nicer," "dependent, submissive, nurturing."[48] Those who did not fit the mold were seen not as disproving the rule but as being themselves dysfunctional.

Unease over societal changes during and after the world wars had encouraged many to strengthen their commitment to this worldview, but the plea to think differently had never gone away. In 1919 Keswick speaker and writer Jessie Penn-Lewis published *The Magna Carta of Woman according to the Scriptures.* In 1940 Congregationalist Mary Church Terrell's autobiography, *A Colored Woman in a White World*, described a life spent fighting to remove the obstacles posed by being black and female and concerns for transmission of faith to the next generation. In 1947 Anglican Dorothy L. Sayers published the essays now collected in the volume *Are Women Human?* In 1957 Lutheran pastor Russell Prohl published *Woman in the Church: A Restudy of Woman's Place in Building the Kingdom.*

A bigger splash had come with the 1963 publication of Betty Friedan's *The Feminine Mystique.* Friedan had brought a version of feminism directly to middle-class American housewives. She argued that the post-war backlash against women working outside the home was designed to be good for the economy, not for people. Rather than pursuing a vocation, women were being encouraged to pour their energy, and their husband's money, into things like smelling nicer than men or keeping a spotless house. The attempt to stretch and narrow themselves to meet these expectations left women "dissatisfied" and "desperate," harming not only women but the children and men they lived with.[49] *The Feminine Mystique* contained a powerful call to middle-class women to rethink themselves and their society.

Elliot had come of age with the post–World War II celebration of the idealized nuclear family, and it appears that she had absorbed these attitudes fairly uncritically. They had never stopped her from doing what she believed needed to be done. When asked to lead church services for the Canadian Sunday School Mission, she had agreed. When asked to teach men in Christian conferences after Jim's death, she had done so. Although her behavior had contradicted what she said she believed the Bible taught, there is no evidence that Elliot had wrestled with her fundamental presuppositions or thoroughly engaged the big picture presented by what are often called the "difficult" passages of Scripture mentioning men and women.

By the time Elliot had returned to the US in 1963 and begun writing *No Graven Image*, it seemed that along with her generally evaluative approach, she might be thinking more, and differently, about the sexes. The novel contains a brief passage critical of men's attitudes toward women within an evangelical context, and all of the positively portrayed Westerners in the story are women. This had not gone unnoticed by readers, including Scanzoni, who had written to say she would appreciate the chance to talk over the subject of "women in the church" with Elliot.

In 1966 Scanzoni had written an article on the subject for *Eternity* magazine, outlining the discussion over the role of women in the American church. "Neither side seems to convince the other," she wrote. "But as the men sit in their theological castles debating women's proper place, Christian women faithfully toil in the vineyards, uneasy about 'breaking a commandment of God,' yet even more fearful lest the work remain undone." She went on to point out "inconsistencies, unanswered questions, and practical problems raised by the stance" of those who wished to limit women's roles, though she qualified this by saying that she did not mean to raise "an impassioned clamor for women's rights or female pastors."[50] After reading it in July 1967, Elliot had written to Scanzoni, "I agree with all you say."[51]

It is difficult to know what this agreement meant for Elliot's thinking at the time. Scanzoni's argument—that women ought to be able to serve God without guilt using whatever gifts he has given them—is gently made. Although, with hindsight, it is clear she was arguing for more involvement of women in the life of the church, if one squints there is *just* room in the piece itself to construe it instead as arguing for men to step up and fulfill their responsibilities.

But whatever Elliot believed about roles in the church, it seems her understanding of roles in marriage was unchanged. Katharine Howard had begun teaching a Bible study for younger women, and Elliot had written to her mother six months after expressing this agreement with Scanzoni, "Tell your 'girls' that marriage is not and never was meant to be a '50-50' proposition! It is one of my pet peeves, that idea, and for years I have considered writing an article on it. Woman was <u>made for man</u>. Yes, she <u>is</u> supposed to 'make all the sacrifices.'"[52] When Scanzoni had a piece published in *Eternity* in the summer of 1968 arguing that many ideas being presented as "Christian" marriage were actually pagan or extrabiblical, and that taking the Scripture in context shows that "Christian marriage should be a relationship in which each partner helps the other to grow in Christ," Elliot had written to say that she "wanted to argue about it," though she hadn't elaborated.[53]

She had continued to read and think about the subject. Later in 1968 she had tackled German theologian Helmut Thielicke's book *The Ethics of Sex*. Thielicke argues that there is "no indication whatsoever of any distinction of rank between man and woman" in the first creation account, that the second creation account describes "fellow humanity" or "partnership" between the man and the woman, and that the earliest suggestion of hierarchy between the sexes appears as "an element of disorder that disturbs the original peace of creation." Jesus, he says, addresses woman "as a human being, as a sister . . . looking beyond the disturbed relationship spoken of in the story of the Fall," and this becomes especially apparent in comparison with contemporary cultural attitudes toward women.[54] Thielicke characterizes Paul's writings on women as a rebuttal of gnostic or naturalistic attitudes that would disenfranchise women as "heirs of God and coheirs with Christ" (Rom. 8:17 HCSB).

In February 1969, a month after her marriage, Elliot had told Scanzoni that Elliot's "own arguments on the subjection of women" were "slightly weakened" by Thielicke's.[55] But in the months that followed, as Elliot worked to adjust herself to Leitch—who would write in *Christianity Today* three years into their marriage that the conversation around women's liberation was "stupid," though he didn't explain why[56]—and embraced Christian Neoplatonism, and listened to a range of feminist voices, it seems she moved back again strongly into the beliefs about the sexes she had absorbed early in life, this time with a considered intellectual justification for her position. And the sense, growing since her visit to Jerusalem, that it was her job not only to report but also to instruct meant she couldn't be silent about her beliefs. Scanzoni's direct appeal for her opinion may even have contributed to her sense that she should speak out. She didn't reply to Scanzoni's September 1970 letter until early the following spring, and then she didn't directly address the question about the term *Christian feminist*. But by then she had begun speaking and writing publicly in opposition to women's liberation.

"I am not sure whether it is of any use at all to go through the engagement calendar and tell you what we've been 'doing,'" Elliot wrote in a family letter in March 1971, "it sounds so chaotic and so few of the names in it would mean anything. We've had the usual number of dinners out . . . and dinners in . . . [and] speaking engagements."[57] For much of the school year, she had primarily taken engagements she could drive to, although she did periodically leave Valerie to cook for Leitch and go out of town overnight, or travel with Leitch on one of his speaking trips while Vandevort came to stay with Valerie. Occasionally both Elliot and Leitch spoke at the same event.

Elliot had given her first speech opposing women's liberation in February. Speaking to a group of students at Gordon College, where both Tom and Van were now working, she had argued "firmly against all W. L. tenets except equal pay for equal work."[58] In March she spoke on the same topic to a group of graduate students at Boston's Park Street Church and signed up to participate in a series of panel discussions on marriage in the Gordon dorms. For about a year, Elliot had been writing a bimonthly column for *Christian Herald*, as well as individual articles for various publications. In a letter to Scanzoni she wrote cheerfully, "If you have seen either of my recent articles on Women's Lib you may not want to hear from me!"[59] She explained that she was at the opposite end of the spectrum from Scanzoni's friend, writer and scholar Nancy Hardesty, who, as Elliot knew, was writing a book with Scanzoni, and instead aligned herself explicitly with the Neoplatonic views of C. S. Lewis. For Lewis, as sociologist Sally K. Gallagher has pointed out, *difference* between the sexes is "at the heart of the created order."[60] Elliot told Scanzoni that, to her, this perspective was unarguable.

Another *Christian Herald* column was about that necessity of a functioning hierarchy, obedience. Elliot argued for "unconditional obedience," "with illustrations from the Dog School" where she had taken MacPhearce. When the article was rejected on the grounds that "that sort of thing can lead to things like My Lai," Elliot sent the piece on to *Eternity*.[61] There seems to be no record as to whether it was accepted. She also wrote a piece for the Gordon-Conwell school paper exhorting women married to ministers not to compare the visible work of their own job (raising children and running the household) with the invisible work of their husband (writing sermons), and not to interrupt him to ask for help because his work has more spiritual value. She covered the main points she had made in her letter to her mother—that "man was not created for woman, but woman for man" (see 1 Cor. 11:9), and thus it is up to woman to adjust, not man.

Elliot was back to work on her novel, which she was thinking of as a story about death. She had also pitched a children's book on Valerie's jungle childhood and was waiting for a response from the publisher. But she seems to have been spread too thin to make progress. It was agonizing to work and work and have nothing to show for it. And then in April her agent ended their business relationship. Robert Lescher, who had started his own agency in 1965, not long before taking on Elliot as an author, explained that he had become too busy to continue acting for her, though it may also have been connected to the long stretch without a book available to shop around. It had been more than two years, the longest gap since Lescher had represented her. Elliot, who already felt like a failure over her inability to finish the novel, was hurt.

As the first sting began to fade, she started to wonder whether she was being steered in a new direction. She and Leitch were already hosting a twice-a-month hymn-singing event in their home for students. They wanted to help them learn some of the theologically dense old hymns that they had found so helpful in their own spiritual formation. Now she was asked to speak at a women's guild meeting at Christ Church, and she took as her subject "the kind of home I came from, viz. a home centered in the Bible, a home where prayer was a kind of permanent background for life, and a place missionaries frequented."[62] She got the impression that approaching the Bible as a guide for daily living was a new idea to many members of her audience, but felt they had responded positively and hoped this would provide new avenues of service. She saw a potential new direction for her writing as well and began to mull over two new books, one on how to discern God's guidance and one about her own life, perhaps her missionary experience before her marriage to Jim.

Elliot noted in her journal that she and Leitch had now been married longer than she and Jim, and she recorded a poignant dream in which Jim came back and she had to decide between the two men. Movingly, in the dream she decided Jim was more interested in other things and unconcerned about whether she chose him or not; she would stay with Add. Although in waking life there continued to be occasional friction in their marriage, on the whole Elliot was deeply happy. In fact, she wrote repeatedly in her journal, she was so happy it seemed almost too good to be true.

The summer of 1971 flew by, filled with travel and guests. Tom and his family came for Sunday tea now and again. They made it to the beach a handful of times. Valerie, now sixteen, learned to drive. They painted the living room raspberry with white trim. Sadly, MacPhearce was hit by a car and killed. Elliot was much affected, writing several times through the course of the summer that she was not yet over his death and puzzling at how she could survive Jim's death and still be overcome by the loss of a pet. They got a new dog, a Sheltie named Tania, but Elliot does not seem ever to have become attached to her, perhaps because she was still grieving so deeply.

Despite her busyness, Elliot took a job as a stylistic consultant for the New York Bible Society's new translation, to be called the New International Version. Jim Elliot's brother-in-law Jerry Hawthorne was on the translation committee, which may have been how Elliot came to take the job. For four to six hours a day over a three-week period, she read the translations of sixteen different books of the Bible and made notes—"suggestions that will presumably make it more readable," as she explained to her family. She had her doubts about both the need for another English translation and about the approach to the task. "How can a committee come up with a good piece of writing? The King James bunch did a fine job, but I think I like JBP because it was done by one man."[63] Nevertheless, she found it interesting to see how the committee approached their task, and she was tickled at being paid—five dollars an hour!—to read the Bible.

Valerie started her senior year of high school in September and filled out an application for Wheaton College. Classes started again for Leitch. Elliot spoke "to the single women students of the seminary (there are 38 of them and 10 showed up) on 'The Place of Women Students in a Predominantly Male Institution.'"[64] It appears that there is no extant copy of this talk, but we can perhaps guess at her views from a later piece of writing: "It would seem that a woman who chooses to go to seminary would know ahead of time that the majority of the students would be men and the program would naturally emphasize this. She would be prepared to be in the minority and accept the limitations imposed by this. Common sense would tell her this."[65]

In October Elliot and Leitch began teaching evening Bible classes to members of Christ Church at the rector's request. Elliot was also offered the use of an office on the Gordon-Conwell campus. At the beginning of the summer she had begun sorting through old letters from 1952 and 1953 for the book on her life in Ecuador, and she was also working on the book on God's guidance. She began taking Leitch to work Mondays, Wednesdays, and Fridays and spending the morning there working on the guidance book, then working on the Ecuador book in her study at home on Tuesday and Thursday mornings. She found it helpful to be away from home "without any phone ringing or any temptations to clean, read the mail, do the ironing, cook, or fiddle with stuff in my desk!"[66] By early November she was finishing a first draft of the guidance book.

As 1971 wound to a close, it became increasingly clear that Katharine Howard, now in her early seventies, would not be able to stay much longer by herself in Little Birdsong. Tom and Elliot were strongly encouraging her to move to Hamilton to be near them, but Katharine was having a difficult time feeling at peace about any of the options. Then she got sick, and the illness just kept hanging on. The family arranged for Leitch, who was in the South for a speaking engagement, to meet her and accompany her back to Massachusetts to spend Christmas.

It was a difficult period. Katharine was sick when she arrived and anxious over her next step. Partway through her stay, Elliot came down with first a stomach bug and then influenza. Tensions between mother and daughter flared. Afterward Elliot wrote to Katharine,

> As I tried to say on the phone, I felt deep regret as soon as you left that I had not been more like the daughter I ought to be. It is unforgivable, but I ask you to forgive me—not that you need to do so in writing, please! Just do it, and I'll try to do better next time, which is what I always resolve. . . . I know I am harsh and unreasonable and distant, and it is enough to make one question the reality of my whole Christian experience. I love you, and am grateful for the kind of mother you've been and the home you gave us.[67]

On New Year's Eve, Elliot recorded her end-of-year reflections in her journal: how unfamiliar illness had seemed, and how it had made her think of what it would be like to die; how she planned to give up journal keeping; how the morrow would be her third wedding anniversary. She ended the little volume by quoting Micah 6:8: "And what does the Lord require of you but to do justice, and to love kindness, and to walk humbly with your God?" She did not believe she had made any progress in living up to these requirements, but she affirmed again her commitment to that aim.

———

The break in journal keeping was short-lived. In March 1972 Elliot began afresh in a new five-by-seven spiral-bound notebook. She felt that most of what she wrote was pointless nonsense but that the act of writing helped her somehow in the living of life. It made a way for her to be alone with her thoughts and make sense of the events of her days, a necessity for an internal processor. And when she looked back over what she had written through the months and years, it helped her see a shape to events of her life.

As she had always done, she would continue to record a jumble of things—current events such as the primary election; family events such as Valerie's acceptance to Wheaton and Leitch's purchase of a new blue Chrysler; professional events such as submission of manuscripts or current projects; things that had stood out to her such as quotations from her reading or observations from people watching. She would make lists of those she was praying for with notes about their needs or hash out things she didn't know how to approach and wanted God's help with.

This last was an important part of her spiritual life. "The necessity of recalling all the things that have any bearing on my need for guidance—the pros and cons of all the possible courses which seem open, the circumstances which look to me significant, the reasons I have for wanting one thing above another—helps me to sort out exactly what it is I am asking." In fact, she felt it was one of the ways that God communicated with her: "And sometimes through this sorting, I see that I ought to ask something quite different. The fact that I am telling God, too, makes them look different. It casts a different light."[68]

This practice was one of the ways of hearing from God that Elliot had put into her book on guidance, just completed. She sent it off to Word Books under the title "To Will Is to Know," taken from Jesus's words: "If any man willeth to do His will, he shall know of the teaching, whether it is of God" (John 7:17 ASV). It was accepted in April with minimal revisions, and would be published a year later as *A Slow and Certain Light: Some Thoughts on the Guidance of God*. She dedicated it to Vandevort, who had been so foundational in the development of her own view of God's guidance.

The slim little volume of Elliot's characteristically deft prose is organized around the premise that usually, when we talk about divine guidance, we want concrete, preferably immediate, direction on what to do in some specific situation, while what God wants is to guide us into knowing God. The book is a consolidation of ideas Elliot had worked out in study and prayer and practice over the course of her adult life. She draws repeatedly on analogies from her experience as a traveler in the thick forests of Ecuador, utterly dependent on a guide who knew the area. When the Bible promises guidance, it is in "promises dependent on the presence of the Guide himself."[69] Repeatedly she discourages developing a checklist to discover God's will and encourages the halting, fumbling practice of learning to know the Guide.

The promises of guidance come with two other conditions. One is to recognize God as who God claims to be rather than as who or what we want God to be. Here again is the theme she found reading Isaiah 43:10 by firelight in Tæwano. "You are my witnesses . . . that you may know and believe me." Recognizing God involves studying the Bible, which shows us both God's character and God's dealings with people. God is so big that we need the whole Bible to begin to have "some inkling" both of the reality of God and of "our own position" in reality—and the whole of our lives in which to do it. "It is a continual fulfillment and a continual attraction."[70]

Then, recognizing who God claims to be—perfect in power, perfect in knowledge, perfect in love—the next condition is, in the words of the old song, "to trust and obey." Elliot, for whom obedience had always been of the first importance, writes poignantly:

> I can't fulfill the conditions. I do not "keep instruction." I hardly listen to it in fact. I am not "godly." I am not good or meek or upright or blameless or truthful or self-sacrificing in any sense at all except a relative one (surely I am no worse than most?). Even a casual look at God's word shows me that a relative goodness won't do. I am none of the things I am told I need to be in order to expect God's guidance.

Thus, she argues, trust and obedience are inseparably intertwined. "We cannot [obey] by ourselves, so we trust God to do [it] for us. . . . The truth is that the whole thing has been done for us—Jesus is our guide, and he is himself the way."[71]

It is important to understand the goal of guidance as well, Elliot says. "Our own goal is to know the right way. We don't like to make mistakes." But God's goal is developing "a lifelong process" aimed at helping us and those around us to get to know the Guide.[72]

In turning to discuss the ways God may offer guidance, Elliot argues that there is no route to the guidance of God that does not require the work of thoughtful discernment from people. "I feel a little wistful now and then," she says, "that God leaves so much up to me. The exercise of the intelligence is taxing." Even supernatural guidance—the pillar of fire that led Israel in the desert, the voice of Balaam's donkey, "dreams and visions"—were "not signs that had been asked for," but signs God had given, unexpectedly, while people were doing the ordinary work of their lives.[73]

Direction may come through circumstances or advice. It may come through the human systems in which we find ourselves; through our own personalities, gifts, and propensities; from an assessment of what we want: "For a long time I took the view that whatever I might want to do could not possibly be what God wanted me to do. That seemed unarguable. I am a sinner, my desires are sinful, 'there is no health in us,' and that's that. I went on the Manichean assumption that I am always and necessarily bent on evil, so it ought to be a relatively simple matter to figure out that the will of God was whatever I didn't want to do." Over time, "a better understanding of Scripture" had helped her to see that because she was made in the image of God she might also, as "a very simple and natural thing," desire good.[74]

The final means of discerning guidance that Elliot presents is that when presented with a choice between two otherwise equal alternatives, we should choose the more difficult path: "'The way that is hard, that leads to life,' Jesus said, so it is likely that he is asking us to will against our will."[75] This is a puzzling assertion, not only because it does not seem that she had used this metric in recent years—for example, in her decision to remarry—but also because it seems counter to the idea that we can discern the guidance of God through our own personality traits and desires. She had abandoned the "Manichean assumption" that her own desires were always wrong, but it seems she had not entirely parted ways with the Stoic ideas imparted by many of the Holiness teachers of her youth. As public theologian Simcha Fisher writes, "We must be *willing* to suffer, but we're not required to seek suffering out. . . . We *are* required to seek *love* out."[76] Here Elliot fails to make this distinction.

Nevertheless, the overall tone of the book is generous and gentle. The section on guidance in one's own context is particularly lovely.

> I grew up in a middle-class fundamentalist family in Philadelphia. . . . I saw a certain kind of Christianity in operation, and to me that was what it meant to be a Christian. It took a while for my imagination to go to work to apply that vision to people in other categories . . . but in the meantime God met me where I was. When I began to learn of the wideness in his mercy, my faith began to grow, and I saw that salvation was a scheme of infinitely vaster dimensions than I had dreamed. And here I had been worrying about whether I would recognize the voice! . . . Whatever our views, they are probably too narrow. . . . But the wonderful thing is that God is willing to start there.[77]

She ends the book by emphasizing, as Vandevort had emphasized to her years before, that "we need not be forever halting and backing up, paralyzed by fear of our own desires," that we can trust our Guide not to let us stray from the path. "Jesus is in the boat with us, no matter how wild the storm is."[78] We need not be afraid.

———

Summer came again. Valerie graduated from high school and was looking forward to college with excitement. Elliot had various speaking trips and engagements. Katharine was with them for the season. Tania was succeeded by a Scottish terrier puppy named MacDuff.[79] In August, the Howard siblings and their spouses and children gathered for a family reunion. For almost a week they stayed in the dorms at Gordon, ate in the college dining room, celebrated the wedding of the eldest Howard grandchild, played games, went swimming, enjoyed the family version of charades (with expressions such as *Metamorphosis of Ovid* and "Put the piano down, Grandma, you're too old to carry a tune"), exercised what Tom called their "gift of laughter" (laughing until they cried at Elliot's pitch-perfect rendition of Britisher Joyce Grenfell's comedy routine "Nursery School"), took a sunset boat ride, and gathered around Tom's piano, brought in for the occasion, to sing hymns.[80] It was a golden hour.

In September, Elliot drove Val to Wheaton and helped her move into the dorm. As she packed for the trip, she experienced the same emotions she had felt at various departures in her own life—leaving for HDA, going to Wheaton, embarking for Ecuador, returning to Shandia after Jim's death, starting on the journey to Tewæno for the first time, moving back to the US, leaving Indinyawi to marry Leitch. In her journal she mused about what exactly that feeling was: not sadness, she decided, but a deep awareness of the importance of the time that was ending. She was deeply thankful for the years spent raising Valerie, full of hope for her future, flooded with nostalgia and affection. But sadness came. "Overcome," as she would write later, she called Vandevort, "the sort of friend you don't have to explain things to," and cried. Van told her, "It's o.k., Bet. It'll be ok."[81] Vandevort's words—reminiscent of Julian of Norwich's words, "all shall be well"—were to Elliot the voice of God, and she was comforted.[82]

Elliot wrote a cheerful family letter in October—this time with an extra copy for Valerie—updating everyone on her travel schedule and social events and announcing that the family had finally made a decision and Katharine would be moving into an apartment nearby.

The next morning in her journal she made brief note of several of the things she had shared in the letter and added that Leitch had a doctor's appointment. For some time he had had a sore on his lip that would not heal.

That afternoon after the appointment she made a second entry, noting the time, 4:45 p.m. The sore was cancerous. Leitch, who had watched his father and first wife die of cancer, had received the news as a death sentence. Twenty-four hours later, he began to have blood in his urine, one of the signs of prostate cancer. Two days after that, Elliot copied into her journal C. S. Lewis's words: "No one ever told me that grief felt so like fear. I am not afraid, but the sensation is like being afraid."[83] Lewis had known fear in the first world war, then grief at the death of his wife. For Elliot the sensations were reversed. She had known grief after Jim's death; now she recognized that fear felt like grief. Though she had been anxious before Jim's last departure from Shandia, she knew now, viscerally, that the worst could happen. And she was afraid.

The rest of the month passed in the effort to keep terror at bay. "Fear, resentment, worry—all very real for both of us, all necessitating coming to Christ."[84] Again and again over the course of a day she took her feelings to Jesus. She meditated on his life, the way he had moved toward crucifixion one day, one act, at a time, resting in the love of his Father. She found it helpful to concentrate on the tasks at hand, and to think of them as a chance to serve. Her disciplined approach left Add aggravated and wounded. As she had done repeatedly throughout her life when relationships were hard, she recorded in her journal the things he said that cut her to the quick, that seemed to mock her efforts to entrust him to God.

Surgery to remove the lip tumor at the beginning of November was followed immediately by a diagnosis of prostate cancer, the cancer that had killed Add's father. That night, with Leitch in the hospital, frightened and angry, and Elliot alone at home, was, as she wrote in her journal, as difficult as any she had ever spent. But there was good news. The prostate cancer was of a slow-growing kind. The urologist was optimistic. And the lab report showed that the lip cancer had not spread to the glands. Leitch had asked her not to make a public fuss about his condition, and at the end of the week she wrote a positive report of events in a family letter, leaving the strong impression that after a difficult week, all was well. They settled in to wait for the next checkups.

Elliot traveled to speak, visited Valerie at Wheaton for Parents' Day, and helped her mother move. She sorted through old family papers and babysat Tom and Lovelace's children and their Yorkie puppy. She read Alan Paton's *Instrument of Thy Peace*, C. S. Lewis's "Work and Prayer" and *Letters to an American Lady*, G. K. Chesterton's *Orthodoxy*. Valerie came home for Christmas, and they hosted the annual caroling party, celebrating the day itself with Katharine, Tom and Ginny, and their families.

Underneath it all ran the current of fear. Add had bleeding that would not stop. He began to worry that the growth on his lip was returning. Elliot lay awake at night wrestling with her thoughts. Some days she would note with surprise that she did not feel afraid. More often she recorded some version of a simple prayer to be rescued from fear. On December

29 a checkup revealed that although the lip still looked good, the prostate cancer was growing. Leitch would start radiation in the new year.

———

January 2, 1973, brought Valerie's departure for Wheaton and Add's first appointment at Massachusetts General Hospital in Boston. Elliot and Leitch were staring down eight weeks of these visits: the drive to the city and back five days a week, the looming expectation of radiation sickness. In her journal, Elliot debated whether to keep a record of the days ahead, ultimately deciding that perhaps doing so would allow her to share encouragement with others in the future. She noted that some days she could work but couldn't avoid tears; others she did not cry but felt lethargic, almost unable to move.

Leitch spent his time in the radiation machine praying for others, but for himself he seemed unable to find comfort. He couldn't sleep, couldn't settle to a task. In the small hours of the morning he spoke of suicide. As the month went on the side-effects of radiation continually worsened. When Elliot tried to share the encouragement she was finding in God, Leitch's response felt angry and cutting; it was as though she were feasting while he lay starving at her door.

In casting about for some way to help, Elliot spoke with friends connected to the medical community. Her old friend Elizabeth "Bunny" Paeth, a doctor, told her that nutrition and frame of mind were the most important part of healing. Elliot read a book by nutritionist Adelle Davis and determined to implement her suggestions. Davis was a proponent of the idea that the right diet can heal most illnesses and prevent them all, and Elliot wanted to believe it. She reasoned that God had designed the human body to work in certain ways; it was only common sense that it would work best within those bounds. She threw out their sugar, flour, and processed foods and put them both on the Adelle Davis diet, which included high doses of vitamins. After three days Elliot felt she saw a change for the better in Leitch's radiation symptoms.

A month into the diet Elliot felt fantastic and believed that Leitch was feeling better too. But a few days later, he seemed worse again. His lip did not seem to be healing, and he began to have pain in other places. He felt too queasy, or it hurt too much to walk; he couldn't concentrate on reading; he couldn't bear company. Worse than his physical pain was his depression. His doctrine made him miserable now. He felt God was indifferent to suffering. To Elliot it seemed as though they were in a strange underwater world, sound blunted, movement slowed—waiting, waiting for the treatment to reach its end, waiting to learn the results, waiting to learn Add's prognosis.

Elliot's journals show a roller coaster of hope and fear. Some days she could work—Harper's had contacted her in January to solicit a book and had sounded interested in her autobiographical "jungle notebook," so when she could, she chipped away at it. Leitch seemed better, then worse, then better, then worse again. His last radiation treatment was on February 22. The next day the doctor told them that the prostate tumor was still too large for surgery. Three days later, the day before Valerie's eighteenth birthday, they learned that the cancer on his lip had returned and another surgery was urgently needed. Elliot wrote in her journal that God was testing her to prove her love.

Desperate to see some improvement, in March she asked a friend to fly to Canada and bring them back an alternative treatment drug called Laetrile. A form of hydrogen cyanide, the drug is still not FDA approved in the US because there is little evidence of effectiveness against cancer in controlled clinical trials. With the Laetrile came a constant flow of contradictory advice from various sources as to diet and vitamin regime, many of which contradicted Adelle Davis. Elliot agonized over the best thing to do. The journal records her daily and sometimes hourly cycling between hope and discouragement as she strained to see improvement and was knocked down by worsening symptoms. Her family letters were still cheerful for the most part, but she acknowledged that Leitch was experiencing "the gamut, I think, of all the awful side effects" of radiation, "pain, nausea, vomiting, diarrhea, sleeplessness, and deep depression. It seems undisputable that the Enemy of Souls uses physical weakness as an opportunity for oppression and spiritual devastation."[85] Elliot believed that these were the result of radiation sickness, not the cancer itself, and was encouraged in this belief by the internist they had begun seeing.

In fact, in April, both the internist and Meir Walters, a family friend who was an MD, examined him and said that he appeared to be cured. Medical paternalism was still the standard of care in America in the early 1970s, and with it the belief that hope was so important to the patient's well-being that doctors should not necessarily disclose the truth about a terminal illness. Years later, Walters would acknowledge that there had never been hope of a cure. The medical records, when Elliot finally had a chance to see them months later, said much the same thing.

Leitch kept losing more weight, feeling more pain. He continued to experience spiritual and emotional despair. Then in May they were told that the lip cancer, a squamous cell carcinoma, had spread wildly. It was in his adrenal glands. He would need another course of radiation, and perhaps disfiguring surgery. Again Elliot was flooded with fear. Again she clung to hope, anticipating looking back on this record of suffering with Leitch after he was once again well, praying for the grace to carry on.

By June 4, Leitch had undergone ten sessions of radiation on his lip. The inside of his mouth was burned. He was suffering and angry, convinced he would be bedridden within weeks, wishing they would just let him die, yet afraid. Elliot noted in her journal that every day he lost a little more ground. He began refusing the food she prepared him, and when she tried to be tender and affectionate he said cruel and cutting things. Walters, who was making house calls for them, remembered: "It was so hard for both of them. It was such a disappointment, you know? A terrible disappointment. . . . And she waited on him hand and foot. And we would work out together what he could eat, and she would go to great lengths to prepare something that would be nourishing for him and strengthening [for] him, and then he would— he wasn't an easy patient, and I can't blame him. It was very hard, what he was going through, but he was hard to take care of. . . . She wouldn't spare herself, up day and night with him."[86] Vandevort was more blunt: "I never saw anybody die with such anger as he had."[87] In her journal, Elliot wrote that her husband was being slowly destroyed before her eyes. She began praying that God would heal him quickly or take him home.

In mid-June, Leitch was hospitalized for dangerously high blood calcium levels. When this was stabilized, he felt somewhat better, but X-rays showed cancer in his bones. His siblings and children came from around the country to see him. Elliot wrote wrenchingly in her journal of her inability to give up hoping, of her wild desire to hold on to her husband, of finding herself bargaining with God to let him stay a little longer.

Leitch came home again at the end of June. Hospice care did not yet exist in the US, and though the oncologist now said Add had perhaps six months to live, they continued his radiation treatment and began chemotherapy. They also encouraged Elliot to make Leitch get up and walk. When she tried, he said horribly hurtful things. She was afraid not to follow doctors' orders, afraid to let him decline more precipitately than he already was, afraid of his harsh words. At other times she felt an urgent need to squeeze the most out of every moment of their time, to make all the time quality time before he was gone beyond her reach. But she came to feel that he needed rest more than she needed to hear his voice. Though Leitch was sunk in black despair, afraid of death and damnation, somehow he continued to dictate his *Christianity Today* column and grade papers.

Tom began coming over daily to help. Katharine and Vandevort ran errands and cleaned. Other friends brought food or came to sit with Add and read aloud. The rector from Christ Church came regularly to celebrate Communion in their home. Ginny came into town and took over much of the housework. Kind letters poured in by every mail. At the end of July, Leitch went back into the hospital for another month. The couple began to plan his funeral, draw up wills and trusts, and make other financial arrangements.[88] Various people wrote and called from around the country to say they were certain Leitch would be healed. Valerie had begun fasting at lunch each day and was confident God would heal her daddy. Elliot prayed that if there was anything getting in the way of Add receiving healing, God would make it known to them.

Leitch came home from the hospital for the last time at the end of August. He was in great pain and could be very unkind. But there were good times too. Sometimes in the evenings they talked over pleasant memories of their life together until the sleeping pills kicked in and Add was able to drift off. Sometimes he was able to receive the comforting words she tried to offer him and to offer kindness in return, telling her how she had helped him. Elliot cried off and on throughout the day. Her mind reached out fumblingly to the future, trying to envision what the moment of separation would be like, trying to plan for the unknowable. But though she no longer believed healing would come, the feeling of fear was finally gone.

By September 13, Leitch's mind had begun to wander. On the sixteenth, Elliot wrote in her journal that their prayers for his peace were still unanswered. The next day, at five minutes till midnight, Addison Hardie Leitch died. He was sixty-four years and eleven months old. Elliot was left alone again, to make sense, again, of the loss of a beloved husband.

————

The next day, September 18, Elliot wrote in her journal the words of Julian of Norwich: "All shall be well, and all shall be well, and all manner of thing shall be well."[89] Then she recorded the events of Add's last day. On another day she wrote that she could not understand how they had endured the past year. The house was full of his absence. Social occasions were full of his absence. The only thing that was not was the reading and writing she had always done alone. Faithful MacDuff was a great comfort.

There was work to be done, and Elliot addressed herself to doing it. There was all the aftermath of death in a bureaucratized state to manage. She hired roofers to begin needed maintenance on the house. She began sorting through their possessions, throwing out things such as Add's toothbrush that weren't needed any longer. Earlier in the month she had put in motion the necessary train of events to have seminary students rent rooms in their home. Leitch would clearly have been unable to work that fall had he lived longer, and it would have provided help with caregiving and housework. Although she no longer needed the help, she saw no reason to change plans, and by the twenty-second, two men had moved in.

But although she was still working to control her response to grief, Elliot had changed since 1956. Add was not there to be hurt any longer if she shared in greater detail what had happened to them, and in her first family letter, written a week after his death, she described his physical and emotional suffering:

We prayed for healing, and we prayed for peace. In the prayers for healing, even when I didn't say it, there was always the footnote "if You want to, Lord. If it would be the good and right thing." I never added any footnotes to the prayers for peace for Add—there was no question in my mind that God would grant that, no matter what physical horrors lay in store for us. Neither prayer was answered. People prayed for me, too, of course—for strength and peace, and God granted both. I said to him "Lord, if You've only got enough for one of us, PLEASE give it to Add. He needs it far worse than I do." God didn't.[90]

Now she could acknowledge, both to herself and others, that her husband had suffered and that she was grieving, in a way she had been unable to do after Jim died.

As the days went on, she pondered the essential loneliness of human suffering, the way Add's suffering and hers, though springing from the same source, had been ultimately incommunicable, separating them long before his death. And then his death had caused, in a sense, her own death as well, the death of "what I was when I was his wife—my body his flesh, my mind the answer to his, my personality molded and changed and nourished by his, my self-image the image I understood him to see." She thought of Jesus's metaphor of a grain of wheat falling to earth and dying. What would come of her loss? "What fruit is it to bring forth?"[91]

Elliot had been greatly helped during Leitch's illness by the life and prayer of Francis of Assisi and had begun pondering the communion of saints and the way she was being helped by the faithfulness of a man dead seven hundred years when she was born. Once Add died, her thoughts turned often toward heaven and eternity, and this idea of the communion of saints, and her own place in it, became even more important to her. She had been a member of the body of Christ before Add's death, and though her loss gave her, perhaps, a new task, she was a member still. She began to pray for the grace to take up her new role.

Everywhere Elliot turned she saw sufferers—unhappy marriages, estranged children, devastating accidents, agonizing illness, depression, bereavement. It seemed that, having found help in her own suffering, perhaps one of her new assignments was to pass along the things that helped her. She wrote a little pamphlet called "Facing the Death of Someone You Love," listing these helps: carving out time to deliberately focus on the person and promises of God; giving thanks—not for the source of suffering, but for that person and those promises; refusing to dwell in self-pity; acceptance; offering the situation to God as a gift; and—here she quoted the prayer of St. Francis—turning to help others.

One of the hard things in the aftermath of death is all the "firsts" that follow. Elliot passed what would have been Leitch's sixty-fifth birthday just a month after his death, then her own birthday, her forty-seventh, a month after that. She and Valerie spent that first Christmas in Michigan with Ginny and her family, their first Christmas not in their own home since they had come back to the US. Then they joined the rest of the Howard siblings and Katharine in Illinois at the tenth InterVarsity Christian Fellowship Urbana Missionary Convention for her first speaking engagement.[92] Dave, who was running the convention, had encouraged his sister to feel free to step back from the commitment, but believing as she did that work and service were balm for a broken heart, she wanted to go ahead.

The title of Elliot's talk was "The Place of Women in World Missions." She began by describing the call both of British missionary Gladys Aylward and the prophet Jeremiah. "In the case of both prophet and parlour maid . . . the issue at stake was identical. The issue was obedience. Questions of intellect and experience, of age and sex, were quite beside the point. God said *do this* and they did it."[93] Jesus had given the Great Commission to both women and men, she said, so the role of women in missions was obedience. Then she discussed women in the Bible and throughout history who had served as witnesses to who God is in a wide range of ways:

> I could go on listing what women have done to prove that they have had an important role in world missions. . . . And besides these names there have surely been tens of thousands of nameless nuns and other anonymous women who have done what God sent them to do—and they've done it without the tub-thumping of modern egalitarian movements. They had a place and they knew they had it because Scripture says they have.[94]

She ended by exhorting her listeners, men and women, to get to know God so that they had something to bear witness *to*, and then to go on and tell people what they've seen. It was a rousing talk, and she received a standing ovation.

The speech dismisses "modern egalitarian movements" because women have served God in the past without them. It does not address the "inconsistencies, unanswered questions, and practical problems" Elliot had once said she saw in arguments opposed to modern egalitarian movements.[95]

"I find clear guidance in Scripture," she says, "about my position in church and home. I find no exemption from the obligations of commitment and obedience. My obligations have certainly varied from time to time and from place to place." She describes the varied situations in which she had found herself on the mission field, emphasizing her own commitment and obedience without addressing the fact that many of the things she had chosen to do were things being opposed by those arguing against egalitarian movements. These things "didn't look to me like a woman's job but God's categories are not always ours. I had to shuffle my categories many times. . . . But it is the same faithful Lord who calls me by name."[96] She does not address whether the disruption of her categories might suggest that they needed to be altered.

Afterward Elliot wrote to her family that "the only word I can think of to describe Urbana is GLORIOUS. I never expect to have another experience like it until we all get to Heaven." Leitch had changed her perspective on church bureaucracy, had "opened my eyes to many things regarding organization that I had been blind to before," and she felt that "he would have just loved everything about that Urbana convention." She was deeply impressed by the scale of Dave's planning and execution and felt that without it, "it is doubtful that the Spirit could have worked as He did—the framework was a necessary of His work."[97] She was moved by the speakers, the singing, the celebration of Communion with fourteen thousand people, the individuals she had met. Afterward she wrote Dave a warm personal letter to say how proud of him she was; in her journal she wrote that the whole convention had seemed designed to comfort and encourage her personally.

The notebook in which she had begun a journal early in 1972 was nearly filled, and as the calendar turned to the new year she closed the little book with words from Psalm 90:1 (GNT), "O Lord, you have always been our home," and a stanza from the prayer of Betty Scott Stam, copied into her childhood Bible: "Work out Thy whole will in my life, at any cost, now & forever."[98]

11

On All Sides

ALMOST TWENTY YEARS LATER, Elliot would write that following Leitch's death, "the Lord in His mercy helped me to see a little more clearly in my second widowhood what I had only dimly descried in the first: a gift, a call, and a vocation, not merely a condition to be endured."[1] The verse in 1 Corinthians came alive for her that said, "Each one must order his life according to the gift the Lord has granted him" (1 Cor. 7:17 NEB). She was deeply grieved by her loss. Sometimes in the grocery store she found herself crying. More than a quarter of a century later, she would still speak of her love for Leitch. But even more deeply, she wanted to do the will of God. So she took her own advice. She focused on the reality of the unseen world, gave thanks for the time she and Add had together, disciplined herself against self-pity, and chose to accept her circumstances as a gift from God, to be offered back to God to use. Both in her community—as a neighbor, church member, and landlord—and more publicly—as a speaker and writer—she set about ordering her life in such a way as to help others as best she knew how.

As 1974 began, Elliot resumed her evening Bible classes at Boston's Park Street Church and her women's Bible classes through Christ Church, now often hosting at her home. People from outside the church began to attend, friends or neighbors of original class members. Elliot's disinterest in small talk and the assurance she projected could be intimidating, but class members came to see beyond her manner, recognizing her concern for them. Decades afterward her students would still remember her careful preparation for teaching, the imaginative homework assignments, the time she spent with them in conversation, and her compassionate support in the difficulties of their lives even when she disagreed with their decisions. She continued to host hymn-singing evenings for students and would periodically invite a group over to drink coffee and listen to a tape of Leitch preaching or a record of late-in-life Christian convert Gert Behanna speaking on men and women.

Elliot put thought into her responsibility toward her lodgers as well. Walter Shepard had moved in the day after Leitch's funeral. He was a twenty-eight-year-old Presbyterian missionary kid who had lived in the Congo until he was fifteen, worked a string of jobs including surveying and airline operations management, and had decided to become a pastor after a car accident caused him to recommit to Christian faith. Lars Gren was a thirty-seven-year-old divorcé who had spent his childhood in Norway, New York, and Mississippi. He had joined the Navy, then worked in farming, restaurants, landscaping, surveying, and as a traveling retail liaison for a women's clothing line, repeatedly questioning whether he was really fulfilling his purpose in life. Now he was enrolled in the seminary's hospital chaplaincy course. When Elliot was home, she cooked the evening meal for Walt and Lars, invited them along to Howard family gatherings, and tried to be available to answer questions, provide a listening ear, and encourage them in pursuing holiness. In turn, they helped with chores, brought her gifts when they came back from school breaks, and chauffeured her to and from the airport when she traveled.

She filled her speaking schedule again. Sometimes she was asked to address a specific topic, and sometimes she would offer a list of topics on which she was prepared to speak so organizers could choose. Locally she spoke to student groups, seminary wives, college chapels, women's groups, novices preparing for religious orders at the Notre Dame Novitiate, and a whole slew of churches. Her travel commitments included a women's retreat in Texas, a missionary conference in New Jersey, a Mennonite women's gathering in Pennsylvania, a "seekers" camping festival in the wilds of Eastern Washington, a summer intensive at Wheaton, and a writers' conference in Wisconsin. She spoke at Eastern College, where she accepted an honorary doctorate, and at the annual convention of the National Association of Evangelicals. After each engagement more and more people came to her, or called, or wrote, asking for advice. After Urbana, the volume of mail had become so great that she began hiring someone to do part-time secretarial work. Though she could easily have decided that personal contacts took too much energy away from speaking and writing, she did her best to respond to each person who reached out.

The summer of 1974 was quiet, with Walt and Lars gone for the long vacation and Val taking classes at Wheaton. It was the first summer of Elliot's life that she had lived alone. In between speaking trips, she swam in the ocean, dog-sat for Eleanor Vandevort, visited her brother Tom and his family in Franconia, took long walks with MacDuff, and worked on her writing. "It has been a lovely peaceful summer," she told her family in a letter. "Never have I had longer, more uninterrupted days to work."[2] She sold several short pieces and finished her "jungle notebook" for Harper's, an extended essay meditating on her first year and four months in Ecuador. The title, *These Strange Ashes,* was taken from a Carmichael poem.

The book would be published the next year as part of Harper's Missionary Classic series. In style, setting, and theme it was reminiscent of *Kinsman.* Elliot was still being asked, she explained in the introduction, to tell her missionary story, and she still had no interest in the usual triumphal tale. The results of her work, measured in books of the Bible translated or people professing Christian faith, were not hers to judge. That story, whatever it was, belonged to the people she had lived with—"or, in the final analysis," to God.[3] All she could try to share was how she herself had been changed.

With a few well-chosen details Elliot affectionately evoked the beauty of the places she had lived, the customs and conditions unfamiliar to most readers, the humorous side of her new life, the naiveté and idealism of her younger self, and the ethical dilemmas inherent in cross-cultural relationships. She described the way those first sixteen months in Ecuador began to break down her tidy categories, her sentimental worldview, and her desire "to foreshorten the promises, to look for some prompt fulfillment of the loss-gain principle" expressed in the Bible.[4] During her time in Ecuador she had begun to believe that the Christian life was not intended to help the Christian get results for God, but to help the Christian get to know God.

Elliot was also preparing for a class she had agreed to teach at Gordon-Conwell in the fall. Titled "Christian Expression," it was "an attempt to teach students the necessity of harmony between content and <u>form</u>" by examining "the presentation of ideas in speech, writing, and behavior."[5] As with her own speaking, writing, and behavior, Elliot hoped to communicate through her teaching a Neoplatonic vision of Christian faith. She would go on to teach the class for the next three years. Though she felt she received a good deal of unspoken opposition from within the seminary, particularly over her beliefs on the roles of men and women, the general response from her students seemed positive.

Once school started, Elliot found that teaching took up a good deal of time. "I teach on Tuesdays, mark papers on Wednesdays, read and make notes for my lecture on Thursdays, try to get it into shape on Friday, and type it up on Monday," she told her family.[6] She only spoke twice during the season. At the time, Wheaton required students to take one quarter off, and Valerie was spending hers at home, sitting in on her mother's class at Gordon-Conwell and her uncle Tom's at Gordon. Elliot found her a great help in managing all the "cleaning, cooking, buying, sewing, helping me entertain and type" required to "keep this show on the road."[7] They hosted a crowd for Thanksgiving dinner, and Elliot invited her whole class for a social evening near the end of the term.

Nineteen-year-old Valerie found time to do more than study and help her mother, however, and in October, Elliot's family letters had begun to contain mention here and there of Val's dates with Walt Shepard. Although she had left for school as he was moving in, they had started getting to know one another during school vacations. When Val was back at school Walt had written to her—a card for Valentine's Day, then for her birthday, letters over the summer. Her decision to spend her quarter off at home had given them the chance to spend more time together. Two days before Christmas, Walt proposed. They planned to marry in May 1976, as soon as Valerie graduated.

At first, Elliot was "stunned" to learn of their plans, but she quickly adjusted. Mother and daughter had been praying for God's guidance in the matter of marriage for Valerie for several years. Valerie, who wanted to raise a large family of children, had been specifically praying since she was in high school that God would allow her to marry a pastor, which was Walt's planned profession. As his landlord, Elliot had gotten a better chance to observe Walt's behavior in daily life than do most prospective in-laws, and she was impressed with what she had seen of his character. The couple's shared life goals and religious beliefs seemed to make them a good fit. It was not hard for Elliot to trust that this was part of God's plan for her daughter. Writing a family letter to announce the couple's engagement, she described herself as "a very happy woman, and a very grateful one."[8]

For some time Elliot had been considering a book on marriage, mentioning it at least as early as the spring of 1971. In the fall of 1974 she had signed a contract with Tyndale House for what she described as "a book on women, marriage, etc."[9] She began writing in January 1975 and would send her manuscript to the publisher late in the year. This project formed the backdrop for the rest of her public work throughout the year.[10]

In May Elliot spoke at Wheaton College on women and liberation.[11] She described how her thinking had been shaped by her experience of Waorani culture and by her Christian faith. Her time with the Waorani had suggested that while sex roles in that culture were different from those in America, they were clear and emphatic. Elliot proposed that difference from the other sex, whatever that difference might be in a given culture, was fundamental to what it means to be female or male. She described hierarchy as part of the divine design and characterized equality as a human idea invented for political purposes. Freedom for the Christian could only come from submitting to God's design, as the freedom of the Waorani way of life had depended on each member submitting to the roles of their society.

Elliot's thinking had been shaped by C. S. Lewis's. Ideas from a talk by Lewis are sprinkled liberally through her speech. Lewis calls equality a "legal fiction," a phrase Elliot quotes. He writes, "I do not believe that God created an egalitarian world. . . . I believe that if we had not fallen . . . patriarchal monarchy would be the sole lawful government." He even suggests that although "artificial equality is necessary in the life of the State, . . . in the Church we strip off this disguise, we recover our real inequalities, and are thereby refreshed and quickened." Rephrasing this, Elliot argued that the women's liberation movement had no place in the church or the home. But she did not reach all of Lewis's conclusions. Lewis goes on to point out that a world in which we are not fallen does not exist, and that the legal fiction is necessary, "not because . . . authority is in itself bad . . . but because fathers and husbands are bad. . . . because priests are wicked men like the rest of us." In the world as it is, he said, the "egalitarian fiction . . . is our only defence against one another's cruelty."[12]

In July Elliot contributed the opposing voice to *Christianity Today*'s for-and-against articles on women's ordination. Pointing out that the argument over ordination was just one facet of the larger conversation about the sexes, she mentions several of the same ideas that had appeared in her chapel address: equality as a political concept only, the importance of difference and hierarchy, submission to the design as a necessary condition for liberation. In this piece she offers brief explanations of *why*: difference is required for "the full expression of the divine image"; men have hierarchical preeminence over women because in Genesis 2, Adam was created first.[13] (She argues the opposite conclusion from the creation order of humans and animals in Genesis 1: that humans are preeminent because they were created last.)

"Historically," Elliot says, "developments in the life of the Church have always been of that which was implicit from the beginning." She acknowledges that women were prophets and judges in the Hebrew Scriptures, characterizing these instances as aberrations from normative patriarchy. Jesus's treatment of women "invested them with a radically new dignity," with not even a suggestion of "inferiority." Paul, she says, followed Jesus in "full acceptance of women as called . . . reconciled, redeemed, members of the holy 'priesthood' of all believers, and full-fledged members of the Church." She distinguishes in Paul's writings between what she called "baptismal order" and the "temporal order of the Church and the home," arguing that he wrote of "full acceptance" of women in the former, but "subjection of women" in the latter. Again she referred to her key phrase from 1 Corinthians 11:9, that woman was made for man. In a startlingly aggressive stance, she wrote, "For those who accept Scripture as authoritative, any attempt to evade or reinterpret this statement is mere tergiversation."

Elliot also argued that the church was not out to suppress women's use of the gifts of God, but rather "to ensure their full and proper use within the divinely given framework." Interpretation of the framework is not up to individuals: "If a woman 'feels called' to do a work that on scriptural grounds is outside the 'idea of God in the making' of her, it is the duty of the Church theologically rather than sociologically to judge her vocation. Service to God is never a purely private matter. No one, merely because he or she has the Spirit, may disregard the judgment of the congregation." Here the institutional emphasis she had learned from Leitch is apparent. In the past, Elliot's own private understanding of God's direction had sometimes trumped "the judgment of the congregation."[14]

At the end of November, Elliot attended the inaugural conference of the Evangelical Women's Caucus and subsequently reviewed the gathering for *The Cambridge Fish*. Speakers included Virginia Ramey Mollenkott, Letha Dawson Scanzoni, and Nancy Hardesty. Elliot's report, "Feminism or Femininity?," argues that the conference had approached the issue from the wrong angle, and that the two questions that ought to have framed discussion were, Should we "change the world to suit the Christian vision, or . . . change Christian vision to suit the world?" and, What does it mean to be a woman? The answers to these questions, she writes, would reveal that "freedom is found on the other side of a very narrow gate—obedience. But that gate leads to a largeness of life undreamed of by the liberators of the world, to a place where the original God-given differentiation between the sexes is not obfuscated but celebrated, where our inequalities are seen as essential to the Image of God."[15]

Elliot rejects the definition of Christian feminism given by Hardesty at the conference: "Christians who believe, first of all, that it is essential for salvation to have a personal relationship with Jesus Christ as Savior and as Lord, and who accept the Bible as the inspired and authoritative word of God. We are also concerned for love and justice between the sexes, and we are committed to find the whole counsel of God on this matter."[16] This statement Elliot calls "applicable to evangelical Christians in general rather than to evangelical Christian feminists." She then describes Christian feminism as a contradiction in terms: "The Biblical feminist vision devalues the form in which divine revelation is given, and the devaluation of form leads ultimately to the destruction of content." It sees "patriarchy not as reflecting God's revelation of Himself, but God's revelation of Himself as reflecting patriarchy, a social system not understood as ordained by God." Most importantly, Elliot argues, it rejects the Trinity, "for there three beings, co-equal and co-eternal, exist in a hierarchical relationship to one another, the Son subjecting Himself in willing and glad filial obedience to the Father who loves the Son and has given all things into His hand. The Holy Spirit takes a place subordinate to that of the Son, witnessing always and only to Him."[17]

At the same time, Elliot wrote to James M. Houston, principal of Regent College in Vancouver, BC, where both she and Hardesty had been invited to teach at a summer intensive the following year, to urge him to rescind Hardesty's invitation. Hardesty had solid evangelical credentials. She had grown up in the Christian and Missionary Alliance, had graduated from Wheaton, and was an assistant editor at *Eternity* and a professor at Trinity College. But Elliot had disagreed with her writing on feminism at least since the spring of 1971. She had read Hardesty and Scanzoni's 1974 book, *All We're Meant to Be*, and attended talks by Hardesty at Gordon-Conwell and at the EWC conference. To Houston, Elliot described Hardesty's position as blasphemous and the conference as nauseous. She was committed to opposing its ideals in every possible way. Houston responded that the committee would withdraw the invitation to Hardesty. He did not address Elliot's concerns or Hardesty's theology, suggesting instead that Hardesty was too emotionally involved to be a good speaker after all.

———

Elliot finished the book on women and marriage late in 1975. With the twentieth anniversary of Jim's death fast approaching, she spent the first week of 1976 reviewing the galleys. Rather than laying out a systematic theology or conducting an academic exploration of the topic, she had structured the book more like a series of literary essays, framed as notes to Valerie ahead of her impending marriage.

The book opens with a celebration of the God who designed human beings and desires our good. Only in this light, Elliot writes, can one address the question of what it means to be a woman: "You can't make proper use of a thing unless you know what it was made for." Women were designed for being "totally other, totally different, totally God's gift to man," and Genesis 2 shows what this difference comprises: "God created male and female, the male to call forth, to lead, initiate and rule, and the female to respond, follow, adapt, submit."[18] This hierarchy is also seen in the doctrine of the Trinity. "Within the Godhead there is both the just and legitimate authority of the Father and the willing and joyful submission of the Son."[19] With a brief section on singleness, these themes make up the first third of the book.[20]

The second portion of the book deals with marriage. Elliot describes four ways to think about a husband and four ways to think about marriage. A husband is "a sinner," "a man," "a husband." He cannot "fulfill all the roles of all the relationships you have had prior to marriage." He needs you "to take care of [him] and to minister to him *as gladly* as a mother ministers to her child," and to "let him 'husband' you" in return. And finally he is an individual, "known fully only to God. There are questions you have no right to ask, matters into which you must not probe." Marriage is "dynamic," either growing or shriveling. It is "a union," husband and wife working together toward the same goal. It is "a mirror," showing where you need to grow. And it is "a vocation," something both spouses have to work at—although "a woman is never a man's life in the same sense that a man is a woman's life, and this is the way it was meant to be."[21]

In the final third of the book, Elliot writes of four things she believes are important to a successful marriage. The first is "acceptance of a divine order." "The man and woman who recognize that they are heirs together of the *grace of life* move in time to the rhythm, accepting their boundaries as do the waves, yielding their self-life to the Will of Life Universal . . . moving always toward the final fulfillment and joy—the perfect Music—which is the will of God."[22]

The second element is sex, which Elliot calls "the most explosively dangerous element in our human nature, the source of the greatest earthly pleasure—even, if you ask me, of the greatest *fun*." Rather than addressing technique ("I'm not going to tell you where, how, or when to do it. I'm not going to tell you what to wear."), she offers a reminder that, "What a real woman wants is a real man. What a real man wants is a real woman. It is masculinity that appeals to a woman. It is femininity that appeals to a man. The more womanly you are, the more manly your husband will want to be."[23]

Loyalty is the third thing Elliot lists, which she describes beautifully as having "faith in the idea that God had when He made him." And fourth, she discusses love—not a feeling, but "self-giving." "Turn your energies to service. Whether your service is to be to a husband and through him and the family and home God gives you to serve the world, or whether you should remain, in the providence of God, single in order to serve the world without the solace of husband, home, and family, you will know fullness of life, fullness of liberty, and (I know whereof I speak) fullness of joy."[24]

Writing a series of essays rather than a treatise made sense for Elliot as a writer. Her early books, apart from *No Graven Image*, had been narrative nonfiction, but for the last few years the essay had been her primary genre. To earn a living she needed to produce new books at a pace that would have made it difficult to undertake detailed research, especially given her speaking schedule. Her calling was still that of the prophet—to show what she herself saw. And she wanted to bring literary quality to Christian writing. *Let Me Be a Woman* is a poetic little book, set against the backdrop of a Cape Cod summer and displaying all the love for and command of language that Philip Howard had bequeathed to his children. However, the style does not lend itself to point-by-point analysis or definition of terms, which can be a weakness when dealing with a controversial topic.

The book's exposition of the Bible can sometimes be uneven. From 1 Corinthians 11, for example, Elliot quotes two verses—"For man was not made from woman, but woman from man. Neither was man created for woman, but woman for man" (vv. 8-9)—concluding, "some texts are susceptible of differing interpretations, but for the life of me I can't see any ambiguities in this one." Paul's writing in 1 Corinthians 7, which apparently gives preference to singleness, she sets in context by quoting and paraphrasing several portions of the chapter and acknowledging "the apparent contradictions in this hard chapter."[25]

The same weakness occurs in her treatment of feminism. Scanzoni and others were writing fairly detailed examinations of the Bible and history, and asking pragmatic questions about women's roles in the church. Elliot did not respond in kind, spending her energy instead on trying to help people catch what she called, "the tremendous hierarchical vision of blessedness."[26] But her decision not to directly address those concerns leaves holes in her presentation of that vision.

Christian feminists argued that societal expectations for femininity were a Procrustean bed, actively harming those who didn't fit "just right." The closest Elliot comes to addressing this is to relay anecdotes about women who fit comfortably within the status quo. She quotes early twentieth-century social scientist Ruth Benedict, who wrote in 1912 that "a great love, a quiet home, and children" are "all that is worthwhile" in a woman's life. She says that Valerie's interest in playing house when she was small came from "a knowledge divinely given on which your imagination . . . went to work." She says the female body conveys the meaning of femininity, and asks rhetorically whether "the idea of you—Valerie—contain[s] the idea of, let's say, 'strapping' or 'husky?' How can we bypass matter in our search for understanding the personality?" Elliot does not address women for whom these things are not true: women who find the contributions they make in a paying job worthwhile; women who, with their own knowledge divinely given spent their girlhood playing wilderness explorers and street hockey; women whose bodies *do* contain the idea of strapping or husky.[27]

Nor does Elliot recognize that many of the things she felt God had called her to had depended on privileges feminists had won for women. The movement that had begun with the Second Great Awakening had helped to create a world in which she could go to the mission field as a single woman. Her father's commitment to higher education for his daughters gave her the exposure to the liberal arts that enriched her life as a wife and mother and the training that allowed her to work as a missionary and a writer.

The contradiction between Elliot's own life and her attitude toward feminism was apparent to many of her friends and acquaintances. It was much discussed among the women of her Bible study. Meir Walters noted that Elliot was determined to be privately submissive to her husband but that there was a disconnect between her public life and her teaching. Olive Liefeld was bemused by an article Elliot wrote in which she argued that women should take their husband's name when they married, although Elliot herself was still publicly using her first husband's name. Vandevort would later say that her friend "was demanding of young women what she . . . had not demanded of herself. . . . And I know, I know that she helped people. There's no question. God does that, you know. . . . It doesn't mean that people weren't helped. But *she* didn't."[28]

———

Let Me Be a Woman was not the only book Elliot was working on during this time. *Christian Herald* ran its own publishing imprint, Christian Herald House, and under this imprimatur published *Twelve Baskets of Crumbs*, a collection of twenty-five of the columns Elliot had written over the last seven years. The essays cover a wide range of subjects—missions, her mother, Gale Cottage, Add's cancer, women's liberation, teaching, speaking, the Waorani, and more—and show the development of the themes that had come to characterize her work. This book was less time consuming, since the only new material Elliot had to supply was the introduction. The two books came out in April, just two weeks apart.

With both manuscripts out of the way, Elliot turned to wedding planning. She was still writing, teaching, speaking, and trying to keep up with the mail. She was still a landlord, though her present renters were late to bed and late to rise, so that she rarely saw them. (Walt and Lars had moved out at the end of the last school year—Walt to Louisiana where he was now working for three different churches, and Lars to other lodging—but other men had moved in at the beginning of the next year.) She accepted an invitation to join the board of Stony Brook School.

In and amongst all of this she was making arrangements for music, flowers, photography, clothes for the wedding party, and hotel reservations for guests. The members of her Bible class volunteered to put on the reception, with help from Lars, who was working for a caterer and could get the equipment for free. When Valerie came home for spring break, mother and daughter went through the house and picked out furniture and equipment that Elliot would give the young couple, including the coffee table Jim had made in Shandia.

Walt came into town a week before the wedding, and there was a flurry of teas, luncheons, last-minute preparations, and finally the rehearsal and dinner. On May 1, 1976, Tom walked Valerie down the aisle, and Jim Hampson, rector of Christ Church, and J. I. Packer, friend of the family, coofficiated the ceremony. Then Val and Walt went off to honeymoon in St. Thomas, and Elliot wrote a family letter pouring out her thankfulness for God's goodness. She was moved to the point of tears for all the help given and love shown to her and Valerie by family, friends, and their church community.

After a flurry of speaking engagements, Elliot spent most of June holed up with her typewriter on the third floor of a vacation house in Franconia, emerging occasionally to swim, hike with MacDuff, or work jigsaw puzzles with her mother and Tom and his family. Packer, who had praised *No Graven Image* enthusiastically, had been urging her to write a new novel, and she was giving it another try. "How's it going?" she wrote rhetorically in a family letter. "No comment."[29]

In July, between speaking events, she visited Val and Walt in their ancient rental house in rural Louisiana. After stopping at home long enough to do laundry and repack, she spent the first half of August in Ecuador, speaking several times, visiting Quito, Shandia—where Valerie's child-size furniture was still in the now-deserted house—Arajuno, Puyupungu, and Tewæno, and spending time with Mary Skinner, Katherine Morgan, Minkaye, Day-omæ, and others she had known. She just missed Rachel Saint, who had left Tewæno twenty-four hours before her arrival.

In Quito, Elliot had a long meeting with the Summer Institute of Linguistics' outgoing Ecuador director John Lindskoog. Lindskoog had written her in February, and although he had been circumspect, he had apologized for his individual role in her departure from Tewæno all those years before. He had not realized, he wrote, just how difficult Saint really was; the events of the past two years had opened his eyes. He had also asked whether Elliot would find it helpful to receive some acknowledgment from SIL in addition to his own mea culpa. There seems to be no record of her response, but they did meet in Quito, and Lindskoog shared more about the circumstances that had led to his apology.

After Elliot's departure, SIL had tried repeatedly over the years to assign Saint a female coworker, in keeping with their company policy. The same possessiveness and stubbornness that Elliot had experienced had thwarted every attempt. Things had come to a head when SIL sent a family—Jim and Kathie Yost and their baby—to live in Tewæno early in 1974. Unlike Saint's earlier SIL coworkers, all linguists or literacy specialists, anthropologist Jim Yost did not defer to the older woman; perhaps in part because unlike them, he had no other job he could get on with despite Saint's interference. Yost's insistence had forced Lindskoog to stop merely hoping the problem would resolve itself, and SIL had started to gently stand up to Saint. However, as Lindskoog now shared with Elliot, after sixty-six years of standing her ground, Saint seemed incapable of compromise. Unable to effect change any other way, SIL had reluctantly chosen to remove her from working directly with the Waorani.

Elliot had always kept up with whatever news was made public about the Waorani, but that had been very little. The fuller picture was, as she wrote in a family letter describing her time in Ecuador, "terribly sad."[30] She gave no other indication as to how Lindskoog's disclosure and apology affected her. Certainly it could have been a relief, even more than fifteen years after the fact, to have confirmation that it hadn't just been *her*. At the same time, it must have been deeply painful to have it confirmed that the people and the work Jim had died for had been left in the hands of someone who seemed to have in many ways squandered the opportunity. As Catherine Peeke, who had worked with Saint and Dayomæ off and on since Hacienda Ila in 1955, had written the summer before, the situation in Tewæno was a "tragedy." Not only were the Waorani in the process of losing their land and many traditional aspects of their culture, but translation "is not going forward and . . . the Wao church is stagnant."[31] Over a period of almost twenty years, Saint and Dayomæ had made drafts of the Gospel of Mark, the book of Acts, and a few small excerpts of other books. Because Saint refused to have them edited, even these were not really complete. Once again, Elliot chose to trust, to see the visible reality—the destruction of so much she had prayed for, so much she loved—in the light of the invisible reality of God's character and God's promises.

———

After Ecuador, Elliot had a quiet month to catch up at home and prepare for the start of the 1976–1977 school year. Her stone patio needed major repairs, and Lars undertook them to save her some money. She bought dictating equipment so her part-time secretary could transcribe letters more easily. Her speech for Urbana '76 (titled "The Glory of God's Will") was due soon, so she chipped away at it and at the novel. She had four lodgers for the fall, including Dave and Phyllis's daughter Beth, who was using her quarter off from Wheaton to attend her aunt's and uncle's respective classes. Elliot continued to take her responsibility to her lodgers seriously. She cooked dinner for the household six nights a week and encouraged the young people to bring something from their reading to share at meals in order to facilitate conversation around worthwhile subjects. She tried to share her beliefs about roles, order, and discipline, made herself available at all hours for questions and conversations. "Pray," she wrote to the family, "that I'll not betray the trust that has been placed in me with this household."[32]

In November, Elliot attended the ordination of one of her former students, VaCountess Johnson. The year before, the Reverend Johnson had been the first black woman to earn a Master of Divinity at Gordon-Conwell, and she was only the fourth woman ordained by the American Baptist Church USA. She would go on to a long life of service, including working with the Evangelical Women's Caucus—a connection she made through Elliot—and teaching at Gordon-Conwell. Though Johnson and Elliot clearly did not see eye to eye on ordination, Johnson had found the older woman "very encouraging to me in terms of making sure I was comfortable on campus and assisting me with my studies." Johnson felt that Elliot "showed me how not to get frustrated about all of the stuff that was happening around us and how to be patient and allow God to step in and deal with certain situations."[33]

December found Elliot adding another board membership to her list of commitments, this time the Episcopal Church's new South American missionary society. Not only did this mean more travel, as meetings were in Pennsylvania, but she was also responsible for interviewing prospective candidates. Beth moved out at the end of the term, and another lodger, Dave, moved in. "My three men are 6'3", 6'4", and 6'5"! Last night Lars (6'2") brought over some hors d'oeuvres and we all sat in the living room with the Christmas candles and the fire."[34] She kept up her usual Christmas traditions but planned to spend the holiday itself in Louisiana with Walt and Val, who were expecting their first baby.

December also found Elliot inundated by requests for a listening ear. "It always seems to be love problems," she wrote ruefully in a family letter. "Girls who are in love, but the man can't make up his mind. Men in love but the girl can't make up her mind. Women who are contemplating divorce, women who are contemplating a second marriage. Broken hearts, anxious minds. It is strange to me how much of this sort of thing has come to my door recently."[35] She did not explain why it struck her as strange. But when she had been engaged in questioning her own cultural religious ideas in the 1960s she had marveled over how many others asking similar questions she seemed to run up against. Perhaps some of the present strangeness lay in the fact that she was starting to do some questioning of her own in matters of the heart.

Lars Gren's arrival with a tray of hors d'oeuvres was only the latest mention of his name in Elliot's family letters. He had invited her and some others to dinner in April, had been instrumental in pulling off Valerie's reception in May, had visited Elliot and the Howards in New Hampshire in June, had helped with her patio in September, and had taken her out to a fancy dinner on Cape Cod in October. Elliot had known for some time that he had begun to see her as more than just a landlord. In fact, that was why she had asked him to find a new place to live at the end of the 1974–1975 school year. Several of her lodgers had chauffeured her and helped around the house while they lived there, but Lars, who now lived just down the road, was still coming by regularly long after moving out. He was also, although she didn't mention this in the family letters, showing up unannounced at her speaking engagements with expensive gifts of jewelry and clothing. She had not been particularly interested in him, but his persistence was beginning to make her wonder if she had been wrong.

———

The year 1977 opened with a whirl of snow, board meetings, missionary screenings, and speaking engagements in Florida. Lars, who was visiting his mother in Palm Beach during his school break, met Elliot at the airport when she arrived. Between her various events he took her sightseeing, to a museum, to a play, to dinner with his mother, and to Vero Beach to visit her own mother. She flew back to Massachusetts at the end of January to tackle the mail, phone calls related to writing and speaking, teaching, amateur counseling sessions for a stream of people seeking help, and various social engagements. She wrote to her family, "It is nice to be wanted, and one of these days I won't be, so I'm grateful while it lasts, but sometimes feel a little breathless."[36]

Lars, too, was soon back in Massachusetts to finish his time at Gordon-Conwell, and, as he would later say, "to find out whether Elisabeth . . . had any interest at all in marriage."[37] He made breakfast on Saturday morning at Elliot's house—Norwegian pancakes—for Elliot, Tom and family, and the current crop of lodgers. A week later he asked her out to dinner, and the next day drove her to her speaking engagement. The week after that, they had dinner together again. During this time he told her, "I would like to be the one building the fences around you, and I want to stand on all sides." In her loneliness for someone to help carry the burden of life, this touched a chord. It was so completely what she felt it meant for a man to *husband* a woman, and such a poetic way of phrasing the idea that as she would later say, it "transformed" the way she saw Lars.[38]

At about the same time, Elliot would later say, she began to believe the Holy Spirit was nudging her, pointing out that she had not asked for God's direction about Lars's interest in her. She had assumed she was done with marriage—after all, not only was she twice widowed, but she had just turned fifty. She asked for forgiveness and instructions. Not long after, her regular Bible reading included 1 Corinthians 12:4–7 (Phillips), which discusses spiritual gifts and the body of Christ: "Men have different gifts. . . . But it is the same God who achieves his purposes through them all." Lars was quite different from Add and Jim; this passage seemed to suggest that he could still be part of God's purposes for her life. Before the end of the month she had approached her friend Miriam Kenyon—one of a handful of people she knew who did not hesitate to argue with her—and then Tom and Lovelace, and asked for their perspective on her and Lars's relationship.

March and the first half of April were taken up with one trip after another. Afterward she lamented how difficult she found it to convey the warmth and friendliness she wanted when meeting so many strangers. She also mentioned that she was trying to find more help, another secretary, perhaps a booking agent. She was spread too thin. "I am feeling the need of some sort of change in 'lifestyle'—can't really handle things very well alone." In May she flew to Louisiana to be present for the birth of Valerie and Walt's baby. Walter Dorman Shepard III had a dimple in his chin just like his grandpa Jim. Elliot was smitten. She had to leave again shortly after his birth to keep a speaking engagement. "How I miss him and them!" she wrote.[39]

After the flurry of the spring, Elliot was home for a long weekend—just enough time to host Lars's mother, Ingrid Gren, for the seminary graduation—before taking off to spend the month of June in the rented cottage on Cape Cod writing. She made her way through several books over the course of the month, ranging from *The Maltese Falcon* to John Updike to the spiritual autobiography of Catholic writer Barbara J. Nauer, with whom she had been corresponding in regard to women's roles. Several of them were lent her by Tom, who was still, she wrote, "without question the primary catalyst in my thinking processes."[40]

Elliot had come to the Cape to escape all the interruptions at home. But Lars, who was spending June painting her kitchen and preparing to move to

Georgia to complete his chaplaincy internship, introduced a new disruption. He had decided he was not going to leave Massachusetts without bringing their relationship to a denouement, and now he came to visit. He brought with him his grandmother's wedding ring to show her he was serious and told her, "I want you for a wife." Elliot replied that she would "think about it and pray about it." And so while she wrote and read and walked MacDuff along the shore, she did.[41]

She must have considered the decision in light of her three-part decision-making framework: "circumstances, the witness of the Word, and . . . peace of mind."[42] Circumstances had thrown them—a Norwegian Georgia Baptist and a Philadelphia Episcopalian—unexpectedly together. Her sense of God's voice through impression and through Scripture seemed to support it. Almost without exception, those she had consulted—her close friends, and, with an exceptional openness to counsel, the women of her Bible class—had responded positively, which was reassuring.[43] Then, too, she had gotten to observe Lars in daily life and seen him interact with her family and friends. She had noted his careful dressing and polished shoes, his thoughtfulness in little things like offering her his arm when there was ice on the ground, his attention to detail in household projects. He had social ease that she lacked—the ability to charm a stranger or work a room—and he wasn't afraid of her or tongue-tied around her as many people were.

And Elliot was tired of being "another strong-minded female," tired of independence and sole responsibility.[44] As a person with great strengths—spiritually, intellectually, in self-discipline, in will, in energy—she seems to have found it hard not to be giving almost all the time. Because she was so strong, it must have been challenging even for close friends to remember that she needed their advice and comfort as much as they needed hers, and she must have been lonely. Marriage must have seemed like the one relationship where she would be able to rest in the shadow of someone stronger than her in all the important ways, would be able to *receive* comfort, help, and intimacy. After two weeks of thinking and praying, she wrote Lars a letter accepting his proposal.

Though Elliot was writing to her mother at least once a week during this time, and a family letter about once a month, she said nothing of all this. Instead, through the rest of the summer and into the fall her letters described travel, speaking events, and social engagements. "You can see

why I don't write many family letters," she wrote after one long stretch away
from home. "Is anything less conducive to correspondence than traveling
around, and could anything be more unutterably boring than itineraries
when it comes to reading material?"[45]

There were bright spots in Elliot's hectic schedule. She and Valerie, with
Walt and little Walter, met in the Pacific Northwest for a visit with the
Elliots, and she reveled in getting to spend time with her grandson. She
found a secretary who could work more hours and set her to typing up Jim's
journals, which she planned to publish. Rereading them as she edited must
have been a bit surreal, so many years later and freshly engaged to another
man. She wrote that she was "enjoying this task very much. . . . Jim's gift
of articulation, imagination, and discerning eye amaze me again in one so
young."[46] Gordon-Conwell had not invited Elliot to teach again for the first
term of the 1977–1978 school year until it was too late for her to reasonably
accept, so that was one thing off her plate. She was down to one renter, a
woman named Cindy, who cleaned the house for her and dog-sat when she
was on the road. And she was able to visit Lars in Georgia in the course of
her autumn travel itinerary.

Nevertheless, at the end of October, after another six weeks of heavy
travel, she again expressed the feeling that she was in over her head:

> Something has got to give—I can't do that sort of schedule and expect to
> do anything else. It is bewildering to know what to do, however, as each
> of the places I went somebody said to me "I <u>know</u> the Lord sent you here,"
> etc. Yes. I pray daily for guidance in saying yes or no to phone calls, letters,
> visits, invitations of any kind. I believe my times are in His hand. I expect
> the Shepherd to lead me in paths of righteousness. I have to trust that He
> does this. Yet I know I must cut back somehow.[47]

Contributing, too, to her sense of weight was the immensity of human
heartache with which her work brought her into contact—the death of
children and spouses, divorce, economic disaster, chronic illness, car accidents, cancer, dark nights of the soul. "In the face of that," she wrote, "what is
there to say but Christ has died, Christ is risen, Christ will come again???"[48]

Lars came back to the Northeast for Thanksgiving, and he and Elliot
spent the holiday in New Hampshire with Tom and Lovelace, where they

announced their engagement. Two weeks later, Elliot wrote a family letter sharing their plans. They would be married on the afternoon of December 21, Elliot's fifty-first birthday, followed by a small reception at a friend's house, and be back from their brief honeymoon in time to spend Christmas with Val and Walt. The newlyweds would move to Georgia in time for Lars to go back to work on January 3. They would not sell the Massachusetts house, since they hoped to move back if Lars could get a job in the area after his internship ended. Ginny and her husband, Bud, in the area on furlough, had agreed to house- and dog-sit, and Ginny would temporarily take over teaching Elliot's Bible class. "I have never been more certain of any step I've taken," Elliot wrote, "and right now I'm 'on tiptoe,' as it were, in anticipation. No, we're not 25 years old. No, it's not the first time for either of us. No, we're not supposed to experience all the same thrills. But what if we do? What if we <u>do</u>?"[49]

———

Lars had lost his temper with Elliot for the first time in the spring of 1975, on the day she asked him to move out of her house, though she didn't know it at the time. They were both working in the kitchen, she cleaning up from breakfast and he making his lunch, when she asked him to look for a new place to live for the coming school year. He would later remember, "I don't know if I said anything at all. I probably said, 'Oh, alright,' or 'Yes,' or something, but my blood pressure went sky high in about two seconds." Then he finished packing his lunch and went to school. When he came back to the house that evening, he had had a chance to cool down. He knocked on the door of her study and asked to talk to her, then told her something like, "You have every right to ask me to leave. There's no problem in that, but I don't appreciate the way you did it. I'm not some kid coming out of high school here. I've been around a little bit. I've been in business. We do things in a more gracious manner."[50] Although Lars had defended her manner to others repeatedly, it was different now that he was on the receiving end. He was nettled by her directness, by that innate *something* in her interpersonal approach that she had lamented and been criticized for her whole life.[51] Finding fault with the way she asked him to leave allowed him to regain a sense of control by putting her in the wrong. For Elliot, who knew nothing of his anger, it must have seemed just another in a long string of "exhortations." In any event, she was his landlord and his elder and thus was in the position of authority. She thanked him politely and, as Lars remembered later, "that was the end of it—we didn't get into any discussion."[52]

The balance of power shifted when they got married. Both believed that in marriage the husband was to be in charge. The first time Lars lost his temper with her after their marriage—apparently on their honeymoon—Elliot knew it. And he lost it again. And again. And again.[53] The events followed the same pattern of anger over perceived loss of control followed by an action designed to reassert control. If the triggering incident occurred publicly or there was some other restraining factor, anger was not always expressed immediately or directly, but control always seemed to be reemphasized. A pair of anecdotes from their wedding day shows this pattern. As the two of them were leaving the sanctuary, they had a choice of directions to turn. Lars started to go one way, and Elliot steered him the other. Friends chuckled over it at the time.[54] But when the newlyweds got back to the house that evening to pick up their luggage, Lars declared himself not ready to leave—not because there was something else he needed to do, but because they weren't leaving until he was good and ready. He told Elliot to call the housesitters she had lined up and tell them to change their plans, a discourtesy that must have embarrassed Elliot, though she did as he said. It was late into the night before the couple made the forty-five-minute drive to Boston, where they would spend their three-night honeymoon. This was the first of many such instances.[55]

In this light, Lars's statement about standing on all sides begins to carry a different weight. The hidden depths it had once suggested seem largely to have stayed locked away, even after the couple were married. Her family and friends felt that they knew Lars as a friendly and jovial man but that their relationship with him never seemed to deepen over time. "Superficially," Dave would say years later, "I know him pretty well. But as far as knowing who he was or what he thought about, I don't really know."[56] And the good humor could be abruptly switched off. Others described conversations in which Lars would suddenly shut down, as if an invisible line had been crossed.[57] Lars himself later acknowledged that long-term relationships had not been a "pattern in life" for him prior to his marriage to Elliot and that he found that a "comfortable" way of operating. He seems to have viewed his repeated outbursts of anger as part of the normal wear and tear of family life.[58]

Elliot was unaware of the extent of Lars's desire for control when she agreed to marry him. It's unclear how much of his background and personality she did understand. His parents, who had owned a small seasonal restaurant on Long Island when he was born and had apparently been the entire staff, had found themselves struggling to keep their business afloat while caring for infant Lars and his older sister. During the off season, when Lars was two months old, they went to visit his mother's parents in Norway, and when they returned to New York they had left Lars with his grandparents. Their busy period was eight months long, so they must have planned for him to stay at least that long, but he would have been three before the Battle of the Atlantic effectively closed shipping, and they had not yet brought him back, so they may have planned all along for him to stay until he was school-aged. Whatever their plans had been, they were interrupted by the Second World War. The visit stretched on for a decade. Lars later remembered the opportunity to grow up with his grandparents as a "special thing," but it must also have been disruptive, and more so when the war ended and he was sent back to the US, a little boy by himself on a big boat. On arrival he had met the parents and sister who must have been strangers, and a little brother he had never seen before. A week later he had started school, "not knowing more than two or three words of English." This, again, he later felt was positive, since total immersion helped him become fluent very quickly. It must also have been stressful at the time.[59]

After operating a series of restaurants in New York, the Grens moved to a farm in Mississippi, then back north to run another restaurant. Lars grew up and joined the Navy, spending two years on active duty and two years in the reserves. He moved to Atlanta, where he worked a string of jobs, never staying at one for more than three or four years. He met Sherry Stanley, and they were married in 1962. There does not appear to be a public record of their divorce, but it must have occurred sometime before Stanley remarried in 1965 or 1966. The pattern of interrupted closeness is apparent. Lars had honed the skills he needed to get along well with new people in social settings, but he does not seem to have developed to the same extent the skills needed for healthy intimacy.

If Elliot's journals from this period ever become available for scholarship, perhaps they will shine more light on what must have been a difficult time. The difference between anticipation and reality would have been a painful disappointment. One of the things she had appreciated in her other marriages had been the opportunity to share the details of her life, the thoughts and feelings that she usually confided only in her journal. But Lars seems to have approached this kind of connection with a take-it-as-read attitude, believing that it's fairly obvious how people are likely to be feeling in a given situation so there's no need to talk about it. If you have a disappointment or a loss, he would later say, "then you pick up your sad feelings and go on and get on with things."[60] And his desire to feel in control affected every aspect of their life together. Reading Elliot's family letters, one can only guess at how she processed the situation: there had been an adjustment period in her marriage with Add—did she hope that more time was all that was needed here? Faced with Mrs. DuBose's anger as a teen, she had not recognized its abusive nature—was she able to view Lars's behavior with more nuance, or did she blame herself? After Jim's death she never seemed able to consider that the couple might have mistaken the guidance of God—how did she understand God's direction and her decision to marry again now?

After Leitch died, Elliot had taken her own advice from her pamphlet on grief. Now, whatever her thoughts and feelings may have been, she seems to have tried to do what she had taught in *Let Me Be a Woman*. Of course Lars was a sinner—there was no other kind of husband available. He was a man, so differences between them were to be expected. Marriage was a mirror, and would show her own need for growth. Despite whatever disappointment she felt, she would "accept the divine order," work to have "faith in the idea that God had when He made" Lars, and practice self-giving love.[61]

Though Elliot would later say that when Lars refused to leave on their honeymoon she realized she had made a mistake, her family letters from this time offer only hints that all was not well: an occasional reference to feeling lonely or unsettled, a tendency to write more warmly than usual to her mother, expressions of thankfulness for days full of work.[62] To her family she attributed this wistfulness to having just moved to a town where she knew no one but Lars and to their frequent separation. The couple had rented a house in the transportation hub of Atlanta so Elliot would be better able to fulfill speaking engagements, but this meant Lars had to commute

100 miles each way to his residency at the infamous Central State Hospital in Milledgeville. Since a Sunday sermon was a part of his duties, his weekends were Thursday and Friday; sometimes he and Elliot were home at the same time and sometimes not. She described their work and their occasional social engagements with Lars's friends in the area, and when she wrote about her new husband she only shared good things.

Sometimes she wrote of him as "a dear husband" or mentioned being glad he was home. Once she said she would marry him again, given the chance. When she visited his patients with him, she noted how he could deal graciously with whatever situation arose, how he "always manages to think of something kind and cheerful to say," even to the people who were angry or verbally abusive toward him, how the nurses clearly appreciated him, how many of his patients recognized him and lit up when he came into the room.[63]

While Lars commuted, preached, made his rounds, and offered comfort, Elliot continued her usual work. She wrote short pieces, including her *Christian Herald* column and another piece for a for-and-against pairing in *Christianity Today*, an article titled "Furnace of the Lord: In Support of the Arabs," which argued on behalf of the Arab point of view and concluded by urging her readers to think critically and to pray, as the Bible says, for the peace of Jerusalem. She spoke all over the country, at everything from women's dinners at small Baptist churches to a 3,500-person *Women Alive* conference. She was in high demand for interviews, including interviews on radio and television programs.

In late March, Lars finished up his time at Central State Hospital. With this commitment out of the way, he started a part-time job working for a friend on a new large-print edition of the King James Bible.[64] The job required a good deal of travel since Lars was to be an agent in contact with translators, publishers, and distributors, but his past sales experience made him well-suited for it, and it was a job he could do as well from Massachusetts as from anywhere. He and Elliot made plans to move back north. In the interim, Lars picked up odd jobs, worked on the rentals he owned in the area, including selling one of the houses, and in April, accompanied Elliot to a speaking engagement, an evening women's meeting at the local Baptist church.

Lars had never heard of Elisabeth Elliot before he had come to Gordon-Conwell. He had never heard of the five men killed in Ecuador in 1956.

He had attended Southern Baptist churches, and their times of missions emphasis had focused exclusively on Southern Baptist missionaries. It hadn't been until he had sat one day idly flipping through a coffee-table book in the living room and realized that the woman in the book and the woman renting him a room must be the same person, that he knew she had ever been a missionary. Mrs. Leitch, as he knew her at the time, was an adjunct professor at the seminary who had written some books and who did some speaking. He hadn't really even known what that entailed. Now he began to ask questions about her work.

He discovered that when Elliot spoke, that was all she did. Sometimes area bookstores had copies of her books available and sometimes they didn't, but she didn't have the bandwidth to arrange for a book table. Lars saw this as a missed opportunity. So before the event at the Baptist church, he ordered in some of her books, telling her, "We'll see what happens."[65] He sold out. The next week he went with her again and sold another batch of books. "Lars is good at it," Elliot wrote in a family letter. "Wish he could always accompany me."[66] The month after that, he flew with her to a conference, taped her talks, and sold tapes. Then he began handling travel arrangements as well. Lars would later remember that the discovery of Elliot's need for an agent and his ability to fill that role "changed the whole aspect of what I was doing." Seeing a choice between continuing to pursue chaplaincy and helping his wife, it seemed "the better of the two to be a support for her."[67]

———

By June 4 Elliot and Lars had sorted through "all his worldly goods (except for those which are at present stored in the basement of 746)," gotten rid of everything that wouldn't fit into two cars and one U-Haul trailer, and made the long drive from Atlanta to Hamilton, arriving at the same time as Valerie and her little family, who had come for a two-week visit while Walt attended a seminar.[68] Elliot reveled in the chance to see her family and friends and her beloved MacDuff again, in having her own furniture, her own study, and her own desk and organizational system back. She hired her niece Pam to do weekly house cleaning and a woman from Christ Church to do part-time secretarial work, went back to teaching her Bible class, attended various social events, wrote her speeches and her column, worked through the galleys for *The Journals of Jim Elliot*, and started research for a new project, a mini-biography of Quaker and Keswick Holiness author Hannah Whitall Smith.

Word Books was putting out a new edition of Whitall Smith's *The Christian's Secret of a Happy Life*, and they had asked Elliot to write an introduction and study guide. Elliot scoured Whitall Smith's published writings and personal letters for information as well as various books about her. She had not written in this genre since *Who Shall Ascend*, and learning about Strachan's life had been rather discouraging than otherwise. Now she found herself braced and cheered. "I have been having a wonderful time reading up on her," Elliot wrote to her family. "She was very funny, as well as being a wonderfully clear thinker and writer."[69] This research also seemed to contribute to a new emphasis that begins to appear in Elliot's writing over the summer of 1978, a stress on the theme of obedience regardless of feelings.

This was not a brand-new idea to Elliot—it's evident in her teenaged desire to have a good attitude, in her focus on the cross in college, in her anguished determination to find exactly the right path regardless of her own desires in the long years between graduation and marriage, in her attitude toward Jim's death. But it finds a new prominence in her thinking in the months after her marriage to Lars. On a trip to visit the Elliots in Portland she saw the fish ladders at Bonneville Dam and thought about the "obedience" of salmon to the spawning instinct, though it comes "at a terrible price."[70] A few weeks later she wrote a speech titled "What If It Doesn't Feel Good?," juxtaposing obedience and emotion. The same theme stood out to her again in her research on Whitall Smith. With the data and sense of personality Elliot gathered, she wrote a twelve-page biography. In her conclusion, she summarized the themes of Whitall Smith's life and writing: "Her emphasis on the sovereignty of God, on His determination to fulfill His promises and to give His children joy, and her down-to-earth insistence on the necessity of action and will as opposed to experience and feeling have heartened and strengthened me."[71] Elliot still believed that the character of God meant obedience was the path to lasting joy, and regardless of her own experiences and feelings, she would still will and act obedience to the best of her understanding.

As summer gave way to fall, Lars was traveling a good deal. When he was home, he worked for the catering company that had employed him when he was a student and took over tasks such as insulating the attic and interviewing a new crop of prospective lodgers. Somehow Elliot's own plate was as full as ever. She agreed to teach at the seminary again, and since it would be under the auspices of a new department she had to design a new course, this time on cross-cultural communication. By the end of September she was writing again of her exhaustion. "I need to rethink this travelling and speaking thing," she said in a family letter. "I hear myself talking as tho' it were someone else who sounds extremely boring and repetitive. People ask the same questions, say the same marvelous things about Jim's testimony, my books, my talks. Pray that I'll 'walk worthy.'"[72]

Elliot marked what would have been her and Jim's twenty-fifth wedding anniversary in October. She had shoulder surgery for bursitis. While she was in recovery she learned that MacDuff had cancer. He had to be put down. She missed him desperately and wanted badly to buy another dog, but Lars did not want one. Elliot never had another dog, though she would speak wistfully of MacDuff for the rest of her life.

In November Elliot was a guest on Pat Robertson's *700 Club*, where she answered questions about the Waorani and the recently published *Journals of Jim Elliot*. She and Lars spent Thanksgiving in New Hampshire with Tom and Lovelace, and Christmas at home with all the usual traditions—except that Val and Walt and little Walter were not there. It was Elliot's second Christmas without her daughter since Valerie had been born.

The new year brought more gains, more losses. Elliot had a new collection of *Christian Herald* essays published under the title *Love Has a Price Tag*, including one in which she meditates on her marriage to Lars as a chance to live out her own teaching and another in which she elegizes MacDuff and shares her hope in the restoration of *all* things. She wrote a three-thousand-word autobiography for the introduction, reiterating her understanding of the "purpose of life": "to learn to know God."[73] Several Gordon-Conwell students started a petition to have her disinvited from teaching at the seminary because of her opposition to feminism. She traveled to England to speak and saw Mary Skinner. Another robbery occurred while she was gone. Ginny and her family decided to stay in the US permanently, and as Ginny would be continuing her work on the Cuyonon language at Gordon, they settled nearby; for the first time in thirty years, Katharine Howard was within Sunday-dinner distance of three of her children. Three Mile Island

and the oil crisis were creating difficulties and worries, and Elliot reminded herself that her hope was in unseen realities. Somehow, she still found time to read and in the course of the year worked her way through such varied material as *New Every Morning*, a devotional book written by her father; *The Habit of Being*, the letters of Flannery O'Connor; and *Counsels of Light and Love* by the mystic St. John of the Cross, with introduction by Thomas Merton.

One particularly special gift was the birth of Val and Walt's second child, Elisabeth. Elliot arrived just after her namesake's birth and spent a few happy days caring for little Walter and doing the cooking so Val could rest with the baby. Another was the purchase of a small house on the Atlantic coast. The rental on Cape Cod had created a desire deep in Elliot to live by the sea, but she had never considered that it might be possible, since coastal properties were in short supply and high demand. Nevertheless, at a friend's suggestion, Elliot had mentioned the idea to God. After praying about it for a while, she hesitantly brought it up to Lars, afraid he would think her discontented. But he responded positively, and through a long series of events they found a place they could afford. The new house was just over 10 miles from Hamilton, a funny little hodge-podge cottage perched on a sloping granite bluff twenty yards above the ocean and secluded by mature trees on the other three sides. The location was perfect, and the house could be remodeled. Elliot named it "the Haven," from Psalm 107:30 (KJV): "He bringeth them unto their desired haven."

The couple decided to rent out their present house and use the money to help pay the mortgage on the Haven. They moved in September, but it was not until November that Elliot had a long enough stretch without other commitments to do the thorough cleaning and organizing that it took to make a place feel like home. "As long as there were closets unexplored, corners piled with unknowns," she wrote in a family letter, "I was ill at ease. . . . Now! We can begin to live." Her desk sat before the picture window in their bedroom, and from the time they moved, her letters began with some description of the view over the ocean. "Outside the window as I type on this cold morning, the sea is grey, white caps break the wrinkled surface and only one little lobster boat lies at anchor far out near the horizon." "Saturday morning. The sea dark grey, energetic, slamming the rocks." "The sea is angry this morning, pounding the rocks, hissing, tossing. The sun is trying to come through a gray sky, making a metallic slick on the gray water." It was a balm for her soul.[74]

As 1979 wound to its end Elliot wrapped up her Christ Church Bible class.[75] It was one small way to lessen the pressure on her time. She sent her novel, which she had worked at off and on for a decade and poured most of her writing time into for the last three-and-a-half years, to a friend with professional editorial experience. "What she had to say was so comprehensively negative" that Elliot gave up on the project entirely.[76] She put the manuscript away in the filing cabinet in case she could mine it for another project later, but the sense that "all those years of work have gone down the drain" was a heavy blow.[77] And perhaps most painfully, she lost the Phillips New Testament she had used since the first summer she and Jim were married, leaving it by accident on a plane. She could buy a new copy, but she could never replace the marginal notes that were a record of her life and of God's voice to her.

———

When, years down the road, Elliot wrote a brief autobiography for her author website, she would sum up the bulk of her life as a quiet time filled with speaking, writing, and family. As she and Lars settled into their marriage, she did more or less the same things from day to day and year to year. The couple developed what Elliot, quoting the Phillips translation of Romans 8:28, called "a pattern for good." When they were home, she set her alarm for 4:50 a.m. so she could enjoy the warmth of her bed for ten minutes before rising. They got up at five o'clock and made the bed together. Elliot had a time of Bible reading and prayer alone in her study, then made breakfast. At eight o'clock, Lars read aloud from the same cricket-chewed *Daily Light* that she had used in Ecuador, and they ate together. Then she would work on writing projects at her desk until time to fix lunch, while he answered the phone and the door and generally tried to protect her concentration. They ate together again at noon, she was back at her desk to deal with mail until dinner, and they had lights out by nine. The couple lived frugally; Elliot made soup with scrap ends a few times a week, dried and reused the paper towels she used to blot lettuce after washing it, made their bread, and line-dried the laundry. Lars made their travel arrangements and promoted her books and tapes, making her work much more widely available and greatly increasing her sales. He also continued to work on the Bible project for several years, to manage various rental houses they owned in Florida and Massachusetts, and occasionally to wait tables for the caterer in Hamilton.

In another sense, Elliot's life was never quiet. Her travel schedule had always been tiring, and, if anything, this intensified after her marriage to Lars. Before, she had found time alone to rest, read, and recharge on flights and in hotel rooms between engagements. Now, on the road as at home, Lars was almost always there. Publicly, he introduced her at the podium, adjusted her microphone, managed the book table, and made sure she ate. He decided when she rested and when she worked and when she socialized. Privately, he was unpredictable, berating her for errors in speaking, taking her to task for her social manner, even critiquing her posture.[78] And he was involved in deciding how many speaking engagements she accepted. Elliot loved New England and her home and sometimes had nightmares about speaking. For some time she had been wanting less time on the road, less time being "on" with strangers, and more time for walks down Old Salem Path to the Shore Road and Sunday dinners with her mother and Tom and Vandevort and the Kenyons. But Lars was, as she once said, "an incurable salesman from way back" who "always kinda hopes for a little bit more" travel.[79] And she worked hard not even to seem to argue or to challenge his authority. The couple began to travel more internationally as well as across the United States, curtailing social engagements and community involvement to make the time. But as Elliot had written in one of the columns reprinted in *Love Has a Price Tag*, "it is always possible to be thankful for what is given rather than to complain about what is not given."[80] She worked, in the words of the psalmist, to "[offer] thanksgiving as [a] sacrifice" (Ps. 50:23).

During those mornings at her desk when she was home, Elliot continued to write, publishing eight more volumes of collected or reprised work, and seven books of new material over the next two decades. All but one dealt with the themes that people continually asked about in letters and phone calls and reception lines after conferences—"love problems," suffering, the roles of men and women—all ultimately boiling down to the question of how to live out Christian discipleship.[81] She never published another novel.

Since Elliot had started studying the writer's craft years before in Ecuador, or perhaps even since Capa had told her in January 1956 that he could never be converted by Christian books, she had been frustrated by much of what was called Christian writing. She had never wanted, as she had once said, to "write 'Christian' books that Van Kampen and Moody would be tickled with."[82] She had deplored the tendency of Christian writers to play it safe and preach to the choir instead of exploring open-ended questions honestly. (She held a particularly dim view of devotional books, not only because so many of them were schmaltzy, but because she believed that Christians ought primarily to read the Bible themselves, not what other people had to say about it.) She had always wanted to be a "real writer," to produce *literature*.[83]

But now that she wasn't having adventures in exotic locales, general-market publishers seemed to have lost interest. This affected the quality of her books. Her editors at Harper's and Doubleday had been some of the biggest names in the business and had pushed her as a writer. She had been dismayed, in working with smaller publishers, to find her work treated as if it was a ninth-grade composition project, with heavy-handed edits that detracted from the beauty and simplicity of her writing. And based on the questions she received and the books that sold, devotionals and how-to manuals seemed to be what much of the Christian reading public wanted.

Even before Leitch died Elliot had realized that a distinct shift had occurred in her career and had prayed for help against the temptation to reorganize her life around regaining literary prominence and financial success. In 1979, reading through Flannery O'Connor's collected letters, Elliot marked a section where O'Connor wrote that being chosen by the Catholic Digest Book Club meant her new book would "reach the pious flotsam and jetsam if nobody else."[84] In the margin Elliot queried whether this described her own public. At the same time, she knew that she had prayed for God's guidance and had done her best to follow it at every step along the path that had brought her to this point. It seemed another opportunity to live by what she had said she believed about obedience, regardless of feelings.

In 1980 Elliot's time teaching at Gordon-Conwell came to an end when she was asked again to prepare a new course from scratch, this time for the missions department. She declined because of the time such preparation would take, though she offered to teach any of her earlier classes again if that was ever of interest. The next year she resigned from the board of the Stony Brook School and accepted a position as writer-in-residence at Gordon, where Tom was teaching. This involved three or four speaking events a year and writing for the school paper, and allowed her to rely to some extent on material she had already developed.[85]

During this period she was also writing a sort of companion volume to *Let Me Be a Woman*. Just as the earlier book had been framed as notes to Valerie, so this, *The Mark of a Man*, was addressed to her nephew Pete DeVries. Although Elliot had seen Ginny's children just a few times in their childhood, nephew and aunt had gotten to know each other better during Pete's college vacations. He had valued her advice and had teased her about writing only to women, and the book was her answer, both to his teasing and to his more serious questions.

In some ways the book runs along a familiar track, arguing that men and women are equal in being created in the image of God and in being morally responsible for their behavior, and unequal in other ways, not because they have different worth but because they are distinct from each other. Again Elliot locates the foundation for what it means to be male or female in Genesis 2, briefly acknowledges singleness, and seats marriage as the penultimate end of humanity.

Some of Elliot's arguments are more carefully nuanced here than they have been in earlier work. She distinguishes between stereotypes and archetypes, suggesting that it is helpful to get rid of stereotypes and harmful to work against archetypes. She refines her argument about creation order, acknowledging that since animals were created before people, if it was all we had to go on, it would not be enough, and arguing that we understand the creation order of Adam and Eve to denote hierarchy because Paul says it does in 1 Timothy. She also acknowledges that she doesn't have all the answers: "I can't pin [masculinity and femininity] down once and for all, or spell out all the ramifications, or dictate the details of how they ought to look in late twentieth-century America. They are, I admit, elusive symbols."[86]

Elliot follows this with a beautiful exposition of the Bible's teaching, juxtaposing "the popular picture of a take-charge man" with the biblical description of a leader, which is "servanthood," "humility," "to lay down a life." Jesus is the perfect leader, and "we see in His earthly life a whole new way of being with people, of loving and serving them at the expense of

Himself. . . . That's what it takes to be fully a man, Pete. You must share the life of Christ." A husband is to sanctify himself for his wife's sake, as Jesus said he had done for his disciples. Even if a wife is not living out the role she is called to, Elliot says, "the standard" for the husband is to love her with "the same sort of love Christ gave. . . . That is the basis for authority. It starts with sacrifice. It is maintained by sacrifice. . . . *Sacrifice* was required of His love for us. Nothing less than sacrifice will be required of us if it is our serious intention to love for a lifetime."[87]

The year 1982 saw the publication of *All That Was Ever Ours*, another collection of *Christian Herald* essays, about half of which had appeared in *Twelve Baskets of Crumbs* while the other dozen were newly collected. That same year she released a sort of primer on Christian discipleship called *Discipline: The Glad Surrender*. This new book emphasizes the joy Elliot felt was to be found in the Christian life. Discipline is not punishment; it is not even an end in itself; it is the path to fulfillment and gladness, a way to practice a joyful response to the love of God. She meditates on seven areas of human life where we can practice that joyful response: body and mind, place (by which she means role not location), time, possessions, work, and feelings. The book ends on a note of gladness in God's love. "He offers us love, acceptance, forgiveness, a weight of glory, fullness of joy. Is it so hard to offer back the gifts that came in the first place from the wounded hands?"[88]

Around this time, it appears that Elliot's *Christian Herald* column came to an end. She had been writing for the publication for more than a decade, and a good deal had changed during that time. As she had moved into more traditionalist positions on several issues, the magazine seemed to have been moving the other way. And the *Herald* had begun to operate at a loss as the US economy moved into a recession and many major magazines found their circulation in steady decline. It's not clear whether Elliot or the *Herald* ended the partnership or how much effect either of these circumstances had on the decision.

The change seems to have coincided with an offer from an ecumenical community called The Word of God to publish a newsletter for Elliot through their affiliate, Servant Publications—the publisher that had brought out *Love Has a Price Tag* a few years before. Begun by charismatic Catholics in the late 1960s, the community seemed to Elliot to share many of her concerns about living as Christians in the modern world. She had been asked to start a newsletter before but had never been able to see a way forward. Now the offer to take care of layout, printing, and distribution removed the primary barrier: time constraints. By publishing bimonthly, writing a short cover article, and filling the rest of the space with excerpts from books she was reading, books she was writing, mail she received, prayer requests for herself and others, family updates, and her upcoming speaking schedule, she could fit the project into the time slot that had been occupied by her *Christian Herald* column. She agreed to do it.

Mindful, perhaps, of Pete's joking complaint, Elliot stressed in the first issue that the new offering was for both men and women. "Not very much of what I have to say applies exclusively to women (can't think of a thing just now that would). I hope that my being a woman will not limit too seriously the readership of my letters. The Bible is a book for men and women. Like Jews and Gentiles, we are fellow-citizens with God's people, members of God's household, bonded together, being built with all the rest into a spiritual dwelling for God."[89] Over the years she would write about all the topics for which she had become known and more, including suffering, obedience, self-discipline, marriage, parenting, aging, prayer, thanksgiving, service, courtesy, ceremony, symbolism, current events, how to structure personal devotional time, the family she grew up in, discerning God's will, and a Christian Neoplatonic worldview.

The newsletter also gave readers glimpses into the ongoing events of Elliot's life. In 1983 she and Lars temporarily moved back into their other house. They had decided the oddly constructed cottage was not a good foundation for remodeling and had it demolished in order to build a new house on the site. It was a long process and a stressful one for Elliot, but by late July 1984 it was almost completed and they were able to move in.

Designed by Elliot, the new house had a view of the sea from every room but the downstairs bathroom. The main floor comprised entry hall, laundry area, bathroom, guest suite, open dining and living room—with stone fireplace, built-in bookshelves, and balcony—and eat-in kitchen with high countertops and the same kind of dual-sided cupboards that Jim had built in Shandia years before, which allowed dishes to be put away in the kitchen and taken out in the dining room. The upstairs held the master suite and separate studies for Elliot and Lars. Elliot hung a few good prints of landscapes and of Capa's work, and displayed a few family photographs, including a three-part frame holding pictures of Jim, Add, and Lars. There was a china cabinet in the dining room and a small curio cabinet in the living room displaying a feather crown, her Kichwa carrying net, and a few other mementos from Ecuador. A nine-foot-long chonta palm lance, given to her by one of the Wao men, was displayed in the hallway. With its white walls and warm wood floors, full of natural light, the house was uncluttered but pleasant and welcoming.

In 1984 Elliot shared with readers the news of the birth of James Elliot Shepard (who joined little Walter, little Elisabeth, and Christiana, born in 1981), and of her own struggle to reconcile herself to using a word processor. She provided updates on her mother, who had had a fall, and on the Waorani, who were struggling with the Ecuadorian government over their historic lands. She also shared excerpts from her new book, *Passion and Purity*. In *Discipline: The Glad Surrender* she had written that every area of life—including sexuality—was to be brought under discipline by the disciple of Jesus. *Passion and Purity* was an expansion of that idea, using as a framework her own romance with Jim so many years before and the letters that came in every mail. "My own love story might be of more or less interest to a few," she wrote. "The 'Dear Abby' sort of letters and my replies might be amusing; but my chief concern is that readers consider the authority of Christ over human passion and set their hearts on purity."[90]

Elliot begins by identifying herself with her letter writers, noting that the longings of their hearts "wake clear echoes of my own." God loves us and gives us good gifts, she writes, and God's will "is a place where a man's heart may safely rest—and a woman's heart, too." Resting in God's will "requires the willingness to bear uncertainty, to carry within oneself the unanswered question, lifting the heart to God about it whenever it intrudes upon one's thoughts." God's gifts to us are given in order to be offered back to God. "God gives us material for sacrifice."[91]

But sacrifice is not an end in itself. "We are not meant to die merely in order to be dead. God could not want that for the creatures to whom He has given the breath of life. *We die in order to live.*" To live with uncertainty and unanswered questions we can choose to live in the present, to receive the good parts of the present as a gift, to remind ourselves of the promises of God to bring about our ultimate good. Then she writes about what not to do—not to lie to yourself about what's really going on by spiritualizing natural desires, not to "trifle with other people's feelings," not (if you're female) to pursue someone you're interested in but to wait patiently, not (if you're male) to dilly-dally forever but to prayerfully discern a path and commit to it, not to indulge in self-pity, not to push the limits on sexual intimacy. She concludes with a chapter on purity in marriage ("giving ourselves to and for each other in obedience to God"), and a chapter on purity as determined not by past sexual activity but by adoption into God's family.[92]

Passion and Purity became one of Elliot's most popular books. She noted that Lars sold "several thousand copies" at the December 28, 1983, Campus Crusade for Christ convention where the book debuted, and that she had "never . . . received so much mail so soon" after a book's publication.[93] Many readers wrote to share how they had been helped by it and many more with fresh requests for individual counsel, hoping that somewhere there was a clear answer for their particular circumstances. Elliot had tried in the book itself to point people to the only possible source of such answers: "You have to ask for help. Help will most certainly be given. . . . We have to keep asking the Savior." But, as she had ruefully acknowledged, "I'm always having to explain to people that when I say there is a simple answer I do not necessarily mean there is an easy answer. It's easy enough to understand. . . . But doing it is just plain hard."[94] It is hard to live with uncertainty and unanswered questions, hard to choose without knowing what the outcome of one's choice will be. A return letter from Elisabeth Elliot made a more recognizable form of guidance.

In fact, so many people wrote to her for help that her next book, *A Lamp for My Feet: The Bible's Light for Daily Living*, published in 1985, described how to seek God's voice in the Bible for oneself. In the introduction Elliot explained that she was often asked for counsel, and that in giving it, "I always go back to my source: 'the path of Thy commandments.'" She was writing because "I desperately want [others] to find what I have found along that path: joy." Formatted as a devotional, the book comprises six months of short daily readings to accompany Bible reading and prayer. They were all drawn from notes taken during her own Bible reading. But she emphasized, strongly, that the goal was not to see things as Elisabeth Elliot had seen them, but to learn to hear the voice of God for oneself. "You may find quite a different lesson in a passage," she wrote. "Let the Spirit of God teach you. I do not mean the book to be read at a single sitting, and I

most emphatically do not mean it to be read *in place* of Bible and meditation. It is only meant to be a help. If you have only five minutes, don't read
my book, read God's. It will be a lamp for your feet."[95]

———

There were, of course, things Elliot did not mention in her newsletter.
Ginny and Bud's divorce after more than twenty-five years of marriage was
one, although she did write in general terms of "the suffering of divorce" and
God's desire "to transform every form of human suffering into something
glorious," to "redeem it," to "bring life out of death."[96] Tom's decision to enter
the Catholic Church was another. These events in her family mattered to her
deeply, but they were not primarily her story. Even if they had been, she had
always been a private person and had no desire to air every corner of her
heart and mind in public. The things she did share were carefully chosen in
hopes of encouraging others to follow Jesus. The things she omitted were
not hidden to create a false impression but because of what Tom would later
call her "pastoral sense of what would be fruitful and helpful" for readers.[97]

Elliot had believed for some time, for example, that it was licit to drink
alcoholic beverages as long as one did not drink to drunkenness. Knowing
that it was a sensitive subject, she did not volunteer the information that she
served alcoholic punch at her annual Christmas party, that she and Tom
would sometimes have a glass of wine, or that Lars enjoyed a beer every
now and again. In the same way, Elliot often recommended and shared
work by Catholic writers that she felt would encourage her readers, but
did not emphasize their Catholicism. She did not draw attention to her
membership in the Episcopal Church, or her appreciation for what Tom
called "the luminous and titanic truth and splendor of the ancient church,"
or her sympathy with his decision to be confirmed.[98]

But she was sympathetic, and the siblings' strong affinity must have
made it poignant for both of them for Tom to take this step without her.
She had followed him into the Episcopal Church, and for fifteen years they
had been members of the same communion. A decade later, Elliot would
characterize her decision to remain as she was as "cowardice," saying that
she had not followed him because "my listeners and readers simply would
not understand" if she did.[99] Tom, whose own move cost him his job at

Gordon College, saw it differently. He attributed his sister's decision to her "determination to be what and where God wanted her to be, and the desire not to cause scandal"—scandal in the Catholic sense of the word, meaning an act that causes others to stumble.[100] Elliot had always taken seriously the responsibility of being a person to whom others looked for guidance.

In 1986 Val and Walt's fifth child was born, Colleen, another "crown of old age," as Elliot wrote, quoting Proverbs 17:6.[101] Six months later, Elliot herself turned sixty. Lars developed glaucoma and embarked upon a lengthy and involved course of treatment that included round-the-clock eye drops and eye surgery. Elliot wrote a pamphlet on chastity for tweens and teens, called *Sex Is a Lot More than Fun*. And she finished a project on which she had been working longer than any of her other published work: *A Chance to Die: The Life and Legacy of Amy Carmichael*. The three-year process had involved far more source material than Elliot had enjoyed access to before. Carmichael had lived to be eighty-three years old and had been a prolific writer. "Every line she wrote is publishable, and she wrote hundreds of thousands of lines," Elliot wrote of the staggering task of sifting her material.[102]

Elliot had traveled to Britain, where Carmichael was born, and to India, where Carmichael's Dohnavur Fellowship was still going strong. At Dohnavur she had been installed in Carmichael's own room to work and given access to Carmichael's books (she had looked carefully through them for marginal notes), notebooks, letters and other documents, as well as having been granted interviews with many who had known Carmichael personally. Although it had been a moving experience to sit where the woman she claimed as a spiritual mother had sat and to handle her belongings, Elliot had been most impressed by the self-giving of the workers who had once been children in Dohnavur, who now cared for a new generation of children. She had written afterward, "Please pray that we may never be the same again."[103]

Despite the wealth of material, Elliot had finally managed to distill all she had read and learned into a finished book. "We read biographies to get out of ourselves and into another's skin," she wrote in the introduction, "to understand the convulsive drama that shapes, motivates, and issues from that other life."

The Christian life comes down to two simple things: trust and obedience. What does that mean exactly? . . . Look at a life. Amy Carmichael set her face toward that other Country. Her education, experience, and environment were incidentals, a mere framework within which she lived for eighty-three years, loved, feared, trusted, suffered, celebrated, failed, triumphed, and died. Through all the lights, poses, moods, and disguises we discern the common human elements that make up all of our lives.[104]

In this shared humanity, Elliot found encouragement: "For a time, I suppose, I thought she must have been perfect, and that was good enough for me. As I grew up I knew she could not have been perfect, and that was better, for it meant that I might possibly walk in her footprints."[105] She wanted to show others that it was possible for them as well.

Elliot did not hesitate to tell the truth, as much of it as she could see, about Carmichael. She discusses the inexplicable nature of Carmichael's long illness, her control issues, the way her separation of husbands and wives harmed families, her colorism, her inconsistencies. She thoroughly explored Carmichael's beliefs on the issue of men's and women's roles, although they largely diverged from her own. But neither was Elliot an iconoclast. "Was Amma 'more human' when she sinned (or was sick or lonely or Victorian) than when she prayed, wrote a poem, rescued a child?" Elliot askes in the epilogue. Her answer is no: each of these things is human, and "the latter perhaps *essentially* more so" because they are ways in which Carmichael was most the person God made her to be.[106] This approach was not always well received. Tom would later remember that Elliot's "direct and factual way of narrating didn't fulfill that . . . set of extravagant and Technicolor expectations on people's part. They wanted Amy Carmichael to be lauded, and elevated." But to Elliot, "the facts of Amy Carmichael's life, and her writing, were the best testimony to who and what Amy Carmichael was."[107]

Three months before *A Chance to Die* was published, Katharine Gillingham Howard died at the age of eighty-seven. Katharine had never been able to settle into life in her apartment in Beverly and had lived in a series of places over the past decade, including a brief stay with Elliot and Lars, time with Tom and Lovelace and then with Dave and Phyllis, and finally at the Quarryville Presbyterian Retirement Community in Pennsylvania. They had been difficult years for everyone. Katharine had suffered a series of falls, resulting in cranial surgery and then hip surgery, and had been increasingly confused and forgetful. But there had been much that was good, as well, and

Elliot wrote an affectionate essay about her mother for newsletter readers and her own mailing list of family and friends, recalling Katharine's sense of humor, her care for her family, her hospitality, her self-discipline, and her commitment to Jesus. All six of her children gathered for her funeral.[108]

———

In 1988's May/June newsletter, Elliot asked her readers to pray about a new venture she had been urged to consider: a radio program for Back to the Bible, a nondenominational organization that had specialized in providing Bible-related programming by shortwave radio for more than fifty years. "I wonder if this may possibly be one of the ways in which I am to obey Hebrews 10:24 (NIV): 'Let us consider how we may spur one another on toward love and good deeds.' Pray that I may not mistake the 'how.'"[109] The program was the vision of a young woman with whom Elliot had been corresponding since the late 1970s. Janet Anderson—Jan, as her friends called her—had written to Elliot as a college student after reading *Let Me Be a Woman* and had been thrilled to receive a personal response. They had met in person at Urbana '79 and again at a conference where Elliot was speaking in the fall of 1987. In the years between, Jan had graduated from college as a radio major, worked for Back to the Bible in Nebraska, for HCJB radio in Quito, and for World Radio Network in Texas. When they had met again, Jan had suggested that Elliot take her message to radio.

Elliot had demurred at first. Her speaking schedule continued to leave her feeling "dusty and parched," and she was in no need of something else to fill her time.[110] But Jan had pointed out that radio would allow Elliot to reach "many more women than was possible in these conference and seminar settings."[111] And the younger woman had kept pursuing the idea, visiting at the Haven and making all the arrangements. By late June, when Elliot visited Back to the Bible's headquarters, Jan had sold her on the vision. The time problem remained a problem—when Elliot announced her decision in the September/October newsletter, she asked for prayer for a secretary who "sees what needs to be done and does it," because "sometimes, like Peter, I feel as though I'm drowning"—but once she had decided this was God's direction, she was determined to obey.[112] Before she left Nebraska she had recorded four hours' worth of material, enough for the first month's programs, and scheduled recording sessions for the rest of the summer.

The program was called *Gateway to Joy*, because Elliot believed that "every experience, if offered to Jesus, can be your gateway to joy." It went on the air at the beginning of October, with seventy-three subscribing radio stations. The producers were amazed at how naturally Elliot took to the new medium—her stamina in recording, her command of a huge amount of material, her almost flawless delivery. Listeners were impressed too. Within a month it was on ninety stations; in less than a year it was on more than one hundred. It would run fifteen minutes a day, five days a week, for almost thirteen years. Four days a week Elliot presented, and the fifth she answered listener questions. Back to the Bible billed the show as a women's program, intended "to invite the Christian woman of today to consider her role and responsibilities in light of biblical principles," but based on the letters Elliot received, many listeners were male. After three years, there was so much correspondence that it was eating deeply into her writing time. After five years, she was receiving more than twenty-eight thousand letters a year just from listeners, and Back to the Bible had a full-time volunteer answering phone calls and mail.

Now more than ever, Elliot found herself responsible for "opportunities I never sought, platforms I never asked for, and influence I hardly know about." She took seriously the words of the apostle James—the instruction to be "doers of the word, and not hearers only," and the warning that those who teach "will be judged with greater strictness" (James 1:22; 3:1)—and she had long prayed that "the words I speak and write may be the words that I also live by. God forbid that I should sin against any by being merely a talker." From the beginning of her career, wanting to be faithful to the call to "write what you see," she had drawn her teaching and writing from what she felt God had shown directly to her, and she prayed for "fresh draughts from the well of Life to give to others." When she was asked to speak on a topic of someone else's choosing, as did periodically happen, she felt that she was "tested along the very lines" of whatever she was preparing to say.[113]

So Elliot's choices of material for *Gateway to Joy* may shed some light on her inner life during this time. She chose as her signature statement for the program a combination of two verses, Jeremiah 31:3 and Deuteronomy 33:27: "You are loved with an 'everlasting love,'—that's what the Bible says—

'and underneath are the everlasting arms.'"[114] She drew her material for the first month of programs from *Let Me Be a Woman*, with its themes of submission and service, and for the next two months she spoke on loneliness.

Elliot had begun writing a new book at the beginning of 1987, just after completing the Carmichael biography. Published in 1988 with the title *Loneliness*, it was a series of essays musing on the universal human experience of loneliness, from causes including moving out on one's own for the first time, one's children moving out, loss of a friend, being rejected, widowed, divorced, or living in a difficult marriage. Solitude and loneliness were not the same thing, she noted, and one could be lonely even in a crowd. But whatever the cause, she wrote, "the answer to our loneliness is *love*—not our finding someone to love us, but our surrendering to the God who has always loved us with an everlasting love."[115]

"Singles always imagine that married people are not lonely," Elliot said in a speech given around this time, "but I can testify that there are different kinds of loneliness."[116] It was the closest she came to sharing the difficulties in her own marriage with her readers and listeners. Occasionally, if she felt it would illustrate God's dealings with her and the principles of obedience she hoped to impart, she would retail anecdotes of times she had been unhappy. But she always focused on her own attitude. She never described the behavior that had caused her unhappiness. The stories were so short on detail that they sounded like the kind of thing that happens in any marriage. Again, this was not because she was trying to create a false impression, but because she was trying to live out the things she had taught.

Nevertheless, things were difficult. Lars monitored Elliot's behavior closely, even checking her odometer after she had driven somewhere without him. He controlled her decisions to the extent that he decided when she could visit with a friend, when she could go out for tea, when she would take a bath. He often reserved his angry outbursts for when they were alone so that she never knew for sure if she had upset him until after the fact.[117]

As time went on, Elliot was clearly suffering the effects of this destructive behavior. She worked hard to keep her pain to herself, but friends who spent time with her in person began to see that she was anxious and tense, not wanting Lars to find out when she made small mistakes such as missing a turn when driving. Others, like Olive Liefeld, who saw Elliot infrequently but had known her for decades, recognized that "our relationship with Betty wasn't the same after she married Lars."[118] But no one seems to have realized the extent of what was happening.

Elliot herself does not necessarily seem to have recognized that the painful incidents she described in her journal were part of a long-term pattern. During her premarital relationship with Lars, she appears to have mistaken love bombing, blame shifting, and refusing to take no for an answer as part of the male drive "to initiate, command, and dominate."[119] Now, in their marriage, Lars forestalled questions about his behavior by making jokes—about how he would "get upset," how he was too stubborn to take Elliot's advice—in public spaces, where social norms made it likely that no one would question him.[120] When no one reacted, it reinforced the idea that his behavior was normal. And the situation was complicated by the fact that there were legitimately good things in their life together. But Elliot was unhappy enough that at least once she privately sought counsel from a friend. It's not clear whom she contacted or exactly how much detail she confided, though it's likely that she was somewhat unclear out of deference to Lars and even out of shame. In any event, the friend responded as if Elliot was experiencing typical marital conflict and encouraged her to work harder at accepting and appreciating Lars.[121]

As she had throughout her life, Elliot turned for comfort to the character of God. In a 1989 series of talks called "Suffering Is Not for Nothing," she says that although nothing explains away or solves the "tremendous mystery" of suffering, "God is God. God is a three-personed God. He loves us. We are not adrift in chaos. To me that is the most fortifying, the most stabilizing, the most peace-giving thing that I know anything about in the universe. Every time things have seemingly fallen apart in my life, I have gone back to those things that do not change. Nothing in the universe can ever change those facts." Although she had told more than one trusted friend that she realized when Lars refused to leave on their honeymoon that she had made a mistake, she no longer believed her mistakes could interfere with the sovereignty of God or the fulfillment of God's promise to bring the best possible good out of the events of her life, whatever they were.[122] There is more to reality than we can see, "this visible world and an invisible kingdom on which the facts of this world are to be interpreted." Although this does not make death or suffering "okay," it offers a lens through which to view our lives. We can find our suffering transfigured into a means of joy if we accept it, give thanks in it, and offer it back to God.

Two years later Elliot would publish a version of this talk as a book called *A Path through Suffering*, blending her own thoughts with a series of meditations on lessons from nature by artist and missionary Lilias Trotter, and pondering again, as she had after Add's death, "the meaning of the cross":

> The disorders and sorrows in my own life, whether attributable solely to my own fault, solely to somebody else's, perhaps to a mixture of both, or to neither, have given me the chance to learn a little more each time of the meaning of the cross. What can I do with the sins of others? Nothing but what I do with my own—and what Jesus did with all of them—take them to the cross. Put them down at the foot and let them stay there. The cross has become my home, my rest, my shelter, my refuge.[123]

Though her marriage and her work were both sources of loneliness and suffering, she really did find joy in offering them to God. In the summer of 1991 she was reading the letters of Brother Lawrence; when he wrote, "I am always happy," she wrote in the margin that so was she, nearly all the time.[124]

Another source of happiness lay in her grandchildren. Walter, Elisabeth, Christiana, James, and Colleen had been joined by Evangeline in 1988. In 1990 the family had grieved the loss of baby Joy, who died before birth. Theodore was born in January 1992, and Sarah would arrive two years later. Elliot laughed at herself in family letters for being a doting grandmother, but she truly found each of her grandchildren delightful. She reveled in the stories Valerie shared and her own times with them and would sometimes call a friend just to share her wonder over them and over God's goodness in these tiny, growing humans. Elliot visited the Shepards as often as possible, fitting in time with them when travel took her to their area and sometimes spending Christmas with them. She and Lars used frequent-flier miles to bring one or sometimes two of the kids at a time to stay with them in the summer. The kids would play outside while Elliot worked, and then Elliot and Lars would take them to the park or out for a picnic afterward. But as often as possible was still comparatively little. Just after Colleen's birth, as Elliot wrote later, she had gotten "the privilege and fun of taking care of four of my grandchildren while their parents were away for a trip and had taken the newborn fifth child with them. That was the only time when I've ever had the chance to do that. My grandchildren live in Southern California and I live in the Northeast. So I'm one of the lonely grandmothers as opposed to the exhausted ones."[125] Over the years she privately noted her sadness over missing her daughter and grandkids again and again, reminding herself of God's promise to bring good out of all things for those who love God.

Elliot's collection of essays from the newsletter, *On Asking God Why* (1989), was followed in 1992 by *The Shaping of a Christian Family*. Frequent questions about parenting came to her from readers and listeners, particularly from those who were raising children but hadn't themselves been raised by Christian parents. She answered their questions to the best of her ability but pointed out that, though "Jim and I had hoped for at least four children," she had only raised one herself, "and that one gave me hardly any reason for serious worry, let alone despair. What 'worked' for her may not work for another child."[126] She looked for other examples to the home she had grown up in. Aware of the human tendency toward rule-making, she wrote in the introduction, "I offer this story of *one* man's family. Some may want to take it as a prescription for theirs, but I do not offer it as such. . . . The Howards sought to learn and apply godly principles from the Bible, and those principles are worth reviewing often, though their application may differ in other homes."[127] Her key principles were revealed in chapter titles such as "He Lived What He Taught Us," "A Habit of Order," "Sacrificial Authority," "Love Is Patient and Kind."

Elliot would labor for four painful years over her next book. (She published *Keep a Quiet Heart*, another collection of essays from the newsletter, in 1994, but these projects required much less energy than the creation of new material.) Every day's mail testified that *Passion and Purity* had whetted, not satisfied, the appetite for her perspective on romantic love. So she set out to write a companion volume on courtship. The term *courtship* subsequently came to have a quite specific connotation in American evangelicalism, but Elliot had been using the word since at least the 1960s for any process through which a man and a woman reach the decision to marry. In the summer of 1994 she wrote in the margin of the book she was reading, Jesuit Jean-Pierre de Caussade's *The Sacrament of the Present Moment*, of her doubts about her book, a sense of futility about her efforts, and a temptation toward despondency. She reminded herself again that her primary task was trusting God. Several months later, she asked newsletter readers to "pray for God's help as I attempt to make the book I am working on *cohere*. It's nothing but a jumble now."[128] Elsewhere she noted repeatedly the considerable struggle she was having with the book and her qualms about it. Although it was the kind of writing that had typically been easier for her, she seems to have struggled with it as much as, or perhaps more than, she had with writing her novel.

As always, one of the reasons for Elliot's difficulty in writing was her speaking schedule. "Speaking is . . . a part of my appointed task," she wrote, but "I believe that my first job is writing."[129] Nevertheless, speaking took the lion's share of her energy. As she said in her "Financial Policy" handout, even one speech took her attention off her writing for several days ahead of time as she got ready for it and several days afterward as she tried to regroup and regain focus. She wrote this to explain her charges: five hundred dollars for the first day (which included two talks and a question-and-answer session), four hundred for the second, three hundred for the third, travel expenses for her—she and Lars paid for his expenses—and a hotel reservation that would accommodate them both, although she accepted engagements pro bono as well.[130] But it also explains some of her difficulty with the new book.

The sheer volume of her correspondence was another factor. She devised an ever-evolving set of tools in an attempt to cope. For business mail she typed sample replies, neatly numbered with a large red marker, for her secretary to use in responding on her behalf to the letters that least needed her personal response. There were at least twenty-one postcard size and thirty-three letter size, covering topics including asking to be taken off a mailing list, declining a speaking engagement either because an invitation was given less than thirteen months in advance or because it was given more than thirteen months in advance, declining to join a board, declining to read a manuscript, and suggestions for how to get published (query a publisher and in the meantime write for magazines).

Personal letters were even more numerous, and more challenging. After a while, Lars began writing a quick postcard of thanks in response to letters that did not ask for counsel, while Elliot responded to those that did. She still prayed for each person who wrote asking for help, but there were far too many for her to write a full, individual response to each one. She developed a file box, organized alphabetically, of form letters sharing her thoughts on topics that she received frequent questions about—abuse, breastfeeding, brain development, call to missions, conception, contraception, dating, death of a pet, divorce and remarriage, fatherhood, finding a wife, head coverings, masturbation, modesty, organization, pornography, psychiatry and psychology, submission, and many more—and she would copy these and send one or more of them with a brief personal note. But even with all these tools, staying on top of the mail took substantial time and energy away from writing.

In 1994, during this period of struggle with the new book, Elliot began what would stretch into a decade of speaking engagements, eventually as many as five times a year, at the brand-new Excellence in Character Educational Leadership (EXCEL) program in Dallas, under the umbrella of Bill Gothard's Institute in Basic Life Principles (IBLP).[131] It's unclear how much Elliot knew about IBLP. It had been almost twenty years since *Eternity* had capped a series of articles raising questions about the organization with a 1977 open letter by Joseph Bayly calling Gothard to account for aspects of his teaching that had led to egregious abuses of power.[132] And it had been almost fifteen years since abuse of power and sexual abuse in the Gothard organization itself had come to light in 1980. The story had been reported in some detail in newspapers across the country and in major Christian publications such as *Eternity* and *Christianity Today*. But Elliot had been intensely busy, and Gothard's damage-control campaign had been successful enough that even those who had attended several IBLP seminars were not necessarily aware of the scandal.

Unless new material comes to light, it seems unlikely that Elliot knew anything of Gothard's track record. She had grown up in a culture that normalized abuse of women, and her advice to individual women whom she knew were being abused is distressing in light of all that is now known about abusive patterns—in the form letter kept in her files as a template, she encouraged her correspondent to "examine your own heart" to see if there is "any way in which you are pushing your husband, challenging or aggravating him," advice that reinforces the misconception that the victim is doing something to deserve abuse and the abuser is justified in lashing out.[133] But Elliot also publicly wrote and spoke clearly in opposition to abuse at least twice during this period. In the 1989 "Suffering Is Not for Nothing" talks she said, "I want to try my best to make very plain what

I mean here when I say 'accept.' I'm not talking about things which can be changed and/or ought to be changed. . . . And there are things which must be changed, such as abuse of persons. So I'm not, I want us to be clear that I'm not saying accept everything, just resign yourself and the worst things that happen, you don't think a thing about it. That is not my purpose in this talk."[134] In a chapter she contributed to the 1991 book *Recovering Biblical Manhood and Womanhood,* she wrote that "the essence of femininity" is "surrender," but that "I do not want to be understood as recommending a woman's surrender to evils such as coercion."[135] This was a more forthright condemnation of abuse than was being taught in many churches at the time.

What Elliot would have known was the information widely advertised about Gothard's programs—that IBLP taught God-ordained hierarchy in the church and home, distinct sex roles, and "remaining pure" sexually; that EXCEL advertised itself as a program to help girls and young women from their mid-teens to early twenties pursue Christian discipleship and develop skills that would help them in their role as women. These sound similar to emphases in her own teaching. Again, there seems to be nothing to indicate that she was aware of problematic specifics of Gothard's teaching, including the way his insistence on simplistic submission encourages an environment that enables abuse. Gothard's ongoing abuse of his own power, particularly over often-underage female staff—including specifically targeting students enrolled in EXCEL—did not come to public attention again until the twenty-tens, after the end of Elliot's public speaking career.

Elliot had tried to make clear that speaking for a particular organization did not necessarily indicate agreement. Without naming any names, she wrote, "Occasionally readers have questioned whether my speaking for certain groups is tantamount to an endorsement. Most emphatically not. I will speak for anyone who will listen. Very few groups I cannot endorse would dream of asking me to speak, but some do. If such groups intend to capitalize on my presence as though it were a seal of approval, I am content to leave that with God."[136] Her decision to maintain personal integrity to the best of her ability and let God worry about the integrity of others had been reached as long ago as the conflict over whether other missions should associate with SIL when their planes were flying Catholic priests in Ecuador. It is an understandable position. If one requires every contact to toe an exact ideological line, one soon finds oneself without contacts. Elliot had long been in the habit of seeking information from a wide range of sources—not only those she knew she agreed with—as her reading lists make clear. She tried to approach ideas critically, keeping what she felt was good and laying aside whatever she felt did not line up with the teaching of the Bible. She wanted her audience to do the same.[137]

Quest for Love finally came out in 1996, two years after Elliot had started speaking at EXCEL. Her goal in writing it, she said in the introduction, was to help readers "toward . . . discernment." *Discernment* is a word that appears repeatedly in the book. Each chapter opens with a Bible passage, quotes heavily from letters she had received or from published accounts of how a Christian found a spouse—sometimes interspersed with Elliot's thoughts on the narrative and sometimes not—and closes with a series of prompts for reflection. "No two stories are alike," she wrote in the intro-duction, "for He knows His sheep, calls them by name, and leads them in paths of righteousness."[138]

The difficulty Elliot had in writing the book is apparent. Her prose is uncharacteristically erratic, sometimes wordy, sometimes terse. Individual chapters cover a bewildering array of themes, some of which appear for the first time in the prompts for reflection at the end. She includes examples of a wide range of choices about romantic relationships and sexual behavior, and it is not always clear which examples she is promoting and which she is deploring. She sometimes seems to deprecate a behavior in one chapter and praise it in the next.

And many of the things she appears to promote are heavily dependent on context in ways that are never acknowledged. To take one example, if a man is dating a string of women for fun and leaving a trail of broken hearts in his wake, it is perhaps appropriate to encourage him to stop dating while he discerns a vocation for singleness or marriage. To tell him that he may be sinning by pursuing close relationships even if he's not engaging in physical intimacy might be the right thing to do. To say the same thing to a scrupulous teenage girl who has never had a relationship with a boy beyond blushing when he says hello to her in the church narthex may encourage her to marry the first young man she gets to know regardless of other considerations, to set her up for a lifetime of feeling guilty should she become friends with a male she does not end up marrying.

The conclusion is the clearest portion of the book and helps to mitigate confusion with a bullet list of twenty-two general principles Elliot had hoped to convey through the stories. Powerfully, twenty of them are applicable to the entire Christian life—maxims such as, "Aim, above all else, at *loving God*," and "Do the next thing."[139] Only two pertain exclusively to sexuality.

The movement that would come to be known as "purity culture" was hitting its stride when *Quest for Love* was published in 1996. Knowing that the Bible spoke directly about sexual behavior and concerned about some of the aftermath of the sexual revolution—high rates of teen pregnancy, for example—evangelical adults were looking for ways to counteract the idea that "anything goes" sexually and to protect the rising generation from engaging in harmful sexual behavior. And evangelical teens were looking for reliable guidance in making good choices. But while the Bible attaches the idea of purity largely to the heart or inner self and deals with purity in every area of life, purity culture tended to reassign the idea of purity specifically to sexual behavior. This unhealthily narrowed the focus of discipleship.

In the conclusion of *Quest for Love*, Elliot contradicts many of the unhealthy attitudes that arise in purity culture.[140] She emphasizes that the first concern of the Christian is to know and love God, that this should be the organizing principle of life. Discerning and obeying the will of God comes under this heading, and living within the traditional Christian sexual ethic is just one area of obedience. Within that area, "there is no single formula" to rely on. The general rules of the Christian life apply here as well as elsewhere. "This book does not offer a prescription for finding a life partner," Elliot writes. "Does the question 'Will this work?' continue to trouble you, as though it were a mechanical contrivance that might malfunction? It is God we are dealing with, a just and merciful Father who is far more interested in our welfare than we are." If we are looking for a checklist that will guarantee a certain outcome, she says, we still have not understood what it means to be human, let alone what it means to be a Christian.[141]

———

Although *Quest for Love* was published in the midst of purity culture's ascendancy, it never achieved the popularity or name recognition of the decades-older *Passion and Purity*, which came to be seen as a foundational document of purity culture. This may have had something to do with the readability of the respective texts. But even more it seems to have been connected to the love stories the books tell. *Quest for Love* features stories from unnamed and perhaps unauthoritative modern letter writers and from nineteenth-century missionary couples such as Adoniram and Nancy Judson or George and Mary Müller, who may seem more authoritative but are also more distant from contemporary sensibilities. *Passion and Purity* tells the love story of a more modern couple, whose spiritual authority seemed gold-sealed by their willingness to die—literally—for Jesus.

Interest in the story of the five men's deaths had never gone away. "I've been traveling for thirty-five years," Elliot would tell Kathryn T. Long, "traveling & speaking, and if I don't say something . . . about the Auca incident, it's sure to come up in the questions."[142] In fact, as Long notes, "each major anniversary—the first, the tenth, the twentieth, and sometimes even the five-year marks in between—led to renewed interest among American evangelicals" and "a new wave of publicity."[143]

In response to reader questions, Elliot periodically shared bits of information over the years about the Waorani and the other widows in her newsletter, continuing to try to balance being respectful to Rachel Saint with telling the truth. In 1981 there had been a twenty-fifth anniversary edition of *Through Gates of Splendor* with a new epilogue that shows this balancing act. There had also been a new book, *Unstilled Voices*, by James and Marti Hefley. Elliot had agreed to be interviewed for the book and had reviewed the parts of the manuscript that contained references to herself. The Heffleys shared more of the complexity of the story than was common, and though Elliot asked the couple to tone down a few minor passages, she had passed the manuscript. It appears the book was not widely noticed, however. The same year, with Saint away from Tewæno for the long haul, SIL had quietly assigned a team to finally translate the New Testament into Wao tededo.

In 1992, for the thirty-sixth anniversary of the men's deaths, Pat Robertson had hosted a reunion of the five widows on the *700 Club*, and that summer the Waorani New Testament was at last completed. Marj and Nate Saint's son, Steve Saint, had begun work on a new documentary called *Beyond the Gates of Splendor*, and Elliot and the other widows agreed to be interviewed for it. In 1994 Elliot had traveled to Ecuador with Lars, visiting Tewæno, "Palm Beach," and her old house in Shandia. Elliot had gotten to see Rachel Saint—who had left SIL in 1982 and was living in a new Wao clearing called Toñæmpade—and give her a hug. Saint had died of cancer later in the year. The fortieth anniversary of the five men's deaths in 1996 brought another special edition of *Through Gates of Splendor*, with yet another new epilogue by Elliot. In January, Elliot and Lars went to Ecuador again, taking Val, Walt, and seventeen-year-old Walter. The family arrived in the country on the anniversary of the day that Jim had left Shandia for the last time and departed on the anniversary of the day that the first body had been found.

———

The intensity of her schedule may not have been the only reason Elliot struggled in the writing of *Quest for Love*. She had turned seventy at the end of the year the book was released. The same year, Phil had been diagnosed with Parkinson's disease and Ginny had undergone treatment for breast cancer. Elliot's teeth had been giving her trouble for thirty years, due perhaps to her nutrition—or dental work—during the years in Ecuador, but otherwise, aside from occasional things such as bursitis and a bout with shingles, she had always been strong and healthy. She was able to hike the muddy trails in Ecuador on the fortieth-anniversary visit with no problem. But halfway through work on the book, she had written in the margin of her devotional that her memory and ability to focus seemed to be failing her. The normal human struggle with concentration during times of stress had always been hers, but the concern about her memory strikes a new note.[144]

It's not clear exactly how this trouble remembering manifested itself or how it affected her over the following months. But by the time Elliot was approaching her seventy-second birthday, things had progressed to the point that she felt she needed to tell Lars. In late 1998 she told him she thought something was wrong. When he asked what she meant, she said she had opened the cupboard to take out some cups, and they were not where they were supposed to be. No one else had been there. She had put them in the wrong place.[145]

This would have been a small thing to many people, but to the orderly Elliot it must have been deeply unsettling. Lars—who, she had once jokingly complained, believed that his desk drawers were only for things he never planned to use—wasn't struck as forcefully by her lapse. "I thought little about it," he would later remember. But a few weeks later she brought it up again. This time she suggested that she consult a neurologist. They chose one out of the yellow pages and made an appointment for January 6, the feast of Epiphany.

When the day came, they drove to the neurologist's office. Lars parked the car and opened his door. "No, don't get out," Elliot said. He later remembered replying, "Why not, I'll go in with you," and her insistence: "No, I'd just like to go in alone."[146]

So Lars waited in the car. Much sooner than he had expected, she was back. He could tell from the look on her face that there was bad news. The doctor had done a basic cognitive assessment, which Elliot had not passed, then told her bluntly, "You have Alzheimer's," and sent her home. Elliot was in shock. Lars would later say it was almost as if she was "unable to take it in." For the first time in the twenty-five years he had known her, she seemed "depressed."[147]

The next morning, in her quiet time, Elliot recorded the date of diagnosis in the margin of her devotional. Finally, alone, she was able to cry. She left the same day on a speaking trip.

In the coming days, Elliot and Lars do not appear to have discussed the situation much. "She came back out," Lars later remembered "and I could see she was upset. So I said, 'Well, what happened?' 'Well,' she said, 'They did these tests, and [the doctor] said, 'Well, you've got Alzheimer's.' I said, 'Oh, man.' And that was the initial situation." This was a continuation of a pattern for them. Although they had been almost constantly together for the past twenty years, they lived separate interior lives. As Lars would later describe their relationship, "We didn't have long sessions of analyzing or sitting around to talk about . . . feelings or something. . . . We didn't sit down for forty-five minutes and just have a general conversation."[148]

Lars seems to have been essentially comfortable with their level of communication. Later he would say that being able to facilitate Elliot's career, to do what seemed to him to "make life a little easier for her," was the highlight of their marriage for him; this was how he expressed his love. He would also say that he had not realized how difficult their life together was for Elliot, and that he regretted not being more affectionate and more open to her input. "And there were certainly times when she should've put me into place and said, 'Look.' She should've been a little bit more assertive in certain ways. Had I discovered [that she was having a hard time] it might've been enough to make me—make me do something else."[149]

It's difficult to know how to understand this. Future access to Elliot's journals may shed more light. On one hand, her understanding of submission in marriage could have affected the situation. She had written before their marriage that "there are times . . . when . . . a wife may offer an alternative viewpoint for her husband's consideration."[150] And early in their marriage she had offered her input—trying, for example, to help Lars organize his study. But it appears that this may have decreased over time. Friends would remember that if something was particularly important to her, she might ask Lars about it briefly, but when he said no, that was the end of it. Her teaching is also suggestive. In the late 1990s, for example, she told women that it was inappropriate to give directions to a man who was driving, even if the woman was the only person in the car who knew how to get where they were going, and that it was never appropriate for a wife to manage the family finances, even if the husband was getting them into financial difficulties. Not only did she draw back as part of submitting to her husband; she also worked to be a help and encouragement to him, for example, leaving him affectionate notes and sharing things that had encouraged her. It is possible that Lars did not know how much his behavior was hurting her.

On the other hand, living a separate interior life must have been to some extent an act of self-preservation for Elliot. Whatever Lars felt he might have done to be a better husband in hindsight, what he *had* done for more than two decades was micromanage her, refuse her input, and get angry with her over things like helping him organize his study after he had asked her to help. If he lost his temper when she was open, it would have provided a strong motivation to reserve a private self.

Elliot had apparently found a sense of comfort and freedom in submitting to Jim and to Add, but she said or wrote several times during her marriage to Lars that submission did not come naturally to her, suggesting that this time things were different. This very difficulty may have made her more scrupulous. Because she saw her marriage as an opportunity to "practice the principles I write about," she disciplined herself to approach potential points of friction between herself and Lars as places for her to submit to him and thus to God.[151] And when, in the pattern of their relationship, every moment was a point of potential friction, an ever-widening circle of behaviors would have been off limits for a submissive wife.

This state of affairs must have made Elliot's illness even more difficult. Her insistence on going in alone to her appointment—contrary to her usual pattern of deferring to Lars—suggests that it was acutely important to her not to have to do the emotional work of hearing bad news and of interacting with him at the same time. Although she had still had to contend with the pressure of other personalities after Jim died and after Add died, she had, in the nature of the case, ultimately been left alone to grieve in her own way and make her own decisions about how she wanted to proceed. Now she was faced with a profound loss and also still responsible to another adult for her response. Some of the difficulty she must have had is apparent in another marginal note in her devotional book five days after her diagnosis, marking her deep relief at the fact that Lars was out of town and she was home, alone.

While there are many gaps in the available details about what came next, it's clear that Elliot responded to her diagnosis as she had responded to suffering again and again through the years. A decade before in *A Path through Suffering*, she had written:

> Old age can seem like a hot wind whistling in from some unseen desert, withering and desiccating with a speed that takes our breath away. Wear and tear make their indelible marks on the face in the mirror which (weirdly and shockingly sometimes) becomes the face of a stranger. Fear grips us as we take note of what has gone and contemplate what is to come. The specters of loneliness, illness, abandonment, and the serial deprivation of our powers stare back at us from the furrowed and sagging face. But God will be there. There is no need to fear the future, *God is already there*.[152]

Now she talked her situation over privately with God, worked to accept it, and got on with the work at hand as well as she could. Her 1999 speaking schedule had been set for a year or more, and she went ahead with it, praying meanwhile about her schedule for 2000. Material for the newsletter and the radio programs continued to come due, and she continued trying to produce it. She made no mention of her personal circumstances, though in retrospect many of the topics she chose—faith in the face of fear, the comfort of the Holy Spirit, a John Greenleaf Whittier poem from Phil beginning, "When on my day of life the night is falling"—are poignant.[153] The couple made no public announcement of her diagnosis. There's nothing to suggest whether this was a plan they discussed or whether it was just what happened as Elliot kept her mouth shut and Lars did what seemed best to him.

Privately, Elliot did tell a few people. The poem that Phil, dealing with his own degenerative diagnosis, had sent her, "sure that it would speak to me as it has to him," suggests she told her siblings at some point during the first year.[154] She must have told a few close friends as well; she and Meir Walters went out to lunch together regularly during the first year, and discussed her situation. Walters's listening ear and understanding friendship were a comfort to Elliot. During this period, Elliot read back through her old family letters, reviewing what she would once have called, in the rich language of the King James, "all the way which the LORD thy God led thee these . . . years in the wilderness" (Deut. 8:2), and noted the evidence of God's past provision for her. She meditated on Scripture—the passage on faith in Hebrews 11, the last weeks of Jesus's life. She made note of the good gifts that still filled her life: foghorns, a storm at sea, "my little study . . . a cozy haven. . . . The lines have certainly fallen unto me in pleasant places (see Psalm 16:6). I have a 'goodly heritage,' for which I am unutterably thankful."[155]

But none of this meant things were easy. Chronic stress disrupts both formation and retrieval of memories, so it's likely that her difficult marriage exacerbated her struggle to remember. And dementia itself involves more than memory loss. The physiological changes it brings—including anxiety, agitation, depression, and sleeplessness—are no respecters of faith or willpower. Elliot felt she was going crazy. Walters would later say, "When she knew that she had this condition . . . there was a year. And she knew what to expect. . . . And that was a terrible year. I would say that's the worst year of her life. . . . It was a test of faith." In the daily devotional she was using that year, Elliot marked a poem by Eliza Scudder called "Thanksgiving." In the margin by the words "the great gifts of thought and reason," she marked the date and asked God not to take these gifts from her, then prayed for the grace to give thanks even in her suffering. Walters called Elliot's response a "typical Elisabeth way of dealing with it. . . . But underneath it was a terror. . . . Oh, it was hard. It was very hard.

She was facing it, which you have to. You have no choice. It was holding on, you know?"[156]

By mid-April, it seems that Elliot and Lars had decided to seek a second opinion. This doctor must have done a better job of doing the requisite testing to rule out other conditions, because there was a period where Elliot was waiting for results. While she waited she pondered the words of nineteenth-century Irish historian William Archer Butler, who wrote, "It was no relief from temporal evils that the Apostle promised. No, the mercy of God might send them to the stake, or the lions; it was still His mercy, if it but kept them 'unspotted from the world'"; and those of Victorian-era Anglican bishop Anthony Wilson Thorold, who wrote, "The highest pinnacle of the spiritual life is not happy joy in unbroken sunshine, but absolute and undoubting trust in the love of God."[157] Although it was couched more gently, the diagnosis when it came was the same.

It's not clear how much Elliot and Lars discussed her condition and their plans for the future after this. Lars would later recount a conversation that stood out to him, saying that they were driving when he realized she was "feeling kind of blue."[158] He pulled over and said, "'Is there something wrong?' And she said, 'Well, I was just thinking about what it will be like and the changes that may be coming.'"[159] He told her, "Well, we don't know what's going to happen. . . . But whatever it is, it'll be all right."[160] He felt that this "seemed to ease the situation and we had very few discussions during the next years about what she could or could not do."[161] It does not seem to have had the same effect for Elliot. She had never seen retirement as a Christian concept, believing she was called to live a life of service as long as she was able. But the prognosis for dementia is clear, and she *did* know what was coming. She could feel herself losing her grip on her abilities, and she was praying for a way to end her public activities. Lars's answer must have seemed like a closed door on any discussion of wrapping up her work. Her decision to let the subject drop seems to have stemmed not from a sense of comfort but from her understanding of submission.

So, to outward appearances, life went on much the same as it always had for a while. Elliot kept trying to do her usual work, and Lars pushed her to do so, hoping to help her hang on to as much as she could for as long as she could. Over the course of 1999 she reread Flannery O'Connor's *Mystery and Manners* and read Jane Austen's *Pride and Prejudice*, apparently for the first time. She made periodic visits to the doctor for monitoring. She tried valiantly to learn to use a computer, although it was a misery to her. She had two books published. *Taking Flight* is aimed at high school and college graduates and comprises brief passages taken from seven of her earlier books. Its sections are loosely grouped by themes, and the brief introduction apparently written by someone at the publisher. *The Music of His Promises* is also a compilation of short meditations, many clearly excerpted from previously published work. There is no introduction and no apparent organizational scheme.

For most of the 1990s Elliot had been reading and rereading a fifty-year-old copy of Mary Wilder Tileston's *Daily Strength for Daily Needs*, its faded cloth spine held together with yellowing tape but pristine on the inside except for her neat, careful notes. Each day's reading consisted of a Scripture verse or two, an excerpt from a poem or hymn, and a slightly longer excerpt from writers such as Fénelon, à Kempis, Madame Guyon, St. Francis de Sales, George Eliot, Marcus Aurelius, and Thomas Carlyle, organized around various themes. In 2000 she switched to Tileston's *Joy and Strength*, constructed along the same lines. She seems to have used this little book until she was no longer able. In it she kept a closely typed three-by-five card with lists of those she prayed for day by day. The margins of these little books, and others she was reading during this time (Fénelon's *Let Go*, Bonhoeffer's *Life Together*), bear in increasingly shaky handwriting a record of her inner life—her prayers for help, her struggle with anxiety, her desire to be "patient under the consciousness of your frailty." In *Let Go* she marked Fénelon's words: "You see, the point is not how you are to be sustained and kept alive, but how you are to give up and die."[162]

Deaths kept coming. Elliot—college debate champion, public speaker for more than sixty years—had always spoken with a minimum of notes, just a few prompts on a three-by-five-inch card. She began needing an outline, then a complete manuscript she could read verbatim. Then even that was not enough to prevent embarrassing lapses. By late 2000 she was increasingly unable to write new material for *Gateway to Joy*, and they were airing reruns more and more. The directors realized that despite Lars's insistence that the show go on, it was time to honor Elliot's request that someone let her know when it was time to stop. They put in motion the necessary steps to transition the show to a new host and a new name. By the time the final programming was recorded in the spring of 2001 (the final program would air in August 2001) Elliot had forgotten that she had asked to stop and was taken aback by the change.

By that summer she was forgetting appointments she had just confirmed, forgetting she had answered letters and answering them again. She told an interviewer that she had resorted to keeping a pencil and paper always with her so that she could make notes when Lars was talking to her. "I can remember all the stuff in the past. I've got all these hymns and stuff in my head that I don't forget. But I can forget what Lars said to me three minutes ago. He'll say, 'You mean, you don't know what I just said?' I have to say, 'Tell me again. Please, tell me again.' Of course it's infuriating to him. It's very difficult for both of us." She asked listeners to pray that she would not become "a crotchety old wife" as she aged.[163] She had worked so hard to be self-controlled; she must have been anxious about how she would behave as the progression of her disease gradually removed her control.

By 2002 the *Elisabeth Elliot Newsletter*, too, was composed largely of recycled content from early issues. Outdated personal notes from Elliot had been replaced by updates from Lars. It might have continued this way indefinitely had not Servant Publications gone out of business in the fall of 2003. The November/December 2003 newsletter issue was the last. The years 2002 and 2003 also brought the publication of Elliot's last two books, both published by Servant. *Secure in the Everlasting Arms* was a final collection of newsletter excerpts, collected by newsletter editor Kathryn Deering. The autobiographical introduction contained anecdotes Elliot hadn't shared before—a time when her little sister had embarrassed her, her fear of Gwynn DuBose. Perhaps they were bubbling up from her deep memory as her brain continued to change. *Be Still My Soul* appears to be another mixture of material she had published before and perhaps some new material, heavily revised to work together as a more coherent whole.

It's not clear how much editorial involvement there was in these books. Some of the work seems beyond Elliot's apparent abilities, but her capacity could be somewhat erratic during this time. During the final recording session for *Gateway to Joy*, Elliot's first session in the studio was fine, the second was so scattered it was unusable, and the final session was the best she'd ever done. Perhaps one of these flashes of light occurred in the writing of the introduction to *Be Still My Soul*, which approaches the almost bare simplicity of Elliot's earlier writing. The piece is a poignant meditation on the self-giving of Mary, the mother of God. "I have spent my life plumbing the depths of what it means to be a Christian. I am, as of this morning, still learning," Elliot begins. She concludes, "We are meant to be chalices, life-bearers. As God's expression of what He is like, we become broken bread and poured-out wine. There is no greater fullness."[164]

These words bring to mind Paul's letter to the Philippians near the end of his own life, in which he writes about being poured out as a drink offering for the encouragement of the church. To many of Elliot's friends, this was what she modeled. Several younger women had come to look up to her over the years as a close friend and spiritual mother, and she had taken those relationships seriously and been nourished by them. She wrote or called regularly, shared passages of Scripture and bits of poetry and books that were meaningful to her, invited them to stay with her or travel with her, introduced them to her other friends, read the books they suggested, brought them gifts, split dessert with them, fixed them peanut-butter-and-honey sandwiches, and prayed for them faithfully. As these women watched her move into dementia, they were struck by the way she continued to live out what she had always said was true. They remembered Elliot's emphasis on accepting the circumstances of life as from the hands of God. "It was painful to watch," Lauren Vandermeer would say. "But it was also a very vivid illustration of the truth of a lot of what she wrote."[165] Donna Otto remembered that Elliot had taught "surrender to Jesus Christ beneath the Cross. And she showed me that, she modeled that, she encouraged it . . . until the end."[166] Arlita Winston said, "I watched her live forgiveness to the end of her days."[167] Jan Anderson Wismer was impressed by Elliot's deep confidence in the love of God. Her offering of her life strengthened and encouraged her friends even as its pouring out grieved them.

As Elliot's abilities decreased, Lars continued to push her to do as much as she could—in fact, more than she could. He loved company and travel and change, and he believed he was treating her, and helping others treat her, as a whole person who was still important. But for Elliot, who was deeply private, who had always been tired by engagement with large groups of strangers, who had suffered periodic bad dreams about public speaking throughout her adult life, who had longed for more time with her daughter and grandchildren, the ongoing struggle to appear in public must have seemed nightmarish. In late 2003, five years post-diagnosis and about to turn seventy-seven, she was still speaking four times in a month in locations as disparate as New Jersey, North Carolina, Virginia, and Massachusetts. As with the radio program and the newsletter, it took outside influence to end Elliot's speaking career. Mike Bell, who was then running the EXCEL program, finally took Lars aside and gently suggested that it was time for Elliot to stop speaking for them. Then the doctor told Lars that their travel schedule was too much for Elliot and suggested that they stop. Finally, part of the way through 2004, Lars canceled the rest of Elliot's engagements and posted an announcement on their website: Elisabeth Elliot had retired from public life.

After 2004, Elliot's life was quieter than it had ever been. "We settled in [at home]," Lars would remember, "and I took care of her, and helped her with the things that she couldn't do."[168] As Elliot gradually lost more and more of her ability to speak, she clung to reminders of God's promises. The hymns she had known since childhood were particularly important to her. Another memory aid was a set of small cards on a wooden stand. Printed on the cards were Bible verses that had always been important to her, with her name inserted into the text: "I am holding you by your hand, Betty—I the Lord your God—and I say to you, don't be afraid, I am here to help you. Isaiah 41:13."[169] The couple still traveled, but trips were less frequent and were now largely social. The only work-related travel they continued was to EXCEL, where they attended as long as the program was running. Lars would play a recording of Elliot speaking and then take questions himself, and Elliot would sit, and occasionally smile at those who came up to say hello.

For the next five years, Lars managed the household, cared for Elliot, and continued to promote her work, maintain her website, and sell her books. He answered her mail by adding a brief personal note of his own to copies on the appropriate topic from Elliot's form letters. Though he was still "stubborn" and "opinionated" with others, he grew more tender toward Elliot as she became more dependent on him and less able to express her own opinions. He verbally expressed affection for her more than he had before, complimented her, and liked giving her things she enjoyed—especially ice cream and chocolate. He took her to the salon regularly to have her hair cut and permed and made sure she was always nicely dressed. Lars's increased warmth seems to have struck an answering note in Elliot. She would smile when he knelt down at her level to talk to her. During this period he took a trip by himself, and when he got home, he remembered later, "I walked down to her . . . and I said, 'Hey!' I said, 'How you doin'?' She smiled and I said, 'You know, I've been away for a little bit!'" In one of her now rare bursts of speech, Elliot replied, "Yes, too long."[170]

In 2009 Elliot tripped and broke her leg. Several weeks later she fell again and broke bones in her foot. Lars decided it was time to get help. He was committed to keeping Elliot at home as long as possible, so he turned to Mike Bell for help in finding women who would be willing to work for them, first as live-in caregivers and then, as time went on, as certified nursing assistants. Over the next years, sixteen women stayed in their home, first singly and then in teams of two. Lars noted that "each one that came knew about Elisabeth by her writings," so she was surrounded by people who respected her.[171] They helped with cooking, laundry, and the mail, as well as giving the physical care Elliot increasingly needed.

As Tom would later say, Lars took "splendid care" of Elliot during this period.[172] He continued to arrange a variety of social occasions. They took a few more big trips—to Peru to visit Bert and Colleen Elliot, to a granddaughter's wedding, to a few book fairs, to visit friends in other parts of the country. Closer to home, they went to church events and to dinner at Ginny's or Tom's or a few local friends' houses. The Shepards came to see them, and Lars invited friends and even sometimes comparative strangers for visits. Elliot particularly enjoyed younger guests and would light up when she saw babies or children. As she lost strength, much of the day began to be devoted to coaxing her to eat—although she still loved sweets, and, no longer worried about self-control, skipped straight to the cookies at tea time. She was still particular about neatness and decorum and would fuss at her caregivers when they went barefoot or tucked their feet up underneath them on the sofa. She still noticed the kinds of things the Howard family had called "little quotes"—accents, turns of speech, anything out of the ordinary or humorous—and although she couldn't say the words anymore, she would still occasionally imitate the sound of a person's voice, no longer cautious about waiting until they weren't there.[173] Some of the caregivers played the piano, and Elliot loved to sit in front of a fire in the big stone fireplace or at the picture window looking out over the sea and hum along with old hymns. She could occasionally say a word here and there—when Lars sneezed she would exclaim, "Goodness!"[174] When a reporter from *World* magazine visited in 2014, Lars spoke of how she had dealt with suffering, including dementia, by accepting it as from the hand of God. "It was something she would rather not have experienced," he said, "but she received it." Elliot nodded and said firmly, "Yes."[175]

Lars believed that Elliot could understand more of what was being said than people assumed. When she could not read any more, he read the Bible to her and reminded her explicitly of the truths she had always clung to. One morning before the caregivers came in to help Elliot get up, he read her the portion from *Daily Light*—on treasures stored in heaven—and reminded her of how she used to teach about the passage. "You often mentioned some of these verses when you spoke," he told her, and described how she had illustrated the weight of glory outweighing our afflictions. "Just think," he told her, "there is a home for you in Heaven—reserved for you—after all of this, whatever the troubles might be or have been."[176] She had been restless when he started talking but seemed to relax as he spoke about the coming glory.

Elliot had never shied away from the thought of death and had emphasized strongly to Lars that "if I ever came in and found her on the floor not to call 911, but just to wait. Valerie and I had agreed to follow this."[177] So when, in the small hours of the morning on Monday, June 15, 2015, Elliot apparently suffered a major stroke, that is what he did. He consulted an MD friend, who supported their decision not to seek treatment and gave them a sense of what to expect. Lars and the caretakers stayed with her and let her know they were there with gentle touch. Lars got Valerie on the phone and put it on speaker so Elliot could hear her daughter's voice. At one point Elliot's namesake, her granddaughter Elisabeth, was on the phone as well. For the next five hours they read to her, sang to her, prayed with her. Her breathing grew shallower and shorter. At 6:15 she opened her eyes, closed them again, smiled, and died. She was eighty-eight years old.

Epilogue

Much We Do Not Know

THE STONE HAD BEEN THROWN, had traced its arc through the air, had slipped quietly beneath the surface of the pond. It was gone, and only gently spreading ripples were left to mark its flight. Eulogies for Elliot appeared in publications from the *New York Times* and the *Wall Street Journal* to the Fredericksburg, Virginia, *Free Lance-Star* and the Washington, Pennsylvania, *Observer-Reporter*, from *Christianity Today* to the *Biblical Recorder*. The funeral took place a week later, at Gordon College, where Elliot had once been writer-in-residence. Lars told the story of his wife's last hours on earth. Phil and Ginny were unable to attend because of their health, but Dave, Tom, and Jim shared memories of an older sister with a hilarious sense of humor, a curious mind, a formidable work ethic, and an active, giving love for her family and her God. Her body was buried at Hamilton Cemetery, not far from the house where she had lived for thirty years, with an uncut boulder of New England granite for a marker. It was engraved with her name, her birth and death dates, and these words from Isaiah 43 (KJV): "When thou passest through the waters, I will be with thee." A month later there was a memorial service in the chapel at Wheaton College, where Valerie, Pete DeVries, and several friends spoke of Elliot as a mother, mentor, writer, speaker, and friend who was indomitable, loving, truthful, and firmly anchored by trust in the goodness of God.

Some ripples from Elliot's life are easily seen. Her 1958 *Life* magazine article about her time with the Waorani was read by 76 percent of American adults. Over the next half-century, her books (more than twenty-five of them, available in thirteen languages), articles, CDs and DVDs, daily devotionals, radio broadcasts, and newsletters reached countless people around the world. During her quiet decade, bits of her story continued to find their way into pastors' sermon illustrations, football coaches' pep talks, family conversations, and youth group breakout sessions. As the Internet became increasingly prominent, references to Elliot blossomed online, everywhere from blogs with only a handful of followers to platforms including *First Things* and *Today's Christian Woman*. Anime bloggers reflected on her decision to live with the Waorani. Hip-hop artist Lecrae wrote a song, "Elisabeth's Interlude," thanking her because she "pointed me to Jesus."[1] Through her role in telling the best-known missionary story of the twentieth century, Elliot became one of the best-known Christians of the twentieth and early twenty-first centuries.

Other ripples are harder to observe. The very ubiquity and familiarity of the story that made Elliot famous have obscured much of her life. On the Sunday afternoon in January 1956 when her first husband died, Elisabeth Elliot had twenty-nine years of living behind her. She lived sixty years after that, fifty-three of them after leaving Ecuador. In the course of her life she saw the first nonstop transatlantic flight and the first flight to the moon, the fall of the Berlin Wall and of the World Trade Center. The personality, heredity, home environment, religious communities, national ethos, and global events that shaped her also shaped the mark she left on the world. Elliot had been developing a practical theology and teaching from it for years prior to publishing her first, best-known, book. In the decades that followed, she continued to revise her theology and to teach it, not only through her extensive published work but through her massive correspondence. Her books are still bought and read; many of her newsletters, speeches, and radio programs are still accessible online. Her influence in the lives of individuals and the life of the church is still unfolding.

And what of the stone itself? Elisabeth Elliot. Elisabeth Gren. Elisabeth Leitch. Betty Elliot. Betty Howard. Bets. Betty. Bet. Elisabeth Howard the Great. For eighty-eight years, five months, and six days, she breathed the air, ate and slept and woke, laughed and cried, worked and played, read and thought and wrote, taught and learned, was mistreated and cared for. She was by turns bold and uncertain, judgmental and understanding, rigid and flexible, ambitious and retiring, foolish and wise, kind and cruel, closed-minded and curious, changeable and faithful, misleading and truthful, sentimental and realistic, traditional and unconventional. She was complicated, which is to say, human. The Sermon on the Mount makes clear that in God's economy, the life and the work, the word and the deed, the intention and the outcome, the public teaching and the private thoughts, are inextricably intertwined, and human beings do not always know what weight to give to any of them. To call your brother a fool can consign you to hell, Jesus says, while a cup of cold water to a child can secure you an eternal reward (see Matt. 5:22; 10:42). Elliot had weaknesses and strengths, she got things right and she got things wrong, and she did not necessarily know which were which. Nor do we. We are too small to see very far.

But there was never any hope for any of us in our ability to reach all the correct doctrinal propositions or to limit ourselves only to the lesser sins. The ripples from our lives matter deeply, but they are not everything. The core of reality lies in the character of God: We are loved with an everlasting love. We are held in the everlasting arms.

In her biography of R. Kenneth Strachan, Elliot wrote:

> God alone can answer the question, Who was he? . . . The answer is beyond us. Here are the data we can deal with. There is much more that we do not know—some of it has been forgotten, some of it hidden, some of it lost—but we look at what we know. We grant that it is not a neat and satisfying picture—there are ironies, contradictions, inconsistencies, imponderables. . . . Will Kenneth Strachan have been welcomed home with a "Well done, good and faithful servant," or will he simply have been welcomed home? The son who delights the father is not first commended for what he has done. He is loved, and Kenneth Strachan was sure of this one thing.[2]

She was describing the reality of the human condition. She was describing herself. For Elisabeth Elliot, the foundation of life was trust in the love of God. Not trust that she would live, as she told her family all those years ago as she set out for Tewæno, not trust that things would go well, but trust in *who God is*. If the great hope of her faith is true, then in the end, the rings spreading out across the surface of the pond, the air displaced by the stone as it flew, the stone itself, are all held in the heart of God, where mercy and justice are never in contradiction, and all things in heaven and earth will finally be made whole.

Acknowledgments

NO LABOR OF ANY KIND happens without the mental and physical labor of homemakers. Although there is more to making a household a nourishing home than physical tasks, none of us would survive to adulthood without the people who ensure that meals are planned and groceries procured and food cooked at intervals, that dishes are washed and the kitchen cleaned, that laundry is washed and dried and washed again. As W. H. Auden said, we are composed of eros and of dust; dust demands this repetitive kind of care.

Because I have for many years been the adult in my own household primarily responsible for orchestrating and carrying out these sorts of tasks, I am particularly aware that this book would never have been begun, let alone completed, without those who not only contributed intellectually to this book in many essential ways but also assumed much of the daily labor necessary for life.

When the opportunity arose to pursue publication for this long-time project, my husband, Dan, did not skip a beat in encouraging me to take it. He has added many of the tasks I used to do to his usual workload to keep our household running while I write. He brings me early-morning tea, makes space for me to breathe, and prays with me and talks me down from the ledge when writing and/or life are hard. Our children, Elijah and Narah, have cheered me on, prayed for me, taken over more chores, been gracious with my absent-mindedness, put the kettle on again, cheered me up with hugs, and read aloud with me in evenings. I am glad, deep in my bones, for the chance to be their mother.

From the very beginnings of this enterprise, my own mother, Carolyn, repeatedly encouraged me, assuring me that it wasn't crazy to research and write a biography while also working as a homeschooling primary parent.

For years she has consistently taken a day a week away from her other work to teach school and feed us and answer her grandchildren's questions so that I could have a day a week to write. Always my first and best reader, she has talked through questions and ideas with me and read every word of the manuscript more times than she probably cares to remember. Thanks to her this book exists—and is far better than it could otherwise have been.

When a publication deadline meant writing would need to become a full-time rather than a part-time job, my father, Randy, came to teach at Sabden Hythe School; in the interstices he washed dishes, brewed endless pots of tea, and served as a consultant on rough-field landing gear. My brother Peter, who lives nearby, has also assumed household tasks for us and has been my research assistant, performing myriad tasks related to the book, which allowed me to concentrate on writing itself. Each of my siblings—Mary, Bill, Noah, and Peter—have voted on titles, read drafts, taken impromptu polls, answered questions, transcribed source materials, and stayed up too late arguing in the kitchen with me, and I am enormously grateful to be their sister.

My father-in-law, David, prayed faithfully that I could meet my publication deadline, and I did. My mother-in-law, Marjie, also prayed—and watched kids, and fed us, and connected me with interview subjects. They have both been endlessly patient with their disappearing daughter-in-law. My uncle, Robin Rathbun, and my cousin, Barry Rathbun, both transcribed source documents and gladdened my heart with their kindness.

Karen Baye, Jasmine Johnson, Cynthia Pederson, Rachel Robinson, Taisha Trigg, and Sarah Williams have encouraged me, prayed for me, cheered me on, fed me, loved my children well, asked questions, listened to me talk about this book endlessly, and offered the hospitality of their own lives. I am nourished by their friendship.

Some of the ideas in this book first appeared in germ in other writing. I am grateful for the opportunity to hone my thinking in essays including "One True Love: In Memory of Elisabeth Elliot," for the Hewitt Homeschooling newsletter and "Our Common Tongue: On Elisabeth Elliot and a *Lingua Cascadia*" for Fuller Seminary's *Christ & Cascadia* in 2015; "'Is This How it Really Was?' Exploring Lives Through Private and Public Writing" at the Oxford Centre for Life Writing in 2016; "From Jim Elliot to John Allen Chau: The Missionary-Martyr Dilemma" for *Christianity Today* in

2018; "A New Set of Spotlights on Elisabeth Elliot: What We Learn About Her Life and Work from Two Releases of Previously Unpublished Writings" and "A Fresh Look at the 5 Missionary Martyrs in Ecuador," review essays for *Christianity Today* and The Gospel Coalition, respectively, in 2019. I'm also grateful to Justin Taylor and everyone at Crossway who have given me the opportunity to develop those ideas further in this book.

Many of the papers of Elisabeth Elliot and other resources pertaining to her life are preserved in the Billy Graham Center Archives at Wheaton College. Katherine Graber and Bob Shuster of the BGC Archives and Keith Call of the Wheaton College Archives were always welcoming and went far out of their way to help me both during and after my time at the archives, and they have graciously answered my numerous questions over the years. Kathy Reeg of the Elisabeth Elliot Foundation was indefatigable in sorting out questions around copyright so that this book could contain direct quotations from Elliot's letters. Janet Anderson Wismer, former producer of *Gateway to Joy*, generously shared with me the results of her own research as well as stories of her personal relationship with Elliot. Kathryn T. Long shared the transcript of her 2001 interview with Elliot and kindly answered my questions. Boone Aldridge, historian with Summer Institute of Linguistics, answered questions, provided access to source materials, and connected me with interview subjects. Annie Elliott, editor with Christian Missions in Many Lands' *Missions* magazine, spent much time providing me with access to back issues of *Fields* and *Voices from the Vineyards* publications. Kristina N. Jones and Leslie M. Van Veen McRoberts with Michigan State University Libraries provided access to Elliot's elusive article in *The Cambridge Fish*; Charles Sullivan and Sarah Burks with the Cambridge Historical Commission provided information on the *Fish* itself. Sarah Stevenson with George Fox University Libraries provided access to material from *The Gospel Message*. Lisa Jacobson with the Presbyterian Historical Society provided access to a document from the papers of Addison H. Leitch despite pandemic shutdowns.

I greatly appreciate the many people who took the time to respond to my questions and suggest directions for research, including Leah H. Edelman at Union Theological Seminary's Burke Library; Gloria Korsman at Andover-Harvard Theological Library; Erica Street at Gordon College's Jenks Library; Michael McVicar at Florida State University; librarians at the

Cambridge Public Library in Cambridge, Massachusetts; Wendi Walker, Jim Bradley, and Oliver Crisp at Fuller Seminary; Joel Carpenter at Calvin College; Bob Krupp at Western Seminary; Gina Zurlo at Boston University; Karen Aberle with the Wetaskiwin & District Heritage Museum; the folks at the BrethrenArchive.org website; and Thomas A. Fudge at the University of New England. April Purtell with Hewitt Homeschooling Resources has been a cheerleader for this project from the beginning and has given me the benefit of her example for almost two decades. Brittany Adams and Katelynne Moxon both assisted me with research in the Billy Graham Center Archives, and Malerie Plaugher and Cassie Hauschildt transcribed oral interviews. Karen Swallow Prior introduced me to Justin Taylor, who was looking for someone to write a biography of Elisabeth Elliot.

In the decade I spent compiling information, I was humbled by the opportunity to talk with many people who spent time with Elliot and her family or in institutions that were important in her life. Some have since died. J.C. Derrick, Pierre Wilds DuBose Jr., Lesa Engelthaler, Karen O'Keefe, Olive Fleming Liefeld, Janet Lingerman, Nancy Mering, Robin Mounce, Steve Nickel, the Reverend VaCountess Johnson, Sally Shupert, Prudy Stinnett, Lauren Vandermeer, and Kristen Wollam all spoke with me about their memories. Danielle Sobie Waters and Kendalyn Staddon, who cared for Elliot in her later years, also shared their recollections with me. The Reverend Johnson also shared her experiences at Gordon-Conwell Seminary. Virginia Embry and Earl Adams spoke with me about their time at Summer Institute of Linguistics. Elna Coley and my dear great-aunt, Ethelyn Eastman Schultz, both class of 1957, shared their memories of Wheaton College.

I was also privileged to talk with several people who knew Elisabeth Elliot particularly long and well. Valerie Elliot Shepard was endlessly patient and gracious during our long correspondence. Meir Walters, Eleanor Vandevort, David Howard, Thomas Howard, and Lars Gren all gave me hours of their time. I enjoyed meeting them more than I can say, and I am deeply honored to have been trusted with their stories. Any mistakes or misjudgments in the book are mine alone. It was wonderful to spend time with many of them in person during a trip to Massachusetts. The Walters family and Donald and Virginia Sohn extended hospitality to me during my stay. Trudy Summers also welcomed me into her home, gave permission to quote from some letters of Eleanor Vandevort's, and has encouraged me more than she knows.

In November 2014, seven months before she died, I met Elisabeth Elliot and spent time in her home over the course of several days. We didn't speak much—she because of dementia and I because of native shyness. But I am thankful for what she wrote years ago about creating biography: the reminder not to censor "anything at all which . . . would contribute to the faithful portrayal" of the subject; the exhortation "to *discover*, not to construct," to tell "the truth."[1] And I am thankful for her reminder, articulated in many different ways over the years, that the foundation of our faith is never in our circumstances and always in the character of God.

Chronological Bibliography of Books by Elisabeth Elliot

Through Gates of Splendor, 1957

Shadow of the Almighty, 1958

The Savage My Kinsman, 1961

No Graven Image, 1966

The Liberty of Obedience: Some Thoughts on Christian Conduct and Service, 1968

Who Shall Ascend: The Life of R. Kenneth Strachan of Costa Rica, 1968

Furnace of the Lord, 1969

A Slow and Certain Light: Some Thoughts on the Guidance of God, 1973

These Strange Ashes, 1975

Twelve Baskets of Crumbs, 1976

Let Me Be a Woman, 1976

The Journals of Jim Elliot, editor, 1978

Love Has a Price Tag, 1979

The Mark of a Man, 1981

All That Was Ever Ours, 1982

Discipline: The Glad Surrender, 1982

Passion and Purity, 1984

A Lamp for My Feet: The Bible's Light for Daily Living, 1985

A Chance to Die: The Life and Legacy of Amy Carmichael, 1987

Loneliness, 1988

On Asking God Why: And Other Reflections on Trusting God in a Twisted World, 1989

A Path through Suffering, 1990

The Shaping of a Christian Family, 1992

Keep a Quiet Heart, 1995

Quest for Love, 1996

Taking Flight, 1999

The Music of His Promises: Listening to God with Love, Trust, and Obedience, 2000

Secure in the Everlasting Arms, 2002

Be Still My Soul, 2003

Selected Bibliography

Sources included here are not directly quoted in the text, but were nonetheless instrumental in the writing of this book.

Books, Articles, and Other Published Materials

"13 Years of Missionary Life in Nasir/South Sudan." Neur Field Notes. Modified August 29, 2003. http://www.dlib.indiana.edu/.

Abbott, Laurence. *Jane Dolinger: The Adventurous Life of an American Travel Writer.* New York: Palgrave Macmillan, 2010.

"Acting Head of Wheaton College Is Now Formally School's 4th President." *Freeport Journal-Standard.* Saturday, May 10, 1941.

Adkinson, Lindsey. "Interim Head of Well Finds Inspiration in Giving." *Brunswick News.* January 22, 2019. https://thebrunswicknews.com/.

Advertisements for vacation packages. *New York Times.* December 20 and 27, 1959, 26–27.

"Albert Carl Koch and NC Techbuilt Houses." NCModernist. Accessed January 7, 2020. http://www.ncmodernist.org/.

Associated Press. "5 U.S. Missionaries Lost; Jungle Murder Feared." *New York Times.* January 11, 1956.

———. "Mission to the Aucas." *Time.* January 23, 1956.

Back, Edith E. "Wheaton." DuPage County Historical Society. Accessed July 22, 2020. http://www.dupagehistory.org/.

Barker, Mary Lou. Unnamed book review. *Tampa Times.* July 20, 1966, 21.

Barlé, Nicole, Camille B. Wortman, and Jessica A. Latack. "Traumatic Bereavement: Basic Research and Clinical Applications." *Journal of Psychotherapy Integration* 27, no. 2 (2017): 127–39.

Barnicle, Mike. Untitled column on the Reverend VaCountess Johnson. *Boston Globe.* January 31, 1977, 3.

Bayly, David, and Tim Bayly. "The death of an Eighteen-Year-Old Brother." *Bayly Blog.* October 8, 2011. http://baylyblog.com/.

Bayly, Joseph. "Basic Conflicts: An Open Letter to Bill Gothard." *Eternity,* June 1977. Accessed August 27, 2020. https://www.recoveringgrace.org/.

Beck, James R. *Dorothy Carey: The Tragic and Untold Story of Mrs. William Carey.* Eugene, OR: Wipf & Stock, 1992.

Bendroth, Margaret Lamberts. "In Memoriam: Nancy A. Hardesty." *Religious Studies News.* American Academy of Religion. https://www.rsnonline.org.

Beyond the Gates of Splendor. Directed by Jim Hanon. Produced by Brent Ryan Green et al. 2002. Oklahoma City, OK: Every Tribe Entertainment, 2005. DVD.

"Beyond Memory Loss: How to Handle the Other Symptoms of Alzheimer's." Johns Hopkins Medicine. Accessed November 10, 2020. https://www.hopkins medicine.org/.

"Bill Gothard Steps Down during Institute Shakeup." *Christianity Today,* August 8, 1980, 46.

"Biographical Note." *Guide to the Addison H. Leitch Papers.* Papers of Addison H. Leitch. https://www.history.pcusa.org/.

Birech, Jeniffer. "Child Marriage: A Cultural Phenomenon." *International Journal of Humanities and Social Science* 3 (September 2013). http://www.ijhssnet.com/.

Blanchard, Charles. *President Blanchard's Autobiography: The Dealings of God with Charles Albert Blanchard, for Many Years a Teacher in Wheaton College, Wheaton, Illinois.* Boone, IA: Western Christian Alliance, 1915.

"Books Published Today." *New York Times.* May 29, 1957, L24.

Boster, James S., James Yost, and Catherine Peeke. "Rage, Revenge, and Religion: Honest Signaling of Aggression and Nonaggression in Waorani Coalitional Violence." *Ethos* 31 (December 2003): 472–73.

"Brief Case." *Eternity.* July–August 1980. https://www.recoveringgrace.org/.

Cain, Susan. *Quiet: The Power of Introverts in a World That Can't Stop Talking.* New York: Broadway Paperbacks, 2013.

Call, Keith. "George W. Griebenow, Nazi Hunter." *ReCollections: Re-telling stories from Buswell Library Special Collections.* May 3, 2017. https://recollections .wheaton.edu/.

———. *Images of America: Wheaton*. Charleston, SC: Arcadia, 2006. Kindle.

Chandler, Russell. "Changing the Masthead at the 'Christian Herald.'" *Christianity Today*, March 26, 1971, 34.

"Charles A. Blanchard." Wheaton History A to Z. Accessed July 16, 2020. http://a2z.my.wheaton.edu/.

"Child among Her Father's Killers: Missionaries Live with Aucas." *Life*, November 24, 1958, 23–29.

Colby, Gerard, and Charlotte Dennett. *Thy Will Be Done: The Conquest of the Amazon: Nelson Rockefeller and Evangelism in the Age of Oil*. New York: HarperCollins, 1996.

Concord Presbyterian Church of Gulf Breeze. "Welcome Walt and Val Shepard." January 21, 2019. https://www.concordpres.com/.

Conroy-Krutz, Emily. "US Foreign Mission Movement 1800–1860." *Oxford Research Encyclopedias*. February 2017. https://www.oxfordre.com.

Coote, Robert T. "Bill Gothard's Seminars Go Marching On." *Eternity*. November 1973. https://www.recoveringgrace.org/.

Cronk, E. C., ed. "Best Methods: Homes for Homeless Missionaries." *The Missionary Review of the World* 47 (January 1924): 456–62.

CT staff. "Operation Auca: Four Years after Martyrdoms: A 1960 Update on Elisabeth Elliot and Her Plan to Bring the Gospel to the Ecuadorian Tribe." *Christianity Today*, January 4, 1960. https://www.christianitytoday.com/.

"Current Population Reports: Consumer Incomes." Bureau of the Census, US Department of Commerce. January 15, 1960. https://www2.census.gov/.

Dailey, Suzanne. "Religious Aspects of Colombia's *La Violencia*: Explanations and Implications." *Journal of Church and State* 15 (Autumn 1973): 381–405.

Davis, Mark. "Quichua/Kichwa and Quechua—Language of the Andes." *Trade and Sustainability*. April 30, 2009. http://www.tradeandsustainability.com/.

Dayton, Donald W. *Discovering an Evangelical Heritage*. New York: Harper & Row, 1976.

———. *From the Margins: A Celebration of the Theological Work of Donald W. Dayton*. Edited by Christian T. Collins Winn. Eugene, OR: Pickwick, 2007.

Deis, Robert. "'Jungle Jane' Dolinger among the Jivaro Head Hunters and Beyond." Men'sPulpMags.com. June 27, 2010. http://www.menspulpmags.com/.

DeVries, Peter. Speaking at Elisabeth Elliot's memorial service. July 26, 2015. https://www.youtube.com/.

"Does Disney Productions have the next Chariots of Fire?" *Christianity Today*, May 20, 1983, 48.

Dolinger, Jane. *The Head with the Long Yellow Hair*. London: Robert Hale Ltd., 1958.

———. *The Jungle Is a Woman*. Chicago: Henry Regnery, 1955.

Doss, Erika, ed. *Looking at Life Magazine*. Washington, DC: Smithsonian Institution Press, 2001.

"Early Marriage: A Harmful Traditional Practice." UNICEF. April 2005. https://www.unicef.org/.

"Echoes of Service Papers." John Rylands University Library. University of Manchester. November 2007. https://www.library.manchester.ac.uk/.

"Ecuador." Mission Aviation Fellowship. Accessed August 27, 2020. https://www.maf-uk.org/.

"Ecuador." Shell Global. Accessed August 27, 2020. https://www.shell.com.

"Ecuador: Dream's End?" *Time*. March 31, 1947.

Elliot, Elisabeth. "An Ordinary Day." *Gateway to Joy*, transcript, Back to the Bible. Accessed September 12, 2020. https://web.archive.org/.

———. *Elisabeth Elliot Newsletter*. September/October 1986. Ann Arbor, MI: Servant Publications.

———. *Elisabeth Elliot Newsletter*. January/February 1989. Ann Arbor, MI: Servant Publications.

———. *Elisabeth Elliot Newsletter*. May/June 1989. Ann Arbor, MI: Servant Publications.

———. *Elisabeth Elliot Newsletter*. January/February 1990. Ann Arbor, MI: Servant Publications.

———. Endorsement. *Homosexuality and the Church: Crisis, Conflict, Compassion*. Richard F. Lovelace. New York: Revell, 1978.

———. "Epilogue II, January 1996." *Through Gates of Splendor: 40th Anniversary Edition*. Wheaton, IL: Tyndale, 1981.

———. "The Courage to Be a Woman." *Revive Our Hearts* podcast. September 1, 2011. Originally aired 2001 on Elisabeth Elliot's radio program *Gateway to Joy*. https://www.reviveourhearts.com/.

Embley, Peter L. "The Origins and Early Development of the Plymouth Brethren." Dissertation, St. Paul's College Cheltenham, 1966. https://bruederbewegung.de/.

Erlandson, Elizabeth. "Radio Role Model." *Back To The Bible Today*. September/October 1993, 3.

"Ex-aide: Gothard Lodge Misused." *The Des Moines Register*. November 23, 1980, 20.

"Explore the Story." Wheaton College. Accessed June 23, 2020. http://stories .wheaton.edu/.

"Financially Pressed Argentine Insists His System Will Work." *San Bernardino Sun*. October 16, 1976. https://www.newspapers.com/.

Fine-Dare, Kathleen S. "From Mestizos to Mashikuna: Global Influences on Discursive, Spatial, and Performed Realizations of Indigeneity in Urban Quito." *Mestizaje and Globalization: Transformations of Identity and Power*. Edited by Stefanie Wickstrom and Philip D. Young. Tucson, AZ: University of Arizona Press, 2014.

Fitzpatrick, Michael. "The Cutter Incident: How America's First Polio Vaccine Led to a Growing Vaccine Crisis." *Journal of the Royal Society of Medicine* 99 (March 2006): 156. https://www.ncbi.nlm.nih.gov/.

Fowlds, Sean. "Servant Publications Folds." *Publishers Weekly*. October 20, 2003. https://www.publishersweekly.com/.

Fox, Bethany McKinney. *Disability and the Way of Jesus*. Downers Grove, IL: InterVarsity Press, 2019.

Franklin, James L. "Reviving Religion of Self-Help." *Boston Globe*. May 24, 1978, 2.

Goerzen, Harold. "Jane Farstad among Many Who Served after 5 Missionaries' Deaths 60 Years Ago." Reach Beyond. January 8, 2016. https:// reachbeyond. org/.

Goetz, Thomas. *The Remedy: Robert Koch, Arthur Conan Doyle, and the Quest to Cure Tuberculosis*. New York, Penguin: 2014.

Gothard, Bill. "Family: Principles of God's Chain-of-Command." *Institute in Basic Youth Conflicts: Research in Principles of Life*. Place of publication not identified: Institute in Basic Youth Conflicts, 1969.

"Gothard's Fast Comeback Overrides Calls for Reform." *Christianity Today*, September 19, 1980, 56.

"'Go Ye and Preach the Gospel': Five Do and Die." *Life*, January 30, 1956, 10–19.

"Grace Line (W. R. Grace & Co.), New York 1882–1969." The Ships List. Modified March 26, 2010. http://www.theshipslist.com/.

Gren, Lars. "A Word from Lars." *Elisabeth Elliot Newsletter*. November/December 1992. Ann Arbor, MI: Servant Publications.

————. "Ramblings from the Cove." Website of Elisabeth Elliot. April 2017. Accessed May 2017. https://elisabethelliot.org/.

Haley, Eleanor. "Grief after Traumatic Loss." What's Your Grief? January 19, 2016. https://whatsyourgrief.com/.

Halliwell, Martin. *American Culture in the 1950s*. Edinburgh: Edinburgh University Press, 2007.

Hambling, David. "This Forgotten 1950s Flying Trick Could Be the Secret of Future Drone Warfare." *Popular Mechanics*. March 21, 2016. https://www.popularmechanics.com/.

Hampden DuBose Academy. *Esse*. Yearbooks. 1959–1963. Zellwood, FL.

Hardesty, Nancy A. "For Men Only?" *Christianity Today*, July 17, 1964, 44.

"History of the Waorani." Association of the Women of the Ecuadorian Amazon, 2009. https://www.amwae.org/ (page discontinued).

"History." Overseas Ministries Study Center. Princeton Theological Seminary. Accessed October 2, 2020. https://www.omsc.org/.

Hitt, Russell. "Shaking the Gothard Chain." *Eternity*. September 1980. https://www.recoveringgrace.org/.

"Home." The Techbuilt House. Accessed January 7, 2020. https://thetechbuilthouse.com/.

Howard, David M. *Hammered as Gold*. New York: Harper & Row, 1969.

————. "Road to Urbana and Beyond." *Missio Nexus*. January 1, 1985. https://missionexus.org/.

Howard, Gail. "Gail Howard's Epilogue." Ecuador Travel Adventures. Accessed September 12, 2020. http://www.ecuadortraveladventures.com.

Howard, Lovelace Oden. Interview with Marcus Grodi. *The Journey Home Program*. November 19, 1999. https://chnetwork.org/.

Howard, Thomas. Interview with Ignatiusinsight.com, "Thomas Howard and the Kindly Light." *Ignatius Insight*. October 2004. ignatiusinsight.com/.

Hulshizer, Steve. "About Us." Plymouth Brethren Writings, 2004. http://www.plymouthbrethren.org/.

"IBLP History." Accessed September 1, 2020. https://iblp.org/.

Igel, Lee H., and Barron H. Lerner. "Moving Past Individual and 'Pure' Autonomy: The Rise of Family-Centered Patient Care." *AMA Journal of Ethics* 18 (January, 2016): 56–62.

"Income of Families and Persons in the United States: 1959." United States Census Bureau. January 5, 1961. https://www.census.gov/.

Internal Revenue Service. *Cumulative List of Organizations Described in Section 170© of the Internal Revenue Code of 1954.* Washington, DC: US Government Printing Office, 1969.

Iseman, Michael D. "Tuberculosis Therapy: Past, Present, and Future." *European Respiratory Journal* 20 (July 2002). https://doi.org/10.1183/09031936.02.00309102.

Jepsen, Diane R. "1978 EEWC Conference Recap." *Christian Feminism Today.* Accessed July 17, 2022. https://eewc.com/women-ministries-christ-report-conference/ (originally published in *Free Indeed* magazine).

"J. Oliver Buswell Jr." PCA Historical Center. Accessed July 16, 2020. https://www.pcahistory.org/.

"J. Oliver Buswell." Wheaton History A to Z. Accessed July 16, 2020. https://a2z.my.wheaton.edu/.

Juskewitch, Justin E., Carmen J. Tapia, and Anthony J. Widenbank. "Lessons from the Salk Polio Vaccine: Methods for and Risks of Rapid Translation." *Clinical and Translational Science* 3 (August 2010): 182–85. https://doi.org/10.1111/j.1752-8062.2010.00205.x.

Kane, Joe. *Savages.* New York: Vintage, 1996.

Kidd, Thomas S. *American Christians and Islam: Evangelical Culture and Muslims from the Colonial Period to the Age of Terrorism.* Princeton, NJ: Princeton University Press, 2009.

Killeen, Allison J. "Biography." *Finding Aid for Nancy A. Hardesty Papers, 1969–2002.* January 2007. https://library.columbia.edu/.

Krapohl, Robert H., and Charles H. Lippy. *The Evangelicals: A Historical, Thematic, and Biographical Guide.* Westport, CT: Greenwood, 1999.

Kübler-Ross, Elisabeth. *On Death and Dying.* New York: Macmillan, 1972.

Laats, Adam. "A February for Fundamentalism." I Love You but You're Going to Hell (blog). February 3, 2015. https://iloveyoubutyouregoingtohell.org/.

Larsen, Timothy. "Women in Public Ministry: A Historic Evangelical Distinctive." *Women, Ministry and the Gospel: Exploring New Paradigms.* Edited by Mark Husbands and Timothy Larsen. Downers Grove, IL: IVP Academic, 2007.

LeBlanc, Doug. "The Decline of Two Historic Magazines." *Christianity Today,* September 14, 1992, 74.

Leitch, Addison H. "So Far and so Fast." *Christianity Today,* April 26, 1968, 46.

———. "Ten Years in the Wrong Direction." *Christianity Today*, September 10, 1971, 55.

———. "The Included Middle." *Christianity Today*, February 2, 1973, 44.

———. "The Primary Task of the Church." *Christianity Today*, October 15, 1956, 11.

———. *Winds of Doctrine: The Theology of Barth, Brunner, Bonhoeffer, Bultmann, Niebuhr, Tillich.* Westwood, NJ: Revell, 1966.

Lemke, Rebecca. "Christianity's Response: A Brief History of Purity Culture." *The Scarlet Virgins.* Norman, OK: Anatole, 2017.

Lindsell, Harold. "Addison H. Leitch: 1908–1973." *Christianity Today*, October 12, 1973, 27.

Lizzie (pseudonym). "Exploited Innocence: Sexual Harassment at HQ," *Recovering Grace.* April 20, 2012. https://www.recoveringgrace.org/.

Long, Kathryn T. "Missionary Realities and the New Evangelicalism in Post-World War II America." *American Evangelicalism: George Marsden and the State of American Religious History.* Edited by Darren Dochuk, Thomas S. Kidd, and Kurt W. Peterson. Notre Dame, IN: University of Notre Dame Press, 2014.

Lyons, Julie. "Virgin Academy." *Dallas Observer*, July 20, 1995. https://www.dallasobserver.com/.

Marrie, Thomas J., ed. *Community-Acquired Pneumonia.* New York: Kluwer Academic, 2001.

Marshall, David L., with Ted T. Cable. *To Timbuktu and Beyond: A Missionary Memoir.* Bloomington, IN: WestBow, 2010.

Martinez, Raul (Qui'chi Patlan). "The Verbal Art of Kichwa Reclamation." *Anthropology News*, September 19, 2019. www.anthropology-news.org/.

"Martyred Missionaries' Widows Return to Carry on God's Work in the Ecuadorian Jungle." *Life*, May 20, 1957.

Matthews, Edward. "The Wesleyan Methodists and Slavery." *New York Times*, April 13, 1860. http://www.nytimes.com/.

Mayo Clinic Staff. "Alzheimer's Disease." December 8, 2018. https://www.mayoclinic.org/.

———. "Memory Loss: When to Seek Help." April 19, 2019. https://www.mayoclinic.org/.

Meyers, Laura Scott. Unnamed book review. *El Paso Herald-Post*, April 2, 1966, 6.

Meyers, Linda. Quoted by Elizabeth Erlandson. "Radio Role Model." *Back to the Bible Today.* September/October 1993, 3.

Minnery, Tom. "Gothard Staffers Ask Hard Questions and Press for Reforms." *Christianity Today*, February 6, 1981, 68.

Murray, John F., Dean E. Schraufnagel, and Philip C. Hopewell. "Treatment of Tuberculosis: A Historical Prospective." *American Thoracic Society Journals* 12 (December 2015). https://doi.org/10.1513/AnnalsATS.201509-632PS.

Nakajima, Satomi, Ito Masaya, Shirai Akemi, and Kanishi Takako. "Complicated Grief in Those Bereaved by Violent Death: The Effects of Post-Traumatic Stress Disorder on Complicated Grief." *Dialogues in Clinical Neuroscience* 14 (June 2012): 210–14.

"National Housing Act (1934)," The Living New Deal. Accessed July 29, 2020. https://livingnewdeal.org/.

Neely, Lois. *Come Up to This Mountain: The Miracle of Clarence W. Jones and the HCJB.* Wheaton, IL: Tyndale, 1980.

Nodjimbadem, Katie. "The Racial Segregation of American Cities Was Anything but Accidental." *Smithsonian Magazine*, May 30, 2017. https://www.smithsonianmag.com/.

Norton, H. Wilbert Sr. "The Student Foreign Missions Fellowship over Fifty-Five Years." *International Bulletin of Missionary Research* 17 (January 1993): 17–21. http://www.internationalbulletin.org/.

Orloff, Leslye E., and Paige Feldman. "Domestic Violence and Sexual Assault Public Policy Timeline Highlighting Accomplishments on Behalf of Immigrants and Women of Color." National Immigrant Women's Advocacy Project, American University, Washington College of Law. February 12, 2007. http://library.niwap.org/.

Orr, Carolyn. "Ecuador Quichua Phonology." *Studies in Ecuadorian Indian Languages: I.* Edited by Benjamin Elson. Norman, OK: Summer Institute of Linguistics, 1962.

"Our History," America's Keswick. Accessed July 22, 2017. https://americaskeswick.org/.

"Our History." Calvert School. Accessed October 13, 2020. https://www.calvertschoolmd.org/.

Oxford Languages. "Quechua." https://languages.oup.com/.

"Papers of Clarence Wesley Jones." Collection 349, Billy Graham Center Archives, Wheaton College, IL. Revised November 18, 2002. https://www2.wheaton.edu/.

"Papers of David Morris Howard Sr." Collection 484, Billy Graham Center Archives, Wheaton College, IL. Revised March 25, 2001. https://www2 .wheaton.edu/.

"Papers of Elisabeth Howard Elliot." Collection 278, Billy Graham Center Archives, Wheaton College, IL. https://web.archive.org/.

Pettengill, S. M. *Newspaper Directory and Advertiser's Handbook for 1878*. New York: S. M. Pettengill & Co., 1878.

Photographer unknown. Postcard showing the Francis Marion Hotel. http:// www.terapeak.com/ (site discontinued).

Praet, Istvan. "Humanity and Life as the Perpetual Maintenance of Specific Efforts: A Reappraisal of Animism." *Biosocial Becomings: Integrating Social and Biological Anthropology*. Edited by Tim Ingold and Gisli Palsson. Cambridge, UK: Cambridge University Press, 2014.

"Prudential Lines." Maritime Timetable Images. Modified June 23, 2019. http:// www.timetableimages.com/.

Ravndal, Christian M. "Journey into the Jungle." *Foreign Service Journal* 36, March 1959.

Records of EFMA. Collection 165, Billy Graham Center Archives, Wheaton College, IL. http://www2.wheaton.edu/.

Rexford, R. W., ed. *National Newspaper Directory and Gazetteer*. Boston: Pettingill, 1892.

Reyes, Eduardo Almeida. "La Danza Del Yumbo en la Comunidad De Rumicucho." *Propuesta Universitaria*, May 2, 2011. http://docenteconvoz.blogspot .com/.

Richards, Leverett G. "Backyard Eagles." *Popular Mechanics*, June 1961, 228.

Richland County, South Carolina, marriage license no. 009639. September 18, 1919, Ewell-DuBose. Accessed September 30, 2015. http://www.richland online.com/.

Ridley, David, ed. *Aspenland II: On Women's Lives and Work in Central Alberta*. Red Deer, Alberta, Canada: Central Alberta Regional Museums Network and Central Alberta Historical Society, 2003.

Robert, Dana Lee. *American Women in Mission: A Social History of Their Thought and Practice*. Macon, GA: Mercer University Press, 1997.

———. "Introduction." *Gospel Bearers, Gender Barriers*. New York: Orbis, 2002.

Rolandsen, Øystein H. and Nicki Kindersley. "The Nasty War: Organized Violence during the Anya–Nya Insurgency in South Sudan, 1963–72."

Journal of African History 60 (March 2019): 87–107. http://doi.org/10.1017/S0021853719000367.

Rosell, Garth M. *A Charge to Keep: Gordon-Conwell Theological Seminary and the Renewal of Evangelicalism*. Eugene, OR: Wipf & Stock, 2020.

Sanders, Coyne Stephen, and Tom Gilbert. *Desilu: The Story of Lucille Ball and Desi Arnaz*. New York: Quill, 1993.

"Santa Rosita, Grace Line Diesel Yacht Boats Ships Original Vintage Postcard." Amazon. Accessed August 24, 2020. https://www.amazon.com/.

Savage, Stephen E. *Rejoicing in Christ: The Biography of Robert Carlton Savage*. Reading, VT: Shadow Rock, 1990.

Scanzoni, Letha Dawson. "The Feminists and the Bible." *Christianity Today*, February 3, 1973, 10.

Scharf, J. Thomas, and Thompson Westcott. *History of Philadelphia, 1609–1884*. Philadelphia: L. H. Everts & Co, 1884.

Schindler, Tom. Cited in "News Feature." *Confident Living: A Ministry of Back to the Bible*. 1988, 32.

"Segregation in America: 'Dragging On and On.'" National Public Radio, February 18, 2011, https://www.npr.org/.

Semenchuk, Paul C. "The Ventnor Arrangement." SMS International. Accessed October 2, 2020. http://www.smsinternational.org/.

"Semiannual Supplement to the Cumulative List of Organizations Contributions to Which Are Deductible Under Section 170 of the Internal Revenue Code of 1954 Covering the Period of July–December 1962." *Internal Revenue Bulletin no. 1962–53*. December 31, 1962. https://books.google.com/.

Shelton, Wayne. "Truth Telling in Medicine: Problems Old and New." Bioethics Today. Albany Medical College. October 23, 2015. Accessed June 19, 2020. https://www.amc.edu/.

Shepard, Valerie Elliot. Personal Facebook page. January 13, 2017. No longer accessible.

———. Testimony to a women's group, Greenville, NC. November 2013. http://www.juanamikels.com/.

"Sherry Stanley Honored." *Atlanta Constitution*. March 7, 1962, 17.

"Sherry Stanley Inspired a Pre-nuptial Party Whirl." *Atlanta Constitution*. February 12, 1962, 18.

Siegel, Reva B. "'The Rule of Love': Wife Beating as Prerogative and Privacy." *Yale Law Journal* 105, no. 2117 (1995–1996). https://digitalcommons.law.yale.edu/.

Skinner, Mary. *If You Came Here to Live*. Bath, UK: Echoes of Service, 1976.

Smalley, Martha Lund. "Guide to the Student Volunteer Movement for Foreign Missions Records." *Archives at Yale*. 1980. https://archives.yale.edu/.

Snyder, Sarah. "The Gothard Ministry's Troubles." *The Atlanta Constitution*, October 11, 1980, 21.

Steinhaus, Mara, and Neetu John. "A Life Not Chosen: Early Marriage and Mental Health." International Center for Research on Women. July 5, 2018. https://www.icrw.org/.

Stidsen, Sille. *The Indigenous World 2007*. Copenhagen: IWGIA, 2007.

Strachan, Harry W. *Finding a Path: Stories from My Life*. Bloomington, IN: iUniverse, 2011.

Strickland, Darby A. *Domestic Abuse: Recognize, Respond, Rescue*. Phillipsburg, NJ: P&R, 2018.

Swart, Morrell F. *The Call of Africa: The Reformed Church in America Mission in the Sub-Sahara, 1948–1998*. Grand Rapids, MI: Eerdmans, 1998.

Thorkelson, Willmar. "Bible Seminar Thriving Despite Sex Scandal." *Minneapolis Star Tribune*, November 7, 1980, 10.

Tolley-Stokes, Rebecca. "Annie Trumbull Slosson." *Early American Nature Writers*. Edited by Daniel Patterson et al. Westport, CT: Greenwood Press, 2008, 321–27.

Tucker, Ruth A. "William Carey's Less-than-Perfect Family Life." *Christianity Today*. Accessed September 16, 2020. https://www.christianity today.com/.

"Tuition and Mandated Fees, Room and Board, and Other Educational Costs at Penn." 2003–. https://archives.upenn.edu/.

TWWK. "Kokoro Connect, Episode 10: Wholly Yours," *Beneath the Tangles: Connecting Anime and Belief in Open Community*. September 9, 2012. https://beneaththetangles.com/.

United States Census Bureau, Population Estimates Program, Population Division. "Historical National Population Estimates, July 1, 1900 to July 1, 1999." Modified June 28, 2000. https://www.census.gov/.

———. *Table MS-2. Estimated Median Age at First Marriage, by Sex: 1890 to the Present*. https://www.census.gov/data/tables/time-series/demo/families/marital.html.

———. *Figure MS-1b. Women's marital status*. https://www.census.gov/data/tables/time-series/demo/families/marital.html.

———. "1975". https://www.census.gov/data/tables/time-series/demo/popest /pre-1980-national.html.

United States Centers for Disease Control and Prevention. "Leading Causes of Death, 1900–1998." Accessed July 12, 2022. http://www.cdc.gov/.

"VaCountess Johnson: Volunteer Minister of Outreach." Staff, First United Methodist Church of Brunswick. https://fumcbrunswick.com/.

Van Der Puy, Abe C. "Through Gates of Splendor." *Reader's Digest*, August 1956, 56–75.

Wagner, Frederick, and William A. Dyrness. "Basic Youth Conflicts: A Closer Look." *Eternity*. November 1973. https://www.recoveringgrace.org/.

Wallis, Ethel Emily, and Mary Angela Bennett. *Two Thousand Tongues to Go: The Story of the Wycliffe Bible Translators*. New York: Harper & Brothers, 1959.

Whitten, Norman E., Dorothea Scott Whitten, and Alfonso Chango. "Return of the Yumbo: The Indigenous Caminata from Amazonia to Andean Quito." *American Ethnologist* 24, no. 2 (1997): 355–91. http://www.jstor.org/.

"Who 'Invented' the TV Dinner?" Library of Congress. November 19, 2019. https://www.loc.gov/.

"Who We Are." The Word of God Community. Accessed August 20, 2020. http://www.thewordofgodcommunity.org/.

Willard, W. Wyeth. *Fire on the Prairie: The Story of Wheaton College*. Wheaton, IL: Van Kampen, 1950.

Wismer, Janet Anderson. Speaking at Elisabeth Elliot's memorial service. July 26, 2015. https://www.youtube.com/.

Worrall, Margaret. *Calvert School: The First Century*. Baltimore, MD: Calvert School, 1996.

Worrall, Simon. "Anthropology beyond the Human: An Amazon Tribe's Deep Connection with the Rain Forest." *National Geographic*, August 4, 2014. www .nationalgeographic.com/.

Archives, Interviews, and Private Collections

Unless otherwise noted, all archival materials are from collection 278, papers of Elisabeth Howard Elliot, Billy Graham Center Archives, Wheaton College, Illinois.

"10th Anniversary Fun Facts." *Gateway to Joy* printed matter. Private collection.

Anonymous 1. Interview with author. May 22, 2020.

Austen, Marjorie. Interview with author. August 26, 2020.

Cavalier, Sally Shupert. Conversation with author. April 29, 2020.

Coley, Elna. Email to Ethelyn Eastman Schultz. October 6, 2017.

DuBose, Pierre Wilds Jr. Interview with author. April 18, 2014.

Elliot, Elisabeth. As told to Anne B. Sawyer. "Writing in the Shadow of the Almighty." *Confident Living*, December 1987, 36–37. Box 16, "My Life and Death."

———. Circular letter. January 1983. Box 5, folder 19.

———. Handwritten note at the top of a program from Church of St. Mary the Virgin. October 1, 1967. Box 16, folder 11.

———. "Head Down, Feet Up." Clipping from Gordon-Conwell Theological Seminary paper. March 1970. Box 5, folder 6.

———. Inscription in *The Music of His Promises*. Private collection.

———. Interview with Andrea Veres for Wheaton College "The Clip." January, 1992. VHS V1.

———. Letter to Ann Curtiss. March 10, 1980. Box 9, folder 4.

———. Letter to B. Clayton Bell. December 6, 1988. Box 9, folder 4.

———. Letter to Cameron Townsend, Rachel Saint, and Sam Saint. April 13, 1958. #15285, William Cameron Townsend Archives, Waxhaw, NC.

———. Letter to Cornell Capa. May 5, 1958. #16056, Townsend Archives.

———. Letters to Janet Anderson Wismer. May 28, 1992, February 21, 2001, March 28, 2001. Private collection.

———. Letter to Jim and Marti Hefley. March 10, 1980. Box 9, folder 4.

———. Letter to Marj Saint and Marilou McCully. October 18, 1958. Folder 6.

———. Letters to Rachel Saint. November 25 and December 20, 1957, and April 9, 1958. #13709, #13659, and #16092. Townsend Archives.

———. Marginal notes in *Daily Strength for Daily Needs*, Mary Wilder Tileston, September 1, 1994, January 6, 7, 11, 1999, April 16 and 17, 1999, November 18, 1999, June 15, 2001. Private collection.

Fields, the. Vol. 15, July 1952. Ford Dodge, IA: Walterick, 1952. Archives of *Missions* magazine/Christian Missions in Many Lands, Belmar, NJ.

Fields, the. Vol. 15, March 1952. Ford Dodge, IA: Walterick, 1952. Archives of *Missions* magazine/Christian Missions in Many Lands, Belmar, NJ.

Fields, the. Vol. 16, January 1953. Ford Dodge, IA: Walterick, 1952. Archives of *Missions* magazine/Christian Missions in Many Lands, Belmar, NJ.

Fields, the. Vol. 17, November 1954. Ford Dodge, IA: Walterick, 1952. Archives of *Missions* magazine/Christian Missions in Many Lands, Belmar, NJ.

Five Missionary Martyrs Fund Receipts. Records of the Evangelical Fellowship of Mission Agencies (EFMA). Collection 165, box 14, folder 1, and box 199, folders 7 and 8, Billy Graham Center Archives, Wheaton College, IL.

Gothard, Bill. Handouts and notes from Institute in Basic Youth Conflicts. September 1971. Private collection.

Hefley, Jim. Letter to Elisabeth Elliot. March 2, 1980. Box 9, folder 4.

Hostetter, Paul. Letters to Elisabeth Elliot. September 7 and September 14, 1968. Box 9, folder 2.

Houston, James M. Letter to Elisabeth Elliot. January 16, 1976. Box 9, folder 3.

Howard, Thomas. Letter to Harold and Luci Shaw. July 8 [no year]. Luci Shaw papers, SC-46, Wheaton College Archives, Wheaton College, IL.

Jones, Martin. Letter to Lars and Elisabeth, cc: Steve Nickel. February 2, 2001. Box 9, folder 6.

Lindskoog, John. Letter to Elisabeth Elliot. February 4, 1976. Box 9, folder 3.

Lingerman, Janet. Interview with author. January 31, 2014.

Long, Kathryn T. Email to author. July 1, 2019.

Moorestown Chronicle. "Philip E. Howard Jr. Third Generation of Family Now Editor Sunday School Times." January 1941. Clipping from Howard, "Omnipotent Hand." Private collection.

Morgan, Katherine. Letter to Philip E. Howard Jr. and Katharine Gillingham Howard. February 1, 1956. Box 4, folder 4.

Mounce, Robin. Interview with author. May 30, 2013.

O'Keefe, Karen. Interview with author. November 22, 2013.

Saint, Marj, quoting Elisabeth Elliot. Letter to Katharine Gillingham Howard, Philip E. Howard Jr., and Sam and Jeanne Saint. November 6, 1958. Box 4, folder 6.

Saint, Marj. Letter to Elisabeth Elliot. November 13, 1960. Box 4, folder 8.

Saint, Rachel. Letter to Lawrence Bradford Saint and Katherine Proctor Saint. October 9, 1958. Box 4, folder 6.

———. Letters to Elisabeth Elliot. December 5 and December 31, 1957. #13687 and #13633, Townsend Archives.

Schultz, Ethelyn Eastman. Interview with author. June 5, 2014.

Schultz-Rathbun, Carolyn. Interview with author. August 26, 2020.

Shuster, Robert. Email to author. July 1, 2015.

Staddon, Kendalyn Kowalchuk. Email to author. March 27, 2014.

"Tarkio College's Memorial Minute to Margaret Heslip Leitch." Papers of Addison H. Leitch, RG 405, Series 6: Miscellaneous 1946–1972, n.d. Box 2, folder 30, Eulogy for Margaret Leitch 1968, Presbyterian Historical Society, Philadelphia, PA.

Taylor, Clyde W. Letter to V. Raymond Edman and William K. Harrison Jr. Subject: "Conference with the 4 Widows in Quito, Ecuador, August 7, 1961." Records of EFMA. Collection 165, box 13, folder 31. Billy Graham Center Archives. Wheaton College, IL.

———. Letter to V. Raymond Edman and William K. Harrison Jr., July 28, 1966.

Trigg, Taisha N. Interview with author. October 29, 2018.

Voices from the Vineyard. 1952. Plymouth Brethren. Archives of *Missions* magazine/Christian Missions in Many Lands, Belmar, NJ.

Wilson, J. Christy Jr. Letter to Elisabeth Elliot. December 16, 1980. Box 9, folder 4.

Wismer, Janet Anderson. Email to author. September 30, 2020.

———. Form letter. November 1988. Private collection.

Notes

Preface
1. Anna Leszkiewicz, "Hermione Lee on How to Write a Life," *New Statesman*, October 21, 2020, https://www.newstatesman.com/; Robert A. Caro, *Working* (New York: Alfred A. Knopf, 2019), 83–84.
2. Catherine L. Albanese et al., *American Christianities: A History of Dominance and Diversity*, ed. Catherine A. Berkus and W. Clark Gilpin (Chapel Hill, NC: University of North Carolina Press, 2011), 12–17.

Prologue: To a Watching World
1. Associated Press, "5 U.S. Missionaries Are Believed Slain," *New York Times*, January 12, 1956; Associated Press, "Four Bodies Found in Ecuador," *New York Times*, January 13, 1956.
2. Scott Seegers, "In the Forests of Fear," *New York Times Magazine*, January 29, 1956, 17.

Chapter 1: Elisabeth Howard the Great
1. Katharine Gillingham Howard, "Upheld by His Righteous Omnipotent Hand," unpublished manuscript (May 12, 1980), typed, 54, private collection.
2. Howard, "Omnipotent Hand," 83.
3. Howard, "Omnipotent Hand," 96.
4. Howard, "Omnipotent Hand," 41.
5. Elisabeth Elliot, *Shaping of a Christian Family* (Grand Rapids, MI: Revell, 1992), 77.
6. Elliot, *Shaping of a Christian Family*, 55.
7. Despite his reluctance to take it on, Philip gave the job all he had while he was there. He was scrupulously honest about being on time, refused to leave even a minute before closing time, and worked at home when he was ill. The *SST* was a nondenominational publication, and Philip was noted for his commitment to preserving that ecumenicism. He used to quote Faber's hymn, "The love of God is broader / Than the measure of our mind," and he taught his children to appreciate the strengths of each denomination rather than criticizing the ways it differed from his own beliefs.
8. Howard, "Omnipotent Hand," 121.
9. Howard, "Omnipotent Hand," 133.
10. Elliot, *Shaping of a Christian Family*, 87.
11. Elliot, *Shaping of a Christian Family*, 90.
12. When Betty Howard was nine, there were forty-two boys in the neighborhood and one other girl, also age nine—her best friend, Essie McCutcheon. "She had me

panting to keep up as she raced through . . . backyards and alleyways. She stood my hair on end with her imaginative stories. . . . All that energy and imagination and know-how!" But that year, Essie died. Betty would mark the anniversary of Essie's death for the rest of her life. Elisabeth Elliot, *A Path through Suffering* (Ventura, CA: Regal, 2003), 21.

13. Elisabeth Elliot, "Some of My Best Friends Are Books," *Twelve Baskets of Crumbs* (New York: Christian Herald, 1976), 89.

14. Their father, Philip Eugene Howard Jr., wrote the editorial notes for the *SST* as well as devotional essays. Many of these essays were collected and published in two books. Like Philip, Charles Gallaudet Trumbull wrote for the *SST* for years and had at least two books published. Annie Trumbull Slosson, who died the year Betty was born, was a founding member of the New York Entomological Society and in her day, a well-known writer in the regionalist movement, outselling Henry James. Slosson's brother, Henry Clay Trumbull, in addition to almost thirty years of writing as the editor of the *SST*, had fifteen books published.

15. "Memory Book," 1938–1940, papers of Elisabeth Howard Elliot, collection 278, box 8, Billy Graham Center Archives, Wheaton College, IL.

16. Elliot, *Shaping of a Christian Family*, 122.

17. Elisabeth Elliot, interview by Robert Shuster, March 26, 1985, collection 278, tape T2, transcript.

Chapter 2: Be, Not Seem

1. Elisabeth Elliot, *The Shaping of a Christian Family* (Grand Rapids, MI: Revell, 1992), 223–24.

2. Elisabeth Elliot, "Miss Andy," *Elisabeth Elliot Newsletter*, September/October (Ann Arbor, MI: Servant, 1997).

3. Photographer(s) unknown, *Aerial view of Lake Margaret and Hampden Dubose Academy; Hasell Hall at the Hampden Dubose Academy; Ewell Hall patio at the Hampden Dubose Academy; Ewell Hall at the Hampden Dubose Academy; Fountain at the end of the formal gardens,* picture postcards, c. 1942; items no. NO44926, NO44935, NO44936, NO44937, NO44938, Florida Photographic Collection; State Archives of Florida, *Florida Memory*, https://floridamemory.com/.

4. Hampden DuBose Academy, *Esse*, yearbook, 1959, http://www.classmates.com/.

5. Mary Anne Phemister, *Lessons from a Broken Chopstick: A Memoir of a Peculiar Childhood* (Garland, TX: Hannibal, 2009), 78, 80–81.

6. Elisabeth Elliot, letter to mother, papers of Elisabeth Howard Elliot, collection 278, box 3, folder 2, Billy Graham Center Archives, Wheaton College, IL. Unless otherwise indicated, subsequent references to Elliot letters in chapter 2 are from collection 278, box 3.

7. Elliot, *Shaping of a Christian Family*, 215.

8. Jon Savage, *Teenage: The Creation of Youth Culture* (New York: Viking), 2007.

9. Elliot, *Shaping of a Christian Family*, 215.

10. Elliot was only five foot ten, but she had grown up hearing herself compared to her six-foot-tall father and was uncomfortably conscious of her height.

11. Although Elisabeth would later remember her teenage years as untroubled, her parents did not have the same perspective at the time. Tom would later remember, "People always looked at her as . . . a daunting figure. Even our parents." Dave would say that in high school, "she was very strong minded. Her making up her mind was not always in accord with how my parents felt. And I remember my mother telling

us later, sort of laughing as we were talking together about our childhood and so on, my mother said . . . there were times where they'd go to bed and be talking together in their bed, and my father would say, 'Well, I guess if we can raise five out of six, that's not a bad percentage.'" Thomas Howard, interview with author, November 6, 2014; David M. Howard, interview with author, November 9, 2016.

12. Elliot, letter to family, September 12, 1943, folder 2.
13. Elliot, letter to family, undated, folder 3.
14. Elliot, letter to parents, March 12, 1944, folder 2.
15. Elisabeth Elliot, *Love Has a Price Tag* (Ann Arbor, MI: Servant, 1979), 6.
16. Elliot, letter to mother, September 19, 1943, folder 2.
17. William Wordsworth, "Personal Talk IV," *The Poetical Works of William Wordsworth* (Paris: A. & W. Galignani, 1828), 118, as quoted by Elliot, letter to mother, January 31, 1944, folder 3.
18. Elliot, letter to mother, January 31, 1944, folder 3.
19. Elliot, letter to family, September 19, 1943, folder 2.
20. Mr. DuBose had an honorary doctorate from what was then Bob Jones College.
21. Elliot, letter to mother, January 12, 1944, folder 3.
22. Elliot, letter to family, October 18, 1943, folder 2.
23. Elliot, letter to parents, February 28, 1944, folder 3.
24. Elliot, letter to family, September 26, 1943, folder 2.
25. Elliot, letter to parents, February 6, 1944, folder 3.
26. Elliot, letter to parents, April 16, 1944, folder 3.
27. Elliot, letter to family, October 31, 1943, folder 2.
28. Elliot, letter to family, November 7, 1943, folder 2.
29. Elliot, letter to family, November 21, 1943, folder 2.
30. Elisabeth Howard Gren, interview with Robert Shuster, March 26, 1985, collection 278, tape T2, transcript, Billy Graham Center Archives, Wheaton College, IL.
31. David M. Howard, interview with Paul Ericksen, March 24, 1993, collection 484, tape T1, Billy Graham Center Archives, Wheaton College, IL.
32. Thomas Howard, interview with author, November 6, 2014.
33. Elliot, letter to parents, May 2, 1944, folder 3.
34. Phemister, *Broken Chopstick*, 80.
35. Elliot, letter to parents, February 20, 1944, folder 3.
36. Elliot, letter to parents, April 2, 194[4], folder 3.
37. Elliot, *Love Has a Price Tag*, 6.
38. Howard, "Omnipotent Hand," 168.
39. Phemister, *Broken Chopstick*, 93–94.
40. William F. Luck Sr. and 68x, "Hampden Dubose Academy, Zellwood, Fl," Hometown Forums.
41. Mickey Roberts Schmale, Jack Shuler, 68x, and trw, "Hampden Dubose Academy, Zellwood, Fl," Hometown Forums.

Chapter 3: For Christ and His Kingdom

1. David M. Howard, interview with author, September 9, 2016.
2. Ethelyn Eastman Schultz, email to author, August 31, 2017.
3. Donald Worster, *A River Running West: The Life of John Wesley Powell* (New York: Oxford University Press, 2001), 56.
4. Robert E. Webber, *The Secular Saint: A Case for Evangelical Social Responsibility* (Eugene, OR: Wipf & Stock, 2004), 173.

5. Jonathan Blanchard, "Public Men and Public Institutions of the Church," lecture, Ripley College, Cincinnati, OH, September 29, 1842.

6. George M. Marsden, *Fundamentalism and American Culture* (New York: Oxford University Press, 2006), 103.

7. Michael S. Hamilton and James A. Mathisen, "Faith and Learning at Wheaton College," in *Models for Christian Higher Education*, ed. Richard T. Hughes and William B. Adrian (Grand Rapids, MI: Eerdmans, 1997), 273.

8. Michael S. Hamilton, *The Fundamentalist Harvard: Wheaton College and the Continuing Vitality of American Evangelicalism* (PhD diss., University of Notre Dame, 1994), 33.

9. Duane Litfin, "Wheaton College President: On V. Raymond Edman, Wheaton's Fourth President," YouTube, from a speech delivered at Wheaton College chapel, January 11, 2010, https://www.youtube.com/.

10. Hamilton and Mathisen, "Faith and Learning at Wheaton," 275.

11. David M. Howard, *From Wheaton to the Nations* (Wheaton, IL: Wheaton College, n.d.), 25.

12. Todd M. Johnson and Gina A. Zurlo, eds., quoting A. T. Pierson, 1876, *World Christian Database* (Leiden/Boston: Brill, 2020), accessed April 2017.

13. Mary Slater, letter to Mr. Palmer and Friends, October 10, 1913, quoted in Dana L. Robert, *American Women in Mission: A Social History of Their Thought and Practice* (Macon, GA: Mercer University Press, 2005), 211.

14. Joel A. Carpenter, "Propagating the Faith Once Delivered: The Fundamentalist Missionary Enterprise, 1920–1945," in *Earthen Vessels, American Evangelicals, and Foreign Missions, 1880–1980*, ed. Joel A. Carpenter and Wilbert R. Shenk (Eugene, OR: Wipf & Stock, 2012), 119, 120.

15. Elliot, letter to parents, September 10, 1944, folder 3. Looking back as an adult, Elliot told an interviewer: "I always took the view throughout my life that wherever I was, I was the only person that didn't know what they were doing. Everybody else knew what they were doing and arriving here was scary and I figured everybody else in the freshman class knew exactly what they were going to do and where they were going. I didn't know anything so I depended heavily, heavily on my big sister to help me out on that." Elisabeth Elliot, interview with Robert Shuster, March 26, 1985, collection 278, tape T2, transcript, Billy Graham Center Archives, Wheaton College, IL, accessed July 21, 2020, https://www2.wheaton.edu/.

16. Elliot, letter to parents, September 10, 1944, folder 3.

17. Elliot, letter to mother, September 20, 1944, folder 3.

18. Elliot, handwritten note on bottom of typed page entitled "Squirm, Worm," collection 278, box 3, folder 3.

19. Elliot, letter to family, October 8, 1944, folder 3.

20. Elliot, letter to family, May 5, 1946, folder 5.

21. Elliot, letter to family, October 27, 1946, folder 5.

22. Elliot, letter to family, April 29, 1948, folder 7. Amy Carmichael died January 18, 1951, so she and Betty were briefly contemporaries. Just before her Wheaton graduation Betty wrote to Carmichael "simply expressing my profound appreciation for all her books have meant to me. Eternity alone can tell what they've done in my life." Elliot, letter to mother, May 25, 1948, folder 7.

23. Elliot, letter to family, April 10, 1945, folder 4.

24. Elliot, letter to family, April 29, 1945, folder 4.

25. Elliot, letter to family, May 12, 1945, folder 4.

26. Elliot, letter to family, September 30, 1945, folder 4.
27. Elliot, interview with Shuster, tape T2.
28. Thomas Howard, interview with author, October 2013.
29. Elliot, letter to family, November 11, 1945, folder 4.
30. Elliot, undated, submitted to a *Kodon* poetry contest, collection 278, box 3, folder 6.
31. Elisabeth Elliot, introduction to *A Chance to Die* (Grand Rapids, MI: Revell, 1996).
32. Elliot, letter to family, January 20, 1947, folder 6; Miss Catherine Cumming was Betty's Sunday school teacher, dorm mother, and friend.
33. Elliot, letter to family, September 12, 1944, folder 3.
34. Elliot, letter to family, January 26, 1945, folder 4.
35. Elliot, letter to family, October 9, 1945, folder 4.
36. Elliot, letter to family, December 2, 1945, folder 4.
37. Elliot, letter to family, March 14, 1945, folder 4.
38. Cited in Valerie Elliot Shepard, *Devotedly* (Nashville, TN: B&H, 2019), 7–8.
39. Elliot, letter to family, December 11, 1944, folder 4.
40. Elliot, letter to family, November 3, 1946, folder 5.
41. Elliot, letter to mother, February 2, 1947, folder 6.
42. Elliot, letters to family, September 20 and 29, 1946, folder 5.
43. Elliot, letter to family, January 13, 1946, folder 5.
44. Elliot, letter to family, September 17, 1945, folder 4.
45. Elliot, letter to mother, May 27, 1945, folder 4.
46. Elliot, letter to family, January 7, 1945, folder 4.
47. Elliot, letter to family, May 5, 1946, folder 5.
48. Elliot, letter to family, May 14, 1947, folder 6.
49. Elliot, letter to family, November 20, 1946, folder 5.
50. Elliot, letter to family, October 6, 1946, folder 5.
51. Shepard, *Devotedly*, 5.
52. Shepard, *Devotedly*, 5.
53. Elliot, letter to family, April 20, 1947, folder 6.
54. Shepard, *Devotedly*, 8.
55. Shepard, *Devotedly*, 10.
56. Elliot, letter to family, April 15, 1947, folder 6.
57. Elliot, letter to family, July 6, 1947, folder 6.
58. Elliot, letter to mother, September 14, 1947, folder 6.
59. She would later say that debate had been "by far the most important training" for her work as a public speaker that she got at Wheaton. Elliot, interview with Shuster, tape T2.
60. Elliot, letter to family, February 17, 1948, folder 7.
61. Shepard, *Devotedly*, 9.
62. Elliot, letter to family, January 13, 1948, folder 7.
63. Elliot, letter to family, March 16, 1948, folder 7.
64. Elliot, letter to family, January 20, 1948, folder 7.
65. Elisabeth Elliot, *Passion and Purity* (Grand Rapids, MI: Revell, 1984), 23.
66. Elliot, letter to family, December 2, 1947, folder 6.
67. Elliot, letter to family, December 14, 1947, folder 6.
68. Elliot, letter to family, December 8, 1947, folder 6.
69. Elliot, *Passion and Purity*, 27.
70. Elliot, letter to family, October 5, 1947, folder 6.
71. Elliot, letter to family, October 20, 1947, folder 6.

72. Elliot, letter to family, November 4, 1947, folder 6.

73. Elisabeth Elliot, *The Shaping of a Christian Family* (Grand Rapids, MI: Revell, 1992), 229.

74. Elliot, letter to family, January 13, 1948, folder 7.

75. Elliot, interview with Shuster, tape T2.

76. Elliot, letter to family, February 11, 1948, folder 7.

77. Eleanor Vandevort, interview with author, November 7, 2014.

78. Shepard, *Devotedly*, 3.

79. Elliot, letter to family, January 20, 1948, folder 7.

80. Elliot, *Passion and Purity*, 34.

81. Elliot, letter to family, November 11, 1947, folder 6.

82. Elliot, letter to mother, September 29, 1947, folder 6.

83. Thomas Howard, interview with author, December 14, 2013.

84. Thomas Howard, interview with author, October, 2013.

85. Elliot, letter to family, October 20, 1947, folder 6.

86. Elliot, letter to family, January 8, 1947, folder 6.

87. Elliot, letter to mother, October 30, 1947, folder 6.

88. Elliot, letter to family, March 7, 1948, folder 7.

89. Elisabeth Elliot, *Shadow of the Almighty* (New York: Harper & Brothers, 1958), 49.

90. David M. Howard, interview with author, September 9, 2016.

91. Elliot, *Shadow of the Almighty*, 51.

92. Elliot, *Passion and Purity*, 32–33.

93. Elliot, *Passion and Purity*, 34.

94. Elliot, letter to family, January 30, 1948, folder 7.

95. Elliot, *Passion and Purity*, 34.

96. Elliot, letter to family, January 30, 1948, folder 7.

97. Elliot, *Passion and Purity*, 33, 43.

98. Shepard, *Devotedly*, 11.

99. Elliot, letter to mother, May 31, 1948, folder 7.

100. Elliot, *Passion and Purity*, 33.

101. Elliot, letter to family, April 6, 1948, folder 7.

102. Elliot, letter to family, February 17, 1946, folder 5.

103. Elliot, letter to family, April 6, 1948, folder 7.

104. The words *colored* and *Negro* were both polite terms in use by black Americans in the 1940s, but the word Betty chose had been widely used with intent to harm for more than a hundred years by the time she was at Wheaton. Randall Kennedy, *Nigger: The Strange Career of a Troublesome Word* (New York: Vintage, 2003), 4; Elliot, letter to family, March 18, 1945, folder 4; Elliot, letter to family, July 20, 1947, folder 6; Elliot, letter to family, April 6, 1948, folder 7; Elliot, letters to family, July 22 and October 29, 1976, box 5, folder 12; Elliot, letter to family, August 25, 1977, box 5, folder 13; Elliot, letters to family, April 4, 17, and 28, 1978, box 5, folder 14.

105. Elliot, letter to mother, May 31, 1948, box 3, folder 7.

106. Elliot, *Passion and Purity*, 44, 49.

107. Elliot, *Passion and Purity*, 54.

108. Katharine Gillingham Howard, "Upheld by His Righteous Omnipotent Hand," unpublished manuscript (May 12, 1980), typed, 54, private collection, 176.

109. Shepard, *Devotedly*, 13, 14.

110. Elliot, interview with Shuster, tape T2.

111. Elliot, letter to family, November 18, 1947, folder 6.

Chapter 4: Red Mud and Hoar Frost

1. The Summer Institute of Linguistics, Camp Wycliffe brochure for Fifteenth Session, Summer 1948, on the campus of the University of Oklahoma, 5–6.
2. Elisabeth Elliot, *Shadow of the Almighty* (New York: Harper & Brothers, 1958), 50, 57.
3. Elisabeth Elliot, letter to family, June 16, 1948, papers of Elisabeth Howard Elliot, collection 278, box 3, folder 8, Billy Graham Center Archives, Wheaton College, IL. Unless otherwise indicated, subsequent references to Elliot letters in chapter 4 are from collection 278, box 3.
4. Valerie Elliot Shepard, *Devotedly* (Nashville, TN: B&H, 2019), 17.
5. Elisabeth Elliot, *Passion and Purity* (Grand Rapids, MI: Revell, 1984), 51–52, 88.
6. Shepard, *Devotedly*, 17.
7. Elliot, letter to family, July 2, 1948, folder 8.
8. Elliot, letter to family, June 16, 1948, folder 8.
9. Elliot, letter to family, July 12, 1948, folder 8.
10. Elliot, letters to family, June 16 and 23, 1948, folder 8.
11. Elliot, letter to family, August 10, 1948, folder 8.
12. Elliot, letter to family, June 23, 1948, folder 8.
13. Elliot, letter to family, July 20, 1948, folder 8.
14. Elliot, letter to family, August 10, 1948, folder 8.
15. Elliot, letter to family, July 20, 1948, folder 8.
16. Elliot, *Passion and Purity*, 70, 87.
17. Elisabeth Elliot, interview with Robert Shuster, March 26, 1985, collection 278, tape T2, transcript, Billy Graham Center Archives, Wheaton College, IL, accessed July 21, 2020, https://www2.wheaton.edu/; Elliot, letter to family, July 20, 1948.
18. Elliot, letter to family, August 5, 1947, folder 6.
19. Elliot, letter to family, July 12, 1948, folder 8.
20. Elliot, letter to family, August 4, 1948, folder 8.
21. Elliot, letter to family, July 12, 1948, folder 8.
22. Elliot, letter to family, July 26, 1948, folder 8.
23. Shepard, *Devotedly*, 23.
24. Elliot, letter to mother, September 27, 1948, folder 9.
25. Elliot, *Passion and Purity*, 118.
26. Shepard, *Devotedly*, 25.
27. Elliot, letters to family, March 11, 1949, folder 10, and undated, from context, likely October 1948, folder 9.
28. Timothy Wray Callaway, *Training Disciplined Soldiers for Christ: The Influence of American Fundamentalism on Prairie Bible Institute (1922-1960)* (Bloomington, IN: WestBow, 2013), xxxvi.
29. Elliot, letters to family, October 6 and 13, 1948, folder 9.
30. Elliot, letter to family, November 4, 1948, folder 9.
31. Elliot, letter to family, July 26, 1948, folder 8.
32. Elliot, letter to family, December 9, 1948, folder 9.
33. Elliot, letter to family, December 9, 1948, folder 9.
34. Elliot, letter to family, December 1, 1948, folder 9.
35. Elliot, letter to family, January 5, 1949, folder 10.
36. Elliot, letter to mother, November 20, 1948, folder 9.
37. Elliot, letter to family, December 1, 1948, folder 9.
38. Elliot, letter to mother, November 20, 1948, folder 9.

39. Elliot, letter to family, December 1, 1948, folder 9.

40. Elliot, letter to family, November 4, 1948, folder 9.

41. Elisabeth Elliot, "Notes on Open Letters: Conscience and Confession," *Sunday School Times*, October 23, 1948, 922, 924–25.

42. Callaway, *Disciplined Soldiers*, 313, 347.

43. L. E. Maxwell, *Born Crucified* (Chicago, IL: Moody, 2010), 40–41, 50.

44. L. E. Maxwell, *Crowded to Christ* (Grand Rapids, MI: Eerdmans, 1950), 77, cited in Callaway, *Disciplined Soldiers*, 235.

45. Elliot, letter to family, October 13, 1948, folder 9.

46. Elliot, letter to family, October 13, 1948, folder 9.

47. *The Free Library*, s.v. "The legacy of Leslie E. Maxwell," accessed July 5, 2018, https://www.thefreelibrary.com/.

48. Elliot, letter to family, January 5, 1949, folder 10.

49. Elliot, letter to family, December 9, 1948, folder 9.

50. Callaway, *Disciplined Soldiers*, 339.

51. Ruth Dearing and James Enns, "Prairie Bible Institute," Central Alberta Museums, accessed August 20, 2020, https://www.unlockthepast.ca/.

52. Timothy Larsen, "Evangelicalism's Strong History of Women in Ministry," *Reformed Journal*, August 31, 2017, https://reformedjournal.com/.

53. Elliot, *Passion and Purity*, 118.

54. Elliot, letter to mother, October 19, 1948, folder 9. The rest of this handwritten letter is in cursive, but the words "desperately wicked" are set out in small caps for emphasis.

55. Elliot, letter to family, November 20, 1948, folder 9.

56. Shepard, *Devotedly*, 35.

57. Elliot, *Shadow of the Almighty*, 95.

58. Shepard, *Devotedly*, 52.

59. Shepard, *Devotedly*, 52.

60. Shepard, *Devotedly*, 54, 58.

61. Elliot, letter to family, March 9, 1949, folder 10.

62. Shepard, *Devotedly*, 49.

63. John Anderson Barbour, *They That Be Wise: The Story of the Canadian Sunday School Mission* (Winnipeg, Manitoba, Canada: Hull, 1951), 34.

64. Elliot, letter to family, March 9, 1949, folder 10.

65. Shepard, *Devotedly*, 49.

66. Elliot, letter to family, March 9, 1949, folder 10.

67. The phrase "thrust out" appears repeatedly in missionary writing from this and earlier time periods. It appears to come from the original Amplified Bible translation of Matt. 9:37–38, in which Jesus says to his disciples, "The harvest is indeed plentiful, but the laborers are few. So pray to the Lord of the harvest to force out and thrust laborers into His harvest." Betty's use of the phrase highlights the cultural assumption that foreign missions are the highest form of Christian work. She is done with school and will be working as a missionary—even as a missionary in another country—but she still sees leaving the North American continent as the real work and her time with the CSSM as a training ground. Elliot, letter to family, March 12, 1949, folder 10.

68. Elliot, letter to family, March 9, 1949, folder 10.

69. Elliot, letter to family, April 17, 1949, folder 10.

70. In contrast to this "spiritualizing," Betty said, the Bible's approach to biography "forces men into the white light of eternal Truth, exposing the naked soul in rugged and stark reality. There is little of the glow of sentimentalism—they are not muffled 'in loving memory.'" Elliot, letter to family, November 4, 1948, folder 9.

71. Elliot, letter to family, February 28, 1949, folder 10.

72. Elliot, *Passion and Purity*, 50; Elliot, *Shadow of the Almighty*, 88.

73. Elliot, *Shadow of the Almighty*, 49.

74. Elliot, letter to family, May 9, 1949, folder 10.

75. Elisabeth Elliot, *Love Has a Price Tag* (Ann Arbor, MI: Servant, 1979), 139.

76. Elliot, letter to family, May 9, 1949, folder 10.

77. Elliot, letter to family, May 9, 1949, folder 10.

78. Elliot, letters to family, May 14 and June 10, 1949, folder 10.

79. Elliot, letter to family, May 20, 1949, folder 10.

80. Elliot, letter to family, July 25, 1949, folder 10.

81. Elliot, letter to family, May 14, 1949, folder 10.

82. Elliot, *Shadow of the Almighty*, 98.

83. Shepard, *Devotedly*, 60.

84. Elliot, letter to family, March 31, 1949, folder 10.

85. Shepard, *Devotedly*, 62.

86. Shepard, *Devotedly*, 62.

87. Elliot, letter to family, undated, summer 1949, folder 10.

88. Elliot, letter to family, undated, summer 1949, folder 10.

89. Elliot, letter to mother, June 9, 1949, folder 10.

90. Elliot, letter to family, May 20, 1949, folder 10.

91. Elliot, letter to family, July 13, 1949, folder 10.

92. Elliot, letter to family, July 13, 1949, folder 10.

93. Elliot, letter to family, July 25, 1949, folder 10.

94. Elliot, *Shadow of the Almighty*, 105.

95. Shepard, *Devotedly*, 64.

96. Elliot, *Passion and Purity*, 139; Elliot, letter to family, August 7, 1949, folder 10.

97. Shepard, *Devotedly*, 71.

98. Shepard, *Devotedly*, 72; Elliot, *Passion and Purity*, 143.

99. Elisabeth Elliot, ed., *The Journals of Jim Elliot* (Grand Rapids, MI: Revell, 2008), 154–56.

100. Elliot, letter to family, dated September 14, 1949, but actually September 15, 1949, folder 10.

101. Things had been serious enough that at least one man had withdrawn his financial support from InterVarsity Christian Fellowship, which was proposing to employ Dave Howard after graduation, after hearing of the way Jim, Dave, and some others had behaved during the renaissance.

102. Shepard, *Devotedly*, 74–75, 77.

103. Shepard, *Devotedly*, 77.

104. Shepard, *Devotedly*, 78.

105. Shepard, *Devotedly*, 79–80.

106. Elliot, *Passion and Purity*, 136.

107. Shepard, *Devotedly*, 82.

108. Shepard, *Devotedly*, 82.

109. Shepard, *Devotedly*, 83.

110. Shepard, *Devotedly*, 83.

111. Shepard, *Devotedly*, 84.
112. Shepard, *Devotedly*, 85.
113. Shepard, *Devotedly*, 82.
114. Shepard, *Devotedly*, 100.
115. Elliot, *Shadow of the Almighty*, 118.
116. Elliot, letter to family, February 16, 1950, folder 11.
117. Elliot, letter to family, March 5, 1950, folder 11.
118. Elliot, letter to family, January 24, 1950, folder 11.
119. Elliot, letter to family, April 17, 1950, folder 11.
120. Elliot, letter to family, March 22, 1950, folder 11.
121. Elliot, letter to family, March 22, 1950, folder 11.
122. Elliot, letter to family, February 26, 1950, folder 11.
123. Shepard, *Devotedly*, 104.
124. David M. Howard, interview with author, November 15, 2013.
125. Shepard, *Devotedly*, 73, 80.
126. David M. Howard, interview with author, November 15, 2013.
127. Jim wrote in his journal in the summer of 1949, "I sense tonight that my desires to be great are likely to frustrate God's intents for good to be done through me." Elliot, *Shadow of the Almighty*, 106.
128. As quoted in Elliot, *Shadow of the Almighty*, 129. Likely Jim's remembering of the American Standard Version.
129. Elisabeth Elliot, *Through Gates of Splendor* (New York: Harper & Brothers, 1957), 21.
130. The summer of 1951 Betty worked at InterVarsity's Pioneer Camp near Port Sydney, Ontario. The job appears to have lasted six or eight weeks. Although Dave was working for InterVarsity at the time, he recalls that Betty likely found out about the job through Phil, who had been heavily involved with Pioneer Camp himself. There is no record in Betty's letters of why her application to the SIM was not accepted or when she made the decision to turn her focus to the Solomon Islands. Dave does not remember her discussing it with the family, saying she was a private person.
131. Shepard, *Devotedly*, 116.
132. Elliot, *Shadow of the Almighty*, 151, 152.
133. Shepard, *Devotedly*, 148, 149.
134. Elliot, *Journals of Jim Elliot*, 344.
135. Shepard, *Devotedly*, 149.
136. Elliot, *Passion and Purity*, 151, 155, 156, 158.
137. Shepard, *Devotedly*, 88.
138. Elliot, *Journals of Jim Elliot*, 191.
139. Elliot, *Journals of Jim Elliot*, 77.
140. Elliot, *Journals of Jim Elliot*, 190–91.
141. Elliot, *Journals of Jim Elliot*, 188.
142. Elliot, *Journals of Jim Elliot*, 268.
143. Beth L. Bailey, *From the Front Porch to the Back Seat: Courtship in Twentieth-Century America* (Baltimore, MD: Johns Hopkins University Press, 1989), 88, 98.
144. Elliot, *Journals of Jim Elliot*, 190–91.
145. Elliot, *Passion and Purity*, 145.
146. Bailey, *Front Porch to Back Seat*, 90.
147. Elliot, *Passion and Purity*, 93.
148. Ken Fleming, *Peter Fleming: A Man of Faith* (Dubuque, IA: ECS Ministries, 2017), 29.
149. David M. Howard, interview with author, November 15, 2013.

150. Olive Fleming Liefeld, *Unfolding Destinies: The Ongoing Story of the Auca Mission* (Grand Rapids, MI: Discovery, 1998), 73.

151. Elliot, *Journals of Jim Elliot*, 344.

152. Elliot, *Journals of Jim Elliot*, 349.

153. Elliot, *Passion and Purity*, 150.

154. Elliot, *Shadow of the Almighty*, 154.

155. Shepard, *Devotedly*, 158.

156. Shepard, *Devotedly*, 204.

157. Elisabeth Elliot, *These Strange Ashes* (New York: Harper & Row, 1975), 2.

158. Shepard, *Devotedly*, 166.

159. Shepard, *Devotedly*, 173.

160. "A Great Woman Has Gone from Us," *The Elisabeth Elliot Newsletter*, January/February (Ann Arbor, MI: Servant, 2001).

161. Shepard, *Devotedly*, 174.

162. Elliot, letter to family, January 12, 1952, folder 12.

163. Shepard, *Devotedly*, 176.

164. Shepard, *Devotedly*, 180.

165. Elliot, letter to family, April 5, 1952, box 4, folder 1.

Chapter 5: In a Different Time, in a Different Place

1. Elisabeth Elliot, letter to family, April 15, 1952, papers of Elisabeth Howard Elliot, collection 278, box 4, folder 1, Billy Graham Center Archives, Wheaton College, IL. Unless otherwise indicated, subsequent references to Elliot letters in chapter 5 are from collection 278, box 4, folder 1.

2. Elliot, letter to family, April 15, 1952.

3. Elisabeth Elliot, *No Graven Image* (New York: Harper & Row, 1966), 2.

4. Elliot, letter to family, April 15, 1952.

5. Valerie Elliot Shepard, *Devotedly* (Nashville, TN: B&H, 2019), 187.

6. Elliot, letter to family, April 16, 1952.

7. Shepard, *Devotedly*, 188.

8. Elliot, letter to family, April 16, 1952.

9. This is exactly what it sounds like: hot chocolate, with pieces of cheese on top instead of marshmallows. The cheese is mild and new, in texture somewhat like cheese curds or mozzarella. As it melts it sinks to the bottom of the mug, and one eats it with a spoon.

10. Elisabeth Elliot, ed., *The Journals of Jim Elliot* (Grand Rapids, MI: Revell, 2008), 402.

11. Pete Fleming, quoted in Olive Fleming Liefeld, *Unfolding Destinies: The Ongoing Story of the Auca Mission* (Grand Rapids, MI: Discovery, 1998), 98.

12. Elliot, letter to family, June 17, 1952.

13. Elliot, letter to family, May 23, 1952.

14. Elliot, letter to family, June 23, 1952.

15. Elliot, letter to family, May 1, 1952.

16. Elliot, letter to family, May 23, 1952.

17. Elliot, letter to family, May 17, 1952.

18. Elliot, letter to family, June 10, 1952.

19. Elisabeth Elliot, *Passion and Purity* (Grand Rapids, MI: Revell, 1984), 60.

20. Elliot, *Journals of Jim Elliot*, 379.

21. Elliot, *Journals of Jim Elliot*, 379.

22. Elliot, letter to family, May 1, 1952.

23. Elliot, *Journals of Jim Elliot*, 388–89.
24. Elliot, *Journals of Jim Elliot*, 390.
25. Elliot, *Journals of Jim Elliot*, 406.
26. Elliot, letter to family, June 10, 1952. Wilfred Tidmarsh used the word *Yumbo* to refer to the Kichwa, and Betty must have picked it up from him. Miguel Cabello de Balboa (1500s) and Juan de Velasco (1700) both wrote of a people group they called the Yumbo, the former of a group living in the Andes, the latter of a group in the Amazon. Historian Eduardo Almeida Reyes identifies this latter group as the ancestors of the Amazonian Kichwa people with whom Tidmarsh had lived, but the Yumbo themselves appear to have faded into history, their healing knowledge and their role in connecting far-flung regions through travel and trade remembered largely in a costumed dance that bears their name.
27. Betty's letters often refer to him as "Dr. Tidmarsh." He had a PhD in geology.
28. Liefeld, *Unfolding Destinies*, 104–5.
29. Elisabeth Elliot, *These Strange Ashes* (New York: Harper & Brothers, 1975), 14–15.
30. Elliot, *Journals of Jim Elliot*, 375.
31. Elliot, *Passion and Purity*, 161.
32. Elliot, letter to family, May 11, 1952.
33. Liefeld, *Unfolding Destinies*, 110.
34. Elliot, *Journals of Jim Elliot*, 402.
35. Liefeld, *Unfolding Destinies*, 113.
36. Olive Fleming Liefeld, interview with author, April 4, 2014.
37. Liefeld, *Unfolding Destinies*, 107–8.
38. Elliot, *Journals of Jim Elliot*, 393.
39. Elliot, *Journals of Jim Elliot*, 394.
40. Elliot, letter to family, June 5, 1952.
41. Elliot, *Journals of Jim Elliot*, 394.
42. Elliot, *Journals of Jim Elliot*, 385, 388, 395–96, 400.
43. Elliot, *Journals of Jim Elliot*, 406–7.
44. He was also an extrovert. During his senior year at Wheaton he wrote, "I am worse than a social animal; I'm a social fiend—I love to be with a gang." Betty would write of him to her mother in the summer of 1953, "Thank you so much for the prints of Jim and me. Doesn't he take wonderful pictures? It's because he's an extrovert and unselfish." Elliot, *Journals of Jim Elliot*, 126; Elliot, letter to family, July 31, 1953.
45. Elliot, *Journals of Jim Elliot*, 403.
46. This difference in processing styles is apparent even in the early days of their relationship. An editorial note in *The Journals of Jim Elliot* records that on May 31, 1948, Jim told Betty that he loved her. The journals hold no record of thoughts about her or of any plans to talk to her prior to that date. This suggests that his decision to share his feelings was not premeditated. And his first journal entry that mentions her (written more than a week after their conversation) says merely, "Mind has been muddy about Betty H. lately and have had trouble in concentration." This suggests, first, that their conversation may not have been as momentous for him as it was for her and, second, that his position in regard to their relationship was not as settled as she had understood it to be. Together with his opening words as recorded in *Passion and Purity*—"We've got to get squared away on how we feel about each other"—these things suggest that what sounded to Betty like a considered declaration of love (which, in turn, according to her family culture, should have meant that he loved her enough to marry her) may have been his attempt to start a

dialogue so that he could decide what to do about his feelings of attraction. Elliot, *Journals of Jim Elliot*, 64; Elliot, *Passion and Purity*, 93.

47. Elliot, *Journals of Jim Elliot*, 386–87.
48. Elliot, *Journals of Jim Elliot*, 390.
49. Elliot, *Journals of Jim Elliot*, 403.
50. Elliot, *Journals of Jim Elliot*, 380.
51. David M. Howard, interview with author, November 15, 2013.
52. Elliot, *Journals of Jim Elliot*, 85, 90, 110.
53. Shepard, *Devotedly*, 54.
54. Elliot, *Journals of Jim Elliot*, 139.
55. Shepard, *Devotedly*, 67.
56. Elliot, *Journals of Jim Elliot*, 149.
57. Elliot, *Journals of Jim Elliot*, 153, 155–56.
58. Elliot, *Journals of Jim Elliot*, 261, 342.
59. Elliot, *Journals of Jim Elliot*, 344, 346, 349.
60. In the fall of 1952, remembering his visit to Birdsong on the way to the East Coast for fundraising, he wrote, "My naiveté and absolute lack of direction or plan in coming to Moorestown amaze me now!" Valerie Elliot Shepard, *Devotedly*, 217, 218.
61. Elisabeth Elliot, *Through Gates of Splendor* (New York: Harper & Brothers, 1957), 28.
62. Shepard, *Devotedly*, 205.
63. Elliot, letter to family, August 31, 1952.
64. Biography was a favorite genre for Betty. After reading a life of nineteenth-century English poet and hymn writer Frances Ridley Havergal in 1951, Betty had written in her journal, "It did what other Christian biographies have done—deepened my hunger for knowing Christ in His fullness, for living wholly 'unto Him who died for us.' I am impressed, always, upon reading of someone who lived a holy life, with the reflection, 'What would be written of me, were I to die today?'" Shepard, *Devotedly*, 129.
65. Elliot, letter to family, October 9, 1952.
66. Elisabeth Elliot, *Shadow of the Almighty* (New York: Harper & Brothers, 1958), 176.
67. Shepard, *Devotedly*, 215.
68. Elliot, letter to family, September 22, 1952.
69. Elliot, letter to family, October 9, 1952.
70. Elliot, letter to family, October 16, 1952.
71. Elliot, letter to family, October 23, 1952.
72. Elliot, letter to family, October 16, 1952.
73. Elliot, letter to family, July 8, 1952.
74. Elliot, letter to family, July 8, 1952.
75. Sheila V. Leech, *God Knows What I'm Doing Here* (Milton Keynes, UK: Authentic Media Ltd., 2017), loc. 568, Kindle.
76. Elliot, *Strange Ashes*, 9.
77. Elliot, letter to family, July 8, 1952.
78. Elliot, letter to family, October 31, 1952.
79. Elliot, letter to family, October 31, 1952.
80. Elliot, *Gates of Splendor*, 31.
81. Elliot, box 4, folder 1. Elisabeth Elliot would marry Addison Leitch in 1969.
82. Tsáchila means "true people," and their language is Tsafiki, "true words." *These Strange Ashes* calls the Tsáchila "Colorados," meaning "dyed red." This name was used by the Spanish Dominicans who came to the area in the 1700s because the Tsáchila dyed their skin and hair red with parts of the achiote plant.

83. Elliot, *Strange Ashes*, 63.

84. It seems likely that this was Bill Cathers, since he was the closest missionary to San Miguel.

85. Elliot, *Strange Ashes*, 105–6, 110–11.

86. Elliot, letter to family, November 7, 1952.

87. Shepard, *Devotedly*, 224.

88. Ondina E. González and Justo L. González, *Christianity in Latin America: A History* (Cambridge, UK: Cambridge University Press, 2008), 170.

89. Elliot, letter to family, May 23, 1952.

90. Elliot, letter to family, September 25, 1952.

91. Amy Carmichael, *Gold Cord* (Fort Washington, PA: Christian Literature Crusade, 1932), 31.

92. Nancy Jiwon Cho argues that Amy Carmichael "attempted to articulate an indigenous Indian theology" in her writing through "obervations" of "landscape, fauna, and flora." Nancy Jiwon Cho, "Prophylactic, Anti-paedophile Hymn-writing in Colonial India: An Introduction to Amy Carmichael (1867–1951) and her Missionary Writings," *The Modern Language Review*, vol. 104 (April 2009): 353–74 (363).

93. Elliot, letter to family, October 6, 1952.

94. Elliot, *Shadow of the Almighty*, 171.

95. Elliot, letter to family, December 2, 1952.

96. Elliot, *Strange Ashes*, 75.

97. Elliot, *Strange Ashes*, 61.

98. Elliot, *Strange Ashes*, 82–84.

99. Elliot, *Strange Ashes*, 113, 108–9, 111, 38.

100. Elliot, letter to family, February 1, 1953.

101. Elliot, *Strange Ashes*, 114–15.

102. Shepard, *Devotedly*, 233.

103. "Excerpts from EH letters, Feb. 1953."

104. Elliot, letter to family, June 23, 1952.

105. Shepard, *Devotedly*, 228.

106. Elliot, *Shadow of the Almighty*, 196.

107. Shepard, *Devotedly*, 236.

108. "Excerpts from EH letters, Feb. 1953."

109. Elliot, *Strange Ashes*, 115.

110. Elliot, *Journals of Jim Elliot*, 445, 446.

111. Elliot, *Strange Ashes*, 124.

112. Elliot, *Journals of Jim Elliot*, 446.

113. Elliot, *Strange Ashes*, 125.

114. Shepard, *Devotedly*, 240.

115. Elliot, *Strange Ashes*, 127.

116. *These Strange Ashes* says she finished on June 16; a letter written at the time says she finished it on June 17.

117. Elliot, letter to family, June 27, 1953.

118. Elliot, letter to family, July 22, 1953.

119. Elliot, letter to family, July 2, 1953.

120. Elliot, letter to family, July 22, 1953.

121. Elliot, letter to family, July 12, 1953.

122. Elliot, letter to family, August 25, 1953.

123. Elliot, letter to family, July 12, 1953.

124. Elliot, letter to family, July 30, 1953.
125. Elliot, letter to family, August 6, 1953.
126. Elliot, *Journals of Jim Elliot*, 450.
127. Liefeld, *Unfolding Destinies*, 147.
128. Elliot, letter to family, July 30, 1953.
129. Elliot, letter to family, July 30, 1953.
130. Elliot, letter to family, March 24, 1953.
131. Elliot, letter to family, August 6, 1953.
132. Elliot, *Journals of Jim Elliot*, 451.
133. Elliot, *Journals of Jim Elliot*, 450.
134. Elliot, letter to family, August 25, 1953.
135. Elliot, letter to family, September 22, 1953.
136. Shepard, *Devotedly*, 262.
137. Elliot, letter to family, September 22, 1953.
138. Elliot, letter to family, October 12, 1953.
139. Elliot, letter to family, October 12, 1953.
140. Elliot, letter to family, October 12, 1953.
141. Elliot, letter to family, October 30, 1953.
142. Elliot, letter to family, November 6, 1953.
143. Elliot, *Journals of Jim Elliot*, 456.
144. Elliot, letter to family, November 19, 1953.
145. Elliot, letter to family, November 22, 1953.
146. Elliot, *Journals of Jim Elliot*, 460.
147. Elliot, letter to family, December 6, 1953.
148. Elliot, letter to family, November 19, 1953.

Chapter 6: Through the Waters
1. Elisabeth Elliot, letter to family, December 17, 1953, collection 278, box 4, folder 1. Until otherwise indicated, subsequent references to Elliot letters in chapter 6 are from collection 278, box 4, folder 2.
2. Elliot, letter to family, December 28, 1953, folder 1. Missionary stories repeatedly record but rarely examine the lack of opportunity available to "pioneer missionaries" to function as the church with other Christians.
3. Elliot, letter to family, March 1, 1954.
4. Thomas Howard, interview with author, October 2013.
5. Valerie Elliot Shepard, *Devotedly* (Nashville, TN: B&H, 2019), 259–60.
6. Elliot, letter to family, March 15, 1954.
7. Elliot, letter to family, March 15, 1954.
8. Elisabeth Elliot, ed., *The Journals of Jim Elliot* (Grand Rapids, MI: Revell, 2008), 299.
9. Elliot, letter to family, April 7, 1954.
10. Elliot, letter to family, March 20, 1954.
11. Elliot, letter to family, April 7, 1954.
12. This account differs in almost every particular from the one which Elisabeth Elliot would later give in *These Strange Ashes*. The book places the event differently chronologically, assigns authorship of the letter to a different writer, and changes the type of vehicle from which they were stolen. And it says that not merely the files but *all* the materials were stolen. Rather than noting that the lost files were largely replaced by the time Betty knew they were gone, the book describes them

as irreplaceable. And it paints a very different picture of Betty's feelings when she learned of the loss:

> Everything I had done in nine months in San Miguel de los Colorados was undone at a stroke.... The tenth Psalm came to my mind: 'Why dost thou hide thyself in times of trouble?' And, as before, I heard no reply to that and other questions. There was no light, no echo, no possible explanation. All the questions as to the validity of my calling, or, much more fundamental, God's interest in the Colorados' salvation, in any missionary work—Bible translation or any other kind—all those questions came again to the fore.

If the letters dated after Betty left San Miguel were, in fact, not in Elisabeth Elliot's possession when she was writing *These Strange Ashes*, these discrepancies can probably be ascribed to the vagaries of memory; after twenty years, one remembers impressions more than detail. This raises the question of what happened between April 1954 and November 1971 that changed the impression left by the loss of the language files from "I'm not too worried about it," to one of devastation and total loss. Elisabeth Elliot, *These Strange Ashes* (New York: Harper & Brothers, 1975), 128–30; Elliot, letter to family, April 7, 1954.

13. Shepard, *Devotedly*, 280.
14. Elliot, letter to family, April 15, 1954.
15. Elisabeth Elliot, *The Savage My Kinsman* (New York: Harper & Row, 1961), 157.
16. Elliot, letter to family, May 30, 1954.
17. Shepard, *Devotedly*, 248, 245, 243.
18. Elliot, letter to family, July 8, 1954.
19. Elliot, letter to family, June 22, 1954.
20. Elliot, letter to family, August 9, 1954.
21. Elliot, letter to family, July 8, 1954.
22. James Hefley and Marti Hefley, *Uncle Cam: The Story of William Cameron Townsend, Founder of the Wycliffe Bible Translators and the Summer Institute of Linguistics* (Huntington Beach, CA: Wycliffe Bible Translators, 1984), 174.
23. Hefley and Hefley, *Uncle Cam*, 113.
24. Elliot, letter to family, July 12, 1954, box 3, folder 2.
25. Shepard, *Devotedly*, 282.
26. Elliot, letter to family, July 19, 1954.
27. Elliot, letter to family, July 27, 1954.
28. Elliot, *Journals of Jim Elliot*, 464.
29. Elliot, letter to family, September 9, 1954.
30. Finally, at Nate's request, they gave Ushpalito to Atanasio. "Nate worried about him chasing the plane, though he never did, actually." Elliot, letter to family, August 8, 1955, folder 3.
31. Elliot, letter to family, July 19, 1954.
32. Elisabeth Elliot, *Let Me Be a Woman: Notes on Womanhood for Valerie* (Wheaton, IL: Tyndale, 1976), 17.
33. Elliot, letter to family, September 9, 1954.
34. Elliot, letter to family, October 8, 1954.
35. Elliot, letter to family, September 9, 1954.
36. Elliot, letter to family, undated, from context, written on or after October 22, 1954.
37. Elliot, letter to family, November 10, 1954.
38. Elliot, letter to family, undated, from context, written on or after October 22, 1954.

39. Elliot, letter to family, October 9, 1954.
40. Shepard, *Devotedly*, 270.
41. Elliot, letter to family, October 28, 1954.
42. Elliot, letter to family, November 21, 1954.
43. Elliot, letter to mother, November 8, 1954.
44. Elliot, letter to mother, November 10, 1954.
45. Elliot, letter to family, November 10, 1954.
46. Elliot, letter to family, September 18, 1956, folder 4.
47. Elliot, *Le Me Be a Woman*, 118–19.
48. Elliot, letter to family, November 29, 1954.
49. Elliot, letter to family, November 29, 1954.
50. Elliot, letter to family, December 18, 1954.
51. Olive Fleming Liefeld, interview with author, April 4, 2014.
52. Elliot, letter to family, December 18, 1954.
53. Elliot, letter to mother, December 9, 1954.
54. Elliot, *Journals of Jim Elliot*, 433–34.
55. Elliot, *Journals of Jim Elliot*, 382.
56. Thomas Howard, interview with author, October 2013.
57. Elliot, *Journals of Jim Elliot*, 382; Thomas Howard, interview with author, November 6, 2014.
58. Elliot, letter to family, December 9, 1954.
59. Thomas Howard, interview with author, November 6, 2014.
60. Elliot, letter to family, December 22, 1954.
61. Elliot, letter to family, December 30, 1954.
62. Elliot, letter to family, January 18, 1955. Until otherwise indicated, subsequent references to Elliot letters in chapter 6 are from collection 278, box 4, folder 3.
63. Elliot, *Journals of Jim Elliot*, 454.
64. Elliot, letter to family, February 21, 1955.
65. Elliot, letter to family, February 21, 1955.
66. Shepard, *Devotedly*, 283.
67. Shepard, *Devotedly*, 283.
68. Elliot, *Let Me Be a Woman*, 17–18.
69. Elliot, letter to family, March 31, 1955.
70. Elliot, letter to family, April 14, 1955.
71. Elliot, letter to family, April 29, 1955.
72. Elliot, letter to family, May 26, 1955.
73. Elliot, letter to family, April 29, 1955.
74. Elliot, letter to family, May 3, 1955.
75. Elliot, letter to family, May 12, 1955.
76. Elliot, letter to family, May 18, 1955.
77. Elliot, letter to family, June 5, 1955.
78. Elliot, letter to family, July 8, 1955.
79. Elliot, letter to family, June 16, 1955.
80. Elliot, letter to family, June 16, 1955.
81. Elliot, *Journals of Jim Elliot*, 467.
82. Elliot, letter to mother, June 16, 1955.
83. Elliot, letter to mother, August 8, 1955.
84. Elliot, letter to mother, August 16, 1955.
85. Elliot, letter to family, September 7, 1955.

86. Olive Fleming Liefeld, *Unfolding Destinies: The Ongoing Story of the Auca Mission* (Grand Rapids, MI: Discovery, 1998), 190.

87. Elliot, letter to family, August 31, 1955.

88. Elliot, letter to mother, September 25, 1955.

89. Elliot, letter to mother, October 6, 1955.

90. Elisabeth Elliot, *Through Gates of Splendor* (New York: Harper & Brothers, 1957), 131.

91. This story has been told and retold for more than fifty years, and some details emerge differently in different tellings. In her 1957 book, *Shadow of the Almighty*, Elisabeth Elliot wrote that the McCullys had told her and Jim the news. Years later, in interviews conducted for the film *Beyond the Gates of Splendor*, she would say that Nate Saint had flown into Shandia for lunch one day and told them then that he had found the tribe and was hoping to put together a team of men to approach them.

92. Liefeld, *Unfolding Destinies*, 183.

93. Elliot, *Gates of Splendor*, 132.

94. Elliot, *Journals of Jim Elliot*, 299.

95. Elisabeth Elliot, *Shadow of the Almighty* (New York: Harper & Brothers, 1958), 232.

96. While the indigenous laborers on Sevilla's plantation were meagerly paid, they were not allowed to leave, and if they managed to escape, they were captured and brought back.

97. Elliot, *Shadow of the Almighty*, 233–34.

98. Although Rachel was in Ecuador in the summer of 1953, a gap in the record of her life makes it unclear what she was doing between then and her move to the plantation.

99. It is difficult to find another explanation for the fact that Rachel Saint appears not to have recognized the word *auca* as a derogatory Kichwa appellation rather than the actual name of the people group. Saint did not speak Kichwa, and although Catherine Peeke did, accounts of their brief time as coworkers in 1955 center Saint so thoroughly that it is impossible to tell what Peeke's involvement may have been.

100. Various accounts make clear that Saint and Peeke left Ila in June of 1955 but don't say why. They do however say that "months of illness" for Rachel followed their departure, suggesting that her illness was the reason they left. Ethel Emily Wallis, *The Dayuma Story* (New York: Harper & Brothers, 1960), 78.

101. Elliot, *Gates of Splendor*, 128.

102. *Beyond the Gates of Splendor*, directed by Jim Hanon, produced by Ryan Green, Bearing Fruit Productions, 2002.

103. Russell T. Hitt, *Jungle Pilot: The Life and Witness of Nate Saint* (Grand Rapids, MI: Zondervan, 1975), 236–37.

104. Hitt, *Jungle Pilot*, 240.

105. Hitt, *Jungle Pilot*, 240.

106. Rosemary Kingsland, *A Saint among Savages* (London: William Collins Sons, 1980), 75.

107. Elliot, *Gates of Splendor*, 139.

108. Elliot, *Journals of Jim Elliot*, 469.

109. Elliot, *Shadow of the Almighty*, 235.

110. Elisabeth Elliot, interviewed in *Beyond the Gates of Splendor*.

111. *Beyond the Gates of Splendor*.

112. Elliot, *Gates of Splendor*, 145.

113. Elliot, *Shadow of the Almighty*, 238.

114. Elliot, letter to family, November 16, 1955.

115. Elliot, *Gates of Splendor*, 149.

116. Elliot, *Journals of Jim Elliot*, 474.

117. Later in the month Betty would write, "Jim and I are reading *Northwest Passage* which you sent us, Mother, and find it extremely interesting and well written. He makes some observations about North American Indians, which hit the nail on the head. He says the most outstanding difference between the Indian and the white man is lack of discipline." She would later disavow this point of view. Elliot, letter to family, December 21, 1955.

118. Elliot, letter to family, December 7, 1955.

119. Elliot, *Gates of Splendor*, 160.

120. Elliot, *Gates of Splendor*, 164.

121. Elliot, *Gates of Splendor*, 165.

122. Elliot, letter to mother, December 13, 1955.

123. Elliot, *Gates of Splendor*, 170–71.

124. *Beyond the Gates of Splendor*.

125. *Beyond the Gates of Splendor*. Ed McCully was six foot two and wore a size 13½ shoe.

126. Elliot, letter to family, December 28, 1955.

127. A few days later, Betty wrote to her mother, "Rachel Saint is coming in to stay with me, but it will be a bit awkward, as of course she knows nothing at all about the attempt to reach the savages. So just what I will be able to learn by way of radio contacts, with her here, I don't know. I suppose Marj will have some kind of code worked out, but I don't know how dumb Rachel is supposed to be, and she will no doubt be suspicious." Elliot, letter to family, January 2, 1956, folder 4.

128. Elliot, *Gates of Splendor*, 174.

129. Elliot, letter to family, December 28, 1955.

130. Liefeld, *Unfolding Destinies*, 198.

131. Elliot, letter to family, January 4, 1956, folder 4. Until otherwise indicated, subsequent references to Elliot letters in chapter 6 are from collection 278, box 4, folder 4.

132. *Beyond the Gates of Splendor*.

133. Elliot, letter to parents, undated.

134. Elliot, *Shadow of the Almighty*, 243.

135. Elliot, letter to family, January 2, 1956.

136. Elliot, *Gates of Splendor*, 177–78.

137. Elliot, *Shadow of the Almighty*, 244.

138. *Beyond the Gates of Splendor*.

139. Elliot, letter to mother, January 6, 1956.

140. The Curaray, the river in which Jim was killed, is a tributary of the Napo, the river that flowed past Shandia.

141. Elliot, *Gates of Splendor*, 196.

142. Years later Betty would later confirm this account, remembering that when Rachel heard Marj's words, "She shot up off that sofa and she said, 'Are those guys in Auca territory?!'" The speed with which Rachel jumped to this conclusion seems to suggest that she had indeed, as Betty had anticipated, been suspicious. *Beyond the Gates of Splendor*.

143. Elliot, letter to family, January 27, 1956.

144. Elliot, *Gates of Splendor*, 196.

145. Elisabeth Elliot, *The Path of Loneliness* (Nashville, TN: Oliver-Nelson Books, 1988), 34.

146. Elliot, letter to family, January 11, 1956. This handwritten letter is in script except for the sentence "There are no regrets," which is emphasized with block printing.

147. Elliot, *Gates of Splendor*, 233.

148. Elliot, *Gates of Splendor*, 249.

149. Frank Drown, *Unmarked Memories* (Monument, CO: SnowFall, 2010), 50.

150. Elliot, *Gates of Splendor*, 259.

151. Elliot, letter to family, January 18, 1956.

152. Elliot, letter to family, January 20, 1956.

153. Elliot, *Path of Loneliness*, 39; Amy Carmichael, "Let Me Not Shrink," *Mountain Breezes: The Collected Poems of Amy Carmichael* (Fort Washington, PA: CLC, 1999), 219.

Chapter 7: An Alien, a Stranger

1. Elisabeth Elliot, letter to family, January 26, 1956, papers of Elisabeth Howard Elliot, collection 278, box 4, folder 4, Billy Graham Center Archives, Wheaton College, IL. Until otherwise indicated, subsequent references to Elliot letters in chapter 7 are from collection 278, box 4, folder 4.

2. Elliot, letter to family, January 27, 1956.

3. Various retellings of the story of what happened on the sandbar on the afternoon of January 8, 1956, have been made, all based on the accounts of various Waorani who have shared their memories of the event over the years. As Kathryn T. Long has pointed out, "Details vary widely in the different stories. The memories of some Waorani have shifted over the years, and all were affected by the chaos of the attack." On any point where the accounts diverge, it is impossible to make a definitive statement about what occurred. Thus this book does not attempt to create a retelling of the story except as it appeared to Elliot at various points in time. To compare or judge between various accounts has been done repeatedly elsewhere, with Long providing perhaps the most reliable "plausible scenario." Kathryn T. Long, *God in the Rainforest* (New York: Oxford University Press, 2019), 20–21.

4. Elliot, letter to family, January 27, 1956.

5. Elliot, letter to family, January 27, 1956.

6. Elliot, letter to family, February 5, 1956.

7. Elliot, letters to family, April 18, May 7, 12, and July 5, 1956.

8. One of the Canadians was Robert Tremblay, who would later add a macabre chapter of his own to the story. The Florida couple must have been Jane Dolinger, a Miami-based adventure-travel writer and softcore pornographer, and her husband Ken Krippene. Although Elliot refers to Dolinger at one point as Jane *Halliday*, the couple's timeline matches references in Elliot's letters. Posing staged pictures as "illustrations" for her sexy travel stories was part of Dolinger's stock-in-trade, and she was unafraid to use and reuse the same material again and again in different "true" stories, as she did with her 1956 stay in Ecuador.

  Among the many pieces based on the trip is a book, *The Head with the Long Yellow Hair*, which recounts Dolinger's search for a blonde shrunken head and a lost Inca emerald mine. The search includes a "solo" trip through Waorani territory, led by Kichwa guides and disguised as a Kichwa woman, but no sign of the people themselves. It also includes a visit with a woman who had escaped from the Waorani, but in Dolinger's account Joaquina, a captured and escaped Kichwa woman, becomes "Ucca," a Wao who has fled her tribe. The purported photo of "Ucca" is cautiously framed but shows her apparently topless and wearing large wooden earplugs. By claiming that her interviewee is a member of the mysterious tribe, Dolinger is able to write about the Waorani with authority, including the (fabricated) presence of witch doctors carrying huge uncut emeralds as a symbol of their power.

Interestingly, despite Dolinger's willingness to play fast and loose with the truth to satisfy her American and Western European audience's desire for an unexplored frontier full of potential for adventure, wealth, and sex, she was faster than the evangelical missionaries to recognize that "auca" is a derogatory Kichwa term and to search for an alternative. She primarily refers to the people as "Aushiri," a name she says was given them by Spanish conquistadors.

9. Elliot, letter to family, April 18, 1956.
10. Elliot, letter to family, May 12, 1956.
11. Valerie Elliot Shepard, *Devotedly* (Nashville, TN: B&H, 2019), 207.
12. Elliot, letter to mother, January 31, 1956.
13. Long, *God in the Rainforest*, 17.
14. Elliot, letter to family, January 27, 1956.
15. Elliot, letter to family, February 8, 1956.
16. Elliot, letter to family, May 12, 1956.
17. Elliot, letter to supporters, January 25, 1956.
18. Elliot, letter to mother, February 15, 1956.
19. Elliot, letter to family, January 20, 1956.
20. Elliot, letter to mother, undated.
21. Elliot, letter to family, January 26, 1956.
22. These underlying assumptions affected Betty's response to others. For example, she worried in family letters that Olive Fleming was "missing the blessings God has for her" in their circumstances and, hoping to be a help, spoke to Olive more than once about the way she was responding to her grief. But Olive would later remember not encouragement but harshness. "At times grief washed over me in waves, and I could not hold back the tears. On one such occasion, Betty, who had remained stoic through the whole ordeal, chided me: 'You are just feeling sorry for yourself,' she said. 'It isn't out of love for Pete that you're crying.'"
    Betty was not the only one who felt that cheerfulness in the face of loss was evidence of God's grace. She later remembered Marj Saint telling one sympathetic visitor who offered "a shoulder to cry on," that she really appreciated it, "but I trust that the Lord is going to give us all grace so that we won't even need any shoulders to cry on." Elliot, letter to family, January 27, 1956; Olive Fleming Liefeld, *Unfolding Destinies: The Ongoing Story of the Auca Mission* (Grand Rapids, MI: Discovery, 1998), 210; Janet Anderson, "Knowing God's Keeping Power," At Your Service: The Life of Marj Saint Van Der Puy, *Confident Living*, April 1998, 5.
23. Elliot, letters to family, January 20 and 31, 1956.
24. Elliot, letter to family, January 27, 1956. A couple of years later, Betty would write in a letter to her mother, "There were times when I wondered if the peace I had after Jim's death was a false one, due to my failure fully to acknowledge to myself that he was dead!" Elliot, letter to family, September 18, 1958, folder 6.
25. Kathryn T. Long, "Cameras 'Never Lie'": The Role of Photography in Telling the Story of American Evangelical Missions," *Church History* 72, no. 4 (2003): 844.
26. Cornell Capa, "Foreword," in Elisabeth Elliot, *The Savage My Kinsman* (New York: Harper & Row, 1961), 12.
27. Elliot, letter to family, January 27, 1956.

28. Elliot, letter to family, August 16, 1956.
29. Elliot, letter to family, February 28, 1956.
30. Elliot, letter to family, March 13, 1956.
31. Elliot, letter to family, February 8, 1956.
32. Elliot, letter to family, February 8, 1956.
33. Elliot, letter to family, April 2, 1956.
34. Elliot, letter to family, May 26, 1956.
35. Elliot, letter to family, May 21, 1956.
36. Elliot, letter to family, May 26, 1956.
37. Elliot, letter to family, June 8, 1956.
38. Elliot, letter to mother, June 8, 1956.
39. Elliot, letter to family, June 21, 1956.
40. Elliot, letter to family, August 4, 1956.
41. Elliot, letter to family, August 11, 1956.
42. Elisabeth Elliot, *Shadow of the Almighty* (New York: Harper & Brothers, 1958), 9.
43. Elliot, letter to family, June 26, 1956.
44. Elliot, letter to mother, August 20, 1956.
45. Elliot, letter to mother, August 29, 1956.
46. Elliot, letter to family, September 11, 1956.
47. Elliot, letter to family, April 25, 1956.
48. Elliot, letter to family, April 5, 1956.
49. Elliot, letter to family, October 9, 1956.
50. Elliot, letter to mother, October 12, 1956.
51. Elliot, letter to mother, October 12, 1956.
52. Elliot, letter to mother, October 12, 1956.
53. Elisabeth Elliot, interview with Kathryn T. Long, June 27, 2001, transcript in email to author, July 1, 2019.
54. Elliot, letter to mother, December 8, 1956.
55. Elliot, letter to mother, February 15, 1956.
56. Elliot, letter to mother, December 31, 1956.
57. Elliot, letter to family, January 8, 1957, folder 5.
58. Elliot, letter to family, January 21, 1957, folder 5.
59. Elliot, letter to family, October 17, 1956.
60. Elliot, letter to family, January 25, 1957, box 4, folder 5. Until otherwise indicated, subsequent references to Elliot letters in chapter 7 are from collection 278, box 4, folder 5.
61. Elliot, letter to mother, January 30, 1957.
62. Elliot, letter to parents, February 8, 1957.
63. Elliot, letter to parents, February 8, 1957.
64. Long, *God in the Rainforest*, 37.
65. Elisabeth Elliot, *Through Gates of Splendor* (New York: Harper & Brothers, 1957), 175, 252.
66. Long, *God in the Rainforest*, 38.
67. Elliot, *Gates of Splendor*, 20, 172–75, 177–78.
68. Elliot, letter to family, November 4, 1948, box 3, folder 9.
69. Long, *God in the Rainforest*, 40.
70. Elisabeth Elliot, ed., *The Journals of Jim Elliot* (Grand Rapids, MI: Revell, 2008), 475.
71. Elliot, letter to family, March 13, 1957.
72. Elliot, letter to family, April 8, 1957.

73. Capa, "Foreword," in *The Savage My Kinsman*, 14.

74. Elliot, letter to family, March 13, 1957.

75. Elisabeth Elliot, speech, National Religious Broadcasters Convention, 1982, records of National Religious Broadcasters, collection 309, tape T259, Billy Graham Center Archives, Wheaton College, IL.

76. Elliot, letter to family, April 8, 1957.

77. Kathryn T. Long has recorded how MAF did not want to risk the bad press they were afraid would be generated if one of their planes crashed in dangerous territory with a female passenger, and also their erroneous belief that all "primitive peoples" were rigidly patriarchal and might therefore respond poorly to hearing a woman's voice over the plane's loudspeaker. Long, *God in the Rainforest*, 55.

78. The evangelical community appears to have been a hotbed of hearsay and rumor. Betty wrote to her parents several times after Jim's death mentioning various rumors connected to his death and their family that were circulating in both Ecuador and the US that, though patently false, she could do nothing to stop.

79. Long, *God in the Rainforest*, 64–65.

80. Elliot, letter to family, October 21, 1957.

81. Elliot, letter to family, November 13, 1957.

82. Tidmarsh had been thinking about how to contact the Waorani for years. Kathryn T. Long notes, "In March 1952, only a month after Pete Fleming and Jim Elliot had arrived in Ecuador, Tidmarsh talked with Fleming about a strategy for contacting the Waorani. With some modifications, the five missionaries of Operation Auca followed the broad contours of Tidmarsh's plan." Long, *God in the Rainforest*, 39.

83. Elliot, letter to family, July 30, 1957.

84. Elliot, letter to family, February 6, 1957.

85. Elliot, letter to family, October 25, 1958, folder 6.

86. Elliot had read the published letters between Katherine Mansfield and her husband John Middleton Murry and wrote that she was very much like Mansfield. She told her family, "I may as well confess that her influence on me is great." In her journal she listed all the things she felt she and Mansfield had in common, including their relationship with a younger brother; their difficulty in sharing emotionally with their mothers; a strong dislike of anything tawdry; a deep capacity for both agony and ardent love; and a feeling that they were outsiders in their family of origin. They also shared a *memento mori* practice that Mansfield described like this: "Whenever I prepare for a journey I prepare as though for death. Should I never return, all is in order. This is what life has taught me." Elliot said that reading Mansfield had wholly transformed the way she thought. Elliot, letter to family, August 13, 1957; The Modern Library (@ModernLibrary), Twitter, October 4, 2019, 1:53p.m., https://twitter.com/.

87. Elliot, letter to family, April 8, 1957.

88. Elliot, letter to family, May 7, 1957.

89. Elliot, letters to family, May 7 and 9, 1957. William Carey was a prolific translator during his time in India, but he did not reach quite these heights. He completed portions of translation in thirty-five dialects and languages. Biographers' exaltation of William Carey and tendency to uncritically accept his treatment of his first wife and their sons were surely a contributing factor in Elliot's attitude toward her own life and work during this time.

90. Elliot, letter to family, May 13, 1957.

91. Elliot, letter to family, May 17, 1957.

92. Elliot, letter to family, May 13, 1957.

93. Elliot, letter to mother, June 12, 1957.

94. Ellen Vaughn, *Becoming Elisabeth Elliot* (Nashville, TN: B&H, 2020), 176; Kathryn Deering photograph of Elisabeth Elliot journal entry, July 6, 1957, papers of Kathryn (Rogers) Deering, collection 670, accession 12–27, disk 1, Billy Graham Center Archives, Wheaton College, IL.

95. Elliot, letter to family, October 30, 1957.

96. Vaughn, *Becoming Elisabeth Elliot*, 186; Deering photo of Elliot journal entry, August 3, 1957.

97. Elliot, letter to family, August 6, 1957.

98. Elliot, letters to family, May 13 and September 10, 1957.

99. Elliot, letter to family, October 16, 1957.

100. Elliot, letter to family, October 30, 1957.

101. The existence of this settlement seems to contradict the general picture of fearsome "auca" killers, but there is apparently no information to further explain the situation. It's unclear why the settlers had chosen that location and why they had been left in peace.

102. Elliot, letter to family, November 13, 1957.

103. Later she began calling them "Molly" and "Sue" as well; no explanation for the dual monikers survives.

104. Vaughn, *Becoming Elisabeth Elliot*, 191; Deering photo of Elliot journal entry, November 15, 1957.

105. Elliot, letter to family, November 15, 1957.

106. Elliot, letter to family, November 18, 1957.

107. Elliot, letter to family, November 22, 1957.

108. Elliot, letter to family, November 22, 1957.

109. Elliot, letter to family, November 26, 1957.

110. Elliot, letter to family, November 26, 1957.

111. Elliot, letter to mother, December 24, 1957.

112. Elliot, letter to family, October 21, 1957.

113. Elliot, letter to family, December 2, 1957.

114. Elliot, letter to family, November 26, 1957.

115. In *God in the Rainforest*, Long records how Sevilla had inexplicably begun to encourage Dayomæ to return to her tribe alone, a dangerous idea at best.

116. Elliot, letter to family, December 8, 1957 [erroneously dated 1057].

117. Elliot, letter to family, January 7, 1958, folder 6. Subsequent references to Elliot letters in chapter 7 are from collection 278, box 4, folder 6.

118. Elliot, letter to family, January 17, 1958.

119. Elliot, letter to family, January 14, 1958.

120. Elliot, letter to family, January 17, 1958.

121. Elliot, letter to family, January 26, 1958.

122. Elliot, letter to family, February 11, 1958.

123. J. Hudson Taylor, *A Retrospect* (Philadelphia: China Inland Mission, n.d.), 15.

124. Elliot, letter to family, Olive Fleming, Marilou McCully, Marjorie Saint, and Barbara Youderian, January 30, 1958.

125. Elliot, letter to family, Olive Fleming, Marilou McCully, Marjorie Saint, and Barbara Youderian, January 30, 1958.

126. Elliot, letter to family, February 24, 1958.

127. Elliot, letter to family, February 24, 1958.

128. Elliot, letter to family, March 3, 1958.

129. Elliot, letter to family, March 3, 1958.

130. Elliot, letter to mother, March 10, 1958.

131. Elliot, letters to family, March 19, 11, and 25, 1958.

132. Elliot, letter to family, April 24, 1958.

133. Elliot, *Shadow of the Almighty*, 109, 114.

134. Elliot, *Shadow of the Almighty*, 13.

135. The words in Jim Elliot's diary are, "He is no fool who gives what he cannot keep to gain that which he cannot lose." Elisabeth Elliot streamlined this very slightly when she quoted it in *Shadow of the Almighty*. "Jim Elliot Quote," Billy Graham Center Archives, rev. January 9, 2016, https://www2.wheaton.edu/; Elliot, *Shadow of the Almighty*, 15, 19, 247; Elliot, ed., *Journals of Jim Elliot*, 174.

136. Elliot, *Shadow of the Almighty*, 236.

137. Elliot, *Shadow of the Almighty*, 247.

138. Elliot, *Gates of Splendor*, 252–53; Elliot, *Shadow of the Almighty*, 246–47, 249.

139. Elliot, letter to family, May 6, 1958.

140. Elliot's letter to her mother, in which she spelled the words "Warani" and "Wa," makes it clear that Rachel Saint also knew this and also disregarded it. In fact, Saint was still stubbornly calling the people "auca" in the 1990s, despite their protestations.

141. James A. Yost, "Who Are the Waorani?," unpublished article, 1974, accessed August 1, 2019, https://www.sil.org/.

142. Elliot, letter to family and friends, May 15, 1958.

143. The traditional daily clothing of the Waorani was a kome, a length of handspun cotton string worn below the natural waist, just where one would put one's hands on one's hips. They also wore balsa wood earplugs, necklaces, and woven armbands. Both women and men wore the kome; men used it as a strap under which to tuck their penis so it would be out of the way when they were doing active work.

144. Elliot, letter to family, May 30, 1958.

145. Elliot, letter to family, June 14, 1958.

146. Elliot, letter to family, June 14, 1958.

147. Long, *God in the Rainforest*, 87.

148. Elliot, letter to parents, June 28, 1958.

149. Elliot, letter to family, July 5, 1958.

150. Elliot, letter to family, July 15, 1958.

151. Elliot, letter to mother, August 6, 1958.

152. Long, *God in the Rainforest*, 89.

153. Elliot, letter to family, August 25, 1958.

154. Elliot, letter to family, September 3, 1958.

155. Elliot, letter to family, September 3, 1958.

156. Elliot, letter to family, September 3, 1958.

Chapter 8: Where Is Rehoboth?

1. Elisabeth Elliot, letter to family, September 26, 1958, papers of Elisabeth Howard Elliot, collection 278, box 4, folder 6, Billy Graham Center Archives, Wheaton College, IL. Unless otherwise indicated, subsequent references to Elliot letters in chapter 8 are from collection 278, box 4.

2. Elliot, letter to supporters, October 4, 1959, folder 6.

3. Elliot, letter to family, October 5, 1958, folder 6.

4. Elliot, letter to family, October 5, 1958, folder 6.

5. Elisabeth Elliot, *The Savage My Kinsman* (New York: Harper & Row, 1961), 81.

6. Elliot, *The Savage My Kinsman*, 92–93.

7. Ellen Vaughn, *Becoming Elisabeth Elliot* (Nashville, TN: B&H, 2020), 214; Deering photo of Elliot journal entry, October 12, 1958.

8. Sedentary cultures are those in which a group of people settles more or less permanently in one location; nomadic cultures are those that regularly move as they hunt and gather, follow flocks or herds, etc. Semisedentary and seminomadic cultures differ in emphasis, but both feature a blend of mobility and settled life.

9. James S. Boster, James Yost, and Catherine Peeke, "Rage, Revenge, and Religion: Honest Signaling of Aggression and Nonaggression in Waorani Coalitional Violence," *Ethos* 31 (December 2003): 492.

10. Elliot, *The Savage My Kinsman*, 155.

11. Clayton Robarchek and Carole Robarchek, "Waorani Grief and the Witch-Killer's Rage: Worldview, Emotion, and Anthropological Explanation," *Ethos* 33 (June 2005): 211–12.

12. Elliot, *The Savage My Kinsman*, 154–55.

13. Elliot, letter to family, October 4, 1958, folder 6.

14. Rachel Saint, letter to Cameron Townsend, December 12, 1958, cited in Kathryn T. Long, *God in the Rainforest* (New York: Oxford University Press, 2019), 109. Long notes: "Saint worried about Elliot's 'tendency to reach the Aucas with love—instead of [with] the Message of the Word' and feared that her questions indicated deeper doubts about basic evangelical doctrines." It is ironic that each of the women seems to have been concerned that the other was communicating an oversimplified version of the faith.

15. Elliot, letter to family, November 14, 1958, folder 6.

16. Elliot, letter to family, November 14, 1958, folder 6.

17. The Modern Library (@ModernLibrary), Twitter, October 4, 2019, 1:53 p.m., https://twitter.com/.

18. Elliot, letter to family, December 28, 1958, folder 6.

19. Elliot, letter to family, December 28, 1958, folder 6.

20. Elliot, letter to family, December 28, 1958, folder 6.

21. Elliot, letter to mother, December 4, 1958, folder 6.

22. Elliot, letter to family, December 31, 1958, folder 6.

23. Elliot, letter to family, February 16, 1959, folder 7.

24. Vaughn, *Becoming Elisabeth Elliot*, 223; Deering photo of Elliot journal entry, March 5, 1959.

25. Elliot, letter to family, March 21, 1959, folder 7.

26. The Greek word *apostle* and the Latin word *missionary* have the same meaning: "sent one." But there is no indication that Elliot ever studied Latin. Her understanding was probably shaped by the institutional English and American use of *missionary* and by her lifelong participation in denominations that primarily taught the Great Commission as applying to every Christian, while treating the title "apostle" as denoting only the twelve disciples plus the apostle Paul, or limiting the use of the term *apostle* to the first century of church history.

27. Elliot, letter to family, April 13, 1959, folder 7.

28. Elliot, letter to family, April 13, 1959, folder 7.

29. Elliot, letter to mother, May 8, 1959, folder 7.

30. Elliot, letter to mother, May 8, 1959, folder 7.

31. Elisabeth Elliot, *Shadow of the Almighty* (New York: Harper & Brothers, 1958), 246.

32. Elliot, letter to mother, February 5, 1956, folder 4.

33. Elliot, letter to family, March 26, 1957, folder 5.

34. Elliot, letter to family, December 20, 1957, folder 5.

35. Elliot, letter to family, January 17, 1958, folder 6.

36. Elliot, letter to family with postscript to mother, October 5, 1958, folder 6.

37. Elliot, letter to mother, May 8, 1959, folder 7.

38. Elliot, letter to mother, May 8, 1959, folder 7.

39. Elliot, letter to family, May 22, 1959, folder 7.

40. Five Missionary Martyrs Fund Receipt Form, Records of EFMA, collection 165, box 3, folder 14, Billy Graham Center Archives, Wheaton College, IL.

41. It would take eleven years and the involvement of lawyers before the women would be able to resolve the situation completely. The men were honest in their keeping of the money; they just didn't trust the women to make decisions with it. In the meantime, they effectively forced the widows to dribble away the money, refusing to hand it out in large amounts when the women had anything in mind they wanted to accomplish and doling it out in small chunks only when the men felt it was appropriate.

42. Elliot, letter to mother, July 23, 1957, folder 5.

43. Marilou McCully, for example, had arranged to appoint her family guardians of one of her children in order to have his medical expenses covered in America rather than applying to the Fund.

44. Elliot, letter to family, May 22, 1959, folder 7.

45. Elliot, letter to family, September 1959, folder 7.

46. Elliot, letter to family, June 2, 1959, folder 7.

47. Elliot, letter to family, September 14, 1959, folder 7.

48. Elliot, letter to family, July 28, 1959, folder 7.

49. Elliot, letter to family, July 27, 1959, folder 7.

50. Vaughn, *Becoming Elisabeth Elliot*, 226; Deering photo of Elliot journal entry, August 18, 1959.

51. Elliot, letter to family, September 14, 1959, folder 7.

52. Elliot, letter to supporters, September 20, 1959, folder 7.

53. CT Staff, "Operation Auca: Four Years After Martyrdoms: A 1960 update on Elisabeth Elliot and Her Plan to Bring the Gospel to the Ecuadorian Tribe," *Christianity Today*, January 4, 1960, https://www.christianitytoday.com/.

54. Elliot, letter to mother, February 1, 1960, folder 8.

55. Elliot, letter to mother, January 21, 1960, folder 8.

56. Elliot, letter to family, February 8, 1960, folder 8.

57. Elliot, letter to family, February 8, 1960, folder 8.

58. Elliot, letter to family, February 8, 1960, folder 8.

59. Elliot, *The Savage My Kinsman*, 16.

60. Elliot, letter to supporters, September 20, 1959, folder 7.

61. Elliot, *The Savage My Kinsman*, 18.

62. Elliot, *The Savage My Kinsman*, 48.

63. Elliot, *The Savage My Kinsman*, 82.

64. Elliot, *The Savage My Kinsman*, 127.

65. Elliot, *The Savage My Kinsman*, 145.

66. Elliot, *The Savage My Kinsman*, 151.

67. Elliot, *The Savage My Kinsman*, 94.

68. Elliot, *The Savage My Kinsman*, 159.

69. Elliot, *The Savage My Kinsman*, 104.

70. William C. Spohn, "The Analogical Imagination," in *Go and Do Likewise: Jesus and Ethics* (New York: Continuum, 2007), 50–66.

71. Elliot, *The Savage My Kinsman*, 104.

72. Henry R. Luce, "The American Century," *Diplomatic History* 23 (April 1999): 159–71, http://www-personal.umich.edu/.

73. Staff, note on contents page, *Life*, November 24, 1958, 2.

74. Elliot, letter to family, May 2, 1960, folder 8.

75. Elliot, letter to family, May 2, 1960, folder 8.

76. Elliot, letter to parents, April 12, 1960, folder 8.

77. Elliot, letter to family, June 4, 1960, folder 8.

78. Elliot, letter to supporters, August 1960, box 5, folder 19.

79. Elliot, letter to supporters, August 1960, box 5, folder 19.

80. Elliot, letter to supporters, August 1960, box 5, folder 19.

81. Elliot, letter to supporters, August 1960, box 5, folder 19.

82. Elliot, letter to family, September 6, 1960, folder 8.

83. Elliot, letter to family, August 31, 1960, folder 8.

84. Elliot, letter to mother, August 31, 1960, folder 8.

85. Elliot, letter to family, September 15, 1960, folder 8.

86. Elliot, letter to family, September 15, 1960, folder 8.

87. The Elisabeth Elliot papers at the Billy Graham Center Archives at Wheaton include a letter from Marj Saint to Elliot sharing how much she appreciates Elliot's friendship and telling her that aside from God's help, Elliot has been her greatest support. Elliot mentioned the letter to her mother as a great comfort and encouragement.

88. Elliot, letter to family, September 22, 1960, folder 8.

89. Elliot, letter to family, October 2, 1960, folder 8.

90. Elliot, letter to family, October 2, 1960, folder 8.

91. Elliot, letter to family, October 16, 1960, folder 8.

92. Elliot, letter to family, October 2, 1960, folder 8.

93. Elliot, letter to family, October 2, 1960, folder 8.

94. Elliot, letter to family, October 6, 1960, folder 8.

95. Calvert School, which had begun in 1896 in Baltimore, Maryland, as a brick-and-mortar school to emulate the traditional German kindergarten, had in 1905 created a program of complete home-instruction materials that appears to have been the first of its kind—for decades the only one of its kind.

96. This marks the end of available material from Elliot's journals until 1964.

97. Elliot, letter to family, November 13, 1960, folder 8.

98. Elliot, letter to mother, December 3, 1960, folder 8.

99. Elliot, letter to family, December 1, 1960, folder 8.

100. Elliot, letter to family, December 16, 1960, folder 8.

101. Elliot, letter to family, December 1, 1960, folder 8.

102. Elliot, letter to family, December 16, 1960, folder 8.

103. Elliot, letter to mother, December 31, 1960, folder 8.

104. Elliot, letter to family, May 20, 1960, folder 8.

105. Elliot, letter to family, June 1, 1960, folder 8.

106. Elliot, letter to family, May 20, 1960, folder 8.

107. Elliot, letter to family, October 16, 1960, folder 8.

108. Elliot, letter to family, January 23, 1961, folder 9.

109. Elliot, letter to family, February 6, 1961, folder 9.

110. Elliot, letter to family, November 13, 27, 1961, folder 9.
111. Elliot, letter to mother, February 27, 1961, folder 9.
112. Elliot, letter to family, February 18, 1961, folder 9.
113. Elliot, letter to family, March 1, 1961, folder 9.
114. Elliot, letter to mother, April 4, 1961, folder 9.
115. Elliot, letter to mother, April 4, 1961, folder 9.
116. Elliot, letter to mother, April 8, 1961, folder 9.
117. Elliot, letter to supporters, April 25, 1961, folder 9.
118. Elliot, letter to family, May 30, 1961, folder 9.
119. Leslie Earl Maxwell of PBI (and a foreshadowing of her own title for her Amy Carmichael biography); Elliot, letter to mother, May 2, 1961, folder 9.
120. Elliot, letter to mother, May 2, 1961, folder 9.
121. Elliot, letter to mother, May 30, 1961, folder 9.
122. Elliot, letter to family, June 28, 1961, folder 9.
123. Elliot, letters to family, June 22 and October 9, 1961, folder 9.
124. Elliot, letter to mother, July 10, 1961, folder 9.
125. Elliot, letter to parents, July 10, 1961; letter to mother, July 27, 1961, folder 9.
126. Elliot, letters to family, August 4 and 10, 1961, folder 9.
127. Elliot, letter to family, September 5, 1961, folder 9.
128. Elliot, letters to family, September 18, 1961 and October 2, 1961, folder 9.
129. Elliot, letters to family, October 13 and 31, 1961, folder 9.
130. Elliot, letter to family, August 10, 1961, folder 9.
131. Elliot, letters to family, November 2 and 13, 1961, folder 9.
132. Elliot, letter to family, November 13, 1961, folder 9.
133. Elliot, letter to family, November 13, 1961, folder 9.
134. Elliot, letter to family, December 3, 1961, folder 9.
135. Elliot, letter to family, November 30, 1961, folder 9.
136. Elisabeth Elliot nominally lived with the Waorani from October 8, 1958, to December 1, 1961. In the first "year," she was present in Tewæno for nine of eleven months, broken into several episodes. (Saint was there for seven, and the two women were there at the same time for four-and-a-half months.) For the second year, from September 10, 1959, to September 21, 1960, Elliot was in the US on furlough. For the third "year," she was in the community for six stints for a total of twelve months out of the fourteen. In the same period, Saint was there for eight-and-a-half months. During this period, the two women overlapped for six months and three weeks, making their total time together in Tewæno just less than a year. Eight weeks were the longest they were ever together at a stretch.
137. Rosemary Kingsland, *A Saint among Savages* (London: William Collins Sons, 1980), 32.
138. It seems that Elliot came to hold this view herself. When Rosemary Kingsland interviewed Elliot for her 1980 book on Rachel Saint, Elliot described Saint as "very possessive of the Aucas." In a 2001 interview with Kathryn T. Long, Elliot summed things up in the same terms, remembering Saint as having resented her presence in the clearing from the beginning and as viewing Elliot as an intruder in her own calling to work alone with the group. For more on Rachel Saint's ongoing challenges in working with other coworkers, see Long's book. Kingsland, *A Saint among Savages*, 98.
139. Long, *God in the Rainforest*, 133.

140. In her important and helpful examination of the relationship between Elliot and Saint in *God in the Rainforest*, Kathryn T. Long rejects the idea that the two women disagreed over the issue of wine in Communion, calling it "embellishment." She also addresses and dismisses the suggestion that the pair disagreed over whether to teach the Waorani that the Bible prohibited polygamy. Long appears to be responding to Rosemary Kingsland's 1980 biography of Rachel Saint, *A Saint among Savages*. Kingsland explains Elliot's departure from Tewæno in terms of disagreement with Saint over what to teach the Waorani—on subjects including sexual behavior and alcoholic beverages.

Kingsland purports to quote Elliot directly. Long cites her own 2001 interview with Elliot, in which Elliot "dismissed these examples as apocryphal." In this interview, Elliot says that she can't remember disagreement on those specific topics and that, because she was working hard to avoid controversial subjects with Saint, it seems unlikely to her that they would have discussed those topics. Long also seems to reject Kingsland's assertions due to a lack of substantiation in available source material, such as Elliot's and Saint's letters from the period.

However, in an October 9, 1961 family letter, Elliot describes a recent disagreement with Saint over the issue of wine in Communion. Saint, likely because of her experience in what she called "drying out drunks" for more than a decade with the Keswick Colony of Mercy, was strongly opposed to the use of alcohol, even in Communion. On a recent visit to the church in Arajuno, Saint had declined to participate in the Lord's Supper over the issue, and she seemed deeply upset that Elliot did not have any qualms about observing the Lord's Supper with believers who used wine for the occasion. Despite Elliot's desire to avoid controversy, the issue was raised by circumstances.

Because this is clearly documented, it does not seem unreasonable to assume that in Long's 2001 interview, seventy-four-year-old Elliot's memory—affected by dementia, and at a remove of forty years from the events themselves and over twenty years from the Kingsland interview—is less reliable on the details of her conflict with Saint than the direct quotations Kingsland attributes to her. Certainly many other statements Kingsland ascribes to Elliot are consonant with the situation as it appears in letters from the time in question: Elliot's careful delineation of the difference between what the Bible says and what evangelical or American culture says; Saint's desire to keep outsiders out of Waorani territory and ongoing concern about sexual behavior among the Waorani; the difference in what the two women believed were make-or-break issues.

There is no surviving documentation in Elliot's letters addressing polygamy directly, but Kingsland's description of Elliot's views is not inconsistent with her documented thinking, whether on Waorani sexual behavior or on other subjects. What's more, Thomas Howard's 1969 book *The Antique Drum* presents an argument for the admissibility of polygamy very much like the one Kingsland quotes Elliot as advancing. Both brother and sister suggest that while monogamy may be the *best* form that marriage can take, there is no clear biblical rule that it is the *only* allowable form. Elliot's letters through the years emphasize repeatedly her strong affinity with Tom and the great similarity in their thinking. So while Kingsland may have given different weight to these topics than Elliot, it is at least possible that polygamy and sexual mores were an area of direct disagreement between the two missionaries. And it is clear that disagreement over the use of wine in Communion is more than apocryphal. Long, *God in the Rainforest*, 132; Rachel Saint, quoted in Kingsland, *A Saint among Savages*, 34.

141. William Wordsworth, "She Dwelt among the Untrodden Ways."

142. Elliot, letter to mother, June 23, 1961, folder 9.

143. Elliot, letter to family, November 29, 1961, folder 9.

144. Elliot, letter to family, February 6, 1961, folder 9.

145. Elisabeth Elliot, interview with Kathryn T. Long, June 27, 2001, transcript in email to author, July 1, 2019.

146. Elliot, letters to family, December 3 and 13, 1961, folder 9.

147. Elliot, letter to family, January 3, 1962, folder 10.

148. Elliot, letter to family, December 13, 1961, folder 9.

149. Elliot, letter to family, October 31, 1962, folder 10.

150. Elliot, letter to family, October 31, 1962, folder 10.

151. Elliot, letter to family, January 23, 1962, folder 10.

152. Elliot, letter to family, May 14, 1963, folder 11.

153. Elliot, letter to family, March 12, 1962, folder 10.

154. Elliot, letter to family, February 28, 1962, folder 10.

155. Elliot, letter to family, January 23, 1962, folder 10.

156. Elliot, letter to family, May 21, 1962, folder 10.

157. Elliot, letters to family, February 5 and May 21, 1962, folder 10.

158. Elliot, letter to family, May 21, 1962, folder 10.

159. Elliot, letter to family, May 21, 1962, folder 10.

160. Elliot, letter to family, July 12, 1962, folder 10.

161. Elliot, letter to family, August 19, 1962, folder 10.

162. Elliot, letter to family, September 27, 1962, folder 10.

163. Elliot, letter to family, February 5, 1962, folder 10.

164. Elliot, letter to mother, October 4, 1962, folder 10.

165. Elliot, letter to family, January 2, 1963, folder 11.

166. Elliot, letter to family, January 8, 1963, folder 11.

167. Elisabeth Elliot, "Introduction," in Matthew Henry, *The Secret of Communion with God,* ed. Elisabeth Elliot (Westwood, NJ: Revell, 1963), 6.

168. Thomas Howard, interview with author, November 6, 2014.

169. Elliot, introduction to *Secret of Communion* by Matthew Henry, 6-7.

170. Elliot, letter to family, October 13, 1961, folder 9.

171. Elliot, letter to family, March 29, 1962, folder 10.

172. Elliot, letter to family, July 24, 1962, folder 10.

173. Elliot, letter to family, January 8, 1963, folder 11.

174. Elliot, letter to family, January 8, 1963, folder 11.

175. Elliot, letters to family, January 6 and 18, 1963, folder 11.

176. Elliot, letter to mother, February 1, 1963, folder 11.

177. Eleanor Vandevort, interview with author, November 7, 2014.

178. Elliot, letter to family, February 11, 1963, folder 11.

179. Elliot, letter to family, February 11, 1963, folder 11.

180. Elliot, letter to family, February 11, 1963, folder 11.

181. Eleanor Vandevort, letter to Addison Hardie Leitch, December 14, 1968, papers of Elisabeth Howard Elliot, collection 278, box 9, folder 19, Billy Graham Center Archives, Wheaton College, IL.

182. Elliot, letter to family, February 25, 1963, folder 11.

183. Elliot, letter to family, February 25, 1963, folder 11.

184. Elliot, letter to family, February 11, 1963, folder 11.

185. Elisabeth Elliot, dedication to *A Slow and Certain Light: Some Thoughts on the Guidance of God* (Waco, TX: Word, 1973).

186. Elliot, letter to family, February 25, 1963, folder 11.

187. Elliot, letter to family, February 25, 1963, folder 11.

188. Elliot, letters to family, February 19 and 25, 1963, folder 11.

189. Elliot, letter to family, March 11, 1963, folder 11.

190. Elliot, letter to family, April 3, 1963, folder 11.

191. Eleanor Vandevort, interview with author, November 7, 2014.

192. Elliot, letter to family, March 23, 1963, folder 11.

193. Elliot, letter to family, April 2, 1963, folder 11.

194. Elliot, letter to family, May 23, 1963, folder 11.

195. Eleanor Vandevort, interview with author, November 7, 2014.

196. Elliot, letter to family, May 29, 1963, folder 11.

197. Jean-Pierre de Caussade, *Sacrament of the Present Moment*, trans. Kitty Muggeridge (San Francisco: HarperSanFrancisco, 1989), 34.

198. Elliot, letter to family, May 29, 1963, folder 11.

199. Elliot, letter to family, May 29, 1963, folder 11.

200. Elliot, letter to family, May 29, 1963, folder 11.

Chapter 9: The Will of God Is Not a Tightrope

1. Again, we can only guess at Elliot's financial situation during this time. Aside from the small loan from her parents, which she paid back within two months, Elliot paid cash for building the house, as she had done to purchase the property. She then owned house and land mortgage free. The average price for TechBuilt houses was $7.50 per square foot, or between $15,000 and $18,000 in 1960s dollars for a house the size of Elliot's. Accounting for inflation as of this writing, that would put the cost of building at about $125,000 to $150,000, not counting the cost of the land.

2. Elisabeth Elliot, letter to family, December 10, 1963, papers of Elisabeth Howard Elliot, collection 278, box 4, folder 11, Billy Graham Center Archives, Wheaton College, IL.

3. Elliot, letter to family, December 10, 1963, folder 11.

4. Katharine Gillingham Howard, "Upheld by His Righteous Omnipotent Hand," unpublished manuscript (May 12, 1980), typed, 204, private collection.

5. Elliot, letter to mother, January 8, 1964, folder 12.

6. Elliot, letter to family, January 17, 1964, folder 12.

7. Elliot, letter to family, January 10, 1964, folder 12.

8. Elliot, letter to family, January 17, 1974, box 5, folder 10.

9. Elliot, letter to family, February 14, 1964, folder 12.

10. Elliot, letter to family, January 17, 1974, box 5, folder 10.

11. Elliot, letter to family, February 14, 1964, folder 12.

12. Elliot, letter to family, March 18, 1964, folder 12.

13. Elliot, letter to family, February 25, 1964, folder 12.

14. Elliot, letter to family, February 14, 1964, folder 12.

15. Elliot, letter to family, February 3, 1964, folder 12.

16. Elliot, letter to family, February 25, 1964, folder 12.

17. Elliot, letter to family, February 25, 1964, folder 12.

18. Elliot, letter to family, February 25, 1964, folder 12. Elliot promised at one point in her family letters to share more about her views on "the ultimate redemption of all creation" but seems to have forgotten about it. Nevertheless, her 1961 response to a letter from her mother makes clear that she saw redemption as more inclusive than the standard evangelical teaching at the time. She quoted 1 Corinthians 15:22, Ephesians 1, and Colossians 1, suggesting reading them in the Phillips translation. In light of these passages, she said, Christians may legitimately refrain from drawing a conclusion on the subject, but she didn't see that they could rule out all possibility of universal reconciliation while taking Scripture seriously.

    The subject did not arise again until 1967, when Tom brought it up again. Elliot replied: "The Scripture plainly says 'those who die without the law, shall be judged without reference to the law,' and we know NOTHING of God's <u>uncovenanted</u> mercies. We are not invited to speculate on them, even, although I do, quite often. We <u>are</u> told that as in Adam all die, even so in Christ shall all be made alive. As for your remark, Mother, that if one is searching for God, He can be trusted to bring that one into contact with the Gospel—I think it would be well to remember that the only ones like that that we <u>hear</u> about, naturally, are those who have eventually had such a contact. We have no way of knowing how many others there are, or whether God might reach them in some other way than 'contact with the Gospel' (ie. What we mean by the Gospel)." Elliot, letter to family, January 23, 1961, folder 9; Elliot, letter to family, February 8, 1967, box 5, folder 3.

19. Elliot, letter to family, February 25, 1964, folder 12. Derr ultimately resigned from MAF.

20. Elliot, letter to family, February 25, 1964, folder 12.

21. Elliot, letter to family, March 9, 1964, folder 12.

22. Elliot, letter to family, March 9, 1964, folder 12.

23. Elliot, letter to family, April 6, 1964, folder 12.

24. Elliot, letter to family, May 18, 1964, folder 12.

25. Joseph Bayly, "Three Sons," *Warhorn* 1, no. 4, accessed January 20, 2020, http://clearnotefellowship.org/.

26. Elliot, letter to family, May 18, 1964, folder 12. Nathan Curtis Bayly outlived his father, though not his mother, dying of cancer in 2001.

27. Howard, "Omnipotent Hand," 199.

28. Elliot, letter to mother, April, 1964, folder 12.

29. Elliot, letter to family, May 4, 1964, folder 12.

30. C. S. Lewis, *The Four Loves* (London: Fontana, 1974), 62.

31. Thomas Howard, *Christ the Tiger: A Postscript to Dogma* (Philadelphia: J. B. Lippincott, 1967), 59, 112.

32. Elliot, letter to family, September 25, 1963, folder 11.

33. Elliot, letter to family, September 25, 1963, folder 11.

34. Elliot, letter to family, September 25, 1963, folder 11.

35. Elliot, letter to family, October 10, 1963, folder 11.

36. Elliot, letter to family, September 25, 1963, folder 11.

37. Elliot, letter to family, March 10, 1964, folder 12.

38. Elliot, letter to family, March 10, 1964, folder 12. Elliot would later endorse Richard F. Lovelace's 1978 book *Homosexuality and the Church: Crisis, Conflict, Compassion*, which explores the historic position of the church and then-present-day discussion around what the Christian scriptures say about sexuality. Lovelace settles on the position that sex is reserved for monogamous, lifelong heterosexual

marriage but calls the straight church to repentance for homophobia and setting a double standard, and ringingly endorses installing what would now be called "Side B" Christians in every area of church leadership.

39. David M. Howard, interview with author, September 9, 2016.
40. Elisabeth Elliot, "Writing as Personal Discovery," Wheaton College Writers Conference, October 1964, papers of Elisabeth Howard Elliot, collection 278, audio tapes, Billy Graham Center Archives, Wheaton College, IL.
41. Elliot, "Writing as Personal Discovery."
42. Elisabeth Elliot, transcript, "Betty Elliot Chapel Message," October 16, 1964, papers of Elisabeth Howard Elliot, collection 278, box 4, folder 12, Billy Graham Center Archives, Wheaton College, IL.
43. Elliot, letter to family, January 15, 1965, box 5, folder 1. Unless otherwise indicated, subsequent references to Elliot letters in chapter 9 are from collection 278, box 5.
44. Elliot, letter to family, February 6, 1965, folder 1.
45. Virginia Mollenkott, interview with Doris Malkamus, September 25, 2004, the Lesbian, Gay, Bisexual and Transgender Religious Archives Network, https://lgbtq religiousarchives.org/.
46. Elliot, letter to family, February 6, 1965, folder 1.
47. Elliot, letter to mother, February 15, 1965, folder 1.
48. Elisabeth Elliot, *No Graven Image* (New York: Haper & Row, 1966), 107, 106.
49. Elliot, *No Graven Image*, 114, 123.
50. Elliot, *No Graven Image*, 146.
51. Elliot, *No Graven Image*, 209.
52. Elliot, *No Graven Image*, 179, 189, 190.
53. Elliot, *No Graven Image*, 179.
54. Elliot, *No Graven Image*, 238. Sparhawk's possible complicity in Pedro's death seems at first to be a departure from the parallels between her story and Elliot's. But in March 1964, *Eternity* magazine had published a piece by Elliot called "The Wake." It told of her own experience at a wake for a baby who had died of neonatal tetanus six days after she had assisted at the delivery. In it she wrote, "I knew that I would have to live with the knowledge that possibly I was responsible for the death of this child."

It is difficult to know whether this story appears in Elliot's family letters. Given her tendency to put parts of stories from different times together to make a more coherent narrative, it's possible that the story told in *Eternity* is a composite, making it harder to identify. However, it was obviously a deeply affecting experience, and may also have come under the category of things she felt she should keep quiet about until she had hashed them out with God.

Neonatal tetanus is transmitted when an infant with no passive immunity from her mother has a wound (often the unhealed umbilicus) that is exposed to *Clostridium tetani* bacteria (perhaps by cutting the umbilical cord or bandaging the stump with unsterile material). This bacteria is present in soil around the world.

Elliot knew about aseptic practices. She was careful to boil her equipment. At one point she had manually replaced a prolapsed and protruding uterus with enough sterile technique that there was no infection, and the patient made a full recovery. Unless something went wrong, which she does not mention in the story, it seems unlikely that she was responsible for introducing the bacteria. But with her imperfect understanding of the pathogenesis of neonatal tetanus, she worried that perhaps "my very presence at the birth [had] introduced foreign germs to which an Indian had no resistance."

While her concern may have been unfounded in this particular case, the problem of coming to help but instead bringing harm was a very real aspect of missionary work, as other cases including contact illness and death among the Waorani show. This was one of the difficult things she had been forced to look in the face during her time in Ecuador. It was part of what she had *seen*, and now she felt it was her job to *show* it. Elisabeth Elliot, "The Wake," *Eternity*, March, 1964.

55. Elliot, *No Graven Image*, 240.
56. Elliot, *No Graven Image*, 242–43.
57. Elliot, *No Graven Image*, 240.
58. Elliot, transcript, "Betty Elliot Chapel Message."
59. Elliot, letter to family, September 8, 1965, folder 1.
60. Elliot, letter to family, April 9, 1965, folder 1.
61. Elisabeth Elliot, *Who Shall Ascend: The Life of R. Kenneth Strachan of Costa Rica* (New York: Harper & Row, 1968), xi; emphasis original.
62. Elliot, letter to family, February 14, 1964, box 4, folder 12.
63. Elliot, letter to family, December 3, 1965, folder 1.
64. Harold Lindsell, "Book Briefs," *Christianity Today*, July 8, 1966, 29.
65. Elliot, letter to family, May 4, 1967, folder 3.
66. Elliot, letter to family, March 19, 1964, box 4, folder 12.
67. C. Peter Wagner, "A New 'Graven Image'?" *Evangelical Missions Quarterly* 3 (1967): 228–33.
68. Elliot, letter to family, May 4, 1967, folder 3; Elliot, postscript to mother, October 25, 1965, folder 2.
69. Elliot, letter to family, August 4, 1966, folder 4.
70. Elliot, letter to family, August 1, 1966, folder 4.
71. Elliot, letter to family, October 10, 1966, folder 4.
72. Elliot, letters to family, October 10 and 25, 1966, folder 4; Elliot, letter to family, October 25, 1966, folder 4.
73. Elliot, letter to family, January 23, 1967, folder 5.
74. Elliot, letter to family, March 6, 1967, folder 5.
75. Elliot, letter to family, May 4, 1967, folder 5.
76. Elliot, *Who Shall Ascend*, xii.
77. Elliot, *Who Shall Ascend*, 159; Elliot, letter to family, May 14, 1968, folder 4.
78. Elliot, *Who Shall Ascend*, 160.
79. "Who Shall Ascend," *Kirkus Reviews*, February 14, 1967.
80. Frank E. Gaebelein, "Book Briefs: The Inner Life of a Missionary," *Christianity Today*, March 1, 1968, 30.
81. Gaebelein, "Book Briefs," 30.
82. David M. Howard, interview with author, September 9, 2016.
83. Elliot, letter to family, September 15, 1967, folder 3.
84. Elisabeth Elliot, "Introduction to the Original Edition," in Eleanor Vandevort, *A Leopard Tamed* (Peabody, MA: Hendrickson), xxii.
85. Elliot, letter to family, October 4, 1967, folder 3.
86. Elliot, letter to family, October 8, 1967, folder 3.
87. Elliot, letter to family, December 5, 1967, folder 3.
88. Elliot, letter to family, October 8, 1967, folder 3.
89. Elliot, letter to family, December 5, 1967, folder 3.
90. Elliot, letter to family, November 4, 1967, folder 3.
91. Elliot, letter to family, October 20, 1967, folder 3.

92. Elliot, letter to family, November 4, 1967, folder 3.

93. Elisabeth Elliot, *Furnace of the Lord* (New York: Doubleday, 1969), 2, 37, 53.

94. One example of the apparently anti-Israel slant in Elliot's letters is the fact that she made no mention of Israeli casualties when the *Eilat* was sunk, and although the ship had been one of only two destroyers in the Israeli navy, she wrote, "The Israelis haven't the slightest fears or doubts for their security." She also assumed, incorrectly, that Israel had been in the wrong—that is, in Egyptian waters—and Egypt justified in firing on the ship. Elisabeth Elliot, letter to family, October 23, 1967, folder 3.

95. Elliot, *Furnace of the Lord*, 101.

96. Elliot, *Furnace of the Lord*, 102.

97. Elliot, *Furnace of the Lord*, 129.

98. Elliot, letter to family, July 10, 1968, folder 4.

99. Elliot, letter to family, August 4, 1968, folder 4.

100. Elliot, letter to family, August 4, 1968, folder 4.

101. Elliot, letter to family, October 1, 1968, folder 4.

102. Elliot, letter to family, October 1, 1968, folder 4.

Chapter 10: Woman Was Made for Man

1. Elisabeth Elliot, letter to Marilou McCully, October 22, 1957, papers of Elisabeth Howard Elliot, collection 278, box 9, folder 1, Billy Graham Center Archives, Wheaton College, IL.

2. Elliot, letter to family, November 15, 1958, box 4, folder 6.

3. Elliot, letter to mother, December 9, 1968, box 5, folder 4.

4. Elliot, letter to family, August 21, 1967, box 5, folder 3.

5. Elliot, letter to mother, December 9, 1968, box 5, folder 4.

6. Kathryn Deering Rogers photograph of Elisabeth Elliot journal entry, June 12, 1968, papers of Kathryn (Rogers) Deering, collection 670, accession 12–27, disk 1, Billy Graham Center Archives, Wheaton College, IL. Unless otherwise indicated, Deering photos noted in chapter 10 are from this source.

7. Deering photo of Elliot journal entry, August 7, 1968.

8. Elisabeth Elliot, *Passion and Purity* (Grand Rapids, MI: Revell, 1984), 51–52.

9. Eleanor Vandevort, letter to Addison Hardie Leitch, December 6, 1968, papers of Elisabeth Howard Elliot, collection 278, box 9, folder 19, Billy Graham Center Archives, Wheaton College, IL.

10. Vandevort, letter to Addison Hardie Leitch.

11. Eleanor Vandevort, interview with author, November 7, 2014.

12. Elisabeth Elliot, letter to Paul Hostetter, September 11, 1968, box 9, folder 2.

13. Elliot, letters to family, December 9, 11, and 26, 1968, box 5, folder 4.

14. Elliot, letter to family, February 7, 1969, box 5, folder 5.

15. Elliot, letter to family, February 21, 1969, box 5, folder 5.

16. Elliot, letter to family, February 21, 1969, box 5, folder 5.

17. Elliot, letter to family, March 4, 1969, box 5, folder 5.

18. Vandevort would later say, "I probably can't make it plain enough to you how appalled I was" by Elliot's about-face on this issue. Eleanor Vandevort, interview with author, November 7, 2014.

19. Elliot, letter to mother, May 19, 1969, box 5, folder 5.

20. Addison H. Leitch, "And that's the Way It Is," *Christianity Today*, September 25, 1970, 64.

21. Elliot, letter to family, February 21, 1969, box 5, folder 5.

22. Elliot, letter to family, February 7, 1969, box 5, folder 5.

23. Elisabeth Elliot, journal entry, 1960, cited in Ellen Vaughn, *Becoming Elisabeth Elliot* (Nashville, TN: B&H, 2020), 187.

24. Elliot's niece Beth Howard observed that Elliot thought about and spoke to men in a way that stood out to her.

25. Elliot, *Passion and Purity*, 102.

26. Elliot, letter to family, January 14, 1969, box 5, folder 5.

27. Elliot, letter to mother, December 19, 1968, box 5, folder 4.

28. Leitch's influence was not the only factor. Others were also dismissive of Vandevort and of the friendship and mutual assistance between the two women, including neighbors, friends, and Paul Hostetter, the other man to propose to Elliot in the summer of 1968. But Leitch, as Elliot's husband, was surely the most influential.

29. Elliot, letter to family, June 15, 1969, box 5, folder 5.

30. Elliot, letter to family, June 15, 1969, box 5, folder 5.

31. Zippy did not make the move from Franconia; Elliot had him put down because they did not want either to fence him in or to pay the three-hundred-dollar fine they would incur if he was found chasing deer. Thomas Howard, *An Antique Drum* (Philadelphia: J. B. Lippincott, 1969), 21–22.

32. Howard, *Antique Drum*, 155, 156.

33. Howard, *Antique Drum*, 21–22, 45–46.

34. Elisabeth Elliot, *Suffering Is Never for Nothing* (Nashville, TN: B&H, n.d.), 14.

35. Elisabeth Elliot, *Twelve Baskets of Crumbs* (New York: Christian Herald, 1976), 173.

36. Elliot, *Twelve Baskets*, 98.

37. Elisabeth Elliot, "Feminism or Femininity?" *The Cambridge Fish* 5 (Winter 1975–1976): 6.

38. Elliot, letter to family, January 29, 1963, box 4, folder 11.

39. Elliot, letter to family, November 10, 1969, box 5, folder 5. Although Leitch joined Elliot and Valerie for Sunday services, he apparently continued to attend presbytery meetings for the Presbyterian church.

40. Thomas Howard, *Evangelical Is Not Enough: Worship of God in Liturgy and Sacrament* (Nashville, TN: Nelson, 1984), 118, 45.

41. Elisabeth Elliot, *Let Me Be a Woman* (Wheaton, IL: Tyndale, 1976), 14.

42. Thomas Howard, *Evangelical Is Not Enough*, 52.

43. Elliot, *Let Me Be a Woman*, 15.

44. Clara Elliot would live another eleven years.

45. Letha Dawson Scanzoni, "A Christian Feminist Remembers Elisabeth Elliot," *Christian Feminism Today*, 2015, 6. Scanzoni was far from alone in this. Lesa Engelthaler, who would become friends with Elliot in the 1990s, recalls devouring everything that Elliot wrote when she was a young adult, noting that Elliot was "iconic" to many women in the sixties and early seventies because she modeled a version of womanhood that was about more than housekeeping. Engelthaler saw pictures of Elliot in her hammock in the jungle and felt she could see a way to be who God had designed her to be. "To read a woman's [work that] was mentally challenging or not saying that everything was about being a wife, that kind of thing," was deeply appealing. Lesa Engelthaler, interview with author, November 20, 2018.

46. Margaret Lamberts Bendroth, *Fundamentalism and Gender: 1875 to the Present* (New Haven, CT: Yale University Press, 1993), 14.

47. "Declaration of Sentiments," *National Park Service: Women's Rights*, https://www.nps.gov/.

48. Hal Boyle, "Feminine Mystique Is Gone," *Central New Jersey Home News,* September 12, 1973, 7; Beth L. Bailey, *From the Front Porch to the Back Seat: Courtship in Twentieth-Century America* (Baltimore, MD: Johns Hopkins University Press, 1989), 98; Parker Kent, "Woman's Place," *Calgary Herald,* April 12, 1960, 4.

49. Betty Friedan, *The Feminine Mystique* (New York: Norton, 2001), 63–65.

50. Letha Dawson Scanzoni, "Woman's Place: Silence or Service?" *Letha's Calling: A Christian Feminist Voice,* originally published as "Elevate Marriage to Partnership" in *Eternity,* February 1966, https://lethadawsonscanzoni.com/.

51. Scanzoni, "A Christian Feminist Remembers," 4–5.

52. Elliot, letter to mother, January 23, 1968, box 5, folder 4. There is also some possibility that Elliot's views were changing between the summer of 1963 and the summer of 1967 but that falling in love with Addison Leitch returned her to her former position. However, if she had been considering writing on the subject for years, it seems more likely that all along, she had believed there was more room for difference of opinion on women's roles in the church than on women's roles in marriage. This is also consistent with her own behavior.

53. Letha Dawson Scanzoni, "Christian Marriage: Patriarchy or Partnership?," April 11, 2010; and "Backstory: 'Elevate Marriage to Partnership' (1968 *Eternity* article)," April 14, 2010, https://lethadawsonscanzoni.com/; Scanzoni, "A Christian Feminist Remembers," 6.

54. Helmut Thielicke, "Introduction," *The Ethics of Sex,* trans. John W. Doberstein (Cambridge, UK: Lutterworth Press, 1964).

55. Scanzoni, "A Christian Feminist Remembers," 6.

56. Addison H. Leitch, "Time to Get Radical," *Christianity Today,* March 12, 1971, 61.

57. Elliot, letter to family, March 16, 1971, box 5, folder 7.

58. Elliot, letter to family, February 23, 1971, box 5, folder 7.

59. Scanzoni, "A Christian Feminist Remembers," 6–7.

60. Sally K. Gallagher, *Evangelical Identity and Gendered Family Life* (New Brunswick, NJ: Rutgers University Press, 2003), 41.

61. Elliot, letter to family, February 10, 1971, box 5, folder 7.

62. Elliot, letter to family, April 14, 1971, box 5, folder 7.

63. Elliot, letter to family, August 18, 1971, box 5, folder 7.

64. Elliot, letter to family, October 1, 1971, box 5, folder 7.

65. Elliot, *Let Me Be a Woman,* 74.

66. Elliot, letter to family, October 1, 1971, box 5, folder 7.

67. Elliot, letter to mother, January 11, 1972, box 5, folder 8.

68. Elisabeth Elliot, dedication, *A Slow and Certain Light: Some Thoughts on the Guidance of God* (Waco, TX: Word, 1973), 46.

69. Elliot, *Slow and Certain Light,* 46.

70. Elliot, *Slow and Certain Light,* 31, 34.

71. Elliot, *Slow and Certain Light,* 30, 38.

72. Elliot, *Slow and Certain Light,* 57, 70.

73. Elliot, *Slow and Certain Light,* 87, 88.

74. Elliot, *Slow and Certain Light,* 99.

75. Elliot, *Slow and Certain Light,* 115.

76. Simcha Fisher, "Does God Get Off On Seeing Us Suffer?" in *Simcha Fisher: I Have to Sit Down,* February 15, 2017, https://www.simchafisher.com/.

77. Elliot, *Slow and Certain Light,* 102.

78. Elliot, *Slow and Certain Light,* 101, 115.

79. Elliot never explained in family letters what happened to Tania.

80. Thomas Howard, interviews with author, November 6, 2014 and December 14, 2013.

81. Elisabeth Elliot, *The Path of Loneliness* (Nashville, TN: Oliver-Nelson, 1988), 113.

82. Julian of Norwich, *Revelations of Divine Love*, ed. Roger Hudleston (Mineola, NY: Dover, 2012), e-book.

83. C. S. Lewis, *A Grief Observed* (New York: Bantam, 1961), 1.

84. Elisabeth Elliot, *A Path through Suffering* (Ventura, CA: Regal, 2003), 141.

85. Elliot, letter to family, March 7, 1973, box 5, folder 9.

86. Meir Walters, interview with author, November 7, 2014.

87. Eleanor Vandevort, interview with author, November 7, 2014.

88. It appears that the couple arranged that Elliot would be at least somewhat supported financially by Leitch's estate until her own death or remarriage, at which time the residue of the estate would go to his daughters.

89. Julian of Norwich, *Revelations of Divine Love*.

90. Elliot, letter to family, September 25, 1973, box 5, folder 9.

91. Elisabeth Elliot, "Unedited Notes and Outline for Unpublished Book on Marriage," accessed August 2010, www.elisabethelliot.org/.

92. The Howard family was recognized on the platform during the convention for their collective contribution to American foreign missions.

93. Elisabeth Elliot, *All That Was Ever Ours* (Old Tappan, NJ: Revell, 1988), 167.

94. Elliot, *All That Was Ever Ours*, 171.

95. Dawson Scanzoni, "Woman's Place: Silence or Service?"

96. Elliot, *All That Was Ever Ours*, 171.

97. Elliot, letter to family, January 7, 1974, box 5, folder 10.

98. Elliot, *Let Me Be a Woman*, 10.

Chapter 11: On All Sides

1. Elisabeth Elliot, *The Path of Loneliness* (Nashville, TN: Oliver-Nelson, 1988), 99.

2. Elisabeth Elliot, letter to family, August 15, 1974, papers of Elisabeth Howard Elliot, collection 278, box 5, folder 10.

3. Elisabeth Elliot, *These Strange Ashes* (New York: Harper & Row, 1975), x.

4. Elliot, *These Strange Ashes*, 131.

5. Elliot, letter to James M. Houston, December 13, 1975, box 9, folder 3.

6. Elliot, letter to family, October 11, 1974, box 5, folder 10.

7. Elliot, letter to family, December 6, 1974, box 5, folder 10.

8. Elliot, letter to family, December 31, 1974, box 5, folder 10.

9. Elliot, letter to family, December 31, 1974, box 5, folder 10.

10. There are no surviving family letters from 1975. Elliot's thinking during this period can be traced through her extant published work and speaking.

11. Elisabeth Elliot Leitch, "Wheaton College Chapel address," May 2, 1975, courtesy Buswell Library, Special Collections, Wheaton College, IL.

12. C. S. Lewis, "Membership," in *The Weight of Glory* (San Francisco: HarperSanFrancisco, 2001), 158–76.

13. Elisabeth Elliot, "Why I Oppose the Ordination of Women," *Christianity Today*, June 6, 1975, https://www.christianitytoday.com/.

14. Elliot, "Why I Oppose," 12–15.

15. Elisabeth Elliot, "Feminism or Femininity?" *The Cambridge Fish*, vol. 5, no. 2 (Winter 1975–1976): 6.

16. Press release, Evangelical Women's Caucus, December 2, 1975, https://eewc.com/.

17. Elliot, "Feminism or Femininity?," 6.
18. Elisabeth Elliot, *Let Me Be a Woman* (Wheaton, IL: Tyndale, 1976), 11, 59, 107.
19. Kathy Kristy, cited in Elliot, *Let Me Be a Woman*, 60.
20. Although the book sets out to address *women*, it ends up dealing almost entirely with marriage. This stems from Elliot's belief that "relatively few women" have to deal with singleness, since "most women marry" early in adulthood (although there were about 110 million American women in 1975, and about 60 percent were married, so that "relatively few women" was about sixty-six million people), and from her personal preference for marriage—she says again that she is better off as a widow than women who have never married. But most of all, Elliot's assertion that "the reflection of the nature of the Trinity in the institution of marriage is the key to the definition of masculinity and femininity" seems to make marriage fundamental to womanness. Elliot, *Let Me Be a Woman*, 33, 38, 55; Kathy Kristy, cited in Elliot, *Let Me Be a Woman*, 60.
21. Elliot, *Let Me Be a Woman*, 78–79, 88, 89, 92, 96, 107, 110, 112, 114.
22. Elliot, *Let Me Be a Woman*, 121, 157.
23. Elliot, *Let Me Be a Woman*, 158, 166.
24. Elliot, *Let Me Be a Woman*, 173, 178, 185.
25. Elliot, *Let Me Be a Woman*, 22, 35, 36.
26. Elliot, "Feminism or Femininity?"
27. Elliot, *Let Me Be a Woman*, 29, 52, 60, 61.
28. Eleanor Vandevort, interview with author, November 7, 2014.
29. Elliot, letter to family, June 11, 1976, box 5, folder 12.
30. Elliot, letter to family, August 16, 1976, box 5, folder 12.
31. Catherine Peeke, letter to Rachel Saint, March 20, 1975, Yost Papers, cited in Kathryn T. Long, *God in the Rainforest* (New York: Oxford University Press, 2019), 208.
32. Elliot, letter to family, Oct 14, 1976, box 5, folder 12.
33. The Reverend VaCountess Johnson, interview with author, August 8, 2020.
34. Elliot, letter to family, December 12, 1976, box 5, folder 12.
35. Elliot, letter to family, December 12, 1976, box 5, folder 12.
36. Elliot, letter to family, January 27, 1977, box 5, folder 14.
37. Lars Gren, interview with author, November 10, 2014.
38. Elisabeth Elliot and Lars Gren, interview, *Family Life Today*, 1999, https://www.familylife.com/.
39. Elliot, letters to family, April 12 and June 7, 1977, box 5, folder 13.
40. Elliot, letter to family, October 31, 1977, box 5, folder 13.
41. Elliot and Gren, interview, *Family Life Today*, 1999.
42. Elliot, letter to family, October 21, 1957, box 5, folder 13.
43. Elliot later noted that one person whose opinion was important to her had not been enthusiastic. Given the long list of names she mentions specifically as having been encouraging, it seems likely that the dissenting voice was Vandevort. This is supported by Lars's memories of that time; he felt that Vandevort had been upset by his pursuit of her friend.
44. Elisabeth Elliot, *Twelve Baskets of Crumbs* (New York: Christian Herald, 1976), 55.
45. Elliot, letter to family, September 19, 1977, box 5, folder 13.
46. Elliot, letter to family, November 18, 1977, box 5, folder 13.
47. Elliot, letter to family, October 31, 1977, box 5, folder 13.
48. Elliot, letter to family, October 31, 1977, box 5, folder 13.
49. Elliot, letter to family, December 2, 1977, box 5, folder 13.
50. Elliot and Gren, interview, *Family Life Today*, 1999.

51. Thomas Howard noted that his sister's manner was constantly causing people to believe she was angry with them, and that this was distressing to her. Elsewhere he would say, "Even back in our childhood church . . . she was never part of the gang. People always looked at her as a kind of obelisk, sort of a daunting figure. Even our parents." Thomas Howard, interview with author, November 6, 2014.

52. Elliot and Gren, interview, *Family Life Today*, 1999.

53. Lars would later remember getting "upset" with Elliot after their marriage for the first time just after they moved to Georgia, but since he seems to have viewed his anger more casually than Elliot, it seems likely that her memory is the more accurate. Lars Gren, interview with author, November 10, 2014.

54. Meir Walters, interview with author, November 7, 2014.

55. Anonymous 2, interview with author, September 21, 2020.

56. David M. Howard, interview with author, September 9, 2016.

57. David M. Howard and Janet Howard, interview with author, August 1, 2019.

58. Lars Gren, interview with author, November 10, 2014.

59. Lars Gren, interview with author, November 10, 2014. There is some possibility that Lars and his older sister were both left with their grandparents. Elliot and Lars had a framed photograph in their living room of Lars and his sister in which he is standing sturdily, so apparently older than when he left the US but still obviously quite young, perhaps around nine to twelve months old. On the other hand, Lars spoke of his time with his grandparents and his return to the US only in the first person, and the exact timing of his move to Norway is somewhat unclear.

60. Lars Gren, interview with author, November 10, 2014.

61. Elliot, *Let Me Be a Woman*, 121, 173.

62. Anonymous 2, interview with author, September 21, 2020.

63. Elliot, letters to family, January 18 and 24, 1978, box 5, folder 14.

64. Elliot never refers to the project by name. It had a new way of translating the names of God, and it printed the words of God in red ink throughout the book; the Sword Study Bible now produced by Whitaker House seems to meet the description she gives.

65. Lars Gren, interview with author, November 10, 2014.

66. Elliot, letter to family, April 17, 1978, box 5, folder 14.

67. Lars Gren, interview with author, November 10, 2014.

68. Elliot, letter to family, May 31, 1978, box 5, folder 14.

69. Elliot, letter to family, August 2, 1978, box 5, folder 14.

70. Elliot, letter to family, July 19, 1978, box 5, folder 14.

71. Elisabeth Elliot, "Introduction," in *The Christian's Secret of a Happy Life* (Waco, TX: Word, 1985), xix.

72. Elliot, letter to family, October 2, 1978, box 5, folder 14.

73. Elisabeth Elliot, *Love Has a Price Tag* (Ann Arbor, MI: Servant, 1979), 10.

74. Elliot, letters to family, October 17, November 10, and December 16, 1979, box 5, folder 15.

75. Elliot had planned for this to be the end of the class forever, but when a young woman from Gordon-Conwell approached her in the late 90s and asked for group discipleship, she agreed. In 1998 and 1999 Elliot was regularly teaching a group of women associated with Gordon-Conwell Seminary in her home.

76. Elliot, letter to family, December 16, 1979, box 5, folder 15.

77. Elisabeth Elliot, "On Asking God Why," in *All That Was Ever Ours* (Old Tappan, NJ: Revell, 1988), 43.

78. Anonymous 2, interview with author, September 21, 2020; Elliot, letter to family, May 31, 1978, box 5, folder 14; Elisabeth Elliot, *Discipline: The Glad Surrender* (Old Tappan, NJ: Revell, 1982), 66.

79. Elliot, circular letter, January, 1981, box 5, folder 19.

80. Elliot, "Provision for Sacrifice," *Love Has a Price Tag*, 96. Comparing the column with Elliot's letters suggests it was originally written in late 1977.

81. Elliot, letter to family, December 12, 1976, box 5, folder 12.

82. Elliot, letter to mother, September 23, 1957, box 4, folder 5. Van Kampen Press published, among other things, the cheery devotionals of V. Raymond Edman.

83. Elliot, letter to mother, September 23, 1957, box 4, folder 5.

84. Flannery O'Connor, *The Habit of Being: Letters of Flannery O'Connor*, ed. Sally Fitzgerald (New York: Farrar, Straus & Giroux, 1979), 488.

85. Letters between Richard F. Gross and Elisabeth Elliot, November 16, 1984, box 9, folder 4. It's not clear how long this position lasted, but it continued at least through 1984, when there is a record of discussion between Elliot and some members of the faculty about the renewal of her contract for 1985. There seems to be no record of how this was resolved.

86. Elisabeth Elliot, *The Mark of a Man* (Grand Rapids, MI: Revell, 1981), 49.

87. Elliot, *Mark of a Man*, 46, 49, 77–78, 95, 105, 107, 143, 146.

88. Elliot, *Discipline*, 155.

89. Elliot, "Why Another Newsletter?" *Elisabeth Elliot Newsletter*, Premier Issue, November 1982.

90. Elisabeth Elliot, *Passion and Purity* (Grand Rapids, MI: Revell, 1984), 12.

91. Elliot, *Passion and Purity*, 47, 59–60, 64.

92. Elliot, *Passion and Purity*, 72, 101, 180; emphasis original.

93. Elliot, *Elisabeth Elliot Newsletter*, May/June 1984 and January/February 1986.

94. Elliot, *Passion and Purity*, 141–42.

95. Elisabeth Elliot, *A Lamp for My Feet* (Ann Arbor, MI: Servant Books, 1985), 11.

96. Elliot, "The Suffering of Divorce," *Elisabeth Elliot Newsletter*, March/April 1985, 1.

97. Thomas Howard, interview with author, October 2013.

98. Thomas Howard, interview with author, October 2013.

99. Heidi Hess Saxton, "Courage to Be Catholic?," *Catholic Exchange*, May 22, 2007.

100. Thomas Howard, interview with author, October 2013. Ironically, she came in for a share of censure anyway, with at least one organization writing after Tom's conversion to inquire not only about her own attitude toward the Catholic Church but also about her personal use of alcohol, and to threaten her with a massive loss in sales should her answers differ from their statement of belief. She replied briefly that she could not in good conscience condemn the use of alcohol more thoroughly than the Bible itself and that she had no plans to enter the Catholic Church. Guy Swartwout, letter to Elisabeth Elliot, August 19, 1985, box 9, folder 4; Elisabeth Elliot, letter to Guy Swartwout, August 27, 1985, box 9, folder 4.

101. Elliot, *Elisabeth Elliot Newsletter*, September/October 1986, 2.

102. Elliot, *Elisabeth Elliot Newsletter*, January/February 1984, 2.

103. Elliot, *Elisabeth Elliot Newsletter*, May/June 1984, 1–2.

104. Elisabeth Elliot, *A Chance to Die* (Grand Rapids, MI: Revell, 1996), 16–17.

105. Elliot, *A Chance to Die*, 15.

106. Elliot, *A Chance to Die*, 378–79.

107. Thomas Howard, interview with author, October 2013.

108. Lars's mother, Ingrid Gren, would die just over a decade later, in April 1998.

109. Elliot, *Elisabeth Elliot Newsletter*, July/August 1988, 3.

110. Elliot, *Elisabeth Elliot Newsletter*, March/April 1985, 3.

111. Janet Anderson, "Your Turn: Janet Anderson," *Our Family Ties*, vol. 3 (July/August 1988), 3.

112. Elliot, *Elisabeth Elliot Newsletter*, September/October 1988.

113. Elliot, *Elisabeth Elliot Newsletter*, November 1982, 2–3, March/April 1985, 3, July/August 1984, 2.

114. Elisabeth Elliot, *Gateway to Joy*.

115. Elliot, *Path of Loneliness*, 158.

116. Elisabeth Elliot, *Suffering Is Never for Nothing* (Nashville, TN: B&H, n.d.), 84.

117. Thomas Howard, letter to Elisabeth Elliot, October 14, 2000, box 9, folder 5; Anonymous 1, interview with author, February 7, 2014; Anonymous 2, interview with author, September 21, 2020.

118. Olive Fleming Liefeld, interview with author, April 4, 2014. Liefeld spoke of Lars as a "gatekeeper" for Elliot's business decisions, although she did not realize the extent of his desire for control. One manifestation of this was that *Through Gates of Splendor*, which had always felt to the other widows (and, the arrangement for the royalties suggests, for Elliot too) like a group project, "really became *her* book" after Lars took over Elliot's business affairs.

119. Elliot, *Let Me Be a Woman*, 148. "Love bombing" describes an attempt to overwhelm a person with gifts, attention, affection, etc., in order to exert control.

120. Lars Gren, cited in Elliot, *Elisabeth Elliot Newsletter*, November/December 1992, 3.

121. Elisabeth Elliot, notes for the unpublished book *Marriage: A Revolution and a Revelation, A Supreme Earthly Test of Discipleship*, accessed September 25, 2020, https://www.schooldrillers.com/ (original at http://elisabethelliot.org/).

122. This is a striking change from Elliot's fear in 1956 that she could thwart God's purposes in Jim's death by making mistakes.

123. Elisabeth Elliot, *A Path through Suffering* (Ventura, CA: Regal, 2003), 185.

124. Brother Lawrence, "Twelfth Letter," *The Brother Lawrence Collection* (Hoboken, NJ: Start Publishing LLC, 2013), e-book.

125. Elliot, *Never for Nothing*, 47.

126. Elliot, *Elisabeth Elliot Newsletter*, January/February 1989, 2.

127. Elisabeth Elliot, *The Shaping of a Christian Family* (Grand Rapids, MI: Revell, 1992), 17.

128. Elliot, *Elisabeth Elliot Newsletter*, March/April 1995.

129. Elisabeth Elliot, "Elisabeth Elliot Financial Policy," private collection.

130. By the mid-90s, the Grens also frequently donated Elliot's fee to various causes they wished to support, sometimes asking the organization at which she was speaking to send the money directly to the recipient on their behalf. Lauren Vandermeer, interview with author, July 2, 2016.

131. Gothard's organization changed names several times, starting in the 1960s under the name Campus Teams, changing to Institute in Basic Youth Conflicts (IBYC) by 1969, and to Institute in Basic Life Principles (IBLP) in, apparently, 1989. The exact dates are unclear because the timeline given on the IBLP website appears to contradict both itself and the copyright on Gothard materials handed out in the early 1970s.

132. Gothard responded publicly to Bayly's letter, minimizing some of the points raised and contradicting others, but people present at his seminars confirm that Gothard did say the things Bayly asked questions about.

133. Elisabeth Elliot, form letter, box 11, folder 8.

134. Elliot, *Never for Nothing*, 51–52.

135. Elisabeth Elliot, "The Essence of Femininity: A Personal Perspective," Recovering Biblical Manhood and Womanhood, accessed September 28, 2020, https://bible.org/.

136. Elliot, *Elisabeth Elliot Newsletter*, November/December 1986.

137. This is clear not only from passages in her books in which she urges discernment but also from her practice in the newsletter of recommending without reservation texts that she had fairly major disagreements with. At least once she recommended a book to readers of her newsletter without qualification—although in a later newsletter, in response to reader questions, she would explain at some length that she disagreed with multiple aspects of the book.

138. Elisabeth Elliot, *Quest for Love* (Grand Rapids, MI: Revell, 1996), 11, 17, 155.

139. Elliot, *Quest for Love*, 269.

140. Elliot contradicted these attitudes wherever she met them. Donna Otto would remember, "She pointed me to Him always, and always away from her. When I met her . . . all I wanted was someone to tell me how to do it. And I would go at the same question with her a dozen different ways. 'Well just tell me what your morning looks like in prayer. What do you do first? Well what do you do in the middle? Well what do you do at the end? And do you do it all seven days?' . . . She always pointed me to Him, she never answered those questions." Donna Otto, speaking at Elisabeth Elliot's memorial service, July 26, 2015, https://www.youtube.com/.

141. Elliot, *Quest for Love*, 268, 270.

142. Elisabeth Elliot, interview with Kathryn T. Long, June 27, 2001, transcript in email to author, July 1, 2019.

143. Long, *God in the Rainforest*, 266.

144. By 2014, research indicated that "by the time somebody starts showing signs or symptoms of memory loss, the Alzheimer's disease pathology has been moving around the brain often for more than a decade." Healthcare Interactive, "Delivering an Alzheimer's Disease Diagnosis," 2014, accessed September 3, 2020, https://www.youtube.com/.

145. Almost fifteen years later, Lars would date the early stages of Elliot's dementia to both the late 1980s and early 1990s and to the late 1990s and early 2000s. Marginal notes in Elliot's daily devotional pin it to the end of 1998.

146. Gren, "Ramblings from the Cove," April 2017.

147. Gren, "Ramblings from the Cove," April 2017.

148. Lars Gren, interview with author, November 10, 2014.

149. Lars Gren, interview with author, November 10, 2014. He did not elaborate on how he had come to his present understanding.

150. Elliot, *Love Has a Price Tag*, 77–78.

151. Elliot, *Passion and Purity*, 12.

152. Elliot, *Path through Suffering*, 156.

153. John Greenleaf Whittier, "When on My Day of Life the Night Is Falling," *Methodist Hymn and Tune Book: Official Hymn Book of the Methodist Church*, https://hymnary.org/.

154. Elliot, *Elisabeth Elliot Newsletter*, November/December 1999.

155. Elliot, *Elisabeth Elliot Newsletter*, September/October 1999.

156. Meir Walters, interview with author, November 7, 2014.

157. William Archer Butler, and Anthony Wilson Thorold, as cited by Mary Wilder Tileston, in *Daily Strength for Daily Needs*, memorial ed., April 16 and 17 (Boston: Little, Brown & Co., n.d.).

158. Lars Gren, interview with author, November 10, 2014.

159. Gren, "Ramblings from the Cove," April 2017.

160. Lars Gren, interview with author, November 10, 2014.

161. Gren, "Ramblings from the Cove," April 2017.

162. Père Hyacinthe Besson, as cited by Mary Wilder Tileston, *Joy and Strength* (Minneapolis: World Wide Publications, 1986), June 10; Francois Fénelon, "Letter Ten," in *Let Go* (New Kensington, PA: Whitaker, 1973).

163. Elisabeth Elliot, interview with Nancy Leigh DeMoss, 2001, https://www.reviveourhearts.com/.

164. Elisabeth Elliot, *Be Still My Soul* (Grand Rapids, MI: Revell, 2003), 7, 11.

165. Lauren Vandermeer, interview with author, July 2, 2016.

166. Donna Otto, speaking at Elisabeth Elliot's memorial service, July 26, 2015, https://www.youtube.com/.

167. Arlita Winston, speaking at Elisabeth Elliot's memorial service.

168. Lars Gren, interview with author, November 10, 2014.

169. Scripture cards, private collection.

170. Lars Gren, interview with author, November 10, 2014.

171. Gren, "Ramblings from the Cove," April 2017.

172. Thomas Howard, interview with author, October 2013.

173. Thomas Howard, interview with author, November 6, 2014.

174. Danielle Sobi Waters, interview with author, February 7, 2014.

175. Lars Gren and Elisabeth Elliot, interview with Tiffany Owens, "Walking through Fire," *World*, March 8, 2014, 57–58.

176. Lars Gren, "Ramblings from the Cove: A Memorable Morning," April 1, 2014.

177. Lars Gren, letter to contact list, July 6, 2015. Even after Elliot's first agony at Jim's death had subsided and she was happily married to Leitch and no longer longed for death, she had noted in her journal that when she reached old age, she did not want medical treatment that would make her live longer.

Epilogue

1. Lecrae, "Elisabeth's Interlude," *So It Continues*, 2012, https://www.youtube.com/.

2. Elisabeth Elliot, *Who Shall Ascend: The Life of R. Kenneth Strachan of Costa Rica* (New York: Harper & Row, 1968), 160–61.

Acknowledgments

1. Elisabeth Elliot, *Shadow of the Almighty* (New York: Harper & Brothers, 1958), 12; Elisabeth Elliot, *Who Shall Ascend: The Life of R. Kenneth Strachan of Costa Rica* (New York: Harper & Row, 1968), xii.

General Index

Scripture Index